D0079199

THE COMPLETE PLAYS OF
WILLIAM WYCHERLEY

GERALD WEALES is Professor of English at the University of Pennsylvania. He received his A.B., A.M. and Ph.D. from Columbia University. His books include *American Drama since World War II; A Play and Its Parts; Religion in Modern English Drama; The Jumping-Off Place: American Drama in the 1960's;* and as editor, *Edwardian Plays* and *Eleven Plays: An Introduction to Drama* (Norton). The author of two children's books and a novel, *Tale for the Bluebird,* he also writes for *The Reporter, Kenyon Review, Hudson Review, Atlantic Monthly, Tulane Drama Review, Drama Survey, Modern Drama,* and *Educational Theatre Journal.* He received the George Jean Nathan Award for Dramatic Criticism for 1965.

The Complete Plays of
WILLIAM WYCHERLEY

LOVE IN A WOOD

THE GENTLEMAN-DANCING-MASTER

THE COUNTRY-WIFE

THE PLAIN-DEALER

EDITED WITH AN INTRODUCTION

NOTES AND VARIANTS BY

GERALD WEALES

The Norton Library

W · W · NORTON & COMPANY · INC ·

NEW YORK

W. W. Norton & Company, Inc. also publishes *The Norton Anthology of English Literature*, edited by M. H. Abrams et al; *The Norton Anthology of Poetry*, edited by Arthur M. Eastman et al; *World Masterpieces*, edited by Maynard Mack et al; *The Norton Reader*, edited by Arthur M. Eastman et al; *The Norton Facsimile of the First Folio of Shakespeare*, prepared by Charlton Hinman; *The Norton Anthology of Modern Poetry*, edited by Richard Ellmann and Robert O'Clair; and the *Norton Critical Editions*.

For
Hennig and Merrie Lou

CONTENTS

INTRODUCTION

The middlebrow or the upper Philistine cannot get rid
of the furtive feeling that a book, to be great, must
deal in great ideas. Oh, I know the type, the dreary
type! He likes a good yarn spiced with social comment:
he likes to recognize his own thoughts and throes in
those of the author; he wants at least one of the
characters to be the author's stooge.

Vladimir Nabokov

William Wycherley's plays are a kind of critical Rorschach. Most Wycherley commentators give direct or
oblique allegiance to one or the other of two main views
of his work. One group, attracted to Horner in *The
Country-Wife*, assumes that Horner is Wycherley and that
the playwright is an amoral libertine whose work expresses his philosophy. The other group, attracted to
Manly in *The Plain-Dealer*, assumes that Manly is Wycherley and that the playwright is a rampaging idealist
whose work expresses his philosophy. There are divisions
within both groups. Some critics admit their attraction to
Horner or Manly and defend the Wycherley they imagine;
others deny the attraction and attack the Wycherley.
These allegiances can be seen even among the most recent critics, who have tried not to be Lord Macaulay or
George B. Churchill, who have used philosophy and
generic analysis to prove that the plays are doctrinaire
comedies of wit, celebrations of the natural over the
artificial, or attempts at formal satire.

If I were to offer a neat theory of my own, I would do
no more than illustrate the paragraph above. It is impossible, however, to write an introduction without making
generalizations. The one that I want most to make is that
Wycherley's plays have a way of slipping out from under

any generalization, that they seem designed to keep the man in the audience (or the reader) from knowing just where he stands in relation to the characters in the play. As an example of how difficult it is to pin Wycherley down, consider Thomas H. Fujimura's comments on Horner in *The Restoration Comedy of Wit*. The thesis of his book demands that Horner, like all of "Wycherley's True-wits," hate the unnatural, the hypocritical, the affected. "This hatred . . . is the motivating force behind Horner's ironic deeds and words." Even if we accept that much of the satire in the play is aimed at affectation (which I do) and that Horner has a great contempt for Lady Fidget (which I am not sure that I do), it is impossible to accept Fujimura's final reading of Horner. Surely if Horner uses his sex to show his hatred of affectation, he is being "unnatural" in a way so gross that Lady Fidget's "preciseness" becomes almost as genteel as she pretends to be. I do not introduce this critical quibble to prove that Fujimura has made a grave misreading of Horner, but to show how difficult it is to place the character. Surely P. F. Vernon is as hard to take when he decides that *The Country-Wife* is a social-problem play about the position of women in Restoration society with Horner just another instance of "the cruelty and indifference of men."

Horner is probably the best character to illustrate the ambiguity that hangs over Wycherley's plays. He is an extremely attractive character for several reasons. The hidden *Playboy* reader in all of us is bound to identify with his sexual triumphs; the audience's fondness for the con man (from Joseph and Odysseus to the King and the Duke in *Huck Finn*) impels it to hope for the success of his scheme. He has a directness which is at once openly appealing (plain dealing is always in fashion) and insidious (we know that his plain dealing is double-dealing —therefore, we can feel superior to his victims). He should, then, be the play's hero, but as we watch him in operation he begins to seem as foolish as the characters he manipulates. His seductions become merely mechanical. He is more like a chain smoker than a great lover. The famous china scene is one of the best jokes in dramatic literature, but we are never sure that Horner is not the butt of it. At the end of Act 2, Sir Jaspar urges Horner and Lady Fidget, "go, go, to your business, I say, pleasure, whilst I go to my pleasure, business." When Sir Jaspar speaks the line, it is the cuckold in him that bears its brunt, but by the end of the play, after Horner has sacrificed social pleasure for sexual and worked so hard for what he has got, the line, in retrospect, is almost a satiric comment on him. My description of Horner implies a greater emphasis on chronology than I intend. He is not unmasked, as Shavian characters so often are; he does not appear to be one thing and turn out to be another. He is several things at once. It is this uncertainty about how we are to react that gives the character, the play, and Wycherley's dramatic work as a whole its peculiar richness.

One of the most sensible comments ever made about Wycherley's work came from John Dennis, in *The Usefulness of the Stage* (1698): "Mr. *Wycherley* being, indeed, almost the only Man alive who has made Comedy instructive in its Fable; almost all the rest, being contented to instruct by their Characters." Dennis, preoccupied with the instructiveness of comedy, did not follow up the critical hint in this casual remark. It is not the fable in itself that gives a Wycherley play its effect; it is, as William Hazlitt implied in *Lectures on the English Comic Writers* (1819), the confrontation of character and incident. All four of Wycherley's plays, like most Restoration comedies, are about the quest for sex (in or out of marriage) and money (in or out of marriage). All four make a point of exposing a variety of kinds of affectation and hypocrisy. Fable should take care of the quest; character, the rest. Things are never so simple in Wycherley. His characters can be divided into three basic groups: the open and obvious comic stereotypes (the fops, the cuckolds, the social pretenders) who can be used for mild satirical points; the Horners and the Freemans, men who have presumably learned how to take care of themselves in a less-than-perfect world; the Christinas and the Fidelias, the refugees from romance, whom some critics accept seriously as vehicles for ideal honor or love. The first group causes few difficulties; the complications arise with the second and third. The Horners, as my description above suggests, succeed in a context that makes one suspicious of their success, and the Fidelias take part in incidents that make dramatic hash of their fine sentiments. One cannot even fall back on end-of-the-play rewards and punishments in a search of sure ground because, just as the incidents becloud the characters, the characters call the working out of the plot in doubt. The end of *The Gentleman-Dancing-Master* is presumably a conventional one, with the young lovers outwitting the stern father and the foolish fiancé, but after watching Hippolita for five acts, one wants to congratulate Monsieur on escaping marriage with her. This "yes-but" effect in all the plays is heightened by Wycherley's casual, even mocking use of literary stereotype and theatrical device. The plays are sprinkled with reminders that we are in a theater, perhaps none more obvious than the one at the end of Act II of *Dancing-Master* when a singer, in no way involved in the action of the play, comes on to perform; "She's come," Hippolita says, "as if she came expresly to sing the new Song . . ." Wycherley's characters, his plots, his subject matter, his theatrical devices are all very much a product of his time, but his double-edged use of them marks him as the most modern—that is, the most accessible to contemporary audiences—of the Restoration dramatists.

For a compact statement of what Wycherley is about in his comedies, one could do worse than borrow Lisideius's definition of a play from John Dryden's *Of Dramatick Poesie* (1668): "A just and lively Image of Humane Nature, representing its Passions and Humours, and the Changes of Fortune to which it is subject; for the Delight and Instruction of Mankind." From Dennis to Vernon, critics—particularly those who are pro-Wycherley—have emphasized Wycherley as a teaching poet, usually underlining the lesson that his plays are supposed to teach ("He took it for granted that the highest function of comedy was to instruct"—Vernon). I do not doubt the seriousness of Wycherley's plays; I simply doubt the explicitness of the lesson. Any image of human nature, particularly one as flexible as that provided by Wycherley's plays, is likely to be instructive if the audience is tough enough to offer itself as target.

In any case, it is the delight and not the instruction that I want to emphasize here. Not that they can be comfortably separated. The intellectual process that lets us perceive a Wycherley play as a whole, with all its contradictions and nuances, may be instructive, but it is also the chief delight that his work provides. There are, however, a great many smaller delights, simpler pleasures to be found in Wycherley. Most critics admit that he can be a very efficient comic writer, although too often they attempt to justify in the name of an artistic, a social, or a moral good the pleasure they take in him. Wycherley's comic talent is not without its imperfections, of which the most obvious, as Hazlitt pointed out, is his tendency to hold onto a joke or a situation long after the life has gone out of it. I am more interested in his abilities than his deficiencies, however, and would like to comment briefly on two of the pleasures that I find in his plays: his "indecency," as Macaulay called it, which is too often attacked, forgiven, or explained away; his stage bits, brief scenes sometimes no more than a line or two long, which —whatever their relation to the play as a whole—have an incidental function as vehicles for the talents of the comic actors who play them.

At Lenny Bruce's first obscenity trial in 1962, the defense plea was that the nightclub performer was a social satirist in the tradition of Aristophanes and Swift and that the offending words were part of his satiric technique. The same defense has been made, too often, of Wycherley. In Wycherley's case, it is a plea that is neither true nor necessary. He does not use his bawdy, as Bruce does his obscene words, for its shock value; he is nearer in spirit to e e cummings in *him*, in which good humor and dramatic context milk the dirty joke of its prurience. Not that Wycherley is incapable of prurience: see "The Answer," his verse reply to "A Letter from Mr. Shadwell to Mr. Wycherley," and his letter to Alexander Pope

(March 22, 1705/6). The effect of even the most outrageous lines or scenes is entirely different in the plays.
For example, take the exchange in Act 4 of *The Country-
Wife* in which Pinchwife, having just inadvertently de-
livered his wife's love letter to Horner, bristles with indignation: "I will not be a Cuckold I say, there will be
danger in making me a Cuckold." "Why," comes Horner's bland reply, "wert thou not well cur'd of thy last
clap?" The success of that line has nothing to do with
Wycherley's presumed moral stance. It is a good line because it works several ways within the play. It is appropriate to the two characters; it reminds the audience of
Pinchwife's rakish past and the ludicrousness of his
present possessiveness even while it illustrates the tired
ironic pose that Horner so often uses. It functions dra-
matically within the play as a whole and within the scene
itself; by exploding the pomposity of Pinchwife's threat,
the line not only strengthens the audience's expectation
that he will be cuckolded, but it gives them the incidental comic pleasure of seeing a windbag punctured.
Most important, however, is the surprise in Horner's line.
If it were blunt and nothing more, it might be as obscene
as Wycherley is sometimes accused of being, and might
evoke only a nervous titter from an audience. It is genu-
inely funny, however, because it hits the audience in two
waves: first, there is the surprise of the word itself,
and then, the delighted recognition of how appropriate
it is. An important element in the total effect is that the
author appears to be using bawdy because he finds it
amusing—and somewhat special by virtue of its directness.
Wycherley ordinarily works in double entendre, as in the
china scene, or by incongruity in which context and line
work together when they appear to be pulling apart, as
when the sanctimonious lecher in *Love in a Wood* enters
Lucy's house with this prayer on his lips: "Peace, Plenty,
and Pastime be within these Walls." I confess that a statement such as F. W. Bateson's comment, in *Essays in
Criticism*, VII (1957), on the china scene appalls me in a
way that nothing in Wycherley can: "The audience, dis-
gusted but fascinated, is quite unable to break away."

To me, the scene is outrageously funny. Unless one approaches Wycherley without the defensiveness of a Bateson, half the fun of his plays will be lost.

The paucity of comment on Wycherley as a writer for actors can probably be explained by the fact that most of his critics are oriented toward literature rather than the stage. The only major drama critic who has written about him at any length is Harley Granville-Barker, who, rather too quickly, dismisses him as a man who "lacks a sense of the theatre." Some of his criticisms are justified (there *are* three acts of exposition in *The Plain-Dealer*), but Granville-Barker appears to be using realistic criteria to judge non-realistic plays. I do not want to suggest that the plays are artificial in the disastrous sense that has been responsible for so many languid Restoration revivals in which archness has been substituted for vitality. They are artificial in the sense that the characters are stereotypical and the exchanges between them are as set as vaudeville comic turns. It is in these set pieces that Wycherley is at his best as a writer for the stage. His visual and verbal sense is superb. He knows the uses of comic contrast—Monsieur vs. Don Diego in *The Gentleman-Dancing-Master*, Sparkish's negligence alongside Pinchwife's rigidity in *The Country-Wife*—and of comic reinforcement—the Alphonse-Gaston routine that Mrs. Joyner and Gripe go through in the first act of *Love in a Wood*, in which they insult one another through compliments. The verbal tag ends that he distributes among his characters (Sir Simon's "faith and troth") may seem a little obvious, but they are the kind of mannerism around which an actor can build a stock character. In other instances, verbal repetition and echo is used both for characterization and direct comic effect:

LADY FIDGET. . . . but indeed, Sir, as perfectly, perfectly, the same Man as before your going into *France*, Sir; as perfectly, perfectly, Sir.
HORNER. As perfectly, perfectly, Madam.

Olivia's repetition of *aversion* in *The Plain-Dealer* works in much the same way.

As an instance of Wycherley's good ear, in a somewhat odd situation, consider the scene in *The Plain-Dealer* in which Fidelia tries to turn Manly against Olivia by repeating the insults that have been heaped upon him:

FIDELIA. She call'd you ten thousand Ruffins.

MANLY. Hold, I say.

FIDELIA. Brutes—

MANLY. Hold.

FIDELIA. Sea-Monsters—

MANLY. Dam your intelligence: hear me a little now.

FIDELIA. Nay, surly Coward she call'd you too.

MANLY. Won't you hold yet? hold, or—

FIDELIA. Nay, Sir, pardon me; I cou'd not but tell you she had the baseness, the injustice, to call you Coward, Sir, Coward, Coward, Sir.

MANLY. Not yet?—

FIDELIA. I've done. Coward, Sir.

That last "Coward, Sir," the malicious afterthought, puts the topping on the whole exchange. Although this scene can be justified in terms of the play as a whole (the feeding of Manly's impatience), I suspect that Wycherley wrote it for its own sake. In the same way, I think that the Harcourt-Alithea-Sparkish scenes in *The Country-Wife* are more important as comic turns than they are as plot sequences. If I were going to criticize Wycherley as a man of the theater, I might do so on the grounds that he is so intent on providing his actors with nice bits that he occasionally interrupts the action of his play to make room for a routine. He is saved from being a writer of revues by the fact that the comic turns tend to have thematic relevance.

A brief introduction can do no more than scratch the surface of Wycherley's virtues as a playwright, and it should do no more with his weaknesses than hide them away in a relative clause here and there. Having scratched and hidden, I am tempted to go on to detailed analysis, thematic and dramatic, but that would demand a great many more pages than are here available to me. A few words will have to suffice. *Love in a Wood* seems to me Wycherley's most underrated play—one whose sardonic tone should appeal to a contemporary audience. The playwright uses a group of interlocking plots which seem designed to illustrate Lady Flippant's "Jone's as good as my Lady in the dark certainly." In a context in which deceit is the norm and lust and greed are the motivations, even Christina's virtue ("faithful Shepherdess," Flippant calls her) becomes a joke, and so it should, since her beloved but jealous Valentine has an opinion of her and all women that places him on a par with Pinchwife. *The Gentleman-Dancing-Master* is Wycherley's most tiresome play since its simple plot is stretched two acts too long to give the comic characters a chance to repeat often funny but monotonous routines; the mechanical delays in the action would only be acceptable if Hippolita were played as an out-and-out adolescent horror, a tease of the most unpleasant kind, and Gerrard as a comic butt. *The Country-Wife,* as Wycherley's best and funniest play, has served so often as an example in this introduction that I will add nothing to my comments on it except a warning to those readers who, like so many critics, are tempted to take Alithea as a character to be admired. As though it were not enough that she remains loyal to Sparkish long after the dullest person in the audience has recognized him for the fool he is, her sententious speech at the end of the play, "Come Brother your Wife is yet innocent . . . ," indicates that she is either as corrupt as Dorilant and the Quack, in covering for Horner, or as stupid as she has often seemed to be. *The Plain-Dealer,* which is too plot-heavy for my taste, is Wycherley's most brutal satire. The world we see is as vile and hypocritical as Manly thinks it is, but from the very beginning (when he receives Widow Blackacre only to get news of Olivia) he is seen as part of that hypocrisy; the ending, by which Manly, who has no discernible virtues, is rewarded with the loving Fidelia and her fortune, is the play's best joke and the most outrageous line may be Fidelia's confession that she has followed him "having in several publick places seen you, and observ'd your actions throughly, with admiration."

These thumbnail descriptions are unlikely to do more than provide the reader with a stick to beat the editor, but, then, every man to his own Rorschach.

TEXTUAL AND
BIBLIOGRAPHICAL NOTES

This edition seeks to provide a text of the Wycherley plays which conforms, as much as possible, with the first editions. Original spelling and punctuation have been retained, with a single exception—*then* has been changed to *than*. A few other silent editorial changes should be noted. I have corrected obvious typographical errors on the basis of errata lists, when they exist, or of later editions. The names of the speakers have been spelled out, as have words (*Ex.*, for instance) in stage directions. I have regularly placed stage directions at the end of the passages to which they refer. This is the general practice in the plays of the period, but in a few instances typography rather than stage action seems to have dictated where the direction falls on the page—sometimes in the middle of the speech to which it refers; it is these that I have moved to the end of the appropriate speeches. Any other changes are indicated in the notes. There, variant readings that seem to me important are also to be found. No attempt has been made to indicate the many variant readings—particularly in spelling and punctuation—of the later editions. Special problems are discussed in the headnotes to each play, where the editions consulted can be found. Aside from those cited, I have made use of the following collections of Wycherley's plays:

The Works of the Ingenious Mr. William Wycherley, London, 1713.

Plays, 2 vols., London, 1720.

The Dramatic Works of Wycherley, Congreve, Vanbrugh and Farquhar, ed. Leigh Hunt, London, 1840.

William Wycherley, ed. W. C. Ward, London, 1888.

The Complete Works of William Wycherley, ed. Montague
  Summers, 4 vols., London, 1924.

Hunt, as editor, was particularly careful about stage directions, providing those that earlier texts had failed to
give, and Summers, for all his idiosyncrasies and his occasional carelessness, was an important source of informa-
tion for explanatory notes.

In connection with each play, references are given in
full at the first mention except for the volumes listed
in the very selective bibliography that follows; these are
identified by author, editor, or title. Dates in all cases
have been converted to conform with the present calendar.

BIBLIOGRAPHY

Churchill, George B., "The Originality of William Wych-
  erley," *Schelling Anniversary Papers,* New York, 1923,
  pp. 65–85.
Connely, Willard, *Brawny Wycherley: First Master in
  English Modern Comedy,* New York, 1930.
Dennis, John. *The Critical Works of John Dennis,* ed. Ed-
  ward Niles Hooker, 2 vols., Baltimore, 1939–43.
Evelyn, John. *The Diary of John Evelyn,* ed. E. S. de
  Beer, 6 vols., Oxford, 1955.
Fujimura, Thomas H., *The Restoration Comedy of Wit,*
  Princeton, New Jersey, 1952.
Granville-Barker, Harley, "Wycherley and Dryden," *On
  Dramatic Method,* New York, 1956, pp. 117–157.
Hazlitt, William, *Lectures on the English Poets and the
  English Comic Writers,* London, 1894.
Holland, Norman N., *The First Modern Comedies: The
  Significance of Etherege, Wycherley and Congreve,*
  Cambridge, Massachusetts, 1959.
The London Stage, 1660–1700, Part 1, ed. William van
  Lennep (Carbondale, Illinois, 1965), of *The London
  Stage, 1660–1800:* A Calendar of Plays, Entertainments
  & Afterpieces, Together with Casts, Box-Receipts and
  Contemporary Comment; Compiled from the Playbills,
  Newspapers and Theatrical Diaries of the Period.

Macaulay, T. Babington, "Comic Dramatists of the Restoration," *Critical and Miscellaneous Essays*, IV, Philadelphia, 1843, pp. 8–66.

Nicoll, Allardyce, *A History of Restoration Drama, 1660–1700*, Cambridge, 1923.

Ogg, David, *England in the Reign of Charles II*, 2 vols., Oxford, 1934.

Pepys, Samuel. *The Diary of Samuel Pepys*, ed. Henry B. Wheatley, 8 vols., London, 1897.

Perromat, Charles, *William Wycherley, Sa Vie - Son Oeuvre*, Paris, 1921.

Pope, Alexander. *The Correspondence of Alexander Pope*, ed. George Sherburn, 5 vols., Oxford, 1956.

Rundle, James Urvin, "Wycherley and Calderón: A Source for *Love in a Wood*," PMLA, LXIV (September 1949), 701–707.

Vernon, P. F., *William Wycherley*, London, 1965.

Vincent, Howard P., "The Death of William Wycherley," *Harvard Studies and Notes in Philology and Literature*, XV (1933), 219–242.

Wilcox, John, *The Relation of Molière to Restoration Comedy*, New York, 1938.

Zimbardo, Rose A., *Wycherley's Drama: A Link in the Development of English Satire*, New Haven, Connecticut, 1965.

I should like to add a note that is neither textual nor bibliographical. This volume owes a great deal to the patience of the University of Pennsylvania library staff, particularly those in the Reference Department, the Rare Book Division, and Furness Memorial Library, and to the helpfulness of colleagues in several departments.

Gerald Weales
Philadelphia
August 23, 1965

LOVE IN A WOOD

Love in a Wood was presumably first performed in 1671 by the King's Company at the Drury Lane Theatre in Bridges Street. On the basis of a reference to Lenten performances in the Dedication, the premiere is assumed to have taken place in the spring; *The London Stage* (1, 181) lists it in March. It was entered in the *Stationers' Register*, October 6, 1671, and listed in the *Term Catalogues*, November 20, 1671; the first quarto is dated 1672 on the title page. There were editions of the play in 1693 and 1694.

The source of the Christina-Valentine-Ranger-Lydia plot, as J. U. Rundle has pointed out, is Calderón's *Mañanas de abril y mayo*, although Rundle, in examining the differences between the two plays, seems unnecessarily disappointed that Wycherley chose to make his own uses of what he borrowed. Leigh Hunt's notion that *Love in a Wood* was suggested by Sir Charles Sedley's *The Mulberry-Garden* (performed and published in 1668) was pretty much exploded by W. C. Ward and Montague Summers, although Willard Connely, in his desperate attempt to find something to put into his biography of the playwright, revived the theory. The similarity between the two plays is that some of the action of Sedley's takes place in the Mulberry Garden and that some of Wycherley's takes place in St. James's Park, where the Mulberry Garden was located, and that mistaken identities or conscious disguises in each case result from the setting. If a park setting were to be taken as evidence of a source, James Shirley's *Hyde Park*, which was revived in July 1668 after the introduction of *The Mulberry-Garden*, might be mentioned, although there is no real similarity between the plays of Shirley and Wycherley. Nor is there a connection in plot between *Love in a Wood* and another of Shirley's plays, *The Changes* (revived April 28, 1668), which, as Samuel Pepys indicates, was known by its subtitle, *Love in a Maze,* although it may have helped Wycherley choose his title. Since "in a wood" is an idiom for "confused," both titles mean the same thing. If *The Mulberry-Garden, Hyde Park,* and *The Changes,* all of which were performed by the King's Company, could be taken as definite influences, however slight, on *Love in a Wood,* it would be a fair guess that Wycherley began work on his play as early as 1668. This is a suggestion, not an assertion. As for other possible sources for the play, it is customary, following Ward, to suggest that Sir Simon dares Lady Flippant to cross the line in Act IV because such dares occur in *Les Cents Nouvelles Nouvelles* (No. 23) and Bandello's *Le Novelle* (I, 53); since the business in Wycherley is used in relation both to the plot and to Lady Flippant's character, its incidental resemblance to possible anecdotal sources is pretty much beside the point.

The epigraph from Horace is from *Ars Poetica,* lines 296–297: "Democritus excludes all sane poets from Helicon." It has nothing to do with the play.

The text for this edition is 1672 Q. I have also consulted 1694 Q. The quartos I used are those in the University of Pennsylvania library. I have regularly changed the lower case "i", as in *i'le,* to the capital, conforming in both instances to the 1694 Q. The lower case "i" turns up primarily in Act IV of 1672 Q which makes me suspect that it was set by a different printer than the other acts or that there was a shortage of capital "I's" in the shop at the time; since the capital "I" used in Act V often differs from that used elsewhere in the play, the second explanation is the more likely. In 1672 Q, a number of speeches, particularly early in the play, were set as though they were verse (see Lady Flippant's third speech), perhaps because the printer was used to setting verse plays. This edition retains the typography of those speeches, but the retention is not meant to imply that Wycherley intended the speeches to be read as verse.

Love in a Wood,

OR,

St James's Park.

A

COMEDY,

As it is Acted at the Theatre Royal, by his
Majesties Servants.

Written by Mr *WYCHERLEY.*

——*Excludit fanos helicone poetas*
Democritus ;—— Horat.

LONDON,

Printed by *J. M.* for *H. Herringman*, at the Sign of the *Blew
Anchor*, in the Lower-Walk of the New Exchange. 1672.

TO HER
GRACE
THE
Dutchess of
CLEAVLAND

MADAM,

*All Authors whatever in their Dedications are Poets;
but I am now to Write to a Lady, who stands as little in
need of Flattery, as her Beauty of Art; otherwise, I shou'd
prove as ill a Poet to her in my Dedication, as to my
Reader in my Play: I can do your Grace no Honour, nor
make you more admirers than you have already; yet I
can do my self the honour to let the world know, I am the
greatest you have; you will pardon me, Madam, for you
know, 'tis very hard for a new Author, and Poet too, to
govern his Ambition; for Poets, let them pass in the world
never so much, for modest, honest men, but begin praise
to others, which concludes in themselves; and are like
Rooks, who lend people money, but to win it back again,
and so leave them in debt to 'em for nothing; they offer
Laurel and Incense to their Hero's, but wear it themselves, and perfume themselves. This is true, Madam,
upon the honest word of an Author, who never yet writ
Dedication; yet though I cannot lye like them, I am as
vain as they, and cannot but publickly give your Grace
my humble acknowledgments for the favours I have receiv'd from you:[1] This, I say, is the Poets Gratitude, which
in plain English, is only Pride and Ambition; and that the
world might know your Grace did me the honour to see
my Play twice together; yet perhaps my Enviers of your
Favour will suggest 'twas in Lent,[2] and therefore for
your Mortification; then, as a jealous Author, I am concern'd not to have your Graces Favours lessen'd, or rather,
my reputation; and to let them know, you were pleas'd,
after that, to command a Copy from me of this Play;
the way without Beauty and Wit, to win a poor Poets
heart. 'Tis a sign your Grace understands nothing better,
than obliging all the world, after the best and most proper
manner; But, Madam, to be obliging to that excess as you*

are, (pardon me, if I tell you, out of my extream concern, and service for your Grace) is a dangerous quality, and may be very incommode to you; for Civility makes Poets as troublesom, as Charity makes Beggers; and your Grace will be hereafter as much pester'd with such scurvy Offerings as this, Poems, Panegyricks, and the like, as you are now with Petitions: And, Madam, take it from me, no man with Papers in's hand, is more dreadful than a Poet, no, not a Lawyer with his Declarations; Your Grace sure did not well consider what you did, in sending for my Play; you little thought I wou'd have had the confidence to send you a Dedication too: But, Madam, you find I am as unreasonable, and have as little conscience, as if I had driven the Poetick trade longer than I have, and ne're consider you had enough of the Play; but (having suffer'd now so severely) I beseech your Grace, have a care for the future, take my Counsel, and be (if you can possible) as proud, and ill-natur'd, as other people of Quality, since your quiet is so much concern'd, and since you have more reason than any to value your self; for you have that perfection of Beauty (without thinking it so) which others of your Sex, but think they have; that Generosity in your Actions, which others of your quality, have only in their Promises; that Spirit, Wit, and Judgment, and all other qualifications, which fit Hero's to command, and wou'd make any but your Grace proud. I begin now elevated by my Subject, to write with the Emotion and Fury of a Poet; yet the integrity of an Historian; and I cou'd never be weary, nay, sure this were my only way, to make my Readers never weary too, though they were a more impatient Generation of people than they are. In Fine, speaking thus of your Grace, I shou'd please all the world but you; therefore I must once observe, and obey you against my will, and say no more, than that I am,

MADAM,
    Your Grace's
        Most obliged, and most
        humble Servant,
WILLIAM WYCHERLEY

PROLOGUE

Custom, which bids the Thief from Cart Harangue,
All those that come to make, and see him hang,
Wills the damn'd Poet (though he knows he's gone)
To greet you, e're his Execution.
  Not having fear of Critick 'fore his eyes,
But still rejecting, wholsome, good advice;
He e'en is come to suffer here to day,
For counterfeiting (as you judge) a Play,
Which is against dread Phœbus highest treason,
Damn'd damning Judges, therefore you have reason;
You he do's mean, who for the self same fault,
That damning Priviledge of yours have bought;[1]
So the huge Bankers when they needs must fail,
Send the small Brothers of their trade to Goal;
Whilst they by breaking Gentlemen, are made,
Then more than any scorn, poor men o'th trade;[2]
You hardn'd Renegado Poets, who
Treat Riming Brother, worse than Turk wou'd do;
But vent your Heathenish rage, hang, draw, and quarter,
His Muse will dye to day a fleering[3] *Martyr;*
Since for ball'd Jest, dull Libel, or Lampoon,
There are who suffer persecution,
With the undaunted briskness of Buffon,
And strict Professors live of Raillery,
Defying Porters Lodge,[4] *or Pillory:*
For those who yet write on our Poets fate,
Shou'd as Co-sufferers commiserate;
But he in vain their pity now wou'd crave,
Who for themselves (alas) no pity have,
And their own gasping credit will not save;
And those, much less, our Criminal wou'd spare,
Who ne'r in Rhyme transgress, (if such there are)
Well then, who nothing hopes, needs nothing fear;
And he, before your cruel Votes shall do it,
By his despair, declares himself no Poet.

THE PERSONS

MR. HART.	MR. RANGER,
MR. BELL.	MR. VINCENT, } Young Gentlemen of the Town.
MR. KINNASTON.	MR. VALENTINE,
MR. LACY.	ALDERMAN GRIPE, seemingly precise, but a covetous, leacherous, old Usurer of the City.
MR. WINTERSELL.	SIR SIMON ADDLEPLOT, a Coxcomb, always in pursuit of Women of great Fortunes.
MR. MOHUN.	MR. DAPPERWIT, a brisk conceited, half-witted fellow of the Town.
MRS. BOUTELL.	CHRISTINA, VALENTINES Mistress.
MRS. BETTY COX.	LYDIA, RANGERS Mistress.
MRS. KNEPP.	MY LADY FLIPPANT, GRIPE'S Sister, an affected Widow, in distress for a Husband, though still declaiming against marriage.
MRS. FARLOWE.	MRS. MARTHA, GRIPE'S Daughter.
MRS. CORY.	MRS. JOYNER, a Match-maker, or precise City Bawd.
MRS. RUTTER.	MRS. CROSSBITE, an old cheating Jilt, and Bawd to her Daughter.
MRS. BETTY SLADE.	MISS LUCY, her Daughter.
MRS. JAMES.	ISABEL, CHRISTINA'S Woman.
MRS. GARTREIGHT.	LEONORE, Servant to LYDIA.

CROSSBITES Landlord, and his Prentices, Servants, Waiters, and other Attendants.

THE SCENE

LONDON.

Crossbite: deceive. The implication is that a crossbiter is one who cheats someone attempting to cheat him. See the couplet in Dapperwit's final speech.

LOVE IN A WOOD
OR
ST JAMES'S PARK

Act I. Scene i.

GRIPES *House in the Evening.*

Enter My Lady FLIPPANT, *Mrs.* JOYNER.

FLIPPANT. Not a Husband to be had for mony.
  Come, come, I might have been a better House-Wife
  for my self (as the World goes now,) if I had dealt for
  an Heir with his Guardian, Uncle, or Mother-in-Law;
  and you are no better than a Chouse, a Cheat.

JOYNER. I a Cheat Madam.

FLIPPANT. I am out of my Mony, and my Patience too.

JOYNER. Do not run out of your patience whatever you do,
  'Tis a necessary virtue for a Widow without
  A Joynture in truly.

FLIPPANT. Vile Woman, though my Fortune be something
  Wasted, my Person's in good repair;
  If I had not depended on you, I had had a Husband
  Before this time; when I gave you the last five pound,
  Did not you promise I should be Marryed by Christmass.

JOYNER. And had kept my promise if you had Cooperated.

FLIPPANT. Cooperated, what should I have done?
  'Tis well known no Woman breathing could use more
  Industry to get her a Husband than I have;
  Has not my Husbands Scutcheon walk'd as much ground
  As the Citizens Signs since the Fire,[1]
  That no quarter of the Town might be ignorant
  Of the Widow *Flippant,*

JOYNER. 'Tis well known Madam indeed.

FLIPPANT. Have I not own'd my self (against my
  Stomach) the relict of a Citizen to credit my Fortune?

JOYNER. 'Tis confest Madam.

FLIPPANT. Have I not constantly kept *Covent-Garden-*
  Church, St. *Martins,* the Play-Houses, *Hide-Park, Mul-*
  bery-Garden, and all other the publick Marts where
  Widows and Mayds are expos'd?[2]

JOYNER. Far be it from me to think you have an
Aversion to a Husband;
But why Madam have you refus'd so many good Offers?

FLIPPANT. Good Offers Mrs. *Joyner*, I'll be sworn
I never had an Offer since my late Husbands; if I had
had an Offer Mrs. *Joyner*; there's the thing Mrs. *Joyner*.

JOYNER. Then your frequent, and publick detestation of
Marriage, is thought real;
And if you have had no Offer, there's the thing Madam.

FLIPPANT. I cannot deny, but I always rail against Marriage
Which is the Widows way to it certainly.

JOYNER. 'Tis the desperate way, of the desperate
Widows, in truly.

FLIPPANT. Wou'd you have us as tractable as the
Wenches that eat Oatmeal; and fool'd like them too.

JOYNER. If no body were wiser than I, I should think,
since the Widow wants the natural alurement which
the Virgin has, you ought to give men all other incour-
agements in truly.

FLIPPANT. Therefore on the contrary, because the Widows Fortune (whether suppos'd, or real) is her chiefest
Bait, the more chary she seems of it, and the more she
withdraws it, the more eagerly the busie gaping frye
will bite: with us Widows Husbands are got like Bish-
opricks, by saying no; and I tell you, a young Heir is
as shie of a Widow, as of a Rook, to my knowledge.

JOYNER. I can alledge nothing against your practice,
But your ill success; and indeed you must use
Another Method with Sir *Simon Addleplot*.

FLIPPANT. Will he be at your House at the hour?

JOYNER. He'll be there by ten, 'tis now nine,
I warrant you he will not fail.

FLIPPANT. I'll warrant you then I will not fail,
For 'tis more than time I were sped.

JOYNER. Mr. *Dapperwit* has not been too busie with you,
I hope your experience has taught you to prevent a
mischance.

FLIPPANT. No, no, my mischance (as you call it) is greater
than that; I have but three Months to reckon, e're I lye

down with my Port and Equipage; and must be deliv-
ered of a Woman, a Foot-man, and a Coach-man. For
my Coach must down, unless I can get Sir *Simon* to
draw with me.

JOYNER. He will payr with you exactly if you knew all.

[*Aside.*

FLIPPANT. Ah Mrs. *Joyner,* nothing grieves me like putting
down my Coach; for the fine Cloathes, the fine Lodgings; let 'em go; for a Lodging is as unnecessary a thing
to a Widow that has a Coach, as a Hat to a Man that
has a good Peruque, for as you see about Town she is
most properly at home in her Coach, she eats, and
drinks, and sleeps in her Coach; and for her Visits she
receives them in the Play-house.

JOYNER. Ay, ay, let the Men keep Lodgings
(As you say Madam) if they will.

> GRIPE *and Sir* SIMON ADDLEPLOT *following him
> as his Man in the Habit of a Clarke at one door,
> and Mrs.* MARTHA *at the other.*

FLIPPANT. Do you think if things had been with me as
they have been, I would ever have hous'd with this
counter fashion Brother of mine, (who hates a Vest[3]
as much as a Surplice) to have my Patches assaulted
every day; at Dinner my Freedom sensured, and my
Visitants shut out of Doors; poor Mr. *Dapperwit* cannot
be admitted.

JOYNER. He knows him too well to keep his Acquaintance.

FLIPPANT. He is a censorious ridged Fop, and knows
nothing.

GRIPE. So, so—   [*Behind.*

JOYNER. Is he here?   [*Aside.*

Nay with your pardon Madam, I must contradict you
there. He is a prying Common-Wealths-man, an im-

Port: retinue.
Patches: small pieces of black
silk pasted to the face, to emphasize a good complexion or
to hide blemishes. Gripe's dis-
approval of patches is another
example of his being *counter
fashion.*

prying: diligently inquiring.
Since the word also had the
meaning that it still has today, Mrs. Joyner's praise of
Gripe, like most of the compliments they exchange for the
rest of the scene, is lightly
masked insult.

placable Majestrate, a sturdy pillar of his cause, and—
[*To my Lady* FLIPPANT.] But oh me is your Worship
so near then? if I had Thought you had heard me—

[*To* GRIPE.

GRIPE. Why, why Mrs. *Joyner*,
  I have said as much of my self e're now,
  And without vanity I profess.

JOYNER. I know your Virtue is proof against Vain-glory;
  But the truth to your face, looks like flattery in your
  Worships servant.

GRIPE. No, no, say what you will of me in that kind,
  Far be it from me to suspect you of flattery.

JOYNER. In truly your Worship knows your self,
  And knows me, for I am none of those—

FLIPPANT. Now they are in—   [*Aside.*
  Mrs. *Joyner* I'll go before to your House,
  You'll be sure to come after me.   [*Exit* FLIPPANT.

JOYNER. Immediately; but as I was saying,
  I am none of those—

GRIPE. No Mrs. *Joyner*, you cannot sew Pillows,
  Under Folks elbows; you cannot hold a Candle to the
  Divel; you cannot tickle a Trout to take him, you—

JOYNER. Lord how well you do know me indeed;
  And you shall see I know your Worship as well,
  You cannot backslide from your Principles;
  You cannot be terrify'd by the laws;
  Nor brib'd to Alegiance by Office or Preferment;
  You—

GRIPE. Hold, hold, my praise must not interrupt yours.

JOYNER. With your Worships pardon, (In truly) I must on.

GRIPE. I am full of your praise, and it will run over.

JOYNER. Nay sweet Sir, you are—

GRIPE. Nay sweet Mrs. *Joyner*, you are—

JOYNER. Nay good your Worship,   [*Stops her mouth*
  you are   *with his Hand-*
GRIPE. I say you are—   *kerchief.*]
JOYNER. I must not be rude with your Worship.

sew: sow. The phrase is a familiar proverb about flatter-ing, as are the others in Gripe's speech.

GRIPE. You are a Nursing mother to the Saints;
  Through you they gather together;
  Through you they fructify and encrease; and through
  you
  The Child cries from out of the Hand-Basket.

JOYNER. Through you Virgins are married or provided
  For as well; through you the Reprobates Wife
  Is made a Saint; and through you the Widow is not
  Disconsolate, nor misses her Husband.

GRIPE. Through you—

JOYNER. Indeed you will put me to the blush.

GRIPE. Blushes are badges of Imperfection,
  Saints have no shame: You are the flowr of
  Matrons Mrs. *Joyner.*

JOYNER. You are the Pink of curtious Aldermen.

GRIPE. You are the Muffler of Secresy.

JOYNER. You are the Head-band of Justice.

GRIPE. Thank you sweet Mrs. *Joyner,* do you think
  So indeed? you are—
  You are the Bonefire of Devotion.

JOYNER. You are the Bellows of Zeal.

GRIPE. You are the Cup-board of Charity.

JOYNER. You are the Fob of Liberality.

GRIPE. You are the Rivet of sanctify'd Love or Wedlock.

JOYNER. You are the Picklock and Dark-Lanthorn of Policy;
  And in a word, a Conventicle of Virtues.

GRIPE. Your Servant, your servant sweet Mrs. *Joyner,*
  You have stopt my mouth.

JOYNER. Your Servant, your servant sweet Alderman,
  I have nothing to say.

SIR SIMON. The half Pullet will be cold Sir.

GRIPE. Mrs. *Joyner* you shall Sup with me.

JOYNER. Indeed I am engag'd to 'Supper with some
  Of your man's Friends; and I came on purpose
  To get leave for him too.

GRIPE. I cannot deny you any thing; but I have forgot to

Fob: not only a small pocket,
as it is today, but also a trick,
a cheat.

tell you what a kind of Fellow my Sisters Dapperwit is; before a full Table of the Coffee-house *Sages* he had the impudence to hold an Argument against me in the defence of Vests and Protections; and therefore I forbid him my house; besides when he came, I was forc'd to lock up my Daughter for fear of him, nay, I think the poor Child her self was afraid of him: come hither Child, were you not afraid of Dapperwit?

MARTHA. Yes indeed, Sir, he is a terrible man.
Yet I durst meet with him in the Piazzo at midnight.
[*Aside.*

GRIPE. He shall never come into my doors again.

MARTHA. Shall Mr. *Dapperwit* never come hither again then?

GRIPE. No, Child.

MARTHA. I am afraid he will.

GRIPE. I warrant thee.

MARTHA. I warrant you then I'le go to him. [*Aside.*
I am glad of that, for I hate him as much as a Bishop.

GRIPE. Thou art no Child of mine, if thou dost not hate Bishops and Wits: Well, Mrs. *Joyner,* I'le keep you no longer. *Jonas,* wait on Mrs. *Joyner.*

JOYNER. Good night to your Worship.

GRIPE. But stay, stay Mrs. *Joyner,* have you spoken with the Widow *Crossbite* about her little Daughter, as I desir'd.

JOYNER. I will to morrow early, it shall be the first thing I'le do after my Prayers.

GRIPE. If *Dapperwit* should contaminate her; I cannot rest till I have redeem'd her from the Jaws of that Lyon, good night.

JOYNER. Good Gentleman. [*Exeunt* GRIPE *and* MARTHA.

Protections: documents guaranteeing immunity from arrest. From Gripe's Puritan standpoint, protections, which the king might grant to those in his service, were as much a sign of court fashion as vests were.

the Piazzo: an open arcade on two sides of Covent Garden, a popular rendezvous. Part of Act 5 of *The Country-Wife* takes place there.

Manent SIR SIMON ADDLEPLOT *and* JOYNER.

SIR SIMON. Hah, hah, ha, Mrs. *Joyner.*

JOYNER. What's the matter, Sir *Simon?*

SIR SIMON. Hah, hah, ha—let us make haste to your House, or I shall burst, faith and troth to see what Fools you and I make of these people.

JOYNER. I will not rob you of any of the credit, I am but a feeble Instrument, you are the Engeneer.

SIR SIMON. Remember what you say now when things succeed, and do not tell me then, I must thank your wit for all.

JOYNER. No in truly, Sir *Simon.*

SIR SIMON. Nay I'm sure *Dapperwit* and I have been partners in many an Intrigue, and he uses to serve me so.

JOYNER. He is an ill man to intrigue with, as you call it.

SIR SIMON. I, so are all your Wits; a pox, if a mans understanding be not so publick as theirs, he cannot do a wise action but they go away with the honour of it, if he be of their acquaintance.

JOYNER. Why do you keep such Acquaintance then?

SIR SIMON. There is a Proverb, Mrs. *Joyner,* You may know him by his Company.

JOYNER. No, no, to be thought a man of parts, you shou'd always keep Company with a man of less wit than your self.

SIR SIMON. That's the hardest thing in the world for me to do, faith and troth.

JOYNER. What, to find a man of less wit than your self? Pardon my Raillery, Sir *Simon.*

SIR SIMON. No, no, I cannot keep Company with a Fool, I wonder how men of parts can do't, there's something in't.

JOYNER. If you cou'd all your wise actions wou'd be your own, and your money wou'd be your own too.

SIR SIMON. Nay, faith and troth that's true; for your Wits are plaguely given to borrow; they'l borrow of their Wench, Coach-man, or Link-boy their hire. Mrs. *Joyner, Dapperwit* has that trick with a vengeance.

JOYNER. Why will you keep Company with him then, I say? for to be plain with you, you have followed him so long, that you are thought but his Culley; for every Wit has his Culley, as every Squire his lead Captain.[4]

SIR SIMON. I his Culley? I his Culley Mrs. *Joyner!* Lord that I should be thought a Culley to any Wit breathing.

JOYNER. Nay do not take it so to heart, for the best Wits Of the Town, are but Culleys themselves.

SIR SIMON. To whom, to whom, to whom, Mrs. *Joyner.*

JOYNER. To Sem'steresses, and Bawds.

SIR SIMON. To your knowledge, Mrs. *Joyner.* There I was with her.[5]

JOYNER. To Taylors and Vintners, but especially to the *French* Houses.

SIR SIMON. But *Dapperwit* is a Culley to none of them for he ticks.

JOYNER. I care not, but I wish you were a Culley to none but me, that's all the hurt I wish you,

SIR SIMON. Thank you Mrs. *Joyner;* well I will throw off *Dapperwits* acquaintance when I am marryed, and will only be a Culley to my Wife, and that's no more than the wisest Husband of 'em all is.

JOYNER. Then you think you shall carry Mrs. *Martha?*

SIR SIMON. Your hundred Guineys are As good as in your Lap.

JOYNER. But I am afraid this double plot of yours Should fail, you wou'd sooner succeed, If you only design'd upon Mrs. *Martha,* Or only upon my Lady *Flippant.*

SIR SIMON. Nay then you are no Woman of Intrigue, faith and troth 'tis good to have two strings to one Bow; if Mrs. *Martha* be coy; I tell the Widow I put on my disguise for her; But if Mrs. *Martha* be kind to *Jonas,* Sir *Simon Addleplot* will be false to the Widow, which is no more than Widows are us'd to, for a promise to a Widow is as seldome kept as a Vow made at Sea, as *Dapperwit* says.

Culley: dupe, sucker.   *ticks:* runs up bills.
French Houses: restaurants.

JOYNER. I am afraid they shou'd discover you.

SIR SIMON. You have nothing to fear, you have your twenty Guineys in your pocket for helping me into my Service,[6] and if I get into Mrs. *Martha's* quarters you have a hundred more, if into the Widdows fifty, happy goe luckey, will her Ladiship be at your house at the hour.

JOYNER. Yes.

SIR SIMON. Then you shall see when I am Sir *Simon Addle-plot* and my self, I'll look like my self, now I am *Jonas* I look like an Ass; you never thought Sir *Simon Addle-plot* cou'd have look'd so like an Ass by his ingenuity.

JOYNER. Pardon me Sir *Simon*.

SIR SIMON. Nay do not flatter faith and troth.

JOYNER. Come let us goe 'tis time.

SIR SIMON. I will carry the Widdow to the French house.

JOYNER. If she will goe.

SIR SIMON. If she will go; why, did you ever know a Widow refuse a treat? no more than a Lawyer a Fee faith and troth; yet I know too.
No treat, sweet words, good meen, but sly Intrigue
That must at length, the jilting Widow fegue. [*Exeunt.*

The Scene changes to the French *House, a Table,*
Wine, and Candles.

Enter VINCENT, RANGER, DAPPERWIT.

DAPPERWIT. Pray, Mr. *Ranger,* let's have no drinking to night.

VINCENT. Pray, Mr. *Ranger,* let's have no *Dapperwit* to night.

RANGER. Nay, nay, *Vincent*.

VINCENT. A pox, I hate his impertinent Chat more than he does the honest *Burgundy*.

DAPPERWIT. But why shou'd you force Wine upon us? we are not all of your gusto.

VINCENT. But why shou'd you force your chaw'd jests, your damn'd ends of your mouldy Lampoones, and last years Sonnets upon us, we are not all of your gusto?

meen: mien.
jilting: teasing.
fegue: whip or beat, but was used, as those words are to-day, in the sense of "get the best of."

DAPPERWIT. The Wine makes me sick, let me perish.

VINCENT. Thy Rhymes make me spew.

RANGER. At Reparty already, come *Vincent,* I know you would rather have him pledge you, here *Dapperwit;* [*Gives him the Glass.*] but why are you so eager to have him drink always.

VINCENT. Because he is so eager to talk always, and there is no other way to silence him.

Waiter to them.

WAITER. Here is a Gentleman desires to speak with Mr. *Vincent.*

VINCENT. I come.   [*Exit* VINCENT.

DAPPERWIT. He may drink because he is obliged to the Bottle, for all the wit and courage he has, 'tis not free and natural like yours.

RANGER. He has more courage than wit, but wants neither.

DAPPERWIT. As a Pump gone dry, if you powr no Water down you will get none out, so—

RANGER. Nay I bar similes too, to night.

DAPPERWIT. Why is not the thought new, don't you apprehend it.

RANGER. Yes, yes, but—

DAPPERWIT. Well, well, will you comply with his sottishness too, and hate brisk things in complaisance to the ignorant dull age? I believe shortly 'twill be as hard to find a patient friend to communicate ones wit to, as a faithful friend to communicate ones secret to. Wit has as few true Judges as painting I see.

RANGER. All people pretend to be judges of both.

DAPPERWIT. I they pretend—but set you aside,
And two more.—

RANGER. But why has *Vincent* neither courage nor wit.

DAPPERWIT. He has no courage because he beat his Wench for giving me *les douces yeux once;* and no wit because he does not comprehend my thoughts; and he is a Son of a Whore for his ignorance; I take ignorance worse from any man than the Lye, because it is as much as to say I am no Wit.

VINCENT *Returns.*

You need not take any notice, though, to him of what
I say.

VINCENT. *Ranger* there is a Woman below, in a Coach
wou'd speak with you.

RANGER. With me. [*Exit* RANGER.

DAPPERWIT. This *Ranger*, Mr. *Vincent*, is as false to his
Friend as his Wench.

VINCENT. You have no reason to say so,
But because he is absent.

DAPPERWIT. 'Tis disobliging to tell a Man of his faults to
his face, if he had but your grave parts, and manly wit,
I shou'd adore him; but a pox he is a meer Buffon, a
Jack-pudding let me perish.

VINCENT. You are an ungrateful fellow, I have heard him
maintain you had wit, which was more than ere you
cou'd do for your self; I thought you had own'd him
your Mæcenas.

DAPPERWIT. A pox he cannot but esteem me, 'tis for his
honour; but I cannot but be just for all that, without
favour or affection, yet I confess I love him so well, that
I wish he had but the hundredth part of your courage.

VINCENT. He has had the courage to save you from many
a beating to my knowledge.

DAPPERWIT. Come, come, I wish the man well, and next
to you, better than any man, and I am sorry to say it, he
has not a courage to snuff a Candle with his fingers;
when he is drunk indeed, he dares get a Clap, or so—
and swear at a Constable.

VINCENT. Detracting Fop, when did you see him desert
his Friend.

DAPPERWIT. You have a rough kind of Raillery Mr. *Vincent,* but since you will have it, (though I love the man
heartily, I say) he deserted me once in breaking of Windows, for fear of the Constable,

RANGER *Returns.*

but you need not take notice to him, of what I tell you;
I hate to put a man to the blush.

RANGER. I have had just now a visit from my Mistress, who is as jealous of me, as a Wife of her Husband when she lies in; My Cosin *Lydia*, you have heard me speak of her.

VINCENT. But she is more troublesom than a Wife that lies in, because she follows you to your haunts; why do you allow her that priviledge before her time?

RANGER. Faith, I may allow her any priviledge and be to hard for her yet; how do you think I have cheated her to night? Women are poor credulous Creatures, easily deceived.

VINCENT. We are poor credulous Creatures, when we think 'em so.

RANGER. Intending a Ramble to St. *James's* Park to night, upon some probable hopes of some fresh Game I have in chase, I appointed her to stay at home, with a promise to come to her within this hour, that she might not foil the scent and prevent my sport.

VINCENT. She'll be even with you when you are married I warrant you: in the mean time here's her health *Dapperwit.*

RANGER. Now had he rather be at the window writing her Anagram in the Glass with his Diamond, or biting his nails in the corner, for a fine thought, to come and divert us with at the Table.

DAPPERWIT. No a pox I have no wit to night, I am as barren and hide-bound as one of your damn'd scribling Poets, who are sotts in company for all their wit, as a Miser poor for all his mony; how do you like the thought.

VINCENT. Drink, drink.

DAPPERWIT. Well I can drink this, because I shall be re-preiv'd presently.

VINCENT. Who will be so civil to us.

DAPPERWIT. Sir *Simon Addleplot*, I have bespoke him a Supper here, for he treats to night a new rich Mistress.

RANGER. That Spark who has his fruitless designs upon the bed-ridden rich Widow, down to the sucking Heiresses in her pissing cloute; He was once the sport, but now the publick grievance of all the fortunes in Town;

for he watches them like a younger Brother that is afraid to be mump'd of his snip, and they cannot steal a Marriage, nor stay their stomachs, but he must know it.

DAPPERWIT. He has now pitch'd his Nets for *Gripe's* Daughter the rich Scrivener, and serves him as a Clerk to get admission to her, which the watchful Fop her Father, denies to all others.

RANGER. I thought you had been nibling at her once, under pretence of love to her Aunt.

DAPPERWIT. I confess I have the same design yet, and *Addleplot* is but my Agent whilst he thinks me his; he brings me Letters constantly from her, and carries mine back.

VINCENT. Still betraying your best friends.

DAPPERWIT. I cannot in honour but betray him (let me perish,) the poor young Wench is taken with my person, and wou'd scratch through fowr walls to come to me.

VINCENT. 'Tis a sign she is kept up close indeed.

DAPPERWIT. Betray him, I'll not be a Traytor to Love for any man.

    Sir SIMON ADDLEPLOT *to them with the Waiter.*

SIR SIMON. Know 'em, you are a sawcy Jack-straw to question me, (faith and troth) I know every body, and every body knows me.

ALL. Sir *Simon*, Sir *Simon*, Sir *Simon*.

RANGER. And you are a welcom man to every body.

SIR SIMON. Now son of a Whore, do I know the Gentlemen? a dog, he wou'd have had a shilling of me before he wou'd let me come to you.

RANGER. The Rogue has been bred at Court sure;
    Get you out Sirrah.

SIR SIMON. He has been bred at a *French* house, where they are more unreasonable.

VINCENT. Here's to you Sir *Simon*.

SIR SIMON. I cannot drink, for I have a Mistress within, though I wou'd not have the people of the house to know it.

mump'd of his snip: cheated
of his share.

RANGER. You need not be asham'd of your Mistresses, for they are commonly rich.

SIR SIMON. And because she is rich, I wou'd conceal her, for I never had a rich Mistress yet, but one or other got her from me presently faith and troth.

RANGER. But this is an ill place to conceal a Mistress in, every Waiter is an Intelligencer to your Rivals.

SIR SIMON. I have 'trick for that, I let no Waiters come into the Room, I'll lay the Cloth my self rather.

RANGER. But who is your Mistress.

SIR SIMON. Your Servant,—your Servant,— Mr. *Ranger*.

VINCENT. Come will you pledge me?

SIR SIMON. No, I'll spare your Wine, if you will spare me *Dapperwits* company, I came for that.

VINCENT. You do us a double favour, to take him and leave the Wine.

SIR SIMON. Come, come *Dapperwit*.

RANGER. Do not go unless he will suffer us to see his Mistress too.   [*Aside*.

SIR SIMON. Come, come man.

DAPPERWIT. Would you have me so incivil as to leave my company; they'll take it ill?

SIR SIMON. I cannot find her talk without thee; pray Gentlemen perswade Mr. *Dapperwit* to go with me.

RANGER. We will not hinder him of better company.

DAPPERWIT. Yours is too good to be left rudely.

SIR SIMON. Nay Gentlemen I wou'd desire your company too, if you knew the Lady.

DAPPERWIT. They know her as well as I, you say I know her not.

SIR SIMON. You are not every body.   [*Aside*.

RANGER. Perhaps we do know the Lady Sir *Simon*.

SIR SIMON. You do not, you do not, none of you ever saw her in your lives; but if you cou'd be secret, and civil.—

RANGER. We have drunk yet but our Bottle a peice.

SIR SIMON. But will you be civil Mr. *Vincent?*

RANGER. He dares not look a Woman in the face under three Bottles.

SIR SIMON. Come along then, but can you be civil Gentle-

men? will you be civil Gentlemen? pray be civil if you
can, and you shall see her.   [*Exit Sir* SIMON.
    Returns with my Lady FLIPPANT *and Mrs.* JOYNER.

DAPPERWIT. How has he got this Jilt[7] here?   [*Aside.*

RANGER. The widow *Flippant!*—   [*Aside.*

VINCENT. Is this the Woman we never saw.   [*Aside.*

FLIPPANT. Does he bring us into company, and *Dapperwit*
one? though I had marryed the Fool, I thought to have
reserv'd the Wit as well as other Ladies.   [*Aside.*

SIR SIMON. Nay, look as long as you will Madam, you will
find them civil Gentlemen and good Company.

FLIPPANT. I am not in doubt of their civility but yours.

JOYNER. You'll never leave snubbing your Servants, did
you not promise to use him kindly.   [*Behind.*

FLIPPANT. 'Tis true.   [*Aside.*
We wanted no good company, Sir *Simon*, as long as we
had yours.

SIR SIMON. But they wanted good company, therefore I
forc'd them to accept of yours.

FLIPPANT. They will not think the Company good they
were forc'd into certainly.

SIR SIMON. A pox I must be using the words in fashion
though I never have any luck with 'em, Mrs. *Joyner*
help me off.

JOYNER. I suppose, Madam, he means the Gentlemen
wanted not inclination to your company, but confidence
to desire so great an honour, therefore he forc'd 'em.

DAPPERWIT. What makes this Bawd here? sure Mistress
you Bawds should be like the small Cards, though at
first you make up the Pack, yet when the play begins,
you should be put out as useless.[8]

JOYNER. Well, well, jibeing companion, you wou'd have
the Pimps kept in only? you would so?

VINCENT. What they are quarrelling?

RANGER. Pimp and Bawd agree now a days like Doctor and
Apothecary.

SIR SIMON. Try Madam if they are not civil Gentlemen,
talk with 'em, while I go lay the cloath no Waiter comes
here: My Mother us'd to tell me, I should avoid all oc-

casions of talking before my Mistress, because silence is a sign of love as well as prudence.   [*Aside.*

FLIPPANT. Methinks you look a little yel- [*Sir* SIMON *lay-* low on't Mr. *Dapperwit;* I hope you   *ing the Cloath.*] do not sensure me because you find me passing away a night with this Fool; he is not a man to be jealous of sure.

DAPPERWIT. You are not a Lady to be jealous of sure.

FLIPPANT. No certainly, but why doe you look as if you were jealous then.

DAPPERWIT. If I had met you in *Wheatstones*-Park[9] with a drunken Foot-Soldier, I should not have been jealous of you.

FLIPPANT. Fye, fye, now you are jealous certainly, for people always when they grow jealous, grow rude; but I can pardon it since it proceeds from love certainly.

DAPPERWIT. I am out of all hopes to be rid of this eternal old acquaintance, when I jear her, she thinks her self prais'd, now I call her Whore in plain english, she thinks I am jealous.   [*Aside.*

FLIPPANT. Sweet Mr. *Dapperwit* be not so sensorious, I speak for your sake, not my own, for jealousie is a great torment, but my honor cannot suffer certainly.

DAPPERWIT. No certainly, but the greatest torment I have is your Love.

FLIPPANT. Alas sweet Mr. *Dapperwit,* indeed Love is a torment, but 'tis a sweet torment; but Jealousie is a bitter torment; I do not go about to cure you of the torment of my love.

DAPPERWIT. 'Tis a sign so.

FLIPPANT. Come, come, look up man, is that a Rival to contest with you?

DAPPERWIT. I will contest with no Rival, not with my old Rival your Coach-man, but they have heartily my resignation, and to do you a favour, but my self a greater, I will help tye the knot you are fumbling for now, betwixt your Culley here, and you.

yellow: jealous.

FLIPPANT. Go, go, I take that kind of jealousie worst of all, to suspect I would be debauch'd to beastly Matrimony; but who are those Gentlemen pray?—are they men of Fortunes Mrs. *Joyner.*

JOYNER. I believe so.

FLIPPANT. Do you believe so indeed; Gentlemen.—
    Advancing towards RANGER *and* VINCENT.

RANGER. If the civility we owe to Ladies, had not controul'd our envy to Mr. *Dapperwit,* we had interrupted e're this your private conversation.

FLIPPANT. Your interruption, Sir, had been most civil, and obliging, for our discourse was of Marriage.

RANGER. That is a subject Madam, as grateful as common.

FLIPPANT. O fye, fye, are you of that opinion too? I cannot suffer any to talk of it in my company.

RANGER. Are you married then Madam?

FLIPPANT. No certainly.

RANGER. I am sure so much Beauty cannot despair of it.

FLIPPANT. Despair of it—

RANGER. Only those that are married, or cannot be married, hate to hear of marriage.

FLIPPANT. Yet you must know, Sir, my aversion to marriage is such, that you nor no man breathing, shall ever perswade me to it.

RANGER. Curs'd be the man shou'd do so rude a thing as to perswade you to any thing against your inclination; I wou'd not do it for the World, Madam.

FLIPPANT. Come, come, though you seem to be a civil Gentleman, I think you no better than your Neighbours; I do not know a man of you all, that will not thrust a Woman up into a corner, and then talk an hour to her impertinently of marriage.

RANGER. You wou'd find me another man in a corner, I assure you, Madam, for you shou'd not have a word of marriage from me, whatsoever you might find in my actions of it; I hate talking as much as you.

FLIPPANT. I hate it extreamly.

RANGER. I am your man then, Madam, for I find just the

same fault with your Sex as you do with ours; I ne're cou'd have to do with a Woman in my life, but still she wou'd be impertinently talking of marriage to me.

FLIPPANT. Observe that, Mrs. *Joyner*. [*Aside*.

DAPPERWIT. Pray Mr. *Ranger* let's go, I had rather drink with Mr. *Vincent*, than stay here with you; besides 'tis Park-time.

RANGER. I come. [*To* DAPPERWIT.

Since you are a Lady that hate marriage, I'll do you the service to withdraw the company, for those that hate marriage, hate loss of time.

FLIPPANT. Will you go then, Sir, but before you go, Sir, pray tell me is your aversion to marriage real?

RANGER. As real as yours.

FLIPPANT. If it were no more real than mine. [*Aside*.

RANGER. Your servant, Madam.

FLIPPANT. But do you hate marriage certainly?

[*Plucks him back*.

RANGER. Certainly.

FLIPPANT. Come, I canot believe it, you dissemble it, only because I pretend it.

RANGER. Do you but pretend it then, Madam?

FLIPPANT. I shall discover my self— [*Aside*.

I mean, because I hold against it, you do the same in complaisance; for I have heard say, cunning men think to bring the coy and untractable women to tameness, as they do some mad people by humoring their frenzies.

RANGER. I am none of those cunning men, yet have too much wit to entertain the presumption of designing upon you.

FLIPPANT. 'Twere no such presumption neither.

DAPPERWIT. Come away, 'sdeath don't you see your danger?

RANGER. Those aims are for Sir *Simon*, good night, Madam.

FLIPPANT. Will you needs go then? the gentlemen are a going, Sir *Simon*, will you let 'em.

SIR SIMON. Nay, Madam, if you cannot keep 'em, how should I?

FLIPPANT. Stay, Sir, because you hate marriage, I'll sing
you a new Song against it.
She Sings.[10]

A S*pouse I do hate,*
For either she's false or she's jealous:
But give us a Mate,
Who nothing will ask us, or tell us.

She stands on no terms,
Nor chaffers by way of Indenture,
Her love for your Farms;
But takes her kind man at a venture.

If all prove not right,
Without an Act, Process, or Warning,
From Wife for a night,
You may be divorc'd in the morning.

When Parents are Slaves,
Their Bratts cannot be any other;
Great Wits, and great Braves,
Have always a Punk to their Mother.

FLIPPANT. Though it be the fashion for women of quality
to sing any Song whatever, because the words are not
distinguish'd; yet I should have blush'd to have done it
now, but for you, Sir.

RANGER. The Song is edifying, the Voice admirable, and
once more, I am your servant, Madam.

FLIPPANT. What, will you go too, Mr. *Dapperwit?*

SIR SIMON. Pray, Mr. *Dapperwit,* do not you go too.

DAPPERWIT. I am engag'd.

SIR SIMON. Well, if we cannot have their company, we will
not have their Room, ours is a private back Room; they
have paid their reckoning, let's go thither again.

FLIPPANT. But pray, sweet Mr. *Dapperwit,* do not go;
keep him Sir *Simon?*

SIR SIMON. I cannot keep him.

                [*Exeunt* VINCENT, RANGER, DAPPERWIT.

It is impossible; (the World is so,)

One cannot keep ones Friend, and Mistress too.

                        [*Exeunt Omnes.*

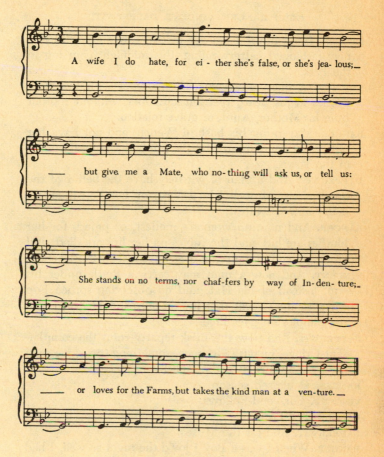

A wife I do hate, for ei-ther she's false, or she's jea-lous;— but give me a Mate, who no-thing will ask us, or tell us: She stands on no terms, nor chaf-fers by way of In-den-ture;— or loves for the Farms, but takes the kind man at a ven-ture.—

St. James's *Park at night.*

Enter RANGER, VINCENT, DAPPERWIT.

RANGER. Hang me if I am not pleas'd extreamly with this new fashioned catterwouling, this midnight coursing in the Park.

VINCENT. A man may come after Supper with his three Bottles in his head, reel himself sober, without reproof from his Mother, Aunt, or grave relation.

RANGER. May bring his bashful Wench, and not have her put out of countenance by the impudent honest women of the Town.

DAPPERWIT. And a man of wit may have the better of the dumb shew, of well trim'd Vest, or fair Perruque; no man's now is whitest.

RANGER. And now no woman's modest, or proud, for her blushes are hid, and the rubies on her lips are died, and all sleepy and glimmering eyes have lost their attraction.

VINCENT. And now a man may carry a Bottle under his arm, instead of his Hat, and no observing spruce Fop will miss the Crevat that lies on ones shoulder, or count the pimples on ones face.

DAPPERWIT. And now the brisk reparty ruins the complaisant Cringe, or wise Grimace, something 'twas, we men of virtue always lov'd the night.

RANGER. O blessed season.

VINCENT. For good-Fellows.

RANGER. For Lovers.

DAPPERWIT. And for the Muses.

RANGER. When I was a Boy I lov'd the night so well, I had a strong vocation to be a Bellman's Apprentice.

VINCENT. I a Drawer.[1]

DAPPERWIT. And I to attend the Waits of *Westminster*,[2] let me perish.

Bellman: night watchman.　　　*Drawer:* bartender.

RANGER. But why do we not do the duty of this and such
　　other places, walk, censure, and speak ill of all we meet?

DAPPERWIT. 'Tis no fault of mine, let me perish.

VINCENT. Fye, fye, Satyrical gentlemen, this is not your
　　time, you cannot distinguish a Friend from a Fop.

DAPPERWIT. No matter, no matter, they will deserve
　　amongst 'em the worst we can say.

RANGER. Who comes here, *Dapperwit?*

DAPPERWIT. By the toss of his head,　[*People walking*
　　training of his feet, and his elbows　*slowly over the*
　　playing at bo-peep behind his back, it　*Stage.*]
　　should be my Lord *Easy.*

RANGER. And who the woman?

DAPPERWIT. My Lord, what d'ye call's Daughter
　　That had a Child by—

VINCENT. *Dapperwit,* hold your tongue?

RANGER. How are you concern'd?

VINCENT. Her Brother's an honest Fellow, and will drink
　　his Glass.

RANGER. Prithee, *Vincent; Dapperwit* did not hinder drink-
　　ing to night, though he speak against it; why then
　　shou'd you interrupt his sport? now let him talk of any
　　body.

VINCENT. So he will, till you cut his throat.

RANGER. Why shou'd you in all ocasions thwart him, con-
　　temn him, and maliciously look grave at his jests only?

VINCENT. Why do's he always rail against my friends then,
　　and my best friend a Beer-glass?

RANGER. *Dapperwit,* be your own Advocate, my Game I
　　think is before me there?　　　　　　　　[*Exit* RANGER.

DAPPERWIT. This *Ranger,* I think has all the ill qualities,
　　of all your Town Fops, leaving his company for a spruce
　　Lord,
　　Or a Wench.

VINCENT. Nay, if you must rail at your own best friends, I
　　may forgive you, railing at mine.

　　LYDIA *and my Lady* FLIPPANT *walking over the* Stage.

LYDIA. False *Ranger,* shall I find thee here?　　　[*Aside.*

VINCENT. Those are women, are they not? [*To* DAPPERWIT.

DAPPERWIT. The least, seems to be my *Lucy* sure. [*Aside.*

VINCENT. Faith, I think I dare speak to a woman in the dark, let's try.

DAPPERWIT. They are persons of quality of my acquaintance; hold.

VINCENT. Nay, if they are persons of quality of your acquaintance, I may be the bolder with 'em.

The Ladies go off, they follow them;
LYDIA *and* FLIPPANT *re-enter.*

LYDIA. I come hither to make a discovery to night.

FLIPPANT. Of my love to you certainly; for no body but you cou'd have debauch'd me to the Park certainly; I wou'd not return another night, if it were to redeem my dear husband from his grave.

LYDIA. I believe you, but to get another Widow.

FLIPPANT. Another Husband, another Husband, foh!

LYDIA. There does not pass a night here, but many a match is made.

FLIPPANT. That a woman of honour shou'd have the word match in her mouth: but I hope, Madam, the fellows do not make honourable Love here, do they? I abominate honourable Love, upon my Honour.

LYDIA. If they should make honourable Love here, I know you would prevent 'em.

VINCENT *and* DAPPERWIT *Re-enter*
and walk slowly towards them.

But here come two men will inform you what they do.

FLIPPANT. Do they come? are they men certainly?

LYDIA. Prepare for an assault, they'l put you to't.

FLIPPANT. Will they put us to't certainly? I was never put to't yet; if they shou'd put us to't, I shou'd drop down, down certainly.

LYDIA. I believe, truly, you wou'd not have power to run away.

FLIPPANT. Therefore I will not stay the push they come, they come, oh the fellows come!

FLIPPANT *runs away,* LYDIA *follows, and* VINCENT,
and DAPPERWIT *after them.*
FLIPPANT *Re-enters at to'ther door alone.*

So I am got off clear, I did not run from the men, but my companion, for all their brags, men have hardly courage to set upon us, when our number is equal; now they shall see I defie 'em, for we women have always most courage when we are alone; but a Pox—the lazie Rogues come not, or they are Drunk and cannot run: Oh drink, abominable drink! instead of inflaming Love, it quenches it, and for one Lover it incourages, it makes a thousand impotent. Curse on all Wine, even Renish-Wine and Sugar—

    Enter ADDLEPLOT *muffled in a Cloak.*

But Fortune will not see me want, here comes a single Bully, I wish he may stand;

    For now anights the jostling Nymph is bolder,
    Than modern Satyr with his Cloak o're shoulder.
Well met Sir.   [*She puts on her Mask.*

SIR SIMON. How shall I know that, forsooth, who are you? do you know me?

FLIPPANT. Who are you? don't you know me?

SIR SIMON. Not I faith and troth.

FLIPPANT. I am glad on't, for no man e're lik'd a woman the better for having known her before.

SIR SIMON. I, but then one can't be so free with a new acquaintance, as with an old one; she may deny one the civility.

FLIPPANT. Not till you ask her.

SIR SIMON. But I am afraid to be deny'd.

FLIPPANT. Let me tell you, Sir, you cannot dis-oblige us women more, than in distrusting us.

SIR SIMON. Pish, what shou'd one ask for, when you know on's meaning? but shall I deal freely with you?

FLIPPANT. I love of my life men should deal freely with me; there are so few men will deal freely with one—

SIR SIMON. Are you not a Fireship? a Punk, Madam?

FLIPPANT. Well, Sir, I love Raillery.

SIR SIMON. Faith and troth I do not railly, I deal freely.

FLIPPANT. This is the time and place for freedom, Sir.

SIR SIMON. Are you handsom?

FLIPPANT. *Jone's* as good as my Lady in the dark certainly; but men that deal freely, never ask questions certainly.

Fireship, Punk: whore.

SIR SIMON. How then! I thought to deal freely, and put a woman to the question, had been all one.

FLIPPANT. But let me tell you, those that deal freely indeed, take a woman by—

SIR SIMON. What, what, what, what?

FLIPPANT. By the hand and lead her aside.

SIR SIMON. Now I understand you come along then.

Enter Torches and Musick at a distance.

FLIPPANT. What unmannerly Rascals are those that bring light into the Park? 'twill not be taken well from 'em by the women certainly; still disappointed—   [*Aside.*

SIR SIMON. Oh the Fidles, the Fidles, I sent for them hither to oblige the women, not offend 'em; for I intend to Serenade the whole Park to night; but my Frolick is not without an intrigue, faith and troth; for I know the Fidles will call the whole Herd of vizard Masks together; and then shall I discover if a stray'd Mistress of mine be not amongst 'em, whom I treated to night at the *French-house;* but as soon as the Jilt had eat up my meat, and drank her two bottles, she run away from me, and left me alone.

FLIPPANT. How! is it he! *Addleplot,* that I cou'd not know him by his faith and troth.   [*Aside.*

SIR SIMON. Now I wou'd understand her tricks, because I intend to Marry her, and shou'd be glad to know what I must trust to.

FLIPPANT. So thou shalt, but not yet.   [*Aside.*

SIR SIMON. Though I can give a great guess already; for if I have any intrigue or sense in me, she is as arrant a Jilt, as ever pull'd pillow from under husbands head (faith and troth) moreover she is bow-legg'd, hopper-hipp'd, and betwixt Pomatum and Spanish Red, has a Complexion like a Holland Cheese,[3] and no more Teeth left, than such as give a Haust-goust[4] to her breath; but she is rich (faith and troth.)

hopper-hipp'd: big-assed.
Pomatum: face cream.
Spanish Red: rouge.

FLIPPANT. Oh Rascal! he has heard some body else say all this of me; but I must not discover my self, lest I should be disappointed of my revenge, for I will marry him.

[*Aside*.

The Torches and Musick approaching.

Exit FLIPPANT.

SIR SIMON. What gone? come then, strike up my lads.

Enter Men and Women in Vizards, and Dance.
ADDLEPLOT *for the most part standing still
in a Cloak and Vizard,
but sometimes going about peeping,
and examining the Womens cloaths;
the Dance ended.*[5]

Exeunt Dancers, Torches, Musick, and ADDLEPLOT.

Enter FLIPPANT, LYDIA, *after them* VINCENT, DAPPERWIT.

FLIPPANT. Nay, if you stay any longer, I must leave you again.   [*To* LYDIA.

VINCENT. We have over-taken them at last again, these are they, they separate too, and that's but a challenge to us.   [FLIPPANT *going off*.

DAPPERWIT. Let me perish Ladies—

LYDIA. Nay, good Madam, let's unite, now here's the common enemy upon us.

VINCENT. Dam me Ladies—

DAPPERWIT. Hold, a Pox you are to rough, let me perish Ladies.

LYDIA. Not for want of breath, Gentlemen, wee'l stay rather.

DAPPERWIT. For want of your favour, rather sweet Ladies.

FLIPPANT. That's *Dapperwit*, false villain; but he must not know I am here; if he should, I should lose his thrice agreeable company, and he would run from me, as fast as from the Bayliffs. What you will not talk with 'em I hope?

LYDIA. Yes, but I will.

FLIPPANT. Then you are a Park-woman certainly, and you will take it kindly if I leave you.

LYDIA. No, you must not leave me.   [*Apart*.

FLIPPANT. Then you must leave them.

LYDIA. I'le see if they are worse company than you first.

FLIPPANT. Monstrous impudence, will you not come?

[*Pulls* LYDIA.

VINCENT. Nay, Madam, I never suffer any violence to be us'd to a woman, but what I do my self; she must stay, and you must not go.

FLIPPANT. Unhand me you rude fellow.

VINCENT. Nay, now I am sure you will stay and be kind; for coyness in a woman is as little sign of true modesty, as huffing in a man, is of true courage.

DAPPERWIT. Use her gently, and speak soft things to her.

LYDIA. Now do I guess I know my Coxcomb.   [*Aside.*
Sir, I am extremely glad I am fallen into the hands of a Gentleman, that can speak soft things; and this is so fine a night to hear soft things in; morning I shou'd have said.

DAPPERWIT. It will not be morning, dear Madam, till you pull off your Mask; that I think was brisk—   [*Aside.*

LYDIA. Indeed, dear Sir, my face would frighten back the Sun.

DAPPERWIT. With glories, more radient than his own;
          I keep up with her I think.   [*Aside.*

LYDIA. But why wou'd you put me to the trouble of lighting the World, when I thought to have gone to sleep?

DAPPERWIT. You only can do it, dear Madam, let me perish.

LYDIA. But why wou'd you (of all men) practice Treason against your friend *Phœbus*, and depose him for a meer stranger?

DAPPERWIT. I think she knows me.   [*Aside.*

LYDIA. But he does not do you justice, I believe, and you are so positively cock-sure of your wit, you wou'd refer to a meer stranger your Plea to the Bay-tree.

DAPPERWIT. She jears me, let me perish.   [*Aside.*

VINCENT. *Dapperwit*, a little of your aid, for my Lady's invincibly dumb.

DAPPERWIT. Wou'd mine had been so too.   [*Aside.*

VINCENT. I have us'd as many arguments to make her speak, as are requisite to make other women hold their tongues.

DAPPERWIT. Well, I am ready to change sides, yet before
I go, Madam; since the Moon consents, now I shou'd see
your face, let me desire you to pull off your Mask,
which to a handsom Lady is a favour, I'm sure.

LYDIA. Truly, Sir, I must not be long in debt to you the
obligation;[6] pray, let me here you recite some of your
verses, which to a Wit, is a favour I'm sure.

DAPPERWIT. Madam, it belongs to your sex to be oblidg'd
first; pull off your Mask, and I'll pull out my paper.

Brisk again of my side.   [*Aside.*

LYDIA. 'Twou'd be in vain, for you wou'd want a Candle
now.

DAPPERWIT. I dare not make use again of the lustre of her
face: [*Aside.*] I'll wait upon you home then, Madam.

LYDIA. Faith no, I believe it will not be much to our advantages, to bring my face, or your Poetry to light, for I
hope, you have yet a pretty good opinion of my face,
and so have I of your wit; but if you are for proving
your wit, why do not you write a Play?

DAPPERWIT. Because 'tis now no more reputation to write a
Play, than it is honour to be a Knight: your true wit
despises the title of Poet, as much as your true gentleman the title of Knight; for as a man may be a Knight
and no Gentleman, so a man may be a Poet and no
Wit, let me perish.

LYDIA. Pray, Sir, how are you dignifi'd or distinguish'd
amongst the rates of Wits? and how many rates are
there?

DAPPERWIT. There are as many degrees of Wits, as of
Lawyers; as there is first your Sollicitor, then your Atur-
ney, then your Pleading-Counsel, then your Chamber-
Counsel, and then your Judge; so there is first your
Court-Wit, your Coffee-Wit, your Poll-Wit or Pollitick-
Wit, your Chamber-Wit or Scribble-Wit, and last of all,
your Judg-Wit or Critick.

LYDIA. But are there as many Wits as Lawyers? Lord,
what will become of us? what employment can they
have? how are they known?

DAPPERWIT. First, your Court-Wit is a fashionable, insinuating, flattering, cringing, grimacing, fellow; and has wit
enough to sollicit a suit of Love; and if he fail, he has
malice enough to ruin the woman with a dull Lampoon,
but he rails still at the man that is absent, for you must
know, all Wits rail; and his wit properly lies in combing
Perruques, matching Ribbonds, and being severe as they
call it, upon other peoples cloaths.

LYDIA. Now, what is the Coffee-Wit?

DAPPERWIT. He is a lying, censorious, gossiping, quibling
wretch, and sets people together by the ears over that
sober drink Coffee;[7] he is a Wit, as he is a commenta-
tor upon the Gazet, and he rails at the Pyrats of *Algiere*,
the Grand Signior of *Constantinople*, and the Christian
Grand Signior.[8]

LYDIA. What kind of man is your Poll-Wit?

DAPPERWIT. He is a fidgeting, busie, dogmatical, hot-
headed Fop, that speaks always in sentences and proverbs, (as others in similitudes) and he rails perpetually
against the present government; his Wit lies in projects
and monopolies, and penning speeches for young
Parliament men.

LYDIA. But what is your Chamber-Wit or Scribble-Wit?

DAPPERWIT. He is a poring, melancholy, modest Sot,
asham'd of the world; he searches all the Records of
Wit, to compile a breviate of them for the use of Players, Printers, Book-sellers, and sometimes Cooks, and
Tabacca-men;[9] he imploys his railing against the ignorance of the age, and all that have more mony
than he.

LYDIA. Now your last.

DAPPERWIT. Your Judg-Wit or Critick, is all these together,
and yet has the wit to be none of them; he can think,
speak, write, as well as all the rest, but scorns (himself
a Judg) to be judg'd by posterity; he rails at all the
other Classes of Wits, and his wit lies in damming all
but himself: he is your true Wit.

Gazet: The London Gazette,   for the most part with news
a semi-official journal, dealing   from abroad.

LYDIA. Then, I suspect you are of his Form.

DAPPERWIT. I cannot deny it, Madam.

VINCENT. *Dapperwit,* you have been all this time on the wrong side, for you love to talk all, and here's a Lady wou'd not have hindred you.

DAPPERWIT. A pox, I have been talking too long indeed here; for Wit is lost upon a silly weak woman, as well as courage. [*Aside.*

VINCENT. I have us'd all common means to move a womans tongue and mask; I call'd her ugly, old, and old acquaintance, and yet she wou'd not disprove me: but here comes *Ranger,* let him try what he can do, for since my Mistress is dogged, I'll go sleep alone. [*Exit.*

RANGER *Enters.*

LYDIA. *Ranger!* 'tis he indeed; I am sorry he is here, but glad I discovered him before I went, yet he must not discover me, lest I should be prevented hereafter, in finding him out, false *Ranger.* [*Aside.*
Nay, if they bring fresh force upon us, Madam, 'tis time to quit the Field. [*Exeunt* LYDIA, FLIPPANT.

RANGER. What, play with your quarrey till it fly from you.

DAPPERWIT. You frightned it away.

RANGER. Ha! is not one of those Ladies in mourning?

DAPPERWIT. All women are so by this light.

RANGER. But you might easily descern it, don't you know her?

DAPPERWIT. No.

RANGER. Did you talk with her?

DAPPERWIT. Yes, she's one of your brisk silly Baggages.

RANGER. 'Tis she, 'tis she, I was afraid I saw her before, let us follow 'em, prithee make haste.
'Tis *Lydia.* [*Aside.*
[*Exeunt.*[10]

LYDIA, *my Lady* FLIPPANT *return at the other door,*
RANGER, DAPPERWIT, *following them at a distance.*

LYDIA. They follow us yet I fear.

FLIPPANT. You do not fear it certainly, otherwise, you wou'd not have encourag'd them.

LYDIA. For heavens sake, Madam, wave your quarrel a little; and let us pass by your Coach, and so on foot to

your acquaintance in the old *Pell-mell;* for I wou'd
not be discover'd by the man that came up last to us.
[*Exeunt.*

The Scene changes to CHRISTINA's *Lodging.*

Enter CHRISTINA, ISABEL.

ISABEL. For Heavens sake undress your self, Madam; they'l
not return to night, all people have left the Park an
hour agoe.

CHRISTINA. What is't a Clock?

ISABEL. 'Tis past one.

CHRISTINA. It cannot be.

ISABEL. I thought, that time had only stolen from happy
Lovers; the Disconsolate have nothing to do but to tell
the Clock.

CHRISTINA. I can only keep account with my misfortunes.

ISABEL. I am glad they are not innumerable.

CHRISTINA. And truly my undergoing so often your impertinency, is not the least of them.

ISABEL. I am then more glad, Madam, for then they cannot
be great, and it is in my power, it seems, to make you
in part happy, if I cou'd but hold this villanous tongue
of mine, but then let the people of the Town hold their
tongues if they will, for I cannot but tell you what they
say.

CHRISTINA. What do they say?

ISABEL. Faith, Madam, I am afraid to tell you, now I think
on't.

CHRISTINA. Is it so ill?

ISABEL. Oh, such base unworthy things.

CHRISTINA. Do they say, I was really *Clerimont's* Wench
as he boasted; and that the ground of the quarrell betwixt *Valentine* and him, was not *Valentines* vindication
of my honour, but *Clerimonts* jealousie of him.

ISABEL. Worse, worse a thousand times, such villanous
things to the utter ruin of your reputation.

old Pell-mell: the present Pall
Mall. The street got its name
from the game which was
originally played there; it was

"old" because the new site of
the game, established after the
Restoration, was the Mall in St.
James's Park.

CHRISTINA. What are they?

ISABEL. Faith, Madam, you'l be angry, 'tis the old trick of Lovers to hate their informers, after they have made 'em such.

CHRISTINA. I will not be angry.

ISABEL. They say then, since Mr. *Valentines* flying into *France*, you are grown mad, have put your self into Mourning, live in a dark room, where you'l see no body, nor take any rest day or night, but rave and talk to your self perpetually.

CHRISTINA. Now what else?

ISABEL. But the surest sign of your madness is, they say, because you are desperately resolv'd (in case my Lord *Clerimont* should dye of his wounds, to Transport your self and Fortune into *France*, to Mr. *Valentine*, a man that has not a groat to return you in exchange.

CHRISTINA. All this hitherto, is true; now to the rest.

ISABEL. Indeed, Madam, I have no more to tell you, I was sorry, I'm sure, to hear so much of any Lady of mine.

CHRISTINA. Insupportable insolence.

ISABEL. This is some revenge for my want of sleep to night; so I hope my old second is come; 'tis seasonable relief.
[*Aside.*

[*Knocking at the door. Exit* ISABEL.

CHRISTINA. Unhappy *Valentine*, cou'dst thou but see how soon thy absence, and mis-fortunes have disbanded all thy Friends, and turn'd thy Slaves all Renegades, thou sure wou'dst prize my only faithful heart.

Enter my Lady FLIPPANT, LYDIA, ISABEL, *to her.*

FLIPPANT. Hail faithful Shepherdess;[11] but truly, I had not kept my word with you, in coming back to night, if it had not been for this Lady, who has her intrigues too with the fellows, as well as you.

LYDIA. Madam, under my Lady *Flippants* protection, I am confident to beg yours; being just now pursu'd out of the Park, by a relation of mine, by whom it imports me extreamly not to be discover'd; but I fear he is now at the door. [*Knocking at the door.*] Let me desire you to deny me to him couragiously, for he will [*To* ISABEL hardly believe he can be mistaken in me. *going out.*]

CHRISTINA. In such an occasion where impudence is requisite, she will serve you, as faithfully as you can wish, Madam.

FLIPPANT. Come, come, Madam, do not upbraid her with her assurance, a qualification that only fits her for a Ladies Service; a fine Woman of the Town, can be no more without a woman that can make an excuse with an assurance, than she can be without a glass certainly.

CHRISTINA. She needs no Advocate.

FLIPPANT. How can any one alone manage an amorous intrigue; though the Birds are tame, some body must help draw the Net; if 'twere not for a Woman that could make an excuse with assurance, how shou'd we whedle, jilt, trace, discover, countermine, undermine, and blow up the stinking fellows, which is all the pleasure I receive, or design by them; for I never admitted a man to my conversation, but for his punishment certainly.

CHRISTINA. No body will doubt that, certainly.

ISABEL *returns.*

ISABEL. Madam, the Gentleman will not be mistaken, he says you are here, he saw you come in; he is your Relation, his name's *Ranger,* and is come to wait upon you home; I had much ado to keep him from coming up.

LYDIA. Madam, for Heavens sake help me, 'tis yet in your power, if but while I retire into your Dining-room, you will please to personate me, and own your self, for her, he pursu'd out of the Park; you are in Mourning too, and your Stature so much mine, it will not contradict you.   [*To* CHRISTINA.

CHRISTINA. I am sorry, Madam, I must dispute any command of yours; I have made a resolution to see the face of no man, till an unfortunate Friend of mine, now out of the Kingdom, return.

LYDIA. By that Friend, and by the hopes you have to see him, let me conjure you to keep me from the sight of mine now; Dear Madam, let your charity prevail over your superstition.

ISABEL. He comes, he comes Madam.

RANGER *enters.*

LYDIA *withdraws and stands unseen at the door.*

RANGER. Ha! this is no *Lydia.*

CHRISTINA. What unworthy defamer has encouraged you to offer me this insolence.

RANGER. She is liker *Lydia* in her style, than her face; I see I am mistaken, but to tell her I follow'd her for another, were an affront, rather than an excuse; she's a glorious creature.   [*Aside.*

CHRISTINA. Tell me, Sir, whence had you reason for this your rude pursuit of me, into my Lodging, my Chamber; why should you follow me?

RANGER. Faith, Madam, because you run away from me.

CHRISTINA. That was no sign of an acquaintance.

RANGER. You'l pardon me Madam.

CHRISTINA. Then it seems you mistook me for another, and the night is your excuse, which blots out all distinctions: but now you are satisfyed in your mistake, I hope, you will go seek out your Woman in another place.

RANGER. Madam, I allow not the excuse you make for me; if I have offended, I will rather be condemned for my love, than pardon'd for my insensibility.

LYDIA. How's that?   [*behind.*

CHRISTINA. What do you say?

RANGER. Though the night had been darker, my heart wou'd not have suffer'd me to follow any one but you; he has been too long acquainted with you, to mistake you.

LYDIA. What means this tenderness; he mistook me for her sure?   [*behind.*

CHRISTINA. What says the Gentleman? did you know me then Sir?

RANGER. Not I, the Devil take me, but I must on now.
                                               [*Aside.*

Cou'd you imagine, Madam, by the innumerable crowd of your admirers, you had left any man free in the Town, or ignorant of the power of your Beauty.

CHRISTINA. I never saw your face before, that I remember.

RANGER. Ah Madam! you wou'd never regard your humb'lest Slave; I was till now a modest Lover.

LYDIA. Falsest of men.   [*behind.*

CHRISTINA. My woman said, you came to seek a Relation here, not a Mistress.

RANGER. I must confess, Madam, I thought you wou'd sooner disprove my dissembled error, than admit my visit; and I was resolv'd to see you.

LYDIA. 'Tis clear.   [*behind.*

RANGER. Indeed, when I follow'd you first out of the Park, I was afraid you might have been a certain Relation of mine, for your Statures and Habits are the same; but when you enter'd here, I was with joy convinc'd: Besides, I would not for the world have given her troublesom love, so much encouragement, to have disturb'd my future addresses to you; for the foolish woman do's perpetually torment me, to make our relation nearer; but never more in vain, than since I have seen you, Madam.

LYDIA. How shall I suffer this? 'tis clear he disappointed me to night for her, and made me stay at home, that I might not disappoint him of her company in the Park.
                                                         [*behind.*

CHRISTINA. I am amaz'd! but let me tell you, Sir, if the Lady were here, I wou'd satisfie her, the sight of me shou'd never frustrate her ambitious designs upon her cruel Kinsman.

LYDIA. I wish you cou'd satisfie me.   [*behind.*

RANGER. If she were here, she wou'd satisfie you, she were not capable of the honour to be taken for you (though in the dark) faith, my Cousin is but a tolerable woman to a man that had not seen you.

CHRISTINA. Sure to my Plague, this is the first time you ever saw me?

RANGER. Sure to the Plague of my poor heart, 'tis not the hundredth time I have seen you; for since the time I saw you first, you have not been at the Park, Play-house, Exchange, or other publick place, but I saw you; for it was my business to watch and follow you.

Exchange: the New Exchange in the Strand, an arcade of shops and a popular spot at the time. Most of the third act of *The Country-Wife* takes place there.

CHRISTINA. Pray, when did you see me last at the Park, Play-house, or Exchange.

RANGER. Some two, three days, or a week ago.

CHRISTINA. I have not been this month out of this Chamber.

LYDIA. That is to delude me.   [*behind.*

CHRISTINA. I knew you were mistaken.

RANGER. You'll pardon a Lovers memory, Madam.
A pox, I have hang'd my self in my own line, one would think, my perpetual ill luck in lying, should break me of the quality; but like a loosing Gamster, I am still for pushing on, till none will trust me.   [*Aside.*

CHRISTINA. Come, Sir, you run out of one error into a greater, you would excuse the rudeness of your mistake, and intrusion at this hour, into my Lodgings, with your gallantry to me, more unseasonable and offensive.

RANGER. Nay, I am in Love I see, for I blush, and have not a word to say for my self.

CHRISTINA. But, Sir, if you will needs play the Gallant, pray leave my House before Morning, lest you should be seen go hence, to the scandal of my honour.

CHRISTINA.[12] Rather than that shou'd be, I'll call up the House and Neighbours to bear witness, I bid you be gon.

RANGER. Since you take a night-visit so ill, Madam, I will never wait upon you again, but by day; I go, that I may hope to return, and for once, I will wish you a good night without me.

CHRISTINA. Good night, for as long as I live. [*Exit* RANGER.

LYDIA. And good night to my Love, I'm sure.   [*Behind.*

CHRISTINA. Though I have done you an inconsiderable service, I assure you, Madam, you are not a little oblig'd to me. Pardon me dear Valentine.   [*Aside.*

LYDIA. I know not yet, whether I am more oblig'd than injur'd; when I do I assure you, Madam, I shall not be insensible of either.

CHRISTINA. I fear, Madam, you are as liable to mistakes, as your Kinsman.

LYDIA. I fear, I am more subject to 'em, it may be for want of sleep, therefore I'll go home.

CHRISTINA. My Lady *Flippant,* good night.

FLIPPANT. Good night, or rather good morrow, faithful Shepherdess.

CHRISTINA. I'll wait of you down.

LYDIA. Your Coach stays yet, I hope.

FLIPPANT. Certainly. [*Exeunt Omnes.*

Enter RANGER, DAPPERWIT.

The Scene, the Street.

DAPPERWIT. I was a faithful Sentinel, no body came out, let me perish.

RANGER. No, no, I hunted upon a wrong scent; I thought I had follow'd a Woman, but found her an Angel.

DAPPERWIT. What is her name?

RANGER. That you must tell me; What very fine woman is there lies hereabouts?

DAPPERWIT. Faith, I know not any, she is I warrant you some fine woman, of a Terms standing or so in the Town;[13] such as seldom appear in publick, but in their Balcones, where they stand so constantly, one would think they had hir'd no other part of the House.

RANGER. And look like the Pictures, which Painters expose to draw in Customers; but I must know who she is, *Vincents* Lodging is hard by, I'll go and enquire of him, and lye with him to night; but if he will not let me, I'll lye with you, for my lodging is too far off—

DAPPERWIT. Then I will go before, and expect you at mine. [*Exeunt.*

The Scene, VINCENTS *Lodging.*

Enter VINCENT, VALENTINE, *in a riding habit, as newly from a Journey.*

VINCENT. Your Mistress, dear *Valentine,* will not be more glad to see you; but my wonder is no less than my joy, that you wou'd return ere you were inform'd *Clerimont* were out of danger; his Surgeons themselves, have not been assur'd of his recovery, till within these two days.

VALENTINE. I fear'd my Mistress, not my Life; my Life I cou'd trust again with my old enemy Fortune; but not longer, my Mistress, in the hands of my greater Enemies, her Relations.

VINCENT. Your fear was in the wrong place then, for though my Lord *Clerimont* live, he and his Relations, may put you in more danger of your life, than your[14] Mistresses Relations can of loosing her.

VALENTINE. Wou'd any cou'd secure me her, I wou'd my self secure my life, for I should value it then.

VINCENT. Come, come, her Relations can do you no hurt; I dare swear, If her Mother shou'd but say, your Hat did not cock handsomly, she wou'd never ask her blessing again.

VALENTINE. Prythee leave thy fooling, and tell me, if since my departure, She has given evidences of her love, to clear those doubts I went away with, for as absence is the bane of common and bastard Love; 'tis the vindication of that, which is true and generous.

VINCENT. Nay, if you cou'd ever doubt her love, you deserve to doubt on; for there is no punishment great enough for jealousie, but jealousie.

VALENTINE. You may remember, I told you before my flight, I had quarrell'd with the defamer of my Mistress, but thought I had kill'd my Rival.

VINCENT. But pray give me now the answer, which the suddenness of your flight deny'd me; how cou'd *Clerimont* hope to subdue her heart, by the assault of her honour?

VALENTINE. Pish, it might be the stratagem of a Rival, to make me desist.

VINCENT. For shame, if 'twere not rather to vindicate her, than satisfie you, I wou'd not tell you, how like a *Penelope* she has behav'd her self in your absence.

VALENTINE. Let me know.

VINCENT. Then know, the next day you went, she put her self into mourning, and—

VALENTINE. That might be for *Clerimont,* thinking him dead, as all the world besides thought.

VINCENT. Still turning the daggers point on your self, hear me out; I say she put her self into mourning for you—

lock'd up her self in her chamber, this month for you—
shut out her barking Relations for you—has not seen the
Sun, or face of man, since she saw you—thinks, and talks
of nothing but you—sends to me daily, to hear of you—
and in short (I think) is mad for you—all this I can
swear, for I am to her so near a Neighbour, and so inquisitive a friend for you—

Servant to them.

SERVANT. Mr. *Ranger,* Sir, is coming up.

VINCENT. What brings him now? he comes to lye with me.

VALENTINE. Who, *Ranger?*

VINCENT. Yes, pray retire a little, till I send him off, unless
you have a mind to have your arrival publish'd to morrow, in the Coffee-houses.

RANGER. What, not yet a-bed? your man is laying you to
sleep with Usquebaugh or Brandy, is he not so?

[VALENTINE *retires to the door behind.*

VINCENT. What Punk will not be troubled with you to
night, therefore I am, is it not so?

RANGER. I have been turn'd out of doors indeed just now,
by a Woman, but such a Woman, *Vincent*—

VINCENT. Yes, yes, your women are always such women.—

RANGER. A Neighbour of yours, and I'm sure the finest
you have.

VINCENT. Prythee do not asperse my Neighbourhood with
your acquaintance; 'twould bring a scandal upon an
Alley.

RANGER. Nay, I do not know her, therefore I come to you.

VINCENT. 'Twas no wonder, she turn'd you out of doors
then; and if she had known you, 'twould have been a
wonder she had let you stay; but where does she live?

RANGER. Five doors off on the right hand.[15]

VINCENT. Pish, pish—

RANGER. What's the matter?

VINCENT. —Does she live there, do you say?

RANGER. Yes, I observ'd them exactly, that my account
from you, might be as exact; do you know who lives
there?

VINCENT. Yes, so well, that I know you are mistaken.

RANGER. Is she not a young Lady scarce eighteen, of extraordinary beauty, her stature next to low, and in mourning?

VALENTINE. What is this?   [Behind.

VINCENT. She is; but if you saw her, you broke in at window.

RANGER. I chas'd her home from the Park, indeed, taking her for another Lady who had some claim to my heart, 'till she shew'd a better title to't.

VINCENT. Hah, hah, hah.

VALENTINE. Was she at Park then? and have I a new Rival?   [Behind.

VINCENT. From the Park did you follow her, do you say? I knew you were mistaken.

RANGER. I tell you I am not.

VINCENT. If you are sure, it was that house, it might be perhaps her woman stollen to the Park, unknown to her Lady.

RANGER. My acquaintance does usually begin with the Maid first, but now 'twas with the Mistress, I assure you.

VINCENT. The Mistress! I tell you, she has not been out of her doors since *Valentines* flight; she is his Mistress, the great Heiress *Christina*.

RANGER. I tell you then again, I followed that *Christina* from the Park home, where I talk'd with her half an hour, and intend to see her to morrow again.

VALENTINE. Would she talk with him too?   [behind.

VINCENT. It cannot be.

RANGER. *Christina*, do you call her? faith I am sorry she is an Heiress, lest it should bring the scandal of interest, and design of lucre upon my Love.

VINCENT. No, no, her face and vertues will free you from that censure; but however, 'tis not fairly done to Rival your friend *Valentine* in his absence; and when he is present, you know 'twil be dangerous, by my Lord *Clerimont's* example; faith if you have seen her, I would not advise you to attempt it again.

RANGER. You may be merry, Sir, you are not in Love; your advise I came not for, nor will I for your assistance; good night.   [Exit RANGER.

VALENTINE. Here's your *Penelope,* the woman that had not
seen the Sun, nor face of Man, since my departure; for
it seems she goes out in the night, when the Sun is absent, and faces are not distinguish'd.

VINCENT. Why, do you believe him?

VALENTINE. Shou'd I believe you?

VINCENT. 'Twere more for your interest, and you wou'd be
less deceiv'd; if you believe him, you must doubt the
chastity of all the fine Women in Town, and five miles
about.

VALENTINE. His reports of them, will little invallidate his
testimony with me.

VINCENT. He spares not the Innocents in Bibs and Aprons
(I'le secure you) he has made (at best) some gross
mistake concerning *Christina,* which to morrow will discover; in the mean time let us go sleep.

VALENTINE. I will not hinder you, because I cannot enjoy
it my self;

Hunger, Revenge, to sleep are petty Foes,

But only Death the jealous Eyes can close.   [*Exeunt.*

ACT III. SCENE I.

CROSSBITES *House.*

Enter Mrs. JOYNER, *Mrs.* CROSSBITE.

JOYNER. Good morrow, Gossip.

CROSSBITE. Good morrow; but why up so early good
Gossip?

JOYNER. My care and passionate concern for you, and
yours, wou'd not let me rest (intruly.)

CROSSBITE. For me and mine?

JOYNER. You know, we have known one another long; I
think it be some nine and thirty years since you were
marryed.

CROSSBITE. Nine and thirty years old Mistress? I'de have
you to know, I am no far born Child; and if the Register

had not been burn'd in the last great fire alas; but my face needs no Register sure: nine and thirty years old said you, Mistress?

JOYNER. I said you had been so long marryed; but, indeed, you bear your years as well as any she in *Pepper-Alley*.[1]

CROSSBITE. Nine and thirty, Mistress.

JOYNER. This it is; a woman now-adays, had rather you should find her faulty with a man, I warrant you, than discover her age, I warrant you.

CROSSBITE. Marry and 'tis the greater secret far; tell a Miser he is rich, and a Woman she is old; you will get no money of him, nor kindness of her: to tell me I was nine and thirty (I say no more) 'twas unneighbourly done of you, Mistress.

JOYNER. My memory confesses my age, it seems, as much as my face, for I thought—

CROSSBITE. Pray talk, nor think no more of any ones Age; but say, what brought you hither so early?

JOYNER. How does my sweet God-daughter? poor wretch.

CROSSBITE. Well, very well.

JOYNER. Ah sweet Creature; alas, alas, I am sorry for her.

CROSSBITE. Why, what has she done to deserve your sorrow, or my reprehension?

LUCY *comes to the door.*

LUCY. What are they talking of me?   [*behind.*

JOYNER. In short, she was seen going into the Meeting-house of the Wicked, otherwise called the Play house, hand in hand, with that vile fellow *Dapperwit.*

CROSSBITE. Mr. *Dapperwit;* let me tell you, if 'twere not for Master *Dapperwit,* we might have liv'd all this Vacation upon Green Cheese, Tripe, and Ox-cheek; if he had it, we should not want it; but poor Gentleman, it often goes hard with him, for he's a Wit.

JOYNER. So then, you are the Dog to be fed, while the house is broken up; I say beware, the sweet bits you swallow, will make your daughters belly swell, Mistress; and after all your Junkets, there will be a bone for you to pick, Mistress.

CROSSBITE. Sure, Master *Dapperwit* is no such manner of man?

JOYNER. He is a Wit, you say, and what are Wits? but contemners of Matrons, Seducers, or Defamers of married Women, and Deflourers of helpless Virgins, even in the Streets, upon the very Bulks; Affronters of midnight Magistracy, and Breakers of Windows in a word.

CROSSBITE. But he is a little-Wit, a modest-wit, and they do no such outragious things, as your great Wits do.

JOYNER. Nay, I dare say, he will not say himself he is a little-Wit, if you ask him.

LUCY. Nay, I cannot hear this with patience;   [*Aside.* with your pardon mother, you are as much mistaken, as my God-mother in *Mr. Dapperwit;* for he is as great a Wit as any, and in what he speaks or writes, as happy as any; I can assure you, he contemns all your tearing Wits, in comparison of himself.

JOYNER. Alas, poor young wretch, I cannot blame thee so much as thy mother, for thou art not thy self; his bewitching Madrigals have charm'd thee into some Heathenish Imp with a hard name.

LUCY. Nymph, you mean God-mother.

JOYNER. But you Gossip, know what's what; yestarday, as I told you, a fine Old Alderman of the City, seeing your Daughter in so ill hands as *Dapperwits,* was Zealously, and in pure Charity, bent upon her redemption; and has sent me to tell you, he will take her into his care, and relieve your necessities, if you think good.

CROSSBITE. Will he relieve all our necessities?

JOYNER. All.

CROSSBITE. Mine, as well as my Daughters?

JOYNER. Yes.

CROSSBITE. Well fare his heart; d'y here Daughter, *Mrs. Joyner* has satisfy'd me clearly; *Dapperwit* is a vile fellow, and in short, you must put an end to that scandalous familiarity between you.

LUCY. Leave sweet *Mr. Dapperwit—* Oh furious in-

Bulks: stalls outside shops.   tearing: grand.

gratitude! was not he the man that gave me my first Farrenden Gown, put me out of Worsted Stockings, and plain Handkerchiefs, taught me to dress, talk, and move well.

CROSSBITE. He has taught you to talk indeed; but Huswife, I will not have my pleasure disputed.

JOYNER. Nay, indeed you are too tart with her, poor sweet Soul.

LUCY. He taught me to rehearse too, wou'd have brought me into the Play-house, where I might have had as good luck as others: I might have had good Cloaths, Plate, Jewels, and things so well about me; that my Neighbours, the little Gentlemens Wives, of Fifteen hundred, or Two thousand pound a year, should have retir'd into the Country, sick with envy, of my prosperity and greatness.

JOYNER. If you follow your mothers counsel, you are like to enjoy all you talk of sooner; than by *Dapperwits* assistance; a poor wretch that goes on tick for the Paper he writes his *Lampoons* on; and the very Ale and Coffee that inspires him as they say.

CROSSBITE. I am credibly informed so, indeed, Madam *Joyner*.

JOYNER. Well, I have discharg'd my Conscience; good morrow to you both.   [*Exeunt.*

Enter DAPPERWIT, RANGER;

CROSSBITES *Dining-room.*

DAPPERWIT. This is the Cabinet, in which I hide my Jewel, a small house, in an obscure, little, retired street too.

RANGER. Vulgarly an Alley.

DAPPERWIT. Nay, I hid my Mistress, with as much care, as a Spark of the Town do's his money from his Dun, after a good hand at Play; and nothing but you cou'd

Farrenden: farandine, cloth, partly silk, partly wool or hair. To get into a gown that was partly silk was, for Lucy, like getting out of worsted stockings, a step toward gentility—in dress, at least. In Act v, however, Mrs. Joyner suggests the jump from farandine to satin.

have wrought upon me for a sight of her, let me perish.

RANGER. My obligation to you is great; do not lessen it by delays, of the favour you promised.

DAPPERWIT. But do not censure my honour, for if you had not been in a desperate condition—for as one nail must beat out another, one poyson expel another, one fire draw out another, one fit of drinking cure the sickness of another; so the Surfeit you took last night of *Christina's* eyes, shall be cured by *Lucy's* this morning, or as—

RANGER. Nay, I bar more similitudes.

DAPPERWIT. What, in my Mistresses lodging? that were as hard as to bar a young Parson in the Pulpit, the fifth of *November*, railing at the Church of *Rome*,[2] or as hard as to put you to bed to *Lucy*, and defend you touching her, or as—

RANGER. Or as hard as to make you hold your tongue— I shall not see your Mistress, I see?

DAPPERWIT. Miss *Lucy*, Miss *Lucy*— [*Knocks at the door, and returns.*] the Devil take me, if good men (I say no more) have not been upon their knees to me, to see her, and you at last must obtain it.

RANGER. I do not believe you.

DAPPERWIT. 'Tis such a she, she is beautiful, without affectation, amorous without impertinency, airy, and brisk without impudence, frolick without rudeness; and in a word, the justest creature breathing to her asignation.[3]

RANGER. You praise her, as if you had a mind to part with her; and yet you resolve, I see, to keep her to your self.

DAPPERWIT. Keep her, poor Creature, she cannot leave me; and rather than leave her, I wou'd leave writing Lampoons or Sonnets almost.

RANGER. Well, I'le leave you with her then.

DAPPERWIT. What, will you go without seeing her?

RANGER. Rather than stay without seeing her.

DAPPERWIT. Yes, yes, you shall see her; but let me perish if I have not been offered a hundred Guinnies, for a sight of her; by—I say no more.

RANGER. I understand you now; [*Aside.*] if the favour be to be purchased, then I'le bid all I have about me for't.

DAPPERWIT. Fye fye, *Mr. Ranger*, you are pleasant i'faith; do you think I would sell the sight of my rarity? like those Gentlemen who hang out Flags at *Charing-cross*,[4] or like—

RANGER. Nay, then I'm gone again.

DAPPERWIT. What, you take it ill I refuse your money? rather than that shou'd be, give us it; but take notice I will borrow it; now I think on't, *Lucy* wants a Gown, and some Knacks.

RANGER. Here.

DAPPERWIT. But I must pay it you again; I will not take it, unless you engage your honour, I shall pay it you again.

RANGER. You must pardon me; I will not engage my honour for such a trifle; go fetch her out.

DAPPERWIT. Well, she's a ravishing Creature, such eyes, and lips, *Mr. Ranger*.

RANGER. Prethee go.

DAPPERWIT. Such neck and breasts, Mr. *Ranger*.

RANGER. Again, prethee go.

DAPPERWIT. Such feet, legs, and thighs, *Mr. Ranger*.

RANGER. Prethee let me see 'em.

DAPPERWIT. And a mouth no bigger than your Ring; I need say no more.

RANGER. Wou'd thou wer't never to speak again.

DAPPERWIT. And then so neat, so sweet a Creature in bed, that to my knowledge, she do's not change her Sheets in half a year.

RANGER. I thank you for that allay to my impatience.

DAPPERWIT. Miss *Lucy*, Miss *Lucy*, Miss.

[*Knocking at the dore.*

RANGER. Will she not open?

DAPPERWIT. I am afraid, my prety Miss is not stirring, and therefore will not admit us.

DAPPERWIT.[5] Fye, Fye, a quibble next your stomach in a morning; what if she shou'd hear us, wou'd you lose a Mistress for a quibble? that's more than I cou'd do, let me perish.

Knacks: trinkets.

RANGER. Is she not gone her walk to Lambs Conduit?

DAPPERWIT. She is within, I hear her.

RANGER. But she will not hear you; she's as deaf, as if you were a Dun or a Constable.

DAPPERWIT. Pish, give her but leave to gape, rub her eyes, and put on her day-Pinner; the long patch under the left eye; awaken the Roses on her cheeks, with some Spanish wool, and warrant her breath with some Lemmon Peil; the dore flies off of the hindges, and she into my arms; she knows there is as much Artifice to keep a victory, as to gain it; and 'tis a sign she values the conquest of my heart.

RANGER. I thought her beauty had not stood in need of Art.

DAPPERWIT. Beauty's a Coward, still without the help of Art, and may have the fortune of a Conquest, but cannot keep it; Beauty and Art can no more be asunder, than Love and Honour.

RANGER. Or to speak more like your self, wit and judgment.

DAPPERWIT. Don't you hear the dore wag yet?

RANGER. Not a whit.

DAPPERWIT. Miss, Miss, 'tis your slave that calls; come, all this tricking for him; lend me your Comb, Mr. *Ranger*.

RANGER. No, I am to be preferred to day, you are to set me off; you are in possession; I will not lend you arms to keep me out—

DAPPERWIT. A Pox, don't let me be ungrateful; if she has smugg'd her self up for me, let me Prune, and Flounce my Perruque a little for her; there's ne're a young fellow in the Town but will do as much, for a meer stranger in the Play-house.

RANGER. A Wits Wig, has the priviledge of being uncomb'd in the very Play-house, or in the presence—

Lambs Conduit: Lamb's Conduit Fields, named for a reservoir and conduit built by William Lamb in 1577, lay north of the City. It was a popular walk for people who lived around Holborn. It would have been quite a stroll for Lucy, if we are to take Mrs. Joyner's Pepper-Alley remark as evidence that the Crossbites lived in Southwark.

DAPPERWIT. But not in the presence of his Mistress; 'tis a greater neglect of her than himself; pray lend me your Comb.

RANGER. I wou'd not have men of Wit, and Courage, make use of every Fops mean Arts, to keep, or gain a Mistress.

DAPPERWIT. But don't you see every day, though a man have ne're so much Wit and Courage, his Mistress will revolt to those Fops that wear, and Comb Peruques well; I'le break off the bargain, and will not receive you, my Partner.

RANGER. Therefore you see I am setting up for my self.
                                        [*Combs his Perruque.*

DAPPERWIT. She comes, she comes, pray, your Comb.
                                  [*Snatches* RANGERS *Comb.*
            Enter Mrs. CROSSBITE *to them.*

CROSSBITE. Bargain, what are you offering us to sale?

DAPPERWIT. A Pox, is't she? here take your Comb again then.   [*Returns the Comb.*

CROSSBITE. Wou'd you sell us? 'tis like you y'fads.

DAPPERWIT. Sell thee, where shou'd we find a Chapman? go prithee mother, call out my dear Miss *Lucy.*

CROSSBITE. Your Miss *Lucy;* I do not wonder you have the Conscience to bargain for us behind our backs, since you have the impudence to claim a propriety in us, to my face.

RANGER. How's this *Dapperwit?*

DAPPERWIT. Come, come, this Gentleman will not think the worse of a Woman, for my acquaintance with her; he has seen me bring your Daughter to the Leur with a Chiney Orange, from one side of the Play-house, to the other.

CROSSBITE. I wou'd have the Gentleman, and you to know, my Daughter is a Girl of reputation, though she has been seen in your company; but is now so sensible of her past danger, that she is resolv'd never more to venture her Pitcher to the Well, as they say.

DAPPERWIT. How's that Widow? I wonder at your new confidence.

Chiney Orange: Dapperwit's lure, the sweet orange (*Citrus sinensis*), a popular fruit, was sold in the theater.

CROSSBITE. I wonder at your old impudence, that where you have had so frequent repulses, you shou'd provoke another, and bring your Friend here to witness your disgrace.

DAPPERWIT. Hark you Widow a little.

CROSSBITE. What, you have Mortgaged my Daughter to that Gentleman; and now wou'd offer me a snip to joyn in the security.

DAPPERWIT. She over-heard me talk of a bargain; 'twas unlucky; [*Aside.*] your wrath is grounded upon a mistake: Miss *Lucy* her self shall be judge, call her out pray.

CROSSBITE. She shall not, she will not come to you.

DAPPERWIT. Till I hear it from her own mouth, I cannot believe it.

CROSSBITE. You shall hear her say't through the dore.

DAPPERWIT. I shall doubt it, unless she say it to my face.

CROSSBITE. Shall we be troubled with you no more then?

DAPPERWIT. If she command my death, I cannot dis-obey her.

CROSSBITE. Come out Child.

[LUCY (*holding down her head*) *to them.*

DAPPERWIT. Your Servant dearest Miss, can you have?—

CROSSBITE. Let me ask her.

DAPPERWIT. No, I'le ask her.

RANGER. I'le throw up Cross or Pile who shall ask her.

DAPPERWIT. Can you have the heart to say, you will never more break a Cheese-cake with me, at New Spring-garden, the Neat-house, or *Chelsey;*[6] never more sit in my lap at a New Play, never more wear a Suit of Knots of my choice; and last of all, never more pass away an afternoon with me again, in the Green Garret? in—do not forget the Green Garret.

LUCY. I wish I had never seen the Green Garret; Demm the Green Garret.

DAPPERWIT. Demm the Green Garret, you are strangely alter'd.

LUCY. Tis you are alter'd.

Cross or Pile: heads or tails.   *Suit of Knots:* bow of ribbons.

DAPPERWIT. You have refus'd *Colby's* Mulberry Garden,[7] and the French-houses, for the Green Garret; and a little something in the Green Garret, pleas'd you more than the best Treat the other places cou'd yield; and can you of a sudden quit the Green Garret?

LUCY. Since you have a design to Pawn me for the Rent, 'tis time to remove my Goods.

DAPPERWIT. Thou art extremely mistaken.

LUCY. Besides, I have heard such strange things of you this morning—

DAPPERWIT. What things?

LUCY. I blush to speak 'em.

DAPPERWIT. I know my Innocence, therefore take my charge as a favour; what have I done?

LUCY. Then know vile Wit, my mother has confess'd just now, thou wer't false to me, to her too certain knowledge; and hast forc'd even her to be false to me too.

DAPPERWIT. Faults in drink, *Lucy,* when we are not our selves, shou'd not condemn us.

LUCY. And now to let me out to hire like Hackney; I tell you my own dear mother shall bargain for me no more; there are as little as I can bargain for themselves now-adays, as well as properer women.

CROSSBITE. Whispering all this while; beware of his snares again, come away Child.

DAPPERWIT. Sweet, dear, *Miss.*

LUCY. Bargain for me; you have reckon'd without your Hostess, as they say, bargain for me, bargain for me.

[*Exit* LUCY.

DAPPERWIT. I must return then, to treat with you.

CROSSBITE. Treat me no treatings, but take a word for all; you shall no more dishonour my Daughter, nor molest my Lodgings, as you have done at all hours.

DAPPERWIT. Do you intend to change 'em, then, to *Bridewel,* or *Longs* powdering-Tub.[8]

Bridewel: Bridewell, originally a house for paupers, had become a house of correction. Since in Charles II's time prostitutes were often held there, Dapperwit is certainly not commenting on Crossbite's economic condition; he is calling her a whore.

CROSSBITE. No, to a Bailifs house, and then you'll be so civil, I presume, as not to trouble us.

RANGER. Here, will you have my Comb again, *Dapperwit?*

DAPPERWIT. A pox, I think women take inconstancy from me, worse than from any man breathing.

CROSSBITE. Pray, Sir, forget me, before you write your next Lampoon.   [*Exit* CROSSBITE.

Sir SIMON ADDLEPLOT *in the dress of a Clark.*

To RANGER *and* DAPPERWIT.

SIR SIMON. Have I found you? have I found you, in your by-walks, faith and troth? I am almost out of breath in following you; Gentlemen when they get into an Alley, walk so fast; as if they had more earnest business there, than in the broad streets.

DAPPERWIT. How came this Sot hither? Fortune has sent him to ease my choler.   [*Aside.*
You impudent Rascal, who are you? that dare intrude thus on us.   [*Strikes him.*

SIR SIMON. Don't you know me, *Dapperwit?* sure you know me.   [*Softly.*

DAPPERWIT. Wilt thou dishonour me with thy acquaintance too? thou rascally, insolent, pen and ink-man.
     [*Strikes him again.*

SIR SIMON. Oh, oh sure, you know me, pray know me.
     [*Speak softly.*

DAPPERWIT. By thy sawcy familiarity, thou shou'dst be a Marker at a Tennis-court, a Barber, or a Slave that fills Coffee.

SIR SIMON. Oh, oh.

DAPPERWIT. What art thou?   [*Kicks him.*

SIR SIMON. Nay, I must not discover my self to *Ranger,* for a kick or two; oh, pray hold, Sir, by that you will know me.   [*Delivers him a Letter.*

DAPPERWIT. How, Sir *Simon!*

SIR SIMON. Mum, mum, make no excuses man, I wou'd not *Ranger* shou'd have known me for five hundred— kicks.

DAPPERWIT. Your disguise is so natural, I protest, it will excuse me.

SIR SIMON. I know that, prythee make no excuses, I say; no ceremony between thee and I man; read the Letter.

DAPPERWIT. What, you have not open'd it?

SIR SIMON. Prythee don't be angry, the Seal is a little crack'd; for I cou'd not help kissing Mrs. *Martha*'s Letter, the word is, now or never, her Father she finds will be abroad all this day, and she longs to see your friend, Sir *Simon Addleplot*: faith, 'tis a pretty jest; While I am with her, and praising my self to her, at no ordinary rate; let thee and I alone, at an intrigue.

DAPPERWIT. Tell her, I will not fail to meet her, at the place, and time, have a care of your charge; and manage your business like your self, for your self.

SIR SIMON. I warrant you.

DAPPERWIT. The gaining *Gripes* Daughter, will make me support the loss of this young Jilt here.   [*Aside.*

RANGER. What fellow's that?

DAPPERWIT. A Servant, to a Friend of mine.

RANGER. Methinks, he something resembles our acquaintance, Sir *Simon,* but it is no complement to tell him so; for that Knight, is the most egregious Coxcomb, that ever plaid with Ladies Fan.

SIR SIMON. So; thanks to my disguise, I know my Enemies.
          [*Aside.*

RANGER. The most incorrigible Ass, beyond the reproof of a kicking Rival, or a frowning Mistress; but if it be possible, thou dost use him worse, than his Mistress, or Rival can; thou dost make such a Culley of him.

SIR SIMON. Do's he think so too?—   [*Aside.*

DAPPERWIT. Go friend, go about your business,
          [*Exit Sir* SIMON.

a pox, you wou'd spoil all, just in the critical time of projection; he brings me here a Summons from his Mistress, to meet her in the evening; will you come to my Wedding?

RANGER. Don't speak so loud, you'll break poor *Lucies* heart; poor creature, she cannot leave you, and rather than leave her, you shou'd leave writing of Lampoons, or Sonnets—almost.

DAPPERWIT. Come, let her go, ungrateful baggage; but

now you talk of Sonnets; I am no living Wit, if her love
has not cost me two thousand Couplets at least.

RANGER. But, what wou'd you give now, for a new Satyr
against women, ready made; 'twou'd be as convenient
to buy, Satyrs against women, ready made, as it is to
buy Crevats ready ty'd.

DAPPERWIT. Or as—

RANGER. Hay, come away, come away, Mr. or as—

[*Exeunt.*

Enter Mrs. JOYNER, GRIPE.

GRIPE. Peace, Plenty, and Pastime be within these Walls.[9]

JOYNER. 'Tis a small House you see, and mean Furniture,
for no Gallants are suffer'd to come hither; she might
have had ere now, as good lodgings, as any in Town;
her *Moreclack*-Hangings,[10] great Glasses, Cabinets,
China embroider'd Beds, *Persia* Carpets, Gold-plate, and
the like, if she would have put her self forward; but
your Worship may please, to make 'em remove to a
place, fit to receive one of your Worships quality; for
this is a little scandalous in truly.

GRIPE. No, no, I like it well enough, I am not dainty; besides privacy, privacy, Mrs. *Joyner,* I love privacy, in
opposition to the Wicked, who hate it?

JOYNER. What do you look for, Sir?   [*Looks about.*

GRIPE. Walls have ears, Walls have ears; but besides, I
look for a private place to retire to, in time of need;
oh her's one convenient.

[*Turns up a Hanging, and discovers the
slender provisions of the Family.*]

JOYNER. But you see poor innocent Souls, to what use they
put it, not to hide Gallants.

GRIPE. Temperance is the nurse of Chastity.

JOYNER. But your Worship may please to mend their fare;
and when you come, may make them entertain you,
better than, you see, they do themselves.

GRIPE. No, I am not dainty, as I told you; I abominate
Entertainments; no Entertainments, pray Mrs. *Joyner.*

JOYNER. No.   [*Aside.*

GRIPE. There can be no entertainment to me, more Luscious and Savoury, than the communion with that little

Gentlewoman; will you call her out, I fast till I see her.

JOYNER. But intruly your Worship, we shou'd have brought
a bottle or two of Rhenish, and some Naples Bisket, to
have entertain'd the young Gentlewoman; 'tis the mode
for Lovers to Treat their Mistresses.

GRIPE. Modes, I tell you *Mrs. Joyner,* I hate Modes and
Forms.

JOYNER. You must send for something to entertain her
with.

GRIPE. Again entertaining; we will be to each other a
Feast.

JOYNER. I shall be asham'd, intruly your Worship; besides,
the young Gentlewoman will despise you.

GRIPE. I shall content her, I warrant you, leave it to me.

JOYNER. I am sure you will not content me, if you will not
content her; 'tis as impossible for a man to love, and be
a miser, as to love and be wise, as they say.   [*Aside.*

GRIPE. While you talk of Treats, you starve my eyes; I
long to see the fair One; fetch her hither.

JOYNER. I am asham'd she shou'd find me so abominable
a lyar; I have so prays'd you to her, and above all your
Vertues, your Liberality; which is so great a Vertue, that
it often excuses Youth, Beauty, Courage, Wit, or any
thing.

GRIPE. Pish, Pish, 'tis the vertue of Fools, every Fool can
have it.

JOYNER. And will your worship want it then? I told her—

GRIPE. Why wou'd you tell her any thing of me? you know
I am a modest man; but come, if you will have me as
extravagant as the wicked; take that, and fetch us a
Treat, as you call it.

JOYNER. Upon my life a Groat, what will this purchase?

GRIPE. Two Black Pots of Ale, and a Cake, at the next
Cellar; come, the Wine has Arsenick in't.

JOYNER. Well, I am mistaken, and my hopes are abus'd;
I never knew any man so mortify'd a Miser, that he
would deny his Letchery any thing; I must be even
with thee then another way.   [*Goes out.*

GRIPE. [*Aside.*] These useful old Women are more exorbi-
tant, and craving in their desires, than the young ones

in theirs; these Prodigals in white Peruques,[11] spoil
'em both; and that's the reason when the Squires come
under my cluchess; I made 'em pay for their folly and
mine, and 'tis but Conscience: Oh here comes the fair
One at last.

Enter JOYNER *leading in* LUCY, *who hangs backward
as she enters.*

LUCY. Oh Lord, there's a man God-mother!

JOYNER. Come in Child, thou art so bashful—

LUCY. My mother is from home too, I dare not.

JOYNER. If she were here, she'd teach you better manners.

LUCY. I'm afraid she'd be angry.

JOYNER. To see you so much an Ass; come along I say.

GRIPE. Nay, speak to her gently; if you won't, I will.

LUCY. Thank you, Sir.

GRIPE. Pretty Innocent, there is I see, one left yet of her
age; what hap have I! sweet, little Gentlewoman, come
and sit down by me.

LUCY. I am better bred, I hope, Sir.

GRIPE. You must sit down by me.

LUCY. I'd rather stand, if you please.

GRIPE. To please me, you must sit, Sweetest.

LUCY. Not before my God-mother, sure.

GRIPE. Wonderment of Innocence!

JOYNER. A poor bashful Girl, Sir; I'm sorry she is not better taught.

GRIPE. I am glad she is not taught; I'le teach her my self.

LUCY. Are you a Dancing-master then, Sir? but if I shou'd
be dull, and not move as you wou'd have me, you wou'd
not beat me, Sir, I hope?

GRIPE. Beat thee, hony Suckle; I'le use thee thus, and
thus, and thus; ah, Mrs. *Joyner,* prethee go fetch our
Treat now.   [*Kisses her.*

JOYNER. A Treat of a Groat, I will not wag.

GRIPE. Why don't you go? here, take more money, and
fetch what you will; take here, half a Crown.

JOYNER. What will half a Crown do?

GRIPE. Take a Crown then, an Angel, a Piece;[12] be gone.

JOYNER. A Treat only will not serve my turn, I must buy
the poor Wretch there some toys.

GRIPE. What toys? what? speak quickly.

JOYNER. Pendents, Neck-laces, Fans, Ribbonds, Poynts, Laces, Stockings, Gloves—

GRIPE. Hold, hold, before it comes to a Gown.

JOYNER. Well remember'd, Sir, indeed she wants a Gown, for she has but that one to her back; for your own sake you should give her a new Gown; for variety of Dresses, rouses desire, and makes an old Mistress seem every day a new one.

GRIPE. For that reason she shall have no new Gown; for I am naturally constant, and as I am still the same, I love she shou'd be still the same; but here take half a piece for the other things.

JOYNER. Half a Piece—

GRIPE. Prethee be gone, take t'other Piece then; two Pieces, three Pieces, five; here, 'tis all I have.

JOYNER. I must have the Broad-Seal Ring too, or I stir not.

GRIPE. Insatiable Woman, will you have that too? Prethee spare me that, 'twas my Grandfathers.

JOYNER. That's false, he had ne're a Coat;[13] so now I go; this is but a violent fit, and will not hold.   [*Aside.*

LUCY. Oh, whither do you go God-mother? will you leave me alone?

JOYNER. The Gentleman will not hurt you; you may venture your self with him alone.

LUCY. I think I may, God-mother; [*Exit* JOYNER.] what, will you lock me in, Sir? don't lock me in, Sir.
                    [*Fumbling at the dore, locks it.*

GRIPE. 'Tis a private lesson, I must teach you fair.

LUCY. I don't see your Fidle, Sir, where is your little Kitt?

GRIPE. I'le shew it thee presently Sweetest;
          Necessity, Mother of invention; [GRIPE *setting a Chair against the dore.*] Come my dearest. [*Takes her in his arms.*]

LUCY. What do you mean, Sir? don't hurt me, Sir, will you— Oh, Oh, you will kill me! murder, murder, oh, oh—help, help, oh—   [*Crys out.*

Coat: coat of arms.

The dore broke open; Enter CROSSBITE, *and two men
in Aprons, her Landlord, and his Prentice.*

CROSSBITE. What, murder my Daughter Villain?

LUCY. I wish he had murder'd me, oh, oh—

CROSSBITE. What has he done?

LUCY. Why wou'd you go out, and leave me alone? unfortunate woman that I am.

GRIPE. How now, what will this end in?   [*Aside.*

CROSSBITE. Who brought him in?

LUCY. That Witch, that Treacherous false Woman, my God-mother, who has betray'd me, sold me to his lust; oh, oh—

CROSSBITE. Have you ravish'd my Daughter then, you old Goat? ravish'd my Daughter, ravish'd my Daughter, speak Villain.

GRIPE. By yea, and by nay,[14] no such matter.

CROSSBITE. A canting Rogue too; take notice Landlord, he has ravish'd my Daughter, you see her all in tears and distraction; and see there the wicked Engine of the filthy execution; [*Pointing to the Chair.*] *Jeremy,* call up my Neighbours, and the Constable, false Villain, thou shalt dye for't.

GRIPE. Hold, hold; nay, I am caught.   [*Aside.*

CROSSBITE. Go, go, make haste—

LUCY. Oh, oh—

CROSSBITE. Poor wretch, go quickly.

GRIPE. Hold, hold; thou young Spawn of the old Serpent; Wicked, as I thought thee Innocent; wilt thou say I wou'd have ravish'd thee?

LUCY. I will swear you did ravish me.

GRIPE. I thought so, Treacherous *Eve,* then I am gone, I must shift as well as I can.   [*Aside.*[15]

LUCY. Oh, oh—

CROSSBITE. Will none of you call up the Neighbours, and the Authority of the Alley?

GRIPE. Hold, I'le give you Twenty Mark[16] among you, to let me go.

CROSSBITE. Villain, nothing shall buy thy life.

LANDLORD. But stay, Mrs. *Crossbite,* let me talk with you.

LUCY. Oh, oh—

LANDLORD. Come, Sir, I am your Friend; in a word, I have appeas'd her, and she shall be contented with a little sum.

GRIPE. What is it? what is it?

LANDLORD. But five hundred pound.

GRIPE. But five hundred pound; hang me then, hang me rather.

LANDLORD. You will say I have been your friend.

PRENTICE. The Constable, and Neighbors are coming.

GRIPE. How, how; will you not take a hundred? pray use conscience in your ways.   [*Kneels to* CROSSBITE.

CROSSBITE. I scorn your money, I will not take a thousand.

GRIPE. My enemies are many, and I shall be a scandal to the Faithful, as a laughing-stock to the wicked; [*Aside.* go, prepare your Engines for my Persecution; I'le give you the best security I can.

LANDLORD. The instruments are drawing in the other room, if you please to go thither.

CROSSBITE. Indeed, now I consider; a Portion will do my Daughter more good, than his death; that wou'd but publish her shame; money will cover it, *probatum est,* as they say—let me tell you, Sir, 'tis a charitable thing to give a young Maid a Portion.   [*Exeunt Omnes.*

The Scene changes to LYDIAS *Lodging.*

Enter LYDIA, *my Lady* FLIPPANT.

LYDIA. 'Tis as hard for a woman to conceal her indignation from her apostate Lover, as to conceal her Love from her faithful servant.

FLIPPANT. Or almost as hard as it is, for the prating fellows now adays, to conceal the favours of obliging Ladies.

LYDIA. If *Ranger* shou'd come up, (I saw him just now in the street) the discovery of my anger to him now, wou'd be as mean as the discovery of my love to him before.

FLIPPANT. Though I did so mean a thing, as to love a fellow, I wou'd not do so mean a thing, as to confess it, certainly, by my trouble to part with him; If I confest Love, it should be before they left me.

LYDIA. So you wou'd deserve to be left, before you were;

but cou'd you ever do so mean a thing, as to confess love to any?

FLIPPANT. Yes; but I never did so mean a thing, as really to love any?

LYDIA. You had once a Husband.

FLIPPANT. Fye, Madam, do you think me so ill bred, as to love a Husband.

LYDIA. You had a Widows heart, before you were a Widow I see.

FLIPPANT. I shou'd rather make an adventure of my honour, with a Gallant, for a Gown, a new Coach, a Necklase, than clap my Husbands cheeks for them, or sit in his lap; I shou'd be as asham'd to be caught in such a posture, with a Husband, as a brisk well bred of the Town, wou'd be, to be caught on his knees at prayers, unless to his Mistress.

To them, RANGER, DAPPERWIT.

LYDIA. Mr. *Ranger,* 'twas obligingly done of you.

RANGER. Indeed Cousin, I had kept my promise with you, last night, but this Gentleman knows—

LYDIA. You mistake me, but you shall not lessen any favour you do me; you are going to excuse your not coming to me last night, when I take it as a particular obligation, that though you threatned me with a visit, upon consideration you were so civil, as not to trouble me.

DAPPERWIT. This is an unlucky morning with me; here's my eternal persecution, the Widow *Flippant.*   [*Aside.*

FLIPPANT. What, Mr. *Dapperwit*!

RANGER. Indeed Cousin, besides my business, another cause, I did not wait on you, was, my apprehension, you were gone to the Park, notwithstanding your promise to the contrary.

LYDIA. Therefore, you went to the Park, to visit me there, notwithstanding your promise to the contrary.

RANGER. Who, I at the Park? when I had promis'd to wait upon you at your lodging; but were you at the Park, Madam?

LYDIA. Who, I at the Park? when I had promis'd to wait for you at home; I was no more at the Park than you were; were you at the Park?

RANGER. The Park had been a dismal desart to me, notwithstanding all the good company in't; if I had wanted yours.

LYDIA. Because it has been the constant endeavour of men, to keep women ignorant, they think us so, but 'tis that encreases our inquisitiveness, and makes us know them ignorant, as false; he is as impudent a dissembler as the widow *Flippant*, who is making her importunate addresses, in vain, for ought I see.   [*Aside*.

FLIPPANT driving DAPPERWIT *from one side
of the Stage, to the other.*

FLIPPANT. Dear, Mr. *Dapperwit*, merciful, Mr. *Dapperwit*.

DAPPERWIT. Unmerciful, Lady *Flippant*.

FLIPPANT. Will you be satisfied?

DAPPERWIT. Won't you be satisfied.

FLIPPANT. That a Wit shou'd be jealous! that a Wit shou'd be jealous! there's never a brisk young fellow in the Town, though no Wit Heaven knows; but thinks too well of himself, to think ill of his Wife, or Mistress; now that a Wit shou'd lessen his opinion of himself, for shame.   [*Aside to* DAPPERWIT.

DAPPERWIT. I promis'd to bring you off, but I find it enough to shift for my self—   [*Softly apart to* RANGER.

LYDIA. What, out of breath, Madam?

FLIPPANT. I have been defending our cause, Madam; I have beat him out of the Pit;[17] I do so mumble these prating, censorious fellows, they call Wits, when I meet with them.

DAPPERWIT. Her Ladyship indeed, is the only thing in Petty-coats, I dread, 'twas well for me there was company in the Room; for I dare no more venture my self with her alone, than a Culley that has been bit, dares venture himself in a Tavern, with an old Rook.

FLIPPANT. I am the revenger of our Sex, certainly.

DAPPERWIT. And the most insatiable one, I ever knew, Madam; I dare not stand your fury longer; Mr. *Ranger*, I will go before and make a new appointment, with your friends that expect you at dinner, at the *French-house*, 'tis fit business, still wait on Love.

mumble: handle roughly.

RANGER. Do so—but now I think on't, Sir *Thomas* goes out of Town this afternoon, and I shall not see him here again these three months.

LYDIA. Nay, pray take him with you, Sir.

FLIPPANT. No, Sir, you shall not take the Gentleman from his Mistress: [do not go yet, sweet Mr. *Dapperwit*.]
[*Aside.*

LYDIA. Take him with you, Sir; I suppose his business may be there, to borrow, or win, mony, and I ought not to be his hinderance; for when he has none, he has his desperate designs upon that little I have; for want of mony, makes as devout Lovers as Christians.

DAPPERWIT. I hope, Madam, he offers you no less security, than his liberty.

LYDIA. His liberty, as poor a pawn to take up mony on, as honour; he is like the desperate Banke-routs of this age, who if they can get peoples fortunes into their hands, care not though they spend them in Goale, all their lives.[18]

FLIPPANT. And the poor crediting Ladies, when they have parted with their mony, must be contented with a pitiful composition or starve for all them.

RANGER. But Widows are commonly so wise, as to be sure their men are solvable, before they trust 'em.

FLIPPANT. Can you blame 'em; I declare, I will trust no man, pray do not take it ill, Gentlemen; Quacks in their Bills, and Poets in the titles of their Plays, do not more disapoint us, than Gallants with their promises; but I trust none.

DAPPERWIT. Nay, she's a very Jew in that particular; to my knowledg, shee'll know her man, over and over again, before she trust him.

RANGER. Well, my dearest Cousin, good morrow; when I stay from you, so long again, blame me to purpose, and be extreamly angry; for nothing can make amends for the loss of your company, but your reprehension of my absence; I'll take such a chiding, as kindly, as *Russian* Wives, do beating.[19]

LYDIA. If you were my Husband, I cou'd not take your absence more kindly, than I do.

RANGER. And if you were my wife, I wou'd trust you as much out of my sight, as I cou'd, to shew my opinion of your virtue.

FLIPPANT. A well-bred Gentleman, I warrant; will you go then cruel Mr. *Dapperwit?*

[*Exeunt* RANGER *and* DAPPERWIT.

LYDIA. Have I not dissembled well, *Leonor?*[20]   [*Apart.*

LEONORE. But, Madam, to what purpose; why do you not put him to his tryal, and see what he can say for himself?

LYDIA. I am afraid lest my proofs, and his guilt, shou'd make him desperate, and so contemn that pardon, which he cou'd not hope for.

LEONORE. 'Tis unjust to condemn him, before you hear him.

LYDIA. I will reprieve him till I have more evidence.

LEONORE. How will you get it?

LYDIA. I will write him a Letter in *Christina's* name, desiring to meet him; when I shall soon discover, if his love to her be of a longer standing, than since last night; and if it be not, I will not longer trust him with the vanity, to think she gave him the occasion, to follow her home from the Park; so will at once dis-abuse him and my self.

LEONORE. What care the jealous take in making sure of ills, which they, but in imagination, cannot undergo.

LYDIA. Misfortunes are least dreadful, when most near.

'Tis less to undergo the ill, than fear.   [*Exeunt.*

ACT IV. SCENE I.

GRIPE'S *House.*

Enter Mrs. JOYNER, *and* GRIPE *in a Blew Gown*[1] *and Night Cap.*

JOYNER. What not well your Worship? this it is, you will be laying out your self beyond your strength; you have taken a Surfeit of the little Gentlewoman, I find; indeed,

you shou'd not have been so immoderate in your embraces, your Worship is something in years, intruly.

GRIPE. Graceless, Perfidious Woman, what mak'st thou
here? art thou not afraid to be us'd like an Informer,
since thou hast made me pay thee for betraying me?

JOYNER. Betray your Worship, what do you mean? I an
Informer, I scorn your words.

GRIPE. Woman, I say again, thou art as Treacherous as
an Informer, and more unreasonable; for he lets us have
something for our money, before he disturbs us.

JOYNER. Your money, I'me sure, was laid out faithfully;
and I went away because I wou'd not disturb you.

GRIPE. I had not grudg'd you the money I gave you, but
the five hundred pound; the five hundred pound, in-
conscionable false woman; the five hundred pound; you
cheated, trappand, rob'd me of the five hundred pound.

JOYNER. I cheat you, I rob you; well, remember what
you say, you shall answer it before Mr. *Double-Cap*,
and the best of—

GRIPE. Oh impudent woman, speak softly!

JOYNER. I will not speak softly, for innocence is loud, as
well as bare-fac'd; is this your return, after you have
made me a meer drudge to your filthy lusts?

GRIPE. Speak softly, my Sister, Daughter and Servants will
hear.

JOYNER. I wou'd have witnesses, to take notice, that you
blast my good name, which was as white as a Tulip,
and as sweet as the head of your Cane; before you
wrought me to the carrying on the work of your fleshly
carnal seekings.

GRIPE. Softly, softly, they are coming in.

Enter FLIPPANT *and* MARTHA.

FLIPPANT. What's the matter Brother?

GRIPE. Nothing, nothing Sister, only the Godly woman is
fallen into a fit of Zeal, against the enormous transgres-
sions of the Age; go, go, you do not love to hear vanity
reprov'd; pray be gone.

JOYNER. Pray stay, Madam, that you may know—

GRIPE. Hold, hold, here are five Guinies for thee, pray
say nothing.   [*Aside. To* JOYNER.

Sister, pray be gone, I say; wou'd you prejudice your
own reputation, to injure mine?

                     [*Exeunt* FLIPPANT *and* MARTHA.

JOYNER. Wou'd you prejudice your own Soul to wrong
my repute, intruly?   [*She seems to weep.*

GRIPE. Pray have me in excuse; indeed, I thought, you
had a share of the five hundred pound, because you
took away my Seal Ring, which they made me send,
together, with a Note to my Cash-keeper for five hundred pound; besides, I thought none, but you, knew it
was my wonted token to send for money by.

JOYNER. 'Twas unlucky I shou'd forget it, and leave it on
the Table; but, oh the Harlotry! did she make that use
of it then? 'twas no wonder you did not stay till I came
back.

GRIPE. I stay'd till the money releas'd me.

JOYNER. Have they the money then? five hundred pound.

GRIPE. Too certain.

JOYNER. They told me not a word of it; and have you
no way to retrive it?

GRIPE. Not any.

JOYNER. I am glad of it;   [*Aside.*
is there no Law but against Saints?

GRIPE. 1 will not for five hundred pound, publish my trans-
gression my self; lest I shou'd be thought to glory in't;
though, I must confess, 'twould tempt a man to conform
to publick praying and sinning; since 'tis so chargeable
to pray, and sin in private.

JOYNER. But are you resolv'd to give off, a loser?

GRIPE. How shall I help it?

JOYNER. Nay, I'le see you shall have, what the young
jade has; for your money, I'le make 'um use some conscience however; take a mans money for nothing?

GRIPE. Thou say'st honestly indeed; and shall I have my
penniworths out of the little Gentlewoman for all this?

JOYNER. I'le be engag'd body for body for her, and you
shall take the forfeiture on me else.

GRIPE. No, no, I'le rather take your word, Mrs. *Joyner.*

JOYNER. Go in and dress your self Smug, and leave the
rest to me.

GRIPE. No man breathing would give off a loser, as she says.   *[Exeunt.*

Enter Sir SIMON ADDLEPLOT, *sitting at a Desk writing
as a Clerk, my Lady* FLIPPANT *jogging him.*

SIR SIMON. 'Tis a Lords Mortgage, and therefore requires the more hast; pray do not jog me, Madam.

FLIPPANT. Dull Rascal.   *[Aside.*

SIR SIMON. They cannot stay for money, as other Folks; if you will not let me make an end on't, I shall loose my expedition fee.

FLIPPANT. There are some Clerks wou'd have understood me before this.   *[Aside.*

SIR SIMON. Nay, pray be quiet, Madam; if you squeeze me so to the wall, I cannot write.

FLIPPANT. 'Tis much for the honour of the Gentlemen of this Age, that we Persons of Quality are forc'd to descend to the importuning of a Clerk, a Butler, Coachman, or Footman; while the Rogues are as dull of apprehension too, as an unfledg'd Country Squire, amongst his Mothers Maids.   *[Aside. Jogs him again.*

SIR SIMON. Again, Let me tell you, Madam, familiarity breeds contempt; you'l never leave, till you have made me sawcy.

FLIPPANT. I wou'd I cou'd see that.

SIR SIMON. I vow and swear then, get you gone; or I'le add a black patch, or two, to those on your face.
I shall have no time to get Mrs. *Martha* out, for her.   *[Aside.*

FLIPPANT. Will you, Sir, will you?   *[Jogs him again.*

SIR SIMON. I must have a plot for her, she is a coy woman. *[Aside.]* I vow and swear if you pass this Creviss, I'le kiss you in plain English.

FLIPPANT. I wou'd I cou'd see that, do you defie me?
    [Steps to him. He kisses her.

SIR SIMON. How's this? I vow and swear, she kisses as tamely as Mrs. *Ticklish,* and with her mouth open too.   *[Aside.*

FLIPPANT. I thought you wou'd have been asham'd, to have done so to your Masters own Sister.

SIR SIMON. I hope you'l be quiet now, Madam?

FLIPPANT. Nay, I'le be reveng'd of you sure.

SIR SIMON. If you come again, I shall do more to you than that; I'le persue my plot, and try if she be honest.

[*Aside.*

FLIPPANT. You do more to me than that; nay, if you'l do more to me, than that—

*She throws down his Ink, and
runs out, he follows her.*

Enter JOYNER.

JOYNER. I must visit my young Clyants in the mean time.

Sir SIMON *returns holding up his hands.*

JOYNER. What's the matter, Sir *Simon?*

SIR SIMON. Lord, who wou'd have thought it?

JOYNER. What aile you, Sir *Simon?*

SIR SIMON. I have made such a discovery, Mrs. *Joyner.*

JOYNER. What is't?

SIR SIMON. Such an one, that makes me at once glad, and sorry; I am sorry my Lady *Flippant* is nought, but I'me glad I know it; thanks still to my disguise.

JOYNER. Fye, fye.

SIR SIMON. Nay, this hand can tell—

JOYNER. But how!

SIR SIMON. She threw down my Ink glass, and ran away into the next room; I follow'd her, and in revenge, threw her down upon the bed; but in short, all that I cou'd do to her, wou'd not make her squeek.

JOYNER. She was out of breath man, she was out of breath.

SIR SIMON. Ah, Mrs. *Joyner,* say no more, say no more of that.

Enter FLIPPANT.

FLIPPANT. You rude, unmannerly Rascal.

JOYNER. You see she complains now.

SIR SIMON. I know why, Mrs. *Joyner,* I know why. [*Apart.*

FLIPPANT. I'le have you turn'd out of the house, you are not fit for my brothers service.

SIR SIMON. Not for yours, you mean, Madam. [*Aside.*

FLIPPANT. I'le go and acquaint my Brother—

JOYNER. Hold, hold, Madam, speak not so loud, 'tis Sir *Simon Addleplot,* your Lover, who has taken this disguise on purpose to be near you; and to watch, and supplant his Rivals.

FLIPPANT. What a beast was I, I cou'd not discover it, you have undone me; why wou'd you not tell me sooner of it. [*Aside to* JOYNER.[2]

JOYNER. I thought he had been discernable enough.

FLIPPANT. I protest I knew him not; for I must confess to you, my eyes are none of the best, since I have us'd the last new wash of Mercury water; what will he think of me?

JOYNER. Let me alone with him; come, come, did you think you cou'd disguise your self from my Ladies knowledg; she knew you man, or else you had ne're had those liberties; alas, poor Lady, she cannot resist you.

FLIPPANT. 'Tis my weakness.

SIR SIMON. How's this? but here comes my Master.

Enter GRIPE *and* MARTHA.

GRIPE. Come, Mrs. *Joyner,* are you ready to go?

JOYNER. I am ever ready when your Worship commands.

FLIPPANT. Brother, if you go to t'other end of the Town, you'l set me down near the Play-house.

GRIPE. The Play-house, do you think I will be seen near the Play-house?

FLIPPANT. You shall set me down in *Lincolns-Inn-Fields* then, for I have earnest business there;[3] (When I come home again, I'le laugh at you soundly, Sir *Simon.*)

[*Apart.*

SIR SIMON. Has *Joyner* betray'd me then? 'tis time to look to my hits. [*Aside.*

GRIPE. *Martha,* be sure you stay within now; if you go out, you shall never come into my dores again.

MARTHA. No, I will not, Sir; I'le ne're come into your dores again, if once I shou'd go out.

GRIPE. 'Tis well said, Girl.

[*Exeunt* GRIPE, JOYNER, FLIPPANT.

SIR SIMON. 'Twas prettily said, I understand you, they are

Mercury water: a mixture of aqua regia and corrosive sublimate, was used as a skin wash. If Lady Flippant got it in her eyes, she has excuse enough for mistaking Sir Simon.

dull, and have no intrigue in 'em; but dear, sweet Mrs. *Martha*, 'tis time we were gone, you have stole away your Scarfs, and Hood from your Maid, I hope.

MARTHA. Nay, I am ready, but—

SIR SIMON. Come, come, Sir *Simon Addleplot*, poor Gentleman, is an impatient man to my knowledge.

MARTHA. Well, my venture is great, I'me sure, for a man I know not; but pray *Jonas* do not deceive me; is he so fine a Gentleman, as you say he is?

SIR SIMON. Pish, pish, he is the—Gentleman of the Town faith, and troth.

MARTHA. But may I take your word *Jonas?*

SIR SIMON. 'Tis not my word, 'tis the word of all the Town.

MARTHA. Excuse me, *Jonas*, for that; I never heard any speak well of him, but Mr. *Dapperwit*, and you.

SIR SIMON. That's because he has been a Rival to all men, and a Gallant to all Ladies; Rivals, and deserted Mistresses, never speak well of a man.

MARTHA. Has he been so general in his Amours, his kindness is not to be vallu'd then?

SIR SIMON. The more by you, because 'tis for you he deserts all the rest, faith and troth.

MARTHA. You plead better for him, than he cou'd for himself; I believe, for indeed they say, he is no better than an Ideot.

SIR SIMON. Then believe me, Madam, for no body knows him better than I; he has as much Wit, Courage, and as good a Meen to the full, as I have; he an Ideot?

MARTHA. The common Gull, so perspicuous a Fop, the women find him out, for none of 'em will marry him.

SIR SIMON. You may see now, how he and you are abus'd; for that he is not Married, is a sign of his Wit; and for being perspicuous, 'tis false, he is as mysterious as a new Parliament man, or a young States-man, newly taken from a Coffee-house, or Tennis-court.

MARTHA. But is it a sign of his Wit because he is not Married?

SIR SIMON. Yes, yes, your Women of the Town ravish your Fops; there's not one about the Town unmarryed, that has any thing.

MARTHA. It may be then he has spent his Estate.

SIR SIMON. How unluckily guess'd.   [*Aside.*

    If he had, he has a head, can retrieve it again.

MARTHA. Besides, they say, he has had the modish distemper.

SIR SIMON. He can cure it with the best *French* Chyrurgion in Town.

MARTHA. Has his practice, on himself, been so much?

SIR SIMON. Come, come.

    Fame, like deserted Jilt, does still belye men,

    Who doubts her man, must be advis'd by *Hymen.*

    For he knows best of any, how to try men.[4]   [*Exeunt.*

The Scene, The Old Pell Mell.

Enter RANGER *and* DAPPERWIT.

RANGER. Now the *Lucy's* have renounc'd us; hey for the *Christina's,* she cannot use me worse, than your honourable Mistress did you.

DAPPERWIT. A Pox, some young Heir, or another, has promis'd her Marriage; there are so many Fools in the world, 'tis impossible for a man of Wit to keep his Wench, from being a Lady, let me perish.

RANGER. But have you no other acquaintance that sticks to her vocation, in spight of temptations of honour, or filthy lucre; I declare, I make honourable Love, meerly out of necessity; as your Rooks play on the square, rather than not play at all.

    To them LEONORE, LYDIAS *woman mask'd,*
      with a Letter in her hand.

DAPPERWIT. Come, the Devil will not lose a Gamester; here's ready money for you, push freely.

RANGER. Thou'rt as well met, as if by assignation. [*To her.*

LEONORE. And you are as well met, as if you were the man I look'd for.

RANGER. Kind Rogue—

LEONORE. Sweet Sir.

RANGER. Come, I am thy Prisoner, (without more words) shew but thy warrant.   [*Goes to pull off her Mask.*

---

modish distemper: venereal disease. French surgeons were presumed to have a specialist's knowledge of it.

LEONORE. You mistake, Sir, here is my Pass.

> [*Gives him the Letter*.

RANGER. A Letter, and directed to me.   [*Reads*.

I cannot put up the injuries, and affronts you did me last night; (a challenge upon my life, and by such a messenger) *therefore conjure you by your Honour, at eight a Clock precisely, this evening, to send your man to St. James's Gate, to wait for me with a Chair, to conduct me, to what place you shall think most fit, for the giving of satisfaction to the injur'd* Christina.

Christina! I am amaz'd! what is't a Clock *Dapperwit?*

DAPPERWIT. It wants not half an hour of eight.

RANGER. Go then back, my pretty Herauld, [*To the Maid*. and tell my fair Enemy, the service she designs my man, is only fit for my Friend here; of whose Faith and Honour, she may be secure of; he shall, immediately, go wait for her at St. *James's* Gate; whilst I go to prepare a place for our ran-counter, and my self to dye at her feet: [*Exit* LEONORE.

Dapperwit, dear *Dapperwit*.

DAPPERWIT. What lucky Surprisal's this?

RANGER. Prethee ask no questions, till I have more leisure, and less astonishment; I know, you will not deny to be an instrument in my happiness.

DAPPERWIT. No, let me perish, I take as much pleasure to bring Lovers together, as an old Woman, that as a Bankrupt Gamester loves to look on, though he has no advantage by the play; or as a Bully that fights not himself, yet takes pleasure to set people together by the ears; or as—

RANGER. S'death, is this a time for similitudes?

DAPPERWIT. You have made me miscarry of a good thought, now let me perish.

RANGER. Go presently to St. *James's* gate, where you are to expect the coming of a Lady, ('tis *Christina*) accompany'd by that woman you saw ev'n now; she will permit you to put her into a Chair, and then conduct her to my lodging, while I go before to remove some Spies, and prepare it for her reception.

DAPPERWIT. Your lodging; had you not better carry her to *Vincent*'s, 'tis hard by, and there a vizard Mask, has as free egress, and regress, as at the Play-house.

RANGER. Faith, though it be not very prudent, yet she shall come thither in my vindication; for he wou'd not believe I had seen her last night.

DAPPERWIT. To have a fine woman, and not tell on't, as you say, Mr. *Ranger*—

RANGER. Go, and bring her to *Vincent*'s lodging, there I'le expect you.　　　　　　　　　　　[*Exeunt severally.*

Enter CHRISTINA, ISABEL, *her Woman.*

ISABEL. This is the door, Madam, here Mr. *Vincent* lodges.

CHRISTINA. 'Tis no matter, we will pass it by, lest the people of our lodging shou'd watch us; but if he shou'd not be here now.

ISABEL. Who, Mr. *Valentine*, Madam? I warrant you, my intelligencer dares not fail me.

CHRISTINA. Did he come last night, said he?

ISABEL. Last night late.

CHRISTINA. And not see me yet; nay, not send to me; 'tis false, he is not come; I wish he were not, I know not which I shou'd take more unkindly from him, exposing his life to his revengeful Enemies; or being almost four and twenty hours so near me, and not let me know't.

ISABEL. A Lovers dangers, are the only secrets kept from his Mistress; he came not to you, because he wou'd not purchase his happiness with your fear and apprehensions.

CHRISTINA. Nay, he is come, I see, since you are come about again of his side.

ISABEL. Will you go in, Madam, and disprove me if you can; 'tis better than standing in the street.

CHRISTINA. We'le go a little farther first, and return.

　　　　　　　　　　　　　　　　　　　　　[*Exeunt.*

VINCENT's *Lodging.*

Enter VINCENT *and* VALENTINE.

VINCENT. I told you I had sent my man, to *Christina*'s, this

vizard Mask: prostitute.

morning, to enquire of her Maid, (who seldom denies him a secret) if her Lady had been at the Park last night; which she peremptorily answered to the contrary, and assur'd him, she had not stirr'd out since your departure.

VALENTINE. Will not Chamber-maids lye, *Vincent?*

VINCENT. Will not *Ranger* lie, *Valentine?*

VALENTINE. The circumstances of his story prov'd it true.

VINCENT. Do you think so old a Master in the faculty, as he, will want the varnish of probability for his lies?

VALENTINE. Do you think a Woman, having the advantage of her Sex, and Education, under such a Mistress, will want impudence to dis-avow a truth, that might be prejudicial to that Mistress?

VINCENT. But if both testimonies are fallible; why will you needs believe his? we are apter to believe the things we wou'd have, than those we wou'd not.

VALENTINE. My ill luck has taught me to credit my misfortunes, and doubt my happiness.

VINCENT. But Fortune we know inconstant.

VALENTINE. And all of her Sex.

VINCENT. Will you judge of Fortune by your experience, and not do your Mistress the same justice? go see her, and satisfie your self and her; for if she be innocent, consider how culpable you are, not only in your censures of her, but in not seeing her since your coming.

VALENTINE. If she be innocent, I shou'd be afraid to surprize her, for her sake; if false, I shou'd be afraid to surprize her, for my own.

VINCENT. To be jealous, and not inquisitive, is as hard as to love extreamly, and not be something jealous.

VALENTINE. Inquisitiveness as seldom cures jealousie, as drinking in a Fever quenches the thirst.

VINCENT. If she were at the Park last night, 'tis probable she'l not miss this; go watch her house, see who goes out, who in; while I in the mean time search out *Ranger;* who, I'le pawn my life, upon more discourse, shall avow his mistake; here he is, go in, how luckily is he come?

Enter RANGER.
VALENTINE *retires to the dore behind,*
over hearing them.

VINCENT. *Ranger,* you have prevented me; I was going to
look you out, between the Scenes at the Play-houses,
the Coffee-house, Tennis-Court, or *Giffords.*[5]

RANGER. Do you want a pretence to go to a Bawdy-house?
but I have other visits to make.

VINCENT. I forget, I shou'd rather have sought you in
Christina's lodgings, ha, ha, ha.

RANGER. Well, well, I am just come to tell you that *Christina*—

VINCENT. Proves not by day-light, the kind Lady you follow'd last night out of the Park.

RANGER. I have better news for you, to my thinking.

VINCENT. What is't?

RANGER. Not that I have been in *Christina's* lodging this
morning; but that she'l be presently here in your lodging with me.

VALENTINE. How!   [*behind.*

VINCENT. You see now, his report was a jest, a meer jest:
Drawing back to the dore, where VALENTINE
stood, and speaking softly to him.
well, must my lodging be your Vaulting School still;
thou hast appointed a Wench to come hither, I find.
                                             [*To* RANGER.

RANGER. A Wench; you seem'd to have more reverence
for *Christina* last night.

VINCENT. Now you talk of *Christina,* prethee tell me what
was the meaning of thy last nights Romance of *Christina.*

RANGER. You shall know the meaning of all, when *Christina*
comes; she'l be here presently.

VINCENT. Who will, *Christina?*

RANGER. Yes, *Christina.*

VINCENT. Ha, ha, ha.

RANGER. Incredulous envy; thou art as envious, as an impotent Letcher at a Wedding.

Vaulting School: brothel.

VINCENT. Thou art either mad, or as vain as a *French-man*, newly return'd home from a *Campagn*, or obliging *England*.[6]

RANGER. Thou art as envious as a Rival; but if thou art mine, there's that will make you desist; [*Gives him the Letter.*] and if you are not my Rival; intrusting you with such a secret, will, I know, oblige you to keep it, and assist me against all other interests.

VINCENT. Do you think I take your secret as an obligation? don't, I know, Lovers, Travellers, and Poets, will give money to be heard; but what's the Paper? a Lampoon upon *Christina*, hatch'd last night betwixt Squire *Dapperwit* and you, because her maid us'd you scurvily.

RANGER. No, 'tis only a Letter from her, to shew, my company was not so disgustful to her last night, but that she desires it again to day.

VALENTINE. A Letter from her.   [*Behind.*

VINCENT. A Letter from *Christina;* [*Reads.*] Ha, ha, ha.

RANGER. Nay, 'tis pleasant.

VINCENT. You mistake, I laugh at you not the Letter.

RANGER. I am like the winning Gamester, so pleas'd with my luck, I will not quarrel with any, who calls me a Fool for't.

VINCENT. Is this the stile of a woman of honour?

RANGER. It may be, for ought you know; I'm sure, 'tis well if your female correspondents can read.

VINCENT. I must confess, I have none of the little Letters, half name, or title, like your Spanish Epistles Dedicatory; but that a man so frequent in honourable Intrigues, as you are, should not know the summons of an impudent common woman, from that of a person of honour.

RANGER. *Christina* is so much a Person of Honour, she'l own what she has writ, when she comes.

VINCENT. But will she come hither indeed?

RANGER. Immediately, you'l excuse my liberty with you; I cou'd not conceal such a happiness, from such a friend as you, lest you shou'd have taken it unkindly.

VINCENT. Faith, you have oblig'd me indeed; for you, and others wou'd often have made me believe your honour-

able Intrigues, but never did me the honour to convince
me of 'em before.

RANGER. You are merry, I find, yet.

VINCENT. When you are happy, I cannot be otherwise.

RANGER. But I lose time, I shou'd lay a little Person[7] in
ambush, that lives hard by, in case *Christina* shou'd be
impatient to be reveng'd of her Friends, as it often happens with a discontented Heiress; Women like old Souldiers, more nimbly execute, than they resolve. [*Aside.*
　　　　　　　　　　　　　　　　　　　　　[*Going out.*

VINCENT. What now, you will not dis-appoint a woman of
Christina's quality?

RANGER. I'le be here before she comes, I warrant you.
　　　　　　　　　　　　　　　　　　　　　[*Exit* RANGER.

VINCENT. I do believe you truly: what think you *Valentine?*

VALENTINE. I think, since she has the courage to challenge
him; she'l have the honour of being first in the Field.

VINCENT. Fye, your opinion of her must be as bad, as
Rangers of himself is good, to think she wou'd write to
him; I long till his *bona-roba* comes, that you may be
both dis-abus'd.

VALENTINE. And I have not patience to stay her coming,
lest you shou'd be dis-abus'd.

　　　　　　　Enter CHRISTINA *and* ISABEL.

VINCENT. Here she is i'faith; I'm glad she's come.

VALENTINE. And I'm sorry; but I will to my post again,
lest she shou'd say she came to me.

VINCENT. By heavens, *Christina* her self, 'tis she! [*Aside.*
　　　　　　　　　　　　　[CHRISTINA *pulls off her Mask.*

VALENTINE. 'Tis she; curs'd be these eyes, more curs'd,
than when they first betray'd me, to that false bewitching face. 　　　　　　　　　　　　　　　　　　　　[*Behind.*

CHRISTINA. You may wonder, Sir, to see me here—

VINCENT. I must confess I do.

CHRISTINA. But the confidence your Friend has in you, is

bona-roba: showy wanton.
The OED quotes John Florio:
"as we say good stuffe."

the cause of mine; and yet some blushes it do's cost
me, to come to seek a man.

VALENTINE. Modest creature.   [*Behind.*

VINCENT. How am I deceiv'd!   [*Aside.*

CHRISTINA. Where is he, Sir, why does he not appear to
keep me in countenance? pray call him, Sir, 'tis something hard if he shou'd know I'm here.

VINCENT. I hardly can, my self, believe you are here,
Madam.

CHRISTINA. If my visit be troublesome, or unseasonable,
'tis your Friends fault, I design'd it not to you, Sir; pray
call him out, that he may excuse it, and take it on himself, together with my shame.

VINCENT. How impatient she is!   [*Aside.*

CHRISTINA. Or do you delay the happiness I ask, to make
it more welcom? I have stay'd too long for it already,
and cannot more desire it; dear Sir, call him out, where
is he? above, or here within? I'le snatch the favour
which you will not give:

> [*Goes to the dore, and discovers* VALENTINE.

What do you hide your self for shame?

VALENTINE. I must confess I do.

CHRISTINA. To see me come hither—

VALENTINE. I acknowledge it.

> [VALENTINE *offers to go out.*

CHRISTINA. Before you came to me; but whither do you
go? come I can forgive you.

VALENTINE. But I cannot forgive you.

CHRISTINA. Whither do you go? you need not forge a quarrel, to prevent mine to you; nor need you try if I wou'd
follow you; you know I will, I have you see.

VALENTINE. That impudence should look so like innocence.

> [*Aside.*

CHRISTINA. Whither wou'd you go? why wou'd you go?

VALENTINE. To call your servant to you.

CHRISTINA. She is here, what wou'd you with her?

VALENTINE. I mean your Lover, the man you came to
meet.

CHRISTINA. Oh heavens! what Lover? what Man? I came
to seek no man but you, whom I had too long lost.

VALENTINE. You cou'd not know that I was here.

CHRISTINA. Ask her, 'twas she that told me.

[*Points to* ISABEL.

VALENTINE. How cou'd she know?

CHRISTINA. That you shall know hereafter.

VALENTINE. No, you thought me too far out of the way, to disturb your assignation; and I assure you, Madam, 'twas my ill fortune, not my design; and that it may appear so, I do withdraw, (as in all good breeding, and civility, I am oblig'd) for sure your wish'd for Lover's coming.

CHRISTINA. What do you mean? are you a weary of that title?

VALENTINE. I am asham'd of it, since it grows common.

[*Going out.*

CHRISTINA. Nay, you will not, shall not go.

VALENTINE. My stay might give him jealousie, and so do you injury, and him the greatest in the world; Heavens forbid! I wou'd not make a man jealous; for though you call a thousand vows, and oaths, and tears, to witness, (as you safely may) that you have not the least of love for me; yet if he ever knew, how I have lov'd you, sure he wou'd not, cou'd not believe you.

CHRISTINA. I do confess, your Riddle is too hard for me to solve; therefore you are oblig'd to do't your self.

VALENTINE. I wish it were capable of any other interpretation, than what you know already.

CHRISTINA. Is this that generous good Valentine, who has disguis'd him so.   [*She weeps.*

VINCENT Nay, I must with-hold you then: [*Stops* VALENTINE *going out.*] methinks she shou'd be innocent; her tongue, and eyes, together, with that floud that swells 'em, do vindicate her heart.

VALENTINE. They shew but their long practice of desimulation.   [*Going out.*

VINCENT. Come back; I hear *Ranger* coming up; stay but till he comes.

VALENTINE. Do you think I have the patience of an Alderman?[8]

VINCENT. You may go out this way, when you will, by the back-stairs; but stay a little, till— Oh, here he comes.

RANGER enters.

VALENTINE. My revenge will now detain me.

[VALENTINE retires again.

Upon RANGERS entrance, CHRISTINA puts on her Mask.

RANGER. What, come already? where is <i>Dapperwit?</i> [<i>Aside.</i> The blessing's double that comes quickly; I did not yet expect you here, otherwise I had not done my self the injury to be absent; but I hope, Madam, I have not made you stay long for me.

CHRISTINA. I have not staid at all for you.

RANGER. I am glad of it, Madam.

CHRISTINA. Is not this that troublesome stranger, who last night follow'd the Lady into my lodgings? 'tis he.

[To ISABEL. Aside.
[Removing from him to t'other side.

RANGER. Why do's she remove so disdainfully from me?

[Aside.

I find you take it ill, I was not at your coming here, Madam.

CHRISTINA. Indeed I do not, you are mistaken, Sir.

RANGER. Confirm me by a smile then, Madam; remove that Cloud, which makes me apprehend [<i>Goes to take off her Mask.</i>] foul weather: Mr. <i>Vincent,</i> pray retire; 'tis you keep on the Ladies Mask, and no displeasure, which she has for me; yet, Madam, you need not distrust his honour, or his faith; but do not keep the Lady under constraint; pray leave us a little Master <i>Vincent.</i>

CHRISTINA. You must not leave us, Sir; wou'd you leave me with a stranger?

VALENTINE. How's that!   [<i>Behind.</i>

RANGER. I've done amiss, I find, to bring her hither,

[Aside.

Madam, I understand you—   [<i>Apart to</i> CHRISTINA.

CHRISTINA. Sir, I do not understand you.

RANGER. You wou'd not be known to Mr. <i>Vincent.</i>

CHRISTINA. 'Tis your acquaintance I wou'd avoid.

RANGER. Dull Brute, that I was, to bring her hither:

[Aside.

I have found my error, Madam; give me but a new appointment, where I may meet you by and by, and straight I will withdraw, as if I knew you not.

[*Softly to her.*

CHRISTINA. Why, do you know me?

RANGER. I must not own it.   [*Aside.*

No Madam, but—   [*Offers to whisper.*

CHRISTINA. Whispering, Sir, argues an old acquaintance; but I have not the vanity to be thought of yours, and resolve you shall never have the disparagement of mine: Mr. *Vincent,* pray let us go in here.

RANGER. How's this! I am undone I see; but if I let her go thus, I shall be an eternal laughing stock to *Vincent.*

VINCENT. Do you not know him, Madam? I thought you had come hither on purpose to meet him.

CHRISTINA. To meet him.

VINCENT. By your own appointment.

CHRISTINA. What strange infatuation do's delude you all? you know, he said, he did not know me.

VINCENT. You writ to him, he has your Letter.

CHRISTINA. Then you know my name sure? yet you confess'd but now, you knew me not.

RANGER. I must confess, your anger has disguis'd you, more than your Mask; for I thought to have met a kinder *Christina* here.

CHRISTINA. Heavens! how cou'd he know me in this place? he watch'd me hither sure; or is there any other of my name, that you may no longer mistake me, for your *Christina?* I'le pull of that which sooths your error.

[*Pulls off her Mask.*

RANGER. Take but t'other vizard off too; I mean your anger, and I'le swear you are the same, and only *Christina,* which I wish'd, and thought to meet here.

CHRISTINA. How cou'd you think to meet me here?

RANGER. By virtue of this your Commission, [*Gives her the Letter.*] which now, I see, was meant a real challenge; for you look, as if you wou'd fight with me.

CHRISTINA. The Paper is a stranger to me, I never writ it; you are abus'd.

VINCENT. *Christina* is a Person of Honour, and will own what she has written, *Ranger*.

RANGER. So, the Comedy begins; I shall be laugh'd at sufficiently, if I do not justifie my self; I must set my impudence to hers, she is resolv'd to deny all I see, and I have lost all hope of her.   [*Aside*.

VINCENT. Come, faith *Ranger*—

RANGER. You will deny too, Madam, that I follow'd you last night from the Park, to your lodging, where I stay'd with you till morning; you never saw me before I warrant?

CHRISTINA. That you rudely intruded, last night, into my lodging, I cannot deny; but I wonder you have the confidence to brag of it; sure you will not of your reception?

RANGER. I never was so ill-bred, as to brag of my reception in a Ladies Chamber; not a word of that, Madam.

VALENTINE. How! if he lies, I revenge her; if it be true, I revenge my self.

VALENTINE *draws his Sword, which* VINCENT *seeing, thrusts him back, and shuts the dore upon him before he was discover'd by* RANGER.

Enter LYDIA *and her Woman, stopping at the dore.*

LYDIA. What do I see! *Christina* with him! a Counter-plot to mine, to make me, and it, ridiculous; 'tis true, I find they have been long acquainted, and I long abus'd; but since she intends a triumph, in spight, as well as shame (not emulation) I retire; she deserves no envy, who will be shortly in my condition; his natural inconstancy, will prove my best revenge on her—on both.

[*Exeunt* LYDIA *with her Woman.*

DAPPERWIT *to them.*

DAPPERWIT. *Christina*'s going away again; what's the matter?

RANGER. What do you mean?

DAPPERWIT. I scarce had paid the Chair-men, and was coming up after her, but I met her on the stairs, in as much haste, as if she had been frightn'd.

RANGER. Who do you talk of?

DAPPERWIT. *Christina*, whom I took up in a Chair, just now at Saint *James*'s Gate.

RANGER. Thou art mad, here she is, this is *Christina*.

DAPPERWIT. I must confess, I did not see her face; but I am sure the Lady is gone, that I brought just now.

RANGER. I tell you, again, this is she; did you bring two?

CHRISTINA. I came in no Chair, had no guide, but my woman there.

VINCENT. When did you bring your Lady, *Dapperwit?*

DAPPERWIT. Ev'n now, just now.

VINCENT. This Lady has been here half an hour.

RANGER. He knows not what he says, he is mad, you are all so, I am so too.

VINCENT. 'Tis the best excuse you can make for your self, and by owning your mistake, you'l shew you are come to your self; I my self saw your woman at the dore, who but look'd in, and then immediately went down again, as your friend *Dapperwit* too affirms.

CHRISTINA. You had best follow her, that look'd for you; and I'le go seek out him, I came to see; Mr. *Vincent*, pray let me in here.

RANGER. 'Tis very fine, wondrous fine!

[CHRISTINA *goes out a little, and returns.*

CHRISTINA. Oh he is gone! Mr. *Vincent*, follow him; he were yet more severe to me, in indangering his life, than in his censures of me; you know the power of his Enemies is great, as their malice; just Heaven preserve him from them, and me from this ill, or unlucky man.

[*Exeunt* CHRISTINA, *her Woman, and* VINCENT.

RANGER. 'Tis well—nay, certainly, I shall never be master of my Senses more; but why do'st thou help to distract me too?

DAPPERWIT. My astonishment was as great as yours, to see her go away again; I wou'd have stay'd her if I cou'd.

RANGER. Yet, again, talking of a woman you met going out, when I talk of *Christina*.

DAPPERWIT. I talk of *Christina* too.

RANGER. She went out just now; the woman you found me with, was she.

DAPPERWIT. That was not the *Christina* I brought just now.

RANGER. You brought her, almost, half an hour ago; s'death, will you give me the lye?

DAPPERWIT. A Lady disappointed by her Gallant, the night before her journey, cou'd not be more touchy with her Maid, or Husband, than you are with me now, after your dis-appointment; but if you thank me so, I'le go serve my self hereafter; for ought I know, I have dis-appointed Mrs. *Martha* for you, and may lose thirty thousand pound by the bargain: farewel, a raving Lover is fit for solitude.   [*Exit* DAPPERWIT.

RANGER. *Lydia*, triumph, I now am thine again; of Intrigues, honourable or dishonourable, and all sorts of rambling, I take my leave; when we are giddy, 'tis time to stand still: why shou'd we be so fond of the by-paths of Love? where we are still way-lay'd, with Surprizes, Trapans, Dangers, and Murdering dis-appointments:

> Just as at Blind-mans Buff, we run at all,
> Whilst those that lead us, laugh to see us fall;
> And when we think, we hold the Lady fast,
> We find it but her Scarf, or Veil, at last.   [*Exit.*[9]

ACT V. SCENE I.

St. James's Park.

Enter Sir SIMON ADDLEPLOT, *leading*
Mrs. MARTHA, DAPPERWIT.

SIR SIMON. At length, you see, I have freed the Captive Lady, for her longing Knight. Mr. *Dapperwit*, who brings off a Plot cleverly now.

DAPPERWIT. I wish our Poets were half so good at it; Mrs. *Martha*, a thousand welcoms—
          [DAPPERWIT *Kisses and Embraces Mrs.* MARTHA.

SIR SIMON. Hold, hold, Sir; your joy is a little too familiar, (faith and troth.)

DAPPERWIT. Will you not let me salute Mrs. *Martha?*

MARTHA. What *Jonas*, do you think I do not know good breeding? must I be taught by you?

SIR SIMON. I wou'd have kept the Maiden-head of your lips, for your sweet Knight, Mrs. *Martha*, that's all; I dare swear, you never kiss'd any man before, but your Father.

MARTHA. My sweet Knight, if he will be a Knight of mine, must be contented with what he finds, as well as other Knights.

SIR SIMON. So smart already, faith and troth!

MARTHA. Dear, Mr. *Dapperwit*, I am over-joy'd to see you; but I thank honest *Jonas* for't.

SIR SIMON. How she hugs him! [*Aside.*

MARTHA. Poor, Mr. *Dapperwit*, I thought I shou'd never have seen you again; but I thank honest *Jonas* there—
[*She hugs* DAPPERWIT.

SIR SIMON. Do not thank me, Mrs. *Martha*, any more than I thank you.

MARTHA. I wou'd not be ungrateful, *Jonas*.

SIR SIMON. Then reserve your kindness, only, for your Worthy Noble, Brave, Heroick Knight; who loves you only, and only deserves your kindness.

MARTHA. I will shew my kindness to my Worthy, Brave, Heroick Knight, in being kind to his Friend, his dear Friend, who help'd him to me.
[*Hugs* DAPPERWIT *again.*

SIR SIMON. But, Mistress *Martha*, he is not to help him always; though he helps him to be married, he is not to help him when he is married.

MARTHA. What, Mr. *Dapperwit*, will you love my worthy Knight, less after marriage, than before? that were against the custom; for marriage gets a man friends, instead of losing those he has.

DAPPERWIT. I will ever be his Servant, and yours; Dear, Madam, do not doubt me.

MARTHA. I do not, sweet, dear, Mr. *Dapperwit*; but I shou'd not have seen you these two days, if it had not been for honest *Jonas*, there— [*She Kisses* DAPPERWIT.

SIR SIMON. For shame, though she be young and foolish, do not you wrong me to my face. [*Apart to* DAPPERWIT.

DAPPERWIT. Wou'd you have me so ill bred, as to repulse

her innocent kindness; what a thing it is to want Wit!

[*Aside.*

SIR SIMON. A Pox, I must make haste to discover my self, or I shall discover, what I wou'd not discover; but if I shou'd discover my self in this habit, 'twou'd not be to my advantage; but I'le go, put on my own cloaths, and look like a Knight: [*Aside.*
Well, Mrs. *Martha,* I'le go seek out your Knight; are you not impatient to see him? [*To her.*

MARTHA. Wives must be obedient, let him take his own time.

SIR SIMON. Can you trust your self, a turn or two, with Master *Dapperwit?*

MARTHA. Yes, yes, *Jonas,* as long as you will.

SIR SIMON. But I wou'd not trust you with him, if I could help it; [*Aside.*
So marry'd Wight, sees what he dares not blame;
And cannot budge for fear, nor stay for shame.

[*Exit* SIR SIMON.

DAPPERWIT. I am glad he is gone, that I may laugh; 'tis such a miracle of Fops, that his conversation shou'd be pleasant to me, even when it hindred me of yours.

MARTHA. Indeed, I'm glad he is gone too, as pleasant as he is.

DAPPERWIT. I know why, I know why, sweet Mrs. *Martha;* I warrant you, you had rather have the Parsons company, than his? now you are out of your Fathers house, 'tis time to leave being a Hypocrite.

MARTHA. Well, for the jests sake, to dis-appoint my Knight, I wou'd not care if I dis-appointed my self of a Ladyship.

DAPPERWIT. Come, I will not keep you on the Tenters, I know you have a mind to make sure of me; I have a little Chaplain, I wish he were a Bishop, or one of the Fryars, to perfect our revenge upon that Zealous Jew, your Father.

MARTHA. Do not speak ill of my Father, he has been your friend, I'm sure.

on the Tenters: in suspense. *Jew:* usurer.
We still say "on tenterhooks."

DAPPERWIT. My Friend—

MARTHA. His hard usage of me, conspir'd with your good Meen, and Wit, and to avoid slavery under him, I stoop to your yoke.

DAPPERWIT. I will be obliged to your Father, for nothing but a portion, nor to you for your love; 'twas due to my merit.

MARTHA. You shew your self Sir *Simons* original, if 'twere not for that vanity—

DAPPERWIT. I shou'd be no wit, 'tis the badge of my calling; for you can no more find a man of wit without vanity, than a fine woman without affectation: But let us go, before the Knight comes again.

MARTHA. Let us go before my Father comes, he soon will have the intelligence.

DAPPERWIT. Stay, let me think a little. [*Pauses.*

MARTHA. What are you thinking of? you shou'd have thought before this time, or, I shou'd have thought rather.

DAPPERWIT. Peace, peace.

MARTHA. What are you thinking of?

DAPPERWIT. I am thinking, what a Wit without vanity is like; he is like—

MARTHA. You do not think we are in a publick place, and may be surpriz'd, and prevented by my Fathers Scouts.

DAPPERWIT. What, wou'd you have me lose my thought?

MARTHA. You wou'd rather lose your Mistress, it seems.

DAPPERWIT. He is like— I think I'm a Sot to night, let me perish.

MARTHA. Nay, if you are so in love with your thought. [*Offers to go.*

DAPPERWIT. Are you so impatient to be my Wife? he is like—he is like—a Picture without shadows, or, or—a Face without Patches—or a Diamond without a Foyl; these are new thoughts now, these are new.

MARTHA. You are wedded already to your thoughts, I see, good night.

DAPPERWIT. Madam, do not take it ill;

For loss of happy thought, there's no amends.

For his new jest, true Wit will lose old Friends.

That's new again, the thought's new.   [*Exeunt.*
Enter GRIPE, *leading Mrs.* LUCY, JOYNER,
CROSSBITE *following.*

GRIPE. Mrs. *Joyner*, I can conform to this mode of publick walking by Moon-light, because one is not known.

LUCY. Why, are you asham'd of your company?

GRIPE. No, Pretty one; because in the dark, or as it were
the dark, there is no envy, nor scandal; I wou'd neither
lose you, nor my reputation.

JOYNER. Your reputation; indeed, your Worship, 'tis well
known, there are as grave men, as your Worship; nay,
men in office too, that adjourn their cares, and businesses, to come and unbend themselves at night here,
with a little vizard mask.

GRIPE. I do believe it, I do believe it, Mrs. *Joyner*.

LUCY. I God-mother, and carries, and treats her at Mulberry Garden.

CROSSBITE. Nay, do's not only treat her, but gives her his
whole gleanings of that day.

GRIPE. They may, they may Mrs. *Crossbite*, they take
above six in the hundred.[1]

CROSSBITE. Nay, there are those of so much worth, and
honour, and love, that they'l take it from their Wives
and Children, to give it to their Misses; now your
Worship has no Wife, and but one Child.

GRIPE. Still for my Edification.   [*Aside.*

JOYNER. That's true indeed, for I know a great Lady, that
cannot follow her Husband abroad to his Haunts, because her Farrendine is so ragged and greasie; whilst
his Mistress is as fine as fippence, in her embroidered
Satens.

GRIPE. Politickly done of him indeed; if the truth were
known, he is a States-man by that, umph—

CROSSBITE. Truly, your women of quality, are very troublesom to their Husbands; I have heard 'em complain, they
will allow them no separate maintainance, though the

---

fine as fippence: fine as five
pence: finely dressed. The
saying is a little like our
"bright as a penny," when it
is used for looks rather than
intelligence, but there are
heavier overtones of pride in
fine as fippence.

honourable Jilts, themselves, will not marry without it.

JOYNER. Come, come, Mistress, sometimes 'tis the craft of those Gentlemen, to complain of their Wives expences, to excuse their own narrowness to their Misses; but your Daughter has a Gallant can make no excuse.

GRIPE. So Mrs. *Joyner*—my friend Mrs. *Joyner*—

CROSSBITE. I hope, indeed, he'l give my Daughter no cause to dun him; for, poor wretch, she is as modest as her Mother.

GRIPE. I profess, I believe it.

LUCY. But, I have the boldness to ask him for a Treat; come Gallant, we must walk towards the Mulberry Gard'n.

GRIPE. So— I am afraid, little Mistress, the rooms are all taken up by this time.

JOYNER. Will you shame your self again? [*Aside to* GRIPE.

LUCY. If the rooms be full, we'l have an arbor.

GRIPE. At this time of night; besides, the Waiters will ne'r come near you.

LUCY. They will be observant of good Customers, as we shall be; come along.

GRIPE. Indeed, and verily, little Mistress, I wou'd go, but that I shou'd be forsworn, if I did.

JOYNER. That's so pitiful an excuse—

GRIPE. In truth, I have forsworn the place, ever since I was pawn'd there for a reckoning.

LUCY. You have broken many an Oath for the good old cause,[2] and will you boggle at one for your poor, little Miss? come along.

Lady FLIPPANT behind.

FLIPPANT. Unfortunate Lady, that I am! I have left the Herd on purpose to be chas'd, and have wandred this hour here; but the Park affords not so much as a Satyr for me, (and that's strange) no Burgundy man, or drunken Scourer will reel my way; the Rag-women, and Synder-women, have better luck than I[3]—but who are these? if this mungril light do's not deceive me, 'tis

---

pawn'd there for a reckoning: left to pay the check.

mungril: mongrel. In this context, light mixed with darkness.

my brother, 'tis he, there's *Joyner* too, and two other
women; I'le follow 'em; it must be he, for this world
hath nothing like him; I know not what the Devil may
be in the other.   [*Exeunt Omnes.*

Enter Sir SIMON ADDLEPLOT *in fine cloaths,* DAPPERWIT,
    and Mrs. MARTHA, *unseen by him at the dore.*

SIR SIMON. Well, after all my seeking, I can find those I
    wou'd not find; I'm sure 'twas old *Gripe*, and *Joyner*
    with him, and the Widow follow'd; he wou'd not have
    been here, but to have sought his Daughter, sure; but
    vigilant *Dapperwit* has spy'd him too, and has, no doubt,
    secur'd her from him.

DAPPERWIT. And you.   [*Behind.*

SIR SIMON. The Rogue is as good at hiding, as I am at steal-
    ing a Mistress; 'tis a vain conceited fellow, yet I think,
    'tis an honest fellow: but again, he is a damnable
    Whoring fellow; and what opportunity this air, and
    darkness may encline 'em to, Heaven knows; for I have
    heard the Rogue say himself, a Lady will no more shew
    her modesty in the dark, than a *Spaniard* his courage.

DAPPERWIT. Ha, ha, ha—

SIR SIMON. Nay, if you are there my true Friend, I'le for-
    give your harkning, if you'l forgive my censures? I speak
    to you, dear, Madam *Martha*; dear, dear— Behold
    your worthy Knight.

MARTHA. That's far from neighbours.

SIR SIMON. Is[4] come to reap the fruit of all his labours.

MARTHA. I cannot see the Knight; well, but I'm sure I hear
    Jonas.

SIR SIMON. I am no *Jonas*, Mrs. *Martha*.

MARTHA. The night is not so dark, nor the Perruque so
    big, but I can discern *Jonas*.

SIR SIMON. Faith and troth, I am the very Sir *Simon Addle-
    plot*, that is to marry you; the same, *Dapperwit* so-
    licited you for; ask him else, my name is not *Jonas*.

MARTHA. You think my youth, and simplicity, capable of
    this cheat; but let me tell you, *Jonas*, 'tis not your bor-

far from neighbours: praise
one's self.

row'd cloaths, and title, shall make me marry my Fathers man.

SIR SIMON. Borrow'd title; I'le be sworn I bought it of my Landress, who was a Court Landress; but, indeed, my cloaths I have not pay'd for, therefore in that sense they are borrow'd.

MARTHA. Prethee, *Jonas*, let the jest end, or I shall be presently in earnest.

SIR SIMON. Pray be in earnest, and let us go; the Parson, and Supper, stay for us, and I am a Knight in earnest.[5]

MARTHA. You a Knight, insolent, sawcy Fool?

SIR SIMON. The Devil take me, Mrs. *Martha*, if I am not a Knight now; a Knight Baronet too: a man ought, I see, to carry his Patent in his Pocket, when he goes to be marry'd, 'tis more necessary than a License; I am a Knight indeed, and, indeed now, Mrs. *Martha*.

MARTHA. Indeed, and indeed, the trick will not pass, *Jonas*.

SIR SIMON. Poor wretch, she's afraid, she shall not be a Lady: come, come, discover the Intrigue, *Dapperwit*—

MARTHA. You need not discover the Intrigue, 'tis apparent already; unworthy Mr. *Dapperwit*, after my confidence repos'd in you; cou'd you be so little generous, as to betray me to my Fathers man? but I'le be even with you.

SIR SIMON. Do not accuse him, poor man, before you hear him; tell her the intrigue man.

DAPPERWIT. A Pox, she will not believe us.

SIR SIMON. Will you not excuse your self? but I must not let it rest so; know then Mrs. *Martha*—

MARTHA. Come, I forgive thee before thy confession, *Jonas*; you never had had the confidence to have design'd this cheat upon me, but from Mr. *Dapperwits* encouragement, 'twas his Plot.

SIR SIMON. Nay, do not do me that wrong, Madam.

MARTHA. But since he has trapan'd me out of my Fathers house, he is like to keep me as long as I live; and so good night, *Jonas*.

Patent: the document conferring his title.

SIR SIMON. Hold, hold, what d'y' mean both? prethee tell
her I am Sir *Simon,* and no *Jonas.*

DAPPERWIT. A Pox, she will not believe us, I tell you.

SIR SIMON. I have provided a Parson, and Supper, at Mulberry Gard'n, and invited all my Friends I cou'd meet
in the Park.

DAPPERWIT. Nay, rather than they shall be dis-appointed,
there shall be a Bride and Bridegroom, to entertain 'em;
Mrs. *Martha,* and I'le go thither presently.

SIR SIMON. Why, shall she be your Bride?

DAPPERWIT. You see she will have it so.

SIR SIMON. Will you make *Dapperwit* your Husband?

MARTHA. Rather than my Fathers man.

SIR SIMON. Oh the Devil—

MARTHA. Nay, come along *Jonas,* you shall make one at
the Wedding, since you help'd contrive it.

SIR SIMON. Will you cheat your self, for fear of being
cheated?

MARTHA. I am desperate now.

SIR SIMON. Wilt thou let her do so ill a thing, *Dapperwit,*
as to marry thee? open her eyes, prethee, and tell her
I am a true Knight.

DAPPERWIT. 'Twou'd be in vain, by my life, you have
carry'd your self so like a natural Clerk—and so adieu
good *Jonas.*   [*Exeunt* MARTHA, *and* DAPPERWIT.

SIR SIMON. What, ruin'd by my own Plot, like an old
Cavalier: yet like him too, I will plot on still,[6] a plot
of prevention, so I have it—her Father was here ev'n
now, I'm sure; well— I'le go tell her Father of her, that
I will;

   And punish so her folly, and his treachery,
   Revenge is sweet, and makes amends for leachery.

                                          [*Exit.*

Enter LYDIA, *and her Woman* LEONORE.

LYDIA. I wish, I had not come hither to night, *Leonore.*

LEONORE. Why did you, Madam? if the place be so dis-
agreeable to you.

LYDIA. We cannot help visiting the place often, where we
have lost any thing we value; I lost *Ranger* here
last night.

LEONORE. You thought you had lost him before, a great while ago; and therefore you ought to be the less troubled.

LYDIA. But 'twas here, I miss'd him first, I'm sure.

LEONORE. Come, Madam, let not the loss vex you, he is not worth the looking after.

LYDIA. It cannot but vex me yet, if I lost him by my own fault.

LEONORE. You had but too much care to keep him.

LYDIA. It often happens, indeed, that too much care, is as bad as negligence; but I had rather be rob'd, than lose what I have carelesly.

LEONORE. But, I believe, you wou'd hang the Thief, if you cou'd.

LYDIA. Not if I cou'd have my own again.

LEONORE. I see, you wou'd be too merciful.

LYDIA. I wish I were try'd.

LEONORE. But, Madam, if you please, we will wave the discourse; for people seldom (I suppose) talk with pleasure, of their real losses.

LYDIA. 'Tis better than to ruminate on them; mine, I'm sure, will not out of my head, nor heart.

LEONORE. Grief is so far from retrieving a loss, that it makes it greater; but the way to lesson it, is, by a comparison with others losses; here are Ladies, in the Park, of your acquaintance, I doubt not, can compare with you; pray, Madam, let us walk and find 'em out.

LYDIA. 'Tis the resentment, you say, makes the loss great, or little; and then I'm sure, there is none like mine; however go on. [*Exeunt.*

Enter VINCENT *and* VALENTINE.

VINCENT. I am glad I have found you, for now I am prepar'd to lead you out of the dark, and all your trouble; I have good news.

VALENTINE. You are as unmerciful, as the Physician, who with new Arts, keeps his miserable Patient alive, and in hopes, when he knows the disease is incurable.

VINCENT. And you, like the melancholy Patient, mistrust, and hate your Physician, because he will not comply with your despair: but I'le cure your jealousie now.

VALENTINE. You know, all Diseases grow worse by relapses.

VINCENT. Trust me once more.

VALENTINE. Well, you may try your experiments upon me.

VINCENT. Just as I shut the dore upon you, the woman, *Ranger*, expected, came up stairs; but finding another woman in discourse with him, went down again, I suppose, as jealous of him, as you of *Christina*.

VALENTINE. How do's it appear she came to *Ranger*?

VINCENT. Thus, *Dapperwit* came up after, who had brought her, just then, in a Chair from St. *James's*, by *Rangers* appointment; and it is certain your *Christina* came to you.

VALENTINE. How can that be? for she knew not I was in the Kingdom.

VINCENT. My man confesses, when I sent him to enquire of her woman, about her Lady's being here in the Park last night; he told her you were come, and she, it seems, told her Mistress.

VALENTINE. That might be—   [*Aside.*
But did not *Christina* confess, *Ranger* was in her lodging last night?

VINCENT. By intrusion, which she had more particularly inform'd me of, if her apprehensions of your danger had not posted me after you; she not having yet (as I suppose) heard of *Clerimonts* recovery: I left her, poor creature, at home, distracted with a thousand fears for your life and love.

VALENTINE. Her love, I'm sure, has cost me more fears, than my life; yet that little danger is not past, (as you think) till the great one be over.

VINCENT. Open but your eyes, and the Fantastick Goblin's vanish'd, and all your idle fears, will turn to shame; for Jealousie, is the basest cowardize.

VALENTINE. I had rather, indeed, blush for my self, than her.

VINCENT. I'm sure you will have more reason—
But is not that *Ranger* there?

RANGER *enters, follow'd by* CHRISTINA *and her
Woman, after them,* LYDIA *and her Woman.*

VALENTINE. I think it is.

VINCENT. I suppose, his friend *Dapperwit* is not far off;
I will examine them both before you, and not leave you
so much, as the shadow of a doubt; *Rangers* astonishment at my lodging, confess'd his mistake.

VALENTINE. His astonishment might proceed from *Christina's* unexpected strangeness to him.

VINCENT. He shall satisfie you now himself to the contrary, I warrant you, have but patience.

VALENTINE. I had rather, indeed, he shou'd satisfie my
doubts, than my revenge; therefore I can have patience.

VINCENT. But what women are those that follow him?

VALENTINE. Stay a little—

RANGER. *Lydia, Lydia*—poor *Lydia.*

LYDIA. If she be my Rival, 'tis some comfort yet, to see
her follow him, rather than he her.   [*To her Maid.*

LEONORE. But if you follow them a little longer, for your
comfort, you shall see them go hand in hand.

CHRISTINA. Sir, Sir—   [*To* RANGER.

LEONORE. She calls to him already.

LYDIA. But he do's not hear, you see; let us go a little
nearer.

VINCENT. Sure it is *Ranger?*

VALENTINE. As sure as the woman that follows him closest,
is *Christina.*

VINCENT. For shame, talk not of *Christina;* I left her just
now at home, surrounded with so many fears and griefs,
she cou'd not stir.

VALENTINE. She is come, it may be, to divert them here
in the Park; I'm sure 'tis she.

VINCENT. When the Moon, at this instant, scarce affords
light enough to distinguish a man from a tree, how can
you know her?

VALENTINE. How can you know *Ranger,* then?

VINCENT. I heard him speak.

VALENTINE. So you may her too; I'le secure you, if you
will draw but a little nearer: she came, doubtless, to
no other end but to speak with him; observe—

CHRISTINA. Sir, I have follow'd you hitherto; [*To* RANGER.
but now, I must desire you to follow me out of the company, for I wou'd not be over-heard, nor disturb'd.

RANGER. Ha! is not this *Christina's* voice? it is I am sure,
I cannot be deceiv'd now—dear Madam—

VINCENT. It is she indeed.   [*Apart to* VALENTINE.

VALENTINE. Is it so?

CHRISTINA. Come, Sir—   [*To* RANGER.

VALENTINE. Nay, I'le follow you too, though not invited.
                                          [*Aside.*

LYDIA. I must not, cannot stay behind. [*Aside.*] [*Exeunt.*
They all go off together in a huddle, hastily;
    CHRISTINA, *her Woman, and* VALENTINE,
            return on the other side.

CHRISTINA. Come along, Sir.

VALENTINE. So I must stick to her when all is done; her
new servant has lost her in the crowd, she has gone too
fast for him; so much my revenge is swifter than his
love: now shall I not only have the deserted Lovers
revenge, of dis-appointing her of her new man; but an
opportunity infallibly at once, to discover her falseness,
and confront her impudence.   [*Aside.*

CHRISTINA. Pray come along, Sir, I am in haste.

VALENTINE. So eager, indeed— I wish that Cloud may yet
with-hold the Moon, that this false Woman, may not
discover me, before I do her.   [*Aside.*

CHRISTINA. Here no one can hear us, and I'm sure we cannot see one another.

VALENTINE. S'death, what have I giddily run my self upon?
'Tis rather a tryal of my self than her;
I cannot undergo it.   [*Aside.*

CHRISTINA. Come nearer, Sir.

VALENTINE. Hell and vengeance, I cannot suffer it, I
cannot.   [*Aside.*

CHRISTINA. Come, come; yet nearer, pray come nearer.

VALENTINE. It is impossible, I cannot hold; I must discover
my self, rather than her infamy.

CHRISTINA. You are conscious, it seems, of the wrong you
have done me, and are asham'd, though in the dark.
                        [*Speaks, walking slowly.*

VALENTINE. How's this! [*Aside.*

CHRISTINA. I'm glad to find it so; for all my business with you, is to show you your late mistakes, and force a confession from you, of those unmannerly injuries you have done me.

VALENTINE. What! I think she's honest; or do's she know me? sure she cannot. [*Aside.*

CHRISTINA. First, your intrusion, last night, into my lodging, which I suppose, has begot your other gross mistakes.

VALENTINE. No, she takes me for *Ranger*, I see again. [*Aside.*

CHRISTINA. You are to know then, (since needs you must) it was not me you follow'd last night to my lodging, from the Park, but some Kinswoman of yours, it seems; whose fear of being discover'd by you, prevail'd with me to personate her, while she withdrew, our Habits and our Statures being much alike; which I did with as much difficulty, as she us'd importunity to make me; and all this, my Lady *Flippant* can witness, who was then with your Cousin.

VALENTINE. I am glad to hear this— [*Aside.*

CHRISTINA. Now, what your claim to me, at Mr. *Vincent's* lodging meant; the letter, and promises, you unworthily, or erroneously lay'd to my charge, you must explain to me and others, or—

VALENTINE. How's this! I hope I shall discover no guilt but my own; she wou'd not speak in threats to a Lover— [*Aside.*

CHRISTINA. Was it because you found me in Mr. *Vincent's* lodgings, you took a liberty to use me, like one of your common Visitants? But know, I came no more to Mr. *Vincent*, than to you; yet, I confess, my visit was intended to a man— A brave man, till you made him use a woman ill, worthy the love of a Princess; till you made him censure mine; good as Angels, till you made him unjust; why—in the name of honour, wou'd you do't?

VALENTINE. How happily, am I dis-appointed! poor injur'd *Christina*. [*Aside.*

CHRISTINA. He wou'd have sought me out first, if you had not made him flye from me; our mutual love, confirm'd by a contract,[7] made our hearts inseparable; till you rudely, if not maliciously, thrust in upon us, and broke the close, and happy knot: I had lost him before for a month, now for ever.   [*She weeps.*

VALENTINE. My joy, and pity, makes me as mute, as my shame; yet I must discover my self.   [*Aside.*

CHRISTINA. Your silence, is a confession of your guilt.

VALENTINE. I own it.   [*Aside.*

CHRISTINA. But that will not serve my turn; for strait you must go clear your self, and me, to him you have injur'd in me; if he has not made too much haste from me, to be found again; you must, I say, for he is a man that will have satisfaction; and in satisfying him, you do me.

VALENTINE. Then he is satisfy'd.

CHRISTINA. How! is it you? then I am not satisfy'd.

VALENTINE. Will you be worse than your word?

CHRISTINA. I gave it not to you.

VALENTINE. Come, dear *Christina*, the Jealous, like the Drunkard, has his punishment, with his offence.

To them VINCENT.

VINCENT. *Valentine*, Mr. *Valentine*.

VALENTINE. *Vincent*—

VINCENT. Where have you been all this while?

VALENTINE *holds* CHRISTINA *by the hand,*
who seems to struggle to get from him.

VALENTINE. Here, with my injur'd *Christina*.

VINCENT. She's behind with *Ranger*, who is forc'd to speak all the tender things himself; for she affords him not a word.

VALENTINE. Pish, pish, *Vincent*, who is blind now? who deceiv'd now?

VINCENT. You are, for I'm sure *Christina* is with him; come back and see.

They go out at one dore, and return at the other.

RANGER *to* LYDIA.

RANGER. Still mock'd, still abus'd! did you not bid me follow you, where we might not be disturb'd, nor over-heard? and now not allow me a word?

VINCENT *to* VALENTINE.

VINCENT. Did you hear him? [*Apart to* VALENTINE.

VALENTINE. Yes, yes, peace— [*Apart to* VINCENT.

RANGER. Disowning your Letter, and me, at *Vincent's* lodging, declaring you came to meet another there, and not me; with a great deal of such affronting unkindness, might be reasonable enough, because you wou'd not intrust *Vincent* with our love; but now, when no body sees us, nor hears us, why this unseasonable shyness?—

LYDIA. It seems, she did not expect him there, but had appointed to meet another; I wish it were so. [*Aside.*

RANGER. I have not Patience; do you design thus to revenge my intrusion into your lodging last night? sure if you had then been displeas'd with my company, you wou'd not have invited your self to't again by a Letter? or is this a punishment for bringing you to a house, so near your own, where, it seems, you were known too? I do confess, it was a fault; but make me suffer any Penance, but your Silence, because it is the certain mark of a Mistress's lasting displeasure—

LYDIA. My —— is not yet come.[8] [*Aside.*

RANGER. Not yet a word? you did not use me so unkindly last night, when you chid me out of your house, and with indignation bid me be gone; now, you bid me follow you, and yet will have nothing to say to me; and I am more deceiv'd this day and night, than I was last night; when, I must confess, I follow'd you for another.—

LYDIA. I'm glad to hear that. [*Aside.*

RANGER. One that wou'd have us'd me better; whose love, I have ungratefully abus'd for yours; yet from no other reason, but my natural inconstancy—

Poor *Lydia, Lydia*— [*Aside.*

LYDIA. He mutter'd my name sure, and with a sigh. [*Aside.*

RANGER. But as last night, by following (as I thought) her, I found you: so this night, by following you in vain, I do resolve, if I can find her again, to keep her for ever.

LYDIA. Now I am obliged, and brought in debt to his inconstancy; faith, now cannot I hold out any longer, I must discover my self. [*Aside.*

RANGER. But, Madam, because I intend to see you no more, I'le take my leave of you for good and all; since you will not speak, I'le try if you will squeek—

[*Goes to throw her down, she squeeks.*

LYDIA. Mr. *Ranger*, Mr. *Ranger*—

VINCENT. Fye, fye, you need not ravish *Christina* sure, that loves you so.

RANGER. Is it she! *Lydia* all this while? how am I gull'd, and *Vincent* in the Plot too?[9]

LYDIA. Now false *Ranger*.

RANGER. Now false *Christina* too; you thought I did not know you now, because I offer'd you such an unusual civility.

LYDIA. You knew me, I warrant you knew too, that I was the *Christina* you follow'd out of the Park last night; that I was the *Christina* that writ the Letter too.

RANGER. Certainly, therefore I wou'd have taken my revenge, you see, for your tricks.

VALENTINE. Is not this the same woman that took refuge in your house last night, Madam?   [*To* CHRISTINA.

CHRISTINA. The very same.

VALENTINE. What, Mr. *Ranger*, we have chop'd, and chang'd, and hid our *Christina's* so long, and often, that at last, we have drawn each of us our own?

RANGER. Mr. *Valentine* in *England!* the truth on't is, you have jugled together, and drawn without my knowledge; but since she will have it so, she shall wear me for good and all now.   [*Goes to take her by the hand.*

LYDIA. Come not near me.

RANGER. Nay, you need not be afraid, I wou'd ravish you, now I know you.

LYDIA. And yet, *Leonore*, I think 'tis but justice, to pardon the fault, I made him commit?

[*Apart to* LEONORE, RANGER *listens.*

RANGER. You consider it right, Cousin; for indeed, you are but merciful to your self in it.

LYDIA. Yet, if I wou'd be rigorous, though I made the blot, your over-sight has lost the game.

RANGER. But 'twas rash womans play, Cousin, and ought not to be play'd again, let me tell you.

[DAPPERWIT *to them.*

DAPPERWIT. Who's there? who's there?

RANGER. *Dapperwit.*

DAPPERWIT. Mr. *Ranger,* I am glad I have met with you; for I have left my Bride just now, in the house at Mulberry Garden, to come and pick up some of my Friends in the Park here, to sup with us.

RANGER. Your Bride! are you marry'd then? where is your Bride?

DAPPERWIT. Here at Mulberry Garden, I say, where you, these Ladies, and Gentlemen, shall all be welcome, if you will afford me the honour of your company.

RANGER. With all our hearts; but who have you marry'd, *Lucy?*

DAPPERWIT. What, do you think I wou'd marry a Wench? I have marry'd an Heiress worth thirty thousand pound, let me perish.

VINCENT. An Heiress worth thirty thousand pound!

DAPPERWIT. Mr. *Vincent,* your servant, you here too?

RANGER. Nay, we are more of your acquaintance here (I think) go, we'le follow you, for if you have not dismiss'd your Parson, perhaps we may make him more work.

[*Exeunt.*

*The Scene changes to the Dining-room,
in Mulberry-Garden-house.*

Enter Sir SIMON ADDLEPLOT, GRIPE, *Mrs.* MARTHA,
JOYNER, CROSSBITE, LUCY.

SIR SIMON. 'Tis as I told you, Sir, you see.

GRIPE. Oh graceless Babe, marry'd to a Wit! an idle, loytering, slandering, foul-mouth'd, beggarly Wit; Oh that my child should ever live to marry a Wit!

JOYNER. Indeed, your Worship had better seen her fairly buried, as they say.

CROSSBITE. If my Daughter, there, shou'd have done so, I wou'd not have gi'n her a groat.

GRIPE. Marry a Wit!

SIR SIMON. Mrs. *Joyner,* do not let me lose the Widow too; for if you do, (betwixt friends) I and my small annuity are both blown up; it will follow my estate.

[*To* JOYNER. *Aside.*

JOYNER. I warrant you.   [*Aside.*

FLIPPANT.[10] Let us make sure of Sir *Simon* to night, or—

[*To* JOYNER. *Aside.*

JOYNER. You need not fear it, like the Lawyers, while my Clients · endeavour to cheat one another; I in justice cheat 'em both.   [*Aside.*

GRIPE. Marry a Wit!

Enter DAPPERWIT, RANGER, *and* LYDIA, VALENTINE, CHRISTINA, *and* VINCENT.

DAPPERWIT *stops 'em, and they stand all behind.*

DAPPERWIT. What is he here, *Lucy* and her Mother?

[*Aside.*

GRIPE. Tell me how thou cam'st to marry a Wit?

MARTHA. Pray be not angry, Sir, and I'le give you a good reason.

GRIPE. Reason for marrying a Wit!

MARTHA. Indeed, I found my self six months gone with Child, and saw no hopes of your getting me a Husband, or else I had not married a Wit, Sir.

JOYNER. Then you were the Wit.   [*Aside.*

GRIPE. Had you that reason? nay, then—

[*Holding up his hands.*

DAPPERWIT. How's that!   [*Aside.*

RANGER. Who wou'd have thought, *Dapperwit,* you wou'd have married a Wench?   [*Aside.*

DAPPERWIT. Well, thirty thousand pound will make me amends; I have known my betters wink, and fall on for five or six. [*To* RANGER.] What, you are come, Sir, to give me joy? [*To* GRIPE *and the rest.*] you Mrs. *Lucy,* you, and you? well, unbid guests are doubly welcom— Sir *Simon,* I made bold to invite these Ladies, and Gentlemen, [*To Sir* SIMON.] for you must know, Mr. *Ranger,* this worthy Sir *Simon,* do's not only give me my Wedding-Supper, but my Mistress too; and is as it were my Father.

SIR SIMON. Then I am as it were a Grand father to your new Wives, *hans en kelder;* to which you are but as it were a Father; there's for you again, Sir—ha ha—

RANGER. Ha, ha, ha—　　　　　　　　　[*To* VINCENT.

DAPPERWIT. Fools sometimes say unhappy things, if we wou'd mind 'em, but—what, Melancholy at your Daughters Wedding, Sir?

GRIPE. How deplorable is my condition?　　　[*Aside.*

DAPPERWIT. Nay, if you will rob me of my Wench, Sir, can you blame me for robbing you of your Daughter? I cannot be without a Woman.

GRIPE. My Daughter, my Reputation, and my Money gone —but the last is dearest to me; yet at once I may retrieve that, and be reveng'd for the loss of the other; and all this by marrying *Lucy* here: I shall get my five hundred pound again, and get Heirs to exclude my Daughter, and frustrate *Dapperwit;* besides, 'tis agreed on all hands, 'tis cheaper keeping a Wife than a Wench.

　　　　　　　　　　　　　　　　　　[*Aside.*

DAPPERWIT. If you are so melancholy, Sir, we will have the Fiddles, and a Dance to divert you; come.

　　　　　　　　　　A Dance.

GRIPE. Indeed, you have put me so upon a merry pin, that I resolve to marry too.

FLIPPANT. Nay, if my Brother come to marrying once, I may too; I swore I wou'd, when he did, little thinking—

SIR SIMON. I take you at your word, Madam.

FLIPPANT. Well, but if I had thought you wou'd have been so quick with me—

GRIPE. Where is your Parson?

DAPPERWIT. What, you wou'd not revenge your self upon the Parson?

GRIPE. No, I wou'd have the Parson revenge me upon you; he shou'd marry me.

DAPPERWIT. I am glad you are so frolick, Sir; but who wou'd you marry?

GRIPE. This innocent Lady.　　　　[*Pointing to* LUCY.

DAPPERWIT. That innocent Lady?

hans en kelder: (Dutch) Jack
in the cellar, an unborn child.

GRIPE. Nay, I am impatient, Mrs. *Joyner,* pray fetch him up, if he be yet in the house.

DAPPERWIT. We were not marry'd here; but you cannot be in earnest.

GRIPE. You'l find it so; since you have rob'd me of my House-keeper, I must get another.

DAPPERWIT. Why? she was my Wench.

GRIPE. I'le make her honest then.

CROSSBITE. Upon my repute he never saw her before: but will your Worship marry my Daughter then?

GRIPE. I promise her, and you, before all this good company, to morrow I will make her my Wife.

DAPPERWIT. How!

RANGER. Our Ladies, Sir, I suppose, expect the same promise from us.   [*To* VALENTINE.

VALENTINE. They may be sure of us without a promise; but let us (if we can) obtain theirs, to be sure of them.

DAPPERWIT. But will you marry her to morrow?—
                                              [*To* GRIPE.

GRIPE. I will verily.

DAPPERWIT. I am undone then, ruin'd let me perish.

SIR SIMON. No, you may hire a little room in *Covent-Garden,* and set up a *Coffee-house;* you, and your Wife, will be sure of the Wits custom.

DAPPERWIT. Abus'd by him, I have abus'd!

> Fortune our foe, we cannot over-wit,
> By none but thee, our projects are Cross-bit.

VALENTINE. Come, dear Madam, what yet angry? jealousie sure is much more pardonable before marriage, than after it; but to morrow, by the help of the Parson, you will put me out of all my fears.

CHRISTINA. I am afraid then you wou'd give me my revenge, and make me jealous of you; and I had rather suspect your faith, than you shou'd mine.

RANGER. Cousin *Lydia,* I had rather suspect your faith too, than you shou'd mine; therefore let us e'en marry to morrow, that I may have my turn of watching, doging, standing under the window at the dore, behind the hanging or—

LYDIA. But if I cou'd be desperate now, and give you up

my liberty; cou'd you find in your heart to quit all other
engagements, and voluntarily turn your self over to one
woman, and she a Wife too? cou'd you away with the
insupportable bondage of Matrimony?

RANGER. You talk of Matrimony as irreverently, as my
Lady *Flippant;* the Bondage of Matrimony, no—

The end of Marriage, now is liberty,
And two are bound—to set each other free.

EPILOGUE

Spoken by DAPPERWIT.[1]

Now my Brisk Brothers of the Pit, you'l say,
I'm come to speak a good word for the Play;
But (Gallants) let me perish, if I do,
For I have Wit, and judgment, just like you;
Wit never partial, judgment free and bold,
For fear or friendship never bought or sold,
Nor by good Nature, e're to be Cajol'd.
Good Nature in a Critick were a crime,
Like mercy in a Judge, and renders him
Guilty of all those faults, he do's forgive:
Besides, if Thief from Gallows you reprieve,
He'll cut your Throat; so Poet sav'd from shame,
In damn'd Lampoon, will murder your good name.
  Yet in true spight to him, and to his Play,
(Good faith) you shou'd not rayl at 'em to day;
But to be more his Foe, seem most his Friend,
And so maliciously, the Play commend,
That he may be betray'd to Writing on,
And Poet let him be, to be undone.

FINIS.

NOTES

1. The conventional dedicatory use of *favour* to mean literary approbation is in this case double entendre; so is much that follows. According to contemporary accounts, Wycherley had become one of the lovers of the Duchess of Cleveland. Since the playwright's biography is more anecdote than fact, John Dennis's version of the first encounter will serve as well as any, and more amusingly than most, to make clear the connection between *Love in a Wood* and the affair between the new dramatist and the new duchess (Barbara Villiers had been given the title on August 3, 1670): "The writing of that Play was likewise the Occasion of his becoming acquainted with one of King *Charles's* Mistresses after a very particular manner. As Mr. *Wycherley* was going thro' *Pall-mall* toward *St. James's* in his Chariot, he met the foresaid Lady in hers, who, thrusting half her Body out of the Chariot, cry'd out aloud to him, *You,* Wycherley, *you are a Son of a Whore,* at the same time laughing aloud and heartily. Perhaps, Sir, if you never heard of this Passage before, you may be surpris'd at so strange a Greeting from one of the most beautiful and best bred Ladies in the World. Mr. *Wycherley* was certainly very much surpris'd at it, yet not so much but he soon apprehended it was spoke with Allusion to the latter End of a Song in the foremention'd Play:

> *When Parents are Slaves*
> *Their Brats cannot be any other,*
> * Great Wits and great Braves,*
> *Have always a Punk to their Mother.*

As, during Mr. *Wycherley's* Surprise, the Chariots drove different ways, they were soon at a considerable Distance from each other, when Mr. *Wycherley* recovering from Surprise, ordered his Coachman to drive back, and to overtake the Lady. As soon as he got over-against her, he said to her, *Madam, you have been pleased to bestow a Title on me which generally belongs to the Fortunate. Will your Ladyship be at the Play to Night? Well,* she reply'd, *what if I am there? Why then I will be there to wait on your Ladyship, tho' I disappoint a very fine Woman who has made me an Assignation. So,* said she, *you are sure to disappoint a Woman who has favour'd you for one who has not. Yes,* he reply'd, *if she who has not favour'd me is the finer Woman of the two. But he who will be constant to your Ladyship, till he can find a finer Woman, is sure to die your Captive.* The Lady blush'd, and bade her Coachman drive away. As she was then in all her Bloom, and the most celebrated Beauty that was then in *England,* or perhaps that has been in *England* since, she was touch'd with the Gallantry of that Compliment. In short, she was that Night in the first Row of the King's Box in *Drury Lane,* and Mr. *Wycherley* in the Pit under her, where he entertained her during the whole Play. And this, Sir, was the beginning of a Correspondence between these two Persons, which afterwards made a great Noise in the Town." (*Original Letters, Familiar, Moral and Critical,* London, 1721, pp. 215–217.)

2. It is primarily on the basis of this remark that the play's premiere is placed uncertainly in March 1671.

PROLOGUE

1. This couplet means more than that other dramatists have earned the right to criticize. Since some playwrights were granted free admission, their writing may have bought their way into the theater.

2. In the 1694 Quarto, the comma is placed between *any* and *Scorn.* This shift does not so much clarify the lines as indicate the difficulties in interpreting the punctuation of the period. The couplet, as it stands, seems to say that they (the small brothers) are made poor men of the trade by the gentlemen who break them rather than by any scorn heaped on them. The 1694 shift suggests that they (the huge bankers), by breaking gentlemen, increase their own reputations and that they scorn the poor men of the trade. Either reading would suit Wycherley's purpose in the Prologue.

3. Since *fleering* means both "smiling flatteringly" and "mocking," Wycherley can suggest the conventional plea for acceptance while he retains the tone of amused contempt that informs the Prologue as a whole.

4. Samuel Pepys reports (April 16, 1667) that "the King was so angry at the liberty taken by Lacy's part to abuse him to his face" at the premiere of Edward Howard's *The Change of Crownes* (April 15) by the King's Company that he made them take off the play. On April 20, Pepys says "That Lacy had been committed to the porter's lodge for his acting his part in the late new play . . ." (Wheatley, VI, 273–274, 277). Since John Lacy was playing Alderman Gripe in Wycherley's play, an inside joke is probably intended as well as a general reference to the persecution of wits. The speaker of the Pro-

logue is not indicated in the published play, but if Thomas Killigrew (the manager of the King's Company) had his wits about him, Lacy would have spoken it. Since his brief incarceration led to a fight with Howard (Lacy hit Howard over the head with his cane) and the temporary closing of the theater, the incident was probably well enough known to have drawn a laugh four years later.

ACT I

1. After the Great Fire of London (September 2–6, 1666) destroyed much of the old City, tradesmen moved out, opened shops in other parts of London; the anonymous author of *The Trade of England Revived* (London, 1681) speaks of shopkeepers "that have (since the fire) set up in Covent-Garden, and on that side of the City" (p. 48). Thus the "Citizens Signs" (outside the shops) may be said to have walked ground. In making her conceit, Lady Flippant balances *Citizens Signs* with *my Husbands Scutcheon*, for a scutcheon, a shield with a coat of arms on it, is a kind of sign. Since she is presumably the walking scutcheon, the phrase takes on amusing overtones. A scutcheon meant not only reputation (by extension from arms), but it had another meaning as well—the metal plate around a keyhole. Whatever the double entendre, the passage means primarily that the Widow Flippant has been doing a great deal of self-advertisement.

2. Hyde Park and the Mulberry Garden were popular gathering places, good spots to initiate flirtations. St. Paul's, Covent Garden, and St. Martin's-in-the-Fields, both fashionable churches, often served the same secular function. Mrs. Cheatly, the bawd of Thomas Shadwell's *The Miser* (1672), trying to arrange an assignation suggests first "the *Mulberry-Garden*" and then "*Covent garden* Church." *The Complete Works of Thomas Shadwell*, London, 1691, 40.

3. Charles II introduced the vest as court dress in October 1666. Pepys, seeing King Charles in his vest for the first time on October 15, described it as "being a long cassocke close to the body, of black cloth, and pinked with white silke under it, and a coat over it . . ." (Wheatley, VI, 21). Gripe, being a Puritan, disapproved of both the court (the vest) and the church (the surplice).

4. A *lead Captain* (or led-captain) attached himself to a squire, earning his position by making himself useful. In *Tom Jones*, Henry Fielding describes "two led Captains, who had before rode with his Lordship": "but they were ready at any Time to have performed the Office of a Footman, or indeed would have condescended lower, for the Honour of his Lord-

ship's Company and for the Convenience of his Table" (London, 1749, IV, 176).

5. This is obviously an aside, although the text gives no stage direction.

6. Mrs. Joyner presumably got Gripe to take on Sir Simon (as Jonas) as a clerk, thus helping him into his service. Considering her profession, *Service* here has an obvious double meaning.

7. Dapperwit means something stronger than the *jilting Widow* of Sir Simon's earlier couplet. One of the meanings of "jilt" is "whore," although the usage is likely to be softer, as we use "tramp" today.

8. "Before you begin the Game at Picket, you must throw of the Pack the *Deuces, Treys, Fours* and *Fives.* . . ." Charles Cotton, *The Compleat Gamester*, London, 1674, p. 80. The author indicates that, besides piquet, a number of other card games—renegado (a kind of ombre), gleek, ruff and honours, whist—were played with stripped decks.

9. Whetstone Park was a tough district, known for its prostitutes. Thomas Shadwell in a verse letter (c. 1671) to Wycherley, asking for news of the town, wants to know "If they break Windows when they're Drunk, / And at late hours, wake *Whetstone's* Punk, / That has all day been hard at Service, / With Clerk and Prentice, *Tim* and *Gervas*" (Summers, II, 244).

10. The song appears as "A Wife I do hate" with music by Pelham Humphrey in *Choice Ayres and Songs,* Fifth Book, London, 1684, pp. 38–39. The words are not exactly the same as those given in the text of the play. See p. 29 for the song, in modern notation.

Act II

1. Vincent, the drinker, seems to have forgotten that they are praising the night and returns to his favorite subject.

2. The City of Westminster, adjacent to London proper (the City), was the site of Whitehall, the King's palace, and the center of government. Cities often maintained a small band of wind instrumentalists at public charge to play on official occasions and in the streets at night: "these are the *City Waits,* who play every Winter's Night thro' the Streets, . . . These are the Topping Tooters of the Town; and have *Gowns, Silver Chains,* and *Salaries,* for playing *Lilla Burlera* to my *Lord Mayors Horse* thro' the City." Ned Ward, *The London-Spy Compleat,* London, 1706, p. 36.

3. This compliment can be read two ways, depending on how one takes *betwixt.* Either the bad complexion is the result of the use of the two cosmetics; or, preferably, the bad complexion can be seen when the face is in its natural state, at that

moment "betwixt," when the pomatum, which has been used to soften the skin, is removed to make way for the rouge. If by *Holland Cheese* Sir Simon means texel, a sheep's milk cheese made in Holland in the seventeenth century, the line is even better; texel is green.

4. From the context, it is clear that *Haust-goust* is a bad smell. The word is probably a corruption of the French *haut goût*, meaning highly seasoned. In Antoine Furetière, *Dictionnaire universel* (Rotterdam, 1708), under *goust* is this phrase: *"Les sauces de trop haut goût sont nuisibles à la santé."*

5. By letting Sir Simon try to find Lady Flippant among the dancers, Wycherley suggests that the dance is relevant to the play's action; in fact, it is not. It is presumably in the play because Restoration audiences loved to see dancing in the theater. See *The London Stage*, I, cviii–cxii, for a discussion of the popularity of dance.

6. 1694 Q: for the obligation.

7. The coffeehouses were relatively new and very popular places for men to meet and talk. As Dapperwit's description of the coffee-wit indicates, the conversation frequently ran to politics—so frequently that there was an attempt to suppress the coffeehouses in 1675. Earlier than that, in a note dated November 23, 1671, Joseph Williamson, secretary to Lord Arlington and the editor of *The London Gazette*, coupled coffeehouses with the Nurseries (training theaters for young actors) as incitements to public unrest and suggested that if they were pulled down "nothing can be more to the establishment of the government." *Calendar of State Papers, Domestic,* ser. 4, XI (London, 1895), p. 581.

8. The *Christian Grand Signior* (Louis XIV of France) was intimately involved with English foreign policy at this time, as the secret and the public treaties of 1670 testify. England's complicated and confused negotiations with the Barbary States erupted momentarily into active war with Algiers in 1669; England, like France and Holland, tried not only to obtain workable agreements with the Barbary States that would let their ships pass freely but also to use the "pirates" against the enemy of the moment. The *Grand Signior of Constantinople* (the Sultan Mahommed IV) was presumably interested in what was going on along the Barbary coast, since that was part of his empire, but Constantinople was not directly involved in English negotiations after the abortive attempts immediately following the Restoration. Dapperwit may have intended three disconnected examples of coffee-wit railing, but he came up with a Mediterranean combination that heightens the suggestion of uninformed wits; the rumors from that part of the world were even less substantial than the ones from directly across the Channel, as the frequently reported death of

John Ward, Consul at Algiers, indicates (see Godfrey Fisher, *Barbary Legend*, Oxford, 1957, pp. 243–244, where some of the quotations are from *The London Gazette's* Mediterranean sources). The juxtaposition of the two Grand Signiors suggests that Wycherley may have been thinking in terms of religions; certainly domestic politics and foreign policy at the time was inextricably bound up in the Catholic-Anglican-Dissenter struggles and the coffee-wits could hardly have been quiet on the subject.

9. Wycherley has a particular kind of book in mind. For example, the *Term Catalogues*, November 22, 1670, lists, for five shillings, "Wit's Interpreter. The English *Parnassus*, or a sure guide to those admirable accomplishments that compleat our English Gentry in the most acceptable qualifications of Discourse, or Writing. The Third Edition, with many new Additions."

10. At the bottom of p. 27 in the 1672 Q, presumably to make room for the catchword, this stage direction is moved up a line so that it looks as though Ranger's aside is spoken after the plural stage direction calls for him to leave the stage with Dapperwit. In 1694 Q, without the excuse of bottom-of-the-page crowding, the order is repeated. The *Exeunt* is here shifted (following Leigh Hunt's edition) so that Ranger can speak his line before he exits.

11. Lady Flippant's mocking greeting almost certainly derives from John Fletcher's *The Faithful Shepherdess*. The play was in the King's Company repertory; we know, from Pepys, that it had been played as recently as February 26, 1669. Zimbardo makes an extended and (to me) completely unconvincing attempt to show that Wycherley's play is a pastoral in conscious imitation of Fletcher's.

12. The repetition of Christina's name here may be a simple typographical error. It is possible, however, that a line has been lost; if so, it is almost certainly another protestation of Ranger's love and his unwillingness to leave.

13. The terms were the periods (four a year) when the superior courts were in session, at which time many people came up to London on business. By counting in terms instead of years, Dapperwit is guessing that the woman is a newcomer to London.

14. 1672 Q: you. 1713 *Works* first adds the missing *r*.

15. This line was provided by the errata list in 1672 Q. In the text there was no line at all, simply a stage direction, *He whispers*. The added line may be necessary to explain the pronoun in Ranger's *Yes, I observ'd them exactly*, but the stage direction suggests a nice bit of business, building from the whisper, to Vincent's *Pish, pish*, to his disbelieving question, to revelation.

Act III

1. In Southwark, the borough across the river from the City. The Pepper Alley Stairs, leading into Pepper Alley, was one of the landing places on the south bank of the Thames. According to Sir Walter Besant (*London in the Time of the Stuarts*, London, 1903, p. 180), Southwark had a reputation for housing some of the least desirable elements in the population. Contemporary sources seem not to have drawn any fine lines between the two sides of the river, but if Besant is correct, Wycherley may intend the street name as an indication of Mrs. Crossbite's character or Mrs. Joyner may intend it as an insult.

2. November 5: Guy Fawkes Day, the anniversary of the unsuccessful Gunpowder Plot (1605), in which Roman Catholic conspirators planned to blow up the Houses of Parliament while the king, lords and commons were assembled.

3. Dapperwit seems to be saying that Lucy is just (in the sense of both "exact" and "suitable") in all her attributes, but the compliment has a double edge. Since assignation, then, as now, meant an illicit meeting, he is also saying that she is a good wench. The line may have a third edge as well, although Dapperwit cannot know it; "just" also means "faithful" and this is what Lucy is about not to be—to Dapperwit and then to Gripe.

4. Dapperwit's use of *rarity*, followed by *hang out Flags*, suggests the setting up of a freak show. In *Memoirs of a Bartholomew Fair* (London, 1859), Henry Morley quotes a 1684 handbill for a giant who may be found at Cow-Lane-End *"where his Picture hangs out"* (p. 318). According to Morley, several Charing Cross coffeehouses had monsters of their own to exhibit—one a midget, one an hermaphrodite—and he quotes a notice from Queen Anne's time which indicates that at Mews' Gate, Charing Cross, one might see "A collection of strange and wonderful creatures from most parts of the world, all alive" (p. 324). If Dapperwit's simile is to make sense, Charing Cross must already have become one of the places for the exhibition of monsters. Even if Lucy is monstrously pretty, the implied comparison in Dapperwit's figure of speech is hardly a compliment.

5. The repeated designation of Dapperwit as speaker and his line beginning *Fye, Fye . . .* suggest that a line of Ranger's is missing, one that would elicit Dapperwit's chiding. As one of the meanings of "quibble" at the time was "quiver," Dapperwit's *quibble next your stomach* hints that the missing line may have contained a double entendre.

6. New Spring Garden at Vauxhall was a gathering place

which offered entertainment, refreshment (Dapperwit's *Cheese-cake*), diverting crowds, and the pleasure of the garden it-self. One attraction of the place for the impecunious Dapperwit may be found in Pepys's description (May 28, 1667): "it is very pleasant and cheap going thither, for a man may go to spend what he will, or nothing, all is one" (Wheatley, VI, 34). The Neat Houses at Chelsea were market gardens that pro-vided a place for a treat. Pepys reports (August 1, 1667) that he took a party "to the Neat Houses in the way to Chelsy; and there, in a box in a tree, we sat and sang, and talked and eat" (Wheatley, VII, 54). One of his guests on this occasion was Mrs. Knepp, who was later to play Lady Flippant.

7. On the basis of this reference and an even less specific line of Estridge's ("he swears hee'l n'er stir / Beyond *Hide-Park* or *Coleby's* at furthest") in Sir Charles Sedley's *The Mulberry-Garden* (London, 1668, p. 5), Montague Summers concludes (I, 252) that Colby (Coleby) ran the dining room in the Mulberry Garden. It is as good a guess as any. The im-portant thing about the line is that Dapperwit is contrast-ing the public pleasures of Colby's with the private pleasures of the Green Garret.

8. Since a powdering-tub was a slang phrase (taken from the curing of meat) for the sweating-tub for the treatment of venereal disease, Dapperwit is saying here what he says with Bridewell. Summers assumes (I, 252) that the reference is to a private house maintained by one of the two Longs mentioned in Henry B. Wheatley's *London Past and Present* (London, 1891)—the owner of Long's Ordinary in Haymarket, or his brother Ben, who ran the Rose Tavern in Covent Garden (actually old Mary Long, the widow of the first Rose Tavern Long, was still alive in 1671). It is just as likely that the pow-dering-tub Long is someone else altogether—or no one at all. If the reference is to one of the Long brothers, it may be an inside joke at the expense of a popular tavernkeeper. If we want to be recherché about it, we might decide that it is not a person but a place and that the reference is to Long Acre, a street between St. Martin's and Drury Lane, where, according to Pepys (February 17, 1663), there were a great many whore-houses.

9. Christ, sending disciples out to teach, enjoined them, "And into whatsoever house ye enter, first say, Peace be to this house" (Luke 10:5); The Book of Common Prayer opens the Order for the Visitation of the Sick with this salutation: "Peace be to this house, and to all that dwell in it." A similar prayer —apparently based on Psalms 122:7, "Peace be within thy walls, and prosperity within thy palaces"—must have been well enough known for Wycherley to make a joke of it. Gripe, as a Puritan, makes the prayer on entering the Crossbite house,

but since he is on lecherous business, the word *Pastime* slips into it. To the ear attuned to a joke, Gripe's prayer may come through as "piece be within these walls."

10. The tapestries made at Mortlake in Surrey in the early seventeenth century were among the best in Europe. The works, founded by James I, never really recovered from the decline that set in during the Commonwealth, but such hangings would certainly have had the kind of high-status sound that Mrs. Joyner intends in her salesman's speech on the kind of price Lucy might command.

11. It was fashionable to powder wigs. Gripe, as an unrelenting Puritan, might wear no wig at all.

12. The value of coins varied from time to time, but in general a crown was five, an angel sometimes as high as ten and a piece twenty-two shillings. The point is that Gripe, in his eagerness, keeps doubling his offer, having gone a long way from the groat (fourpence) treat that he first offered.

13. Mrs. Joyner is saying that the grandfather was no gentleman, but she may also be saying that he was so poor that he could not afford a coat to cover him. In either case, she is telling Gripe, whose usury-made money presumably bought him the coat of arms on his broad seal ring, that he need not put on airs with her.

14. The phrase "by yea and nay" was a form of declaration, not technically an oath, used by Quakers. It came to suggest equivocation and "yea-and-nay" became a pejorative term for Quaker. By extension, it could be used for any Puritan. The comic point of the line is that it identifies Gripe as a Puritan, as many of the lines in the play do, and through the suggestion of equivocation emphasizes the distance between his actions and his presumed principles.

15. There is no reason why this line should be spoken as an aside. The stage direction is not in 1694 Q.

16. A mark was worth less than a pound. They are going to demand more than twenty-five times what Gripe offers.

17. Lady Flippant's metaphor of victory comes from animal baiting, probably from the cockfighting popular at the time, but it implies also the pit in the theater, the proper site for a wit combat.

18. Bankrupt, at this time was often used to designate a debtor who had got into that state through riotous living. Amid the confusion of pronouns in this line, it should be clear that it is the bankrupt who is to get the fortune and the owner of the fortune who is to spend the rest of his life in jail.

19. A popular myth about Russian women, still current in seventeenth-century England, was that a wife took regular beatings as assurance of her husband's affection. In *Britain's Discovery of Russia, 1553–1815* (New York, 1958), M. S.

Anderson cites (p. 690) a number of examples of books that repeated the myth, including *A Geographical Description of the World,* which was published in London in 1671, the year this play was first produced.

20. Wycherley nowhere provides a stage direction to indicate when Leonore enters. Leigh Hunt sensibly brings her on with Lydia and Lady Flippant at the beginning of their scene together.

Act IV

1. Blue, at this time, was a kind of material (an ordinary woolen weave presumably), and it is difficult to know whether Wycherley is describing the color of Gripe's gown or what it is made of. His mentioning a character's dress at all is so unusual that one is tempted to search for significance. Gripe's *Blew Gown* might be the dress of an almoner or even of a prostitute in a house of correction, since the phrase had both usages. The *Blew* might suggest a servant (as in "blue coat") or the man who dressed with Puritanical plainness (as in "blue stocking"). Although any of these could be made to fit Gripe and his situation, such readings would work (if at all) only in a verbal context, for surely the phrases were better known than the costumes that gave them birth. The joke (if there is one) is purely visual, arising out of the audience's recognition of Gripe's costume. A simple reading is probably in order. Gripe's costume and Mrs. Joyner's opening line, an inquiry after his health, suggest that he has taken to his bed to recover from the swindling of Act III.

2. Although Wycherley supplies only this one stage direction, it should be clear from the context that from Mrs. Joyner's speech beginning *Hold, hold, Madam . . .* through her *Let me alone with him* Lady Flippant and Mrs. Joyner are speaking out of Sir Simon's hearing. On *come, come,* Sir Simon is brought back into the conversation.

3. Her earnest business is to go to the playhouse. The Duke's Company then occupied the theater at Lincoln's Inn Fields.

4. Since Hymen—then as now—is the virginal membrane as well as the god of marriage, there is a double entendre in Sir Simon's tercet.

5. Mother Gifford was one of the most famous madams of the period, often referred to in the comedies. Modish in *The Mulberry-Garden* (see Act III, n. 15) says, "There's as hard drinking in Gentlemens Houses / Nowadays, as at Taverns, and as hot service / In many a Ladys Chamber, as at *Giffords*" (p. 47).

6. The vanity of the Frenchman might be pretty much the same whether *obliging* is a gerund or an adjective in this

sentence—whether he returns from "obliging England" (binding her by some promise or contract) or from "obliging (complaisant, accommodating) England." The second is the more attractive reading since it enforces the many possibilities of *Campagn*—military, political, sexual.

7. W. C. Ward changes *person* to *parson*. The lines make a great deal more sense in his version. Since Ranger is on the way to Christina's when he receives the letter, there can be no prior assignation with a *little Person* that has to be cried off. On the other hand Ranger might find it useful to keep a *little parson* on tap, for the most likely revenge Christina could take on her friends (on Valentine) would be to marry someone else. Whether it is a person or a parson Ranger sets out to find, the motivation in the line is Wycherley's rather than his character's; the playwright needs to get Ranger offstage so that Christina can play her scene with Vincent.

8. The Court of Aldermen, with the Lord Mayor, was the chief governing body of the City of London. An alderman's duties were so demanding that many merchants refused to serve. The implication of Valentine's line is that, unlike him, an alderman can listen to anything.

9. 1672 Q: *Exeunt*. This error, repeated in later editions, was finally corrected in the 1720 *Plays*.

Act V

1. By law (1660), the legal rate of interest to moneylenders was 6 percent; anything above that was usury. It is typical of Gripe that in a single canting sentence he is able to plead poverty and respectability.

2. The Good Old Cause was a common phrase for the Puritan Rebellion, used seriously or satirically depending on the user's bias. In 1659, both the anonymous *The Good Old Cause Explained* and John Rogers' *Mr. Prynne's Good Old Cause* were published. That the phrase was current well beyond the production of *Love in a Wood* can be seen in the fact that Aphra Behn wrote a play in 1681 which she called *The Roundheads; or, The Good Old Cause*.

3. The cinder-woman's job was to rake ashes and take out the cinders. Lady Flippant's complaint is that the pickers of rags and cinders turn up more that is useful to their purposes than she has been able to pick up in Mulberry Garden for hers.

4. 1672 Q: I's. This seems to me a simple typographical error, but since it was not corrected until the 1720 *Plays*, I list it as a variant reading.

5. The play on *in earnest* in this passage suggests that Wycherley is making use of a common confusion that supposed that "earnest" (money paid as a bond) derived from the idea of a bargain made "in earnest" (seriously). The import of

the whole exchange is that Sir Simon purchased his title; that his laundress was his influence is a comment on the morals—economic as well as social—of the court.

6. After the Restoration, Parliament provided for the return of confiscated court and church lands, but did nothing to compensate the individual landowner who had been forced to sell his land, whether to support the cause or to pay the heavy fines imposed on him. The resentment of the old Cavaliers influenced political alignments throughout Charles's reign. See Ogg, I, 162–165.

7. This suggests a formal betrothal, although Valentine's later lines about securing a promise of the ladies (if we take them as anything other than the playwright's bringing the play to a neat and formal ending) calls such a reading in doubt.

8. In 1672 Q there is a space after *my* which looks as though a word has been left out accidentally. In later editions a —— has been added, as though the omission were intentional, some hesitation in Lydia's line. To judge from the available space in 1672 Q and the sense of the passage, the missing word is *time*.

9. Although Wycherley provides no stage direction with this line, it is plainly an aside, as Leigh Hunt indicates.

10. There is no stage direction to indicate Lady Flippant's entrance. Leigh Hunt sensibly brings her in with the rest of the party at the beginning of the scene.

EPILOGUE

1. In contrast to the Prologue, which might be spoken by any member of the cast, as actor rather than character, the Epilogue, in content and in style, plainly belongs to Dapperwit.

THE
GENTLEMAN-DANCING-MASTER

The Gentleman-Dancing-Master was performed on February 6, 1672, by the Duke's Company at the Dorset Garden Theatre; it is uncertain whether this was the premiere. It was entered in the *Stationers' Register,* September 18, 1672, and listed in the *Term Catalogues,* November 21, 1672; the first quarto is dated 1673 on the title page. There were editions of the play in 1693 and 1702.

The disguise implied by Wycherley's title is borrowed from Calderón's *El Maestro de Danzar,* but both W. C. Ward and Montague Summers have pointed out how superficial the debt to the Spanish play is. John Wilcox rightly dismisses as unimportant the possible borrowings from Molière.

The epigraph from Horace is from *Satires* I. x. 7–8: "It is not enough to make the hearer laugh out loud; although there is a certain merit even in this." The quotation, following a reference to farces, may be Wycherley's way of indicating that this is his most farcical play. He sensibly carries the quotation no further; the next line, a call for conciseness, would hardly be suitable for a play which has more overextended jokes than any other of the playwright's works.

The text for this edition is 1673 Q. I have also consulted 1693 Q. The quartos I used are those in the University of Pennsylvania library. I have made no attempt to bring order to the chaos of Monsieur's speech; the accents—all grave (`)—have been left where they fell in 1673 Q. In retaining the variant spellings, I faced the problem of Gerrard-Gerard and Flirt-Flirte. In each case I chose the first form, the one more frequently used, in spelling out the abbreviated identifications of the speakers.

THE
GENTLEMAN
Dancing-Master.

A
COMEDY,

Acted at the
DUKE'S THEATRE.

By Mr. *Wycherley.*

Horat.——— *Non satis est risu diducere rictum*
Auditoris : & est quædam tamen hìc quoq; virtus.

LONDON,

Printed by *J. M.* for *Henry Herringman* and *Thomas Dring* at the Sign of the
Blew Anchor in the Lower Walk of the *New Exchange*, and at the Sign
of the *White Lyon* in *Fleetstreet* near *Chancery-lane* end. 1673.

PROLOGUE

To the CITY,[1]

Newly after the Removal of the Dukes Company from
Lincoln-Inn-fields to their new Theatre, near
Salisbury-Court.[2]

Our Author (like us) finding 'twould scarce do,
At t'other end o'th' Town, is come to you:[3]
And since 'tis his last Tryal, has that Wit
To throw himself on a substantial Pit,
Where needy Wit, or Critick dare not come,
Lest Neighbour i'the Cloak, with looks so grum,
Shou'd prove a Dunne;
Where Punk *in Vizor dare not rant and tear*
To put us out, since Bridewel[4] *is so near;*
In short, we shall be heard, he understood,
If not, shall be admir'd, and that's as good;
For you to senseless Plays have still been kind,
Nay where no sense was, you a Jest wou'd find:
And never was it heard of, that the City
Did ever take occasion to be witty
Upon dull Poet, or stiff Players Action,
But still with claps oppos'd the hissing Faction.
But if you hiss'd, 'twas at the Pit, not Stage,
So with the Poet, damn'd the damning Age,
And still we know are ready to ingage
Against the flouting, ticking Gentry, who
Citizen, Player, Poet, wou'd undo,
The Poet, no; unless by commendation;
For on the Change, Wits have no reputation;
And rather than be branded for a Wit,
He with you, able men, wou'd credit get.

last: latest.
Punk: whore.
ticking Gentry: men who
pushed their way into the
playhouse without paying.

Change: Royal Exchange,
where the merchants carried
out their business.
grum: morose, surly.

THE PERSONS

MR. GERARD, }
MR. MARTIN. } Young Gentlemen of the Town, and Friends.

MR. PARRIS *or* MONSIEUR DE PARIS. A vain Coxcomb, and rich City-Heir, newly returned from FRANCE, and mightily affected with the FRENCH Language and Fashions.

MR. JAMES FORMAL *or* DON DIEGO. An old rich SPANISH Merchant newly returned home, as much affected with the Habit and Customs of SPAIN, and Uncle to DE PARIS.

MRS. HIPPOLITA. FORMAL's Daughter.

MRS. CAUTION. FORMAL's Sister, an impertinent precise Old Woman.

PRUE. HIPPOLITA's Maid.

MRS. FLIRT. }
MRS. FLOUNCE. } Two Common Women of the Town.

A little BLACK-A-MORE, Lacquey to FORMAL.

A Parson.

A French Scullion.

Servants, Waiter, and Attendants.

SCENE LONDON.

THE
GENTLEMAN-
DANCING-MASTER

Act I. Scene i.

DON DIEGO'S *House in the Evening.*

Enter HIPPOLITA *and* PRUE *her Maid.*

HIPPOLITA. To confine a Woman just in her rambling Age! take away her liberty at the very time she shou'd use it! O barbarous Aunt! O unnatural Father! to shut up a poor Girl at fourteen, and hinder her budding; all things are ripen'd by the Sun; to shut up a poor Girl at four-teen!—

PRUE. 'Tis true, Miss, two poor young Creatures as we are!

HIPPOLITA. Not suffer'd to see a play in a twelve-month!—

PRUE. Nor to go to *Ponchinello* nor Paradise![1]—

HIPPOLITA. Nor to take a Ramble to the Park nor Mul-berry-gar'n!—

PRUE. Nor to *Tatnam-Court* nor *Islington!*[2]—

HIPPOLITA. Nor to eat a Sillybub in new Spring-gar'n[3] with a Cousin!—

PRUE. Nor to drink a pint of Wine with a Friend at the Prince in the Sun![4]—

HIPPOLITA. Nor to hear a Fiddle in good Company.

PRUE. Nor to hear the Organs and Tongs at the Gun in *Moorfields!*[5]—

HIPPOLITA. Nay, not suffer'd to go to Church, because the men are sometimes there! little did I think I should ever have long'd to go to Church!

PRUE. Or I either, but between two Maids!—

HIPPOLITA. Not see a man!—

PRUE. Nor come near a man!—

HIPPOLITA. Nor hear of a man—

PRUE. No, Miss, but to be deny'd a man! and to have no use at all of a man!—

Park: St. James's Park. See
Love . . . , i, n. 2.

HIPPOLITA. Hold, hold—your resentment is as much greater
than mine, as your experience has been greater; but all
this while, what do we make of my Cousin, my Husband elect (as my Aunt says) we have had his Company these three days. Is he no man?

PRUE. No faith, he's but a *Monsieur*, but you'll resolve
your self that question within these three days: for by
that time, he'll be your Husband, if your Father come
to night?—

HIPPOLITA. Or if I provide not my self with another in the
mean time! For Fathers seldom chuse well, and I will
no more take my Fathers choice in a Husband, than I
would in a Gown or a Suit of Knots: so that if that
Cousin of mine were not an ill contriv'd ugly-Freekish-
fool in being my Fathers choice, I shou'd hate him;
besides, he has almost made me out of love with mirth
and good humour, for he debases it as much as a Jack-
pudding; and Civility and good Breeding more than a
City Dancing-Master.—

PRUE. What, won't you marry him then, Madam?

HIPPOLITA. Wou'dst thou have me marry a Fool! an Idiot?

PRUE. Lord! 'tis a sign you have been kept up indeed!
and know little of the World to refuse a man for a Husband only, because he's a Fool. Methinks he's a pretty
apish kind of a Gentleman, like other Gentlemen, and
handsom enough to lye with in the dark; when Husbands take their priviledges, and for the day-times you
may take the priviledge of a Wife.

HIPPOLITA. Excellent Governess, you do understand the
World, I see.

PRUE. Then you shou'd be guided by me.

HIPPOLITA. Art thou in earnest then, damn'd Jade? wou'dst
thou have me marry him? well—there are more poor
young Women undone and married to filthy Fellows,
by the treachery and evil counsel of Chamber-maids,
than by the obstinacy and covetousness of Parents.

PRUE. Does not your Father come on purpose out of *Spain*
to marry you to him? Can you release your self from
your Aunt or Father any other way? Have you a mind

Suit of Knots: bow of ribbons.   *Jack-pudding:* buffoon, clown.

to be shut up as long as you live? For my part (though you can hold out upon the Lime from the Walls here, Salt, old Shoes, and Oat-meal) I cannot live so, I must confess my patience is worn out—

HIPPOLITA. Alas! alas! poor *Prue*! your stomach lies another way, I will take pity of you, and get me a Husband very suddenly, who may have a Servant at your service; but rather than marry my Cousin, I will be a Nun in the new Protestant Nunnery[6] they talk of, where (they say) there will be no hopes of coming near a man.

PRUE. But you can marry no body but your Cousin, Miss, your Father you expect to night, and be certain his *Spanish* policy and wariness, which has kept you up so close ever since you came from *Hackney*-School,[7] will make sure of you within a day or two at farthest—

HIPPOLITA. Then 'tis time to think how to prevent him— stay—

PRUE. In vain, vain Miss!

HIPPOLITA. If we knew but any man, any man, though he were but a little handsomer than the Devil, so that he were a Gentleman.

PRUE. What if you did know any man, if you had an opportunity; cou'd you have confidence to speak to a man first? But if you cou'd, how cou'd you come to him, or he to you? nay how cou'd you send to him? for though you cou'd write, which your Father in his *Spanish* prudence wou'd never permit you to learn, who shou'd carry the Letter? but we need not be concern'd for that, since we know not to whom to send it.

HIPPOLITA. Stay!—it must be so—I'le try however—

Enter MONSIEUR DE PARIS.

MONSIEUR. Servitèur, Servitèur, la Cousinè, I come to give the *bon Soir*, as the *French* say.

HIPPOLITA. O Cousin, you know him, the fine Gentleman they talk of so much in Town.

PRUE. What! will you talk to him of any man else?

MONSIEUR. I know all the beaux monde Cousinè.

HIPPOLITA. Mister—

MONSIEUR. Monsieur Taileur! Monsieur *Esmit*, Monsieur—

HIPPOLITA. These are *French*-men—

MONSIEUR. Non, non, vou'd you have me say Mr. *Taylor*, Mr. *Smith*, fie, fie, teste[8] nòn—

HIPPOLITA. But don't you know the brave Gentleman they talk of so much in Town?

MONSIEUR. Who, Monsieur *Gerrard*?

HIPPOLITA. What kind of man is that Mr. *Gerrard*? and then I'le tell you.

MONSIEUR. Why—he is truly a pretty man, a pretty man— a pretty so so—kind of man, for an *English*-man.

HIPPOLITA. How! a pretty man?

MONSIEUR. Why, he is conveniently tall—but—

HIPPOLITA. But, what?

MONSIEUR. And not ill-shap'd—but—

HIPPOLITA. But what?

MONSIEUR. And handsom, as 'tis thought—but—

HIPPOLITA. But, what are your Exceptions to him?

MONSIEUR. I can't tell you, because they are innumerable, innumerable mon foy.

HIPPOLITA. Has he Wit?

MONSIEUR. Ay, ay, they say he's witty, brave and dè bèl humeùr and well-bred with all that—but—

HIPPOLITA. But what? he wants Judgment?

MONSIEUR. Non, non, they say he has good sense and judgment, but it is according to the account *Englis'*— for—

HIPPOLITA. For what?

MONSIEUR. For Jarniè—if I think it—

HIPPOLITA. Why?

MONSIEUR. Why—why his Taylor lives within *Ludgate*[9]— his Valet dè Chambrè is no *French*-man—and he has been seen at noon-day to go into an *English* Eating-house—

HIPPOLITA. Say you so, Cousin?

MONSIEUR. Then for being well-bred you shall judge—first he can't dance a step, nor sing a *French* Song, nor swear a *French* Oatè, nor use the polite *French* word in his Conversation; and in fine, can't play at Hombrè—but

Jarniè: a telescoping of "je renie Dieu."

speaks base good *Englis'* with the commune homebred
pronunciation, and in fine, to say no more, he ne're carries a Snuff-box about with him.[10]

HIPPOLITA. Indeed—

MONSIEUR. And yet this man has been abroad as much
as any man, and does not make the least shew of it,
but a little in his Meen, not at all in his discour Jerniè;
he never talks so much as of St. *Peters* Church, and
Rome, the Escurial, or *Madrid*, nay not so much as of
Henry IV. of *Pont-Neuf*, *Paris*, and the new *Louvre*,
nor of the *Grand Roy*.[11]

HIPPOLITA. 'Tis for his commendation, if he does not talk
of his Travels.

MONSIEUR. Auh, auh—Cousinè—he is conscious himself of
his wants, because he is very envious, for he cannot
endure me—

HIPPOLITA. He shall be my man then for that.   [*aside*.
Ay, ay, 'tis the same, *Prue*. No I know he can't endure
you, Cousin—

MONSIEUR. How do you know it—who never stir out. Testè
non—

HIPPOLITA. Well—dear Cousin—if you will promise me
never to tell my Aunt, I'le tell you—

MONSIEUR. I won't, I won't, Jarniè—

HIPPOLITA. Nor to be concern'd your self so as to make a
quarrel of it.

MONSIEUR. Non, non—

HIPPOLITA. Upon the word of a Gentleman.

MONSIEUR. Foy de Chevalier, I will not quarrel.

PRUE. Lord, Miss! I wonder you won't believe him without more ado?

HIPPOLITA. Then he has the hatred of a Rival for you.

MONSIEUR. Mal à peste.

HIPPOLITA. You know my Chamber is backward, and has
a door into the Gallery, which looks into the back-yard
of a Tavern, whence Mr. *Gerrard* once spying me at the
Window, has often since attempted to come in at that
Window by the help of the Leads of a low Building

Meen: mien.   *Leads:* strips of lead were
                                 used as roofing.

adjoyning, and indeed 'twas as much as my Maid and I cou'd do to keep him out—

MONSIEUR. Aù lè Coquin!—

HIPPOLITA. But nothing is stronger than aversion; for I hate him perfectly, even as much as I love you—

PRUE. I believe so faith—but what design have we now on foot? [*aside*.

HIPPOLITA. This discovery is an Argument sure of my love to you—

MONSIEUR. Ay, ay; say no more, Cousin, I doubt not your amourè for me, because I doubt not your judgment. But what's to be done with this Fanfaron—I know where he eats to night—I'le go find him out ventrè bleù—

HIPPOLITA. Oh my dear Cousin, you will not make a quarrel of it? I thought what your promise wou'd come to!

MONSIEUR. Wou'd you have a man of Honour—

HIPPOLITA. Keep his promise?

MONSIEUR. And lose his Mistress, that were not for my honour, ma foy—

HIPPOLITA. Cousin, though you do me the injury to think I cou'd be false—do not do your self the injury to think any one cou'd be false to you—will you be afraid of losing your Mistress; to shew such a fear to your Rival, were for his honour, and not for yours sure.

MONSIEUR. Nay, Cousin, I'de have you know I was never afraid of losing my Mistress in earnest— Let me see the man can get my Mistress from me, Jarniè—but he that loves must seem a little jealous.

HIPPOLITA. Not to his Rival, those that have Jealousie, hide it from their Rivals.

MONSIEUR. But there are some who say Jealousie is no more to be hid than a Cough; but it shou'd never be discovered in me, if I had it, because it is not *French*, it is not *French* at all—ventrè—bleu—

HIPPOLITA. No, you shou'd railly your Rival, and rather make a Jest of your Quarrel to him, and that I suppose is *French* too—

MONSIEUR. 'Tis so, 'tis so, Cousin, 'tis the veritable *French* Method; for your *Englis*, for want of Wit, drive every

thing to a serious grum quarrel, and then wou'd make
a Jest on't, when 'tis too late, when they can't laugh,
Jarniè!—

HIPPOLITA. Yes, yes, I wou'd have you railly him soundly,
do not spare him a jot—but shall you see him to night?

MONSIEUR. Ay, ay—

HIPPOLITA. Yes! pray be sure to see him for the Jest's sake—

MONSIEUR. I will—for I love a Jestè as well as any bel Es-
prit of 'em all—da.

HIPPOLITA. Ay, and railly him soundly; be sure you railly
him soundly, and tell him, just thus—that the Lady he
has so long courted, from the great Window of the *Ship*-
Tavern,[12] is to be your Wife to morrow, unless he come
at his wonted hour of six in the morning to her Window
to forbid the Banes; for 'tis the first and last time of
asking: and if he come not, let him for ever hereafter
stay away and hold his tongue.

MONSIEUR. Hah, ha, ha, a vèr good Jestè, testè bleu.

HIPPOLITA. And if the Fool shou'd come again, I wou'd tell
him his own, I warrant you, Cousin; my Gentleman
shou'd be satisfied for good and all, I'de secure him.

MONSIEUR. Bòn, Bòn.

PRUE. Well, well! young Mistress, you were not at *Hackney*-School for nothing I see; nor taken away for nothing: a Woman may soon be too old, but is never too
young to shift for her self? [*aside.*

MONSIEUR. Hah, ah, ah, Cousin, dòu art a merry Grigg—
ma foy—I long to be with *Gerrard,* and I am the best
at improving a Jestè—I shall have such divertisement to
night testè bleù.

HIPPOLITA. He'll deny, 'may be at first, that he never[13]
courted any such Lady.

MONSIEUR. Nay, I am sure he'll be asham'd of it: I shall
make him look so sillily, testè nòn—I long to find him
out, adieu, adieu, la Cousinè.

HIPPOLITA. Shall you be sure to find him?

MONSIEUR. Indubitablemènt I'le search the Town over but
I'le find him, hah, ha, ha— *Exit* MONSIEUR *and returns.*

But I'm afrait, Cousinè, if I should tell him you are to
be my Wife to morrow, he wou'd not come, now I am
for having him come for the Jest's sake—ventrè—

HIPPOLITA. So am I, Cousin, for having him come too for
the Jest's sake.

MONSIEUR. Well, well! leave it to me! ha, ha, ha.

Enter Mrs. CAUTION.

CAUTION. What's all this gigling here?

MONSIEUR. Hay, do you tinkè we'll tell you, no faìt, I warrant you testè nòn, ha, ha, ha—

HIPPOLITA. My Cousin is over-joy'd, I suppose, that my Father is to come to night.

CAUTION. I am afraid he will not come to night—but you'll
stay and see, Nephew.

MONSIEUR. Non, non: I am to sup at tother end of the
Town to night—la, la, la, la—ra, ra, ra—

Exit MONSIEUR *singing.*

CAUTION. I wish the *French* Levity of this Young man
may agree with your Fathers *Spanish* Gravity.

HIPPOLITA. Just as your crabbed old age and my youth
agree.[14]

CAUTION. Well, Malapert! I know you hate me, because I
have been the Guardian of your Reputation. But your
Husband may thank me one day.

HIPPOLITA. If he be not a Fool, he would rather be oblig'd
to me for my vertue than to you, since, at long run he
must whether he will or no.

CAUTION. So, so!—

HIPPOLITA. Nay, now I think on't; I'de have you to know
the poor man, whoso'ere he is, will have little cause to
thank you.

CAUTION. No—

HIPPOLITA. No; for I never lived so wicked a life, as I have
done this twelve-month, since I have not seen a man.

CAUTION. How! how! If you have not seen a man, how
cou'd you be wicked? how cou'd you do any ill?

HIPPOLITA. No, I have done no ill, but I have paid it with
thinking.

CAUTION. O that's no hurt; to think is no hurt; the ancient,
grave, and godly cannot help thoughts.

HIPPOLITA. I warrant, you have had 'em your self, Aunt.

CAUTION. Yes, yes! when I cannot sleep.

HIPPOLITA. Ha, ha— I believe it, but know I have had those thoughts sleeping and waking: for I have dream't of a man.

CAUTION. No matter, no matter, so that it was but a dream, I have dream't my self; for you must know Widows are mightily given to dream, insomuch that a dream is waggishly call'd the Widows Comfort.

HIPPOLITA. But I did not only dream Ih—[15]   [*sighs.*

CAUTION. How, how! did you more than dream! speak, young Harlotry; confess, did you do more than dream? how could you do more than dream in this house? speak! confess.

HIPPOLITA. Well! I will then. Indeed, Aunt, I did not only dream, but I was pleased with my dream when I wak'd.

CAUTION. Oh is that all? nay, if a dream only will please you, you are a modest young Woman still but have a care of a Vision.

HIPPOLITA. I; but to be delighted when we wake with a naughty dream, is a sin, Aunt; and I am so very scrupulous, that I wou'd as soon consent to a naughty man as to a naughty dream.

CAUTION. I do believe you.

HIPPOLITA. I am for going into the Throng of Temptations.

CAUTION. There I believe you agen.

HIPPOLITA. And making my self so familiar with them, that I wou'd not be concern'd for 'em a whit.

CAUTION. There I do not believe you.

HIPPOLITA. And would take all the innocent liberty of the Town, to tattle to your men under a Vizard in the Playhouses, and meet 'em at night in Masquerade.

CAUTION. There I do believe you again, I know you wou'd be masquerading; but worse wou'd come on't, as it has done to others, who have been in a Masquerade, and are now Virgins but in Masquerade, and will not be their own Women agen as long as they live. The Children of this Age must be wise Children indeed, if they know their Fathers, since their Mothers themselves cannot inform 'em! O the fatal Liberty of this masquerading Age,[16] when I was a young Woman.

HIPPOLITA. Come, come, do not blaspheme this masquerading Age, like an ill-bred City Dame, whose Husband is half broke by living in *Coven-Garden,* or who has been turn'd out of the *Temple* or *Lincolns-Inn*[17] upon a masquerading Night: by what I've heard 'tis a pleasant-well-bred-complacent-free-frolick-good-natur'd-pretty-Age; and if you do not like it, leave it to us that do.

CAUTION. Lord! how impudently you talk, Niece, I'm sure I remember when I was a Maid.

HIPPOLITA. Can you remember it, reverent Aunt?

CAUTION. Yes, modest Niece, that a raw young thing though almost at Womans estate, that was then at 30 or 35 years of age, would not so much as have look'd upon a man.

HIPPOLITA. Above her Fathers Butler or Coach-man.

CAUTION. Still taking me up! well thou art a mad Girl, and so good night. We may go to bed, for I suppose now your Father will not come to night.

HIPPOLITA. I am sorry for it, for I long to see him. [*Exit* CAUTION.][18] But I lye; I had rather see *Gerrard* here, and yet I know not how I shall like him: if he has wit he will come, and if he has none he wou'd not be welcome.   [*aside.*[19]] [*Exeunt* HIPPOLITA *and* PRUE.

SCENE *changes to the* French-House,
a Table, Bottles, and Candles.

Enter Mr. GERRARD, MARTIN, *and* MONSIEUR DE PARIS.

MONSIEUR. 'Tis ver veritablè, Jarniè, what the *French* say of you *English,* you use the debauch so much, it cannot have with you the *French* operation, you are never enjoyeè; but come, let us for once be enfinement gal-

---

broke: occasionally used as it is today to mean "penniless," but in this context it probably derives from the verb "to broke," meaning "to act as a go-between." For a husband to take a house in Covent Garden, the phrase suggests, is almost to act as pimp for his wife.

French-House: restaurant.

liard, and sing a *French* Sonnet, [*sings*][20] *la boutelle, la boutelle, glou, glou.*

MARTIN *to Gerrard.* What a melodious Fop it is?

MONSIEUR. Auh—you have no Complaisance.

GERRARD. No, we can't sing, but we'll drink to you the Ladies health, whom (you say) I have so long courted at her Window.

MONSIEUR. Ay, there is your Complaisance; all your *English* Complaisance is pledging Complaisance, ventrè— but if I do you reason here, [*Takes the Glass*] will you do me reason to a little *French* Chanson aboirè— I shall begin to you— *La boutellè, la boutellè*— [*sings.*

MARTIN *to Gerrard.* I had rather keep Company with a Set of wide-mouth'd-drunken Cathedral Choristers.

GERRARD. Come, Sir, drink, and he shall do you reason to your *French* Song:[21] since you stand upon't sing him *Arthur* of *Bradely*, or, *I am the Duke of Norfolk.*[22]

MONSIEUR. Auh, Testè bleu, an *English* Catch fie, fie, ventrè—

GERRARD. He can sing no damn'd *French* Song.

MONSIEUR. Nor can I drink the damn'd *Englis'* Wine.

[*Sets down the Glass.*

GERRARD. Yes, to that Ladies health, who has commanded me to wait upon her to morrow at her Window, which looks (you say) into the inward Yard of the *Ship*-Tavern, near the end of what dee call't street.

MONSIEUR. Ay ay, do you not know her, not you (vert & bleu)

GERRARD. But 'pray repeat agen what she said.

MONSIEUR. Why, she said, she is to be marry'd to morrow to a person of Honour, a brave Gentleman, that shall be nameless, and so, and so forth (little does he think who 'tis)   [*aside.*

GERRARD. And what else?

MONSIEUR. That if you make not your appearance before her Window to morrow at your wonted hour of six in the morning to forbid the Banes, you must for ever

Sonnet: little song.   *vert & bleu:* vertubleu (from vertu Dieu).

hereafter stay away and hold your tongue, for 'tis the
first and last time of asking, ha, ha, ha!

GERRARD. 'Tis all a Riddle to me; I should be unwilling
to be fool'd by this Coxcomb.   [*aside*.

MONSIEUR. I won't tell him all she said, lest he shou'd
not go, I wou'd fain have him go for the Jest's sake—
ha, ha, ha.   [*aside*.

GERRARD. Her name is, you say *Hippolita* Daughter to a
rich *Spanish* Merchant.

MONSIEUR. Ay, ay, you don't know her, not you à d'autrè
à d'autrè ma foy—ha, ha, ha.

GERRARD. Well! I will be an easie Fool for once.

MARTIN. By all means go.

MONSIEUR. Ay, ay, by all means go—hah, ha, ha.

GERRARD. To be caught in a Fools Trap— I'le venture it.
[*aside*.
Come, 'tis her health.   [*Drinks to him*.

MONSIEUR. And to your good reception—testè bleu—ha,
ha, ha.

GERRARD. Well, Monsieur! I'le say this for thee, thou hast
made the best use of three months at *Paris* as ever
English Squire did.

MONSIEUR. Considering I was in a dam' *Englis'* pention too.

MARTIN. Yet you have convers'd with some *French*, I
see; Foot-men I suppose at the Fencing-School, I judge
it by your oaths.

MONSIEUR. *French* Foot-men! well, well, I had rather have
the conversation of a *French* Foot-man than of an *English* Esquire, there's for you da—

MARTIN. I beg your pardon, *Monsieur:* I did not think
the *French* Foot-men had been so much your Friends.

GERRARD. Yes, yes, I warrant they have oblig'd him at
Paris much more than any of their Masters did. Well,
there shall be no more said against the *French* Foot-
men.

MONSIEUR. Non de Grace—you are alway turning the
Nation *Francez* into redicule, dat Nation so accomplie,
dat Nation which you imitate, so, dat in the conclusion
you buttè turn your self into rediculè ma foy: if you
are for de raillery, abuse the *Duch*, why not abuse the

Duch? les grossè Villaines, Pandars, Insolents; but here in your *England* ma foy, you have more honeùr, respectè, and estimation for de Dushè Swabber, who come to cheat your Nation, den for de Franch-Footman, who come to oblige your Nation.[23]

MARTIN. Our Nation! then you disowne it for yours, it seems.

MONSIEUR. Well! wàt of dàt; are you the disobligeè by datè?

GERRARD. No, Monsieur, far from it; you cou'd not oblige us, nor your Country any other way than by disowning it.

MONSIEUR. It is de Brutalè Country, which abuse de *France*, an' reverencè de *Dushe: I vill maintain, sustain, and justifie dat one little Franch-Foot-man have more honeur, courage, and generosity, more good blood in his vaineè, an' mush more good manners an' civility den all de State General togedèr,* Jarniè—dey are only wise and valiant wèn dey are drunkeè.

GERRARD. That is always.

MONSIEUR. But dey are never honestè wèn dey are drunkeè; dey are de only Rogue in de Varldè, who are not honestè wèn dey are drunk—ma foy.

GERRARD. I find you are well acquainted with them, Monsieur.

MONSIEUR. Ay, ay, I have made the tourè of *Holland,* but it was èn postè, derè was no staying for me, testè non—for de Gentleman can no more live derè den de Toad in *Ir'land,* ma foy; for I did not see on' Chevalier in de whole Cuntreè: alway, *you know de Rebel hate de gens de quality;* besides, *I had make sufficient observation of the Canaile barbare de first nighteè of my arrival at Amsterdammè. I did visit you must know one of de Principal of de Stat General, to whom I had recommendation from England, and did find his Excellence weighing Sope,* Jarniè—ha, ha, ha.

State General: States-General here means Holland; as it is used in Monsieur's long speech, describing the chandler, it means the governing body, made up of representatives of the provincial estates.

GERRARD. Weighing Sope!

MONSIEUR. Weighing Sopè, ma foy, for he was a whole Sale Chandeleer, and his Lady was taking the Tale of Chandels wid her own witer hands, ma foy, and de young Lady, his Excellence Daughters stringing Harring, stringing Harring, Jarniè—

GERRARD. So—h—and what were his Sons doing?

MONSIEUR. Auh—his Son (for he had but one) was making de Toure of *France, Espaigne, Italy,* an' *Germany* in a Coach and six, or rader now I think on't, gone of an Embassy hidèr to derè Master *Cromwell,*[24] whom dey did love and fear, because he was some-tingè de greater Rebel butè now I talk of de Rebellè, none but de Rebel can love de Rebellè, and so mush for you and your Friend the *Dushe* I'le say no more, and pray do you say no more of my Friend de *Franch,* not so mush as of my Friend the *Franch*-Foot-man—da—

GERRARD. No, no; but, Monsieur, now give me leave to admire thee, that in three months at *Paris* you could renounce your Language, Drinking and your Country (for which we are not angry with you as I said) and come home so perfect a *French*-man, that the Dreymen of your Fathers own Brew-house wou'd be ready to knock thee in the head.

MONSIEUR. Vèl, vèl, my Father was a Merchant of his own Beer, as the Noblessè of *France* of their own Wine: but I can forgive you that Raillery, that Bob, since you say I have the Eyrè *Francèz.* But have I the Eyrè *Francèz?*

GERRARD. As much as any *French*-Footman of 'em all.

MONSIEUR. And do I speak agreeable ill *Englis'* enough?

GERRARD. Very ill.

MONSIEUR. Veritablemènt!

GERRARD. Veritablemènt.

MONSIEUR. For you must know, 'tis as ill breeding now to speak good *Englis',* as to write good *Englis',* good sense, or a good hand.

Bob: bitter jest.

GERRARD. But indeed, methinks, you are not slovenly
enough for a *French*-man.

MONSIEUR. Slovenly! you mean negligent?

GERRARD. No, I mean slovenly.

MONSIEUR. Then I will be more slovenly.

GERRARD. You know, to be a perfect *French*-man, you
must never be silent, never sit still, and never be clean.

MARTIN. But you have forgot one main qualification of a
true *French*-man, he shou'd never be sound, that is, be
very pockie too.

MONSIEUR. Oh! if dat be all, I am very pockie; pockie
enough Jarnie, that is the only *French* qualification
may be had without going to *Paris,* mon foy.

Enter a WAITER.

WAITER. Here are a couple of Ladies coming up to you,
Sir.

GERRARD. To us! did you appoint any to come hither,
Martin?

MARTIN. Not I.

GERRARD. Nor you, Monsieur!

MONSIEUR. Nor I.

GERRARD. Sirrah, tell your Master, if he cannot protect
us from the Constable, and these midnight-Coursers,
'tis not a House for us.

MARTIN. Tell 'em you have no body in the house, and
shut the doors.

WAITER. They'll not be satisfi'd with that, they'll break
open the door, they search'd last night all over the
house for my Lord *Fisk* and Sir *Jeffery Jantee,* who
were fain to hide themselves in the Bar under my Mistresses Chair and Peticoats.

MONSIEUR. Wat do the Women hunt out the men so now?

MARTIN. Ay, ay, things are alter'd since you went to *Paris,*
there's hardly a young man in Town dares be known
of his Lodging for 'em.

GERRARD. Bailiffs, Pursevants, or a City-Constable are
modest people in comparison of them.

MARTIN. And we are not so much afraid to be taken up

pockie: infected with the pox,   *Pursevant:* summons deliverer.
syphilitic.

by the Watch, as by the taring midnight Ramblers or Houza-Women.

MONSIEUR. Jarnie—ha, ha, ha.

GERRARD. Where are they? I hope they are gone agen?

WAITER. No, Sir, they are below at the Stair-foot, only swearing at their Coach-man.

GERRARD. Come, you Rogue! they are in Fee with you Waiters, and no Gentleman can come hither, but they have the intelligence straight.

WAITER. Intelligence from us, Sir, they shou'd never come here if we cou'd help it. I am sure we wish 'em choak'd when we see them come in; for they bring such good stomachs from St. *James*'s Park or rambling about in the streets, that we poor Waiters have not a bit left; 'tis well if we can keep our money in our Pockets for 'em; I am sure I have paid seventeen and six pence in half Crowns for Coach-hire at several times for a little damn'd taring Lady, and when I ask't her for it agen one morning in her Chamber, she bid me pay my self, for she had no money: but I wanted the Courage of a Gentleman; besides the Lord that kept her, was a good Customer to our house, and my Friend, and I made a Conscience of wronging him.

GERRARD. A man of Honour!

MONSIEUR. Vert & bleu, pleasènt, pleasènt, mon foy.

GERRARD. Go, go, Sirrah, shut the door, I hear 'em coming up.

WAITER. Indeed I dare not; they'll kick me down stairs, if I should.

GERRARD. Go you, Rascal, I say.

The WAITER *shuts the door, 'tis thrust open agen,*
    Enter FLOUNCE *and* FLIRTE *in Vizards,*
   striking the WAITER, *and come up to the Table.*

GERRARD. *Flounce* and *Flirte* upon my life.   [*aside.*
Ladies, I am sorry you have no Volunteers in your Service; this is meer pressing, and argues a great necessity you have for men.

---

taring: tearing, violent.   *Houza:* huzza, one given to noisy or riotous conduct.

FLOUNCE. You need not be afraid, Sir, we will use no violence to you, you are not fit for our Service; we know you—

FLIRT. The hot Service you have been in formerly, makes you unfit for ours now; besides, you begin to be something too old for us we are for the brisk Hoaza's of seventeen or eighteen.

GERRARD. Nay 'faith, I am not too old yet, but an old acquaintance will make any man old; besides, to tell you the truth, you are come a little too early for me, for I am not drunk yet; but there are your brisk young men who are always drunk, and perhaps have the happiness not to know you.

FLOUNCE. The happiness not to know us!

FLIRT. The happiness not to know us!

GERRARD. Be not angry, Ladies; 'tis rather happiness to have pleasure to come, than to have it past, and therefore these Gentlemen are happy in not knowing you.

MARTIN. I'de have you to know, I do know the Ladies too, and I will not lose the honour of the Ladies acquaintance for any thing.

FLOUNCE. Not for the pleasure of beginning an acquaintance with us, as Mr. *Gerrard* says: but it is the general vanity of you Town-Fops to lay claim to all good acquaintance and persons of Honour; you cannot let a Woman pass in the *Mall* at midnight, but dam you, you know her strait, you know her; but you wou'd be damn'd before you wou'd say so much for one in a Mercers Shop.

GERRARD. He has spoken it in a *French*-house, where he has very good credit, and I dare swear you may make him eat his words.

MONSIEUR. She does want a Gown indeèt: [*Peeping under her Scarff.*] she is in her dishabilieè, this dishabilieè is a great Mode in *England;* the Women love the dishabilieè as well as the men, ma foy.

FLIRT. Well: if we should stay and sup with you, I warrant

Mall: a shaded walk in St. James's Park. See *Love in a Wood,* II, p. 40.

you wou'd be bragging of it to morrow amongst your
Comrades that you had the Company of two Women
of Quality at the *French*-house and name us.

MARTIN. Pleasant Jilts.   [*aside*.

GERRARD. No upon our Honours, we wou'd not brag of
your Company.

FLOUNCE. Upon your Honours?

MARTIN. No faith.

FLOUNCE. Come, we will venture to sit down then: yet
I know the vanity of you men; you cou'd not contain
your selves from bragging.

GERRARD. No, no! you Women now adays have found
out the pleasure of bragging, and will allow it the men
no longer.

MARTIN. Therefore indeed we dare not stay to sup with
you; for you wou'd be sure to tell on't.

GERRARD. And we are Young-men who stand upon our
Reputations.

FLOUNCE. You are very pleasant, Gentlemen.

MARTIN. For my part I am to be marry'd shortly, and
know 'twould quickly come to my Mistresses's ear.

GERRARD. And for my part I must go visit to morrow morning by times a new City-Mistress, and you know they
are as inquisitive as precise in the City.

FLIRT. Come, come! pray leave this fooling; sit down
agen, and let us bespeak Supper.

GERRARD. No 'faith, I dare not.

MARTIN. Besides, we have supp'd.

FLOUNCE. No matter, we only desire you shou'd look on,
while we eat, and put the glass about, or so.

                              GERRARD *and* MARTIN *offer to go out*.

FLIRT. Pray, stay.

GERRARD. Upon my life I dare not.

FLOUNCE. Upon our Honours we will not tell, if you are
in earnest.

GERRARD. P'shaw, p'shaw—I know the vanity of you
Women, you cou'd not contain your selves from
bragging.

by times: early.

MONSIEUR. Ma foy! is it certain! ha, ha, ha! hark you, Madam! can't you fare well, but you must cry Roast-meat?[25]
You'll spoil your Trade by bragging of your gains,
The silent Sow (Madam) does eat most Grains.
—da—

FLIRT. Your Servant, Monsieur Fop.

FLOUNCE. Nay, faith, do not go, we will no more tell—

MONSIEUR. Than you would of a Clapè, if you had it, dat's the only secret you can keep, Jarnie.

MARTIN. I am glad we are rid of these Jilts.

GERRARD. And we have taken a very ridiculous occasion.

MONSIEUR. Wàt! must we leave the Lady then, dìs is dam Civilitie *Englis'* mon foy.

FLIRT. Nay, Sir, you have too much of the *French* Eyre to have so little honour and good breeding.

[*Pulling him back.*

MONSIEUR. Deè, you tinkè so then, sweet Madam, I have mush of de *French* Eyre?

FLIRT. More than any *French*-man breathing.

MONSIEUR. Auh, you are the curtoise Dame, mort-bleu, I shall stay then, if you think so. Monsieur *Gerrard*, you will be certain to see the Lady to morrow, pray not forget, ha, ha, ha.

GERRARD. No, no Sir.

MARTIN. You will go then?

GERRARD. I will go on a Fools Errant for once.

[*Exeunt* GERRARD *and* MARTIN.

FLOUNCE. What will you eat, Sir?

MONSIEUR. Wàt you please, Madamè.

FLOUNCE. De Heare, Waiter, then some young Partridge.

WAITER. What else, Madam?

FLIRT. Some Ruffes.

WAITER. What else, Madam?

FLOUNCE. Some young Pheasants.

WAITER. What else, Madam?

FLIRT. Some young Rabits, I love Rabits.

Ruffes: a ruff is both the male of a shorebird and a European freshwater fish. Since the girls are ordering birds, presumably the first is intended.

WAITER. What else, Madam?

FLOUNCE. Stay—

MONSIEUR. Dìs *Englis'* Waiter wit his wat else Madam
will ruine me, testè non.   [*aside.*

WAITER. What else, Madam?

MONSIEUR. Wàt else Madam agen! call up the *French*
Waiter.

WAITER. What else, Madam?

MONSIEUR. Again, call up the *French* Waiter or Quesi-
nièr, mort-testè-ventrè, vitè, vitè— Auh, Madam, the
stupidity of the *Englis'* Waiter, I hate the *Englis'* Waiter,
mon foy.   [*Exit* WAITER.

FLIRT. Be not in passion, dear Monsieur.

MONSIEUR. I kiss your hand obligeant, Madam.

Enter a French SCULLION.

Cherè Pierot,[26] Serviteur, Serviteur, or ca a manger.
[*Kisses the* SCULLION.

SCULLION. En voulez vous de Cram Schiquin.[27]

FLOUNCE. Yes.

SCULLION. De Partrish, de Faysan, de Quailles.

MONSIEUR. This Bougre vel ruinè me too, but he speak
wit dàt bel Eyrè and gracè. I cannot bid him hold
his tongue, ventre, c'est assey, Pierot, vat-èn.
[*Exit* SCULLION *and returns.*

SCULLION. And de litèl plate dè—

MONSIEUR. Jarnie, vat-èn.   [*Exit* SCULLION *and returns.*

SCULLION. And de litèl plate dè—

MONSIEUR. De grace go dy way.
[*Exit* SCULLION *and returns.*

SCULLION. And de litèl dè—

MONSIEUR. De Fourmage, de Brie, vat-èn, go, go.

FLOUNCE. What's that Cheese that stinks?

MONSIEUR. Ay, ay, be sure it stinkè extrementè, Pierot
vat-èn; but stay till I drink dy health, here's to dat
pretty Fellow's health, Madam.

FLIRT. Must we drink the Scullions health?

MONSIEUR. Auh, you will not be disobligeant, Madam, he
is the Quisinier for a King, nay for a Cardinal or
French Abbot.   [*drinks.*

FLOUNCE. But how shall we divertise our selves till Supper be ready?

FLIRT. Can we have better Divertisement than this Gentleman?

FLOUNCE. But I think we had better carry the Gentleman home with us, and because it is already late sup at home, and divertise the Gentleman at Cards, till it be ready de hear Waiter, let it be brought when 'tis ready to my Lodging hard by in *Mustard*-Alley, at the Sign of the *Crooked-Billet*.[28]

MONSIEUR. At the *Crook-Billet!*

FLIRT. Come, Sir, come.

MONSIEUR. Mort-bleu, I have take the Vow (since my last Clap) never to go again to the Bourdel.

FLOUNCE. What is the Bourdel?

MONSIEUR. How call you the name of your House?

FLIRT. The *Crooked-Billet*.

MONSIEUR. No, no, the—the Bawdy-house, vert & bleu.

FLOUNCE. How our Lodging! we'd have you to know—

MONSIEUR. Auh, mort-bleu, I wou'd not know it, de *Crookè-Billet*, hah, ha.

FLIRT. Come, Sir.

MONSIEUR. Besides, if I go wit you to the Bourdel, you will tell, mort-bleu.

FLOUNCE. Fie, fie, come along.

MONSIEUR. Beside, I am to be marry'd within these two days, if you shou'd tell now.

FLIRT. Come, come along, we will not tell.

MONSIEUR. But will you promise then to have the care of my honour, pray, good Madam, have de care of my honeùr, pray have de care of my honeùr. Will you have care of my honeùr? pray have de care of my honeùr, and do not tell, if you can help it; pray, dear Madam, do not tell.   [*Kneels to 'em.*

FLIRT. I wou'd not tell for fear of losing you, my Love for you will make me secret.

MONSIEUR. Why, do you love me?

FLIRT. Indeed I cannot help telling you now what my modesty ought to conceal, but my eyes wou'd disclose it too. I have a passion for you, Sir.

MONSIEUR. A passion for me!

FLIRT. An extreme passion, dear Sir, you are so *French,* so mightily *French,* so agreeable *French;* but I'le tell you more of my heart at home: come along.

MONSIEUR. But is your patiòn sincere?

FLIRT. The truest in the World.

MONSIEUR. Well then I'le venture my body wit thee for one night.

FLIRT. For one night, don't you believe that, and so you wou'd leave me to morrow; but I love you so, I cannot part with you, you must keep me for good and all, if you will have me. I can't leave you for my heart.

MONSIEUR. How keep, Jarniè, de Whore *Englis'* have notingè but keepè, keepè in derè mouths now a-days, testè nòn: formerly 'twas enough to keep de shild, ma foy.

FLIRT. Nay, I will be kept else—but come we'll talk on't at home.

MONSIEUR. Umh—so, so, ver vèl de Amourè of de Whore does alway end in keep, ha, keep, ma foy, keep, ha—

The Punck that entertains you wit' her passion,
Is like kind Host who makes the Invitation,
At your own cost, to his fort bon Collation. [*Exeunt.*

ACT II. SCENE I.

DON DIEGO's *House in the Morning.*

Enter DON DIEGO *in the* Spanish *Habit,*
Mrs. CAUTION *his Sister.*

DON DIEGO. Have you had a *Spanish* care of the Honour of my Family, that is to say, have you kept up my Daughter close in my absence? as I directed.

CAUTION. I have, Sir; but it was as much as I cou'd do.

DON DIEGO. I knew that; for 'twas as much I cou'd do to keep up her Mother. I that have been in *Spain* look you.

CAUTION. Nay, 'tis a hard task to keep up an *English* Woman.

DON DIEGO. As hard as it is for those who are not kept up to be honest, look you con *Licentia* Sister.

CAUTION. How now, Brother! I am sure my Husband never kept me up.

DON DIEGO. I knew that, therefore I cryed con *Licentia* Sister, as the *Spaniards* have it.

CAUTION. But you *Spaniards* are too censorious, Brother.

DON DIEGO. You *English* Women, Sister, give us too much cause (look you) but you are sure my Daughter has not seen a man since my departure.

CAUTION. No, not so much as a Church-man.

DON DIEGO. As a Church-man (*Voto*) I thank you for that, not a Church-man! not a Church-man!

CAUTION. No, not so much as a Church-man; but of any, one wou'd think one might trust a Church-man.

DON DIEGO. No, we are bold enough in trusting them with our Souls, I'le never trust 'em with the body of my Daughter, look you, *Guarda,* you see what comes of trusting Church-men here in *England;* and 'tis because the Women govern the Families, that Chaplains are so much in fashion. Trust a Church-man—trust a Coward with your honour, a Fool with your secret, a Gamester with your purse, as soon as a Priest with your Wife or Daughter, look you, *Guarda,* I am no Fool, look you.

CAUTION. Nay, I know you are a wise man, Brother.

DON DIEGO. Why, Sister, I have been fifteen years in *Spain* for it, at several times look you: Now in *Spain* he is wise enough that is grave, politick enough, that says little; and honourable enough that is jealous; and though I say it that shou'd not say it, I am as grave, grum, and jealous, as any *Spaniard* breathing.

CAUTION. I know you are, Brother.

DON DIEGO. And I will be a *Spaniard* in every thing still, and will not conform, not I, to their ill-favour'd *English* Customs, for I will wear my *Spanish* Habit still,[1] I will stroke my *Spanish* Whiskers still,[2] and I will eat my *Spanish* Olio still;[3] and my Daughter shall go a Maid to her Husbands bed, let the *English* Custom be what 'twill: I wou'd fain see any finical cunning in-

finical: affected, foppish.

sinuating Monsieur, of the age debauch, or steal away my Daughter; but well, has she seen my Cousin? How long has he been in *England?*

CAUTION. These three days.

DON DIEGO. And she has seen him, has she? I was contented he shou'd see her, intending him for her Husband: but she has seen no body else upon your certain knowledge?

CAUTION. No, no, alas! how shou'd she? 'tis impossible she shou'd.

DON DIEGO. Where is her Chamber? pray let me see her.

CAUTION. You'll find her, poor Creature, asleep, I warrant you; or if awake, thinking no hurt, nor of your coming this morning.

DON DIEGO. Let us go to her, I long to see her, poor innocent Wretch.   [*Exeunt.*

Enter HIPPOLITA, GERRARD, *and* PRUE *at a distance.*

GERRARD. Am I not come upon your own Summons, Madam? and yet receive me so?

HIPPOLITA. My Summons, Sir, no I assure you; and if you do not like your reception, I cannot help it; for I am not us'd to receive men, I'de have you to know.

GERRARD. She is beautiful beyond all things I ever saw.
                                                         [*aside.*

HIPPOLITA. I like him extremely.   [*aside.*

GERRARD. Come, fairest, why do you frown?

HIPPOLITA. Because I am angry.

GERRARD. I am come on purpose to please you then, do not receive me so unkindly.

HIPPOLITA. I tell you, I do not use to receive men; there has not been a man in the house before, but my Cousin, this twelve-month, I'de have you to know.

GERRARD. Then you ought to bid me the more welcome, I'de have you to know.

HIPPOLITA. What do you mock me too? I know I am but a home-bred-simple Girl; but I thought you Gallants of the Town had been better bred, than to mock a poor Girl in her Fathers own house. I have heard indeed 'tis a part of good breeding to mock people behind their backs, but not to their faces.

GERRARD. Pretty Creature! she has not only the Beauty but the Innocency of an Angel. [*aside.*

Mock you, dear Miss! no, I only repeated the words, because they were yours, sweet Miss, what we like we imitate.

HIPPOLITA. Dear Miss! sweet Miss! how came you and I so well acquainted? This is one of your confident Tricks too, as I have been told, you'll be acquainted with a Woman in the time you can help her over a Bench in the Play-house, or to her Coach: but I need not wonder at your confidence, since you cou'd come in at the great Gallery-window just now. But pray who shall pay for the glass you have broken?

GERRARD. Pretty Creature! your Father might have made the Window bigger then, since he has so fine a Daughter, and will not allow people to come in at the door to her.

HIPPOLITA. A pleasant man! well, tis harder playing the Hypocrite with him, I see, than with my Aunt or Father; and if dissimulation were not very natural to a Woman, I'm sure I cou'd not use it at this time; but the mask of simplicity and innocency is as useful to an intriguing Woman, as the mask of Religion to a States-man, they say. [*aside.*

GERRARD. Why do you look away, dearest Miss?

HIPPOLITA. Because you quarrell'd with me just now for frowning upon you, and I cannot help it, if I look upon you.

GERRARD. O let me see that Face at any rate.

HIPPOLITA. Wou'd you have me frown upon you? for I shall be sure to do't.

GERRARD. Come, I'le stand fair: you have done your worst to my heart already.

HIPPOLITA. Now I dare not look upon him, lest I shou'd not be able to keep my word. [*aside.*

GERRARD. Come, I am ready, and yet I am afraid of her frowns. [*aside.*

Come, look, Ih—am ready, Ih—am ready.

HIPPOLITA. But I am not ready.   [*aside.*

GERRARD. Turn, dear Miss, Come, Ih–am ready.

HIPPOLITA. Are you ready then, I'le look?

[*Turns upon him.*

No faith, I can't frown upon him, if I shou'd be hang'd.

[*aside.*

GERRARD. Dear Miss, I thank you, that look has no terrour in't.

HIPPOLITA. No, I cannot frown for my heart; for blushing,
I don't use to look upon men, you must know.

GERRARD. If it were possible any thing cou'd, those blushes
wou'd add to her Beauty: well, bashfulness is the only
out-of-fashion-thing that is agreeable.   [*aside.*

HIPPOLITA. Ih–h–like this man strangely, I was going
to say lov'd him. Courage then, *Hippolita,* make use
of the only opportunity thou canst have to enfranchize
thy self: Women formerly (they say) never knew how
to make use of their time till it was past; but let it not
be said so of a young Woman of this Age; my damn'd
Aunt will be stirring presently: well then, courage, I
say, *Hippolita,* thou art full fourteen years old, shift for
thy self.   [*aside.*

GERRARD. So, I have look'd upon her so long, till I am
grown bashful too; Love and Modesty come together
like Money and Covetousness, and the more we have,
the less we can shew it. I dare not look her in the face
now, nor speak a word.   [*aside.*

HIPPOLITA. What, Sir, methinks you look away now.

GERRARD. Because you wou'd not look upon me, Miss.

HIPPOLITA. Nay, I hope you can't look me in the face,
since you have done so rude a thing as to come in at
the Window upon me; come, come, when once we
Women find the men bashful, then we take heart; now
I can look upon you as long as you will; let's see if you
can frown upon me now!

GERRARD. Lovely Innocency! No, you may swear I can't
frown upon you, Miss.

HIPPOLITA. So I knew you were asham'd of what you
have done; well, since you are asham'd, and because

you did not come of your own head, but were sent by my Cousin, you say.

GERRARD. Which I wonder at.   [*aside.*

HIPPOLITA. For all these reasons I do forgive you.

GERRARD. In token of your forgiveness then (dearest Miss) let me have the honour to kiss your hand.

HIPPOLITA. Nay, there 'tis you men are like our little Shock-dogs, if we don't keep you off from us, but use you a little kindly, you grow so fidling, and so troublesom, there is no enduring you.

GERRARD. O dear Miss, if I am like your Shock-dog, let it be in his priviledges.

HIPPOLITA. Why, I'de have you know he does not lye with me.

GERRARD. 'Twas well guess'd, Miss, for one so innocent.

HIPPOLITA. No, I always kick him off from the Bed, and never will let him come near it; for of late indeed (I do not know what's the reason) I don't much care for my Shock-dog nor my Babies.

GERRARD. O then, Miss, I may have hopes; for after the Shock-dog and the Babies, 'tis the mans turn to be belov'd.

HIPPOLITA. Why cou'd you be so good-natur'd as to come after my Shock-dog in my Love? it may be indeed, rather than after one of your Brother men.

GERRARD. Hah, ha, ha—poor Creature, a Wonder of Innocency.

HIPPOLITA. But I see you are humble, because you wou'd kiss my hand.

GERRARD. No, I am ambitious therefore.

HIPPOLITA. Well, all this fooling but loses time, I must make better use of it. [*aside.*] I cou'd let you kiss my hand, but then I'm afraid you wou'd take hold of me and carry me away.

GERRARD. Indeed I wou'd not.

HIPPOLITA. Come! I know you wou'd.

GERRARD. Truly I wou'd not.

Babies: dolls.

HIPPOLITA. You wou'd, you wou'd, I know you wou'd.

GERRARD. I'le swear I wo' not—by—

HIPPOLITA. Nay, don't swear, for you'll be the apter to do it then, I wou'd not have him forswear it neither; he does not like me sure well enough to carry me away.

[aside.

GERRARD. Dear Miss, let me kiss your hand.

HIPPOLITA. I am sure you wou'd carry me away, if I shou'd.

GERRARD. Be not afraid of it.

HIPPOLITA. Nay! I am afraid of the contrary; either he dislikes me, and therefore will not be troubled with me, or what is as bad, he loves me, and is dull, or fearful to displease me.   [aside.

GERRARD. Trust me, sweetest; I can use no violence to you.

HIPPOLITA. Nay, I am sure you wou'd carry me away, what shou'd you come in at the Window for, if you did not mean to steal me?

GERRARD. If I shou'd endeavour it, you might cry out, and I shou'd be prevented.

HIPPOLITA. Dull, dull man of the Town, are all like thee. He is as dull as a Country Squire at Questions and Commands. [aside.] No, if I shou'd cry out never so loud; this is quite at the further end of the house, and there no body cou'd hear me.

GERRARD. I will not give you the occasion, Dearest.

HIPPOLITA. Well! I will quicken thy sense, if it be possible. [aside.] Nay, I know you come to steal me away; because I am an Heiress, and have twelve hundred pound a' year, lately left me by my Mothers Brother, which my Father cannot meddle with, and which is the chiefest reason (I suppose) why he keeps me up so close.

GERRARD. Ha!   [aside.

Questions and Commands: a game in which one person addresses foolish questions and commands to each of the other players. Judging by a line of Sweetissa's in Fielding's *The Grub-Street Opera* (1731), kisses could be commanded: "If ever I suffer'd William to kiss me in my life, unless when we have been at questions and commands, . . ." *The Dramatic Works of Henry Fielding, Esq.*, II, London, 1755, p. 45.

HIPPOLITA. So—this has made him consider, O money, pow-
erful money! how the ugly, old, crooked, straight, handsom young Women are beholding to thee?

GERRARD. Twelve hundred pound a year—

HIPPOLITA. Besides, I have been told my Fortune, and
the Woman said I shou'd be stoln away, because she
says 'tis the Fate of Heiresses to be stoln away.

GERRARD. Twelve hundred pound a year—   [*aside.*

HIPPOLITA. Nay more, she described the man to me, that
was to do it, and he was as like you as cou'd be! have
you any Brothers?

GERRARD. Not any! 'twas I, I warrant you, Sweetest.

HIPPOLITA. So he understands himself now.

GERRARD. Well, Madam, since 'twas foretold you, what
do you think on't? 'tis in vain, you know, to resist Fate.

HIPPOLITA. I do know indeed they say, 'tis to no purpose:
besides, the Woman that told me my Fortune, or you
have bewitch'd me. Ih—think.   [*sighs.*

GERRARD. My Soul, my Life, 'tis you have Charms power-
ful as numberless, especially those of your innocency
irresistable, and do surprise the wary'st Heart; such
mine was, while I cou'd call it mine, but now 'tis yours
for ever.

HIPPOLITA. Well, well, get you gone then, I'le keep it
safe for your sake.

GERRARD. Nay, you must go with me, sweetest.

HIPPOLITA. Well, I see you will part with the Jewel; but
you'll have the keeping of the Cabinet to which you
commit it.

GERRARD. Come, come, my Dearest, let us be gone: Fortune as well as Women must be taken in the humour.
      Enter PRUE *running hastily to stop 'em,* DON DIEGO
            and Mrs. CAUTION *immediately after.*[4]

PRUE. O Miss, Miss! your Father, it seems, is just now
arriv'd, and here is coming in upon you.

HIPPOLITA. My Father!

DON DIEGO. My Daughter! and a man!

CAUTION. A man! a man in the house!

GERRARD. Ha!—what mean these! a *Spaniard.*

HIPPOLITA. What shall I do? stay—nay, pray stir not from me; but lead me about, as if you lead me a Corant.
[*Leads her about.*

DON DIEGO. Is this your Government, Sister, and this your innocent Charge, that has not seen the face of a man this twelve-month *En horâ mala.*

CAUTION. O sure it is not a man, it cannot be a man!
[*Puts on her Spectacles.*

DON DIEGO. It cannot be a man! if he be not a man he's a Devil; he has her lovingly by the hand too, Valga me el Cielo.

HIPPOLITA. Do not seem to mind them, but dance on, or lead me about still.

GERRARD. What de'e mean by't?   [*apart to* HIPPOLITA.

DON DIEGO. Hey! they are frolick, a dancing.

CAUTION. Indeed they are dancing, I think, why Niece.

DON DIEGO. Nay, hold a little: I'le make 'em dance in the Devils name, but it shall not be la Gailliarda!
[*Draws his Sword,* CAUTION *holds him.*

CAUTION. O Niece! why Niece!

GERRARD. Do you hear her? what do you mean?
[*apart to* HIPPOLITA.

HIPPOLITA. Take no notice of them; but walk about still, and sing a little, sing a Corant.

GERRARD. I can't sing; but I'le hum, if you will.

DON DIEGO. Are you so merry? well, I'le be with you en hora mala.

Corant: the courante was an intricate dance, characterized by a running or sliding step. It was danced slowly and with great deliberation, which makes it particularly suitable here. Not only is the conversation between Gerrard and Hippolita possible, but the gravity of the dance should heighten the effect of arrogance and so feed Don Diego's outrage. The courante is said to have begun as a pantomime play without words.

See Ardern Holt, *How to Dance the Revived Ancient Dances,* London, 1907, p. 48. If so, in this scene it regains some of its original function.

Gailliarda: the galliard was a spirited dance, often following the stately pavane. According to Holt (p. 42), it was said to be an invention of the Devil. Don Diego's line sounds as though he had heard that story.

CAUTION. Oh Niece, Niece, why Niece, Oh—

DON DIEGO. Why, Daughter, my dainty Daughter, my shame, my ruine, my plague.

Strugling gets from CAUTION, *goes towards 'em with his Sword drawn.*

HIPPOLITA. Mind him not, but dance and sing on.

GERRARD. A pretty time to dance and sing indeed, when I have a *Spaniard* with naked Toledo at my tail: no, pray excuse me, Miss, from fooling any longer.

HIPPOLITA. O my Father! my Father! poor Father! you are welcome, pray give me your blessing. [*Turning about.*

DON DIEGO. My blessing en hora mala.

HIPPOLITA. What, am I not your Daughter, Sir?

DON DIEGO. My Daughter, mi mal, mi muertè.

HIPPOLITA. My name's *Hippolita*, Sir, I don't owne your *Spanish* names; but pray, Father, why do you frighten one so! you know I don't love to see a Sword: what do you mean to do with that ugly thing out?

DON DIEGO. I'le shew you, Trayidor Ladron, demi honra,[5] thou dy'st.   [*Runs at* GERRARD.

GERRARD. Not if I can help it, good *Don;* but by the names you give me, I find you mistake your man, I suppose some *Spaniard* has affronted you.   [*Draws.*

DON DIEGO. None but thee, Ladron, and thou dy'st for't.
                                                        [*Fight.*

CAUTION. Oh, oh, oh—help, help, help.

HIPPOLITA. Oh—what will you kill my poor Dancing-master?   [*Kneels.*

DON DIEGO. A Dancing-master, he's a Fencing-master rather, I think. But is he your Dancing-master? Umph—

GERRARD. So much Wit and Innocency were never together before.   [*aside.*

DON DIEGO. Is he a Dancing-master?   [*Pausing.*

CAUTION. Is he a Dancing-master? He does not look like a Dancing-master.

HIPPOLITA. Pish—you don't know a Dancing-master, you have not seen one these threescore years, I warrant.

CAUTION. No matter; but he does not look like a Dancing-master.

DON DIEGO. Nay, nay, Dancing-masters look like Gentle-men, enough, Sister; but he's no Dancing-master by drawing his Sword so briskly: those tripping out-sides of Gentlemen are like Gentlemen enough in every thing but in drawing a Sword, and since he is a Gentleman, he shall dye by mine.

HIPPOLITA. Oh, hold, hold.   [*Fight agen.*

CAUTION. Hold, hold! pray, Brother, let's talk with him a little first, I warrant you I shall trap him, and if he confesses, you may kill him; for those that confess, they say, ought to be hang'd—let's see—

GERRARD. Poor *Hippolita,* I wish I had not had this occasion of admiring thy Wit; I have increased my Love, whilst I have lost my hopes, the common Fate of poor Lovers.   [*aside.*

CAUTION. Come, you are guilty by that hanging down of your head. Speak, are you a Dancing-master? Speak, speak, a Dancing-master?

GERRARD. Yes, forsooth, I am a Dancing-master, ay, ay—

DON DIEGO. How do'st it appear?

HIPPOLITA. Why there is his Fiddle, there upon the Table, Father.

CAUTION. No busie-body, but it is not—that is my Nephews Fiddle.

HIPPOLITA. Why, he lent it to my Cousin; I tell you it is his.

CAUTION. Nay, it may be indeed, he might lend it him, for ought I know.

DON DIEGO. I, I, but ask him, Sister, if he be a Dancing-master, where?

CAUTION. Pray, Brother, let me alone with him, I know what to ask him, sure!

DON DIEGO. What will you be wiser than I? nay, then stand away. Come, if you are a Dancing-master; where's your School? adondè, adondè.

CAUTION. Why, he'l say, may be he has ne're a one.

DON DIEGO. Who ask'd you, nimble Chaps? So you have put an Excuse in his head.

Chaps: jaws.

GERRARD. Indeed, Sir, 'tis no Excuse, I have no School.

CAUTION. Well! but who sent you, how came you hither?

GERRARD. There I am puzl'd indeed.   [*aside.*

CAUTION. How came you hither, I say? how—

GERRARD. Why, how, how, how shou'd I come hither?

DON DIEGO. Ay, how shou'd he come hither? upon his Legs.

CAUTION. So, so, now you have put an Excuse in his head too, that you have, so you have, but stay—

DON DIEGO. Nay, with your favour, Mistress, I'le ask him now.

CAUTION. Y facks; but you shan't, I'le ask him, and ask you no favour that I will.

DON DIEGO. Y fackins; but you shan't ask him, if you go there to look you, you Prattle-box you, I'le ask him.

CAUTION. I will ask him, I say, come.

DON DIEGO. Where.

CAUTION. What.

DON DIEGO. Mine's a shrewd question.

CAUTION. Mine's as shrewd as yours.

DON DIEGO. Nay then we shall have it come, answer me, where's your Lodging? come, come, Sir.

CAUTION. A shrewd question indeed, at the Surgeons Arms I warrant in—for 'tis Spring-time, you know.

DON DIEGO. Must you make lyes for him?

CAUTION. But come, Sir, what's your Name? answer me to that, come.

DON DIEGO. His Name, why 'tis an easie matter to tell you a false Name, I hope.

CAUTION. So, must you teach him to cheat us?

DON DIEGO. Why did you say my questions were not shrewd questions then?

CAUTION. And why wou'd you not let me ask him the question then? Brother, Brother, ever while you live for all your *Spanish* wisdom, let an old Woman make discoveries, the young Fellows cannot cheat us in any thing, I'de have you to know; set your old Woman still to grope out an Intrigue, because you know the Mother

Y facks . . . Y fackins: in
faith—a mild oath.

found her Daughter in the Oven:[6] a word to the wise
Brother.

DON DIEGO. Come, come, leave this tattling; he has dishonour'd my Family, debauch'd my Daughter, and what
if he cou'd excuse himself? the *Spanish* Proverb says,
Excuses neither satisfie Creditors nor the injur'd; the
wounds of Honour must have blood and wounds, St.
Jago para mi.

Kisses the Cross of his Sword, and runs at GERRARD.

HIPPOLITA. Oh hold! dear Father, and I'le confess all.

GERRARD. She will not, sure, after all.   [*aside.*

HIPPOLITA. My Cousin sent him, because, as he said, he
wou'd have me recover my Dancing a little before our
Wedding, having made a Vow he wou'd never marry a
Wife who cou'd not dance a Corant. I am sure I was
unwilling, but he wou'd have him come, saying, I was
to be his Wife, as soon as you came, and therefore expected obedience from me.

DON DIEGO. Indeed the venture is most his, and the shame
wou'd be most his; for I know here in *England* 'tis not
the custom for the Father to be much concern'd what
the Daughter does, but I will be a *Spaniard* still.

HIPPOLITA. Did not you hear him say last night he wou'd
send me one this morning?

CAUTION. No not I sure. If I had, he had never come here.

HIPPOLITA. Indeed, Aunt, you grow old, I see, your memory fails you very much. Did not you hear him, *Prue,*
say he wou'd send him to me?

PRUE. Yes I'le be sworn did I.

HIPPOLITA. Look you there, Aunt.

CAUTION. I wonder I should not remember it.

DON DIEGO. Come, come, you are a doting old Fool.

CAUTION. So, so, the fault will be mine now. But pray,
Mistress, how did he come in: I am sure I had the Keys
of the Doors, which till your Father came in, were not
open'd to day.

HIPPOLITA. He came in just after my Father, I suppose.

St. Jago: St. James the Apos-
tle. James Formal swears by
his name saint, just as he got
his Spanish name, Diego, by
translating his first name.

CAUTION. It might be indeed while the Porters brought in the things, and I was talking with you.

DON DIEGO. O might he so, forsooth; you are a brave Governantè, look you, you a *Duenna voto*—and not know who comes in and out.

CAUTION. So, 'twas my fault, I know.

DON DIEGO. Your Maid was in the Room with you! was she not, Child?

HIPPOLITA. Yes indeed, and indeed, Father, all the while.

DON DIEGO. Well, Child, I am satisfi'd then; but I hope he does not use the Dancing-masters tricks of squeezing your hands, setting your Legs and Feet, by handling your Thighs, and seeing your Legs.[7]

HIPPOLITA. No indeed, Father; I'de give him a Box on the Ear, if he shou'd.

DON DIEGO. Poor Innocent! Well I am contented you shou'd learn to dance; since, for ought I know, you shall be marry'd to morrow, or the next day at farthest, by that time you may recover a Corant, a Sarabrand[8] I wou'd say; and since your Cousin too will have a dancing Wife, it shall be so, and I'le see you dance my self, you shall be my Charge these two days, and then I dare venture you in the hand of any Dancing-master, even a sawcy *French* Dancing-master, look you.

CAUTION. Well, have a care though; for this man is not dress'd like a Dancing-master.

DON DIEGO. Go, go, you dote, are they not (for the most part) better dress'd and prouder than many a good Gentleman? you wou'd be wiser than I wou'd you? Querno[9]—

CAUTION. Well, I say only look to't, look to't.

DON DIEGO. Hey, hey! come, Friend, to your bus'ness, teach her, her Lesson over again, let's see.

HIPPOLITA. Come, Master.

DON DIEGO. Come, come, let's see your *English* Method, I understand something of Dancing my self—come.

HIPPOLITA. Come, Master.

GERRARD. I shall betray you yet, dearest Miss, for I know not a step, I cou'd never dance. [*apart to* HIPPOLITA.

HIPPOLITA. No!

DON DIEGO. Come, come, Child.

HIPPOLITA. Indeed I'm asham'd, Father.

DON DIEGO. You must not be asham'd, Child, you'll never dance well, if you are asham'd.

HIPPOLITA. Indeed I can't help it, Father.

DON DIEGO. Come, come, I say, go to't.

HIPPOLITA. Indeed I can't, Father, before you; 'tis my first Lesson, and I shall do it so ill: pray, good Father, go into the next Room for this once, and the next time my Master comes, you shall see I shall be confident enough.

DON DIEGO. Poor-foolish-innocent Creature; well, well, I will, Child, who but a *Spanish* kind of a Father cou'd have so innocent a Daughter? In *England,* well I wou'd fain see any one steal or debauch my Daughter from me.

HIPPOLITA. Nay, won't you go, Father!

DON DIEGO. Yes, yes, I go, Child, we will all go but your Maid; you can dance before your Maid.

HIPPOLITA. Yes, yes, Father, a Maid at most times with her Mistress is no body.

[*Exeunt* DIEGO *and Mrs.* CAUTION.

GERRARD. He peeps yet at the door.

HIPPOLITA. Nay, Father, you peep, indeed you must not see me, when we have done you shall come in.

[*She pulls the door to.*

PRUE.[10] Indeed, little Mistress, like the young Kitten, you see, you play'd with your prey, till you had almost lost it!

HIPPOLITA. 'Tis true, a good old Mouser like you, had taken it up,[11] and run away with it presently.

GERRARD. Let me adore you, dearest Miss, and give you—

[*Going to embrace her.*

HIPPOLITA. No, no, embracing good Mr. that ought to be the last Lesson you are to teach me, I have heard.

GERRARD. Though an after Game be the more tedious and dangerous, 'tis won, Miss, with the more honour

after Game: a second game played to reverse or improve the outcome of the first.

and pleasure; for all that I repent we were put to't; the coming in of your Father as he did, was the most unlucky thing that ever befel me.

HIPPOLITA. What, then you think I would have gone with you.

GERRARD. Yes, and will go with me yet, I hope, courage, Miss, we have yet an opportunity, and the Gallery-window is yet open.

HIPPOLITA. No, no, if I went, I would go for good and all; but now my Father will soon come in again, and may quickly overtake us; besides, now I think on't, you are a Stranger to me. I know not where you live, nor whither you might carry me; for ought I know, you might be a Spirit, and carry me to *Barbadoes*.[12]

GERRARD. No, dear Miss, I would carry you to Court, the Play-houses, and Hide-Park—

HIPPOLITA. Nay, I know 'tis the trick of all you that spirit Women away to speak 'em mighty fair at first; but when you have got 'em in your Clutches: you carry 'em into *York-shire*, *Wales*, or *Cornwall*, which is as bad as to *Barbadoes*, and rather than be served so, I would be a Pris'ner in *London* still as I am.

GERRARD. I see the Air of this Town without the pleasures of it, is enough to infect Women with an aversion for the Country. Well, Miss, since it seems you have some diffidence in me, give me leave to visit you as your Dancing-master, now you have honour'd me with the Character, and under that, I may have your Fathers permission to see you, till you may better know me and my heart, and have a better opportunity to reward it.

HIPPOLITA. I am afraid, to know your heart, would require a great deal of time, and my Father intends to marry me very suddenly to my Cousin who sent you hither.

GERRARD. Pray, sweet Miss, then let us make the better use of our time, if it be short: but how shall we do with that Cousin of yours in the mean time, we must needs charm him?

HIPPOLITA. Leave that to me!

GERRARD. But what's worse! how shall I be able to act a Dancing-master? who ever wanted inclination and patience to learn my self.

HIPPOLITA. A Dancing-School in half an hour will furnish you with terms of the Art. Besides, Love (as I have heard say) supplies his Scholars with all sorts of Capacities they have need of in spight of Nature, but what has Love to do with you?

GERRARD. Love indeed has made a grave Gouty Statesman fight Duels; the Souldier flye from his Colours, a Pedant a fine Gentleman; nay, and the very Lawyer a Poet, and therefore may make me a Dancing-master.

HIPPOLITA. If he were your Master.

GERRARD. I'm sure, dearest Miss, there is nothing else which I cannot do for you already, and therefore may hope to succeed in that.

Enter DON DIEGO.

DON DIEGO. Come, have you done?

HIPPOLITA. O! my Father agen.

DON DIEGO. Come, now let us see you dance.

HIPPOLITA. Indeed I am not perfect yet, pray excuse me till the next time my Master comes: but when must he come agen, Father?

DON DIEGO. Let me see, Friend, you must needs come after Dinner agen, and then at night agen, and so three times to morrow too. If she be not marry'd to morrow (which I am to consider of) she will dance a Corant in twice or thrice teaching more, will she not? for 'tis but a twelve-month since she came from *Hackney-School.*

GERRARD. We will lose no time I warrant you, Sir, if she be to be marry'd to morrow.

DON DIEGO. Truly, I think she may be marry'd to morrow, therefore I would not have you lose any time, look you.

GERRARD. You need not caution me I warrant you, Sir, sweet Scholar, your humble Servant, I will not fail you immediately after Dinner.

DON DIEGO. No, no, pray do not, and I will not fail to satisfie you very well, look you.

HIPPOLITA. He does not doubt his reward, Father, for his pains. If you shou'd not, I wou'd make that good to him.

DON DIEGO. Come, let us go into your Aunt, I must talk with you both together, Child.

[*Exeunt* GERRARD, DON DIEGO.

HIPPOLITA. I follow you, Sir.

PRUE. Here's the Gentlewoman o'th next house come to see you, Mistress.

HIPPOLITA. She's come, as if she came expresly to sing the new Song she sung last night,[13] I must hear it, for 'tis to my purpose now.   [*aside.*

Madam, your Servant, I dream't all night of the Song you sung last; the new Song against delays in Love: pray let's hear it again.

SINGS.

1.

Since we poor slavish Women know
Our men we cannot pick and choose,
To him we like, why say we no?
And both our time and Lover lose.

With feign'd repulses and delays
A Lovers appetite we pall;
And if too long the Gallant stays,
His stomach's gone for good and all.

2.

Or our impatient am'rous Guest,
Unknown to us, away may steal,
And rather than stay for a Feast,
Take up with some coorse, ready meal.

When opportunity is kind,
Let prudent Woman be so too;
And if the man be to your mind,
Till needs you must, ne're let him go.

3.

The Match soon made is happy still,
For only Love has there to do;
Let no one marry 'gainst her will,
But stand off, when her Parents woo.

And only to their Suits be coy,
*   For she whom Joynter can obtain*
To let a Fop her Bed enjoy,
*   Is but a lawful Wench for gain.*

Since we, poor sla-vish _ wo-men, know, our Men we can-not pick and chuse: To   him   we Love, why   say   we, No?   and both our time and la-bour lose.   By our put offs, and fond de-lays   a Lo-vers ap-pe-tite   we pall; and if   too long the Gal-lant stays, his sto-machs gone for _ good and all.

Joynter: jointure, estate settled on a woman at marriage.

PRUE. Your Father calls for you, Miss.   [*steps to the door.*

HIPPOLITA. I come, I come. I must be obedient as long as
I am with him.   [*pausing.*

> *Our Parents who restrain our liberty,*
> *But take the course to make us sooner free,*
> *Though all we gain be but new slavery;*
> *We leave our Fathers, and to Husbands fly.*
>   [*Exeunt.*

Act III. Scene i.

DON DIEGO'S *House.*

Enter MONSIEUR, HIPPOLITA, *and* PRUE.

MONSIEUR. Serviteur, Serviteur, la Cousin, your Maid told
me she watch'd at the stair-foot for my coming, because you had a mind to speak wit me before I saw your
Fadèr, it seem.

HIPPOLITA. I wou'd so indeed, Cousin.

MONSIEUR. Or ca, Or ca, I know your affair, it is to tell me
wat recreation you adè with Monsieur *Gerrard;* but did
he come I was afrait he wou'd not come.

HIPPOLITA. Yes, yes, he did come.

MONSIEUR. Ha, ha, ha—and were you not infiniment divertiseè and pleasè, confess.

HIPPOLITA. I was indeed, Cousin, I was very well pleas'd.

MONSIEUR. I do tinkè so. I did tinkè to come and be
divertiseè my self this morning with the sight of his
reception; but I did ran'counter last night wit dam Company dàt keep me up so late I cou'd not rise in dè
morning. Mala-pestè de Puteins—

HIPPOLITA. Indeed we wanted you here mightily, Cousin.

MONSIEUR. To elpè you to laugh; for if I adde been here,
I had made such recreation wid dàt Coxcomb *Gerrard.*

HIPPOLITA. Indeed, Cousin! you need not have any subject
or property to make one laugh, you are so pleasant your
self, and when you are but alone, you wou'd make one
burst.

MONSIEUR. Am I so happy, Cousin? then in the bòn quality of making people laugh.

HIPPOLITA. Mighty happy, Cousin.

MONSIEUR. De gracè.

HIPPOLITA. Indeed!

MONSIEUR. Nay, sans vanitiè I observe wheresoe're I come I make every body merry, sans vanitiè—da—

HIPPOLITA. I do believe you do.

MONSIEUR. Nay, as I marchè in de street I can make de dull Apprenty laugh and sneer.

HIPPOLITA. This Fool, I see, is as apt as an ill Poet to mistake the contempt and scorn of people for applause and admiration.   [aside.

MONSIEUR. Ah, Cousin, you see wàt it is to have been in *France;* before I went into *France* I cou'd get no body to laugh at me, ma foy.

HIPPOLITA. No! truly Cousin, I think you deserv'd it before, but you are improv'd indeed by going into *France.*

MONSIEUR. Ay, ay, the *Franch* Education make us propre à tout; beside, Cousin, you must know to play the Fool is the Science in *France,* and I diddè go to the *Italian* Academy at *Paris* thrice a week to learn to play de Fool of Signior *Scaramouchè,*[1] who is the most excellent Personage in the World for dat Noble Science. *Angel* is a dam *English* Fool to him.

HIPPOLITA. Methinks now *Angel* is a very good Fool.

MONSIEUR. Nauh, nauh, *Nokes* is a better Fool,[2] but indeed the *Englis'* are not fit to be Fools; here are vèr few good Fools. 'Tis true, you have many a young Cavalier, who go over into *France* to learn to be the Buffoon; but for all dat, dey return but mauvais Buffoon. Jarniè.

HIPPOLITA. I'm sure, Cousin, you have lost no time there.

MONSIEUR. Auh lè bravè *Scaramouchè.*

HIPPOLITA. But is it a Science in *France,* Cousin? and is there an Academy for Fooling: sure none go to it but Players.

MONSIEUR. Dey are Comedians dàt are de Matrès, but all the beaux monde go to learn, as they do here of *Angel* and *Nokes;* for if you did go abroad into Company, you wou'd find the best almost of de Nation conning in all places the Lessons which dey have learnt of the Fools, dere Matrès, *Nokes* and *Angel*.

HIPPOLITA. Indeed!

MONSIEUR. Yes, yes, dey are the Gens de quality that practise dat Science most, and the most ambitieux; for Fools and Buffoons have been always most welcome to Courts, and desir'd in all Companies. Auh to be de Fool, de Buffoon, is to be de greatè Personagè.

HIPPOLITA. Fools have Fortune, they say indeed.

MONSIEUR. So say old *Sequè*.[3]

HIPPOLITA. Well, Cousin (not to make you proud) you are the greatest Fool in *England*, I am sure.

MONSIEUR. Non, non, de gracè, non, *Nokes* dè Comedian is a pretty man, a pretty man for a Comedian, da—

HIPPOLITA. You are modest, Cousin; but least my Father shou'd come in presently (which he will do as soon as he knows you are here) I must give you a Caution, which 'tis fit you shou'd have before you see him.

MONSIEUR. Well, vèl, Cousin, vat is dat?

HIPPOLITA. You must know then (as commonly the conclusion of all mirth is sad) after I had a good while pleas'd my self in jesting and leading the poor Gentleman you sent into a Fools Paradise, and almost made him believe I wou'd go away with him, my Father coming home this morning, came in upon us, and caught him with me.

MONSIEUR. Mala-pestè.

HIPPOLITA. And drew his Sword upon him, and wou'd have kill'd him; for you know my Fathers *Spanish* fierceness and Jealousie.

MONSIEUR. But how did he come off then? testè nòn.

HIPPOLITA. In short, I was fain to bring him off by saying he was my Dancing-master.

MONSIEUR. Hah, ha, ha, vèr good Jestè.

HIPPOLITA. I was unwilling to have the poor man kill'd you know for our foolish Frolick with him; but then upon my Aunts and Fathers inquiry, how he came in, and who sent him; I was forc'd to say you did, desiring I shou'd be able to dance a Corant before our Wedding.

MONSIEUR. A vèr good Jest—da—still bettrè as bettrè.

HIPPOLITA. Now all that I am to desire of you, is to owne
you sent him, that I may not be caught in a lye.

MONSIEUR. Yes, yes, a ver good Jest, *Gerrard,* a Mastrè de
Dance, hah, ha, ha.

HIPPOLITA. Nay, the Jest is like to be better yet; for my
Father himself has oblig'd him now to come and teach
me: So that now he must take the Dancing-master upon
him, and come three or four times to me before our
Wedding, lest my Father, if he shou'd come no more,
shou'd be suspicious I had told him a lye: and (for
ought I know) if he shou'd know or but guess he were
not a Dancing-master, in his *Spanish* strictness and
Punctillioes of Honour he might kill me as the shame
and stain of his Honour and Family, which he talks of
so much. Now you know the jealous cruel Fathers in
Spain serve their poor innocent Daughters often so, and
he is more than a *Spaniard.*

MONSIEUR. Non, non, fear noting, I warrant you he shall
come as often as you will to the house, and your Father
shall never know who he is till we are marry'd; but then
I'le tell him all for the Jests sake.

HIPPOLITA. But will you keep my Counsel, dear Cousin,
till we are marry'd?

MONSIEUR. Poor, dear Fool, I warrant thee, mon foy.

HIPPOLITA. Nay, what a Fool am I indeed, for you wou'd
not have me kill'd: you love me too well sure, to be an
Instrument of my death;

  Enter DON DIEGO *walking gravely, a little Black*
    behind him. Mrs. CAUTION.

But here comes my Father, remember.

MONSIEUR. I would no more tell him of it, than I would tell
you if I had been with a Wench, Jarnie—she's afraid to
be kill'd, poor Wretch, and he's a capricious jealous Fop
enough to do't, but here he comes.   [*aside.*
I'le keep thy Counsel I warrant thee, my dear Soul,
mon petit Cœùr.

HIPPOLITA. Peace, peace, my Father's coming this way.

MONSIEUR. I, but by his march he won't be near enough
to hear us this half hour, hah, ha, ha.

  DON DIEGO *walks leisurely round the* MONSIEUR,

*surveying him, and shrugging up his shoulders
whilst* MONSIEUR *makes Legs and Faces.*

DON DIEGO. Is that thing my Cousin, Sister?　　　[*aside.*

CAUTION. 'Tis he, Sir.

DON DIEGO. Cousin, I'm sorry to see you.

MONSIEUR. Is that a *Spanish* Complement?

DON DIEGO. So much disguis'd, Cousin.

MONSIEUR. Oh! is it out at last, ventrè?　　　[*aside.*[4]
Serviteur, Serviteur, a Monseur mon Oncle, and I am
glad to see you here within doors, most *Spanish* Oncle,
ha, ha, ha. But I should be sorry to see you in the
streets, teste non.

DON DIEGO. Why soh—would you be asham'd of me,
hah—(voto a St. *Jago*) wou'd you? hauh—

MONSIEUR. I it may be you wou'd be asham'd your self,
Monseur mon Oncle, of the great Train you wou'd get
to wait upon your *Spanish* Hose, puh—the Boys wou'd
follow you, and hoot at you (vert & bleu) pardonè my
Franch Franchise, Monsieur mon Oncle.

HIPPOLITA. We shall have sport anon, betwixt these two
Contraries.　　　[*apart to* PRUE.

DON DIEGO. Do'st thou call me Monseur (voto a St. *Jago*.)

MONSIEUR. No, I did not call you Monseur voto a St. *Jago*,
Sir, I know you are my Uncle Mr. *James Formal*—da—

DON DIEGO. But I can hardly know you are my Cousin, Mr.
Nathaniel Paris; but call me Sir *Don Diego* hencefor-
ward, look you, and no Monsieur, call me Monsieur
Guarda.

MONSIEUR. I confess my errour, Sir; for none but a blind
man wou'd call you Monsieur, ha, ha, ha— But pray do
not call me neder *Paris,* but de *Paris,* de *Paris* (si vou

---

makes Legs: makes a leg:
bows.

Spanish Hose: a kind of
breeches worn with a doublet.
Stretching from the waistline
to below the knees, they nar-
rowed along the thighs, being
shaped to fit the figure. They
are contrasted here, and elsewhere in the play, with Mon-

sieur's pantaloons. These were
petticoat breeches with im-
mensely wide legs, pleated
into the waist and reaching to
the knees; they resembled a
short skirt. John Evelyn re-
acted to them as "a kind of
Hermaphrodite and of neither
sex." *Tyrannus,* p. 25.

Franchise: frankness.

plai'st) Monseur de *Paris!* Call me Monseur and welcome, da—

DON DIEGO. Monsieur de *Pantalloòns* then voto—

MONSIEUR. Monsieur de *Pantalloons!* a pretty name, a
pretty name, ma foy, da—bein trove de *Pantalloons;*
how much betrè dèn your de la *Fountaines,* de la
Rivieres, de la *Roches,* and all the *De's* in *France*—da—
well; but have you not the admiration for my *Pantalloon, Don Diego* mon Oncle?

DON DIEGO. I am astonish'd at them verde deramentè,[5]
they are wonderfully ridiculous.

MONSIEUR. Redicule, redicule! ah—'tis well you are my
Uncle, da— Redicule, ah—is dere any ting in de Universe so jenti as de *Pantalloons?* any ting so ravisaunt as
de *Pantallons?* Auh—I cou'd kneel down and varship a
pair of jenti *Pantalloons?* vat, vat, you wou'd have me
have de admiration for dis outward skin of your Thigh,
which you call *Spanish* Hose, fie, fie, fie—ha, ha, ha.

DON DIEGO. Do'st thou deride my *Spanish* Hose? young
Man, hauh.

MONSIEUR. In comparison of *Pantalloon* I do undervalue
'em indeet, *Don Diegue* mon Oncle, ha, ha, ha.

DON DIEGO. Thou art then a gavanho[6] de malo gusto, look
you.

MONSIEUR. You may call me vàt you vìl, Oncle *Don
Diegue;* but I must needs say, your *Spanish* Hose are
scurvy Hose, ugly Hose, lousie Hose, and stinking Hose.

DON DIEGO. Do not provoke me, *Boracho.*

[*Puts his hand to his Sword.*

MONSIEUR. Indeet for lousie I recant dat Epithete, for
dere is scarce room in 'em for dat little Animal, ha,
ha, ha. But for stinking Hose, dat Epithete may stand;
for how can dey chuse but stink, since dey are so
furieusmentè close to your *Spanish* Tail, da.

HIPPOLITA. Ha, ha, ridiculous.   [*aside.*

DON DIEGO. Do not provoke me, I say, En horâ malâ.

[*Seems to draw.*

MONSIEUR. Nay, Oncle, I am sorry you are in de pation;
but I must live and dye for de *Pantalloon* against de
Spanish Hose, da.

DON DIEGO. You are a rash young Man, and while you wear Pantalloons, you are beneath my passion, voto—Auh—they make thee look and waddle (with all those gew-gaw Ribbons) like a great old Fat, slovenly Water-dog.

MONSIEUR. And your *Spanish* Hose, and your Nose in the Air, make you look like a great grisled-long-*Irish*-Grey-hound, reaching a Crust off from a high Shelf, ha, ha, ha.

DON DIEGO. Bueno, Bueno.

CAUTION. What have you a mind to ruine your self, and break off the Match?

MONSIEUR. Pshaw—wàt do you telle me of de Matchè? deè tinke I will not vindicate Pantalloons, Morbleu?

DON DIEGO. Well! he is a lost young Man, I see, and desperately far gone in the Epidemick Malady of our Nation, the affectation of the worst of *French* Vanities: but I must be wiser than him, as I am a *Spaniard* look you *Don Diego,* and endeavour to reclaim him by Art and fair means (look you, *Don Diego*) if not he shall never marry my Daughter look you, *Don Diego,* though he be my own Sister's Son, and has two thousand five hundred seventy three pound Starling twelve shillings and two pence a year Penny-rent, Segouaramentè.

> [*aside.*

Come Young-man, since you are so obstinate, we will refer our difference to Arbitration, your Mistress my Daughter shall be Umpire betwixt us, concerning *Spanish* Hose and Pantalloons.

MONSIEUR. Pantalloons and *Spanish* Hose (si vous plaist.)

DON DIEGO. Your Mistress is the fittest Judge of your Dress, sure?

MONSIEUR. I know ver vel, dat most of the Jeunesse of *England't* will not change the Ribband upon de Crevat widout the consultation of dere Matress, but I am no *Anglois* da—nor shall I make de reference of my Dress to any in the Universe, da—I judg'd by any in *England,* teste non. I wou'd not be judg'd by an *English* Looking-glass, Jarnie.

Penny-rent: income in money.

DON DIEGO. Be not positivo, Young-man.

CAUTION. Nay, pray refer it, Cousin, pray do.

MONSIEUR. Non, non, your Servant, your Servant, Aunt.

DON DIEGO. But pray be not so positive, come hither, Daughter, tell me which is best.

HIPPOLITA. Indeed, Father, you have kept me in universal ignorance, I know nothing.

MONSIEUR. And do you tink I shall refer an Affair of dat consequence to a poor young ting who have not see the Varld, da, I am wiser than so voto?[7]

DON DIEGO. Well, in short, if you will not be wiser, and leave off your *French* Dress, Stammering, and Tricks, look you, you shall be a Fool and go without Daughter, voto.

MONSIEUR. How, must I leave off my Janti *Franch* Accoustrements, and speak base *Englis,* too, or not marry my Cousin! mon Oncle *Don Diego.* Do not break off the Match, do not; for know I will not leave off my Pantalloon and *Franch* Pronuntiation for ne're a Cousin in *England't,* da.

DON DIEGO. I tell you again, he that marry's my Daughter shall at least look like a wise man, for he shall wear the *Spanish* Habit, I am a *Spanish* Positivo.

MONSIEUR. Ver vèl, ver vèl! and I am a *Franch* Positivo.

DON DIEGO. Then I am Definitivo; and if you do not go immediately into your Chamber, and put on a *Spanish* Habit, I have brought over on purpose for your Wedding Cloaths, and put off all these *French* Fopperies and Vanidades with all your Grimaces, Agreeables, Adorables, ma Foys, and Jernies. I swear you shall never marry my Daughter (and by an Oath by *Spaniard* never broken) by my Whiskers and Snuff-box.[8]

MONSIEUR. O hold, do not swear, Uncle, for I love your Daughter furiesmènt.

DON DIEGO. If you love her, you'l obey me.

MONSIEUR. Auh, wat vil become of me! but have the consideration, must I leave off all the *Franch* Beautes, Graces, and Embellisemènts, bote of my Person and Language.

[*Exeunt* HIPPOLITA, *Mrs.* CAUTION, *and* PRUE *laughing.*

DON DIEGO. I will have it so.

MONSIEUR. I am ruinne den undonne, have some consideration for me, for dere is not the least Ribbon of my Garniture, but is as dear to me as your Daughter, Jernie—

DON DIEGO. Then you do not deserve her, and for that reason I will be satisfi'd you love her better, or you shall not have her, for I am positivo.

MONSIEUR. Vil you breake mine Arte! pray have de consideration for me.

DON DIEGO. I say agen, you shall be dress'd before night from Top to Toe in the *Spanish* Habit, or you shall never marry my Daughter, look you.

MONSIEUR. If you will not have de consideration for me, have de consideration for your Daughter; for she have de passionate Amour for me, and like 'me in dis Habite betre den in yours, da—

DON DIEGO. What I have said I have said, and I am uno Positivo.

MONSIEUR. Will you not so mush as allow me one little *Franch* Oate?

DON DIEGO. No, you shall look like a *Spaniard*, but speak and swear like an *English* man, look you.

MONSIEUR. Helas, helas, den I shall take my leave, mort, teste, ventre, Jernie, teste-bleu, ventre-bleu, ma foy, certes.

DON DIEGO. *Pedro, Sanchez,* wait upon this Cavaliero into his Chamber with those things I ordered you to take out of the Trunks, [*Calls at the door.*] I wou'd have you a little accustomed to your Cloaths before your Wedding; for if you comply with me, you shall marry my Daughter to morrow, look you.

MONSIEUR. Adieu then, dear Pantalloon! dear Beltè! dear Sword![9] dear Perruque! and dear Chappeaux, Re-

Chappeaux Retrouseè: chapeau retrousé: cocked hat. On June 3, 1667, Pepys reports seeing "a brisk young fellow, with his hat cocked like a fool behind, as the present fashion among the blades is . . ." (Wheatley, VI, 349).

trouseè, and dear Shoe, Garni;[10] adieu, adieu, adieu,
helas, helas, helas, will you have yet no pitie.

DON DIEGO. I am a *Spanish* Positivo, look you.

MONSIEUR. And more cruel than de *Spanish* Inquisitiono,
to compel a man to a Habit against his conscience,
helas, helas, helas.   [*Exit* MONSIEUR.

Enter PRUE *and* GERRARD.

PRUE. Here is the Dancing-master, shall I call my Mistress,
Sir?

DON DIEGO. Yes.   [*Exit* PRUE.[11]

O you are as punctual as a *Spaniard:* I love your punctual men, nay, I think 'tis before your time something.

GERRARD. Nay, I am resolv'd your Daughter, Sir, shall lose
no time by my fault.

DON DIEGO. So, so, tis well.

GERRARD. I were a very unworthy man, if I should not
be punctual with her, Sir.

DON DIEGO. You speak honestly, very honestly, Friend;
and I believe a very honest man, though a Dancing-
master.

GERRARD. I am very glad you think me so, Sir.

DON DIEGO. What you are but a Young-man, are you
marry'd yet?

GERRARD. No, Sir, but I hope I shall, Sir, very suddenly,
if things hit right.

DON DIEGO. What the old Folks her Friends are wary,
and cannot agree with you so soon as the Daughter
can?

GERRARD. Yes, Sir, the Father hinders it a little at present;
but the Daughter I hope is resolv'd, and then we shall
do well enough.

DON DIEGO. What! you do not steal her, according to the
laudable Custom of some of your Brother-Dancing-
masters?

GERRARD. No, no, Sir, steal her, Sir, steal her, you are
pleas'd to be merry, Sir, ha, ha, ha.

I cannot but laugh at that question.   [*aside.*

DON DIEGO. No, Sir, methinks you are pleas'd to be merry;
but you say the Father does not consent.

GERRARD. Not yet, Sir; but 'twill be no matter whether he does or no.

DON DIEGO. Was she one of your Scholars? if she were, 'tis a hundred to ten but you steal her.

GERRARD. I shall not be able to hold laughing.

[*aside, laughs.*

DON DIEGO. Nay, nay, I find by your laughing you steal her, she was your Scholar, was she not?

GERRARD. Yes, Sir, she was the first I ever had, and may be the last too; for she has a Fortune (if I can get her) will keep me from teaching to dance any more.

DON DIEGO. So, so, then she is your Scholar still it seems, and she has a good Portion, I am glad on't, nay, I knew you stole her.

GERRARD. My laughing may give him suspicions, yet I cannot hold.   [*aside.*

DON DIEGO. What, you laugh I warrant to think how the young Baggage and you will mump the poor old Father; but if all her dependence for a Fortune be upon the Father, he may chance to mump you both, and spoil the Jest.

GERRARD. I hope it will not be in his power, Sir, ha, ha, ha. I shall laugh too much anon.   [*aside.*
Pray, Sir, be pleas'd to call for your Daughter, I am impatient till she comes; for time was never more precious with me and with her too, it ought to be so, sure, since you say she is to be marry'd to morrow.

DON DIEGO. She ought to bestir her, as you say indeed, wuh, Daughter, Daughter, *Prue, Hippolita:* Come away, Child, why do you stay so long?

[*Calls at the door.*

Enter HIPPOLITA, PRUE, *and* CAUTION.

HIPPOLITA. Your Servant, Master! indeed I am asham'd you have stay'd for me.

GERRARD. O good Madam, 'tis my Duty, I know you came as soon as you cou'd.

HIPPOLITA. I knew my Father was with you, therefore I did not make altogether so much haste as I might; but if you had been alone, nothing shou'd have kept

mump: cheat.

me from you, I wou'd not have been so rude as to have made you stay a minute for me, I warrant you.

DON DIEGO. Come, fidle, fadle, what a deal of Ceremony there is betwixt your Dancing-master and you, Querno—

HIPPOLITA. Lord, Sir, I hope you'l allow me to shew my respect to my Master, for I have a great respect for my Master.

GERRARD. And I am very proud of my Scholar, and am a very great Honourer of my Scholar.

DON DIEGO. Come, come, Friend, about your bus'ness, and honour the King.[12] Your Dancing-masters and Barbers are such finical smooth-tongu'd, tatling Fellows, and if you set 'em once a talking, they'll ne're a done, no more than when you set 'em a fidling: indeed all that deal with Fiddles are given to impertinency.

                              [*To Mrs.* CAUTION.

CAUTION. Well! well! this is an impertinent Fellow, without being a Dancing-master: he's no more a Dancing-master than I am a Maid.

DON DIEGO. What! will you still be wiser than I? voto. Come, come about with my Daughter, man.

PRUE. So he wou'd, I warrant you, if your Worship wou'd let him alone.

DON DIEGO. How now Mrs. Nimble-Chaps?

GERRARD. Well, though I have got a little Canting at the Dancing-School since I was here, yet I do all so bunglingly, he'll discover me.   [*aside to* HIPPOLITA.

HIPPOLITA. Try, come take my hand, Master.

CAUTION. Look you, Brother, the impudent Harletry gives him her hand.

DON DIEGO. Can he dance with her without holding her by the hand?

HIPPOLITA. Here take my hand, Master.

GERRARD. I wish it were for good and all. [*aside to her.*

HIPPOLITA. You Dancing-masters are always so hasty, so nimble.

fidling: since "to fiddle" means "to cheat" and "to caress a woman familiarly," the double-entendre possibilities in this line are manifold.

DON DIEGO. Voto a St. *Jago,* not that I can see, about, about with her, man.

GERRARD. Indeed, Sir, I cannot about with her as I wou'd do, unless you will please to go out a little, Sir; for I see she is bashful still before you, Sir.

DON DIEGO. Hey, hey, more fooling yet, come, come, about with her.

HIPPOLITA. Nay, indeed, Father, I am asham'd and cannot help it.

DON DIEGO. But you shall help it, for I will not stir: move her, I say, begin Hussie, move when he'll have you.

PRUE. I cannot but laugh at that, ha, ha, ha.   [*aside.*

GERRARD. Come then, Madam, since it must be so let us try, but I shall discover all, One, two, and Coupee.
[*apart to* HIPPOLITA.

CAUTION. Nay de' see how he squeezes her hand, Brother, O the lewd Villain!

DON DIEGO. Come, move, I say, and mind her not.

GERRARD. One, two, three, four, and turn round.

CAUTION. De' see again he took her by the bare Arm.

DON DIEGO. Come, move on, she's mad.

GERRARD. One, two, and a Coupee.

DON DIEGO. Come. One, two, turn out your Toes.

CAUTION. There, there, he pinch'd her by the Thigh, will you suffer it?

GERRARD. One, two, three, and fall back.

DON DIEGO. Fall back, fall back, back, some of you are forward enough to fall[13] back.

GERRARD. Back, Madam.

DON DIEGO. Fall back when he bids you, Hussie.

CAUTION. How! how! fall back, fall back, marry, but she shall not fall back when he bids her.

DON DIEGO. I say she shall, Huswife, come.

GERRARD. She will, she will, I warrant you, Sir, if you won't be angry with her.

CAUTION. Do you know what he means by that now, you a *Spaniard?*

Coupee: a coupée is a dance step in which one foot cuts or displaces the other.

DON DIEGO. How's that, I not a *Spaniard?* say such a word again.

GERRARD. Come forward, Madam, three steps agen.

CAUTION. See, see, she squeezes his hand now, O the debauch'd Harletry!

DON DIEGO. So, so, mind her not, she moves forward pretty well; but you must move as well backward as forward, or you'll never do any thing to purpose.

CAUTION. Do you know what you say, Brother, your self now? are you at your beastliness before your young Daughter?

PRUE. Ha, ha, ha.

DON DIEGO. How now, Mistress, are you so merry? is this your staid Maid as you call her, Sister impertinent?

GERRARD. I have not much to say to you, Miss; but I shall not have an opportunity to do it, unless we can get your Father out.   [*aside to* HIPPOLITA.

DON DIEGO. Come about agen with her.

CAUTION. Look you, there she squeezes his hand hard again.

HIPPOLITA. Indeed and indeed, Father, my Aunt puts me quite out, I cannot dance while she looks on for my heart, she makes me asham'd and afraid together.

GERRARD. Indeed if you wou'd please to take her out, Sir, I am sure I shou'd make my Scholar do better, than when you are present, Sir, pray, Sir, be pleased for this time to take her away; for the next time I hope I shall order it so, we shall trouble neither of you.

CAUTION. No, no, Brother, stir not, they have a mind to be left alone. Come, there's a beastly Trick in't: he's no Dancing-master I tell you.

GERRARD. Dam'd Jade, she'll discover us.
                              [*aside to* HIPPOLITA.

DON DIEGO. What will you teach me? nay then I will go out, and you shall go out too, look you.

CAUTION. I will not go out, look you.

DON DIEGO. Come, come, thou art a sensorious wicked Woman, and you shall disturb them no longer.

CAUTION. What will you bawd for your Daughter?

DON DIEGO. Ay, ay, come go out, out, out.

CAUTION. I will not go out, I will not go out, my conscience will not suffer me; for I know by experience what will follow.

GERRARD. I warrant you, Sir, we'll make good use of our time when you are gone.

CAUTION. Do you hear him again, don't you know what he means?   [*Exit* DON DIEGO *thrusting* CAUTION *out.*

HIPPOLITA. 'Tis very well, you are a fine Gentleman to abuse my poor Father so.

GERRARD. 'Tis but by your Example, Miss.

HIPPOLITA. Well I am his Daughter, and may make the bolder with him, I hope.

GERRARD. And I am his Son-in-law, that shall be; and therefore may claim my Priviledge too of making bold with him, I hope.

HIPPOLITA. Methinks you shou'd be contented in making bold with his Daughter; for you have made very bold with her, sure.

GERRARD. I hope I shall make bolder with her yet.

HIPPOLITA. I do not doubt your confidence, for you are a Dancing-master.

GERRARD. Why, Miss? I hope you wou'd not have me a fine senseless Whining, modest Lover; for modesty in a man is as ill as the want of it in a Woman.

HIPPOLITA. I thank you for that, Sir, now you have made bold with me indeed; but if I am such a confident Piece, I am sure you made me so; if you had not had the confidence to come in at the Window, I had not had the confidence to look upon a man: I am sure I cou'd not look upon a man before.

GERRARD. But that I humbly conceive, sweet Miss, was your Fathers fault, because you had not a man to look upon. But, dearest Miss, I do not think you confident, you are only innocent; for that which wou'd be called confidence, nay impudence in a Woman of years, is called innocency in one of your age; and the more impudent you appear, the more innocent you are thought.

HIPPOLITA. Say you so! has Youth such Priviledges? I do

not wonder then most Women seem impudent, since it is to be thought younger than they are it seems; but indeed, Master you are as great an Encourager of impudence I see, as if you were a Dancing-master in good earnest.

GERRARD. Yes, yes, a young thing may do any thing, may leap out of the Window, and go away with her Dancing-master, if she please.

HIPPOLITA. So, so, the use follows the Doctrine very suddenly.

GERRARD. Well, Dearest, pray let us make the use we shou'd of it, lest your Father shou'd make too bold with us, and come in before we wou'd have him.

HIPPOLITA. Indeed old Relations are apt to take that ill-bred freedom of pressing into young Company at unseasonable hours.

GERRARD. Come, dear Miss, let me tell you how I have design'd matters; for in talking of any thing else we lose time and opportunity: people abroad indeed say the *English* Women are the worst in the World in using an opportunity, they love tittle tattle and Ceremony.

HIPPOLITA. 'Tis because I warrant opportunities are not so scarce here as abroad, they have more here than they can use; but let people abroad say what they will of *English* Women, because they do not know 'em, but what say people at home?

GERRARD. Pretty Innocent, ha, ha, ha. Well I say you will not make use of your opportunity.

HIPPOLITA. I say you have no reason to say so yet.

GERRARD. Well, then anon at nine of the Clock at night I'le try you; for I have already bespoke a Parson, and have taken up the three back Rooms of the Tavern, which front upon the Gallery-window, that no body may see us escape, and I have appointed (precisely betwixt eight and nine of the Clock when it is dark) a Coach and Six to wait at the Tavern-door for us.

HIPPOLITA. A Coach and Six, a Coach and Six, do you say? nay then I see you are resolv'd to carry me away; for a Coach and Six, though there were not a man

but the Coach-man with it, wou'd carry away any
young Girl of my Age in *England,* a Coach and Six!

GERRARD. Then you will be sure to be ready to go with
me.

HIPPOLITA. What young Woman of the Town cou'd ever
say no to a Coach and Six, unless it were going into the
Country: a Coach and Six, 'tis not in the power of
fourteen year old to resist it.

GERRARD. You will be sure to be ready?

HIPPOLITA. You are sure 'tis a Coach and Six?

GERRARD. I warrant you, Miss.

HIPPOLITA. I warrant you then they'll carry us merrily
away: a Coach and Six?

GERRARD. But have you charm'd your Cousin the *Monsieur*
(as you said you wou'd) that he in the mean time say
nothing to prevent us?

HIPPOLITA. I warrant you.

Enter to 'em DON DIEGO *and Mrs.* CAUTION *pressing in.*

CAUTION. I will come in.

DON DIEGO. Well, I hope by this time you have given her
full instructions, you have told her what and how to do,
you have done all.

GERRARD. We have just done indeed, Sir.

HIPPOLITA. Ay, Sir, we have just done, Sir.

CAUTION. And I fear just undone, Sir.

GERRARD. De' hear that dam'd Witch. [*aside to* HIPPOLITA.

DON DIEGO. Come leave your sensorious prating, thou
hast been a false right Woman thy self in thy Youth,
I warrant you.

CAUTION. I right! I right! I scorn your words, I'de have
you to know, and 'tis well known. I right! no 'tis your
dainty Minx, that Jillflirt your Daughter here that is
right, do you see how her Hankerchief is ruffled, and
what a heat she's in?

DON DIEGO. She has been dancing.

CAUTION. Ay, ay, *Adam* and *Eves* Dance, or the beginning of the World, de' see how she pants?

DON DIEGO. She has not been us'd to motion.

right Woman: loose woman.

CAUTION. Motion, motion, motion de' call it? no indeed, I
   kept her from motion till now, motion with a vengeance.

DON DIEGO. You put the poor bashful Girl to the blush,
   you see, hold your peace.

CAUTION. 'Tis her guilt, not her modesty, marry.

DON DIEGO. Come, come, mind her not, Child, come,
   Master, let me see her dance now the whole Dance
   roundly together, come sing to her.

GERRARD. Faith, we shall be discovered after all, you
   know I cannot sing a Note, Miss. [*aside to* HIPPOLITA.

DON DIEGO. Come, come, man.

HIPPOLITA. Indeed, Father, my Master's in haste now, pray
   let it alone till anon at night, when you say he is to
   come again, and then you shall see me dance it to the
   Violin, pray stay till then, Father.

DON DIEGO. I will not be put off so, come begin.

HIPPOLITA. Pray, Father.

DON DIEGO. Come, sing to her, come begin.

GERRARD. Pray, Sir, excuse me till anon, I am in some haste.

DON DIEGO. I say begin, I will not excuse you, come take
   her by the hand, and about with her.

CAUTION. I say he shall not take her by the hand, he shall
   touch her no more; while I am here there shall be no
   more squeesing and tickling her palm, good Mr. Dancing-master, stand off.   [*Thrusts* GERRARD *away.*

DON DIEGO. Get you out, Mrs. *Impertinence*, take her by
   the hand, I say.

CAUTION. Stand off, I say, he shall not touch her, he has
   touch'd her too much already.

DON DIEGO. If patience were not a *Spanish* Vertue, I
   wou'd lay it aside now. I say let 'em dance.

CAUTION. I say they shall not dance.

HIPPOLITA. Pray, Father, since you see my Aunts obstinacy,
   let us alone till anon, when you may keep her out.

DON DIEGO. Well then, Friend, do not fail to come.

HIPPOLITA. Nay, if he fail me at last.

DON DIEGO. Be sure you come, for she's to be marry'd to
   morrow, do you know it?

GERRARD. Yes, yes, Sir, sweet Scholar, your humble Servant, till night, and think in the mean time of the instructions I have given you, that you may be the readier when I come.

DON DIEGO. I, Girl, be sure you do, and do you be sure to come.

CAUTION. You need not be so concern'd, he'll be sure to come, I warrant you; but if I cou'd help it, he shou'd never set foot agen in the house.

DON DIEGO. You wou'd frighten the poor Dancing-master from the house; but be sure you come for all her.

GERRARD. Yes, Sir.

But this Jade will pay me when I am gone.　　　[*aside.*

CAUTION. Hold, hold, Sir, I must let you out, and I wish I cou'd keep you out. He a Dancing-master, he's a Chouce, a Cheat, a meer Cheat, and that you'll find.

DON DIEGO. I find any man a Cheat! I cheated by any man! I scorn your words, I that have so much *Spanish* Care, Circumspection, and Prudence, cheated by a man: do you think I who have been in *Spain,* look you, and have kept up my Daughter a twelve-month, for fear of being cheated of her, look you? I cheated of her!

CAUTION. Well, say no more.

[*Exeunt* DON DIEGO, HIPPOLITA, CAUTION *and* PRUE.

GERRARD. Well, old Formality, if you had not kept up your Daughter, I am sure I had never cheated you of her.　　　[*aside.*[14]

> *The wary Fool is by his care betray'd,*
> *As Cuckolds by their Jealousie are made.*
>
> 　　　　　　　　　　　　　　　[*Exit.*[15]

Act IV. Scene i.

Enter MONSIEUR DE PARIS *without a Perruque with a*
Spanish *Hat, a* Spanish *Doublet, Stockins, and*
Shooes, but in Pantalloons, a Waste-Belt, and a
Spanish *Dagger in't, and a Crevat about his Neck.*

Enter HIPPOLITA *and* PRUE *behind laughing.*

MONSIEUR. To see wat a Fool Love do make of one,
Jernie. It do metamorphose de brave man into de Beast,
de Sotte, de Animal.

HIPPOLITA. Ha, ha, ha.

MONSIEUR. Nay, you may laugh, 'tis ver vel, I am become
as redicule for you as can be, mort-bleu. I have deform
my self into an ugly *Spaniard.*

HIPPOLITA. Why, do you call this disguising your self like
a *Spaniard* while you wear Pantalloons still and the
Crevat.

MONSIEUR. But is here not the double Doublet and the
Spanish Dagger aussy.

HIPPOLITA. But 'tis as long as the *French* Sword, and worn
like it. But where's your *Spanish* Beard, the thing of
most consequence?

MONSIEUR. Jernie, do you tink Beards are as easie to be
had as in de Play-houses, non; but if here be no the
ugly-long-*Spanish* Beard, here are, I am certain, the
ugly-long-*Spanish* Ear.

HIPPOLITA. That's very true, ha, ha, ha.

MONSIEUR. Auh de ingrate! dat de Woman is, when we
poor men are your Gallants you laugh at us your selves,
and wen we are your Husband, you make all the Warld

Spanish Hat: perhaps the flat-crowned hat Ned Ward mentioned; see Act III, n. 8. The sugar loaf hat, which was high crowned but with a brim only moderately wide, would also have served as a contrast to Monsieur's cocked hat.

Spanish Ear: presumably he is wearing an earring. They were popular in England up until the Commonwealth, but men no longer wore them at this time.

laugh at us, Jernie. Love, dam Love, it make the man more redicule than poverty Poetry, or a new Title of Honeur, Jernie.

Enter DON DIEGO and CAUTION.

DON DIEGO. What at your Jernies still? voto.

MONSIEUR. Why, Oncle, you are at your voto's still.

DON DIEGO. Nay, I'le allow you to be at your voto's too, but not to make the incongruous Match of *Spanish* Doublet and *French* Pantalloons.

[Holding his Hat before his Pantalloons.[1]

MONSIEUR. Nay, pray dear Oncle, let me unite *France* and *Spain*, 'tis the Mode of *France* now, Jarnie, voto.[2]

DON DIEGO. Well, I see I must pronounce, I told you, if you were not drest in the *Spanish* Habit to night, you shou'd not marry my Daughter to morrow, look you.

MONSIEUR. Well, am I not habiliee in de *Spanish* Habit, my Doublet, Ear, and Hat, Leg and Feet are *Spanish*, that dey are.

DON DIEGO. I told you I was a *Spanish* Positivo, voto.

MONSIEUR. Vil you not spare my Pantalloon (begar) I will give you one little finger to excuse my Pantalloon, da—

DON DIEGO. I have said, look you.

MONSIEUR. Auh chere Pantalloons, speak for my Pantalloons, Cousin, my poor Pantalloons are as dear to me as de Scarff to de Countree Capitaine, or de new made Officer: therefore have de compassion for my Pantalloons, *Don Diego,* mon Oncle, helas, helas, helas.

[Kneels to DON DIEGO.

DON DIEGO. I have said, look you, your Dress must be *Spanish,* and your Language *English,* I am uno Positivo.

MONSIEUR. And must speak base good *English* too, ah la pitiee, helas.

DON DIEGO. It must be done, and I will see this great change 'ere it be dark, voto—your time is not long, look to't, look you.

Scarff: the scarf was a broad band worn diagonally across the body from one shoulder to the opposite hip or around the waist. Its importance in this context is that it was an indication of military rank.

MONSIEUR. Helas, helas, helas, dat *Espaigne* shou'd conquer la *France* in *England,* helas, helas, helas.

[*Exit* MONSIEUR.

DON DIEGO. You see what pains I take to make him the more agreeable to you, Daughter.

HIPPOLITA. But indeed and indeed, Father, you wash the Black-a-more white, in endeavouring to make a *Spaniard* of a *Monsieur,* nay an *English Monsieur*[3] too, consider that, Father; for when once they have taken the *French* plie (as they call it) they are never to be made so much as *English* men again, I have heard say.

DON DIEGO. What, I warrant, you are like the rest of the young silly Baggages of *England,* that like nothing but what is *French.* You wou'd not have him reform'd, you wou'd have a *Monsieur* to your Husband, wou'd you, Querno?

HIPPOLITA. No indeed, Father, I wou'd not have a *Monsieur* to my Husband, not I indeed, and I am sure you'll never make my Cousin otherwise.

DON DIEGO. I warrant you.

HIPPOLITA. You can't, you can't, indeed Father: and you have sworn, you know, he shall never have me, if he does not leave off his Monsieurship. Now as I told you, 'tis as hard for him to cease being a *Monsieur,* as 'tis for you to break a *Spanish* Oath, so that I am not in any great danger of having a *Monsieur* to my Husband.

DON DIEGO. Well; but you shall have him for your Husband, look you.

HIPPOLITA. Then you will break your *Spanish* Oath.

DON DIEGO. No, I will break him of his *French* Tricks, and you shall have him for your Husband, Querno.

HIPPOLITA. Indeed and indeed, Father, I shall not have him.

DON DIEGO. Indeed you shall, Daughter.

HIPPOLITA. Well, you shall see, Father.

CAUTION. No I warrant you, she will not have him, she'll

---

plie: the phrase "prendre le pli" is used in the sense of forming unalterable habits; presumably one becomes like a cloth with a crease that cannot be ironed out.

have her Dancing-master rather: I know her meaning, I understand her.

DON DIEGO. Thou malicious foolish Woman, you understand her! but I do understand her, she says I will not break my Oath, nor he his *French* Customs, so through our difference she thinks she shall not have him, but she shall.

HIPPOLITA. But I shan't.

CAUTION. I know she will not have him, because she hates him.

DON DIEGO. I tell you, if she does hate him, 'tis a sign she will have him for her Husband; for 'tis not one of a thousand that marries the man she loves, look you. Besides, 'tis all one whether she loves him now or not; for as soon as she's marry'd, she'd be sure to hate him: that's the reason we wise *Spaniards* are jealous and only expecte, nay will be sure our Wives shall fear us, look you.

HIPPOLITA. Pray, good Father and Aunt, do not dispute about nothing, for I am sure he will never be my Husband to hate.

CAUTION. I am of your opinion indeed, I understand you, I can see as far as another.

DON DIEGO. You, you cannot see so much as through your Spectacles, but I understand her, 'tis her meer desire to Marriage makes her say she shall not have him; for your poor young things, when they are once in the teens, think they shall never be marry'd.

HIPPOLITA. Well, Father, think you what you will, but I know what I think.

Enter MONSIEUR *in the* Spanish *Habit entire only with a Crevat, and follow'd by the little Black-a-more with a Golilia in his hand.*

Golilia: the golilla, or standing band, was a semi-circular collar with a curved edge standing up in the back of the head and straight horizontal edges in front. A wire underpropping, a rebato, kept it in place. Monsieur's cravat was soft neckwear by comparison; it would have been worn either in a bow beneath the chin or loosely knotted with the long ends, probably fringed, hanging down. The conflict between Don Diego's *Golilia* and Monsieur's *Crevat* is the play's best indication of the contrast between the stiff-

DON DIEGO. Come, did not I tell you, you shou'd have him, look you there, he has comply'd with me, and is a perfect *Spaniard.*

MONSIEUR. Ay, ay, I am ugly Rogue enough, now sure, for my Cousin; but 'tis your Father's fault, Cousin, that you han't the handsomest best dress'd man in the Nation, a man bein mise.

DON DIEGO. Yet agen at your *French?* and a Crevat on still (voto a St. *Jago*) off, off with it.

MONSIEUR. Nay I will ever hereafter speak clownish good *English,* do but spare me my Crevat.

DON DIEGO. I am uno Positivo, look you.

MONSIEUR. Let me not put on that *Spanish* yoke, but spare me my Crevat; for I love Crevat furiesment.

DON DIEGO. Agen at your Furiesments!

MONSIEUR. Indeed I have forgot my self, but have some mercy.   [*Kneels.*

DON DIEGO. Off, off, off with it I say, come refuse the Ornamento principal of the *Spanish* Habit.

Takes him by the Crevat, pulls it off, and the BLACK *puts on the Golilia.*

MONSIEUR. Will you have no mercy, no pity, alas, alas, alas, Oh I had rather put on the *English* Pillory than this *Spanish* Golilia, for 'twill be all a case I'm sure; for when I go abroad, I shall soon have a Crowd of Boys about me, peppering me with rotten Eggs and Turneps, helas, helas.   [DON DIEGO *puts on the Golilia.*[4]

DON DIEGO. Helas again?

MONSIEUR. Alas, alas, alas.

HIPPOLITA. ⎰I shall dye; ⎱
PRUE.   ⎱I shall burst,⎰ } ha, ha, ha.

MONSIEUR. Ay, ay, you see what I am come to for your sake, Cousin, and Uncle, pray take notice how ridiculous I am grown to my Cousin that loves me above all the World? she can no more forbear laughing at me, I vow and swear, than if I were as arrant a *Spaniard* as your self.

---

ness of Don Diego and the affected nonchalance of Monsieur.

DON DIEGO. Be a *Spaniard* like me, and ne're think people laugh at you: there was never a *Spaniard* that thought any one laugh'd at him; but what do you laugh at a Golilia, Baggage?

Come, Sirrah-Black, now do you teach him to walk with the verdadero gesto, gracia, and Gravidad of a true *Castilian*.

MONSIEUR. Must I have my Dancing-master too? come little Master then, lead on.

> BLACK *struts about the Stage, the* MONSIEUR *follows him, imitating awkerdly all he does.*

DON DIEGO. Malo, malo, with your Hat on your Pole, as if it hung upon a Pin; the *French* and *English* wear their Hats, as if their Horns would not suffer 'em to come over their Foreheads, voto—

MONSIEUR. 'Tis true, there are some well-bred Gentlemen have so much Reverence for their Perruque, that they wou'd refuse to be Grandees of your *Spain,* for fear of putting on their Hats, I vow and swear.

DON DIEGO. Come, Black, teach him now to make a *Spanish* Leg.

MONSIEUR. Ha, ha, ha, your *Spanish* Leg is an *English* Courtsie, I vow and swear, hah, hah, ha.

DON DIEGO. Well, the Hood does not make the Monk, the Ass was an Ass still, though he had the Lyons Skin on;[5] this will be a light *French* Fool, in spight of the grave *Spanish* Habit, look you. But, Black, do what you can, make the most of him, walk him about.

PRUE. Here are the people, Sir, you sent to speak with about Provisions for the Wedding, and here are your Cloaths brought home too, Mistress.

> [PRUE *goes to the door, and returns.*

DON DIEGO. Well, I come, Black, do what you can with him, walk him about.

MONSIEUR. Indeed, Uncle, if I were as you, I would not

Pole: head; *Pin:* peg. The wig was swept up high at the forehead and was occasionally teased into two small horns of hair, so that it would be impossible for a hat to sit square on the head. In Don Diego's speech, however, the horns suggest the cuckold as well.

have the grave *Spanish* Habit so travesty'd, I shall disgrace it and my little Black Master too, I vow and swear.

DON DIEGO. Learn, learn of him, improve your self by him, and do you walk him, walk him about soundly. Come, Sister and Daughter, I must have your Judgments, though I shall not need 'em, look you, walk him, see you walk him. [*Exeunt* DON DIEGO, HIPPOLITA *and* CAUTION.

MONSIEUR. Jernie, he does not only make a *Spaniard* of me, but a *Spanish* Jennit, in giving me to his Lacquey to walk; but come a long, little Master.

The BLACK *instructs the* MONSIEUR *on one side of the Stage,* PRUE *standing on the other.*

PRUE. O the unfortunate condition of us poor Chambermaids, who have all the carking and caring, the watching and sitting up, the trouble and danger of our Mistresses Intrigues! whilst they go away with all the pleasure; and if they can get their man in a corner, 'tis well enough, they ne're think of the poor watchful Chamber-maid, who sits knocking her heels in the cold, for want of better exercise in some melancholy Lobby or Entry, when she cou'd imploy her time every whit as well as her Mistress for all her Quality, if she were but put to't.   [*aside.*

BLACK. Hold up your head, hold up your head, Sir, a stooping *Spaniard,* Malo.

MONSIEUR. True, a *Spaniard* scorns to look upon the ground.

PRUE. We can shift for our Mistresses, and not for our selves, mine has got a handsom proper Young-man, and is just going to make the most of him, whilst I must be left in the Lurch here with a Couple of ugly little Black-a-more Boys in Bonets[6] and an old wither'd *Spanish* Eunuch, not a Servant else in the house, nor have I hopes of any comfortable Society at all.   [*aside.*

BLACK. Now let me see you make your Visit-Leg thus.

MONSIEUR. Auh, teste non, ha, ha, ha.

BLACK. What, a *Spaniard,* and laugh aloud! no; if you laugh thus only so—now your Salutation in the street as you pass by your Acquaintance, look you, thus—if to a Woman, thus, putting your Hat upon your heart; if to a man, thus with a nod, so—but frown a little more, frown. But if to a Woman you wou'd be very cere- monious too, thus—so—your Neck nearer your shoulder, so— Now if you wou'd speak contemptibly of any man or thing, do thus with your hand—so—and shrug up your shoulders, till they hide your Ears.

[MONSIEUR *imitating the* BLACK.

Now walk agen.

[*The* BLACK *and the* MONSIEUR *walk off the Stage.*

PRUE. All my hopes are in that Coxcomb there; I must take up with my Mistress's leavings, though we Chamber- maids are wont to be before-hand with them: but he is the dullest, modestest Fool, for a Frenchifi'd Fool, as ever I saw; for no body cou'd be more coming to him than I have been (though I say it) and yet I am ne're the nearer. I have stollen away his Hankerchief, and told him of it, and yet he wou'd never so much as strug- gle with me to get it again.[7] I have pull'd off his Perruque, unty'd his Ribbons, and have been very bold with him, yet he would never be so with me; nay, I have pinch'd him, punch'd him, and tickl'd him, and yet he would never do the like for me.

[*The* BLACK *and* MONSIEUR *return.*

BLACK. Nay, thus, thus, Sir.

PRUE. And to make my person more acceptable to him, I have us'd Art, as they say; for every night since he came, I have worn the Forehead-piece of Bees-wax and Hogs-grease, and every morning wash'd with Butter- milk and wild Tansie,[8] and have put on every day for his only sake my Sunday's Bow-dy-Stockins, and have new chalk'd my Shoos, and's constantly as the morning came; nay, I have taken an occasion to garter my Stockins before him, as if unawares of him; for a good Leg and Foot, with good Shoos and Stockins, are very provoking, as they say, but the Devil a bit wou'd he be provok'd; but I must think of a way.

Bow-dy: scarlet. The word derives from Bow-dye, a scar- let dye made at Bow.

BLACK. Thus, thus.

MONSIEUR. What so—well, well, I have Lessons enow for
this time. Little Master, I will have no more, lest the
multiplicity of 'em make me forget 'em, da—
Prue, art thou there, and so pensive? what art thou
thinking of?

PRUE. Indeed I am asham'd to tell your Worship.

MONSIEUR. What asham'd! wer't thou thinking then of my
beastliness? ha, ha, ha.

PRUE. Nay, then I am forc'd to tell your Worship in my
own vindication.

MONSIEUR. Come then.

PRUE. But indeed your Worship— I'm asham'd that I am,
though it was nothing but of a dream I had of your
sweet Worship last night.

MONSIEUR. Of my sweet Worship! I warrant it was a sweet
dream then, what was it? ha, ha, ha.

PRUE. Nay, indeed I have told your Worship enough already, you may guess the rest.

MONSIEUR. I cannot guess, ha, ha, ha, what shou'd it be?
prethee let's know the rest.

PRUE. Wou'd you have me so impudent?

MONSIEUR. Impudent! ha, ha, ha, nay prethee tell me, for
I can't guess, da—

PRUE. Nay, 'tis always so; for want of the mens guessing,
the poor Women are forc'd to be impudent, but I am
still asham'd.

MONSIEUR. I will know it, speak.

PRUE. Why then methoughts last night you came up into
my Chamber in your Shirt, when I was in Bed, and that
you might easily do; for I have ne're a Lock to my door:
now I warrant I am as red as my Petticoat.

MONSIEUR. No, thou'rt as yellow as e're thou wert.

PRUE. Yellow, Sir!

MONSIEUR. Ay, ay; but let's hear the Dream out.

PRUE. Why, can't you guess the rest now?

MONSIEUR. No not I, I vow and swear, come let's hear.

PRUE. But can't you guess in earnest?

MONSIEUR. Not I, the Devil eat me.

PRUE. Not guess yet! why then methoughts you came to bed to me? Now am I as read as my Petticoat again.

MONSIEUR. Ha, ha, ha, well, and what then? ha, ha, ha.

PRUE. Nay, now I know by your Worship's laughing, you guess what you did: I'm sure I cry'd out, and wak'd all in tears, with these words in my mouth, You have undone me, you have undone me! your Worship has undone me.

MONSIEUR. Hah, ha, ha; but you wak'd and found it was but a Dream.

PRUE. Indeed it was so lively, I know not whether 'twas a Dream or no: but if you were not there, I'le undertake you may come when you will, and do any thing to me you will, I sleep so fast.

MONSIEUR. No, no, I don't believe that.

PRUE. Indeed you may, your Worship—

MONSIEUR. It cannot be.

PRUE. Insensible Beast! he will not understand me yet, and one wou'd think I speak plain enough.   [*aside*.

MONSIEUR. Well, but *Prue*, what art thou thinking of?

PRUE. Of the Dream, whether it were a Dream or no.

MONSIEUR. 'Twas a Dream I warrant thee.

PRUE. Was it? I am hugeous glad it was a Dream.

MONSIEUR. Ay, ay, it was a Dream; and I am hugeous glad it was a Dream too.

PRUE. But now I have told your Worship, my door hath neither Lock nor Latch to it: if you shou'd be so naughty as to come one night, and prove the dream true—I am so afraid on't.

MONSIEUR. Ne're fear it, dreams go by the contraries.

PRUE. Then by that I should come into your Worship's Chamber, and come to bed to your Worship. Now am I as red as my Petticoat again, I warrant.

MONSIEUR. No, thou art no redder than a Brick unburnt, *Prue*.

PRUE. But if I shou'd do such a trick in my sleep, your Worship wou'd not censure a poor harmless Maid, I hope; for I am apt to walk in my sleep.

MONSIEUR. Well then, *Prue*, because thou shalt not shame

thy self (poor Wench) I'le be sure to lock my door every
night fast.

PRUE. So, so, this way I find will not do, I must come
roundly and down-right to the bus'ness, like other
Women, or—[9]

Enter GERRARD.

MONSIEUR. O the Dancing-master!

PRUE. Dear Sir, I have something to say to you in your
Ear, which I am asham'd to speak aloud.

MONSIEUR. Another time, another time, *Prue,* but now go
call your Mistress to her Dancing-master, go, go.

PRUE. Nay, pray hear me, Sir, first.

MONSIEUR. Another time, another time, *Prue,* prethee be
gone.

PRUE. Nay, I beseech your Worship hear me.

MONSIEUR. No, prethee be gone.

PRUE. Nay, I am e'en well enough serv'd for not speaking
my mind when I had an opportunity. Well, I must be
playing the modest Woman, forsooth; a Womans hypocrisie in this case does only deceive her self.[10]

[*Exit* PRUE.

MONSIEUR. O the brave Dancing-master, the fine Dancing-
master, your Servant, your Servant.

GERRARD. Your Servant, Sir, I protest I did not know you
at first. I am afraid this Fool shou'd spoil all, notwithstanding *Hippolita*'s care and management, yet I ought
to trust her; but a Secret is more safe with a treacherous
Knave than a talkative Fool.   [*aside.*

MONSIEUR. Come, Sir, you must know a little Brother
Dancing-master of yours, Walking-master I shou'd have
said; for he teaches me to walk and make Legs by the
by: Pray know him, Sir, salute him, Sir; you Christian
Dancing-masters are so proud.

GERRARD. But, Monsieur, what strange Metamorphosis is
this? you look like a *Spaniard,* and talk like an *English-*
man again, which I thought had been impossible.

MONSIEUR. Nothing impossible to Love, I must do't, or lose
my Mistress your pretty Scholar, for 'tis I am to have
her; you may remember I told you she was to be marry'd
to a great man, a man of Honour and Quality.

GERRARD. But does she enjoyn you to this severe penance, such I am sure it is to you.

MONSIEUR. No, no, 'tis by the compulsion of the starch'd Fop her Father, who is so arrant a *Spaniard,* he wou'd kill you and his Daughter, if he knew who you were; therefore have a special care to dissemble well.

[*draws him aside.*

GERRARD. I warrant you.

MONSIEUR. Dear *Gerrard,* go little Master and call my Cousin, tell her, her Dancing-master is here.

[*Exit* BLACK.

I say, dear *Gerrard,* faith I'm obliged to you for the trouble you have had: when I sent you, I intended a Jest indeed, but did not think it wou'd have been so dangerous a Jest; therefore pray forgive me.

GERRARD. I do, do heartily forgive you.

MONSIEUR. But can you forgive me, for sending you at first, like a Fool as I was, 'twas ill done of me; can you forgive me?

GERRARD. Yes, yes, I do forgive you.

MONSIEUR. Well, thou art a generous man, I vow and swear, to come and take upon you this trouble, danger, and shame, to be thought a paltry Dancing-master, and all this to preserve a Ladies honour and life, who intended to abuse you; but I take the obligation upon me.

GERRARD. Pish, pish, you are not obliged to me at all.

MONSIEUR. Faith but I am strangely obliged to you.

GERRARD. Faith but you are not.

MONSIEUR. I vow and swear but I am.

GERRARD. I swear you are not.

MONSIEUR. Nay, thou art so generous a Dancing-master— ha, ha, ha.

Enter DON DIEGO, HIPPOLITA, CAUTION, *and* PRUE.

DON DIEGO. You shall not come in, Sister.

CAUTION. I will come in.

DON DIEGO. You will not be civil.

CAUTION. I'm sure they will not be civil, if I do not come in, I must, I will.

DON DIEGO. Well, honest Friend, you are very punctual,

which is a rare Vertue in a Dancing-master, I take notice of it, and will remember it; I will, look you.

MONSIEUR. So silly-damn'd-politick *Spanish* Uncle, ha, ha,
ha.   [*aside.*

GERRARD. My fine Scholar, Sir, there, shall never have reason (as I told you) Sir, to say I am not a punctual man,
for I am more her Servant than to any Scholar I ever
had.

MONSIEUR. Well said, i'faith, thou dost make a pretty Fool
of him, I vow and swear; but I wonder people can be
made such Fools of, ha, ha, ha.   [*aside.*

HIPPOLITA. Well, Master, I thank you, and I hope I shall
be a grateful kind Scholar to you.

MONSIEUR. Ha, ha, ha, cunning little Jilt, what a Fool she
makes of him too: I wonder people can be made such
Fools of, I vow and swear, ha, ha, ha.   [*aside.*

HIPPOLITA. Indeed it shall go hard but I'le be a grateful
kind Scholar to you.

CAUTION. As kind as ever your Mother was to your Father,
I warrant.

DON DIEGO. How; agen with your senseless suspicions.

MONSIEUR. Pish, pish, Aunt, ha, ha, ha, she's a Fool another way; she thinks she loves him, ha, ha, ha. Lord,
that people shou'd be such Fools!   [*aside.*

CAUTION. Come, come, I cannot but speak, I tell you beware in time; for he is no Dancing-master, but some
debauch'd person who will mump you of your Daughter.

DON DIEGO. Will you be wiser than I still? Mump me of
my Daughter! I wou'd I cou'd see any one mump me of
my Daughter.

CAUTION. And mump you of your Mistress too, young
Spaniard.

MONSIEUR. Ha, ha, ha, will you be wiser than I too, voto.
Mump me of my Mistress! I wou'd I cou'd see any one
mump me of my Mistress.   [*To* CAUTION.
I am afraid this dam'd old Aunt shou'd discover us, I
vow and swear; be careful therefore and resolute.

                    [*aside to* GERRARD *and* HIPPOLITA.

CAUTION. He, he does not go about his bus'ness like a
Dancing-master, he'll ne're teach her to dance, but he'll

teach her no goodness soon enough I warrant: he a Dancing-master!

MONSIEUR. I, the Devil eat me, if he be not the best Dancing-master in *England* now. Was not that well said, Cousin? was it not? for he's a Gentleman Dancing-master, you know.   [*aside to* GERRARD *and* HIPPOLITA.

DON DIEGO. You know him, Cousin, very well, Cousin, you sent him to my Daughter?

MONSIEUR. Yes, yes, Uncle, know him.

We'll ne're be discovered, I warrant, ha, ha, ha. [*aside.*

CAUTION. But will you be made a Fool of too?

MONSIEUR. Ay, ay, Aunt, ne're trouble your self.

DON DIEGO. Come, Friend, about your bus'ness, about with my Daughter.

HIPPOLITA. Nay, pray, Father, be pleas'd to go out a little, and let us but practise a while, and then you shall see me dance the whole Dance to the Violin.

DON DIEGO. Tittle, tattle, more fooling still! did not you say when your Master was here last, I shou'd see you dance to the Violin when he came agen.

HIPPOLITA. So I did, Father; but let me practise a little first before, that I may be perfect. Besides, my Aunt is here, and she will put me out, you know I cannot dance before her.

DON DIEGO. Fidle, fadle.

MONSIEUR. They're afraid to be discovered by *Gerards* bungling, I see. Come, come, Uncle, turn out, let 'em practise.   [*aside.*

DON DIEGO. I won't (voto a St. *Jago*) what a fooling's here?

MONSIEUR. Come, come, let 'em practise, turn out, turn out, Uncle.

DON DIEGO. Why, can't she practise it before me?

MONSIEUR. Come, Dancers and Singers are sometimes humorsom; besides, 'twill be more grateful to you, to see it danc'd all at once to the Violin. Come, turn out, turn out, I say.

DON DIEGO. What a fooling's here still amongst you, voto?

MONSIEUR. So there he is with you, voto, turn out, turn out, I vow and swear you shall turn out.

[*Takes him by the shoulder.*

DON DIEGO. Well, shall I see her dance it to the Violin at last?

GERRARD. Yes, yes, Sir, what do you think I teach her for?
[*Exit* DON DIEGO.

MONSIEUR. Go, go, turn out, and you too, Aunt.

CAUTION. Seriously, Nephew, I shall not budge, royally I shall not.

MONSIEUR. Royally you must, Aunt, come.

CAUTION. Pray hear me, Nephew.

MONSIEUR. I will not hear you.

CAUTION. 'Tis for your sake I stay, I must not suffer you to be wrong'd.

MONSIEUR. Come, no wheedling, Aunt, come away.

CAUTION. That slippery Fellow will do't.

MONSIEUR. Let him do't.

CAUTION. Indeed he will do't, royally he will.

MONSIEUR. Well let him do't, royally.

CAUTION. He will wrong you.

MONSIEUR. Well, let him, I say, I have a mind to be wrong'd, what's that to you, I will be wrong'd, if you go thereto, I vow and swear.

CAUTION. You shall not be wrong'd.

MONSIEUR. I will.

CAUTION. You shall not.   [DON DIEGO *returns.*

DON DIEGO. What's the matter? won't she be rul'd? come, come away, you shall not disturb 'em.
[DON DIEGO *and* MONSIEUR *thrust* CAUTION *out.*

CAUTION. De' see how they laugh at you both, well, go to, the Troth-telling *Trojan* Gentlewoman of old was ne're believ'd, till the Town was taken, rumag'd, and ransak'd, even, even so—

MONSIEUR. Hah, hah, ha, turn out.   [*Exit* CAUTION.[11]
Lord, that people shou'd be such arrant Cuddens, ha, ha, ha; but I may stay, may I not?

HIPPOLITA. No, no, I'de have you go out and hold the door, Cousin, or else my Father will come in agen before his time.

MONSIEUR. I will, I will then, sweet Cousin, 'twas well

Troth-telling Trojan Gentle-   *Cuddens:* fools.
woman: Cassandra.

thought on, that was well thought on indeed for me to hold the door.

HIPPOLITA. But be sure you keep him out, Cousin, till we knock.

MONSIEUR. I warrant you, Cousin, Lord, that people shou'd be made such Fools of, ha, ha, ha.   [*Exit* MONSIEUR.

GERRARD. So, so, to make him hold the door, while I steal his Mistress is not unpleasant.

HIPPOLITA. Ay, but wou'd you do so ill a thing, so treacherous a thing? faith 'tis not well.

GERRARD. Faith I can't help it. Since 'tis for your sake, come, Sweetest, is not this our way into the Gallery?

HIPPOLITA. Yes, but it goes against my Conscience to be accessary to so ill a thing; you say you do it for my sake?

GERRARD. Alas, poor Miss! 'tis not against your Conscience, but against your modesty, you think to do it franckly.

HIPPOLITA. Nay, if it be against my modesty too, I can't do it indeed.

GERRARD. Come, come, Miss, let us make haste, all's ready.

HIPPOLITA. Nay, faith, I can't satisfie my scruple.

GERRARD. Come, Dearest, this is not a time for scruples nor modesty; modesty between Lovers is as impertinent as Ceremony between Friends, and modesty is now as unseasonable as on the Wedding night: come away, my Dearest.

HIPPOLITA. Whither?

GERRARD. Nay sure, we have lost too much time already: Is that a proper Question now? if you wou'd know, come along, for I have all ready.

HIPPOLITA. But I am not ready.

GERRARD. Truly, Miss, we shall have your Father come in upon us, and prevent us agen, as he did in the morning.

HIPPOLITA. 'Twas well for me he did; for on my Conscience if he had not come in, I had gone clear away with you when I was in the humour.

GERRARD. Come, Dearest, you wou'd frighten me as if you were not yet in the same humour. Come, come away, the Coach and Six is ready.

HIPPOLITA. 'Tis too late to take the Air, and I am not ready.

GERRARD. You were ready in the morning.

HIPPOLITA. I, so I was.

GERRARD. Come, come, Miss, indeed the Jest begins to be none.

HIPPOLITA. What, I warrant you think me in jest then?

GERRARD. In jest, certainly; but it begins to be troublesom.

HIPPOLITA. But, Sir, you cou'd believe I was in earnest in the morning, when I but seemed to be ready to go with you; and why won't you believe me now, when I declare to the contrary? I take it unkindly, that the longer I am acquainted with you, you shou'd have the less confidence in me.

GERRARD. For Heaven's sake, Miss, lose no more time thus, your Father will come in upon us, as he did—

HIPPOLITA. Let him, if he will.

GERRARD. He'll hinder our design.

HIPPOLITA. No, he will not, for mine is to stay here now.

GERRARD. Are you in earnest?

HIPPOLITA. You'll find it so.

GERRARD. How! why you confess'd but now you wou'd have gone with me in the morning.

HIPPOLITA. I was in the humour then.

GERRARD. And I hope you are in the same still, you cannot change so soon.

HIPPOLITA. Why, is it not a whole day ago?

GERRARD. What, are you not a day in the same humour?

HIPPOLITA. Lord! that you who know the Town (they say) shou'd think any Woman could be a whole day together in an humor, ha, ha, ha.

GERRARD. Hey! this begins to be pleasant: What, won't you go with me then after all?

HIPPOLITA. No indeed, Sir, I desire to be excus'd.

GERRARD. Then you have abus'd me all this while?

HIPPOLITA. It may be so.

GERRARD. Cou'd all that so natural Innocency be dissembl'd? faith it cou'd not, dearest Miss.

HIPPOLITA. Faith it was, dear Master.

GERRARD. Was it, faith?

HIPPOLITA. Methinks you might believe me without an Oath: you saw I cou'd dissemble with my Father, why shou'd you think I cou'd not with you?

GERRARD. So young a Wheadle?

HIPPOLITA. Ay, a meer damn'd Jade I am.

GERRARD. And I have been abus'd, you say?

HIPPOLITA. 'Tis well you can believe it at last.

GERRARD. And I must never hope for you?

HIPPOLITA. Wou'd you have me abuse you again?

GERRARD. Then you will not go with me?

HIPPOLITA. No; but for your comfort your loss will not be great, and that you may not resent it, for once I'le be ingenuous and disabuse you; I am no Heiress, as I told you, to twelve hundred pound a year. I was only a lying Jade then, now you will part with me willingly I doubt not.

GERRARD. I wish I cou'd.   *[sighs.*

HIPPOLITA. Come, now I find 'tis your turn to dissemble; but men use to dissemble for money, will you dissemble for nothing?

GERRARD. 'Tis too late for me to dissemble.

HIPPOLITA. Don't you dissemble, faith?

GERRARD. Nay, this is too cruel.

HIPPOLITA. What, wou'd you take me without the twelve hundred pound a year? wou'd you be such a Fool as to steal a Woman with nothing?

GERRARD. I'le convince you, for you shall go with me; and since you are twelve hundred pound a year the lighter, you'll be the easier carried away.

        [He takes her in his Arms, she struggles.

PRUE. What, he takes her away against her will, I find I must knock for my Master then.   *[She knocks.*

    Enter DON DIEGO *and Mrs.* CAUTION.

HIPPOLITA. My Father, my Father is here.

GERRARD. Prevented again! *[*GERRARD *sets her down again.*

DON DIEGO. What, you have done I hope now, Friend, for good and all?

GERRARD. Yes, yes, we have done for good and all indeed.

DON DIEGO. How now! you seem to be out of humour, Friend.

GERRARD. Yes, so I am, I can't help it.

CAUTION. He's a Dissembler in his very Throat, Brother.

Wheadle: wheedler, coaxer.   *Jade:* minx.

HIPPOLITA. Pray do not carry things so as to discover your self, if it be but for my sake, good Master.

[*aside to* GERRARD.

GERRARD. She is grown impudent.   [*aside.*

CAUTION. See, see, they whisper, Brother, to steal a Kiss under a Wisper, O the Harletry!

DON DIEGO. What's the matter, Friend?

HIPPOLITA. I say for my sake be in humour, and do not discover your self, but be as patient as a Dancing-master still.   [*To* GERRARD.

DON DIEGO. What, she is wispering to him indeed! what's the matter? I will know it, Friend, look you.

GERRARD. Will you know it?[12]

DON DIEGO. Yes, I will know it.

GERRARD. Why, if you will know it, then she wou'd not do as I wou'd have her, and whisper'd me to desire me not to discover it to you.

DON DIEGO. What, Hussy, wou'd you not do as he'd have you! I'le make you do as he'd have you.

GERRARD. I wish you wou'd.

CAUTION. 'Tis a lye, she'll do all he'll have her do, and more too, to my knowledge.

DON DIEGO. Come, tell me what 'twas then she wou'd not do, come do it, Hussy, or—
Come, take her by the hand, Friend, come, begin, let's see if she will not do any thing now I am here.

HIPPOLITA. Come, pray be in humour, Master.

GERRARD. I cannot dissemble like you.

DON DIEGO. What, she can't dissemble already, can she?

CAUTION. Yes but she can, but 'tis with you she dissembles; for they are not fallen out, as we think, for I'le be sworn I saw her just now give him the languishing Eye, as they call it, that is, the Whitings Eye, of old called the Sheeps Eye. I'le be sworn I saw it with these two Eyes, that I did.

HIPPOLITA. You'll betray us, have a care, good Master.

[*aside to* GERRARD.

GERRARD. Hold your peace, I say, silly Woman.

DON DIEGO. But does she dissemble already? how do you mean?

GERRARD. She pretends she can't do what she shou'd do, and that she is not in humour, the common Excuse of Women for not doing what they shou'd do.

DON DIEGO. Come, I'le put her in humour; dance, I say, come, about with her, Master.

GERRARD. I am in a pretty humour to dance.   [*aside.*
I cannot fool any longer, since you have fool'd me.
[*To* HIPPOLITA.

HIPPOLITA. You wou'd not be so ungenerous, as to betray the Woman that hated you, I do not do that yet; for Heaven's sake for this once be more obedient to my desires than your passion.

DON DIEGO. What is she humoursom still? But methinks you look your self as if you were in an ill humour; but about with her.

GERRARD. I am in no good Dancing humour indeed.

Enter MONSIEUR.

MONSIEUR. Well, how goes the Dancing forward? what my Aunt here to disturb 'em again?

DON DIEGO. Come, come.   [GERRARD *leads her about.*

CAUTION. I say stand off, thou shalt not come near, avoid, Satan, as they say.

DON DIEGO. Nay then we shall have it, Nephew, hold her a little, that she may not disturb 'em, come, now away with her.

GERRARD. One, two, and a Coupee.
Fool'd and abus'd.   [*aside.*

CAUTION. Wilt thou lay violent hands upon thy own natural Aunt, Wretch?   [*The* MONSIEUR *holding* CAUTION.

DON DIEGO. Come, about with her.

GERRARD. One, two, three, four, and turn round.
By such a piece of Innocency.   [*aside.*

CAUTION. Dost thou see, Fool, how he squeezes her hand?

MONSIEUR. That won't do, Aunt.

HIPPOLITA. Pray, Master, have patience, and let's mind our business.

DON DIEGO. Why did you anger him then, Hussy, look you?

CAUTION. Do you see how she smiles in his face, and squeezes his hand now?

MONSIEUR. Your Servant, Aunt, that won't do, I say.

HIPPOLITA. Have patience, Master.

GERRARD. I am become her sport, [*aside*.] one, two, three, Death, Hell, and the Devil.

DON DIEGO. Ay, they are three indeed; but pray have patience.

CAUTION. Do you see how she leers upon him and clings to him, can you suffer it?

MONSIEUR. Ay, ay.

GERRARD. One, two, and a slur; can you be so unconcern'd after all?

DON DIEGO. What, is she unconcern'd! Hussy, mind your bus'ness.

GERRARD. One, two, three, and turn round, one, two, fall back, Hell and Damnation.

DON DIEGO. Ay, people, fall back indeed into Hell and Damnation, Heav'n knows.

GERRARD. One, two, three, and your Honour: I can fool no longer.

CAUTION. Nor will I be withel'd any longer like a poor Hen in her Pen, while the Kite is carrying away her Chicken before her face.

DON DIEGO. What have you done? Well then let's see her dance it now to the Violin.

MONSIEUR. Ay, ay, let's see her dance it to the Violin.

GERRARD. Another time, another time.

DON DIEGO. Don't you believe that, Friend; these Dancing-masters make no bones of breaking their words. Did not you promise just now I shou'd see her dance it to the Violin, and that I will too, before I stir.

GERRARD. Let *Monsieur* play then while I dance with her, she can't dance alone.

MONSIEUR. I can't play at all, I'm but a Learner; but if you'll play, I'le dance with her.

GERRARD. I can't play neither.

DON DIEGO. What a Dancing-master, and not play!

CAUTION. Ay, you see what a Dancing-master he is. 'Tis as I told you, I warrant: A Dancing-master, and not play upon the Fiddle!

DON DIEGO. How!

slur: gliding step.

HIPPOLITA. O you have betray'd us all! if you confess that, you undo us for ever.   [*apart to* GERRARD.

GERRARD. I cannot play, what wou'd you have me say?

MONSIEUR. I vow and swear we are all undone, if you cannot play.

DON DIEGO. What, are you a Dancing-master, and cannot play! umph—

HIPPOLITA. He is only out of humour, Sir; here, Master, I know you will play for me yet, for he has an excellent hand.   [*She offers* GERRARD *the Violin.*

MONSIEUR. Ay, that he has.

    At giving a box on the Ear.   [*aside.*

DON DIEGO. Why does he not play then?

HIPPOLITA. Here, Master, pray play for my sake.
        [*Gives* GERRARD *the Violin.*

GERRARD. What wou'd you have me do with it? I cannot play a stroke.

HIPPOLITA. No, stay then, seem to tune it, and break the strings.   [*apart to* GERRARD.

GERRARD. Come then.

    Next to the Devil's the Invention of Women, they'll no more want an excuse to cheat a Father with, than an opportunity to abuse a Husband.   [*aside.*

    But what do you give me such a dam'd Fiddle with rotten strings for?

    Windes up the strings till they break, and throws the Violin on the ground.

DON DIEGO. Hey-day, the Dancing-master is frantick.

MONSIEUR. Ha, ha, ha, that people shou'd be made such Fools of.[13]

CAUTION. He broke the strings on purpose, because he cou'd not play, you are blind, Brother.

DON DIEGO. What, will you see further than I? look you.

HIPPOLITA. But pray, Master, why in such haste?

GERRARD. Because you have done with me.

DON DIEGO. But don't you intend to come to morrow agen?

GERRARD. Your Daughter does not desire it.

DON DIEGO. No matter, I do, I must be your pay Master I'm sure, I wou'd have you come betimes too, not only to make her perfect; but since you have so good a hand upon the Violin to play your part with half a dozen of Musicians more, whom I wou'd have you bring with you; for we will have a very merry Wedding, though a very private one; you'll be sure to come?

GERRARD. Your Daughter does not desire it.

DON DIEGO. Come, come, Baggage, you shall desire it of him, he is your Master.

HIPPOLITA. My Father will have me desire it of you, it seems.

GERRARD. But you'll make a Fool of me agen: if I shou'd come, wou'd you not?

HIPPOLITA. If I shou'd tell you so, you'd be sure not to come.

DON DIEGO. Come, come, she shall not make a Fool of you, upon my word: I'le secure you, she shall do what you'll have her.

MONSIEUR. Ha, ha, ha, so, so, silly *Don.*   [*aside.*

GERRARD. But, Madam, will you have me come?

HIPPOLITA. I'd have you to know for my part, I care not whether you come or no; there are other Dancing-masters to be had, it is my Fathers request to you: all that I have to say to you, is a little good advice, which (because I will not shame you) I'le give you in private.
                                        [*whispers* GERRARD.

CAUTION. What, will you let her whisper with him too?

DON DIEGO. Nay, if you find fault with it, they shall whisper; though I did not like it before, I'le ha' no body wiser than my self; but do you think if 'twere any hurt, she wou'd whisper it to him before us?

CAUTION. If it be no hurt, why does she not speak aloud?

DON DIEGO. Because she says she will not put the man out of Countenance.

CAUTION. Hey-day, put a Dancing-master out of countenance!

DON DIEGO. You say he is no Dancing-master.

CAUTION. Yes, for his impudence, he may be a Dancing-master.

DON DIEGO. Well, well, let her whisper before me as much as she will to night, since she is to be marry'd to morrow, especially since her Husband that shall be stands by consenting too.

MONSIEUR. Ay, ay, let 'em whisper (as you say) as much as they will before we marry.

She's making more sport with him, I warrant; but I wonder how people can be fool'd so, ha, ha, ha. [*aside.*

DON DIEGO. Well, a Penny for the secret, Daughter.

HIPPOLITA. Indeed, Father, you shall have it for nothing to morrow.

DON DIEGO. Well, Friend, you will not fail to come.

GERRARD. No, no, Sir.

Yet I am a Fool, if I do. [*aside.*

DON DIEGO. And be sure you bring the Fiddlers with you, as I bid you.

HIPPOLITA. Yes, be sure you bring the Fiddlers with you, as I bid you.

CAUTION. So, so, He'll fiddle your Daughter out of the house, must you have Fiddles, with a fiddle, faddle.

MONSIEUR. Lord! that people shou'd be made such Fools of, hah, hah.[14]

[*Exeunt* DON DIEGO, HIPPOLITA, MONSIEUR, CAUTION
and PRUE.

GERRARD. Fortune we sooner may than Woman trust
    To her confiding Gallant, she is just;
    But falser Woman only him deceives,
    Who to her Tongue and Eyes most
        credit gives.   *Exit.*

ACT V. SCENE I.

Enter MONSIEUR *and* BLACK *stalking over the Stage,
to them Mr.* GERARD.

MONSIEUR. Good morrow to thee noble Dancing-master, ha, ha, ha, your little black Brother here my Master I see, is the more diligent man of the two; but why do you come so late? what you begin to neglect your Scholar, do you?

Little black Master (con Licentia) pray get you out of the Room. [*Exit* BLACK.

What, out of humour, man! a Dancing master shou'd
be like his Fiddle, always in Tune. Come, my Cousin
has made an Ass of thee, what then, I know it.

GERRARD. Does he know it?   [*aside.*

MONSIEUR. But prethee don't be angry, 'twas agreed upon
betwixt us, before I sent you to make a Fool of thee,
ha, ha, ha.

GERRARD. Was it so?

MONSIEUR. I knew you would be apt to entertain vain
hopes from the Summons of a Lady; but faith the design was but to make a Fool of thee, as you find.

GERRARD. 'Tis very well.

MONSIEUR. But indeed I did not think the Jest wou'd have
lasted so long, and that my Cousin wou'd have made a
Dancing-master of you, ha, ha, ha.

GERRARD. The Fool has reason, I find, and I am the Coxcomb while I thought him so.   [*aside.*

MONSIEUR. Come, I see you are uneasie, and the Jest of
being a Dancing master grows tedious to you; but have
a little patience, the Parson is sent for, and when once
my Cousin and I are marry'd, my Uncle may know who
you are.

GERRARD. I am certainly abus'd.

MONSIEUR. What do you say?   [MONSIEUR *listens.*

GERRARD. Meerly fool'd.   [*aside.*

MONSIEUR. Why do you doubt it? ha, ha, ha.

GERRARD. Can it be?   [*aside.*

MONSIEUR. Pish, pish, she told me yesterday as soon as
you were gone, that she had led you into a Fools Paradise, and made you believe she wou'd go away with
you, ha, ha, ha.

GERRARD. Did she so! I am no longer to doubt it then?
                                                  [*aside.*

MONSIEUR. Ay, ay, she makes a meer Fool of thee, I vow
and swear; but don't be concern'd, there's hardly a man
of a thousand but has been made a Fool of by some
Woman or other: I have been made a Fool of my self,
man, by the Women, I have, I vow and swear, I have.

GERRARD. Well, you have, I believe it, for you are a Coxcomb.

MONSIEUR. Lord! you need not be so touchy with one, I tell you but the truth for your good, for though she does, I wou'd not fool you any longer; but prethee don't be troubl'd at what can't be help'd. Women are made on purpose to fool men; when they are Children, they fool their Fathers; and when they have taken their leaves of their Hanging-sleeves, they fool their Gallants or Dancing-masters, ha, ha, ha.

GERRARD. Hark you, Sir, to be fool'd by a woman you say is not to be help'd; but I will not be fool'd by a Fool.

MONSIEUR. You shew your English breeding now, an English Rival is so dull and brutish as not to understand raillery, but what is spoken in your passion, I'le take no notice of, for I am your friend, and would not have you my Rival to make your self ridiculous. Come, prethee, prethee, don't be so concern'd; for as I was saying, women first fool their Fathers, then their Gallants, and then their Husbands; so that it will be my turn to be fool'd too; (for your comfort) and when they come to be Widows, they would fool the Devil I vow and swear. Come, come, dear *Gerard,* prethee don't be out of humour and look so sillily.

GERRARD. Prethee do not talk so sillily.

MONSIEUR. Nay, faith I am resolv'd to beat you out of this ill humour.

GERRARD. Faith, I am afraid I shall first beat you into an ill humour.

MONSIEUR. Ha, ha, ha, that thou should'st be gull'd so by a little Gipsey, who left off her Bib but yesterday; faith I can't but laugh at thee.

GERRARD. Faith then I shall make your mirth (as being too violent) conclude in some little mis-fortune to you. The Fool begins to be tyrannical.

MONSIEUR. Ha, ha, ha, poor angry *Dancing-Master;* prethee match my Spanish pumps and legs with one of your best and newest Sarabands; ha, ha, ha, come—

Hanging-sleeves: loose open sleeves hanging down from the arm, worn by children or young people.

Gipsey: Gypsy, a mildly contemptuous term for a deceitful woman.

GERRARD. I will match your Spanish ear thus, Sir, and
  make you Dance thus.   [*strikes and kicks him.*

MONSIEUR. How! sa, sa, sa, then I'le make you Dance
  thus. [MONSIEUR *draws his Sword and runs at him, but*
  GERRARD *drawing he retires.*] Hold, hold a little, a desperate disappointed Lover will cut his own throat, then
  sure he will make nothing of cutting his Rivals throat.
                                           [*Aside.*

GERRARD. Consideration is an enemy to fighting; if you
  have a mind to revenge your self, your Sword's in
  your hand.

MONSIEUR. Pray, Sir, hold your peace; I'le ne'r take my
  Rivals counsel be't what 'twill, I know what you wou'd
  be at; you are disappointed of your Mistress, and cou'd
  hang your self, and therefore will not fear hanging; but
  I am a successful Lover, and need neither hang for you
  nor my Mistress; nay, if I should kill you, I know I
  should do you a kindness; therefore e'en live to dye
  daily with envy of my happiness; but if you will needs
  dye, kill your self and be damn'd for me I vow and
  swear.

GERRARD. But won't you fight for your Mistress?

MONSIEUR. I tell you, you shall not have the honour to be
  kill'd for her; besides, I will not be hit in the teeth by
  her as long as I live with the great love you had for
  her. Women speak well of their dead Husbands, what
  will they do of their dead Gallants?

GERRARD. But if you will not fight for her, you shall Dance
  for her, since you desir'd me to teach you to Dance too;
  I'le teach you to Dance thus—

          [*Strikes his Sword at his legs,* MONSIEUR *leaps.*

MONSIEUR. Nay, if it be for the sake of my Mistress, there's
  nothing I will refuse to do.

GERRARD. Nay, you must Dance on.

MONSIEUR. Ay, ay for my Mistress and Sing too, la, la, la,
  ra, la.

            Enter HIPPOLITA *and* PRUE.

HIPPOLITA. What Swords drawn betwixt you too? what's
  the matter?

MONSIEUR. Is she here?   [*Aside.*
   Come put up your Sword; you see this is no place for
   us; but the Devil eat me, if you shall not eat my Sword
   but—

HIPPOLITA. What's the matter Cousin?

MONSIEUR. Nothing, nothing Cousin; but your presence is
   a sanctuary for my greatest enemy, or else, *teste non.*

HIPPOLITA. What, you have not hurt my Cousin, Sir, I
   hope?   [*To* GERRARD.

GERRARD. How she's concern'd for him; nay, then I need
   not doubt, my fears are true.   [*Aside.*

MONSIEUR. What was that you said Cousin! hurt me, ha,
   ha, ha, hurt me! if any man hurt me, he must do it
   basely; he shall ne'r do it when my Sword's drawn, sa,
   sa, sa.

HIPPOLITA. Because you will ne'r draw your Sword perhaps.

MONSIEUR. Scurvily guess'd.   [*Aside.*
   You Ladies may say any thing; but, Cousin, pray do not
   you talk of Swords and fighting, meddle with your Gui-
   tar, and talk of dancing with your Dancing-master there,
   ha, ha, ha.

HIPPOLITA. But I am afraid you have hurt my Master,
   Cousin, he says nothing; can he draw his breath?

MONSIEUR. No, 'tis you have hurt your Master, Cousin, in
   the very heart, Cousin, and therefore he wou'd hurt
   me; for Love is a disease makes people as malicious as
   the Plague does.

HIPPOLITA. Indeed, poor Master, something does ail you.

MONSIEUR. Nay, nay, Cousin, faith don't abuse him any
   longer, he's an honest Gentleman, and has been long of
   my acquaintance, and a man of tolerable sense to take
   him out of his Love; but prethee, Cousin, don't drive
   the Jest too far for my sake.

GERRARD. He counsels you well, pleasant-cunning-jilting-
   Miss for his sake; for if I am your divertisement, it shall
   be at his cost, since he's your Gallant in favour.

HIPPOLITA. I don't understand you.

MONSIEUR. But I do, a pox take him, and the Custom that
   so orders it, forsooth; that if a Lady abuse or affront a

man, presently the Gallant must be beaten, nay, what's more unreasonable, if a Woman abuse her Husband, the poor Cuckold must bear the shame as well as the injury.   [*aside*.

HIPPOLITA. But what's the matter, Master? what was it you said?

GERRARD. I say pleasant, cunning, jilting Lady, though you make him a Cuckold, it will not be revenge enough for me upon him for marrying you.

HIPPOLITA. How, my surly, huffing, jealous, sensless sawcy Master?

MONSIEUR. Nay, nay, faith give losers leave to speak, losers of Mistresses especially, ha, ha, ha. Besides, your anger is too great a favour for him, I scorn to honour him with mine, you see.

HIPPOLITA. I tell you, my sawcy Master, my Cousin shall never be made that monstrous thing (you mention) by me.

MONSIEUR. Thank you, I vow and swear, Cousin, no, no, I never thought I should.

GERRARD. Sure you marry him by the sage Maxime of your Sex, which is, Wittals make the best Husbands, that is, Cuckolds.

HIPPOLITA. Indeed, Master, whatsoever you think, I wou'd sooner chuse you for that purpose than him.

MONSIEUR. Ha, ha, ha, there she was with him, i'faith, I thank you for that, Cousin, I vow and swear.

HIPPOLITA. Nay, he shall thank me for that too; but how came you two to quarrel? I thought, Cousin, you had had more wit than to quarrel, or more kindness for me than to quarrel here: what if my Father hearing the Bustle shou'd have come in, he wou'd soon have discover'd our false Dancing-master (for passion un-masks every man) and then the result of your quarrel had been my ruine.

MONSIEUR. Nay, you had both felt his desperate, deadly, daunting Dagger; there are your dès for you.

HIPPOLITA. Go, go presently therefore, and hinder my Father from coming in, whilst I put my Master into a better humour, that we may not be discover'd, to the prevention of our Wedding, or worse, when he comes, go, go.

MONSIEUR. Well, well, I will, Cousin.

HIPPOLITA. Be sure you let him not come in this good while.

MONSIEUR. No, no, I warrant you.

[MONSIEUR *goes out and returns.*

But if he shou'd come before I wou'd have him, I'le come before him and cough and hawk soundly, that you may not be surprised. Won't that do well, Cousin?

HIPPOLITA. Very well, pray be gone.   [*Exit* MONSIEUR. Well, Master, since I find you are quarrelsom and melancholy, and wou'd have taken me away without a Portion, three infallible signs of a true Lover, faith here's my hand now in earnest, to lead me a Dance as long as I live.

GERRARD. How's this? you surprise me as much as when first I found so much Beauty and Wit in Company with so much Innocency. But, Dearest, I would be assur'd of what you say, and yet dare not ask the question. You h— do not abuse me again, you h— will fool me no more sure.

HIPPOLITA. Yes but I will sure.

GERRARD. How! nay, I was afraid on't.

HIPPOLITA. For I say you are to be my Husband, and you say Husbands must be Wittals and some strange things to boot.

GERRARD. Well, I will take my Fortune.

HIPPOLITA. But have a care, rash man.

GERRARD. I will venture.

HIPPOLITA. At your peril, remember I wish'd you to have a care, fore-warn'd, fore-arm'd.

PRUE. Indeed now that's fair; for most men are fore-arm'd before they are warn'd.

HIPPOLITA. Plain dealing is some kind of honesty however, and few women wou'd have said so much.

GERRARD. None but those who wou'd delight in a Husbands jealousie, as the proof of his love and her honour.

HIPPOLITA. Hold, Sir, let us have a good understanding betwixt one another at first, that we may be long

Friends; I differ from you in the point, for a Husbands jealousie, which cunning men wou'd pass upon their Wives for a Complement, is the worst can be made 'em, for indeed it is a Complement to their Beauty, but an affront to their Honour.

GERRARD. But, Madam—

HIPPOLITA. So that upon the whole matter I conclude, jealousie in a Gallant is humble true Love, and the height of respect, and only an undervaluing of himself to overvalue her; but in a Husband 'tis arrant sawciness, cowardise, and ill breeding, and not to be suffer'd.

GERRARD. I stand corrected gracious Miss.

HIPPOLITA. Well! but have you brought the Gentlemen Fidlers with you as I desired?

GERRARD. They are below.

HIPPOLITA. Are they arm'd well?

GERRARD. Yes, they have Instruments too that are not of wood; but what will you do with them?

HIPPOLITA. What did you think I intended to do with them? when I whisper'd you to bring Gentlemen of your acquaintance instead of Fidlers, as my Father desir'd you to bring; pray what did you think I intended?

GERRARD. Faith, e'en to make fools of the Gentlemen-Fidlers, as you had done of your Gentleman Dancing-Master.

HIPPOLITA. I intended 'em for our guard and defence against my Fathers *Spanish* and *Guiny* force, when we were to make our retreat from hence, and to help us to take the keys from my Aunt, who has been the watchful Porter of this house this twelve-month; and this design (if your heart do not fail you) we will put in execution, as soon as you have given your friends below instructions.

GERRARD. Are you sure your heart will stand right still? you flinch'd last night, when I little expected it, I am sure.

HIPPOLITA. The time last night, was not so proper for us

Guiny: African. Guinea was often used not only to identify a specific area, but as a general term for the West African coast.

as now, for reasons I will give you; but besides that, I confess I had a mind to try whether your interest did not sway you more than your love; whether the twelve hundred pounds a year I told you of, had not made a greater impression in your heart than *Hippolita;* but finding it otherwise—yet hold, perhaps upon consideration you are grown wiser; can you yet, as I said, be so desperate, so out of fashion, as to steal a woman with nothing?

GERRARD. With you I can want nothing, nor can be made by any thing more rich or happy.

HIPPOLITA. Think well again; can you take me without the twelve hundred pounds a year; the twelve hundred pounds a year?

GERRARD. Indeed, Miss, now you begin to be unkind again, and use me worse than e're you did.

HIPPOLITA. Well, though you are so modest a Gentleman as to suffer a Wife to be put upon you with nothing, I have more conscience than to do it: I have the twelve hundred pounds a year out of my Father's power, which is yours, and I am sorry it is not the *Indies* to mend your bargain.

GERRARD. Dear Miss, you but encrease my fears, and not my wealth: pray let us make haste away, I desire but to be secure of you; come, what are you thinking of?

HIPPOLITA. I am thinking if some little filching inquisitive Poet shou'd get my story, and represent it on the Stage; what those Ladies, who are never precise but at a Play, wou'd say of me now; that I were a confident coming piece I warrant, and they wou'd damn the poor Poet for libelling the Sex; but sure though I give my self and fortune away franckly, without the consent of my Friends, my confidence is less than theirs, who stand off only for separate maintenance.

GERRARD. They wou'd be Widows before their time, have a Husband and no Husband: but let us be gone, lest fortune shou'd recant my happiness. Now you are fix'd my dearest Miss.　　　　　　　　[*He kisses her hand.*

Enter MONSIEUR *coughing, and* DON DIEGO.

HIPPOLITA. Oh here's my Father!

DON DIEGO. How now Sir! what kissing her hand? what means that friend, ha! Daughter ha! do you permit this insolence ha! (*voto à mi honrâ.*)

GERRARD. We are prevented again.

HIPPOLITA. Ha, ha, ha, you are so full of your *Spanish* Jealousie, Father, why you must know he's a City Danc-ing-master, and they, forsooth, think it fine to kiss the hand at the Honour before the Corant.

MONSIEUR. Ay, ay, ay, Uncle, don't you know that?

DON DIEGO. Go to, go to, you are an easie *French* Fool, there's more in it than so, look you.

MONSIEUR. I vow and swear there's nothing more in't, if you'll believe one.
Did not I cough and hawk? a jealous prudent Husband cou'd not cough and hawk louder at the approach of his Wifes Chamber in visiting-time, and yet you wou'd not hear me, he'll make now ado about nothing, and you'll be discover'd both.
[*aside to* HIPPOLITA *and* GERRARD.

DON DIEGO. Umph, umph, no, no, I see it plain, he is no Dancing-master, now I have found it out, and I think I can see as far into matters as another: I have found it now, look you.

GERRARD. My fear was prophetical.

HIPPOLITA. What shall we do? nay, pray, Sir, do not stir yet.   [GERRARD *offers to go out with her.*
Enter Mrs. CAUTION.

CAUTION. What's the matter, Brother? what's the matter?

DON DIEGO. I have found it out, Sister, I have found it out, Sister, this Villain here is no Dancing-master, but a dis-honourer of my House and Daughter, I caught him kiss-ing her hand.

MONSIEUR. Pish, pish, you are a strange *Spanish* kind of an Uncle, that you are, a dishonourer of your Daugh-ter, because he kissed her hand; pray how cou'd he honour her more? he kiss't her hand, you see, while he was making his Honour to her.

DON DIEGO. You are an unthinking, shallow, *French* Fop, voto— But I tell you, Sister, I have thought of it, and have found it out, he is no Dancing-master, Sister. Do you remember the whispering last night? I have found out the meaning of that too, and I tell you, Sister, he's no Dancing-master, I have found it out.

CAUTION. You found it out, marry come up, did not I tell you always he was no Dancing-master?

DON DIEGO. You tell me, you silly Woman, what then? what of that? you tell me, de' think I heeded what you told me? but I tell you now I have found it out.

CAUTION. I say I found it out.

DON DIEGO. I say 'tis false, Gossip, I found him out.

CAUTION. I say I found him out first, say you what you will.

DON DIEGO. Sister *Mum,* not such a word again, guarda— you found him out.

CAUTION. Nay, I must submit, or dissemble like other prudent Women, or—

DON DIEGO. Come, come, Sister, take it from me, he is no Dancing-master.

CAUTION. O yes, he is a Dancing-master.

DON DIEGO. What will you be wiser than I every way? remember the whispering, I say.

CAUTION. So, he thinks I speak in earnest, then I'le fit him still. [*aside.*] But what do you talk of their whispering, they wou'd not whisper any ill before us sure.

DON DIEGO. Will you still be an Idiot, a Dolt, and see nothing.

MONSIEUR. Lord! you'll be wiser than all the World, will you? are we not all against you? pshaw, pshaw, I ne're saw such a Donissimo as you are, I vow and swear.

DON DIEGO. No, Sister, he's no Dancing-master; for now I think on't too, he cou'd not play upon the Fiddle.

CAUTION. Pish, pish, what Dancing-master can play upon a Fiddle without strings?

DON DIEGO. Again, I tell you he broke 'em on purpose, because he cou'd not play; I have found it out now, Sister.

CAUTION. Nay, you see farther than I, Brother.

[GERRARD *offers to lead her out.*

HIPPOLITA. For Heaven's sake stir not yet.

DON DIEGO. Besides, if you remember they were perpetually putting me out of the Room, that was, Sister, because they had a mind to be alone, I have found that out too: Now, Sister, look you, he is no Dancing-master.

CAUTION. But has he not given her Lesson often before you.

DON DIEGO. I but, Sister, he did not go about his bus'ness like a Dancing-master; but go, go down to the dore, some body rings.   [*Exit* CAUTION.

MONSIEUR. I vow and swear Uncle he is a Dancing-master; pray be appeas'd, Lord de'e think I'de tell you a lye?

DON DIEGO. If it prove to be a lye, and you do not confess it, though you are my next Heir after my Daughter, I will disown thee as much as I do her, for thy folly and treachery to thy self, as well as me; you may have her, but never my estate look you.

MONSIEUR. How! I must look to my hits then.   [*Aside.*

DON DIEGO. Look to't.

MONSIEUR. Then I had best confess all, before he discover all, which he will soon do.

Enter PARSON.

O here's the Parson too! he won't be in choler nor brandish Toledo before the Parson sure?   [*Aside.*
Well, Uncle, I must confess, rather than lose your favour, he is no Dancing-master.

DON DIEGO. No.

GERRARD. What has the Fool betray'd us then at last? nay, then 'tis time to be gone; come away Miss. [*Going out.*

DON DIEGO. Nay, Sir, if you pass this way, my *Toledo* will pass that way look you.

[*Thrusts at him with his Sword.*

HIPPOLITA. O hold Mr. *Gerrard*, hold Father!

MONSIEUR. I tell you Uncle he's an honest Gentleman, means no hurt, and came hither but upon a frolick of mine and your Daughters.   [*Stops his Uncle.*

DON DIEGO. Ladron, Trayidor.

MONSIEUR. I tell you all's but a jest, a meer jest I vow and swear.

DON DIEGO. A jest, jest with my honour voto, ha! no Family to dishonour but the Grave, Wise, Noble, Honourable, Illustrious, Puissant, and right Worshipful Family of the Formals; nay, I am contented to reprieve you, till you know who you have dishonoured, and convict you of

the greatness of your crime before you die; we are descended look you—

MONSIEUR. Nay, pray Uncle hear me.

DON DIEGO. I say, we are descended.

MONSIEUR. 'Tis no matter for that.

DON DIEGO. And my great, great, great Grandfather was.

MONSIEUR. Well, well, I have something to say more to the
purpose.

DON DIEGO. My great, great, great Grandfather, I say, was—

MONSIEUR. Well, a Pin-maker in—

DON DIEGO. But he was a Gentleman for all that Fop, for
he was a Serjeant to a Company of the Train-bands,
and my great, great, great Grandfather[1] was.

MONSIEUR. Was his Son, what then? won't you let me
clear this Gentleman?

DON DIEGO. He was, he was—

MONSIEUR. He was a Felt-maker, his Son a Wine-cooper,
your Father a Vintner, and so you came to be a Canary-
Merchant.

DON DIEGO. But we were still Gentlemen, for our Coat was
as the Heralds say—was—

MONSIEUR. Was, your sign was the Three Tuns, and the
Field Canary; now let me tell you this honest Gentleman—

DON DIEGO. Now that you shou'd dare to dishonour this
Family; by the Graves of my Ancestors in Great Saint
Ellens Church—

MONSIEUR. Yard.

DON DIEGO. Thou shalt dye fort't ladron.

[*Runs at* GERARD.

Train-bands: trained companies of citizen soldiers.

Canary-Merchant: Canary
was a sweet wine from the
Canary Islands. Don Diego
presumably is more than a
wine importer; a Canary-merchant would have been generally involved in the West
African trade.

Great Saint Ellens Church:
Great St. Helen's, Bishopgate

Street. In the church there
are monuments to a number
of sixteenth-century mer-
chants, including Sir Thomas
Gresham, who founded the
Royal Exchange. When Mon-
sieur places the graves of Don
Diego's ancestors in the yard
instead of the church itself,
he pares the Formal family
tree of its loftier branches.

MONSIEUR. Hold, hold Uncle, are you mad?

HIPPOLITA. Oh, oh.

MONSIEUR. Nay then, by your own *Spanish* rules of honour (though he be my Rival) I must help him, since I brought him into danger.   [*Draws his sword.*
Sure he will not shew his valour upon his Nephew and Son-in-Law, otherwise I shou'd be afraid of shewing mine.   [*Aside.*
Here Mr. *Gerrard,* go in here, nay, you shall go in Mr. *Gerrard,* I'le secure you all; and Parson do you go in too with 'em; for I see you are afraid of a Sword and the other World, though you talk of it so familiarly, and make it so fine a place.

Opens a dore, and thrusts GERRARD, HIPPOLITA *and* PARSON *in, then shuts it, and guards it with his Sword.*

DON DIEGO. Tu quoque Brute.

MONSIEUR. Nay, now Uncle you must understand reason; what, you are not only a *Don,* but you are a *Don Quixot* too I vow and swear.

DON DIEGO. Thou spot, sploach of my Family and blood; I will have his blood look you.

MONSIEUR. Pray good Spanish Uncle, have but patience to hear me; suppose— I say, suppose he had done, done, done the feat to your Daughter.

DON DIEGO. How, done the feat, done the feat, done the feat, *En horâ Malâ.*

MONSIEUR. I say, suppose, suppose—

DON DIEGO. Suppose—

MONSIEUR. I say, suppose he had, for I do but suppose it; well, I am ready to marry her however; now Marriage is as good a Solder for crack'd female-honour, as blood, and can't you suffer the shame but for a quarter of an hour, till the Parson has marry'd us, and then if there be any shame, it becomes mine; for here in *England,* the Father has nothing to do with the Daughters business, honour, what de'e call't, when once she's marry'd, de'e see.

DON DIEGO. *England!* what de'e tell me of *England?* I'le be a *Spaniard* still, voto a mi hora, and I will be reveng'd,

Pedro, Juan, Sanches.   [*Calls at the dore.*
Enter MRS. CAUTION *follow'd by* FLIRT *and* FLOUNCE
in vizard Masks.

CAUTION. What's the matter Brother?

DON DIEGO. *Pedro, Sanchez, Juan,* but who are these Sister? are they not men in womens cloaths? what make they here?

CAUTION. They are relations, they say, of my Cousins, who press'd in when I let in the Parson, they say my Cousin invited 'em to his Wedding.

MONSIEUR. Two of my relations, ha—they are my Cousins indeed of the other night; a Pox take 'em, but that's no Curse for 'em; a Plague take 'em then, but how came they here?

DON DIEGO. Now must I have witnesses too of the dishonour of my Family; it were Spanish prudence to dispatch 'em away out of the house, before I begin my revenge.
                                        [*Aside.*
What are you? what make you here? who wou'd you speak with?

FLIRT. With *Monsieur.*

DON DIEGO. Here he is.

MONSIEUR. Now will these Jades discredit me, and spoil my match just in the coupling minute.

DON DIEGO. Do you know 'em?

MONSIEUR. Yes, Sir, sure, I know 'em. Pray, Ladies, say as I say, or you will spoil my Wedding, for I am just going to be marry'd, and if my Uncle, or Mistress should know who you are, it might break of the match.
                                        [*Aside to 'em.*

FLOUNCE. We come on purpose to break the match.

MONSIEUR. How!

FLIRT. Why, de'e think to marry and leave us so in the lurch?

MONSIEUR. What do the Jades mean?   [*Aside.*

DON DIEGO. Come, who are they? what wou'd they have? if they come to the Wedding, Ladies, I assure you there will be none to day here.

MONSIEUR. They won't trouble you, Sir, they are going again. Ladies, you hear what my Uncle says; I know you won't trouble him. I wish I were well rid of 'em. [*Aside.*

FLOUNCE. You shall not think to put us off so.   [*Aside.*

DON DIEGO. Who are they? what are their names?

FLIRT. We are, Sir—

MONSIEUR. Nay, for Heaven's sake don't tell who you are, for you will undo me, and spoil my match infallibly.

[*Aside to 'em.*

FLOUNCE. We care not, 'tis our business to spoil matches.

MONSIEUR. You need not, for, I believe, marry'd men are your best customers, for greedy Batchelors take up with their Wives.

DON DIEGO. Come, pray Ladies, if you have no business here, be pleas'd to retire, for few of us are in humour to be so civil to you, as you may deserve.

MONSIEUR. Ay, prethee dear Jades get you gone.

FLIRT. We will not stir.

DON DIEGO. Who are they I say, fool, and why don't they go?

FLOUNCE. We are, Sir—

MONSIEUR. Hold, hold.

They are persons of honour and quality, and—

FLIRT. We are no persons of honour and quality, Sir, we are—

MONSIEUR. They are modest Ladies, and being in a kind of disguise, will not own their quality.

FLOUNCE. We modest Ladies!

MONSIEUR. Why? sometimes you are in the humour to pass for women of honour and quality; prethee, dear Jades, let your modesty and greatness come upon you now.

[*Aside to 'em.*

FLIRT. Come, Sir, not to delude you, as he wou'd have us, we are—

MONSIEUR. Hold, hold—

FLIRT. The other night at the French house—

MONSIEUR. Hold, I say, 'tis even true as *Gerrard* says, the women will tell I see.

FLOUNCE. If you wou'd have her silent, stop her mouth with that ring.   [*Takes off his ring and gives it her.*

MONSIEUR. Will that do't, here, here—

'Tis worth one hundred and fifty pounds; but I must not lose my match, I must not lose a Trout for a Fly.

That men shou'd live to hire women to silence.

Enter GERRARD, HIPPOLITA, PARSON *and* PRUE.

DON DIEGO. Oh, are you come agen!

[*Draws his Sword and runs*

MONSIEUR. Oh, hold, hold Uncle!

at 'em, MONSIEUR *holds him.*]

What are you mad, *Gerrard,* to expose your self to a new danger? why wou'd you come out yet?

GERRARD. Because our danger now is over, I thank the Parson there. And now we must beg—

[GERRARD *and* HIPPOLITA *kneel.*

MONSIEUR. Nay, faith Uncle, forgive him now, since he asks you forgiveness upon his knees, and my poor Cousin too.

HIPPOLITA. You are mistaken, Cousin; we ask him blessing, and you forgiveness.

MONSIEUR. How, how, how! what do you talk of blessing? what do you ask your Father blessing, and he asks me forgiveness? But why shou'd he ask me forgiveness?

HIPPOLITA. Because he asks my Father blessing.

MONSIEUR. Pish, pish, I don't understand you I vow and swear.

HIPPOLITA. The Parson will expound to you, Cousin.

MONSIEUR. Hey! what say you to it, Parson?

PARSON. They are marry'd, Sir.

MONSIEUR. Marry'd!

CAUTION. Marry'd! so I told you what 'twou'd come to.

DON DIEGO. You told us—

MONSIEUR. Nay, she is setting up for the reputation of a Witch.

DON DIEGO. Marry'd *Juan, Sanchez, Petro,* arm, arm, arm.

CAUTION. A Witch, a Witch!

HIPPOLITA. Nay, indeed Father, now we are marry'd, you had better call the Fiddles: Call 'em *Prue* quickly.

[*Exit* PRUE.

MONSIEUR. Who do you say marry'd, man?

PARSON. Was I not sent for on purpose to marry 'em? why shou'd you wonder at it?

MONSIEUR. No, no, you were to marry me, man, to her; I knew there was a mistake in't some how; you were meerly mistaken, therefore you must do your business over again for me now: The Parson was mistaken, Uncle, it seems, ha, ha, ha.

CAUTION. I suppose five or six Guinies made him make the mistake, which will not be rectify'd now Nephew; they'll marry all that come near 'em, and for a Guiny or two, care not what mischief they do Nephew.

DON DIEGO. Marry'd *Pedro, Sanchez?*

MONSIEUR. How, and must she be his Wife then for ever and ever? have I held the dore then for this, like a fool as I was?

CAUTION. Yes, indeed.

MONSIEUR. Have I worn Golillia here for this? little Breeches for this?

CAUTION. Yes, truly.

MONSIEUR. And put on the Spanish honour with the habit, in defending my Rival; nay, then I'le have another turn of honour in revenge. Come, Uncle, I'm of your side now, sa, sa, sa, but let's stay for our force, *Sanchez, Juan, Petro,* arm, arm, arm.

Enter two BLACKS, *and the* SPANIARD *follow'd by* PRUE, MARTIN, *and five other Gentlemen like Fiddlers.*

DON DIEGO. Murder the Villain, kill him.

> [*Running all upon* GERRARD.

MARTIN. Hold, hold, Sir.

DON DIEGO. How now, who sent for you, Friends?

MARTIN. We Fiddlers, Sir, often come unsent for.

DON DIEGO. And you are often kick'd down stairs for't too.

MARTIN. No, Sir, our Company was never kick'd I think.

DON DIEGO. Fiddlers, and not kick'd? then to preserve your Virgin honour, get you down stairs quickly; for we are not at present dispos'd much for mirth, voto.

MONSIEUR. *peeping.* A pox, is it you, *Martin?* nay, Uncle, then 'tis in vain; for they won't be kick'd down stairs, to my knowledge. They are Gentlemen Fiddlers, forsooth, a pox on all Gentlemen Fiddlers and Gentlemen Dancing-masters say I.

DON DIEGO. How! ha.   [*Pausing.*

MONSIEUR. Well, *Flirt,* now I am a Match for thee, now I
may keep you, and there's little difference betwixt keeping a Wench and Marriage, only Marriage is a little the
cheaper; but the other is the more honourable now,
vert & bleu, nay now I may swear a *French* Oath too.
Come, come, I am thine, let us strike up the Bargain,
thine according to the honourable Institution of Keeping, come.

FLIRT. Nay hold, Sir, two words to the Bargain, first I
have ne're a Lawyer here to draw Articles and Settlements.

MONSIEUR. How! is the World come to that? a man cannot
keep a Wench without Articles and Settlements, nay
then 'tis e'en as bad as Marriage indeed, and there's no
difference betwixt a Wife and a Wench.

FLIRT. Only in Cohabitation, for the first Article shall be
against Cohabitation; we Mistresses suffer no Cohabitation.

MONSIEUR. Nor Wives neither now.

FLIRT. Then separate Maintenance, in case you shou'd take
a Wife, or I a new Friend.

MONSIEUR. How! that too? then you are every whit as
bad as a Wife.

FLIRT. Then my House in Town, and yours in the Country, if you will.

MONSIEUR. A meer Wife.

FLIRT. Then my Coach apart, as well as my Bed apart.

MONSIEUR. As bad as a Wife still.

FLIRT. But take notice I will have no little, dirty, second-hand Charriot new forbish'd, but a large, sociable,
well painted Coach, nor will I keep it till it be as well
known as my self, and it come to be call'd *Flirt*-Coach;
nor will I have such pitiful Horses as cannot carry me
every night to the *Park;* for I will not miss a night in the
Park, I'd have you to know.

MONSIEUR. 'Tis very well, you must have your great, gilt,
fine, painted Coaches, I'm sure they are grown so common already amongst you, that Ladies of Quality begin
to take up with Hackneys agen, Jarnie; but what else?

FLIRT. Then, that you do not think I will be serv'd by a

little dirty Boy in a Bonnet, but a couple of handsom, lusty, cleanly Footmen, fit to serve Ladies of Quality, and do their business as they shou'd do.

MONSIEUR. What then?

FLIRT. Then, that you never grow jealous of them.

MONSIEUR. Why will you make so much of them?

FLIRT. I delight to be kind to my Servants.

MONSIEUR. Well, is this all?

FLIRT. No then, that when you come to my house, you never presume to touch a Key, lift up a Latch, or thrust a Door, without knocking before hand; and that you ask no questions, if you see a stray Piece of Plate, Cabinet, or Looking-glass in my house.

MONSIEUR. Just a Wife in every thing; but what else?

FLIRT. Then, that you take no acquaintaince with me abroad, nor bring me home any when you are drunk, whom you will not be willing to see there, when you are sober.

MONSIEUR. But what allowance? let's come to the main bus'ness, the money.

FLIRT. Stay, let me think, first for advance-money five hundred pound for Pins.

MONSIEUR. A very Wife.

FLIRT. Then you must take the Lease of my House, and furnish it as becomes one of my Quality; for don't you think we'll take up with your old Queen *Elizabeth* Furniture, as your Wives do.

MONSIEUR. Indeed there she is least like a Wife, as she says.

FLIRT. Then, for House-keeping, Servant-wages, Cloaths, and the rest, I'le be contented with a thousand pound a year present maintenance, and but three hundred pound a year separate maintenance for my life, when our Love grows cold; but I am contented with a thousand pound a year, because for Pendants, Neck-laces, and all sorts of Jewels, and such Trifles, nay and some Plate, I will shift my self as I can, make shifts, which you shall not take any notice of.

old Queen Elizabeth: old-fashioned.

MONSIEUR. A thousand pound a year! what will wenching come to? Time was, a man might have fared as well at a much cheaper rate; and a Lady of ones affections, instead of a House wou'd have been contented with a little Chamber three pair of Stairs backward, with a little Closet or Larder to't; and instead of variety of new Gowns and rich Petticoats, with her Dishabiliee or Flame-colour Gown call'd *Indian,* and Slippers of the same,[2] wou'd have been contented for a twelve-month; and instead of Visits and gadding to Plays, wou'd have entertain'd her self at home with St. *George* for *England,* the Knight of the Sun, or the Practice of Piety;[3] and instead of sending her Wine and Meat from the *French-*houses, wou'd have been contented, if you had given her (poor Wretch) but credit at the next Chandlers and Checker'd Cellar; and then instead of a Coach, wou'd have been well satisfi'd to have gone out and taken the Air for three or four hours in the Evening in the Balcony, poor Soul. Well, *Flirt,* however we'll agree; 'tis but three hundred pound a year separate maintenance, you say, when I am weary of thee and the Charge.

DON DIEGO. Rob'd of my Honour, my Daughter, and my Revenge too! Oh my dear Honour! nothing vexes me but that the World should say, I had not *Spanish* Policy enough to keep my Daughter from being debauch'd from me; but methinks my *Spanish* Policy might help me yet: I have it so—I will cheat 'em all; for I will declare I understood the whole Plot and Contrivance, and conniv'd at it, finding my Cousin a Fool, and not answering my expectation. Well; but then if I approve of the Match, I must give this Mock-Dancing-master my Estate, especially since half he wou'd have in right

Checker'd Cellar: alehouse. In *The London and Lacedemonian Oracles* Tom Brown asks the question, "What is the reason why a Chequer is plac'd at Alehouse Doors?" and gives this answer, ". . . Alehouses in the days of yore were places of Gaming, where our sober Ancestors used to pass away an Afternoon or so at Chess." Thomas Brown, *Works,* III, London, 1708, pp. 140–141.

of my Daughter, and in spight of me. Well, I am resolv'd to turn the Cheat upon themselves, and give
them my Consent and Estate.[4]

MONSIEUR. Come, come, ne're be troubl'd, Uncle, 'twas a
Combination you see, of all these Heads and your
Daughters; you know what I mean, Uncle, not to be
thwarted or govern'd by all the *Spanish* Policy in
Christendom. I'm sure my *French* Policy wou'd not have
govern'd her; so, since I have scap'd her, I am glad I
have scap'd her, Jernie.

CAUTION. Come, Brother, you are wiser than I, you see,
ay, ay.

DON DIEGO. No, you think you are wiser than I now, in
earnest; but know, while I was thought a Gull, I gull'd
you all, and made them and you think I knew nothing
of the Contrivance. Confess, did not you think verily,
that I knew nothing of it, and that I was a Gull?

CAUTION. Yes indeed, Brother, I did think verily you were
a Gull.

HIPPOLITA. How's this?   [*listning*.

DON DIEGO. Alas, alas, all the sputter I made was but to
make this Young-man my Cousin believe, when the
thing shou'd be effected, that it was not with my con-
nivence or consent; but since he is so well satisfi'd, I
owne it. For do you think I wou'd ever have suffer'd
her to marry a *Monsieur*, a *Monsieur Guarda*. Besides,
it had been but a beastly incestuous kind of a Match,
voto—

CAUTION. Nay, then I see, Brother, you were wiser than
I indeed.

GERRARD. So, so.   [*aside*.

CAUTION. Nay, Young-man, you have danc'd a fair Dance
for your self royally, and now you may go jig it together
till you are both weary; and though you were so eager
to have him, Mrs. *Minx*, you'll soon have your belly-full
of him, let me tell you, Mistress.

PRUE. Hah, ha.

MONSIEUR. How, Uncle! what was't you said? Nay if I had
your *Spanish* Policy against me, it was no wonder I
miss'd of my aim, mon foy.

DON DIEGO. I was resolv'd too, my Daughter shou'd not marry a Coward, therefore made the more ado to try you, Sir, but I find you are a brisk man of honour, firm, stiff Spanish honour; and that you may see I deceiv'd you all a long, and you not me; ay, and am able to deceive you still; for, I know, now you think that I will give you little or nothing with my Daughter (like other Fathers) since you have marry'd her without my consent; but, I say, I'le deceive you now, for you shall have the most part of my Estate in present, and the rest at my death; there's for you, I think I have deceiv'd you now look you.

GERRARD. No, indeed, Sir, you have not deceiv'd me, for I never suspected your love to your Daughter, nor your Generosity.

DON DIEGO. How, Sir! have a care of saying I have not deceiv'd you, lest I deceive you another way; guarda— pray, Gentlemen, do not think any man cou'd deceive me look you; that any man could steal my Daughter look you, without my connivance.

> The less we speak, the more we think,
> And he sees most, that seems to wink.

HIPPOLITA. So, so, now I cou'd give you my blessing, Father, now you are a good complaisant Father, indeed.

> When Children marry, Parents shou'd obey,
> Since Love claims more Obedience far than they.

> [*Exeunt Omnes.*

EPILOGUE

Spoken by FLIRT

The Ladies first I am to Compliment,
Whom (if he cou'd) the Poet wou'd content,
But to their pleasure then they must consent;

Most spoil their sport still by their modesty,
And when they shou'd be pleas'd, cry out O fie,
And the least smooty jest will ne're pass by:

But *Citty Damsel* ne're had confidence,
At smooty *Play* to take the least offence,
But mercy shews, to shew her innocence.

   Yet lest the *Merchants Daughters* shou'd to day
Be scandaliz'd, not at our harmless *Play;*
But our *Hippolita, since* she's like one
Of us bold *Flirts,* of t'other end o'th' *Town;*
Our *Poet* sending to you (*though unknown*)
His best respects by me, do's frankly own
The character to be unnatural;
Hippolita is not like you at all;
You, while your *Lovers* court you, still look grum,
And far from wooing, when they woo, cry mum;
And if some of you, e're were stol'n away,
Your *Portion's* fault 'twas only I dare say:
Thus much for him the *Poet* bid me speak,
Now to the men, I my own mind will break;
You good men o'th' *Exchange,* on *whom alone*
We must depend, when *Sparks* to *Sea* are gone;[1]
Into the *Pit* already you are come,
'Tis but a step more to our *Tyring-room;*
Where none of us but will be wondrous sweet
Upon an able *Love* of *Lumber-street:*
You we had rather see between our *Scenes,*
Than spend-thrift *Fops* with better *Cloaths* and meens;
Instead of *Lac'd-coats, Belts,* and *Pantalloons,*
Your *Velvet Jumps, Gold Chains,* and grave *Fur Gowns,*
Instead of *Perriwigs,* and broad *cock'd Hats,*
Your *Sattin Caps,* small *Cuffs,* and vast *Crevats;*[2]
For you are fair and square in all your dealings,
You never cheat your *Doxies* with guilt *Shillings;*
You ne're will break our *Windows,* then you are
Fit to make love, while our *Houzaas* make war;

Lumber-street: Lombard Street was where the bankers had their headquarters. In *The Little London Directory of 1677* (London, 1863), which purports to list "all the Goldsmiths that keep Running Cashes," twenty-seven out of forty-four men (or partners) worked from Lombard addresses.

guilt: gilt. To pass off a silver coin as a gold one.

And since all Gentlemen must pack to Sea,
Our Gallants, and our Judges you must be;
We therefore, and our Poet, do submit
To all the Chamlet Cloaks now i'the Pit.

FINIS.

Chamlet: Camlet gets its name from camel's hair although, at this time, it was often Angora goat hair. Here contrasted to the fancier cloaks of the sparks.

NOTES

1. By addressing his Prologue to the City, a collective noun standing for the solid, middle-class merchants who did business there, Wycherley is able not only to recognize the location of the new theater, but to make satiric capital of the popular contrast between the City and the self-styled fashionable world. In praising the former at the expense of the latter, he manages to attack the wits directly and at the same time make the City men sound stupid.

2. Dorset Garden Theatre. It opened on November 9, 1671, with Dryden's *Sir Martin Mar-all.* According to John Downes in *Roscius Anglicanus,* Wycherley's was the third new play performed there (London, 1708, p. 32: facsimile ed., London, 1886).

3. The speaker, as representative of the Duke's Company, is saying simply that they moved from the theater in Lincoln's Inn Fields to accommodate their audience. The remark about the author may be more complicated. In saying that it (the play presumably) would not do at the other end of town, Wycherley seems to be suggesting that a play which centers, however satirically, on a rich merchant and his foibles needs the City audience to whom the Prologue is directed. Actually, the audience at the new theater must have been pretty much the one that went to the Drury Lane in Bridges Street and to Lincoln's Inn Fields. For this reason, I suspect that the line is an oblique reference to the fact that Wycherley has switched acting companies. This is the only one of his four plays not performed by the King's Company and no one has been able to explain why he should have made the change for this play. There may be a quarrel between him and the managers of the King's Company behind the " 'twould scarce do," but if so it was patched up by the time *The Country-Wife* was performed in 1675. It is sometimes suggested that the change had to do with the fire that destroyed the Drury Lane in January 1672 and forced the King's Company to make its temporary home in the theater that the Duke's Company had just vacated in Lincoln's Inn Fields. If this were true, however, it seems likely that some reference to the fire would have got into the Prologue.

4. See *Love in a Wood,* III, p. 59.

Act I

1. Anthony Devolto (Antonio di Voto) ran a punchinello booth at Charing Cross. See *Calendar of State Papers, Domestic*, ser. 4, XII (London, 1897), p. 75 (January 9, 1672). Pepys mentioned going "to Polichinelli at Charing Crosse, which is prettier and prettier" on March 20, 1667 (Wheatley, VI, 231). On September 23, 1673, John Evelyn wrote: "we went to see *Paradise*, a roome in *Hatton Garden* furnished with the representations of all sorts of animals, handsomely painted on boards or cloth, & so cut out & made to stand & move, fly, crawll, roare & make their severall cries, as was not unpretty: though in it selfe a meere bauble . . . " (de Beer, IV, 24).

2. Tottenham Court Road was a market road with Tottenham Fields at hand; Islington, a country village within easy reach of the city. Both provided public entertainment and were suitable spots for Hippolita's ramble. On April 1, 1662, Pepys took a party "to Islington, and then, after a walk in the fields, I took them to the great cheese-cake house and entertained them . . ." (Wheatley, II, 213–214).

3. To make a plain syllabub, according to the recipe of Sir Kenelm Digby, "Take a pint of verjuyce in a boul, milk the Cow to the verjuyce; take off the Curd, and take sweet Cream, and beat them together with a little Sack and Sugar; put it into your Syllabub-pot; then strew Sugar on it, and so send it to the Table." *The Closet of the Eminently Learned Sir Kenelme Digby Kt. Opened*, London, 1677, p. 114. He gives several more elegant recipes, but a plain syllabub is probably what one would get at New Spring Garden, for which see *Love in a Wood*, iii, n. 6.

4. Given the pleasures that the two girls list, a particular tavern may well be intended. Summers makes an unsubstantiated guess (I, 258), but I can find no reference to a tavern of this name. Since the sign for a Sun Tavern sometimes had the face of a man with rays going out from it, Prince in the Sun could be an alternative name for a coffeehouse or tavern better known simply as Sun.

5. Summers tells us (I, 258) that the Gun was a well-known tavern, but he offers no evidence to prove his statement. From the context we can assume that it was an establishment ("one half *Tavern* and t'other *Musick-House*") rather like the one Ned Ward visited in Wapping a few years later where he "heard *Fiddlers* and *Hoitboys*, together with a Hum-drum *Organ*." An organ in a tavern, then, is a possibility, but since Prue uses the plural, she may intend the word in a general sense, meaning wind instrument or pipe. Certainly the tongs are a less elegant instrument than the others Ward mentions. Francis W. Galpin in *Old English Instruments of Music*

(London, 1910, p. 259) suggests that ordinary tongs, those used in a fireplace for instance, were used to tap out a rude music. Its quality is clear from a remark of Thomas Rymer's in *Tragedies of the Last Age* (1677): "When we would listen to a *Lute*, our ears are rapt with the *tintamar* and twang of the *Tongs* and *Jewstrumps.*" *The Critical Works of Thomas Rymer*, ed. Curt A. Zimansky, New Haven, 1956, p. 74. In terms of aesthetic pleasure, the Gun may not have been very different from the tavern Ward visited because he reports "such incomparable Musick, that had the Harmonious Grunt-ing of a *Hog* been added as a *Bass* to a Ravishing Concert of Caterwauling Performers, in the height of the Extasie, the unusualness of the sound could not have render'd it, to a Nice Ear, more engaging." *The London-Spy Compleat*, London, 1706, p. 329. In any case, the point is that Prue's taste in music is a little on the primitive side, that this pleasure, like the others in the catalogue that she and Hippolita make, is as uncomplicated as their desire for a man. With words like *organ, tongs* and *gun* in the sentence, my suspicion is that, for Wycherley, if not for Prue, there was an implied rela-tionship between the two pleasures.

6. English men and women with an attraction to the clois-tered life often went abroad at this time to live in English Catholic monasteries and convents; as a result there was talk of Protestant nunneries. *An Academy or Colledge: Wherein Young Ladies and Gentlewomen May at a very moderate Ex-pence be duly instructed in the true Protestant Religion* was published in London in 1671. Written by Edward Cham-berlayne, it was in effect a brochure for a proposed school, designed to provide a virtuous Christian education for young ladies which could not be found in the "Maiden Schools" in the London suburbs (such as the one Hippolita went to) and could be found abroad only by facing the dangers of *"Romish Superstitions"* (p. 3). He cites the need for "excellent Seminar-ies and Nurseries, out of which Persons of Honour and Worth may at all time make choice of Vertuous Wives; but also Provision (whereof there is great want in *England*) may be made for sober, pious, elder Virgins and Widdows, who desire to separate themselves from the vanities of the World, and yet employ their Talents for the benefit of the Publick" (pp. 4–5). He then invites "any Devout Widdows or Elder Virgins, who intend not to marry, desire to be admitted Fellows and Assistants in this Government, and to lead the rest of their dayes without cares and troubles of the World, to live with honour and reputation, to devote themselves to the service of God and the good of their Countrey . . ." to give their names to certain stationers (p. 6). The academy apparently never opened; Chamberlayne must have suspected that it would not

for he provides that subscription money shall be returned with 5% interest, "in case of want of necessary provision and contribution, this laudable Design should not go on (which God forbid)" (p. 9).

7. Richard Steele, in *The Tatler*, No. 83, proposing to write a treatise "wherein I shall lay down Rules when a young Stripling is to say, No, and a young Virgin, Yes," adds "For the Publication of this Discourse, I wait only for Subscription from the Under-graduates of each University, and the young Ladies in the Boarding-Schools of *Hackney* and *Chelsea*" (October 19, 1709). Forty years earlier, on April 21, 1667, Pepys mentions going "to Hackney church. . . . That which we went chiefly to see was the young ladies of the schools, whereof there is great store, very pretty . . ." (Wheatley, VI, 279).

8. Most of Monsieur's French is recognizable through the seventeenth-century spelling and his mispronunciation. It consists mainly of expletives, mildly blasphemous oaths like *'sdeath* and *'sblood,* which euphemistically swallow or disguise the mention of God. *Teste* is presumably *tête,* used as Silvestre uses it in *Les Fourberies de Scapin* (II, 6), where he piles one expletive on another: "Par la mort! par la tête! par la ventre!"; "Ah! tête! ah! ventre!" Molière, *Oeuvres Complètes,* Paris, 1956, II, 694–695. *Ventre* in a variety of forms is also a favorite of Monsieur's.

9. "This str. and the hill are of late Years, much inhabited by Mercers and Woolen-Drapers, and the str. was more so about 100 years ago." *A New View of London,* I, London, 1708, p. 50. In short, Gerrard does not have a French tailor.

10. At this distance it is difficult to sort out the niceties of social behavior, to tell how many of Monsieur's accusations reflect affectations recently borrowed from France and how many are English usages adopted as French by a foolish young man who also gives a mistaken French accent to English words. Ombre, originally a Spanish card game, must have been as much English as French by this time, for it was very fashionable in England; Charles Cotton, *The Compleat Gamester,* London, 1674, which often indicates the popularity of a game within a particular group, makes no mention of France in the description of ombre. The snuffbox, on the other hand, may have been a sure sign of the Frenchified fop. By the time Sganarelle came on in the first act of Molière's *Dom Juan* (1665), flashing his snuffbox and speaking his praise of tobacco, the snuffbox was firmly established in France. It was apparently at home in England by the 1690s; at least, it was used casually in the comedies of that decade. Brisk in William Congreve's *The Double-Dealer* (1693) borrows Lord Froth's pocket-glass because "I broke my Glass that was in the Lid of my Snuff-Box" (London, 1694, p. 9). Tattle in Congreve's

Love for Love (1695) makes Miss Prue a present of a snuff-
box.

11. The standard place-name dropping of the tourist. John
Lauder, who was in Paris in 1665, reports, "While I was at
Paris I went and saw the new Bridge, and Henry 4 his stately
statue in brasse sent as a present by the King of Denmark. . . .
I saw also that vast stupendious building, the Louwre, which
hath layd many kings in their graves and yet stands unfin-
ished. . . ." *Journals of Sir John Lauder*, Edinburgh, 1900,
pp. 4–5. Monsieur apparently calls the Louvre new because the
celebrated colonnade on the east façade was built between
1666 and 1670. *Grand Roy* is Louis XIV.

12. Although Summers suggests (I, 260) the possibility that
a specific Ship Tavern is intended and offers a candidate, his
hesitation is justified. Later in the act (p. 140) Wycherley
seems to go out of his way to avoid a particular location
when he has Gerrard place the tavern in *what dee call't
street*. Since this tavern—unlike the allusions at the opening
of the act—is plainly a plot device rather than local color,
Wycherley presumably is using a common name for a tavern.
Jacob Henry Burns, *A Descriptive Catalogue of the London
Traders, Tavern, and Coffee-House Tokens Current in the
Seventeenth Century* (London, 1855), has sixteen entries under "Ship sailing" in the Index of Signs.

13. 1693 Q: ever.

14. "Crabbed age and youth cannot live together." *The Passionate Pilgrime* [xii], line 57.

15. 1693 Q: in—. This line is repeated in most of the later
editions. W. C. Ward drops the *in* and ends the sentence
"dream—". Summers finally restores the *Ih—* which is plainly
intended to represent the sigh. In the scene between Gerrard
and Hippolita in the next act, *Ih—* is used as a hesitation in
speech, a lingering over the first person pronoun while the
speaker decides how and whether to go on.

16. 1673 Q: no punctuation. Since the clause beginning
when is obviously a new thought, I put in a comma, following
1720 *Plays*.

17. Middle Temple, Inner Temple, and Lincoln's Inn were
three of the four Inns of Court, where young men studied law.
A masquerading City Dame, going there at night, might, to
paraphrase Hippolita, be taking the "not so innocent liberty of
the Town." The speech as a whole accuses Mrs. Caution of
being jealous and hypocritical in censuring the age.

18. In 1673 Q this stage direction follows Mrs. Caution's
last speech. It seems clear, however, that Hippolita would not
have spoken her filial first sentence unless her aunt were still
on stage.

19. An unnecessary stage direction. Since there is no one on

stage but Hippolita and Prue, there is no reason for the speech to be an aside.

20. In 1673 Q this was printed as though it were part of Monsieur's speech, an error repeated in later editions. 1720 *Plays* rightly prints it as a stage direction.

21. 1673 Q: no punctuation. Something is needed to break the speech, half of which is directed to Monsieur, half to Martin; the colon is used in 1720 *Plays*.

22. "The Ballad of Arthur of Bradley" is a very English song about a rural wedding; a version of it is printed in *An Antidote against Melancholy*, London, 1661, pp. 21–25 (Collier's Reprints). A tune for "Paul's Steeple, or I Am the Duke of Norfolk" is printed in William Chappell, *Old English Popular Music*, I, London, 1893, pp. 282–283. Although the original ballad is lost, it presumably is English enough to elicit Monsieur's *"Auh."*

23. The third Anglo-Dutch War, which was about to begin (March 17, 1672), had been in the making for months. See *Calendar of State Papers, Domestic,* ser. 4, XI (London, 1895), pp. 525, 563, 581. Despite this fact, Monsieur's abuse of the Dutch here and in the next few pages is a conventional national-stereotype joke more than it is a political comment. At least, it is difficult to guess how an audience would be expected to react to the political connotations. Although the English merchants resented the Dutch success as traders, they were more like them, in their style of living and their religion, than they were like the French—at least those whom Monsieur tries to imitate.

24. The reference to Cromwell, "whom dey did love and fear," makes specific the similarity between the independent, Protestant merchant classes of the two countries; Monsieur, the son of a brewer, just back from three months in an English pension in Paris, is not much different from the Dutch chandler's son off on the Grand Tour. In so far as the scene has any political relevance, it seems to be aimed not at the Dutch but at the City men, so ambiguously praised in the Prologue and the Epilogue, who were not very enthusiastic about this war which, unlike the earlier Dutch wars, was designed less to secure British trade than to give Charles II the opportunity to make England once again a Catholic country; see Ogg, I, 322–356. It is clear that Wycherley expects the audience both to enjoy the abuse of the Dutch (Gerrard joins in it) and to recognize that Monsieur deserves some of the same abuse, but to read political meaning into the scene is very difficult; Monsieur's affectations are French and although it is his pretensions that are the main butt of the joke, some of the satiric reaction is bound to rub off on the French themselves.

25. Cf. the lines from Wycherley's *"Upon the Favour of a Cook-Maid"* from *Miscellany Poems:* "Thy Kindness, 'twere ungrateful to deny, / And I cannot ev'n with a Cook-Maid Lie, / But (if I like her) Roast-meat must I cry" (Summers, III, 245–246).

26. Pierrot here may be no more than a simple diminutive, Peterkin. Since Monsieur mentions *Scaramouchè* at the beginning of Act III, the temptation is to find a commedia reference with Pierrot also. Giuseppe Giaratone, a member of the Italian Company in Paris at this time, is generally supposed to have first introduced Pierrot into the commedia in *La Suite du Festin de Pierre* in 1673—too late for Monsieur to mention the name here. Still, Molière's *Dom Juan ou Le Festin de Pierre* (1665), on which *La Suite* was based, had a Pierrot. It is possible that Monsieur's use of the name is to indicate not simply his Frenchness but his familiarity with Paris and its fashionable pleasures.

27. Kenelm Digby offers "An excellent way to Cram Chicken": "Stone a pound of Raisins of the Sun, and beat them in a Mortar to pulp; pour a quart of milk upon them, and let them soak so all night. Next morning stir them well together, and put to them so much crums of grated stale white bread as to bring it to a soft paste, work all well together, and lay it in the trough before the Chicken (which must not be above six in a pen, and keep it very clean) and let a candle be by them all night. The delight of this meat will make them eat continually; and they will be so fat (when they are but of the bigness of a Black-bird) that they will not be able to stand, but lie down on their bellies to eat." *The Closet,* pp. 224–225.

28. Summers (I, 261) has discovered a Mustard Alley in Southwark in a mid-eighteenth-century directory, but the 1708 *New View of London* does not list one. I doubt that a specific street is intended. Although Eric Partridge labels *mustard-pot,* meaning the female pudenda, as a usage dating from the nineteenth century, it is a credible guess that the mustard was being cut long before that. I suspect that the names of both the street and the inn refer to the girls' profession. Although the Crooked Billet was a common sign for a tavern, Monsieur's exclamatory repetition of the name suggests that there is special significance in it.

Act II

1. "We deride the *Spaniard* for his odd shape, not for his Constancy to it." John Evelyn, *Tyrannus Or the Mode,* London, 1661, p. 15 (Luttrell Reprints, No. 11, Oxford, 1951).

2. Although *Whiskers,* at this time, was more likely to mean

"moustache" than "beard," Hippolita's reference to *Spanish beard* at the beginning of Act IV suggests that a beard may be intended. If so, it may be a square, full beard, also known as the "Cathedral beard"; see C. Willett and Phyllis Cunnington, *Handbook of English Costume in the Seventeenth Century*, London, 1960, pp. 73, 165. In either case, it is unfashionable as Englishmen tended to go clean-shaven at this period.

3. Spanish olio was not that un-English. Pepys was treated to one at the Mulberry Garden on April 5, 1669 (Wheatley, VIII, 284). Kenelm Digby gives a recipe for "A plain but good Spanish Oglia," of, among other ingredients, beef, mutton, veal, bacon, capon, pigeons, onions, cabbage, and chickpeas ("If you have *Garavanzas,* put them in . . ."). *The Closet,* pp. 157–158.

4. Prue has not been offstage. Leigh Hunt changed the stage direction to read, "As they are going out, Prue runs hastily to them," and moved the entrance of Don Diego and Mrs. Caution to follow Hippolita's *My Father!* His change not only removes the contradiction, but makes a sensible suggestion about staging.

5. 1673 Q: demi houra. It was Ward who decided that the *n* had been turned upside down. Certainly the exclamation, "give me honor," makes sense in the context, and *honra* appears elsewhere in the play.

6. This line probably refers to the old proverb: the old woman would never have looked in the oven for her daughter, if she had not been there herself. It is impossible, however, to escape the suspicion (unconfirmed in reference sources) that "oven" may have been used, as it is familiarly today, to imply "womb": she's got one in the oven.

7. Although later editions have continued to print the line as it here appears, I suspect that it should read "feeling your Legs." The context makes such a reading feasible, and the similarity between the *f* and the old style *s* and the fact that the word was broken in 1673 Q before the -*ing* makes a typographical error quite possible.

8. Don Diego seems to be using *Sarabrand* as though it were a synonym for courante. They were two different dances. The saraband began as a wild Spanish dance, but became slow and stately when it was taken over by the French court of Louis XIII. It is this quality that would attract Don Diego and that might make him confuse it with the courante. The similarity between the two dances can be seen in an exchange from Sir Charles Sedley's *The Grumbler.* Lolive (as a dancing master): "You wou'd have a grave, serious Dance, perhaps?" Grichard: "Yes, a serious one, if there be any, but very serious." Lolive: "Well, the Courante, the Bocane, the Sarabande?" *Works*, II, London, 1722, p. 183.

9. Ward: cuerno.

10. The exchange between Prue and Hippolita is surely spoken out of Gerrard's hearing, although there is no stage direction to indicate it.

11. 1673 Q: it taken up.

12. A spirit was a kidnaper. "Affidavits of Mary, wife of Mark Collins, and Thomas Stone against William Haverland, 'generally called a spirit.' Also of William Haverland against John Steward for spiriting persons to Barbadoes, Virginia, Jamaica, and other places . . ." January–February, 1671. *Calendar of State Papers, Colonial,* IX (London, 1893), p. 521.

13. Although the song has some thematic relevance to the play, the singer has no connection with the plot; for this reason, presumably, Wycherley makes a joke of her entrance. He provides no stage direction to bring her on; Leigh Hunt provides one before Hippolita's *Madam, your Servant, . . .* The song, with music by John Bannister, can be found in *Choice Songs and Ayres,* London, 1673, p. 22, and *Choice Ayres, Songs & Dialogues,* Second Edition, London, 1675, pp. 18–19. The words are not exactly the same as those given in the text of the play. See p. 169 for the song, in modern notation.

ACT III

1. Tiberio Fiorillo, probably the most famous Scaramuccia ever, was at this time playing with the *Comédie Italienne* in Paris.

2. John Genest assumes that Nokes played the part of Monsieur ("There would have been no fun, unless Nokes had acted the part himself") and that Angel played Don Diego. *Some Account of the English Stage from the Restoration in 1660 to 1830,* Bath, 1832, I, p. 137. James Nokes and Edward Angel were both members of the Duke's Company for the 1671–72 season (*The London Stage,* I, p. 186). Nokes was an extremely popular comedian for whom John Dryden presumably wrote the comic lead in *Sir Martin Mar-all* (1688); see Downes, *Roscius Anglicanus,* p. 28. Downes also describes at length (p. 29) a French-costume clown bit that Nokes did as Sir Arthur Addle in a production of John Caryll's *Sir Salomon,* put on in Dover when the English court went to welcome the king's sister, the Duchess of Orléans in May 1670. That Nokes and Angel customarily played together is also clear from Downes's description of a production of Roger Boyle's *Guzman:* "There being an odd sort of Duel in it, between Mr. *Nokes* and Mr. *Angel,* both Comicks meeting in the Field to fight . . ." (p. 28). Common sense and circumstantial evidence conspire to second Genest's suggestion.

3. "Fools have fortune" was a widely popular proverb. Since Seneca seems to have touched most of the bromidic bases, he

may well have used it, but if so I have no idea where. Monsieur is not notoriously a bookish boy, so I tend to doubt the allusion.

4. 1673 Q assigns this *aside* to Don Diego's speech, although Monsieur's lines plainly indicate that he hears and reacts to his uncle's words. 1720 *Plays* moves the stage direction to Monsieur's first sentence.

5. Ward: verdaderamente.

6. Ward suggests that he means "gabacho," which, since it means a Frenchified person, is certainly suitable.

7. Either Wycherley or Monsieur, in the urgency of the argument, has forgotten that Monsieur's affectation is French. He has borrowed his uncle's *voto*.

8. "we were got amongst a parcel of *Lank-Hair'd Formalists*, in *Flat Crowned Hats*, and *Short Cloaks*, walking with as much State and Gravity, as a Snail o'er the Leaf of a *Cabbage*, with a Box of *Tobacco-dust* in one hand, the other employed in charging their *Nostrils*, from whence it drops into their *Mustachoes*, which are always as full of *Snuff* as a *Beaus Wig* is full of *Powder*; . . . these, my Friend told me, were *Spaniards*." Ned Ward, p. 69.

9. Downes, describing the production of *Sir Salomon* at Dover (see n. 2), tells this story: "The *French* Court wearing the Excessive short Lac'd Coats; some Scarlet, some Blew, with Broad wast Belts; Mr. *Nokes* having at that time one shorter than the *French* Fashion, to Act Sir *Arthur Addle* in; the Duke of *Monmouth* gave Mr. *Nokes* his Sword and Belt from his Side, and Buckled it on himself, on purpose to Ape the *French*: That Mr. *Nokes* lookt more like a Drest up Ape, than a Sir *Arthur*: Which upon his first Entrance on the Stage, put the King and Court to an Excessive Laughter; at which the *French* look'd very Shaggrin, to see themselves Ap'd by such a Buffoon as Sir Arthur: Mr. *Nokes* kept the Dukes Sword to his Dying Day." Downes, p. 29.

10. 1673 Q: *Jernie*. The errata list changes this to *Garni*, although later editions (except Summers) retain the original reading. I assume that he is using *Shoe, Garni* to balance *Chappeaux, Retrouseè* and that he is describing a kind of dress. It may be too late in the century for the elaborate shoe ornamentation, such as roses that covered the laces or heavy embroidery, but ribbons were still used, sometimes attached to the toes. A decorated shoe is almost certainly intended.

11. In 1673 Q the stage direction follows Prue's speech. Leigh Hunt sensibly directs that she wait on stage until she gets Don Diego's *Yes*.

12. It is clear enough in this speech that Don Diego is telling them to get on with the dance, but the precise meaning of *honour the King* escapes me. It may be a way of telling him to

bow and her to curtsy, for the courante figure opens with the performing of such "honours." It is possible—but a little far-fetched—that the line is addressed to Gerrard in his guise as dancing-master and that Don Diego is telling him to honor the king's picture on coins, that is, to earn his money. "King's picture" was current slang for "money."

13. This *fall* is not in 1673 Q. The comic repetition of the phrase "fall back" seems to call for it, so I have followed 1693 Q by adding it.

14. Since Gerrard is the only person on stage, this direction is unnecessary.

15. 1673 Q: *Exeunt.*

ACT IV

1. The stage direction refers to Monsieur.

2. Monsieur's line is presumably political. The War of Devolution, which ended with the Treaty of Aix-la-Chapelle (May 2, 1668), grew out of Louis XIV's claim to certain Spanish territories in the right of his wife, Maria Theresa, upon whom the ownership was supposed to have devolved. Although the Treaty was worded vaguely enough to give the French king an excuse to occupy a number of Spanish towns and villages a dozen years later and although it left to France the conquests it had made in Flanders in the campaign of 1667, it was unpopular in France because several captured towns and the province of Franche Comté were restored to Spain.

3. James Howard's *The English Mounsieur* (London, 1674) had been in the repertory of the King's Company since 1666; we know from Pepys that it had been revived as recently as April 7, 1668.

4. Since the servant has already put the golilla on Monsieur in the stage direction above, this one is unnecessary unless we assume that Monsieur, in his anguish, has pulled it off again. Such staging would be desirable if the scene is to be milked of every possible comic effect implicit in the struggle between the two affectations.

5. Familiar proverbs about clothes not making the man. John Evelyn in *Tyrannus* writes, "Though I would not judge of the Monk by the Hood he wears" (p. 3). The story of the ass that wore the lion's skin is one of Aesop's fables; translations and verse renderings of Aesop were popular at the time. La Fontaine retold the story (Book V, Fable 21) in his *Fables* (1668).

6. Summers (I, 266) suggests turbans. Flirt's speech in the next act about not being served by a "Boy in a Bonnet" (p. 231) seems to indicate that a servant's cap is intended.

7. The *it* was not in 1673 Q; added 1693 Q.

8. Prue is obviously trying to improve her complexion. Sir Kenelm Digby offers a recipe for "Another Excellent Ointment for Wounds or Sores in Man or Beast" which begins "Take Rosin, yellow Wax, of each a like quantity: Melt it with a soft fire, then put in it half a pound of Hogs-grease . . ." *Choice and Experimented Receipts in Physick and Chirurgery*, 2d ed., London, 1675, p. 56. Prue's beeswax and hogs-grease salve may be a variation. Although Digby does not recommend buttermilk and tansy for the complexion, the section of his *Remedes Souverains et Secrets Experimentez* (Paris, 1639) dealing with *"Secrets pour la Conservation de la Beauté Des Dames"* does contain a great number of recipes that make use of milk, cream, or goat's milk and a wide variety of herbal waters mixed on occasion with less attractive substances—pigeon's entrails (p. 280).

9. Leigh Hunt rightly labels this line an aside.

10. Hunt: *aside.*

11. In 1673 Q this stage direction follows Mrs. Caution's speech. It is clear that Monsieur's line is directed at her; following Leigh Hunt, I have moved the direction to the present position. Hunt also provides for Don Diego's exit at this point. Certainly, he is not on stage to hear Monsieur's lines that follow.

12. 1673 Q: know to it.

13. Hunt: *aside.*

14. Hunt: *aside.*

Act V

1. There is one *great* too many for this grandfather. Leigh Hunt drops one in his edition, but since Don Diego, in his excitement, could easily have over-*great*ed, I let it stand.

2. Both men and women wore Indian gowns, informal dress. The name presumably has to do with the color and design of the cloth. The reference to undress here means that mistresses were once content to stay at home and so needed no *variety of new Gowns.*

3. Lewis Bayly's *The Practise of Piety* was published early in the seventeenth century (the 3d edition, the earliest known, is 1612) and was reprinted more than fifty times during the century. The other home pleasures that Monsieur mentions are more difficult to identify. Summers assumes (I, 267) that *St. George for England* refers to the ballad which was often printed in anthologies during the Restoration, for instance in *An Antidote against Melancholy*, pp. 34–36. His is a reasonable guess based on the popularity of the ballad, but the context suggests a book. Donald Wing, *Short-Title Catalogue, 1641–1700* (New York, 1945), lists one publication with this name

(*St. George for England: or, a relation,* London, 1661), but there were no later editions and it could hardly have been easily recognized ten years after its publication. Monsieur may well be referring to Richard Johnson's *The Most Famous History of the Seven Champions of Christendom* (1596), in which St. George figures prominently; there were editions in 1660 and 1670. Jerry Blackacre, in *The Plain-Dealer,* asks for it under a garbled title. See p. 448. Summers suggests (I, 268) that *the Knight of the Sun* refers to the hero of Diego Ortuñez de Calahorra, *The Mirrour of Princely deedes and Knighthood,* the first part of which was translated into English and published in London c. 1580. A number of parts of *The Mirrour* were published in the sixteenth century, but Wing lists none for the Restoration. Once again, there is a problem of popularity. Unfortunately, I have no candidate to replace Summers's knight.

4. 1720 *Plays: aside.*

EPILOGUE

1. The war with the Dutch was about to begin.

2. It is fitting that the Epilogue to a play so concerned with fashion should make use of the same kind of comparison. In *Collin's Walk Through London and Westminster* (London, 1690), Thomas D'Urfey describes aldermen "Wrapp'd round in Furr from arm to arm" (p. 70) and speaks of "Sheriffs with Gold Chain" (p. 63). John Evelyn, commenting on some aldermen removed from office (October 4, 1683), sees them "wearing no more Gownes or Chaines of Gold" (de Beer, IV, 342). A jump was a short coat worn during the seventeenth century. The satin cap emphasizes the absence of the perriwig because caps were not worn over wigs. The small cuff refers by contraries to a fashion of the period, deep cuffs, turned back and buttoned to the sleeve in front but open in the back. If the cravats of City men were vaster than those of sparks, I have found no evidence of it; perhaps Wycherley wanted a rhyme for *hats.*

THE COUNTRY-WIFE

The Country-Wife was performed on January 12, 1675, by the King's Company at the Theatre Royal, Drury Lane; this is generally accepted as the premiere. It was entered in the *Stationers' Register,* January 13, 1675, and listed in the *Term Catalogues,* May 10, 1675; the first quarto is dated 1675 on the title page. There were editions of the play in 1683, 1688, and two in 1695.

It is generally assumed that two plays of Molière, *L'École des Maris* and *L'École des Femmes,* influenced Wycherley in the writing of *The Country-Wife,* but the two dramatists are so different that the incidental borrowings are relatively unimportant. In *Maris* Sganarelle, like Pinchwife, does mistakenly carry a letter to his fiancée's lover, and Isabelle, like Mrs. Pinchwife, does disguise herself as her sister to escape her domestic imprisonment, but the dramatists use the incidents differently. Except that *Femmes* is about an innocent young bride-to-be who outwits an older, presumably wiser man, there is even less similarity between it and *Wife.* There are echoes of Molière lines in those of Wycherley, but a comparison of Pinchwife's first-act praise of marrying a silly wife with that of Arnolphe in Act 1 of *Femmes* indicates that in even so obvious a case ("a free adaptation": Wilcox, p. 88) the differences in tone are great. Wycherley supposedly borrowed the device of Horner's disability from Terence's *The Eunuch.*

The epigraph from Horace is from *Epistles* II. i. 76–78: "I am offended when something is blamed, not because it is grossly and inelegantly composed, but because it is modern; when for the ancients, not indulgence, but honors and rewards are demanded." If the quotation has particular meaning for this play, it may be the author's suggestion that his play deserves commendation for making rich use, dramatic and satiric, of a device which in Terence is little more than a trick. John Dryden's *Of Dramatick Poesie* comes to mind. In it, Eugenius, the defender of the moderns, quotes the first two lines of this Horatian epigraph, and both he and Crites, the defender of the ancients, turn to *The Eunuch* for several of their examples. It is Eugenius "who seem'd to have the better of the Argument." (London, 1668, p. 26.)

The text for this edition is 1675 Q, the copy in the Yale University library. I also consulted the University of Pennsylvania copies of 1683 Q, 1688 Q, and 1695 Q. This last is the edition listed as item 1326 in Gertrude L. Woodward and James G. McManaway, *A Check List of English Plays, 1671–1700*, Chicago, 1945, p. 145. Robert N. E. Megaw has argued that the order of the two 1695 quartos is reversed in *Check List*, that 1325 is a faulty edition based on 1326; see "The Two 1695 Editions of Wycherley's *Country-Wife*," *Studies in Bibliography*, III (1950–51), 252–253. Megaw assumes that 1326 was based on 1688 Q; Fujimura (p. ix) that it was based on 1683 Q. Since 1688 was a paginal reprint of 1683, there is a strong similarity between them. Although I am accepting Megaw's conclusion for the sake of this textual note, it seems to me just as reasonable to assume that 1325 was a faulty edition of the play and that 1326 was a second edition issued the same year which went back to an earlier one (choose your quarto) to make corrections. I have also consulted the copy of 1695 Q-2 in the Yale University library. I have made use of several recent editions of *The Country-Wife: Bell's British Theatre*, Vol. 17, London, 1780; George B. Churchill (ed.), *The Country Wife and The Plain Dealer*, New York, 1924, pp. 1–187; Ursula Todd-Naylor (ed.), *Smith College Studies in Modern Languages*, XII (1930–31), Nos. 1–3; Thomas H. Fujimura (ed.), Lincoln, Nebraska, 1965. In retaining the variant spellings, I faced the problem of Jaspar-Jasper and Dainty-Daynty. In each case I chose the first form, the one that appears in the list of

Persons. I chose Pinchwife, an occasional usage in 1675 Q, instead of the customary Mr. Pinchwife to indicate him as speaker on the assumption that the reader could thus distinguish more clearly between him and Mrs. Pinchwife.

THE
Country-Wife,
A
COMEDY,

Acted at the

THEATRE ROYAL.

Written by Mr. *Wycherley.*

Indignior quicquam reprehendi, non quia crasse
Compositum illepidéve putetur, sed quia nuper:
Nec veniam Antiquis, sed honorem & præmia posci.

Horat.

LONDON,

Printed for *Thomas Dring*, at the *Harrow*, at the
Corner of *Chancery-Lane* in *Fleet-ftreet.* 1675.

spoken by MR. HART.

Poets like Cudgel'd Bullys, never do
At first, or second blow, submit to you;
But will provoke you still, and ne're have done,
Till you are weary first, with laying on:
The late so bafled Scribler of this day,[1]
Though he stands trembling, bids me boldly say,
What we, before most Playes are us'd to do,
For Poets out of fear, first draw on you;
In a fierce Prologue, the still Pit defie,
And e're you speak, like Castril, *give the lye;*[2]
But though our Bayses[3] *Batles oft I've fought,*
And with bruis'd knuckles, their dear Conquests bought;
Nay, never yet fear'd Odds upon the Stage,
In Prologue dare not Hector with the Age,
But wou'd take Quarter from your saving hands,
Though Bayse[4] *within all yielding Countermands,*
Says you Confed'rate Wits no Quarter give,
Ther'fore his Play shan't ask your leave to live:
Well, let the vain rash Fop, by huffing so,
Think to obtain the better terms of you;
But we the Actors humbly will submit,
Now, and at any time, to a full Pit;
Nay, often we anticipate your rage,
And murder Poets for you, on our Stage:
We set no Guards upon our Tyring-Room;
But when with flying Colours, there you come,
We patiently you see, give up to you,
Our Poets, Virgins, nay our Matrons too.

THE PERSONS

MR. HORNER,	MR. HART:
MR. HARCOURT,	MR. KENASTON.
MR. DORILANT,	MR. LYDAL.
MR. PINCHWIFE,	MR. MOHUN.
MR. SPARKISH,	MR. HAYNES.
SIR JASPAR FIDGET,	MR. CARTWRIGHT.
MRS. MARGERY PINCHWIFE,	MRS. BOWTEL.
MRS. ALITHEA,	MRS. JAMES.
MY LADY FIDGET,	MRS. KNEP.
MRS. DAINTY FIDGET,	MRS. CORBET.
MRS. SQUEAMISH.	MRS. WYATT.
OLD LADY SQUEAMISH.	MRS. RUTTER.

Waiters, Servants, *and* Attendants.

A BOY.	
A QUACK,	MR. SCHOTTEREL.
LUCY, ALITHEA'S MAID,	MRS. CORY.

THE SCENE
LONDON.

ACT 1. SCENE I.

Enter HORNER, *and* QUACK *following him at a distance.*

HORNER. A Quack is as fit for a Pimp, as a Midwife for a
Bawd; they are still but in their way, both helpers of
Nature.—[*aside.*]— Well, my dear Doctor, hast thou
done what I desired.

QUACK. I have undone you for ever with the Women, and
reported you throughout the whole Town as bad as an
Eunuch, with as much trouble as if I had made you one
in earnest.

HORNER. But have you told all the Midwives you know, the
Orange Wenches at the Playhouses, the City Husbands,
and old Fumbling Keepers of this end of the Town, for
they'l be the readiest to report it.

QUACK. I have told all the Chamber-maids, Waiting
women, Tyre women, and Old women of my acquaintance; nay, and whisper'd it as a secret to'em, and to
the Whisperers of *Whitehal;* so that you need not
doubt 'twill spread, and you will be as odious to the
handsome young Women, as—

HORNER. As the small Pox.— Well—

QUACK. And to the married Women of this end of the
Town, as—

HORNER. As the great ones; nay, as their own Husbands.

QUACK. And to the City Dames as Annis-seed *Robin*
of filthy and contemptible memory; and they will

Tyre women: lady's maids.
Whitehal: Whitehall, the
King's palace, where people
wandered in and out of the
public rooms all day and
where the royal household itself had a staff of several
hundred, could be expected to
have more than its share of
whisperers.

great ones: great pox: syph-
ilis.
Annis-seed Robin: an hermaphrodite. On the occasion
of Robin's death Charles Cotton wrote "On Annel-seed
Robin, the Hermophrodite."
Poems on Several Occasions,
London, 1687, pp. 457–458.

frighten their Children with your name, especially their Females.

HORNER. And cry *Horner's* coming to carry you away: I am only afraid 'twill not be believ'd; you told'em 'twas by an *English-French* disaster, and an *English-French* Chirurgeon, who has given me at once, not only a Cure, but an Antidote for the future, against that damn'd malady, and that worse distemper, love, and all other Womens evils.

QUACK. Your late journey into *France* has made it the more credible, and your being here a fortnight before you appear'd in publick, looks as if you apprehended the shame, which I wonder you do not: Well I have been hired by young Gallants to bely'em t'other way; but you are the first wou'd be thought a Man unfit for Women.

HORNER. Dear Mr. Doctor, let vain Rogues be contented only to be thought abler Men than they are, generally 'tis all the pleasure they have, but mine lyes another way.

QUACK. You take, methinks, a very preposterous way to it, and as ridiculous as if we Operators in Physick, shou'd put forth Bills to disparage our Medicaments, with hopes to gain Customers.

HORNER. Doctor, there are Quacks in love, as well as Physick, who get but the fewer and worse Patients, for their boasting; a good name is seldom got by giving it ones self, and Women no more than honour are compass'd by bragging: Come, come Doctor, the wisest Lawyer never discovers the merits of his cause till the tryal; the wealthiest Man conceals his riches, and the cunning Gamster his play; Shy Husbands and Keepers like old Rooks are not to be cheated, but by a new unpractis'd trick; false friendship will pass now no more than false dice upon'em, no, not in the City.

Enter BOY.

BOY. There are two Ladies and a Gentleman coming up.[1]

HORNER. A Pox, some unbelieving Sisters of my former acquaintance, who I am afraid, expect their sense shou'd be satisfy'd of the falsity of the report.

No—this formal Fool and [*Enter Sir* JASPAR FIDGET,
Women! *Lady* FIDGET, *and Mrs.*
QUACK. His Wife and Sister. DAINTY FIDGET.]

SIR JASPAR. My Coach breaking just now before your door
Sir, I look upon as an occasional repremand to me Sir,
for not kissing your hands Sir, since your coming out of
France Sir; and so my disaster Sir, has been my good
fortune Sir; and this is my Wife, and Sister Sir.

HORNER. What then, Sir?

SIR JASPAR. My Lady, and Sister, Sir.—Wife, this is Master
Horner.

LADY FIDGET. Master *Horner*, Husband!

SIR JASPAR. My Lady, my Lady *Fidget*, Sir.

HORNER. So, Sir.

SIR JASPAR. Won't you be acquainted with her Sir?
[So the report is true, I find by his coldness or aversion
to the Sex; but I'll play the wag with him.] [*Aside.*
Pray salute my Wife, my Lady, Sir.

HORNER. I will kiss no Mans Wife, Sir, for him, Sir; I have
taken my eternal leave, Sir, of the Sex already, Sir.

SIR JASPAR. Hah, hah, hah; I'll plague him yet. [*aside.*
Not know my Wife, Sir?

HORNER. I do know your Wife, Sir, she's a Woman, Sir,
and consequently a Monster, Sir, a greater Monster than
a Husband, Sir.

SIR JASPAR. A Husband; how, Sir?

HORNER. So, Sir; [*makes horns.*][2] but I make no more
Cuckholds, Sir.

SIR JASPAR. Hah, hah, hah, *Mercury, Mercury.*[3]

LADY FIDGET. Pray, Sir *Jaspar*, let us be gone from this
rude fellow.

DAINTY. Who, by his breeding, wou'd think, he had
ever been in *France*?

LADY FIDGET. Foh, he's but too much a French fellow, such
as hate Women of quality and virtue, for their love to
their Husbands, Sr. *Jaspar;* a Woman is hated by'em as
much for loving her Husband, as for loving their Money:
But pray, let's be gone.

HORNER. You do well, Madam, for I have nothing that you
came for: I have brought over not so much as a Bawdy

Picture, new Postures,[4] nor the second Part of the *Es-cole de Filles;*[5] Nor—

QUACK. Hold for shame, Sir; what d'y mean? you'l ruine your self for ever with the Sex—   [*apart to* HORNER.

SIR JASPAR. Hah, hah, hah, he hates Women perfectly I find.

DAINTY. What pitty 'tis he shou'd.

LADY FIDGET. Ay, he's a base rude Fellow for't; but af-fectation makes not a Woman more odious to them, than Virtue.

HORNER. Because your Virtue is your greatest affectation, Madam.

LADY FIDGET. How, you sawcy Fellow, wou'd you wrong my honour?

HORNER. If I cou'd.

LADY FIDGET. How d'y mean, Sir?

SIR JASPAR. Hah, hah, hah, no he can't wrong your Lady-ships honour, upon my honour; he poor Man—hark you in your ear—a meer Eunuch.

LADY FIDGET. O filthy French Beast, foh, foh; why do we stay? let's be gone; I can't endure the sight of him.

SIR JASPAR. Stay, but till the Chairs come, they'l be here presently.

LADY FIDGET. No, no.

SIR JASPAR. Nor can I stay longer; 'tis—let me see, a quar-ter and a half quarter of a minute past eleven; the Coun-cil will be sate, I must away: business must be preferr'd always before Love and Ceremony with the wise Mr. *Horner.*

HORNER. And the Impotent Sir *Jaspar.*

SIR JASPAR. Ay, ay, the impotent Master *Horner,* hah, ha, ha.

LADY FIDGET. What leave us with a filthy Man alone in his lodgings?

SIR JASPAR. He's an innocent Man now, you know; pray stay, I'll hasten the Chaires to you. —Mr. *Horner* your Servant, I shou'd be glad to see you at my house; pray, come and dine with me, and play at Cards with my Wife after dinner, you are fit for Women at that game; yet hah, ha— ['Tis as much a Husbands prudence to pro-

vide innocent diversion for a Wife, as to hinder her un-
lawful pleasures; and he had better employ her, than
let her employ her self. [*Aside.*

Farewel. [*Exit Sir* JASPAR.

HORNER. Your Servant Sr. *Jaspar.*

LADY FIDGET. I will not stay with him, foh—

HORNER. Nay, Madam, I beseech you stay, if it be but to
see, I can be as civil to Ladies yet, as they wou'd desire.

LADY FIDGET. No, no, foh, you cannot be civil to Ladies.

DAINTY. You as civil as Ladies wou'd desire.

LADY FIDGET. No, no, no, foh, foh, foh.

[*Exeunt Ladie* FIDGET *and* DAINTY.

QUACK. Now I think, I, or you your self rather, have done
your business with the Women.

HORNER. Thou art an Ass, don't you see already upon the
report and my carriage, this grave Man of business
leaves his Wife in my lodgings, invites me to his house
and wife, who before wou'd not be acquainted with me
out of jealousy.

QUACK. Nay, by this means you may be the more acquainted with the Husbands, but the less with the
Wives.

HORNER. Let me alone, if I can but abuse the Husbands,
I'll soon disabuse the Wives: Stay—I'll reckon you up
the advantages, I am like to have by my Stratagem:
First, I shall be rid of all my old Acquaintances, the
most insatiable sorts of Duns, that invade our Lodgings
in a morning: And next, to the pleasure of making a
New Mistriss, is that of being rid of an old One, and of
all old Debts; Love when it comes to be so, is paid the
most unwillingly.

QUACK. Well, you may be so rid of your old Acquaintances;
but how will you get any new Ones?

HORNER. Doctor, thou wilt never make a good Chymist,
thou art so incredulous and impatient; ask but all the
young Fellows of the Town, if they do not loose more
time like Huntsmen, in starting the game, than in running it down; one knows not where to find'em, who will,
or will not; Women of Quality are so civil, you can
hardly distinguish love from good breeding, and a Man

is often mistaken; but now I can be sure, she that shews an aversion to me loves the sport, as those Women that are gone, whom I warrant to be right: And then the next thing, is your Women of Honour, as you call'em, are only chary of their reputations, not their Persons, and 'tis scandal they wou'd avoid, not Men: Now may I have, by the reputation of an Eunuch, the Priviledges of One; and be seen in a Ladies Chamber, in a morning as early as her Husband; kiss Virgins before their Parents, or Lovers; and may be in short the *Pas par tout* of the Town. Now Doctor.

QUACK. Nay, now you shall be the Doctor; and your Process is so new, that we do not know but it may succeed.

HORNER. Not so new neither, *Probatum est*[6] Doctor.

QUACK. Well, I wish you luck and many Patients whil'st I go to mine.   [*Exit* QUACK.

Enter HARCOURT, *and* DORILANT *to* HORNER.

HARCOURT. Come, your appearance at the Play yesterday, has I hope hardned you for the future against the Womens contempt, and the Mens raillery; and now you'l abroad as you were wont.

HORNER. Did I not bear it bravely?

DORILANT. With a most Theatrical impudence; nay more than the Orange-wenches shew there, or a drunken vizard Mask, or a great belly'd Actress; nay, or the most impudent of Creatures, an ill Poet; or what is yet more impudent, a second-hand Critick.

HORNER. But what say the Ladies, have they no pitty?

HARCOURT. What Ladies? the vizard Masques you know never pitty a Man when all's gone, though in their Service.

DORILANT. And for the Women in the boxes, you'd never pitty them, when 'twas in your power.

HARCOURT. They say 'tis pitty, but all that deal with common Women shou'd be serv'd so.

DORILANT. Nay, I dare swear, they won't admit you to play at Cards with them, go to Plays with'em, or do the little duties which other Shadows of men, are wont to do for'em.

right woman: loose woman.   *vizard Mask*: prostitute.

HORNER. Who do you call Shadows of Men?

DORILANT. Half Men.

HORNER. What Boyes?

DORILANT. Ay your old Boyes, old *beaux Garcons,* who like superannuated Stallions are suffer'd to run, feed, and whinney with the Mares as long as they live, though they can do nothing else.

HORNER. Well a Pox on love and wenching, Women serve but to keep a Man from better Company; though I can't enjoy them, I shall you the more: good fellowship and friendship, are lasting, rational and manly pleasures.

HARCOURT. For all that give me some of those pleasures, you call effeminate too, they help to relish one another.

HORNER. They disturb one another.

HARCOURT. No, Mistresses are like Books; if you pore upon them too much, they doze you, and make you unfit for Company; but if us'd discreetly, you are the fitter for conversation by'em.

DORILANT. A Mistress shou'd be like a little Country retreat near the Town, not to dwell in constantly, but only for a night and away; to tast the Town the better when a Man returns.

HORNER. I tell you, 'tis as hard to be a good Fellow, a good Friend, and a Lover of Women, as 'tis to be a good Fellow, a good Friend, and a Lover of Money: You cannot follow both, then choose your side; Wine gives you liberty, Love takes it away.

DORILANT. Gad, he's in the right on't.

HORNER. Wine gives you joy, Love grief and tortures; besides the Chirurgeon's.[7] Wine makes us witty, Love only Sots: Wine makes us sleep, Love breaks it.

DORILANT. By the World he has reason, *Harcourt.*

HORNER. Wine makes—

DORILANT. Ay, Wine makes us—makes us Princes, Love makes us Beggars, poor Rogues, y gad—and Wine—

HORNER. So, there's one converted.— No, no, Love and Wine, Oil and Vinegar.

HARCOURT. I grant it; Love will still be uppermost.

---

beaux Garcons: fops.   *doze:* confuse, bewilder.

HORNER. Come, for my part I will have only those glorious, manly pleasures of being very drunk, and very slovenly.

Enter BOY.

BOY. Mr. *Sparkish* is below, Sir.[8]

HARCOURT. What, my dear Friend! a Rogue that is fond of me, only I think for abusing him.

DORILANT. No, he can no more think the Men laugh at him, than that Women jilt him, his opinion of himself is so good.

HORNER. Well, there's another pleasure by drinking, I thought not of; I shall loose his acquaintance, because he cannot drink; and you know 'tis a very hard thing to be rid of him, for he's one of those nauseous offerers at wit, who like the worst Fidlers run themselves into all Companies.

HARCOURT. One, that by being in the Company of Men of sense wou'd pass for one.

HORNER. And may so to the short-sighted World, as a false Jewel amongst true ones, is not discern'd at a distance; his Company is as troublesome to us, as a Cuckolds, when you have a mind to his Wife's.

HARCOURT. No, the Rogue will not let us enjoy one another, but ravishes our conversation, though he signifies no more to't, than Sir *Martin Mar-all's* gaping, and auker'd thrumming upon the Lute, does to his Man's Voice, and Musick.[9]

DORILANT. And to pass for a wit in Town, shewes himself a fool every night to us, that are guilty of the plot.

HORNER. Such wits as he, are, to a Company of reasonable Men, like Rooks to the Gamesters, who only fill a room at the Table, but are so far from contributing to the play, that they only serve to spoil the fancy of those that do.

DORILANT. Nay, they are us'd like Rooks too, snub'd, check'd, and abus'd; yet the Rogues will hang on.

HORNER. A Pox on'em, and all that force Nature, and wou'd be still what she forbids'em; Affectation is her greatest Monster.

auker'd: awkward.

HARCOURT. Most Men are the contraries to that they wou'd seem; your bully you see, is a Coward with a long Sword; the little humbly fawning Physician with his Ebony cane, is he that destroys Men.

DORILANT. The Usurer, a poor Rogue, possess'd of moldy Bonds, and Mortgages; and we they call Spend-thrifts, are only wealthy, who lay out his money upon daily new purchases of pleasure.

HORNER. Ay, your errantest cheat, is your Trustee, or Executor; your jealous Man, the greatest Cuckhold; your Church-man, the greatest Atheist; and your noisy pert Rogue of a wit, the greatest Fop, dullest Ass, and worst Company as you shall see: For here he comes.

Enter SPARKISH *to them.*

SPARKISH. How is't, Sparks, how is't? Well Faith, *Harry,* I must railly thee a little, ha, ha, ha, upon the report in Town of thee, ha, ha, ha, I can't hold y Faith; shall I speak?

HORNER. Yes, but you'l be so bitter then.

SPARKISH. Honest *Dick* and *Franck* here shall answer for me, I will not be extream bitter by the Univers.

HARCOURT. We will be bound in ten thousand pound Bond, he shall not be bitter at all.

DORILANT. Nor sharp, nor sweet.

HORNER. What, not down right insipid?

SPARKISH. Nay then, since you are so brisk, and provoke me, take what follows; you must know, I was discoursing and raillying with some Ladies yesterday, and they hapned to talk of the fine new signes in Town.

HORNER. Very fine Ladies I believe.

SPARKISH. Said I, I know where the best new sign is. Where, says one of the Ladies? In *Covent-Garden,* I reply'd. Said another, In what street? In *Russel-street,* answer'd I. Lord says another, I'm sure there was ne're

---

Russel-street: Russell Street, off the east side of Covent Garden. Wycherley presumably let Horner live there to make the joke about the sign more appropriate; there were a number of well-known taverns and coffeehouses in both Covent Garden and Russell Street.

a fine new sign there yesterday. Yes, but there was, said I again, and it came out of *France,* and has been there a fortnight.

DORILANT. A Pox I can hear no more, prethee.

HORNER. No hear him out; let him tune his crowd a while.

HARCOURT. The worst Musick the greatest preparation.

SPARKISH. Nay faith, I'll make you laugh. It cannot be, says a third Lady. Yes, yes, quoth I again. Says a fourth Lady,

HORNER. Look to't, we'l have no more Ladies.

SPARKISH. No.—then mark, mark, now, said I to the fourth, did you never see Mr. *Horner;* he lodges in *Russel-street,* and he's a sign of a Man, you know, since he came out of *France,* heh, hah, he.

HORNER. But the Divel take me, if thine be the sign of a jest.

SPARKISH. With that they all fell a laughing, till they be-piss'd themselves; what, but it do's not move you, me-thinks? well see one had as good go to Law without a witness, as break a jest without a laugher on ones side. —Come, come Sparks, but where do we dine, I have left at *Whitehal* an Earl to dine with you.

DORILANT. Why, I thought thou hadst lov'd a Man with a title better, than a Suit with a French trimming to't.

HARCOURT. Go, to him again.

SPARKISH. No, Sir, a wit to me is the greatest title in the World.

HORNER. But go dine with your Earl, Sir, he may be ex-ceptious; we are your Friends, and will not take it ill to be left, I do assure you.

HARCOURT. Nay, faith he shall go to him.

SPARKISH. Nay, pray Gentlemen.

DORILANT. We'l thrust you out, if you wo'not, what disap-point any Body for us.

SPARKISH. Nay, dear Gentlemen hear me.

HORNER. No, no, Sir, by no means; pray go Sir.

SPARKISH. Why, dear Rogues.　　　　*[They all thrust him*

DORILANT. No, no.　　　　　　　　*out of the room.*

ALL. Ha, ha, ha.　　　　　　　　　*[*SPARKISH *returns.*

crowd: fiddle.　　　　　　　　*exceptious:* peevish.

SPARKISH. But, Sparks, pray hear me; what d'ye think I'll eat then with gay shallow Fops, and silent Coxcombs? I think wit as necessary at dinner as a glass of good wine, and that's the reason I never have any stomach when I eat alone.— Come, but where do we dine?

HORNER. Ev'n where you will.

SPARKISH. At *Chateline's.*

DORILANT. Yes, if you will.

SPARKISH. Or at the *Cock.*

DORILANT. Yes, if you please.

SPARKISH. Or at the *Dog* and *Partridg.*[10]

HORNER. Ay, if you have mind to't, for we shall dine at neither.

SPARKISH. Pshaw, with your fooling we shall loose the new Play; and I wou'd no more miss seing a new Play the first day, than I wou'd miss setting in the wits Row; therefore I'll go fetch my Mistriss and away.

[*Exit* SPARKISH.

Manent HORNER, HARCOURT, DORILANT;
Enter to them Mr. PINCHWIFE.

HORNER. Who have we here, *Pinchwife?*

PINCHWIFE. Gentlemen, your humble Servant.

HORNER. Well, *Jack,* by thy long absence from the Town, the grumness of thy countenance, and the slovenlyness of thy habit; I shou'd give thee joy, shou'd I not, of Marriage?

PINCHWIFE. [Death does he know I'm married too? I thought to have conceal'd it from him at least.] [*Aside.* My long stay in the Country will excuse my dress, and I have a suit of Law, that brings me up to Town, that puts me out of humour; besides I must give *Sparkish* to morrow five thousand pound to lye with my Sister.

HORNER. Nay, you Country Gentlemen rather than not purchase, will buy any thing, and he is a crackt title, if we may quibble: Well, but am I to give thee joy, I heard thou wert marry'd.

PINCHWIFE. What then?

HORNER. Why, the next thing that is to be heard, is thou'rt a Cuckold.

grumness: moroseness.

PINCHWIFE. Insupportable name.   [*Aside.*

HORNER. But I did not expect Marriage from such a Whoremaster as you, one that knew the Town so much, and Women so well.

PINCHWIFE. Why, I have marry'd no *London* Wife.

HORNER. Pshaw, that's all one, that grave circumspection in marrying a Country Wife, is like refusing a deceitful pamper'd *Smithfield* Jade,[11] to go and be cheated by a Friend in the Country.

PINCHWIFE. A Pox on him and his Simile.   [*Aside.*
At least we are a little surer of the breed there, know what her keeping has been, whether soyl'd or unsound.

HORNER. Come, come, I have known a clap gotten in *Wales*, and there are Cozens, Justices, Clarks, and Chaplains in the Country, I won't say Coach-men, but she's handsome and young.

PINCHWIFE. I'll answer as I shou'd do.   [*Aside.*
No, no, she has no beauty, but her youth; no attraction, but her modesty, wholesome, homely, and huswifely, that's all.

DORILANT. He talks as like a Grasier as he looks.

PINCHWIFE. She's too auker'd, ill favour'd, and silly to bring to Town.

HARCOURT. Then methinks you shou'd bring her, to be taught breeding.

PINCHWIFE. To be taught; no, Sir, I thank you, good Wives, and private Souldiers shou'd be ignorant.—[I'll keep her from your instructions, I warrant you.[12]

HARCOURT. The Rogue is as jealous, as if his wife were not ignorant.   [*Aside.*

HORNER. Why, if she be ill favour'd, there will be less danger here for you, than by leaving her in the Country; we have such variety of dainties, that we are seldom hungry.

DORILANT. But they have alwayes coarse, constant, swinging stomachs in the Country.

HARCOURT. Foul Feeders indeed.

DORILANT. And your Hospitality is great there.

Grasier: grazier, one who fattens cattle for market. Used here as we would use "horse-trader."

HARCOURT. Open house, every Man's welcome.

PINCHWIFE. So, so, Gentlemen.

HORNER. But prethee, why woud'st thou marry her? if she be ugly, ill-bred, and silly, she must be rich then.

PINCHWIFE. As rich as if she brought me twenty thousand pound out of this Town; for she'l be as sure not to spend her moderate portion, as a *London* Baggage wou'd be to spend hers, let it be what it wou'd; so 'tis all one: then because shes ugly, she's the likelyer to be my own; and being ill-bred, she'l hate conversation; and since silly and innocent, will not know the difference betwixt a Man of one and twenty, and one of forty.

HORNER. Nine—to my knowledge; but if she be silly, she'l expect as much from a Man of forty nine, as from him of one and twenty: But methinks wit is more necessary than beauty, and I think no young Woman ugly that has it, and no handsome Woman agreable without it.

PINCHWIFE. 'Tis my maxime, he's a Fool that marrys, but he's a greater that does not marry a Fool; what is wit in a Wife good for, but to make a Man a Cuckold?

HORNER. Yes, to keep it from his knowledge.

PINCHWIFE. A Fool cannot contrive to make her husband a Cuckold.

HORNER. No, but she'l club with a Man that can; and what is worse, if she cannot make her Husband a Cuckold, she'l make him jealous, and pass for one, and then 'tis all one.

PINCHWIFE. Well, well, I'll take care for one, my Wife shall make me no Cuckold, though she had your help Mr. *Horner;* I understand the Town, Sir.

DORILANT. His help! [*Aside.*

HARCOURT. He's come newly to Town it seems, and has not heard how things are with him. [*Aside.*

HORNER. But tell me, has Marriage cured thee of whoring, which it seldom does.

HARCOURT. 'Tis more than age can do.

HORNER. No, the word is, I'll marry and live honest; but a Marriage vow is like a penitent Gamesters Oath, and entring into Bonds, and penalties to stint himself to such a particular small sum at play for the future, which makes him but the more eager, and not being able to hold out, looses his Money again, and his forfeit to boot.

DORILANT. Ay, ay, a Gamester will be a Gamester, whilst his Money lasts; and a Whoremaster, whilst his vigour.

HARCOURT. Nay, I have known'em, when they are broke and can loose no more, keep a fumbling with the Box in their hands to fool with only, and hinder other Gamesters.

DORILANT. That had wherewithal to make lusty stakes.

PINCHWIFE. Well, Gentlemen, you may laugh at me, but you shall never lye with my Wife, I know the Town.

HORNER. But prethee, was not the way you were in better, is not keeping better than Marriage?

PINCHWIFE. A Pox on't, the Jades wou'd jilt me, I cou'd never keep a Whore to my self.

HORNER. So then you only marry'd to keep a Whore to your self; well, but let me tell you, Women, as you say, are like Souldiers made constant and loyal by good pay, rather than by Oaths and Covenants, therefore I'd advise my Friends to keep rather than marry; since too I find by your example, it does not serve ones turn, for I saw you yesterday in the eighteen penny place with a pretty Country-wench.

PINCHWIFE. How the Divel, did he see my Wife then? I sate there that she might not be seen; but she shall never go to a play again.   [*Aside.*

HORNER. What dost thou blush at nine and forty, for having been seen with a Wench?

DORILANT. No Faith, I warrant 'twas his Wife, which he seated there out of sight, for he's a cunning Rogue, and understands the Town.

HARCOURT. He blushes, then 'twas his Wife; for Men are now more ashamed to be seen with them in publick, than with a Wench.

eighteen penny place: seat in the middle gallery. Since that part of the theater was notorious for the whores who frequented it, a man might be expected to seat his wife elsewhere. Still, it is the best place to keep her from being seen by the gallants, who would have been in the pit or the boxes.

PINCHWIFE. Hell and damnation, I'm undone, since *Horner* has seen her, and they know 'twas she. [*Aside.*

HORNER. But prethee, was it thy Wife? she was exceedingly pretty; I was in love with her at that distance.

PINCHWIFE. You are like never to be nearer to her. Your Servant Gentlemen. [*Offers to go.*

HORNER. Nay, prethee stay.

PINCHWIFE. I cannot, I will not.

HORNER. Come you shall dine with us.

PINCHWIFE. I have din'd already.

HORNER. Come, I know thou hast not; I'll treat thee dear Rogue, thou sha't spend none of thy *Hampshire* Money to day.

PINCHWIFE. Treat me; so he uses me already like his Cuckold. [*Aside.*

HORNER. Nay, you shall not go.

PINCHWIFE. I must, I have business at home.

[*Exit* PINCHWIFE.

HARCOURT. To beat his Wife, he's as jealous of her, as a *Cheapside* Husband of a *Covent-garden* Wife.[13]

HORNER. Why, 'tis as hard to find an old Whoremaster without jealousy and the gout, as a young one without fear or the Pox.

As Gout in Age, from Pox in Youth proceeds;
So Wenching past, then jealousy succeeds:
The worst disease that Love and Wenching breeds.

ACT 2. SCENE I.

Mrs. MARGERY PINCHWIFE, *and* ALITHEA: *Mr.* PINCHWIFE
peeping behind at the door.

MRS. PINCHWIFE. Pray, Sister, where are the best Fields and Woods, to walk in in *London?*

ALITHEA. A pretty Question; why, Sister! *Mulberry Garden,* and St. *James's Park;* and for close walks the *New Exchange.*[1]

MRS. PINCHWIFE. Pray, Sister, tell me why my Husband looks so grum here in Town? and keeps me up so close, and will not let me go a walking, nor let me wear my best Gown yesterday?

ALITHEA. O he's jealous, Sister.

MRS. PINCHWIFE. Jealous, what's that?

ALITHEA. He's afraid you shou'd love another Man.

MRS. PINCHWIFE. How shou'd he be afraid of my loving another man, when he will not let me see any but himself.

ALITHEA. Did he not carry you yesterday to a Play?

MRS. PINCHWIFE. Ay, but we sate amongst ugly People, he wou'd not let me come near the Gentry, who sate under us, so that I cou'd not see'em: He told me, none but naughty Women sate there, whom they tous'd and mous'd; but I wou'd have ventur'd for all that.

ALITHEA. But how did you like the Play?

MRS. PINCHWIFE. Indeed I was aweary of the Play, but I lik'd hugeously the Actors; they are the goodlyest proper'st Men, Sister.

ALITHEA. O but you must not like the Actors, Sister.

MRS. PINCHWIFE. Ay, how shou'd I help it, Sister? Pray, Sister, when my Husband comes in, will you ask leave for me to go a walking?

ALITHEA. A walking, hah, ha; Lord, a Country Gentlewomans leasure[2] is the drudgery of a foot-post; and she requires as much airing as her Husbands Horses.

[*Aside.*

Enter Mr. PINCHWIFE *to them.*

But here comes your Husband; I'll ask, though I'm sure he'l not grant it.

MRS. PINCHWIFE. He says he won't let me go abroad, for fear of catching the Pox.

ALITHEA. Fye, the small Pox you shou'd say.

---

tous'd and mous'd: tousled and mousled (or muzzled). The OED describes both words as meaning to pull about roughly but good-naturedly. The phrase apparently had a wide range of meanings, as we use "tease" today, from simply picking at a person to mild sex play. See Mrs. Pinchwife's description of Horner's kiss in Act 4 (p. 318): *Why he put the tip of his tongue between my lips, and so musl'd me.*

foot-post: a messenger who travels on foot.

MRS. PINCHWIFE. Oh my dear, dear Bud, welcome home; why dost thou look so fropish, who has nanger'd thee?

PINCHWIFE. Your a Fool.

[*Mrs.* PINCHWIFE *goes aside, & cryes.*

ALITHEA. Faith so she is, for crying for no fault, poor tender Creature!

PINCHWIFE. What you wou'd have her as impudent as your self, as errant a Jilflirt, a gadder, a Magpy, and to say all a meer notorious Town-Woman?

ALITHEA. Brother, you are my only Censurer; and the honour of your Family shall sooner suffer in your Wife there, than in me, though I take the innocent liberty of the Town.

PINCHWIFE. Hark you Mistriss, do not talk so before my Wife, the innocent liberty of the Town!

ALITHEA. Why, pray, who boasts of any intrigue with me? what Lampoon has made my name notorious? what ill Women frequent my Lodgings? I keep no Company with any Women of scandalous reputations.

PINCHWIFE. No, you keep the Men of scandalous reputations Company.

ALITHEA. Where? wou'd you not have me civil? answer'em in a Box at the Plays? in the drawing room at *Whitehal?* in St. *James's Park? Mulberry-garden?* or—

PINCHWIFE. Hold, hold, do not teach my Wife, where the Men are to be found; I believe she's the worse for your Town documents already; I bid you keep her in ignorance as I do.

MRS. PINCHWIFE. Indeed be not angry with her Bud, she will tell me nothing of the Town, though I ask her a thousand times a day.

PINCHWIFE. Then you are very inquisitive to know, I find?

MRS. PINCHWIFE. Not I indeed, Dear, I hate *London;* our Place-house in the Country is worth a thousand of't, wou'd I were there again.

PINCHWIFE. So you shall I warrant; but were you not talking of Plays, and Players, when I came in? you are her encourager in such discourses.

fropish: peevish.
Place-house: country-house and its surroundings, the chief house on an estate.

MRS. PINCHWIFE. No indeed, Dear, she chid me just now for liking the Player Men.

PINCHWIFE. Nay, if she be so innocent as to own to me her liking them, there is no hurt in't—   [*Aside.* Come my poor Rogue, but thou lik'st none better than me?

MRS. PINCHWIFE. Yes indeed, but I do, the Player Men are finer Folks.

PINCHWIFE. But you love none better than me?

MRS. PINCHWIFE. You are mine own Dear Bud, and I know you, I hate a Stranger.

PINCHWIFE. Ay, my Dear, you must love me only, and not be like the naughty Town Women, who only hate their Husbands, and love every Man else, love Plays, Visits, fine Coaches, fine Cloaths, Fidles, Balls, Treates, and so lead a wicked Town-life.

MRS. PINCHWIFE. Nay, if to enjoy all these things be a Town-life, *London* is not so bad a place, Dear.

PINCHWIFE. How! if you love me, you must hate *London.*

ALITHEA. The Fool has forbid me discovering to her the pleasures of the Town, and he is now setting her a gog upon them himself.

MRS. PINCHWIFE. But, Husband, do the Town-women love the Player Men too?

PINCHWIFE. Yes, I warrant you.

MRS. PINCHWIFE. Ay, I warrant you.

PINCHWIFE. Why, you do not, I hope?

MRS. PINCHWIFE. No, no, Bud; but why have we no Player-men in the Country?

PINCHWIFE. Ha— Mrs. Minx, ask me no more to go to a Play.

MRS. PINCHWIFE. Nay, why, Love? I did not care for going; but when you forbid me, you make me as't were desire it.

ALITHEA. So 'twill be in other things, I warrant.   [*Aside.*

MRS. PINCHWIFE. Pray, let me go to a Play, Dear.

PINCHWIFE. Hold your Peace, I wo'not.

MRS. PINCHWIFE. Why, Love?

PINCHWIFE. Why, I'll tell you.

ALITHEA. Nay if he tell her, she'l give him more cause
to forbid her that place.   [*Aside.*

MRS. PINCHWIFE. Pray, why, Dear?

PINCHWIFE. First, you like the Actors, and the Gallants
may like you.

MRS. PINCHWIFE. What, a homely Country Girl? no Bud,
no body will like me.

PINCHWIFE. I tell you, yes, they may.

MRS. PINCHWIFE. No, no, you jest—I won't believe you,
I will go.

PINCHWIFE. I tell you then, that one of the lewdest Fellows in Town, who saw you there, told me he was in
love with you.

MRS. PINCHWIFE. Indeed! who, who, pray who wast?

PINCHWIFE. I've gone too far, and slipt before I was aware;
how overjoy'd she is!   [*Aside.*

MRS. PINCHWIFE. Was it any *Hampshire* Gallant, any of
our Neighbours? I promise you, I am beholding to
him.

PINCHWIFE. I promise you, you lye; for he wou'd but ruin
you, as he has done hundreds: he has no other love for
Women, but that, such as he, look upon Women like
Basilicks, but to destroy'em.

MRS. PINCHWIFE. Ay, but if he loves me, why shou'd he
ruin me? answer me to that: methinks he shou'd not, I
wou'd do him no harm.

ALITHEA. Hah, ha, ha.

PINCHWIFE. 'Tis very well; but I'll keep him from doing
you any harm, or me either.

                    Enter SPARKISH *and* HARCOURT.

But here comes Company, get you in, get you in.

MRS. PINCHWIFE. But pray, Husband, is he a pretty Gentleman, that loves me?

PINCHWIFE. In baggage, in.

                    [*Thrusts her in: shuts the door.*

What all the lewd Libertines of the Town brought to
my Lodging, by this easie Coxcomb! S'death I'll not
suffer it.

SPARKISH. Here *Harcourt,* do you approve my choice?

Dear, little Rogue, I told you, I'd bring you acquainted
with all my Friends, the wits, and—

[HARCOURT *salutes her.*

PINCHWIFE. Ay, they shall know her, as well as you your
self will, I warrant you.

SPARKISH. This is one of those, my pretty Rogue, that are
to dance at your Wedding to morrow; and him you
must bid welcom ever, to what you and I have.

PINCHWIFE. Monstrous!—   [*Aside.*

SPARKISH. *Harcourt* how dost thou like her, Faith? Nay,
Dear, do not look down; I should hate to have a Wife
of mine out of countenance at any thing.

PINCHWIFE. Wonderful!

SPARKISH. Tell me, I say, *Harcourt,* how dost thou like
her? thou hast star'd upon her enough, to resolve me.

HARCOURT. So infinitely well, that I cou'd wish I had a
Mistriss too, that might differ from her in nothing, but
her love and engagement to you.

ALITHEA. Sir, Master *Sparkish* has often told me, that his
Acquaintance were all Wits and Raillieurs, and now
I find it.

SPARKISH. No, by the Universe, Madam, he does not railly
now; you may believe him: I do assure you, he is the
honestest, worthyest, true hearted Gentleman— A man
of such perfect honour, he wou'd say nothing to a
Lady, he does not mean.

PINCHWIFE. Praising another Man to his Mistriss!

HARCOURT. Sir, you are so beyond expectation obliging,
that—

SPARKISH. Nay, I gad, I am sure you do admire her extreamly, I see't in your eyes.— He does admire you
Madam.— By the World, don't you?

HARCOURT. Yes, above the World, or, the most glorious
part of it, her whole Sex; and till now I never thought
I shou'd have envy'd you, or any Man about to marry,
but you have the best excuse for Marriage I ever knew.

ALITHEA. Nay, now, Sir, I'm satisfied you are of the Society
of the Wits, and Raillieurs, since you cannot spare your
Friend, even when he is but too civil to you; but the
surest sign is, since you are an Enemy to Marriage, for

that I hear you hate as much as business or bad Wine.

HARCOURT. Truly, Madam, I never was an Enemy to Marriage, till now, because Marriage was never an Enemy to me before.

ALITHEA. But why, Sir, is Marriage an Enemy to you now? Because it robs you of your Friend here; for you look upon a Friend married, as one gone into a Monastery, that is dead to the World.

HARCOURT. 'Tis indeed, because you marry him; I see Madam, you can guess my meaning: I do confess heartily and openly, I wish it were in my power to break the Match, by Heavens I wou'd.

SPARKISH. Poor *Franck!*

ALITHEA. Wou'd you be so unkind to me?

HARCOURT. No, no, 'tis not because I wou'd be unkind to you.

SPARKISH. Poor *Franck*, no gad, 'tis only his kindness to me.

PINCHWIFE. Great kindness to you indeed; insensible Fop, let a Man make love to his Wife to his face.   [*Aside.*

SPARKISH. Come dear *Franck*, for all my Wife there that shall be, thou shalt enjoy me sometimes dear Rogue; by my honour, we Men of wit condole for our deceased Brother in Marriage, as much as for one dead in earnest: I think that was prettily said of me, ha *Harcourt?*— But come *Franck*, be not melancholy for me.

HARCOURT. No, I assure you I am not melancholy for you.

SPARKISH. Prethee, *Frank*, dost think my Wife that shall be there a fine Person?

HARCOURT. I cou'd gaze upon her, till I became as blind as you are.

SPARKISH. How, as I am! how!

HARCOURT. Because you are a Lover, and true Lovers are blind, stockblind.

SPARKISH. True, true; but by the World, she has wit too, as well as beauty: go, go with her into a corner, and trye if she has wit, talk to her any thing, she's bashful before me.

stockblind: as blind as a stock, a lifeless thing. "Stock" had come to mean a stupid person.

HARCOURT. Indeed if a Woman wants wit in a corner, she has it no where.

ALITHEA. Sir, you dispose of me a little before your time.—
[*Aside to* SPARKISH.

SPARKISH. Nay, nay, Madam let me have an earnest of your obedience, or—go, go, Madam—
[HARCOURT *courts* ALITHEA *aside.*

PINCHWIFE. How, Sir, if you are not concern'd for the honour of a Wife, I am for that of a Sister; he shall not debauch her: be a Pander to your own Wife, bring Men to her, let'em make love before your face, thrust'em into a corner together, then leav'em in private! is this your Town wit and conduct?

SPARKISH. Hah, ha, ha, a silly wise Rogue, wou'd make one laugh more than a stark Fool, hah, ha: I shall burst. Nay, you shall not disturb'em; I'll vex thee, by the World. [*Struggles with* PINCHWIFE *to keep him from* HARCOURT *and* ALITHEA.

ALITHEA. The writings are drawn, Sir, settlements made; 'tis too late, Sir, and past all revocation.

HARCOURT. Then so is my death.

ALITHEA. I wou'd not be unjust to him.

HARCOURT. Then why to me so?

ALITHEA. I have no obligation to you.

HARCOURT. My love.

ALITHEA. I had his before.

HARCOURT. You never had it; he wants you see jealousie, the only infallible sign of it.

ALITHEA. Love proceeds from esteem; he cannot distrust my virtue, besides he loves me, or he wou'd not marry me.

HARCOURT. Marrying you, is no more sign of his love, than bribing your Woman, that he may marry you, is a sign of his generosity: Marriage is rather a sign of interest, than love; and he that marries a fortune, covets a Mistress, not loves her: But if you take Marriage for a sign of love, take it from me immediately.

ALITHEA. No, now you have put a scruple in my head; but in short, Sir, to end our dispute, I must marry him, my reputation wou'd suffer in the World else.

HARCOURT. No, if you do marry him, with your pardon, Madam, your reputation suffers in the World, and you wou'd be thought in necessity for a cloak.

ALITHEA. Nay, now you are rude, Sir.— Mr. *Sparkish*, pray come hither, your Friend here is very troublesom, and very loving.

HARCOURT. Hold, hold—   [*Aside to* ALITHEA.

PINCHWIFE. D'ye hear that?

SPARKISH. Why, d'ye think I'll seem to be jealous, like a Country Bumpkin?

PINCHWIFE. No, rather be a Cuckold, like a credulous Cit.

HARCOURT. Madam, you wou'd not have been so little generous as to have told him.

ALITHEA. Yes, since you cou'd be so little generous, as to wrong him.

HARCOURT. Wrong him, no Man can do't, he's beneath an injury; a Bubble, a Coward, a sensless Idiot, a Wretch so contemptible to all the World but you, that—

ALITHEA. Hold, do not rail at him, for since he is like to be my Husband, I am resolv'd to like him: Nay, I think I am oblig'd to tell him, you are not his Friend.— Master *Sparkish*, Master *Sparkish*.

SPARKISH. What, what; now dear Rogue, has not she wit?

HARCOURT. Not so much as I thought, and hoped she had.
     [*Speaks surlily*.

ALITHEA. Mr. *Sparkish*, do you bring People to rail at you?

HARCOURT. Madam—

SPARKISH. How! no, but if he does rail at me, 'tis but in jest I warrant; what we wits do for one another, and never take any notice of it.

ALITHEA. He spoke so scurrilously of you, I had no patience to hear him; besides he has been making love to me.

HARCOURT. True damn'd tell-tale-Woman.   [*Aside*.

Cit: citizen. Used contemptuously to differentiate between the City merchant and the aristocrat.

a Bubble: a dupe. See the conversation in Act 3 (p. 296) for related uses of "bubble."

SPARKISH. Pshaw, to shew his parts—we wits rail and make love often, but to shew our parts; as we have no affections, so we have no malice, we—

ALITHEA. He said, you were a Wretch, below an injury.

SPARKISH. Pshaw.

HARCOURT. Damn'd, sensless, impudent, virtuous Jade; well since she won't let me have her, she'l do as good, she'l make me hate her.

ALITHEA. A Common Bubble.

SPARKISH. Pshaw.

ALITHEA. A Coward.

SPARKISH. Pshaw, pshaw.

ALITHEA. A sensless driveling Idiot.

SPARKISH. How, did he disparage my parts? Nay, then my honour's concern'd, I can't put up that, Sir; by the World, Brother help me to kill him; [I may draw now, since we have the odds of him:—'tis a good occasion too before my Mistriss]—   [*Aside.*
[*Offers to draw.*

ALITHEA. Hold, hold.

SPARKISH. What, what.

ALITHEA. I must not let'em kill the Gentleman neither, for his kindness to me; I am so far from hating him, that I wish my Gallant had his person and understanding:—
[Nay if my honour—   [*Aside.*

SPARKISH. I'll be thy death.

ALITHEA. Hold, hold, indeed to tell the truth, the Gentleman said after all, that what he spoke, was but out of friendship to you.

SPARKISH. How! say, I am, I am a Fool, that is no wit, out of friendship to me.

ALITHEA. Yes, to try whether I was concern'd enough for you, and made love to me only to be satisfy'd of my virtue, for your sake.

HARCOURT. Kind however—   [*Aside.*

SPARKISH. Nay, if it were so, my dear Rogue, I ask thee pardon; but why wou'd not you tell me so, faith.

HARCOURT. Because I did not think on't, faith.

SPARKISH. Come, *Horner* does not come, *Harcourt,* let's be gone to the new Play.— Come Madam.

ALITHEA. I will not go, if you intend to leave me alone in the Box, and run into the pit, as you use to do.

SPARKISH. Pshaw, I'll leave *Harcourt* with you in the Box, to entertain you, and that's as good; if I sate in the Box, I shou'd be thought no Judge, but of trimmings. —Come away *Harcourt,* lead her down.

[*Exeunt* SPARKISH, HARCOURT, *and* ALITHEA.

PINCHWIFE. Well, go thy wayes, for the flower of the true Town Fops, such as spend their Estates, before they come to'em, and are Cuckolds before they'r married. But let me go look to my own Free-hold— How—

Enter my Lady FIDGET, *Mistriss* DAINTY FIDGET, *and Mistriss* SQUEAMISH.

LADY FIDGET. Your Servant, Sir, where is your Lady? we are come to wait upon her to the new Play.

PINCHWIFE. New Play!

LADY FIDGET. And my Husband will wait upon you presently.

PINCHWIFE. Damn your civility— [*Aside.*
Madam, by no means, I will not see Sir *Jaspar* here, till I have waited upon him at home; nor shall my Wife see you, till she has waited upon your Ladyship at your lodgings.

LADY FIDGET. Now we are here, Sir—

PINCHWIFE. No, Madam.

DAINTY. Pray, let us see her.

SQUEAMISH. We will not stir, till we see her.

PINCHWIFE. A Pox on you all—[*Aside.*] she has lock'd the door, and is gone abroad. [*Goes to the door, and returns.*]

LADY FIDGET. No, you have lock'd the door, and she's within.

DAINTY. They told us below, she was here.

PINCHWIFE. [Will nothing do?][3]— Well it must out then, to tell you the truth, Ladies, which I was afraid to let you know before, least it might endanger your lives, my Wife has just now the Small Pox come out upon her, do not be frighten'd; but pray, be gone

Ladies, you shall not stay here in danger of your lives; pray get you gone Ladies.

LADY FIDGET. No, no, we have all had'em.

SQUEAMISH. Alack, alack.

DAINTY. Come, come, we must see how it goes with her, I understand the disease.

LADY FIDGET. Come.

PINCHWIFE. Well, there is no being too hard for Women at their own weapon, lying, therefore I'll quit the Field.

[*Aside.*

[*Exit* PINCHWIFE.

SQUEAMISH. Here's an example of jealousy.

LADY FIDGET. Indeed as the World goes, I wonder there are no more jealous, since Wives are so neglected.

DAINTY. Pshaw, as the World goes, to what end shou'd they be jealous.

LADY FIDGET. Foh, 'tis a nasty World.

SQUEAMISH. That Men of parts, great acquaintance, and quality shou'd take up with, and spend themselves and fortunes, in keeping little Play-house Creatures, foh.

LADY FIDGET. Nay, that Women of understanding, great acquaintance, and good quality, shou'd fall a keeping too of little Creatures, foh.

SQUEAMISH. Why, 'tis the Men of qualities fault, they never visit Women of honour, and reputation, as they us'd to do; and have not so much as common civility, for Ladies of our rank, but use us with the same indifferency, and ill breeding, as if we were all marry'd to'em.

LADY FIDGET. She says true, 'tis an errant shame Women of quality shou'd be so slighted; methinks, birth, birth, shou'd go for something; I have known Men admired, courted, and followed for their titles only.

SQUEAMISH. Ay, one wou'd think Men of honour shou'd not love no more, than marry out of their own rank.

DAINTY. Fye, fye upon'em, they are come to think cross breeding for themselves best, as well as for their Dogs, and Horses.

LADY FIDGET. They are Dogs, and Horses for't.

SQUEAMISH. One wou'd think if not for love, for vanity a little.

DAINTY. Nay, they do satisfy their vanity upon us sometimes; and are kind to us in their report, tell all the
World they lye with us.

LADY FIDGET. Damn'd Rascals, that we shou'd be only
wrong'd by'em; to report a Man has had a Person,
when he has not had a Person, is the greatest wrong
in the whole World, that can be done to a person.

SQUEAMISH. Well, 'tis an errant shame, Noble Persons
shou'd be so wrong'd, and neglected.

LADY FIDGET. But still 'tis an erranter shame for a Noble
Person, to neglect her own honour, and defame her own
Noble Person, with little inconsiderable Fellows, foh!—

DAINTY. I suppose the crime against our honour, is the
same with a Man of quality as with another.

LADY FIDGET. How! no sure the Man of quality is likest
one's Husband, and therefore the fault shou'd be the
less.

DAINTY. But then the pleasure shou'd be the less.

LADY FIDGET. Fye, fye, fye, for shame Sister, whither
shall we ramble? be continent in your discourse, or I
shall hate you.

DAINTY. Besides an intrigue is so much the more notorious
for the man's quality.

SQUEAMISH. 'Tis true, no body takes notice of a private
Man, and therefore with him, 'tis more secret, and the
crime's the less, when 'tis not known.

LADY FIDGET. You say true; y faith I think you are in the
right on't: 'tis not an injury to a Husband, till it be an
injury to our honours; so that a Woman of honour
looses no honour with a private Person; and to say
truth—

DAINTY. So the little Fellow is grown a private Person—
with her—   [*Apart to* SQUEAMISH.

LADY FIDGET. But still my dear, dear Honour.

Enter Sir JASPAR, HORNER, DORILANT.

SIR JASPAR. Ay, my dear, dear of honour, thou hast still
so much honour in thy mouth—

HORNER. That she has none elsewhere—   [*Aside.*

LADY FIDGET. Oh, what d'ye mean to bring in these upon
us?

DAINTY. Foh, these are as bad as Wits.

SQUEAMISH. Foh!

LADY FIDGET. Let us leave the Room.

SIR JASPAR. Stay, stay, faith to tell you the naked truth.

LADY FIDGET. Fye, Sir *Jaspar*, do not use that word naked.

SIR JASPAR. Well, well, in short I have business at *Whitehal*, and cannot go to the play with you, therefore wou'd have you go—

LADY FIDGET. With those two to a Play?

SIR JASPAR. No, not with t'other, but with Mr. *Horner*, there can be no more scandal to go with him, than with Mr. *Tatle*, or Master *Limberham*.[4]

LADY FIDGET. With that nasty Fellow! no—no.

SIR JASPAR. Nay, prethee Dear, hear me.

[*Whispers to Lady* FIDGET.[5]

HORNER. Ladies.   [HORNER, DORILANT *drawing near*
DAINTY. Stand off.   SQUEAMISH, *and* DAINTY.]

SQUEAMISH. Do not approach us.

DAINTY. You heard with the wits, you are obscenity all over.

SQUEAMISH. And I wou'd as soon look upon a Picture of *Adam* and *Eve*, without fig leaves, as any of you, if I cou'd help it, therefore keep off, and do not make us sick.

DORILANT. What a Divel are these?

HORNER. Why, these are pretenders to honour, as criticks to wit, only by censuring others; and as every raw peevish, out-of-humour'd, affected, dull, Tea-drinking, Arithmetical Fop sets up for a wit, by railing at men of sence, so these for honour, by railing at the Court, and Ladies of as great honour, as quality.

SIR JASPAR. Come, Mr. *Horner,* I must desire you to go with these Ladies to the Play, Sir.

HORNER. I! Sir.

SIR JASPAR. Ay, ay, come, Sir.

HORNER. I must beg your pardon, Sir, and theirs, I will not be seen in Womens Company in publick again for the World.

heard: herd.

SIR JASPAR. Ha, ha, strange Aversion!

SQUEAMISH. No, he's for Womens company in private.

SIR JASPAR. He—poor Man—he! hah, ha, ha.

DAINTY. 'Tis a greater shame amongst lew'd fellows to be seen in virtuous Womens company, than for the Women to be seen with them.

HORNER. Indeed, Madam, the time was I only hated virtuous Women, but now I hate the other too; I beg your pardon Ladies.

LADY FIDGET. You are very obliging, Sir, because we wou'd not be troubled with you.

SIR JASPAR. In sober sadness he shall go.

DORILANT. Nay, if he wo'not, I am ready to wait upon the Ladies; and I think I am the fitter Man.

SIR JASPAR. You, Sir, no I thank you for that—Master *Horner* is a privileg'd Man amongst the virtuous Ladies, 'twill be a great while before you are so; heh, he, he, he's my Wive's Gallant, heh, he, he; no pray withdraw, Sir, for as I take it, the virtuous Ladies have no business with you.

DORILANT. And I am sure, he can have none with them: 'tis strange a Man can't come amongst virtuous Women now, but upon the same terms, as Men are admitted into the great Turks Seraglio; but Heavens keep me, from being an hombre Player with'em: but where is *Pinchwife*— [*Exit* DORILANT.

SIR JASPAR. Come, come, Man; what avoid the sweet society of Woman-kind? that sweet, soft, gentle, tame, noble Creature Woman, made for Man's Companion—

HORNER. So is that soft, gentle, tame, and more noble Creature a Spaniel, and has all their tricks, can fawn, lye down, suffer beating, and fawn the more; barks at your Friends, when they come to see you; makes your bed hard, gives you Fleas, and the mange some-

hombre Player: Ombre was a fashionable card game, and the tame male companions of the ladies, as the next few speeches indicate, were expected to play cards with them. This game, however, gives Dorilant a chance for a double entendre: to say that he does not want to play at being a man with them.

times: and all the difference is, the Spaniel's the more
faithful Animal, and fawns but upon one Master.

SIR JASPAR. Heh, he, he.

SQUEAMISH. O the rude Beast.

DAINTY. Insolent brute.

LADY FIDGET. Brute! stinking mortify'd rotten French
Weather, to dare—

SIR JASPAR. Hold, an't please your Ladyship; for shame
Master, *Horner* your Mother was a Woman— [Now
shall I never reconcile'em]   [*Aside.*
Hark you, Madam, take my advice in your anger; you
know you often want one to make up your droling
pack of hombre Players; and you may cheat him easily,
for he's an ill Gamester, and consequently loves play:
Besides you know, you have but two old civil Gentlemen (with stinking breaths too) to wait upon you
abroad, take in the third, into your service; the other
are but crazy: and a Lady shou'd have a supernumerary
Gentleman-Usher, as a supernumerary Coach-horse,
least sometimes you shou'd be forc'd to stay at home.

LADY FIDGET. But are you sure he loves play, and has
money?

SIR JASPAR. He loves play as much as you, and has money
as much as I.

LADY FIDGET. Then I am contented to make him pay for
his scurrillity; money makes up in a measure all other
wants in Men.— Those whom we cannot make hold for
Gallants, we make fine.   [*Aside.*

SIR JASPAR. So, so; now to mollify, to wheedle him,—
                                                    [*Aside.*

Master *Horner* will you never keep civil Company, methinks 'tis time now, since you are only fit for them:
Come, come, Man you must e'en fall to visiting our

Weather: wether.
droling: drolling, clownish.
crazy: broken down, frail,
sickly.
Usher: male attendant for a
lady.
fine: pay the penalty. The
phrase was used particularly
in cases in which men paid
to avoid the duties of an
office, which makes it particularly appropriate here,
considering the one duty of a
gallant that Horner presumably cannot carry out.

Wives, eating at our Tables, drinking Tea with our virtuous Relations after dinner, dealing Cards to'em, reading Plays, and Gazets to'em, picking Fleas out of their shocks for'em, collecting Receipts, New Songs, Women, Pages, and Footmen for'em.

HORNER. I hope they'l afford me better employment, Sir.

SIR JASPAR. Heh, he, he, 'tis fit you know your work before you come into your place; and since you are unprovided of a Lady to flatter, and a good house to eat at, pray frequent mine, and call my Wife Mistriss, and she shall call you Gallant, according to the custom.

HORNER. Who I?—

SIR JASPAR. Faith, thou sha't for my sake, come for my sake only.

HORNER. For your sake—

SIR JASPAR. Come, come, here's a Gamester for you, let him be a little familiar sometimes; nay, what if a little rude; Gamesters may be rude with Ladies, you know.

LADY FIDGET. Yes, losing Gamesters have a privilege with Women.

HORNER. I alwayes thought the contrary, that the winning Gamester had most privilege with Women, for when you have lost your money to a Man, you'l loose any thing you have, all you have, they say, and he may use you as he pleases.

SIR JASPAR. Heh, he, he, well, win or loose you shall have your liberty with her.

LADY FIDGET. As he behaves himself; and for your sake I'll give him admittance and freedom.

HORNER. All sorts of freedom, Madam?

SIR JASPAR. Ay, ay, ay, all sorts of freedom thou can'st take, and so go to her, begin thy new employment; wheedle her, jest with her, and be better acquainted one with another.

HORNER. I think I know her already, therefore may venter with her, my secret for hers—   [*Aside.*

[HORNER, *and Lady* FIDGET *whisper.*

SIR JASPAR. Sister *Cuz,* I have provided an innocent Play-fellow for you there.

DAINTY. Who he!

SQUEAMISH. There's a Play-fellow indeed.

SIR JASPAR. Yes sure, what he is good enough to play at Cards, Blind-mans buff, or the fool with sometimes.

SQUEAMISH. Foh, we'l have no such Play-fellows.

DAINTY. No, Sir, you shan't choose Play-fellows for us, we thank you.

SIR JASPAR. Nay, pray hear me. [*Whispering to them.*

LADY FIDGET. But, poor Gentleman, cou'd you be so generous? so truly a Man of honour, as for the sakes of us Women of honour, to cause your self to be reported no Man? No Man! and to suffer your self the greatest shame that cou'd fall upon a Man, that none might fall upon us Women by your conversation; but indeed, Sir, as perfectly, perfectly, the same Man as before your going into *France*, Sir; as perfectly, perfectly, Sir.

HORNER. As perfectly, perfectly, Madam; nay, I scorn you shou'd take my word; I desire to be try'd only, Madam.

LADY FIDGET. Well, that's spoken again like a Man of honour, all Men of honour desire to come to the test: But indeed, generally you Men report such things of your selves, one does not know how, or whom to believe; and it is come to that pass, we dare not take your words, no more than your Taylors, without some staid Servant of yours be bound with you; but I have so strong a faith in your honour, dear, dear, noble Sir, that I'd forfeit mine for yours at any time, dear Sir.

HORNER. No, Madam, you shou'd not need to forfeit it for me, I have given you security already to save you harmless my late reputation being so well known in the World, Madam.

LADY FIDGET. But if upon any future falling out, or upon a suspition of my taking the trust out of your hands, to employ some other, you your self shou'd betray your trust, dear Sir; I mean, if you'l give me leave to speak obscenely, you might tell, dear Sir.

HORNER. If I did, no body wou'd believe me; the reputation of impotency is as hardly recover'd again in the World, as that of cowardise, dear Madam.

LADY FIDGET. Nay then, as one may say, you may do your worst, dear, dear, Sir.

SIR JASPAR. Come, is your Ladyship reconciled to him yet? have you agreed on matters? for I must be gone to *Whitehal.*

LADY FIDGET. Why, indeed, Sir *Jaspar,* Master *Horner* is a thousand, thousand times a better Man, than I thought him: Cosen *Squeamish,* Sister *Dainty,* I can name him now, truly not long ago you know, I thought his very name obscenity, and I wou'd as soon have lain with him, as have nam'd him.

SIR JASPAR. Very likely, poor Madam.

DAINTY. I believe it.

SQUEAMISH. No doubt on't.

SIR JASPAR. Well, well—that your Ladyship is as virtuous as any she,—I know, and him all the Town knows—heh, he, he; therefore now you like him, get you gone to your business together; go, go, to your business, I say, pleasure, whilst I go to my pleasure, business.

LADY FIDGET. Come then dear Gallant.

HORNER. Come away, my dearest Mistriss.

SIR JASPAR. So, so, why 'tis as I'd have it. [*Exit Sir* JASPAR.

HORNER. And as I'd have it.

LADY FIDGET.
　　Who for his business, from his Wife will run;
　　Takes the best care, to have her bus'ness done.
　　　　　　　　　　　　　　　　　　　　[*Exeunt omnes.*

ACT 3. SCENE 1.

ALITHEA, *and Mrs.* PINCHWIFE.

ALITHEA. Sister, what ailes you, you are grown melancholy?

MRS. PINCHWIFE. Wou'd it not make any one melancholy, to see you go every day fluttering about abroad, whil'st I must stay at home like a poor lonely, sullen Bird in a cage?

ALITHEA. Ay, Sister, but you came young, and just from the nest to your cage, so that I thought you lik'd it; and cou'd be as chearful in't, as others that took their flight themselves early, and are hopping abroad in the open Air.

MRS. PINCHWIFE. Nay, I confess I was quiet enough, till my Husband told me, what pure lives, the *London* Ladies live abroad, with their dancing, meetings, and junketings, and drest every day in their best gowns; and I warrant you, play at nine Pins every day of the week, so they do.

Enter Mr. PINCHWIFE.

PINCHWIFE. Come, what's here to do? you are putting the Town pleasures in her head, and setting her a longing.

ALITHEA. Yes, after Nine-pins; you suffer none to give her those longings, you mean, but your self.

PINCHWIFE. I tell her of the vanities of the Town like a Confessor.

ALITHEA. A Confessor! just such a Confessor, as he that by forbidding a silly Oastler to grease the Horses teeth, taught him to do't.

PINCHWIFE. Come Mistriss *Flippant*, good Precepts are lost, when bad Examples are still before us; the liberty you take abroad makes her hanker after it; and out of humour at home, poor Wretch! she desired not to come to *London*, I wou'd bring her.

ALITHEA. Very well.

PINCHWIFE. She has been this week in Town, and never desired, till this afternoon, to go abroad.

ALITHEA. Was she not at a Play yesterday?

PINCHWIFE. Yes, but she ne'er ask'd me; I was my self the cause of her going.

ALITHEA. Then if she ask you again, you are the cause of her asking, and not my example.

PINCHWIFE. Well, to morrow night I shall be rid of you; and the next day before 'tis light, she and I'll be rid of the Town, and my dreadful apprehensions: Come, be not melancholly, for thou sha't go into the Country after to morrow, Dearest.

ALITHEA. Great comfort.

MRS. PINCHWIFE. Pish, what d'ye tell me of the Country for?

PINCHWIFE. How's this! what, pish at the Country?

MRS. PINCHWIFE. Let me alone, I am not well.

PINCHWIFE. O, if that be all—what ailes my dearest?

MRS. PINCHWIFE. Truly I don't know; but I have not been well, since you told me there was a Gallant at the Play in love with me.

PINCHWIFE. Ha—

ALITHEA. That's by my example too.

PINCHWIFE. Nay, if you are not well, but are so concern'd, because a lew'd Fellow chanc'd to lye, and say he lik'd you, you'l make me sick too.

MRS. PINCHWIFE. Of what sickness?

PINCHWIFE. O, of that which is worse than the Plague, Jealousy.

MRS. PINCHWIFE. Pish, you jear, I'm sure there's no such disease in our Receipt-book at home.

PINCHWIFE. No, thou never met'st with it, poor Innocent —well, if thou Cuckold me, 'twill be my own fault—for Cuckolds and Bastards, are generally makers of their own fortune.   [*Aside.*

MRS. PINCHWIFE. Well, but pray Bud, let's go to a Play to night.

PINCHWIFE. 'Tis just done, she comes from it; but why are you so eager to see a Play?

MRS. PINCHWIFE. Faith Dear, not that I care one pin for their talk there; but I like to look upon the Player-men, and wou'd see, if I cou'd, the Gallant you say loves me; that's all dear Bud.

PINCHWIFE. Is that all dear Bud?

ALITHEA. This proceeds from my example.

MRS. PINCHWIFE. But if the Play be done, let's go abroad however, dear Bud.

PINCHWIFE. Come have a little patience, and thou shalt go into the Country on Friday.

MRS. PINCHWIFE. Therefore I wou'd see first some sights, to tell my Neighbours of. Nay, I will go abroad, that's once.

ALITHEA. I'm the cause of this desire too.

PINCHWIFE. But now I think on't, who was the cause of *Horners* coming to my Lodging to day? that was you.

ALITHEA. No, you, because you wou'd not let him see your handsome Wife out of your Lodging.

MRS. PINCHWIFE. Why, O Lord! did the Gentleman come hither to see me indeed?

PINCHWIFE. No, no;— You are not cause of that damn'd question too, Mistriss *Alithea?*—[Well she's in the right of it; he is in love with my Wife—and comes after her—'tis so—but I'll nip his love in the bud; least he should follow us into the Country, and break his Chariot-wheel near our house, on purpose for an excuse to come to't; but I think I know the Town. [*Aside.*

MRS. PINCHWIFE. Come, pray Bud, let's go abroad before 'tis late; for I will go, that's flat and plain.

PINCHWIFE. So! the obstinacy already of a Town-wife, and I must, whilst she's here, humour her like one. [*Aside.* Sister, how shall we do, that she may not be seen, or known?

ALITHEA. Let her put on her Mask.

PINCHWIFE. Pshaw, a Mask makes People but the more inquisitive, and is as ridiculous a disguise, as a stage-beard; her shape, stature, habit will be known: and if we shou'd meet with *Horner,* he wou'd be sure to take acquaintance with us, must wish her joy, kiss her, talk to her, leer upon her, and the Devil and all; no I'll not use her to a Mask, 'tis dangerous; for Masks have made more Cuckolds, than the best faces that ever were known.

ALITHEA. How will you do then?

MRS. PINCHWIFE. Nay, shall we go? the *Exchange* will be shut, and I have a mind to see that.

PINCHWIFE. So—I have it—I'll dress her up in the Suit, we are to carry down to her Brother, little Sir *James;* nay, I understand the Town tricks: Come let's go dress her; a Mask! no—a Woman mask'd, like a cover'd Dish, gives a Man curiosity, and appetite, when, it may be, uncover'd, 'twou'd turn his stomack; no, no.

ALITHEA. Indeed your comparison is something a greasie

one: but I had a gentle Gallant, us'd to say, a Beauty mask'd, like the Sun in Eclipse, gathers together more gazers, than if it shin'd out.　　　　　　[*Exeunt.*

The Scene changes to the new Exchange: *Enter*
HORNER, HARCOURT, DORILANT.

DORILANT. Engag'd to Women, and not Sup with us?

HORNER. Ay, a Pox on'em all.

HARCOURT. You were much a more reasonable Man in the morning, and had as noble resolutions against'em, as a Widdower of a weeks liberty.

DORILANT. Did I ever think, to see you keep company with Women in vain.

HORNER. In vain! no—'tis, since I can't love'em, to be re-veng'd on'em.

HARCOURT. Now your Sting is gone, you look'd in the Box amongst all those Women, like a drone in the hive, all upon you; shov'd and ill-us'd by'em all, and thrust from one side to t'other.

DORILANT. Yet he must be buzzing amongst'em still, like other old beetle-headed, lycorish drones; avoid'em, and hate'em as they hate you.

HORNER. Because I do hate'em, and wou'd hate'em yet more, I'll frequent'em; you may see by Marriage, noth-ing makes a Man hate a Woman more, than her con-stant conversation: In short, I converse with'em, as you do with rich Fools, to laugh at'em, and use'em ill.

DORILANT. But I wou'd no more Sup with Women, unless I cou'd lye with'em, than Sup with a rich Coxcomb, unless I cou'd cheat him.

HORNER. Yes, I have known thee Sup with a Fool, for his drinking, if he cou'd set out your hand that way only, you were satisfy'd; and if he were a Wine-swallowing mouth 'twas enough.

HARCOURT. Yes, a Man drink's often with a Fool, as he

beetle-headed: block-headed. *set out* in the sense of "equip," "furnish." Churchill suggests (p. 183) that the line means that Dorilant will be satisfied if he is supplied with a glass instead of money or the means to get it (dice, cards) which he would hold if he cheated a rich fool.

tosses with a Marker, only to keep his hand in Ure; but do the Ladies drink?

HORNER. Yes, Sir, and I shall have the pleasure at least of laying 'em flat with a Bottle; and bring as much scandal that way upon 'em, as formerly t'other.

HARCOURT. Perhaps you may prove as weak a Brother amongst 'em that way, as t'other.

DORILANT. Foh, drinking with Women, is as unnatural, as scolding with 'em; but 'tis a pleasure of decay'd Fornicators, and the basest way of quenching Love.

HARCOURT. Nay, 'tis drowning Love, instead of quenching it; but leave us for civil Women too!

DORILANT. Ay, when he can't be the better for 'em; we hardly pardon a Man, that leaves his Friend for a Wench, and that's a pretty lawful call.

HORNER. Faith, I wou'd not leave you for 'em, if they wou'd not drink.

DORILANT. Who wou'd disappoint his Company at *Lewis's*,[1] for a Gossiping?

HARCOURT. Foh, Wine and Women good apart, together as nauseous as Sack and Sugar:[2] But hark you, Sir, before you go, a little of your advice, an old maim'd General, when unfit for action is fittest for Counsel; I have other designs upon Women, than eating and drinking with them: I am in love with *Sparkish's* Mistriss, whom he is to marry to morrow, now how shall I get her?

Enter SPARKISH, *looking about.*

HORNER. Why, here comes one will help you to her.

HARCOURT. He! he, I tell you, is my Rival, and will hinder my love.

HORNER. No, a foolish Rival, and a jealous Huband assist their Rivals designs; for they are sure to make their Women hate them, which is the first step to their love, for another Man.

HARCOURT. But I cannot come near his Mistriss, but in his company.

tosses with a Marker, . . . in Ure: plays with the scorekeeper for practice.

HORNER. Still the better for you, for Fools are most easily cheated, when they themselves are accessaries; and he is to be bubled of his Mistriss, as of his Money, the common Mistriss, by keeping him company.

SPARKISH. Who is that, that is to be bubled? Faith let me snack, I han't met with a buble since Christmas: gad; I think bubles are like their Brother Woodcocks, go out with the cold weather.

HARCOURT. A Pox, he did not hear all I hope.

[*Apart to* HORNER.

SPARKISH. Come, you bubling Rogues you, where do we sup— Oh, *Harcourt,* my Mistriss tells me, you have been making fierce love to her all the Play long, hah, ha— but I—

HARCOURT. I make love to her?

SPARKISH. Nay, I forgive thee; for I think I know thee, and I know her, but I am sure I know my self.

HARCOURT. Did she tell you so? I see all Women are like these of the *Exchange,* who to enhance the price of their commodities, report to their fond Customers offers which were never made'em.

HORNER. Ay, Women are as apt to tell before the intrigue, as Men after it, and so shew themselves the vainer Sex; but hast thou a Mistriss, *Sparkish?* 'tis as hard for me to believe it, as that thou ever hadst a buble, as you brag'd just now.

SPARKISH. O your Servant, Sir; are you at your raillery, Sir? but we were some of us beforehand with you to day at the Play: the Wits were something bold with you, Sir; did you not hear us laugh?

HARCOURT. Yes, But I thought you had gone to Plays, to laugh at the Poets wit, not at your own.

SPARKISH. Your Servant, Sir, no I thank you; gad I go to a Play as to a Country-treat, I carry my own wine to one, and my own wit to t'other, or else I'm sure I shou'd not be merry at either; and the reason why we are so often lowder, than the Players, is, because we think we speak more wit, and so become the Poets Rivals in his

snack: share.

audience: for to tell you the truth, we hate the silly Rogues; nay, so much that we find fault even with their Bawdy upon the Stage, whilst we talk nothing else in the Pit as lowd.

HORNER. But, why should'st thou hate the silly Poets, thou hast too much wit to be one, and they like Whores are only hated by each other; and thou dost scorn writing, I'am sure.

SPARKISH. Yes, I'd have you to know, I scorn writing; but Women, Women, that make Men do all foolish things, make'em write Songs too; every body does it: 'tis ev'n as common with Lovers, as playing with fans; and you can no more help Rhyming to your *Phyllis*, than drinking to your *Phyllis*.[3]

HARCOURT. Nay, Poetry in love is no more to be avoided, than jealousy.

DORILANT. But the Poets damn'd your Songs, did they?

SPARKISH. Damn the Poets, they turn'd'em into Burlesque, as they call it; that Burlesque is a *Hocus-Pocus*-trick, they have got, which by the virtue of *Hictius doctius, topsey turvey*, they make a wise and witty Man in the World, a Fool upon the Stage you know not how; and 'tis therefore I hate'em too, for I know not but it may be my own case; for they'l put a Man into a Play for looking a Squint: Their Predecessors were contented to make Serving-men only their Stage-Fools, but these Rogues must have Gentlemen, with a Pox to'em, nay Knights: and indeed you shall hardly see a Fool upon the Stage, but he's a Knight; and to tell you the truth, they have kept me these six years from being a Knight in earnest, for fear of being knighted in a Play, and dubb'd a Fool.

DORILANT. Blame'em not, they must follow their Copy, the Age.

HARCOURT. But why should'st thou be afraid of being in a Play, who expose your self every day in the Play-houses, and as publick Places.

Hictius doctius: term used by jugglers.

HORNER. 'Tis but being on the Stage, instead of standing on a Bench in the Pit.

DORILANT. Don't you give money to Painters to draw you like? and are you afraid of your Pictures, at length in a Play-house, where all your Mistresses may see you.

SPARKISH. A Pox, Painters don't draw the Small Pox, or Pimples in ones face; come damn all your silly Authors whatever, all Books and Booksellers, by the World, and all Readers, courteous or uncourteous.

HARCOURT. But, who comes here, *Sparkish?*

Enter Mr. PINCHWIFE, *and his Wife in Mans Cloaths,*
ALITHEA, LUCY *her Maid.*

SPARKISH. Oh hide me, there's my Mistriss too.

[SPARKISH *hides himself behind* HARCOURT.

HARCOURT. She sees you.

SPARKISH. But I will not see her, 'tis time to go to *Whitehal,* and I must not fail the drawing Room.

HARCOURT. Pray, first carry me, and reconcile me to her.

SPARKISH. Another time, faith the King will have sup't.[4]

HARCOURT. Not with the worse stomach for thy absence; thou art one of those Fools, that think their attendance at the King's Meals, as necessary as his Physicians, when you are more troublesom to him, than his Doctors, or his Dogs.

SPARKISH. Pshaw, I know my interest, Sir, prethee hide me.

HORNER. Your Servant, *Pinchwife,*—what he knows us not—

PINCHWIFE. Come along. [*To his Wife aside.*

MRS. PINCHWIFE. Pray, have you any Ballads, give me sixpenny worth?

CLASP.[5] We have no Ballads.

MRS. PINCHWIFE. Then give me *Covent-garden*-Drollery, and a Play or two— Oh here's *Tarugos* Wiles, and the Slighted Maiden, I'll have them.[6]

PINCHWIFE. No, Playes are not for your reading; come along, will you discover your self? [*Apart to her.*

HORNER. Who is that pretty Youth with him, *Sparkish?*

SPARKISH. I believe his Wife's Brother, because he's something like her, but I never saw her but once.

HORNER. Extreamly handsom, I have seen a face like it too; let us follow'em.

> [*Exeunt* PINCHWIFE, *Mistriss* PINCHWIFE. ALITHEA,
> LUCY, HORNER, DORILANT *following them.*

HARCOURT. Come, *Sparkish,* your Mistriss saw you, and will be angry you go not to her; besides I wou'd fain be reconcil'd to her, which none but you can do, dear Friend.

SPARKISH. Well that's a better reason, dear Friend; I wou'd not go near her now, for her's, or my own sake, but I can deny you nothing; for though I have known thee a great while, never go, if I do not love thee, as well as a new Acquaintance.

HARCOURT. I am oblig'd to you indeed, dear Friend, I wou'd be well with her only, to be well with thee still; for these tyes to Wives usually dissolve all tyes to Friends: I wou'd be contented, she shou'd enjoy you a nights, but I wou'd have you to my self a dayes, as I have had, dear Friend.

SPARKISH. And thou shalt enjoy me a dayes, dear, dear Friend, never stir; and I'll be divorced from her, sooner than from thee; come along—

HARCOURT. So we are hard put to't, when we make our Rival our Procurer; but neither she, nor her Brother, wou'd let me come near her now: when all's done, a Rival is the best cloak to steal to a Mistress under, without suspicion; and when we have once got to her as we desire, we throw him off like other Cloaks.   [*Aside.*

> [*Exit* SPARKISH, *and* HARCOURT *following him.*
> *Re-enter* Mr. PINCHWIFE, *Mistress* PINCHWIFE *in*
> *Man's Cloaths.*

PINCHWIFE. Sister, if you will not go, we must leave you—
                                        [*To* ALITHEA.[7]
The Fool her Gallant, and she, will muster up all the young santerers of this place, and they will leave their dear Seamstresses to follow us; what a swarm of Cuckolds, and Cuckold-makers are here?   [*Aside.*
Come let's be gone Mistriss *Margery.*

MRS. PINCHWIFE. Don't you believe that, I han't half my belly full of sights yet.

PINCHWIFE. Then walk this way.

MRS. PINCHWIFE. Lord, what a power of brave signs are here! stay—the Bull's-head, the Rams-head, and the Stags-head, Dear—

PINCHWIFE. Nay, if every Husbands proper sign here were visible, they wou'd be all alike.

MRS. PINCHWIFE. What d'ye mean by that, Bud?

PINCHWIFE. 'Tis no matter—no matter, Bud.

MRS. PINCHWIFE. Pray tell me; nay, I will know.

PINCHWIFE. They wou'd be all Bulls, Stags, and Rams heads.   [*Exeunt Mr.* PINCHWIFE, *Mrs.* PINCHWIFE.
  Re-enter SPARKISH, HARCOURT, ALITHEA, LUCY,
  at t'other door.[8]

SPARKISH. Come, dear Madam, for my sake you shall be reconciled to him.

ALITHEA. For your sake I hate him.

HARCOURT. That's something too cruel, Madam, to hate me for his sake.

SPARKISH. Ay indeed, Madam, too, too cruel to me, to hate my Friend for my sake.

ALITHEA. I hate him because he is your Enemy; and you ought to hate him too, for making love to me, if you love me.

SPARKISH. That's a good one, I hate a Man for loving you; if he did love you, 'tis but what he can't help, and 'tis your fault not his, if he admires you: I hate a Man for being of my opinion, I'll ne'er do't, by the World.

ALITHEA. Is it for your honour or mine, to suffer a Man to make love to me, who am to marry you to morrow?

SPARKISH. Is it for your honour or mine, to have me jealous? That he makes love to you, is a sign you are handsome; and that I am not jealous, is a sign you are virtuous, that I think is for your honour.

ALITHEA. But 'tis your honour too, I am concerned for.

HARCOURT. But why, dearest Madam, will you be more concern'd for his honour, than he is himself; let his honour alone for my sake, and his,[9] he, he, has no honour—

SPARKISH. How's that?

HARCOURT. But what, my dear Friend can guard himself.

SPARKISH. O ho—that's right again.

HARCOURT. Your care of his honour argues his neglect of it, which is no honour to my dear Friend here; therefore once more, let his honour go which way it will, dear Madam.

SPARKISH. Ay, ay, were it for my honour to marry a Woman, whose virtue I suspected, and cou'd not trust her in a Friends hands?

ALITHEA. Are you not afraid to loose me?

HARCOURT. He afraid to loose you, Madam! No, no—you may see how the most estimable, and most glorious Creature in the World, is valued by him; will you not see it?

SPARKISH. Right, honest *Franck*, I have that noble value for her, that I cannot be jealous of her.

ALITHEA. You mistake him, he means you care not for me, nor who has me.

SPARKISH. Lord, Madam, I see you are jealous; will you wrest a poor Mans meaning from his words?

ALITHEA. You astonish me, Sir, with your want of jealousie.

SPARKISH. And you make me guiddy, Madam, with your jealousie, and fears, and virtue, and honour; gad, I see virtue makes a Woman as troublesome, as a little reading, or learning.

ALITHEA. Monstrous!

LUCY. [Well to see what easie Husbands these Women of quality can meet with, a poor Chamber-maid can never have such Lady-like luck; besides he's thrown away upon her, she'l make no use of her fortune, her blessing, none to a Gentleman, for a pure Cuckold, for it requires good breeding to be a Cuckold. [*Behind.*

ALITHEA. I tell you then plainly, he pursues me to marry me.

SPARKISH. Pshaw—

HARCOURT. Come, Madam, you see you strive in vain to make him jealous of me; my dear Friend is the kindest Creature in the World to me.

---

jealous: vehement in feeling. Alithea uses the word in its more conventional meaning; the two meanings give Wych- erley a chance for the kind of echo effect of which he is so fond.

SPARKISH. Poor fellow.

HARCOURT. But his kindness only is not enough for me, without your favour; your good opinion, dear Madam, 'tis that must perfect my happiness: good Gentleman he believes all I say, wou'd you wou'd do so, jealous of me! I wou'd not wrong him nor you for the World.

SPARKISH. Look you there; hear him, hear him, and do not walk away so.   [ALITHEA *walks carelessly, to and fro.*

HARCOURT. I love you, Madam, so—

SPARKISH. How's that! Nay—now you begin to go too far indeed.

HARCOURT. So much I confess, I say I love you, that I wou'd not have you miserable, and cast your self away upon so unworthy, and inconsiderable a thing, as what you see here.

   [*Clapping his hand on his breast, points at* SPARKISH.

SPARKISH. No faith, I believe thou woud'st not, now his meaning is plain: but I knew before thou woud'st not wrong me nor her.

HARCOURT. No, no, Heavens forbid, the glory of her Sex shou'd fall so low as into the embraces of such a contemptible Wretch, the last of Mankind—my dear Friend here—I injure him.   [*Embracing* SPARKISH.

ALITHEA. Very well.

SPARKISH. No, no, dear Friend, I knew it Madam, you see he will rather wrong himself than me, in giving himself such names.

ALITHEA. Do not you understand him yet?

SPARKISH. Yes, how modestly he speaks of himself, poor Fellow.

ALITHEA. Methinks he speaks impudently of your self, since—before your self too, insomuch that I can no longer suffer his scurrilous abusiveness to you, no more than his love to me.   [*Offers to go.*

SPARKISH. Nay, nay, Madam, pray stay, his love to you: Lord, Madam, has he not spoke yet plain enough?

ALITHEA. Yes indeed, I shou'd think so.

SPARKISH. Well then, by the World, a Man can't speak civilly to a Woman now, but presently she says, he makes love to her: Nay, Madam, you shall stay, with your pardon, since you have not yet understood him, till he has made an eclaircisment of his love to you, that is what kind of love it is; answer to thy Catechisme: Friend, do you love my Mistriss here?

HARCOURT. Yes, I wish she wou'd not doubt it.

SPARKISH. But how do you love her?

HARCOURT. With all my Soul.

ALITHEA. I thank him, methinks he speaks plain enough now.

SPARKISH. You are out still.   [*to* ALITHEA.
But with what kind of love, *Harcourt?*

HARCOURT. With the best, and truest love in the World.

SPARKISH. Look you there then, that is with no matrimonial love, I'm sure.

ALITHEA. How's that, do you say matrimonial love is not best?

SPARKISH. Gad, I went too far e're I was aware:[10] But speak for thy self *Harcourt,* you said you wou'd not wrong me, nor her.

HARCOURT. No, no, Madam, e'n take him for Heaven's sake.

SPARKISH. Look you there, Madam.

HARCOURT. Who shou'd in all justice be yours, he that loves you most.   [*Claps his hand on his breast.*

ALITHEA. Look you there, Mr. *Sparkish,* who's that?

SPARKISH. Who shou'd it be? go on *Harcourt.*

HARCOURT. Who loves you more than Women, Titles, or fortune Fools.   [*Points at* SPARKISH.

SPARKISH. Look you there, he means me stil, for he points at me.

ALITHEA. Ridiculous!

HARCOURT. Who can only match your Faith, and constancy in love.

SPARKISH. Ay.

HARCOURT. Who knows, if it be possible, how to value so much beauty and virtue.

SPARKISH. Ay.

HARCOURT. Whose love can no more be equall'd in the world, than that Heavenly form of yours.

SPARKISH. No—

HARCOURT. Who cou'd no more suffer a Rival, than your absence, and yet cou'd no more suspect your virtue, than his own constancy in his love to you.

SPARKISH. No—

HARCOURT. Who in fine loves you better than his eyes, that first made him love you.

SPARKISH. Ay—nay, Madam, faith you shan't go, till—

ALITHEA. Have a care, lest you make me stay too long—

SPARKISH. But till he has saluted you; that I may be assur'd you are friends, after his honest advice and declaration: Come pray, Madam, be friends with him.

Enter Master PINCHWIFE, *Mistriss* PINCHWIFE.

ALITHEA. You must pardon me, Sir, that I am not yet so obedient to you.

PINCHWIFE. What, invite your Wife to kiss Men? Monstrous, are you not asham'd? I will never forgive you.

SPARKISH. Are you not asham'd, that I shou'd have more confidence in the chastity of your Family, than you have; you must not teach me, I am a man of honour, Sir, though I am frank and free; I am frank, Sir—

PINCHWIFE. Very frank, Sir, to share your Wife with your friends.

SPARKISH. He is an humble, menial Friend, such as reconciles the differences of the Marriage-bed; you know Man and Wife do not alwayes agree, I design him for that use, therefore wou'd have him well with my Wife.

PINCHWIFE. A menial Friend—you will get a great many menial Friends, by shewing your Wife as you do.

SPARKISH. What then, it may be I have a pleasure in't, as I have to shew fine Clothes, at a Play-house the first day, and count money before poor Rogues.

PINCHWIFE. He that shews his wife, or money will be in danger of having them borrowed sometimes.

SPARKISH. I love to be envy'd, and wou'd not marry a Wife, that I alone cou'd love; loving alone is as dull, as eating alone; is it not a frank age, and I am a frank Person? and to tell you the truth, it may be I love to

frank and free: frank here means "free" in all its senses; as the wordplay continues,

Sparkish uses *frank* to mean "open," "candid"; Pinchwife, to mean "generous."

have Rivals in a Wife, they make her seem to a Man still, but as a kept Mistriss; and so good night, for I must to *Whitehal*. Madam, I hope you are now reconcil'd to my Friend; and so I wish you a good night, Madam, and sleep if you can, for to morrow you know I must visit you early with a Canonical Gentleman. Good night dear *Harcourt*.   [*Exit* SPARKISH.

HARCOURT. Madam, I hope you will not refuse my visit to morrow, if it shou'd be earlyer, with a Canonical Gentleman, than Mr. *Sparkish*'s.

PINCHWIFE. This Gentle-woman is yet under my care, therefore you must yet forbear your freedom with her, Sir.   [*Coming between* ALITHEA *and* HARCOURT.

HARCOURT. Must, Sir—

PINCHWIFE. Yes, Sir, she is my Sister.

HARCOURT. 'Tis well she is, Sir—for I must be her Servant, Sir. Madam—

PINCHWIFE. Come away Sister, we had been gone, if it had not been for you, and so avoided these lewd Rakehells, who seem to haunt us.

> *Enter* HORNER, DORILANT *to them.*

HORNER. How now *Pinchwife?*

PINCHWIFE. Your Servant.[11]

HORNER. What, I see a little time in the Country makes a Man turn wild and unsociable, and only fit to converse with his Horses, Dogs, and his Herds.

PINCHWIFE. I have business, Sir, and must mind it; your business is pleasure, therefore you and I must go different wayes.

HORNER. Well, you may go on, but this pretty young Gen-tleman—   [*Takes hold of Mrs.* PINCHWIFE.

HARCOURT. The Lady—

DORILANT. And the Maid—

HORNER. Shall stay with us, for I suppose their business is the same with ours, pleasure.

PINCHWIFE. 'Sdeath he knows her, she carries it so sillily, yet if he does not, I shou'd be more silly to discover it first.   [*Aside.*

ALITHEA. Pray, let us go, Sir.

PINCHWIFE. Come, come—

HORNER. Had you not rather stay with us?

[*to Mrs.* PINCHWIFE.

Prethee *Pinchwife*, who is this pretty young Gentleman?

PINCHWIFE. One to whom I'm a guardian.

[I wish I cou'd keep her out of your hands—   [*Aside.*

HORNER. Who is he? I never saw any thing so pretty in all my life.

PINCHWIFE. Pshaw, do not look upon him so much, he's a poor bashful youth, you'l put him out of countenance. Come away Brother.   [*Offers to take her away.*

HORNER. O your Brother!

PINCHWIFE. Yes, my Wifes Brother; come, come, she'l stay supper for us.

HORNER. I thought so, for he is very like her I saw you at the Play with, whom I told you, I was in love with.

MRS. PINCHWIFE. O Jeminy! is this he that was in love with me, I am glad on't I vow, for he's a curious fine Gentleman, and I love him already too.   [*Aside.*
Is this he Bud?   [*to Mr.* PINCHWIFE.

PINCHWIFE. Come away, come away.   [*To his Wife.*

HORNER. Why, what hast are you in? why wont you let me talk with him?

PINCHWIFE. Because you'l debauch him, he's yet young and innocent, and I wou'd not have him debauch'd for any thing in the World.
How she gazes on him! the Divel—   [*Aside.*

HORNER. *Harcourt, Dorilant*, look you here, this is the likeness of that Dowdey he told us of, his Wife, did you ever see a lovelyer Creature? the Rogue has reason to be jealous of his Wife, since she is like him, for she wou'd make all that see her, in love with her.

HARCOURT. And as I remember now, she is as like him here as can be.

DORILANT. She is indeed very pretty, if she be like him.

HORNER. Very pretty, a very pretty commendation—she is a glorious Creature, beautiful beyond all things I ever beheld.

PINCHWIFE. So, so.

HARCOURT. More beautiful than a Poets first Mistriss of Imagination.

HORNER. Or another Mans last Mistriss of flesh and blood.

MRS. PINCHWIFE. Nay, now you jeer, Sir; pray don't jeer me—

PINCHWIFE. Come, come. [By Heavens she'l discover her self.   [Aside.

HORNER. I speak of your Sister, Sir.

PINCHWIFE. Ay, but saying she was handsom, if like him, made him blush. [I am upon a wrack—   [Aside.

HORNER. Methinks he is so handsom, he shou'd not be a Man.

PINCHWIFE. O there 'tis out, he has discovered her, I am not able to suffer any longer.
[Come, come away, I say—   [To his Wife.

HORNER. Nay, by your leave, Sir, he shall not go yet—
Harcourt, Dorilant, let us torment this jealous Rogue a little.   [To them.

HARCOURT. } How?
DORILANT. }

HORNER. I'll shew you.

PINCHWIFE. Come, pray let him go, I cannot stay fooling any longer; I tell you his Sister stays supper for us.

HORNER. Do's she, come then we'l all go sup with her and thee.

PINCHWIFE. No, now I think on't, having staid so long for us, I warrant she's gone to bed— [I wish she and I were well out of their hands—   [Aside.
Come, I must rise early to morrow, come.

HORNER. Well then, if she be gone to bed, I wish her and you a good night. But pray, young Gentleman, present my humble service to her.

MRS. PINCHWIFE. Thank you heartily, Sir.

PINCHWIFE. S'death, she will discover her self yet in spight of me.   [Aside.
He is something more civil to you, for your kindness to his Sister, than I am, it seems.

HORNER. Tell her, dear sweet little Gentleman, for all your Brother there, that you have reviv'd the love, I had for her at first sight in the Play-house.

MRS. PINCHWIFE. But did you love her indeed, and indeed?

PINCHWIFE. So, so. [*Aside.*
Away, I say.

HORNER. Nay stay; yes indeed, and indeed, pray do you tell her so, and give her this kiss from me. [*Kisses her.*

PINCHWIFE. O Heavens! what do I suffer; now 'tis too plain he knows her, and yet— [*Aside.*

HORNER. And this, and this— [*Kisses her again.*

MRS. PINCHWIFE. What do you kiss me for, I am no Woman.

PINCHWIFE. So—there 'tis out. [*Aside.*
Come, I cannot, nor will stay any longer.

HORNER. Nay, they shall send your Lady a kiss too; here *Harcourt, Dorilant,* will you not? [*They kiss her.*

PINCHWIFE. How, do I suffer this? was I not accusing another just now, for this rascally patience, in permitting his Wife to be kiss'd before his face? ten thousand ulcers gnaw away their lips. [*Aside.*
Come, come.

HORNER. Good night dear little Gentleman; Madam goodnight; farewel *Pinchwife.* [Did not I tell you, I wou'd raise his jealous gall. [*Apart to* HARCOURT *and* DORILANT.
[*Exeunt* HORNER, HARCOURT, *and* DORILANT.

PINCHWIFE. So they are gone at last; stay, let me see first if the Coach be at this door. [*Exit.*

HORNER. What not gone yet? will you be sure to do as I desired you, sweet Sir?
[HORNER, HARCOURT, DORILANT *return.*

MRS. PINCHWIFE. Sweet Sir, but what will you give me then?

HORNER. Any thing, come away into the next walk.
[*Exit* HORNER, *haling away Mrs.* PINCHWIFE.

ALITHEA. Hold, hold,—what d'ye do?

LUCY. Stay, stay, hold—

HARCOURT. Hold Madam, hold, let him present him, he'l come presently; nay, I will never let you go, till you answer my question. [ALITHEA, LUCY *strugling*

LUCY. For God's sake, Sir, I must *with* HARCOURT,
follow'em. *and* DORILANT.

DORILANT. No, I have something to present you with too, you shan't follow them.

PINCHWIFE returns.

PINCHWIFE. Where?—how?—what's become of? gone—whither?

LUCY. He's only gone with the Gentleman, who will give him something, an't please your Worship.

PINCHWIFE. Something—give him something, with a Pox —where are they?

ALITHEA. In the next walk only, Brother.

PINCHWIFE. Only, only; where, where?

Exit PINCHWIFE, and returns presently, then goes out again.

HARCOURT. What's the matter with him? why so much concern'd? but dearest Madam—

ALITHEA. Pray, let me go, Sir, I have said, and suffer'd enough already.

HARCOURT. Then you will not look upon, nor pitty my sufferings?

ALITHEA. To look upon'em, when I cannot help'em, were cruelty, not pitty, therefore I will never see you more.

HARCOURT. Let me then, Madam, have my priviledge of a banished Lover, complaining or railing, and giving you but a farewell reason; why, if you cannot condescend to marry me, you shou'd not take that wretch my Rival.

ALITHEA. He only, not you, since my honour is engag'd so far to him, can give me a reason, why I shou'd not marry him; but if he be true, and what I think him to me, I must be so to him; your Servant, Sir.

HARCOURT. Have Women only constancy when 'tis a vice, and like fortune only true to fools?

DORILANT. Thou sha't not stir thou robust Creature, you see I can deal with you, therefore you shou'd stay the rather, and be kind.

[To LUCY, who struggles to get from him.
Enter PINCHWIFE.

PINCHWIFE. Gone, gone, not to be found; quite gone, ten thousand plagues go with'em; which way went they?

ALITHEA. But into t'other walk, Brother.

LUCY. Their business will be done presently sure, an't please your Worship, it can't be long in doing I'm sure on't.

ALITHEA. Are they not there?

PINCHWIFE. No, you know where they are, you infamous Wretch, Eternal shame of your Family, which you do not dishonour enough your self, you think, but you must help her to do it too, thou legion of Bawds.

ALITHEA. Good Brother.

PINCHWIFE. Damn'd, damn'd Sister.

ALITHEA. Look you here, she's coming.

Enter Mistriss PINCHWIFE *in Mans cloaths, running with her hat under her arm, full of Oranges and dried fruit,* HORNER *following.*

MRS. PINCHWIFE. O dear Bud, look you here what I have got, see.

PINCHWIFE. And what I have got here too, which you can't see. *[Aside rubbing his forehead.*

MRS. PINCHWIFE. The fine Gentleman has given me better things yet.

PINCHWIFE. Has he so? [Out of breath and colour'd— I must hold yet. *[Aside.*

HORNER. I have only given your little Brother an Orange, Sir.

PINCHWIFE. Thank you, Sir. *[To* HORNER. You have only squeez'd my Orange, I suppose, and given it me again; yet I must have a City-patience. *[Aside.* Come, come away— *[To his Wife.*

MRS. PINCHWIFE. Stay, till I have put up my fine things, Bud.

Enter Sir JASPAR FIDGET.

SIR JASPAR. O Master *Horner,* come, come, the Ladies stay for you; your Mistriss, my Wife, wonders you make not more hast to her.

HORNER. I have staid this half hour for you here, and 'tis your fault I am not now with your Wife.

SIR JASPAR. But pray, don't let her know so much, the

City-patience: the patience of a City husband who dares not admit openly that he knows himself a cuckold.

truth on't is, I was advancing a certain Project to his
Majesty, about—I'll tell you.

HORNER. No, let's go, and hear it at your house: Good
night sweet little Gentleman; one kiss more, you'l remember me now I hope.   [*Kisses her.*

DORILANT. What, Sir *Jaspar*, will you separate Friends?
he promis'd to sup with us; and if you take him to your
house, you'l be in danger of our company too.

SIR JASPAR. Alas Gentlemen my house is not fit for you,
there are none but civil Women there, which are not
for your turn; he you know can bear with the society
of civil Women, now, ha, ha, ha; besides he's one of
my Family;—he's—heh, heh, heh.

DORILANT. What is he?

SIR JASPAR. Faith my Eunuch, since you'l have it, heh,
he, he.   [*Exeunt*[12] *Sir* JASPAR FIDGET, *and* HORNER.

DORILANT. I rather wish thou wert his, or my Cuckold:
Harcourt, what a good Cuckold is lost there, for want
of a Man to make him one; thee and I cannot have
Horners privilege, who can make use of it.

HARCOURT. Ay, to poor *Horner* 'tis like coming to an
estate at threescore, when a Man can't be the better
for't.

PINCHWIFE. Come.

MRS. PINCHWIFE. Presently Bud.

DORILANT. Come let us go too: Madam, your Servant.
[*To* ALITHEA.] Good night Strapper.—   [*To* LUCY.

HARCOURT. Madam, though you will not let me have a
good day, or night, I wish you one; but dare not name
the other half of my wish.

ALITHEA. Good night, Sir, for ever.

MRS. PINCHWIFE. I don't know where to put this here,
dear Bud, you shall eat it; nay, you shall have part of
the fine Gentlemans good things, or treat as you call it,
when we come home.

PINCHWIFE. Indeed I deserve it, since I furnish'd the best
part of it.   [*Strikes away the Orange.*

The Gallant treates, presents, and gives the Ball;
But 'tis the absent Cuckold, pays for all.

In PINCHWIFE'S *house in the morning.*

LUCY, ALITHEA *dress'd in new Cloths.*

LUCY. Well—Madam, now have I dress'd you, and set you out with so many ornaments, and spent upon you ounces of essence, and pulvilio; and all this for no other purpose, but as People adorn, and perfume a Corps, for a stinking second-hand-grave, such or as bad I think Master *Sparkish*'s bed.

ALITHEA. Hold your peace.

LUCY. Nay, Madam, I will ask you the reason, why you wou'd banish poor Master *Harcourt* for ever from your sight? how cou'd you be so hard-hearted?

ALITHEA. 'Twas because I was not hard-hearted.

LUCY. No, no; 'twas stark love and kindness, I warrant.

ALITHEA. It was so; I wou'd see him no more, because I love him.

LUCY. Hey day, a very pretty reason.

ALITHEA. You do not understand me.

LUCY. I wish you may your self.

ALITHEA. I was engag'd to marry, you see, another man, whom my justice will not suffer me to deceive, or injure.

LUCY. Can there be a greater cheat, or wrong done to a Man, than to give him your person, without your heart, I shou'd make a conscience of it.

ALITHEA. I'll retrieve it for him after I am married a while.

LUCY. The Woman that marries to love better, will be as much mistaken, as the Wencher that marries to live better. No, Madam, marrying to encrease love, is like gaming to become rich; alas you only loose, what little stock you had before.

ALITHEA. I find by your Rhetorick you have been brib'd to betray me.

LUCY. Only by his merit, that has brib'd your heart you

pulvilio: a perfumed powder.   women apparently used it ad
Men used it on their wigs;   libitum.

see against your word, and rigid honour; but what a
Divel is this honour? 'tis sure a disease in the head, like
the Megrim, or Falling-sickness, that alwayes hurries
People away to do themselves mischief; Men loose
their lives by it: Women what's dearer to'em, their love,
the life of life.

ALITHEA. Come, pray talk you no more of honour, nor
Master *Harcourt;* I wish the other wou'd come, to secure my fidelity to him, and his right in me.

LUCY. You will marry him then?

ALITHEA. Certainly, I have given him already my word,
and will my hand too, to make it good when he comes.

LUCY. Well, I wish I may never stick pin more, if he be
not an errant Natural, to t'other fine Gentleman.

ALITHEA. I own he wants the wit of *Harcourt,* which I
will dispense withal, for another want he has, which is
want of jealousie, which men of wit seldom want.

LUCY. Lord, Madam, what shou'd you do with a fool to
your Husband, you intend to be honest don't you? then
that husbandly virtue, credulity, is thrown away upon
you.

ALITHEA. He only that could suspect my virtue, shou'd
have cause to do it; 'tis *Sparkish*'s confidence in my
truth, that obliges me to be so faithful to him.

LUCY. You are not sure his opinion may last.

ALITHEA. I am satisfied, 'tis impossible for him to be jealous, after the proofs I have had of him: Jealousie in a
Husband, Heaven defend me from it, it begets a thousand plagues to a poor Woman, the loss of her honour,
her quiet, and her—

LUCY. And her pleasure.

ALITHEA. What d'ye mean, Impertinent?

LUCY. Liberty is a great pleasure, Madam.

ALITHEA. I say loss of her honour, her quiet, nay, her life
sometimes; and what's as bad almost, the loss of this
Town, that is, she is sent into the Country, which is
the last ill usage of a Husband to a Wife, I think.

LUCY. O do's the wind lye there?   [*Aside.*
Then of necessity, Madam, you think a man must carry
his Wife into the Country, if he be wise; the Country

is as terrible I find to our young English Ladies, as a
Monastery to those abroad: and on my Virginity, I
think they wou'd rather marry a *London*-Goaler, than a
high Sheriff of a County, since neither can stir from his
employment: formerly Women of wit married Fools,
for a great Estate, a fine seat, or the like; but now 'tis
for a pretty seat only in *Lincoln's Inn-fields*, St. *James's-
fields*, or the *Pall-mall*.[1]

Enter to them SPARKISH, *and* HARCOURT
dress'd like a Parson.

SPARKISH. Madam, your humble Servant, a happy day to
you, and to us all.

HARCOURT. Amen.—

ALITHEA. Who have we here?

SPARKISH. My Chaplain faith—O Madam, poor *Harcourt*
remembers his humble service to you; and in obedience
to your last commands, refrains coming into your sight.

ALITHEA. Is not that he?

SPARKISH. No, fye no; but to shew that he ne're intended
to hinder our Match has sent his Brother here to joyn
our hands: when I get me a Wife, I must get her a
Chaplain, according to the Custom; this is his Brother,
and my Chaplain.

ALITHEA. His Brother?

LUCY. And your Chaplain, to preach in your Pulpit then—
[*Aside.*

ALITHEA. His Brother!

SPARKISH. Nay, I knew you wou'd not believe it; I told
you, Sir, she wou'd take you for your Brother *Frank*.

ALITHEA. Believe it!

LUCY. His Brother! hah, ha, he, he has a trick left still it
seems—   [*Aside.*

SPARKISH. Come my dearest, pray let us go to Church before the Canonical hour[2] is past.

ALITHEA. For shame you are abus'd still.

SPARKISH. By the World 'tis strange now you are so incredulous.

ALITHEA. 'Tis strange you are so credulous.

SPARKISH. Dearest of my life, hear me, I tell you this is
Ned Harcourt of *Cambridge*, by the world, you see he

has a sneaking Colledg look; 'tis true he's something like his Brother *Frank,* and they differ from each other no more than in their age, for they were Twins.

LUCY. Hah, ha, he.

ALITHEA. Your Servant, Sir, I cannot be so deceiv'd, though you are; but come let's hear, how do you know what you affirm so confidently?

SPARKISH. Why, I'll tell you all; *Frank Harcourt* coming to me this morning, to wish me joy and present his service to you: I ask'd him, if he cou'd help me to a Parson; whereupon he told me, he had a Brother in Town who was in Orders, and he went straight away, and sent him, you see there, to me.

ALITHEA. Yes, *Frank* goes, and puts on a black-coat, then tell's you, he is *Ned,* that's all you have for't.

SPARKISH. Pshaw, pshaw, I tell you by the same token, the Midwife put her Garter about *Frank's* neck, to know'em asunder, they were so like.

ALITHEA. *Frank* tell's you this too.

SPARKISH. Ay, and *Ned* there too; nay, they are both in a Story.

ALITHEA. So, so, very foolish.

SPARKISH. Lord, if you won't believe one, you had best trye him by your Chamber-maid there; for Chamber-maids must needs know Chaplains from other Men, they are so us'd to'em.

LUCY. Let's see; nay, I'll be sworn he has the Canonical smirk, and the filthy, clammy palm of a Chaplain.

ALITHEA. Well, most reverend Doctor, pray let us make an end of this fooling.

HARCOURT. With all my soul, Divine, Heavenly Creature, when you please.

ALITHEA. He speaks like a Chaplain indeed.

SPARKISH. Why, was there not, soul, Divine, Heavenly, in what he said.

ALITHEA. Once more, most impertinent Black-coat, cease your persecution, and let us have a Conclusion of this ridiculous love.

HARCOURT. I had forgot, I must sute my Stile to my Coat, or I wear it in vain.   [*Aside.*

ALITHEA. I have no more patience left, let us make once
an end of this troublesome Love, I say.

HARCOURT. So be it, Seraphick Lady, when your Honour
shall think it meet, and convenient so to do.

SPARKISH. Gad I'm sure none but a Chaplain cou'd speak
so, I think.

ALITHEA. Let me tell you Sir, this dull trick will not serve
your turn, though you delay our marriage, you shall
not hinder it.

HARCOURT. Far be it from me, Munificent Patroness, to delay your Marriage, I desire nothing more than to marry
you presently, which I might do, if you your self wou'd;
for my Noble, Good-natur'd and thrice Generous Patron
here wou'd not hinder it.

SPARKISH. No, poor man, not I faith.

HARCOURT. And now, Madam, let me tell you plainly, no
body else shall marry you by Heavens, I'll die first, for
I'm sure I shou'd die after it.

LUCY. How his Love has made him forget his Function,
as I have seen it in real Parsons.[3]

ALITHEA. That was spoken like a Chaplain too, now you
understand him, I hope.

SPARKISH. Poor man, he takes it hainously to be refus'd;
I can't blame him, 'tis putting an indignity upon him
not to be suffer'd, but you'l pardon me Madam, it shan't
be, he shall marry us, come away, pray Madam.

LUCY. Hah, ha, he, more ado! 'tis late.[4]

ALITHEA. Invincible stupidity, I tell you he wou'd marry
me, as your Rival, not as your Chaplain.

SPARKISH. Come, come Madam.   [*Pulling her away.*

LUCY. I pray Madam, do not refuse this Reverend Divine, the honour and satisfaction of marrying you; for
I dare say, he has set his heart upon't, good Doctor.

ALITHEA. What can you hope, or design by this?

HARCOURT. I cou'd answer her, a reprieve for a day only,
often revokes a hasty doom; at worst, if she will not
take mercy on me, and let me marry her, I have at least
the Lovers second pleasure, hindring my Rivals enjoyment, though but for a time.

SPARKISH. Come Madam, 'tis e'ne twelve a clock, and my Mother charg'd me never to be married out of the Canonical hours; come, come, Lord here's such a deal of modesty, I warrant the first day.

LUCY. Yes, an't please your Worship, married women shew all their Modesty the first day, because married men shew all their love the first day.

[*Exeunt* SPARKISH, ALITHEA, HARCOURT, *and* LUCY.

The Scene changes to a Bed-chamber, where appear
PINCHWIFE, *Mrs.* PINCHWIFE.

PINCHWIFE. Come tell me, I say.

MRS. PINCHWIFE. Lord, han't I told it an hundred times over.

PINCHWIFE. I wou'd try, if in the repetition of the ungrateful tale, I cou'd find her altering it in the least circumstance, for if her story be false, she is so too. [*Aside.* Come how was't Baggage?

MRS. PINCHWIFE. Lord, what pleasure you take to hear it sure!

PINCHWIFE. No, you take more in telling it I find, but speak how was't?

MRS. PINCHWIFE. He carried me up into the house, next to the Exchange.

PINCHWIFE. So, and you two were only in the room.

MRS. PINCHWIFE. Yes, for he sent away a youth that was there, for some dryed fruit, and China Oranges.

PINCHWIFE. Did he so? Damn him for it—and for—

MRS. PINCHWIFE. But presently came up the Gentlewoman of the house.

PINCHWIFE. O 'twas well she did, but what did he do whilst the fruit came?

MRS. PINCHWIFE. He kiss'd me an hundred times, and told me he fancied he kiss'd my fine Sister, meaning me you

---

e'ne twelve a clock: unless Sparkish is using "even" in an unusual way—to mean "almost"—he is saying that it is now twelve o'clock; he has missed his canonical hours.

China Oranges: the sweet orange, supposedly originally from China. This familiar seventeenth-century name is reflected in its scientific name: *Citrus sinensis.*

know, whom he said he lov'd with all his Soul, and bid
me be sure to tell her so, and to desire her to be at her
window, by eleven of the clock this morning, and he
wou'd walk under it at that time.

PINCHWIFE. And he was as good as his word, very punctual, a pox reward him for't.   [*Aside.*

MRS. PINCHWIFE. Well, and he said if you were not within,
he wou'd come up to her, meaning me you know,
Bud, still.

PINCHWIFE. So—he knew her certainly, but for this confession, I am oblig'd to her simplicity.   [*Aside.*
But what you stood very still, when he kiss'd you?

MRS. PINCHWIFE. Yes I warrant you, wou'd you have
had me discover'd my self?

PINCHWIFE. But you told me, he did some beastliness to
you, as you call'd it, what was't?

MRS. PINCHWIFE. Why, he put—

PINCHWIFE. What?

MRS. PINCHWIFE. Why he put the tip of his tongue between
my lips, and so musl'd me—and I said, I'd bite it.

PINCHWIFE. An eternal canker seize it, for a dog.

MRS. PINCHWIFE. Nay, you need not be so angry with him
neither, for to say truth, he has the sweetest breath I
ever knew.

PINCHWIFE. The Devil—you were satisfied with it then, and
wou'd do it again.

MRS. PINCHWIFE. Not unless he shou'd force me.

PINCHWIFE. Force you, changeling! I tell you no woman
can be forced.

MRS. PINCHWIFE. Yes, but she may sure, by such a one as
he, for he's a proper, goodly strong man, 'tis hard, let
me tell you, to resist him.

PINCHWIFE. So, 'tis plain she loves him, yet she has not
love enough to make her conceal it from me, but the
sight of him will increase her aversion for me, and love
for him; and that love instruct her how to deceive me,
and satisfie him, all Ideot as she is: Love, 'twas he gave
women first their craft, their art of deluding; out of
natures hands, they came plain, open, silly and fit for

slaves, as she and Heaven intended 'em; but damn'd
Love— Well— I must strangle that little Monster, whilest
I can deal with him.

Go fetch Pen, Ink and Paper out of the next room:

mrs. pinchwife. Yes Bud.   [*Exit Mrs.* pinchwife.

pinchwife. Why should Women have more invention in
love than men? It can only be, because they have more
desires, more sollicting passions, more lust, and more of
the Devil.   [*Aside.*

Mistris pinchwife *returns.*

Come, Minks, sit down and write.

mrs. pinchwife. Ay, dear Bud, but I can't do't very well.

pinchwife. I wish you cou'd not at all.

mrs. pinchwife. But what shou'd I write for?

pinchwife. I'll have you write a Letter to your Lover.

mrs. pinchwife. O Lord, to the fine Gentleman a Letter!

pinchwife. Yes, to the fine Gentleman.

mrs. pinchwife. Lord, you do but jeer; sure you jest.

pinchwife. I am not so merry, come write as I bid you.

mrs. pinchwife. What, do you think I am a fool?

pinchwife. She's afraid I would not dictate any love to
him, therefore she's unwilling; but you had best begin.

mrs. pinchwife. Indeed, and indeed, but I won't, so I
won't.

pinchwife. Why?

mrs. pinchwife. Because he's in Town, you may send for
him if you will.

pinchwife. Very well, you wou'd have him brought to
you; is it come to this? I say take the pen and write,
or you'll provoke me.

mrs. pinchwife. Lord, what d'ye make a fool of me for?
Don't I know that Letters are never writ, but from the
Countrey to *London,* and from *London* into the Countrey; now he's in Town, and I am in Town too; therefore I can't write to him you know.

pinchwife. So I am glad it is no worse, she is innocent
enough yet.   [*Aside.*
Yes you may when your Husband bids you write Letters to people that are in Town.

mrs. pinchwife. O may I so! Then I'm satisfied.

PINCHWIFE. Come begin— Sir—   [*Dictates*.

MRS. PINCHWIFE. Shan't I say, Dear Sir? You know one
says always something more than bare Sir.

PINCHWIFE. Write as I bid you, or I will write Whore with
this Penknife in your Face.

MRS. PINCHWIFE. Nay good Bud— Sir—   [*She writes*.

PINCHWIFE. Though I suffer'd last night your nauseous,
loath'd Kisses and Embraces— Write.

MRS. PINCHWIFE. Nay, why shou'd I say so, you know I
told you, he had a sweet breath.

PINCHWIFE. Write.

MRS. PINCHWIFE. Let me but put out, loath'd.

PINCHWIFE. Write I say.

MRS. PINCHWIFE. Well then.   [*Writes*.

PINCHWIFE. Let's see what have you writ?

Though I suffer'd last night your kisses and embraces—
                              [*Takes the paper, and reads*.

Thou impudent creature, where is nauseous and loath'd?

MRS. PINCHWIFE. I can't abide to write such filthy words.

PINCHWIFE. Once more write as I'd have you, and question
it not, or I will spoil thy writing with this, I will stab
out those eyes that cause my mischief.

                              [*Holds up the penknife*.

MRS. PINCHWIFE. O Lord, I will.

PINCHWIFE. So—so— Let's see now!   [*Reads*.

Though I suffer'd last night your nauseous, loath'd
kisses, and embraces; Go on— Yet I would not have you
presume that you shall ever repeat them— So—

                              [*She writes*.

MRS. PINCHWIFE. I have writ it.

PINCHWIFE. On then— I then conceal'd my self from your
knowledge, to avoid your insolencies—   [*She writes*.

MRS. PINCHWIFE. So—

PINCHWIFE. The same reason now I am out of your hands—
                              [*She writes*.

MRS. PINCHWIFE. So—

PINCHWIFE. Makes me own to you my unfortunate, though
innocent frolick, of being in man's cloths.

                              [*She writes*.

MRS. PINCHWIFE. So—

PINCHWIFE. That you may for ever more cease to pursue her, who hates and detests you— [*She writes on.*

MRS. PINCHWIFE. So—h— [*Sighs.*

PINCHWIFE. What do you sigh?—detests you—as much as she loves her Husband and her Honour—

MRS. PINCHWIFE. I vow Husband he'll ne'er believe, I shou'd write such a Letter.

PINCHWIFE. What he'd expect a kinder from you? come now your name only.

MRS. PINCHWIFE. What, shan't I say your most faithful, humble Servant till death?

PINCHWIFE. No, tormenting Fiend; her stile I find wou'd be very soft. [*Aside.*

Come wrap it up now, whilest I go fetch wax and a candle; and write on the back side, for Mr. *Horner.* [*Exit* PINCHWIFE.

MRS. PINCHWIFE. For Mr. *Horner*— So, I am glad he has told me his name; Dear Mr. *Horner,* but why should I send thee such a Letter, that will vex thee, and make thee angry with me;—well I will not send it— Ay but then my husband will kill me—for I see plainly, he won't let me love Mr. *Horner*—but what care I for my Husband—I won't so I won't send poor Mr. *Horner* such a Letter—but then my Husband— But oh—what if I writ at bottom, my Husband made me write it— Ay but then my Husband wou'd see't— Can one have no shift, ah, a *London* woman wou'd have had a hundred presently; stay—what if I shou'd write a Letter, and wrap it up like this, and write upon't too; ay but then my Husband wou'd see't— I don't know what to do— But yet y vads I'll try, so I will—for I will not send this Letter to poor Mr. *Horner,* come what will on't.

Dear, Sweet Mr. *Horner*— So— [*She writes, and repeats what she hath writ.*] my Husband wou'd have me send you a base, rude, unmannerly Letter—but I won't —so—and wou'd have me forbid you loving me—but I wont—so—and wou'd have me say to you, I hate you poor Mr. *Horner*—but I won't tell a lye for him—*there*— for I'm sure if you and I were in the Countrey at cards

y vads: in faith.

together,—*so*—I cou'd not help treading on your Toe
under the Table—*so*—or rubbing knees with you, and
staring in your face, 'till you saw me—*very well*—and
then looking down, and blushing for an hour together
—*so*—but I must make haste before my Husband come;
and now he has taught me to write Letters: You shall
have longer ones from me, who am

> Dear, dear, poor dear Mr. *Horner,* your most
>> Humble Friend, and Servant to command
>>> 'till death, *Margery Pinchwife.*

Stay I must give him a hint at bottom—*so*—now
wrap it up just like t'other—*so*—now write for Mr.
Horner,— But oh now what shall I do with it? for here
comes my Husband.

Enter PINCHWIFE.

PINCHWIFE. I have been detained by a Sparkish Coxcomb,
who pretended a visit to me; but I fear 'twas to my
Wife.   [*Aside.*
What, have you done?

MRS. PINCHWIFE. Ay, ay Bud, just now.

PINCHWIFE. Let's see't, what d'ye tremble for; what, you
wou'd not have it go?

MRS. PINCHWIFE. Here.— No I must not give him that,[5]
[*He opens, and reads the first Letter.*] so I had been
served if I had given him this.   [*Aside.*

PINCHWIFE. Come, where's the Wax and Seal?

MRS. PINCHWIFE. Lord, what shall I do now? Nay then I
have it—   [*Aside.*
Pray let me see't, Lord you think me so errand a fool, I
cannot seal a Letter, I will do't, so I will.

> [*Snatches the Letter from him, changes it for
> the other, seals it, and delivers it to him.*

PINCHWIFE. Nay, I believe you will learn that, and other
things too, which I wou'd not have you.

MRS. PINCHWIFE. So, han't I done it curiously?
I think I have, there's my Letter going to Mr. *Horner;*
since he'll needs have me send Letters to Folks. [*Aside.*

PINCHWIFE. 'Tis very well, but I warrant, you wou'd not
have it go now?

MRS. PINCHWIFE. Yes indeed, but I wou'd, Bud, now.

PINCHWIFE. Well you are a good Girl then, come let me
lock you up in your chamber, 'till I come back; and
be sure you come not within three strides of the window, when I am gone; for I have a spye in the street.

[*Exit Mrs.* PINCHWIFE.

[PINCHWIFE *locks the door.*

At least, 'tis fit she think so, if we do not cheat women,
they'll cheat us; and fraud may be justly used with secret
enemies, of which a Wife is the most dangerous; and
he that has a handsome one to keep, and a Frontier
Town, must provide against treachery, rather than open
Force— Now I have secur'd all within, I'll deal with the
Foe without with false intelligence.

[*Holds up the Letter.*

[*Exit* PINCHWIFE.

The Scene changes to HORNER'S *Lodging.*

QUACK *and* HORNER.

QUACK. Well Sir, how fadges the new design; have you not
the luck of all your brother Projectors, to deceive only
your self at last.

HORNER. No, good *Domine* Doctor, I deceive you it
seems, and others too; for the grave Matrons, and old
ridgid Husbands think me as unfit for love, as they are;
but their Wives, Sisters and Daughters, know some of
'em better things already.

QUACK. Already!

HORNER. Already, I say; last night I was drunk with half a
dozen of your civil persons, as you call 'em, and people
of Honour, and so was made free of their Society, and
dressing rooms for ever hereafter; and am already come
to the privileges of sleeping upon their Pallats, warming
Smocks, tying Shooes and Garters, and the like Doctor,
already, already Doctor.

QUACK. You have made use of your time, Sir.

HORNER. I tell thee, I am now no more interruption to 'em,
when they sing, or talk bawdy, than a little squab
French Page, who speaks no English.

QUACK. But do civil persons, and women of Honour drink, and sing bawdy Songs?

HORNER. O amongst Friends, amongst Friends; for your Bigots in Honour, are just like those in Religion; they fear the eye of the world, more than the eye of Heaven, and think there is no virtue, but railing at vice; and no sin, but giving scandal: They rail at a poor, little, kept Player, and keep themselves some young, modest Pulpit Comedian to be privy to their sins in their Closets, not to tell 'em of them in their Chappels.

QUACK. Nay, the truth on't is, Priests amongst the women now, have quite got the better of us Lay Confessors, Physicians.

HORNER. And they are rather their Patients, but—

Enter my Lady FIDGET, *looking about her.*

Now we talk of women of Honour, here comes one, step behind the Screen there, and but observe; if I have not particular privileges, with the women of reputation already, Doctor, already.

LADY FIDGET. Well *Horner*, am not I a woman of Honour? you see I'm as good as my word.

HORNER. And you shall see Madam, I'll not be behind hand with you in honour; and I'll be as good as my word too, if you please but to withdraw into the next room.

LADY FIDGET. But first, my dear Sir, you must promise to have a care of my dear Honour.

HORNER. If you talk a word more of your Honour, you'll make me incapable to wrong it; to talk of Honour in the mysteries of Love, is like talking of Heaven, or the Deity in an operation of Witchcraft, just when you are employing the Devil, it makes the charm impotent.

LADY FIDGET. Nay, fie, let us not be smooty; but you talk of mysteries, and bewitching to me, I don't understand you.

HORNER. I tell you Madam, the word money in a Mistresses mouth, at such a nick of time, is not a more disheartning sound to a younger Brother,[6] than that of Honour to an eager Lover like my self.

LADY FIDGET. But you can't blame a Lady of my reputation to be chary.

HORNER. Chary—I have been chary of it already, by the report I have caus'd of my self.

LADY FIDGET. Ay, but if you shou'd ever let other women know that dear secret, it would come out; nay, you must have a great care of your conduct; for my acquaintance are so censorious, (oh 'tis a wicked censorious world, Mr. *Horner*) I say, are so censorious, and detracting, that perhaps they'll talk to the prejudice of my Honour, though you shou'd not let them know the dear secret.

HORNER. Nay Madam, rather than they shall prejudice your Honour, I'll prejudice theirs; and to serve you, I'll lye with 'em all, make the secret their own, and then they'll keep it: I am a *Machiavel* in love Madam.

LADY FIDGET. O, no Sir, not that way.

HORNER. Nay, the Devil take me, if censorious women are to be silenc'd any other way.

LADY FIDGET. A secret is better kept I hope, by a single person, than a multitude; therefore pray do not trust any body else with it, dear, dear Mr. *Horner*.

[*Embracing him.*

Enter Sir JASPAR FIDGET.

SIR JASPAR. How now!

LADY FIDGET. O my Husband—prevented—and what's almost as bad, found with my arms about another man—that will appear too much—what shall I say? [*Aside.* Sir *Jaspar* come hither, I am trying if Mr. *Horner* were ticklish, and he's as ticklish as can be, I love to torment the confounded Toad; let you and I tickle him.

SIR JASPAR. No, your Ladyship will tickle him better without me, I suppose, but is this your buying China, I thought you had been at the China House?

HORNER. China-House, that's my Cue, I must take it.

[*Aside.*

A Pox, can't you keep your impertinent Wives at home? some men are troubled with the Husbands, but I with the Wives; but I'd have you to know, since I cannot be your Journey-man by night, I will not be your drudge by day, to squire your wife about, and be your man of straw, or scare-crow only to Pyes and Jays; that would be nibling at your forbidden fruit; I shall be shortly the Hackney Gentleman-Usher of the Town.

SIR JASPAR. Heh, heh, he, poor fellow he's in the right on't faith, to squire women about for other folks, is as ungrateful an employment, as to tell money for other folks; [*Aside.*] heh, he, he, ben't angry *Horner*—

LADY FIDGET. No, 'tis I have more reason to be angry, who am left by you, to go abroad indecently alone; or, what is more indecent, to pin my self upon such ill bred people of your acquaintance, as this is.

SIR JASPAR. Nay, pr'ythee what has he done?

LADY FIDGET. Nay, he has done nothing.

SIR JASPAR. But what d'ye take ill, if he has done nothing?

LADY FIDGET. Hah, hah, hah, Faith, I can't but laugh however; why d'ye think the unmannerly toad wou'd not come down to me to the Coach, I was fain to come up to fetch him, or go without him, which I was resolved not to do; for he knows China very well, and has himself very good, but will not let me see it, lest I should beg some; but I will find it out, and have what I came for yet.   [*Exit* LADY FIDGET, *and locks the door,*
                              followed by HORNER *to the door.*

HORNER. Lock the door Madam— [*Apart to Lady* FIDGET.] So, she has got into my chamber, and lock'd me out; oh the impertinency of woman-kind! Well Sir *Jaspar*, plain dealing is a Jewel; if ever you suffer your Wife to trouble me again here, she shall carry you home a pair of Horns, by my Lord Major she shall; though I cannot furnish you my self, you are sure, yet I'll find a way.

SIR JASPAR. Hah, ha, he, at my first coming in, and finding her arms about him, tickling him it seems, I was half jealous, but now I see my folly.   [*Aside.*
Heh, he, he, poor *Horner.*

HORNER. Nay, though you laugh now, 'twill be my turn e're long: Oh women, more impertinent, more cunning, and more mischievous than their Monkeys, and to me

Major: mayor.

almost as ugly—now is she throwing my things about, and rifling all I have, but I'll get into her the back way, and so rifle her for it—

SIR JASPAR. Hah, ha, ha, poor angry *Horner*.

HORNER. Stay here a little, I'll ferret her out to you presently, I warrant.   [*Exit* HORNER *at t'other door*.

SIR JASPAR. Wife, my Lady *Fidget*, Wife, he is coming into you the back way. [*Sir* JASPAR *calls through the door to his Wife, she answers from within*.

LADY FIDGET. Let him come, and welcome, which way he will.

SIR JASPAR. He'll catch you, and use you roughly, and be too strong for you.

LADY FIDGET. Don't you trouble your self, let him if he can.

QUACK. [*Behind*] This indeed, I cou'd not have believ'd from him, nor any but my own eyes.

Enter Mistris SQUEAMISH.

SQUEAMISH. Where's this Woman-hater, this Toad, this ugly, greasie, dirty Sloven?

SIR JASPAR. So the women all will have him ugly, methinks he is a comely person; but his wants make his form contemptible to 'em; and 'tis e'en as my Wife said yesterday, talking of him, that a proper handsome Eunuch, was as ridiculous a thing, as a Gigantick Coward.

SQUEAMISH. Sir *Jaspar*, your Servant, where is the odious Beast?

SIR JASPAR. He's within in his chamber, with my Wife; she's playing the wag with him.

SQUEAMISH. Is she so, and he's a clownish beast, he'll give her no quarter, he'll play the wag with her again, let me tell you; come, let's go help her— What, the door's lock't?

SIR JASPAR. Ay, my Wife lock't it—

SQUEAMISH. Did she so, let us break it open then?

SIR JASPAR. No, no, he'll do her no hurt.

SQUEAMISH. No— But is there no other way to get into 'em, whither goes this? I will disturb 'em.   [*Aside*.
                [*Exit* SQUEAMISH *at another door*.

Enter old Lady SQUEAMISH.

LADY SQUEAMISH. Where is this Harlotry, this Impudent Baggage, this rambling Tomrigg? O Sir *Jaspar*, I'm glad to see you here, did you not see my vil'd Grandchild come in hither just now?

SIR JASPAR. Yes.

LADY SQUEAMISH. Ay, but where is she then? where is she? Lord Sir *Jaspar* I have e'ne ratled my self to pieces in pursuit of her, but can you tell what she makes here, they say below, no woman lodges here.

SIR JASPAR. No.

LADY SQUEAMISH. No— What does she here then? say if it be not a womans lodging, what makes she here? but are you sure no woman lodges here?

SIR JASPAR. No, nor no man neither, this is Mr. *Horners* Lodging.

LADY SQUEAMISH. Is it so are you sure?

SIR JASPAR. Yes, yes.

LADY SQUEAMISH. So then there's no hurt in't I hope, but where is he?

SIR JASPAR. He's in the next room with my Wife.

LADY SQUEAMISH. Nay if you trust him with your wife, I may with my Biddy, they say he's a merry harmless man now, e'ne as harmless a man as ever came out of *Italy* with a good voice,[7] and as pretty harmless company for a Lady, as a Snake without his teeth.

SIR JASPAR. Ay, ay poor man.

Enter Mrs. SQUEAMISH.

SQUEAMISH. I can't find 'em— Oh are you here, Grandmother, I follow'd you must know my Lady *Fidget*

Tomrigg: a tomrig could be either a tomboy or a strumpet; Squeamish is a bit of both.

vil'd: an old form of "vile," the word usually used in modern-spelling editions, following the reading of Hunt. Since there is an apostrophe in the word as it stands here, it may

be intended as a past participle of the obsolescent verb "vile" meaning "defile." In old Lady Squeamish's eyes her granddaughter would be defiled by entering a man's lodgings. Bell gives "wild," of which "vild" was an old form and which is also suitable to the character.

hither, 'tis the prettyest lodging, and I have been staring on the prettyest Pictures.

Enter Lady FIDGET *with a piece of China in her hand, and* HORNER *following.*

LADY FIDGET. And I have been toyling and moyling, for the pretti'st piece of China, my Dear.

HORNER. Nay she has been too hard for me do what I cou'd.

SQUEAMISH. Oh Lord I'le have some China too, good Mr. *Horner,* don't think to give other people China, and me none, come in with me too.

HORNER. Upon my honour I have none left now.

SQUEAMISH. Nay, nay I have known you deny your China before now, but you shan't put me off so, come—

HORNER. This Lady had the last there.

LADY FIDGET. Yes indeed Madam, to my certain knowledge he has no more left.

SQUEAMISH. O but it may be he may have some you could not find.

LADY FIDGET. What d'y think if he had had any left, I would not have had it too, for we women of quality never think we have China enough.

HORNER. Do not take it ill, I cannot make China for you all, but I will have a Rol-waggon[8] for you too, another time.

SQUEAMISH. Thank you dear Toad.   [*To* HORNER *aside.*

LADY FIDGET. What do you mean by that promise?

HORNER. Alas she has an innocent, literal understanding.
                                    [*Apart to Lady* FIDGET.

LADY SQUEAMISH. Poor Mr. *Horner,* he has enough to doe to please you all, I see.

HORNER. Ay Madam, you see how they use me.

LADY SQUEAMISH. Poor Gentleman I pitty you.

HORNER. I thank you Madam, I could never find pitty, but from such reverend Ladies as you are, the young ones will never spare a man.

SQUEAMISH. Come come, Beast, and go dine with us, for we shall want a man at Hombre after dinner.

HORNER. That's all their use of me Madam you see.

SQUEAMISH. Come Sloven, I'le lead you to be sure of you.
[*Pulls him by the Crevat.*

LADY SQUEAMISH. Alas poor man how she tuggs him, kiss, kiss her, that's the way to make such nice women quiet.

HORNER. No Madam, that Remedy is worse than the Torment, they know I dare suffer any thing rather than do it.

LADY SQUEAMISH. Prythee kiss her, and I'le give you her Picture in little, that you admir'd so last night, prythee do.

HORNER. Well nothing but that could bribe me, I love a woman only in Effigie, and good Painting as much as I hate them— I'le do't, for I cou'd adore the Devil well painted. [*Kisses Mrs.* SQUEAMISH.

SQUEAMISH. Foh, you filthy Toad, nay now I've done jesting.

LADY SQUEAMISH. Ha, ha, ha, I told you so.

SQUEAMISH. Foh a kiss of his—

SIR JASPAR. Has no more hurt in't, than one of my Spaniels.

SQUEAMISH. Nor no more good neither.

QUACK. I will now believe any thing he tells me. [*Behind.*

Enter Mr. PINCHWIFE.

LADY FIDGET. O Lord here's a man, Sir *Jaspar,* my Mask, my Mask, I would not be seen here for the world.

SIR JASPAR. What not when I am with you.

LADY FIDGET. No, no my honour—let's be gone.

SQUEAMISH. Oh Grandmother, let us be gone, make hast, make hast, I know not how he may censure us.

LADY FIDGET. Be found in the lodging of any thing like a man, away.

Exeunt Sir JASPAR, *Lady* FIDGET, *Old Lady* SQUEAMISH, *Mrs.* SQUEAMISH.

QUACK. What's here another Cuckold—he looks like one, and none else sure have any business with him.
[*Behind.*

HORNER. Well what brings my dear friend hither?

PINCHWIFE. Your impertinency.

HORNER. My impertinency—why you Gentlemen that have got handsome Wives, think you have a privilege of say-

ing any thing to your friends, and are as brutish, as if
you were our Creditors.

PINCHWIFE. No Sir, I'le ne're trust you any way.

HORNER. But why not, dear *Jack*, why diffide in me, thou
knowst so well.

PINCHWIFE. Because I do know you so well.

HORNER. Han't I been always thy friend honest *Jack*, always ready to serve thee, in love, or battle, before thou
wert married, and am so still.

PINCHWIFE. I believe so you wou'd be my second now indeed.

HORNER. Well then dear *Jack*, why so unkind, so grum, so
strange to me, come prythee kiss me deare Rogue, gad
I was always I say, and am still as much thy Servant as—

PINCHWIFE. As I am yours Sir. What you wou'd send a kiss
to my Wife, is that it?

HORNER. So there 'tis—a man can't shew his friendship to
a married man, but presently he talks of his wife to you,
prythee let thy Wife alone, and let thee and I be all
one, as we were wont, what thou art as shye of my
kindness, as a Lumbard-street Alderman of a Courtiers
civility at Lockets.[9]

PINCHWIFE. But you are over kind to me, as kind, as if I
were your Cuckold already, yet I must confess you ought
to be kind and civil to me, since I am so kind, so civil
to you, as to bring you this, look you there Sir.

[*Delivers him a Letter.*

HORNER. What is't?

PINCHWIFE. Only a Love Letter Sir.

HORNER. From whom—how, this is from your Wife—hum
—and hum—   [*Reads.*

PINCHWIFE. Even from my Wife Sir, am I not wondrous
kind and civil to you, now too?
But you'l not think her so.   [*Aside.*

HORNER. Ha, is this a trick of his or hers.   [*Aside.*

PINCHWIFE. The Gentleman's surpriz'd I find, what you expected a kinder Letter?

HORNER. No faith not I, how cou'd I.

diffide in: distrust.

PINCHWIFE. Yes yes, I'm sure you did, a man so well made as you are must needs be disappointed, if the women declare not their passion at first sight or opportunity.

HORNER. But what should this mean? stay the Postscript. Be sure you love me whatsoever my husband says to the contrary, and let him not see this, lest he should come home, and pinch me, or kill my Squirrel.

[*Reads aside.*

It seems he knows not what the Letter contains. [*Aside.*

PINCHWIFE. Come ne're wonder at it so much.

HORNER. Faith I can't help it.

PINCHWIFE. Now I think I have deserv'd your infinite friendship, and kindness, and have shewed my self sufficiently an obliging kind friend and husband, am I not so, to bring a Letter from my Wife to her Gallant?

HORNER. Ay, the Devil take me, art thou, the most obliging, kind friend and husband in the world, ha, ha.

PINCHWIFE. Well you may be merry Sir, but in short I must tell you Sir, my honour will suffer no jesting.

HORNER. What do'st thou mean?

PINCHWIFE. Does the Letter want a Comment? then know Sir, though I have been so civil a husband, as to bring you a Letter from my Wife, to let you kiss and court her to my face, I will not be a Cuckold Sir, I will not.

HORNER. Thou art mad with jealousie, I never saw thy Wife in my life, but at the Play yesterday, and I know not if it were she or no, I court her, kiss her!

PINCHWIFE. I will not be a Cuckold I say, there will be danger in making me a Cuckold.

HORNER. Why, wert thou not well cur'd of thy last clap?

PINCHWIFE. I weare a Sword.

HORNER. It should be taken from thee, lest thou should'st do thy self a mischiefe with it, thou art mad, Man.

PINCHWIFE. As mad as I am, and as merry as you are, I must have more reason from you e're we part, I say again though you kiss'd, and courted last night my Wife in man's clothes, as she confesses in her Letter.

HORNER. Ha—   [*Aside.*

PINCHWIFE. Both she and I say you must not design it

again, for you have mistaken your woman, as you have
done your man.

HORNER. Oh—I understand something now—   [*Aside.*
Was that thy Wife? why would'st thou not tell me 'twas
she? faith my freedome with her was your fault, not
mine.

PINCHWIFE. Faith so 'twas—   [*Aside.*

HORNER. Fye, I'de never do't to a woman before her husbands face, sure.

PINCHWIFE. But I had rather you should do't to my wife
before my face, than behind my back, and that you
shall never doe.

HORNER. No—you will hinder me.

PINCHWIFE. If I would not hinder you, you see by her Letter, she wou'd.

HORNER. Well, I must e'ne acquiess then, and be contented
with what she writes.

PINCHWIFE. I'le assure you 'twas voluntarily writ, I had no
hand in't you may believe me.

HORNER. I do believe thee, faith.

PINCHWIFE. And believe her too, for she's an innocent creature, has no dissembling in her, and so fare you well Sir.

HORNER. Pray however present my humble service to her,
and tell her I will obey her Letter to a tittle, and fulfill
her desires be what they will, or with what difficulty
soever I do't, and you shall be no more jealous of me,
I warrant her, and you—

PINCHWIFE. Well then fare you well, and play with any
mans honour but mine, kiss any mans wife but mine,
and welcome—   [*Exit Mr.* PINCHWIFE.

HORNER. Ha, ha, ha, Doctor.

QUACK. It seems he has not heard the report of you, or
does not believe it.

HORNER. Ha, ha, now Doctor what think you?

QUACK. Pray let's see the Letter—hum—for—deare—love
you—   [*Reads the Letter.*

HORNER. I wonder how she cou'd contrive it! what say'st
thou to't, 'tis an Original.

QUACK. So are your Cuckolds too Originals: for they are
like no other common Cuckolds, and I will henceforth

believe it not impossible for you to Cuckold the Grand
Signior amidst his Guards of Eunuchs, that I say—

HORNER. And I say for the Letter, 'tis the first love Letter
that ever was without Flames, Darts, Fates, Destinies,
Lying and Dissembling in't.

Enter SPARKISH *pulling in Mr.* PINCHWIFE.

SPARKISH. Come back, you are a pretty Brother-in-law,
neither go to Church, nor to dinner with your Sister
Bride.

PINCHWIFE. My Sister denies her marriage, and you see is
gone away from you dissatisfy'd.

SPARKISH. Pshaw, upon a foolish scruple, that our Parson
was not in lawful Orders, and did not say all the Common Prayer, but 'tis her modesty only I believe, but let
women be never so modest the first day, they'l be sure
to come to themselves by night, and I shall have enough
of her then; in the mean time, *Harry Horner*, you must
dine with me, I keep my wedding at my Aunts in the
Piazza.[10]

HORNER. Thy wedding, what stale Maid has liv'd to de-
spaire of a husband, or what young one of a Gallant?

SPARKISH. O your Servant Sir—this Gentlemans Sister
then— No stale Maid.

HORNER. I'm sorry for't.

PINCHWIFE. How comes he so concern'd for her— [*Aside.*

SPARKISH. You sorry for't, why do you know any ill by her?

HORNER. No, I know none but by thee, 'tis for her sake, not
yours, and another mans sake that might have hop'd, I
thought—

SPARKISH. Another Man, another man, what is his Name?

HORNER. Nay since 'tis past he shall be nameless.

Poor *Harcourt* I am sorry thou hast mist her—   [*Aside.*

PINCHWIFE. He seems to be much troubled at the match—
[*Aside.*

SPARKISH. Prythee tell me—nay you shan't go Brother.

PINCHWIFE. I must of necessity, but I'le come to you to
dinner.   [*Exit* PINCHWIFE.

Grand Signior: the Sultan in
Constantinople.

SPARKISH. But *Harry,* what have I a Rival in my Wife already? but withal my heart, for he may be of use to me hereafter, for though my hunger is now my sawce, and I can fall on heartily without, but the time will come, when a Rival will be as good sawce for a married man to a wife, as an Orange to Veale.[11]

HORNER. O thou damn'd Rogue, thou hast set my teeth on edge with thy Orange.

SPARKISH. Then let's to dinner, there I was with you againe, come.

HORNER. But who dines with thee?

SPARKISH. My Friends and Relations, my Brother *Pinchwife* you see of your acquantance.

HORNER. And his Wife.

SPARKISH. No gad, he'l nere let her come amongst us good fellows, your stingy country Coxcomb keeps his wife from his friends, as he does his little Firkin of Ale, for his own drinking, and a Gentleman can't get a smack on't, but his servants, when his back is turn'd broach it at their pleasures, and dust it away, ha, ha, ha, gad I am witty, I think, considering I was married to day, by the world, but come—

HORNER. No, I will not dine with you, unless you can fetch her too.

SPARKISH. Pshaw what pleasure can'st thou have with women now, *Harry?*

HORNER. My eyes are not gone, I love a good prospect yet, and will not dine with you, unless she does too, go fetch her therefore, but do not tell her husband, 'tis for my sake.

SPARKISH. Well I'le go try what I can do, in the mean time come away to my Aunts lodging, 'tis in the way to *Pinchwifes.*

HORNER. The poor woman has call'd for aid, and stretch'd forth her hand Doctor, I cannot but help her over the Pale out of the Bryars.[12]

             [*Exeunt* SPARKISH, HORNER, QUACK.

dust it away: drink it quickly, toss it off.

The Scene changes to PINCHWIFES *house.*

Mrs. PINCHWIFE *alone leaning on her elbow.*

A Table, Pen, Ink, and Paper.

MRS. PINCHWIFE. Well 'tis e'ne so, I have got the *London* disease, they call Love, I am sick of my Husband, and for my Gallant; I have heard this distemper, call'd a Feaver, but methinks 'tis liker an Ague, for when I think of my Husband, I tremble and am in a cold sweat, and have inclinations to vomit, but when I think of my Gallant, dear Mr. *Horner,* my hot fit comes, and I am all in a Feaver, indeed, & as in other Feavers, my own Chamber is tedious to me, and I would fain be remov'd to his, and then methinks I shou'd be well; ah poor Mr. *Horner,* well I cannot, will not stay here, therefore I'le make an end of my Letter to him, which shall be a finer Letter than my last, because I have studied it like any thing; O Sick, Sick!   [*Takes the Pen and writes.*

Enter Mr. PINCHWIFE *who seeing her writing steales softly behind her, and looking over her shoulder, snatches the paper from her.*

PINCHWIFE. What writing more Letters?

MRS. PINCHWIFE. O Lord Budd, why d'ye fright me so?

She offers to run out: he stops her, and reads.

PINCHWIFE. How's this! nay you shall not stir Madam.

Deare, Deare, deare, Mr *Horner*—very well—I have taught you to write Letters to good purpose—but let's see't.

First I am to beg your pardon for my boldness in writing to you, which I'de have you to know, I would not have done, had not you said first you lov'd me so extreamly, which if you doe, you will never suffer me to lye in the arms of another man, whom I loath, nauseate, and detest— [Now you can write these filthy words] but what follows— Therefore I hope you will speedily find some way to free me from this unfortunate match, which was never, I assure you, of my choice, but I'm afraid 'tis already too far gone; however if you love me, as I do you, you will try what you can do, but you must

help me away before to morrow, or else alass I shall be
for ever out of your reach, for I can defer no longer our
—our— [*The Letter concludes.*] what is to follow our—
speak what? our Journey into the Country I suppose—
Oh Woman, damn'd Woman, and Love, damn'd Love,
their old Tempter, for this is one of his miracles, in a
moment, he can make those blind that cou'd see, and
those see that were blind, those dumb that could speak,
and those prattle who were dumb before, nay what is
more than all, make these dow-bak'd, sensless, indocile
animals, Women, too hard for us their Politick Lords and
Rulers in a moment; But make an end of your Letter,
and then I'le make an end of you thus, and all my
plagues together.   [*Draws his Sword.*

MRS. PINCHWIFE. O Lord, O Lord you are such a Passionate
Man, Budd.

Enter SPARKISH.

SPARKISH. How now what's here to doe.

PINCHWIFE. This Fool here now!

SPARKISH. What drawn upon your Wife? you shou'd never
do that but at night in the dark when you can't hurt her,
this is my Sister in Law is it not? [*Pulls aside her Hand-
kercheife.*] ay faith e'ne our Country *Margery*, one may
know her, come she and you must go dine with me,
dinner's ready, come, but where's my Wife, is she not
come home yet, where is she?

PINCHWIFE. Making you a Cuckold, 'tis that they all doe,
as soon as they can.

SPARKISH. What the Wedding day? no, a Wife that designs
to make a Cully of her Husband, will be sure to let him
win the first stake of love, by the world, but come they
stay dinner for us, come I'le lead down our *Margery*.

PINCHWIFE.[13] No— Sir go we'l follow you.

SPARKISH. I will not wag without you.

dow-bak'd: dough-baked: fee-
ble-minded. I cannot help
feeling that "docile" would
be more appropriate than *indocile* in this list of adjectives, unless *indocile* in the
sense of "difficult to teach"
serves Pinchwife's rhetorical
purpose.

PINCHWIFE. This Coxcomb is a sensible torment to me amidst the greatest in the world.[14]

SPARKISH. Come, come Madam *Margery*.

PINCHWIFE. No I'le lead her my way, what wou'd you treat your friends with mine, for want of your own Wife?

[*Leads her to t'other door, and locks her in and returns.*

I am contented my rage shou'd take breath—   [*Aside.*

SPARKISH. I told *Horner* this.

PINCHWIFE. Come now.

SPARKISH. Lord, how shye you are of your Wife, but let me tell you Brother, we men of wit have amongst us a saying, that Cuckolding like the small Pox comes with a fear, and you may keep your Wife as much as you will out of danger of infection, but if her constitution incline her to't, she'l have it sooner or later by the world, say they.

PINCHWIFE. What a thing is a Cuckold, that every fool can make him ridiculous—   [*Aside.*

Well Sir— But let me advise you, now you are come to be concern'd, because you suspect the danger, not to neglect the means to prevent it, especially when the greatest share of the Malady will light upon your own head, for—

How'sere the kind Wife's Belly comes to swell.
The Husband breeds for her, and first is ill.

Act 5. Scene i.

Mr. PINCHWIFES *House.*

Enter Mr. PINCHWIFE *and Mrs.* PINCHWIFE, *a Table and Candle.*

PINCHWIFE. Come take the Pen and make an end of the Letter, just as you intended, if you are false in a tittle, I shall soon perceive it, and punish you with this as you

sensible: acutely felt.
breeds: used here in the sense of developing an outgrowth (teeth, wings, etc.). The husband breeds horns, the malady that lights upon his head, before the wife's belly shows the results.

deserve, [*Lays his hand on his Sword.*] write what was to follow—let's see—

[You must make haste and help me away before to morrow, or else I shall be for ever out of your reach, for I can defer no longer our—] What follows our?—

MRS. PINCHWIFE. Must all out then Budd?— Look you there then.   [*Mrs.* PINCHWIFE *takes the Pen and writes.*

PINCHWIFE. Let's see— [For I can defer no longer our— Wedding— Your slighted *Alithea*] What's the meaning of this, my Sisters name to't, speak, unriddle?

MRS. PINCHWIFE. Yes indeed Budd.

PINCHWIFE. But why her name to't speak—speak I say?

MRS. PINCHWIFE. Ay but you'l tell her then again, if you wou'd not tell her again.

PINCHWIFE. I will not, I am stunn'd, my head turns round, speak.

MRS. PINCHWIFE. Won't you tell her indeed, and indeed.

PINCHWIFE. No, speak I say.

MRS. PINCHWIFE. She'l be angry with me, but I had rather she should be angry with me than you Budd; and to tell you the truth, 'twas she made me write the Letter, and taught me what I should write.

PINCHWIFE. Ha—I thought the stile was somewhat better than her own,[1] but how cou'd she come to you to teach you, since I had lock'd you up alone.

MRS. PINCHWIFE. O through the key hole Budd.

PINCHWIFE. But why should she make you write a Letter for her to him, since she can write her self?

MRS. PINCHWIFE. Why she said because—for I was unwilling to do it.

PINCHWIFE. Because what—because.

MRS. PINCHWIFE. Because lest Mr. *Horner* should be cruel, and refuse her, or vaine afterwards, and shew the Letter, she might disown it, the hand not being hers.

PINCHWIFE. How's this? ha—then I think I shall come to my self again— This changeling cou'd not invent this lye, but if she cou'd, why should she? she might think I should soon discover it—stay—now I think on't too, *Horner* said he was sorry she had married *Sparkish*, and

her disowning her marriage to me, makes me think she
has evaded it, for *Horner's* sake, yet why should she
take this course, but men in love are fools, women may
well be so.—   [*Aside.*
But hark you Madam, your Sister went out in the morning, and I have not seen her within since.

MRS. PINCHWIFE. A lack a day she has been crying all day
above it seems in a corner.

PINCHWIFE. Where is she, let me speak with her.

MRS. PINCHWIFE. O Lord then he'l discover all—   [*Aside.*
Pray hold Budd, what d'y mean to discover me, she'l
know I have told you then, pray Budd let me talk with
her first—

PINCHWIFE. I must speak with her to know whether *Horner*
ever made her any promise; and whether she be married
to *Sparkish* or no.

MRS. PINCHWIFE. Pray dear Budd don't, till I have spoken
with her and told her that I have told you all, for she'll
kill me else.

PINCHWIFE. Go then and bid her come out to me.

MRS. PINCHWIFE. Yes, yes Budd—

PINCHWIFE. Let me see—

MRS. PINCHWIFE. I'le go, but she is not within to come to
him, I have just got time to know of *Lucy* her Maid,
who first set me on work, what lye I shall tell next, for
I am e'ne at my wits end—[2]   [*Exit Mrs.* PINCHWIFE.

PINCHWIFE. Well I resolve it, *Horner* shall have her, I'd
rather give him my Sister than lend him my Wife, and
such an alliance will prevent his pretensions to my Wife
sure,—I'le make him of kinn to her, and then he won't
care for her.   [*Mrs.* PINCHWIFE *returns.*

MRS. PINCHWIFE. O Lord Budd I told you what anger you
would make me with my Sister.

PINCHWIFE. Won't she come hither?

MRS. PINCHWIFE. No no, alack a day, she's asham'd to look
you in the face, and she says if you go in to her, she'l
run away down stairs, and shamefully go her self to Mr.
Horner, who has promis'd her marriage she says, and she
will have no other, so she won't—

PINCHWIFE. Did he so—promise her marriage—then she shall have no other, go tell her so, and if she will come and discourse with me a little concerning the means, I will about it immediately, go— [*Exit Mrs.* PINCHWIFE. His estate is equal to *Sparkish's*, and his extraction as much better than his, as his parts are, but my chief reason is, I'd rather be of kin to him by the name of Brother-in-law, than that of Cuckold—

[*Enter Mrs.* PINCHWIFE.

Well what says she now?

MRS. PINCHWIFE. Why she says she would only have you lead her to *Horners* lodging—with whom she first will discourse the matter before she talk with you, which yet she cannot doe; for alack poor creature, she says she can't so much as look you in the face, therefore she'l come to you in a mask, and you must excuse her if she make you no answer to any question of yours, till you have brought her to Mr. *Horner,* and if you will not chide her, nor question her, she'l come out to you immediately.

PINCHWIFE. Let her come I will not speak a word to her, nor require a word from her.

MRS. PINCHWIFE. Oh I forgot, besides she says, she cannot look you in the face, though through a mask, therefore wou'd desire you to put out the Candle.

PINCHWIFE. I agree to all, let her make haste— [*Exit Mrs.* PINCHWIFE, *puts out the Candle.*] there 'tis out— My case is something better, I'd rather fight with *Horner* for not lying with my Sister, than for lying with my Wife, and of the two I had rather find my Sister too forward than my Wife; I expected no other from her free education, as she calls it, and her passion for the Town— well— Wife and Sister are names which make us expect Love and duty, pleasure and comfort, but we find 'em plagues and torments, and are equally, though differently troublesome to their keeper; for we have as much a-doe to get people to lye with our Sisters, as to keep 'em from lying with our Wives.

Enter Mrs. PINCHWIFE *Masked, and in Hoods*
and Scarves, and a night Gown[3] and Petticoat
of ALITHEAS *in the dark.*

What are you come Sister? let us go then—but first let
    me lock up my Wife, Mrs. *Margery* where are you?

MRS. PINCHWIFE. Here Budd.

PINCHWIFE. Come hither, that I may lock you up, get you
    in, [*Locks the door.*] Come Sister where are you now?
    Mrs. PINCHWIFE *gives him her hand, but when he lets*
    her go, she steals softly on t'other side of him, and is
    lead away by him for his Sister ALITHEA.

The scene changes to HORNERS *Lodging.*

QUACK, HORNER.

QUACK. What all alone, not so much as one of your Cuck-
    olds here, nor one of their Wives! they use to take their
    turns with you, as if they were to watch you.

HORNER. Yes it often happens, that a Cuckold is but his
    Wifes spye, and is more upon family duty, when he is
    with her gallant abroad hindring his pleasure, than when
    he is at home with her playing the Gallant, but the
    hardest duty a married woman imposes upon a lover is,
    keeping her husband company always.

QUACK. And his fondness wearies you almost as soon as
    hers.

HORNER. A Pox, keeping a Cuckold company after you
    have had his Wife, is as tiresome as the company of a
    Country Squire to a witty fellow of the Town, when he
    has got all his Mony.

QUACK. And as at first a man makes a friend of the Hus-
    band to get the Wife, so at last you are faine to fall out
    with the Wife to be rid of the Husband.

HORNER. Ay, most Cuckold-makers are true Courtiers,
    when once a poor man has crack'd his credit for 'em,
    they can't abide to come neer him.

QUACK. But at first to draw him in are so sweet, so kind, so
    dear, just as you are to *Pinchwife,* but what becomes of
    that intrigue with his Wife?

HORNER. A Pox he's as surly as an Alderman that has been

bit, and since he's so coy, his Wife's kindness is in vain, for she's a silly innocent.

QUACK. Did she not send you a Letter by him?

HORNER. Yes, but that's a riddle I have not yet solv'd—allow the poor creature to be willing, she is silly too, and he keeps her up so close—

QUACK. Yes, so close that he makes her but the more willing, and adds but revenge to her love, which two when met seldome faile of satisfying each other one way or other.

HORNER. What here's the man we are talking of I think.

Enter Mr. PINCHWIFE *leading in his Wife*
Masqued, Muffled, and in her Sisters Gown.

HORNER. Pshaw.

QUACK. Bringing his Wife to you is the next thing to bringing a Love Letter from her.

HORNER. What means this?

PINCHWIFE. The last time you know Sir I brought you a love Letter, now you see a Mistress, I think you'l say I am a civil man to you.

HORNER. Ay the Devil take me will I say thou art the civillest man I ever met with, and I have known some; I fancy, I understand thee now, better than I did the Letter, but hark thee in thy eare—

PINCHWIFE. What?

HORNER. Nothing but the usual question man, is she sound on thy word?

PINCHWIFE. What you take her for a Wench and me for a Pimp?

HORNER. Pshaw, wench and Pimp, paw words, I know thou art an honest fellow, and hast a great acquaintance among the Ladies, and perhaps hast made love for me rather than let me make love to thy Wife—

PINCHWIFE. Come Sir, in short, I am for no fooling.

HORNER. Nor I neither, therefore prythee let's see her face presently, make her show man, art thou sure I don't know her?

PINCHWIFE. I am sure you doe know her.

HORNER. A Pox why dost thou bring her to me then?

paw: naughty.

PINCHWIFE. Because she's a Relation of mine.

HORNER. Is she faith man, then thou art still more civil and obliging, dear Rogue.

PINCHWIFE. Who desir'd me to bring her to you.

HORNER. Then she is obliging, dear Rogue.

PINCHWIFE. You'l make her welcome for my sake I hope.

HORNER. I hope she is handsome enough to make her self wellcome; prythee let her unmask.

PINCHWIFE. Doe you speak to her, she wou'd never be rul'd by me.

HORNER. Madam— [*Mrs.* PINCHWIFE *whispers to* HORNER. She says she must speak with me in private, withdraw prythee.

PINCHWIFE. She's unwilling it seems I shou'd know all her undecent conduct in this business—   [*Aside.*
Well then Ile leave you together, and hope when I am gone you'l agree, if not you and I shan't agree Sir.—

HORNER. What means the Fool?[4]—if she and I agree 'tis no matter what you and I do.

Whispers to Mrs. PINCHWIFE, *who makes signs with her hand for him to be gone.*[5]

PINCHWIFE. In the mean time I'le fetch a Parson, and find out *Sparkish* and disabuse him.
You wou'd have me fetch a Parson, would you not, well then— Now I think I am rid of her, and shall have no more trouble with her— Our Sisters and Daughters like Usurers money, are safest, when put out; but our Wifes, like their writings, never safe, but in our Closets under Lock and Key.   [*Exit Mr.* PINCHWIFE.

Enter BOY.

BOY. Sir *Jaspar Fidget* Sir is coming up.

HORNER. Here's the trouble of a Cuckold, now we are talking of, a pox on him, has he not enough to doe to hinder his Wifes sport, but he must other women's too.— Step in here Madam.   [*Exit Mrs.* PINCHWIFE.

Enter Sir JASPAR.

SIR JASPAR. My best and dearest Friend.

HORNER. The old stile Doctor—[6]

their writings: the documents
that attest to the loans.

Well be short, for I am busie, what would your impertinent Wife have now?

SIR JASPAR. Well guess'd y' faith, for I do come from her.

HORNER. To invite me to supper, tell her I can't come, go.

SIR JASPAR. Nay, now you are out faith, for my Lady and
the whole knot of the virtuous gang, as they call themselves, are resolv'd upon a frolick of coming to you to
night in a Masquerade, and are all drest already.

HORNER. I shan't be at home.

SIR JASPAR. Lord how churlish he is to women—nay prythee don't disappoint 'em, they'l think 'tis my fault, prythee don't, I'le send in the Banquet and the Fiddles,
but make no noise on't, for the poor virtuous Rogues
would not have it known for the world, that they go a
Masquerading, and they would come to no mans Ball,
but yours.

HORNER. Well, well—get you gone, and tell 'em if they
come, 'twill be at the peril of their honour and yours.

SIR JASPAR. Heh, he, he—we'l trust you for that, farewell—
                                        [*Exit Sir* JASPAR.

HORNER. Doctor anon you too shall be my guest.
    But now I'm going to a private feast.

The Scene changes to the Piazza of Covent Garden.
                SPARKISH, PINCHWIFE.
        SPARKISH *with the Letter in his hand.*

SPARKISH. But who would have thought a woman could
have been false to me, by the world, I could not have
thought it.

PINCHWIFE. You were for giving and taking liberty, she has
taken it only Sir, now you find in that Letter, you are a
frank person, and so is she you see there.

SPARKISH. Nay if this be her hand—for I never saw it.

PINCHWIFE. 'Tis no matter whether that be her hand or no,
I am sure this hand at her desire lead her to Mr. *Horner*,
with whom I left her just now, to go fetch a Parson to
'em at their desire too, to deprive you of her for ever,
for it seems yours was but a mock marriage.

SPARKISH. Indeed she wou'd needs have it that 'twas *Har-*

court himself in a Parsons habit, that married us, but
I'm sure he told me 'twas his Brother Ned.

PINCHWIFE. O there 'tis out and you were deceiv'd not she,
for you are such a frank person—but I must be gone—
you'l find her at Mr. *Horners,* goe and believe your eyes.

[*Exit Mr.* PINCHWIFE.

SPARKISH. Nay I'le to her, and call her as many Crocodiles,
Syrens, Harpies, and other heathenish names, as a Poet
would do a Mistress, who had refus'd to heare his suit,
nay more his Verses on her.

But stay, is not that she following a Torch at t'other end
of the Piazza, and from *Horners* certainly—'tis so—

Enter ALITHEA *following a Torch, and* LUCY *behind.*

You are well met Madam though you don't think so;
what you have made a short visit to Mr. *Horner,* but I
suppose you'l return to him presently, by that time the
Parson can be with him.

ALITHEA. Mr. *Horner,* and the Parson Sir—

SPARKISH. Come Madam no more dissembling, no more jilting for I am no more a frank person.

ALITHEA. How's this.

LUCY. So 'twill work I see— [*Aside.*

SPARKISH. Cou'd you find out no easie Country Fool to
abuse? none but me, a Gentleman of wit and pleasure
about the Town, but it was your pride to be too hard
for a man of parts, unworthy false woman, false as a
friend that lends a man mony to lose, false as dice, who
undoe those that trust all they have to 'em.

LUCY. He has been a great bubble by his similes as they
say— [*Aside.*

ALITHEA. You have been too merry Sir at your wedding
dinner sure.

SPARKISH. What d'y mock me too?

ALITHEA. Or you have been deluded.

SPARKISH. By you.

ALITHEA. Let me understand you.

SPARKISH. Have you the confidence, I should call it something else, since you know your guilt, to stand my just
reproaches? you did not write an impudent Letter to
Mr. *Horner,* who I find now has club'd with you in de-

luding me with his aversion for women, that I might not forsooth suspect him for my Rival.

LUCY. D'y think the Gentleman can be jealous now Madam—   [*Aside.*

ALITHEA. I write a Letter to Mr. *Horner*!

SPARKISH. Nay Madam, do not deny it, your Brother shew'd it me just now, and told me likewise he left you at *Horners* lodging to fetch a Parson to marry you to him, and I wish you joy Madam, joy, joy, and to him too much joy, and to my self more joy for not marrying you.

ALITHEA. So I find my Brother would break off the match, and I can consent to't, since I see this Gentleman can be made jealous.   [*Aside.*
O *Lucy*, by his rude usage and jealousie, he makes me almost afraid I am married to him, art thou sure 'twas *Harcourt* himself and no Parson that married us.

SPARKISH. No Madam I thank you, I suppose that was a contrivance too of Mr. *Horners* and yours, to make *Harcourt* play the Parson, but I would as little as you have him one now, no not for the world, for shall I tell you another truth, I never had any passion for you, 'till now, for now I hate you, 'tis true I might have married your portion, as other men of parts of the Town do sometimes, and so your Servant, and to shew my unconcernedness, I'le come to your wedding, and resign you with as much joy as I would a stale wench to a new Cully, nay with as much joy as I would after the first night, if I had been married to you, there's for you, and so your Servant, Servant.   [*Exit* SPARKISH.

ALITHEA. How was I deceiv'd in a man!

LUCY. You'l believe then a fool may be made jealous now? for that easiness in him that suffers him to be led by a Wife, will likewise permit him to be perswaded against her by others.

ALITHEA. But marry Mr. *Horner*, my brother does not intend it sure; if I thought he did, I would take thy advice, and Mr. *Harcourt* for my Husband, and now I wish, that if there be any over-wise woman of the Town, who like me would marry a fool, for fortune, liberty, or title, first that her husband may love Play, and be a Cully to all the Town, but her, and suffer none but fortune to be mistress of his purse, then if for liberty, that he may send her into the Country under the conduct of some housewifely mother-in law; and if for title, may the world give 'em none but that of Cuckold.

LUCY. And for her greater curse Madam, may he not deserve it.

ALITHEA. Away impertinent—is not this my old Lady *Lanterlus*?

LUCY. Yes Madam. [and here I hope we shall find Mr. *Harcourt*— [*Aside.*

[*Exeunt* ALITHEA, LUCY.

The Scene changes again to HORNER'S *Lodging.*

HORNER, LADY FIDGET, *Mrs.* DAYNTY FIDGET,
Mrs. SQUEAMISH, *a Table, Banquet,*
and Bottles.

HORNER. A Pox they are come too soon—before I have sent back my new—Mistress, all I have now to do, is to lock her in, that they may not see her— [*Aside.*

LADY FIDGET. That we may be sure of our wellcome, we have brought our entertainment with us, and are resolv'd to treat thee, dear Toad.

DAINTY. And that we may be merry to purpose, have left Sir *Jaspar* and my old Lady *Squeamish* quarrelling at home at Baggammon.

SQUEAMISH. Therefore let us make use of our time, lest they should chance to interrupt us.

LADY FIDGET. Let us sit then.

HORNER. First that you may be private, let me lock this door, and that, and I'le wait upon you presently.

LADY FIDGET. No Sir, shut 'em only and your lips for ever, for we must trust you as much as our women.

HORNER. You know all vanity's kill'd in me, I have no occasion for talking.

Lanterlus: Lanterloo: a card
game. Also called loo; see
Epilogue.

LADY FIDGET. Now Ladies, supposing we had drank each of us our two Bottles, let us speak the truth of our hearts.

DAINTY and SQUEAMISH. Agreed.

LADY FIDGET. By this brimmer, for truth is no where else to be found, [Not in thy heart false man.

[*Aside to* HORNER.

HORNER. You have found me a true man I'm sure.

[*Aside to Lady* FIDGET.

LADY FIDGET. Not every way—   [*Aside to* HORNER.
But let us sit and be merry.

Lady FIDGET sings.

1.

Why should our damn'd Tyrants oblige us to live.
On the pittance of Pleasure which they only give.
  We must not rejoyce,
  With Wine and with noise.
In vaine we must wake in a dull bed alone.
Whilst to our warm Rival the Bottle, they're gone.
  Then lay aside charms,
  *And take up these arms**   *The Glasses.

2.

'Tis Wine only gives 'em their Courage and Wit,
Because we live sober to men we submit.
  If for Beauties you'd pass.
  Take a lick of the Glass.
'Twill mend your complexions, and when they are gone,
The best red we have is the red of the Grape.
  Then Sisters lay't on.
  And dam a good shape.

DAINTY. Dear Brimmer, well in token of our openness and plain dealing, let us throw our Masques over our heads.

HORNER. So 'twill come to the Glasses anon.

SQUEAMISH. Lovely Brimmer, let me enjoy him first.

LADY FIDGET. No, I never part with a Gallant, till I've try'd him. Dear Brimmer that mak'st our Husbands short sighted.

DAINTY. And our bashful gallants bold.

SQUEAMISH. And for want of a Gallant, the Butler lovely in our eyes, drink Eunuch.

LADY FIDGET. Drink thou representative of a Husband, damn a Husband.

DAINTY. And as it were a Husband, an old keeper.

SQUEAMISH. And an old Grandmother.

HORNER. And an English Bawd, and a French Chirurgion.

LADY FIDGET. Ay we have all reason to curse 'em.

HORNER. For my sake Ladies.

LADY FIDGET. No, for our own, for the first spoils all young gallants industry.

DAINTY. And the others art makes 'em bold only with common women.

SQUEAMISH. And rather run the hazard of the vile distemper amongst them, than of a denial amongst us.

DAINTY. The filthy Toads chuse Mistresses now, as they do Stuffs, for having been fancy'd and worn by others.

SQUEAMISH. For being common and cheap.

LADY FIDGET. Whilst women of quality, like the richest Stuffs, lye untumbled, and unask'd for.

HORNER. Ay neat, and cheap, and new often they think best.

DAINTY. No Sir, the Beasts will be known by a Mistriss longer than by a suit.

SQUEAMISH. And 'tis not for cheapness neither.

LADY FIDGET. No, for the vain fopps will take up Druggets, and embroider 'em, but I wonder at the depraved appetites of witty men, they use to be out of the common road, and hate imitation, pray tell me beast, when you were a man, why you rather chose to club with a multitude in a common house, for an entertainment, than to be the only guest at a good Table.

HORNER. Why faith ceremony and expectation are unsufferable to those that are sharp bent, people always eat with the best stomach at an ordinary, where every man is snatching for the best bit.

LADY FIDGET. Though he get a cut over the fingers—but I have heard people eat most heartily of another man's meat, that is, what they do not pay for.

HORNER. When they are sure of their wellcome and freedome, for ceremony in love and eating, is as ridiculous
as in fighting, falling on briskly is all should be done in
those occasions.

LADY FIDGET. Well then let me tell you Sir, there is no
where more freedome than in our houses, and we take
freedom from a young person as a sign of good breeding,
and a person may be as free as he pleases with us, as
frolick, as gamesome, as wild as he will.

HORNER. Han't I heard you all declaim against wild men.

LADY FIDGET. Yes, but for all that, we think wildness in a
man, as desireable a quality, as in a Duck, or Rabbet; a
tame man, foh.

HORNER. I know not, but your Reputations frightned me,
as much as your Faces invited me.

LADY FIDGET. Our Reputation, Lord! Why should you not
think, that we women make use of our Reputation, as
you men of yours, only to deceive the world with less
suspicion; our virtue is like the State-man's Religion, the
Quakers Word, the Gamesters Oath, and the Great
Man's Honour, but to cheat those that trust us.

SQUEAMISH. And that Demureness, Coyness, and Modesty,
that you see in our Faces in the Boxes at Plays, is as
much a sign of a kind woman, as a Vizard-mask in the
Pit.

DAINTY. For I assure you, women are least mask'd, when
they have the Velvet Vizard on.

LADY FIDGET. You wou'd have found us modest women in
our denyals only.

SQUEAMISH. Our bashfulness is only the reflection of the
Men's.

DAINTY. We blush, when they are shame-fac'd.

HORNER. I beg your pardon Ladies, I was deceiv'd in you
devilishly, but why, that mighty pretence to Honour?

LADY FIDGET. We have told you; but sometimes 'twas for
the same reason you men pretend business often, to
avoid ill company, to enjoy the better, and more privately those you love.

HORNER. But why, wou'd you ne'er give a Friend a wink
then?

LADY FIDGET. Faith, your Reputation frightned us as much, as ours did you, you were so notoriously lewd.

HORNER. And you so seemingly honest.

LADY FIDGET. Was that all that deterr'd you?

HORNER. And so expensive—you allow freedom you say.

LADY FIDGET. Ay, ay.

HORNER. That I was afraid of losing my little money, as well as my little time, both which my other pleasures required.

LADY FIDGET. Money, foh—you talk like a little fellow now, do such as we expect money?

HORNER. I beg your pardon, Madam, I must confess, I have heard that great Ladies, like great Merchants, set but the higher prizes upon what they have, because they are not in necessity of taking the first offer.

DAINTY. Such as we, make sale of our hearts?

SQUEAMISH. We brib'd for our Love? Foh.

HORNER. With your pardon, Ladies, I know, like great men in Offices, you seem to exact flattery and attendance only from your Followers, but you have receivers about you, and such fees to pay, a man is afraid to pass your Grants; besides we must let you win at Cards, or we lose your hearts; and if you make an assignation, 'tis at a Goldsmiths, Jewellers, or China house, where for your Honour, you deposit to him, he must pawn his, to the punctual Citt, and so paying for what you take up, pays for what he takes up.

DAINTY. Wou'd you not have us assur'd of our Gallants Love?

SQUEAMISH. For Love is better known by Liberality, than by Jealousie.

LADY FIDGET. For one may be dissembled, the other not —but my Jealousie can be no longer dissembled, and they are telling-ripe: [*Aside.*

Come here's to our Gallants in waiting, whom we must name, and I'll begin, this is my false Rogue.

[*Claps him on the back.*

prizes: prices.
pass your Grants: here, accept your gifts; perhaps

"grant" in the obsolescent meaning, "accomplish," "execute."

SQUEAMISH. How!

HORNER. So all will out now—

SQUEAMISH. Did you not tell me, 'twas for my sake only, you reported your self no man? [*Aside to* HORNER.

DAINTY. Oh Wretch! did you not swear to me, 'twas for my Love, and Honour, you pass'd for that thing you do? [*Aside to* HORNER.

HORNER. So, so.

LADY FIDGET. Come, speak Ladies, this is my false Villain.

SQUEAMISH. And mine too.

DAINTY. And mine.

HORNER. Well then, you are all three my false Rogues too, and there's an end on't.

LADY FIDGET. Well then, there's no remedy, Sister Sharers, let us not fall out, but have a care of our Honour; though we get no Presents, no Jewels of him, we are savers of our Honour, the Jewel of most value and use, which shines yet to the world unsuspected, though it be counterfeit.

HORNER. Nay, and is e'en as good, as if it were true, provided the world think so; for Honour, like Beauty now, only depends on the opinion of others.

LADY FIDGET. Well Harry Common, I hope you can be true to three, swear, but 'tis no purpose, to require your Oath; for you are as often forsworn, as you swear to new women.

HORNER. Come, faith Madam, let us e'en pardon one another, for all the difference I find betwixt we men, and you women, we forswear our selves at the beginning of an Amour, you, as long as it lasts.

Enter Sir JASPAR FIDGET, *and old Lady* SQUEAMISH.

SIR JASPAR. Oh my Lady *Fidget*, was this your cunning, to come to Mr. *Horner* without me; but you have been no where else I hope.

LADY FIDGET. No, Sir *Jaspar*.

LADY SQUEAMISH. And you came straight hither Biddy.

SQUEAMISH. Yes indeed, Lady Grandmother.

SIR JASPAR. 'Tis well, 'tis well, I knew when once they were throughly acquainted with poor *Horner*, they'd ne'er be from him; you may let her masquerade it with

my Wife, and *Horner*, and I warrant her Reputation
safe.

Enter BOY.

BOY. O Sir, here's the Gentleman come, whom you bid me
not suffer to come up, without giving you notice, with a
Lady too, and other Gentlemen—

HORNER. Do you all go in there, whil'st I send 'em away,
and Boy, do you desire 'em to stay below 'til I come,
which shall be immediately.

[*Exeunt Sir* JASPAR, *Lady* SQUEAMISH, *Lady*
FIDGET, *Mistris* DAINTY, SQUEAMISH.

BOY. Yes Sir.   [*Exit.*

[*Exit* HORNER *at t'other door, and returns*
with Mistris PINCHWIFE.

HORNER. You wou'd not take my advice to be gone home,
before your Husband came back, he'll now discover all,
yet pray my Dearest be perswaded to go home, and
leave the rest to my management, I'll let you down the
back way.

MRS. PINCHWIFE. I don't know the way home, so I don't.

HORNER. My man shall wait upon you.

MRS. PINCHWIFE. No, don't you believe, that I'll go at all;
what are you weary of me already?

HORNER. No my life, 'tis that I may love you long, 'tis to
secure my love, and your Reputation with your Husband, he'll never receive you again else.

MRS. PINCHWIFE. What care I, d'ye think to frighten me
with that? I don't intend to go to him again; you shall
be my Husband now.

HORNER. I cannot be your Husband, Dearest, since you are
married to him.

MRS. PINCHWIFE. O wou'd you make me believe that—
don't I see every day at *London* here, women leave
their first Husbands, and go, and live with other men as
their Wives, pish, pshaw, you'd make me angry, but
that I love you so mainly.

HORNER. So, they are coming up— In again, in, I hear 'em:

[*Exit Mistris* PINCHWIFE.

Well, a silly Mistriss, is like a weak place, soon got, soon
lost, a man has scarce time for plunder; she betrays her

Husband, first to her Gallant, and then her Gallant, to her Husband.

Enter PINCHWIFE, ALITHEA, HARCOURT, SPARKISH, LUCY, *and a Parson.*

PINCHWIFE. Come Madam, 'tis not the sudden change of your dress, the confidence of your asseverations, and your false witness there, shall perswade me, I did not bring you hither, just now; here's my witness, who cannot deny it, since you must be confronted— Mr. *Horner,* did not I bring this Lady to you just now?

HORNER. Now must I wrong one woman for anothers sake, but that's no new thing with me; for in these cases I am still on the criminal's side, against the innocent.   [*Aside.*

ALITHEA. Pray, speak Sir.

HORNER. It must be so— I must be impudent, and try my luck, impudence uses to be too hard for truth.   [*Aside.*

PINCHWIFE. What, you are studying an evasion, or excuse for her, speak Sir.

HORNER. No faith, I am something backward only, to speak in womens affairs or disputes.

PINCHWIFE. She bids you speak.

ALITHEA. Ay, pray Sir do, pray satisfie him.

HORNER. Then truly, you did bring that Lady to me just now.

PINCHWIFE. O ho—

ALITHEA. How Sir—

HARCOURT. How, *Horner!*

ALITHEA. What mean you Sir, I always took you for a man of Honour?

HORNER. Ay, so much a man of Honour, that I must save my Mistriss, I thank you, come what will on't.   [*Aside.*

SPARKISH. So if I had had her, she'd have made me believe, the Moon had been made of a Christmas pye.

LUCY. Now cou'd I speak, if I durst, and 'solve the Riddle, who am the Author of it.   [*Aside.*

ALITHEA. O unfortunate Woman! a combination against my Honour, which most concerns me now, because you share in my disgrace, Sir, and it is your censure which I must now suffer, that troubles me, not theirs.

HARCOURT. Madam, then have no trouble, you shall now see 'tis possible for me to love too, without being jealous, I will not only believe your innocence my self, but make all the world believe it—

Horner I must now be concern'd for this Ladies Honour.

[*Apart to* HORNER.

HORNER. And I must be concern'd for a Ladies Honour too.

HARCOURT. This Lady has her Honour, and I will protect it.

HORNER. My Lady has not her Honour, but has given it me to keep, and I will preserve it.

HARCOURT. I understand you not.

HORNER. I wou'd not have you.

MRS. PINCHWIFE. What's the matter with 'em all.

[*Mistress* PINCHWIFE *peeping in behind.*

PINCHWIFE. Come, come, Mr. *Horner*, no more disputing, here's the Parson, I brought him not in vain.

HARCOURT.[7] No Sir, I'll employ him, if this Lady please.

PINCHWIFE. How, what d'ye mean?

SPARKISH. Ay, what does he mean?

HORNER. Why, I have resign'd your Sister to him, he has my consent.

PINCHWIFE. But he has not mine Sir, a womans injur'd Honour, no more than a man's, can be repair'd or satisfied by any, but him that first wrong'd it; and you shall marry her presently, or— [*Lays his hand on his Sword.*

Enter to them Mistress PINCHWIFE.

MRS. PINCHWIFE. O Lord, they'll kill poor Mr. *Horner*, besides he shan't marry her, whilest I stand by, and look on, I'll not lose my second Husband so.

PINCHWIFE. What do I see?

ALITHEA. My Sister in my cloaths!

SPARKISH. Ha!

MRS. PINCHWIFE. Nay, pray now don't quarrel about finding work for the Parson, he shall marry me to Mr. *Horner;* for now I believe, you have enough of me.

[*To Mr.* PINCHWIFE.

HORNER. Damn'd, damn'd loving Changeling.

MRS. PINCHWIFE. Pray Sister, pardon me for telling so many lyes of you.

HARCOURT.[8] I suppose the Riddle is plain now.

LUCY. No, that must be my work, good Sir, hear me.

Kneels to Mr. PINCHWIFE, *who stands doggedly,*
with his hat over his eyes.

PINCHWIFE. I will never hear woman again, but make 'em
all silent, thus—   [*Offers to draw upon his Wife.*

HORNER. No, that must not be.

PINCHWIFE. You then shall go first, 'tis all one to me.

[*Offers to draw on* HORNER, *stopt by* HARCOURT.

HARCOURT. Hold—

Enter Sir JASPAR FIDGET, *Lady* FIDGET, *Lady* SQUEAMISH,
Mrs. DAINTY FIDGET, *Mrs.* SQUEAMISH.

SIR JASPAR. What's the matter, what's the matter, pray
what's the matter Sir, I beseech you communicate Sir.

PINCHWIFE. Why my Wife has communicated Sir, as your
Wife may have done too Sir, if she knows him Sir—

SIR JASPAR. Pshaw, with him, ha, ha, he.

PINCHWIFE. D'ye mock me Sir, a Cuckold is a kind of a
wild Beast, have a care Sir—

SIR JASPAR. No sure, you mock me Sir—he cuckold you!
it can't be, ha, ha, he, why, I'll tell you Sir.

[*Offers to whisper.*

PINCHWIFE. I tell you again, he has whor'd my Wife, and
yours too, if he knows her, and all the women he comes
near; 'tis not his dissembling, his hypocrisie can wheedle
me.

SIR JASPAR. How does he dissemble, is he a Hypocrite?
nay then—how—Wife—Sister is he an Hypocrite?

LADY SQUEAMISH. An Hypocrite, a dissembler, speak young
Harlotry, speak how?

SIR JASPAR. Nay then—O my head too—O thou libidinous
Lady!

LADY SQUEAMISH. O thou Harloting, Harlotry, hast thou
don't then?

SIR JASPAR. Speak good *Horner,* art thou a dissembler, a
Rogue? hast thou—

HORNER. Soh—

LUCY. I'll fetch you off, and her too, if she will but hold
her tongue.   [*Apart to* HORNER.

HORNER. Canst thou? I'll give thee—   [*Apart to* LUCY.

LUCY to MR. PINCHWIFE. Pray have but patience to hear me
Sir, who am the unfortunate cause of all this confusion,
your Wife is innocent, I only culpable; for I put her
upon telling you all these lyes, concerning my Mistress,
in order to the breaking off the match, between Mr.
Sparkish and her, to make way for Mr. *Harcourt.*

SPARKISH. Did you so eternal Rotten-tooth, then it seems
my Mistress was not false to me, I was only deceiv'd by
you, brother that shou'd have been, now man of conduct, who is a frank person now, to bring your Wife to
her Lover—ha—

LUCY. I assure you Sir, she came not to Mr. *Horner* out of
love, for she loves him no more—

MRS. PINCHWIFE. Hold, I told lyes for you, but you shall
tell none for me, for I do love Mr. *Horner* with all my
soul, and no body shall say me nay; pray don't you go
to make poor Mr. *Horner* believe to the contrary, 'tis
spitefully done of you, I'm sure.

HORNER. Peace, Dear Ideot. [*Aside to Mrs.* PINCHWIFE.

MRS. PINCHWIFE. Nay, I will not peace.

PINCHWIFE. Not 'til I make you.

Enter DORILANT, QUACK.

DORILANT. *Horner,* your Servant, I am the Doctors Guest,
he must excuse our intrusion.

QUACK. But what's the matter Gentlemen, for Heavens
sake, what's the matter?

HORNER. Oh 'tis well you are come—'tis a censorious world
we live in, you may have brought me a reprieve, or else
I had died for a crime, I never committed, and these
innocent Ladies had suffer'd with me, therefore pray
satisfie these worthy, honourable, jealous Gentlemen—
that—   [*Whispers.*

QUACK. O I understand you, is that all— Sir *Jasper,* by
heavens and upon the word of a Physician Sir,—
                              [*Whispers to Sir* JASPER.

SIR JASPAR. Nay I do believe you truly—pardon me my
virtuous Lady, and dear of honour.

LADY SQUEAMISH. What then all's right again.

SIR JASPAR. Ay, ay, and now let us satisfie him too.

[*They whisper with Mr.* PINCHWIFE.

PINCHWIFE. An Eunuch! pray no fooling with me.

QUACK. I'le bring half the Chirurgions in Town to swear it.

PINCHWIFE. They—they'l sweare a man that bled to death through his wounds died of an Apoplexy.[9]

QUACK. Pray hear me Sir—why all the Town has heard the report of him.

PINCHWIFE. But does all the Town believe it.

QUACK. Pray inquire a little, and first of all these.

PINCHWIFE. I'm sure when I left the Town he was the lewdest fellow in't.

QUACK. I tell you Sir he has been in *France* since, pray ask but these Ladies and Gentlemen, your friend Mr. *Dorilant,* Gentlemen and Ladies, han't you all heard the late sad report of poor Mr. *Horner.*

ALL LADIES. Ay, ay, ay.

DORILANT. Why thou jealous Fool do'st thou doubt it, he's an errant French Capon.

MRS. PINCHWIFE. 'Tis false Sir, you shall not disparage poor Mr. *Horner,* for to my certain knowledge—

LUCY. O hold—

SQUEAMISH. Stop her mouth—   [*Aside to* LUCY.

LADY FIDGET.[10] Upon my honour Sir, 'tis as true.

[*To* PINCHWIFE.

DAINTY. D'y think we would have been seen in his company—

SQUEAMISH. Trust our unspotted reputations with him!

LADY FIDGET. This you get, and we too, by trusting your secret to a fool—   [*Aside to* HORNER.

HORNER. Peace Madam,—well Doctor is not this a good design that carryes a man on unsuspected, and brings him off safe.—   [*Aside to* QUACK.

PINCHWIFE. Well, if this were true, but my Wife— [*Aside.*

[DORILANT *whispers with Mrs.* PINCHWIFE.

ALITHEA. Come Brother your Wife is yet innocent you see, but have a care of too strong an imagination, least like

an overconcern'd timerous Gamester by fancying an unlucky cast it should come, Women and Fortune are
truest still to those that trust 'em.

LUCY. And any wild thing grows but the more fierce and
hungry for being kept up, and more dangerous to the
Keeper.

ALITHEA. There's doctrine for all Husbands Mr. *Harcourt*.

HARCOURT. I edifie Madam so much, that I am impatient
till I am one.

DORILANT. And I edifie so much by example I will never
be one.

SPARKISH.[11] And because I will not disparage my parts I'le
ne're be one.

HORNER. And I alass can't be one.

PINCHWIFE. But I must be one—against my will to a Country-Wife, with a Country-murrain to me.

MRS. PINCHWIFE. And I must be a Country Wife still too I
find, for I can't like a City one, be rid of my musty Husband and doe what I list.   [*Aside*.

HORNER. Now Sir I must pronounce your Wife Innocent,
though I blush whilst I do it, and I am the only man by
her now expos'd to shame, which I will straight drown
in Wine, as you shall your suspition, and the Ladies
troubles we'l divert with a Ballet, Doctor where are your
Maskers.

LUCY. Indeed she's Innocent Sir, I am her witness, and her
end of coming out was but to see her Sisters Wedding,
and what she has said to your face of her love to Mr.
Horner was but the usual innocent revenge on a Husbands jealousie, was it not Madam speak—

MRS. PINCHWIFE. Since you'l have me tell more lyes—
                          [*Aside to* LUCY *and* HORNER.
Yes indeed Budd.

PINCHWIFE.   For my own sake fain I wou'd all believe.
              Cuckolds like Lovers shou'd themselves de-
                 ceive.
                   But—sighs—
              His honour is least safe, (too late I find)
              Who trusts it with a foolish Wife or Friend.

A Dance of Cuckolds.[12]

HORNER. Vain Fopps, but court, and dress, and keep a
          puther,
          To pass for Womens men, with one another.
          But he who aimes by women to be priz'd,
          First by the men you see must be despis'd.

FINIS.

EPILOGUE

spoken by Mrs. KNEP.[1]

Now you the Vigorous, who dayly here
O're Vizard-Mask, in publick domineer,
And what you'd doe to her if in Place where;
Nay have the confidence, to cry come out,
Yet when she says lead on, you are not stout;
But to your well-drest Brother straight turn round
And cry, Pox on her Ned, she can't be sound:
Then slink away, a fresh one to ingage,
With so much seeming heat and loving Rage,
You'd frighten listning Actress on the Stage:
Till she at last has seen you huffing come,
And talk of keeping in the Tyreing-Room,
Yet cannot be provok'd to lead her home:
Next you Fallstaffs of fifty, who beset
Your Buckram Maidenheads, which your friends get;
And whilst to them, you of Atchievements boast,
They share the booty, and laugh at your cost.[2]
In fine, you Essens't Boyes, both Old and Young,
Who wou'd be thought so eager, brisk, and strong,
Yet do the Ladies, not their Husbands, wrong:
Whose Purses for your manhood make excuse,
And keep your Flanders Mares[3] *for shew, not use;*
Encourag'd by our Womans Man to day,

puther: pother.

A Horners *part may vainly think to Play;*
And may Intreagues so bashfully disown
That they may doubted be by few or none,
May kiss the Cards at Picquet, Hombre,—Lu,
And so be thought to kiss the Lady too;
But Gallants, have a care faith, what you do.
The World, which to no man his due will give,
You by experience know you can deceive,
And men may still believe you Vigorous,
But then we Women,—there's no cous'ning us.

FINIS.

NOTES

1. John Downes says of *The Gentleman-Dancing-Master*, "it lasted but 6 Days, being like't but indifferently, it was laid by to make Room for other new ones." *Roscius Anglicanus*, London, 1708, p. 32.

2. Kastril is "the angry Boy" in Ben Jonson's *The Alchemist*. The line refers to an exchange between him and Subtle in Act IV, Scene 2: KAS: You lie. SUB: How, child of wrath and anger! the loud lie? / For what, my sodaine Boy? KAS: Nay, that looke you too, / I am afore-hand. *The Works of Benjamin Jonson*, London, 1616, p. 652.

3. Bayes, the poet of George Villiers' *The Rehearsal* (1671), was primarily a lampoon of John Dryden; the name became so identified with Dryden that he used it to describe himself in the Epilogue to *All for Love* (1677). Charles Hart had often fought Bayes's battles. He was Cortez in Dryden's *The Indian Emperour* (1665); Porphyrius in *Tyrannic Love* (1669); and Almanzor in the plays mentioned here, the two parts of *The Conquest of Granada* (1670–71).

4. Here Bayes, used in the general sense of "poet," refers to Wycherley.

Act 1

1. The Boy presumably exits after his announcement. Leigh Hunt provides a stage direction here.

2. In 1675 Q and later editions this stage direction falls at the end of Horner's line. I have moved it to the present position to emphasize that it is the physical action to accompany *So, Sir*.

3. Mercury was used in the treatment of venereal disease.

4. Pietro Aretino wrote his *Sonetti lussuriosi* (c. 1524) to accompany the engravings that Marcantonio Raimondi made from sixteen drawings by Giulio Romano, depicting sexual activity. As a result, the name "Aretine's postures" became attached to a genre of such engravings popular in England in the seventeenth century. Thomas D'Urfey in *Collin's Walk Through London and Westminster* (London, 1690) has Major reprimand Collin's prudishness: "Why? what a Devil had it

been / To thee, if *Peter Aretine* / With all his Nudities, and Postures, / Had deck'd the Walls or inward Cloyster?" (p. 57.) As an example of the confusion of Aretino with the artist, consider D'Urfey's annotation of his poem in which he describes Aretine as "A Famous *Italian* Poet and Painter, who for Publishing a Book of Shameful Nudities and Postures, was doom'd by the Senate to have his Eyes put out" (pp. 197–198).

5. On January 13, 1668, Pepys reports that he "stopped at Martin's, my bookseller, where I saw the French book which I did think to have had for my wife to translate, called 'L'escholle des filles,' but when I come to look in it, it is the most bawdy, lewd book that ever I saw . . . so that I was ashamed of reading in it . . ." (Wheatley, VII, 279). On February 8, he "bought the idle, rogueish book . . . in plain binding, avoiding the buying of it better bound, because I resolve, as soon as I have read it, to burn it, that it may not stand in the list of books, nor among them, to disgrace them if it should be found" (VII, 310). The next day, the Lord's Day, he was reading it in his office, finding it "a mighty lewd book, but yet not amiss for a sober man once to read over to inform himself in the villainy of the world" (VII, 311). *Escole des filles, ou la philosophie des dames, divisée en deux dialogues* (that may explain why Horner mentions a second part) was published at Fribourg in 1668. Its author is known variously as Mililot, Millot, Milot, and Hélot. There was supposed to have been an earlier, suppressed edition in 1655.

6. Horner may mean no more than that the reactions of Sir Jaspar and his ladies have proved the worth of his scheme. The *not so new* seems to imply a more general reference, an inside joke of some kind. Wycherley suggests in "The World Unmask'd," one of the *Miscellany Poems* (1704), that the practice is common: "Young Lusty Whore-masters, for Fumblers too, / And Impotent, with Men will often go, / But with their Women to have more to do" (Summers, IV, 4). The testimony of the poem may be beside the point since, although it is not dated, it quite likely postdates the play.

7. 1675 Q: *besides the Chirurgeon's Wine makes us witty.* In 1720 *Plays* the passage reads: "Wine gives you Joy; Love Grief and Tortures, besides Surgeons: Wine makes us witty. . . ." I have accepted the 1720 reading, but retained the original spelling which provides that *chirurgeon's* be possessive rather than plural; the Churchill edition recognizes that the possessive was intended.

8. Hunt adds an *exit*.

9. Warner in Act v of John Dryden's *Sir Martin Mar-all* (1667) advises his master, "get up into your Window, and set two Candles by you, take my Land-lords Lute in your hand, and fumble on't, and make grimmaces with your mouth, as if

you sung; in the mean time, I'll play in the next Room in the dark, and consequently your Mistress, who will come to her Balcone over against you, will think it to be you . . ." (London, 1668, p. 53). Sir Martin's attempts are as unsuccessful as Harcourt's description implies. The Dryden play was a popular one. It had been revived as recently as October 21, 1673. The mention of it in *The Country-Wife* may have reminded the Duke's Company that it was in the repertory for it was revived on January 21, 1675, nine days after the first recorded performance of Wycherley's play.

10. The three places Sparkish mentions were well-known restaurants. On March 13, 1668, Pepys reports "at noon, all of us to Chatelin's the French house in Covent Garden, to dinner" (Wheatley, VII, 361). Any of several Cock Taverns may be intended. The one in Bow Street, Covent Garden, is the likeliest candidate since Wycherley set part of Act v of *The Plain-Dealer* there, but the Cock Alehouse in Fleet Street and the Cock Tavern and Ordinary at Charing Cross are possibilities. Of the latter, Pepys says (March 15, 1669), "to the Cocke, at the end of Suffolke Streete, where I never was, a great ordinary, mightily cried up . . ." (VIII, 261). Bridget in Thomas Shadwell's *The Sullen Lovers* tells her mistress, "Oh, Madam, we must go to the Setting Dog and Partridge to supper to night, Master *Whiskin* came to invite us, there will be the Blades, and we shall have a Ball" (London, 1668, p. 31).

11. The horse market in Smithfield had a reputation for sharp dealing, as can be seen in two lines from the Epilogue to Dryden's *The Kind Keeper* (1678): "This Town two Bargains has, not worth one farthing, / A *Smithfield* Horse, and Wife of *Covent-Garden*" (London, 1680, p. 66). Since a jade was not only a worn-out horse, but a disreputable woman, Horner's simile is an apt one.

12. Plainly an aside. Churchill provides a stage direction. It may be that the *Aside* marking Harcourt's line, which might be spoken openly, really belongs to Pinchwife.

13. Cheapside was known for its silk mercers and linen drapers. Here, the phrase describes a merchant husband with a would-be fashionable wife. For an opinion of *Covent-Garden* wives, see the Dryden quote, n. 11.

Act 2

1. Both St. James's Park and the Mulberry Garden, which was in the Park, were popular gathering places. Part of Act II and all of Act v of *Love in a Wood* take place in the Park, which gives its name, as subtitle, to Wycherley's play. The New Exchange was an arcade of shops in the Strand; Mrs. Pinchwife gets there in Act 3.

2. 1683 Q: pleasure. This is the customary reading of the line. The spelling of "leisure" with the *ea* and the word's falling at the beginning of the line in 1675 Q suggest that the *p* may have been dropped. Churchill gives a compromised reading—(p)leasure—and Todd-Naylor reverts to *leasure*.

3. Plainly an aside. Bell adds the stage direction.

4. Names for the *old Boyes,* the *superannuated Stallions,* mentioned in Act 1 (p. 264), whose presence cannot endanger the ladies' reputations. Dryden later used Limberham as the name of the "tame, foolish Keeper" in *The Kind Keeper; or, Mr. Limberham* (1678); at the beginning of Act II, he is explaining to his Tricksy, "Nay, but dear sweet honey *Pug,* forgive me but this once : it may be any man's case, when his desires are too vehement" (p. 14). Tattle in William Congreve's *Love for Love* (1695) is another kind of joke.

5. As Sir Jaspar has told his wife Horner's secret in Act 1 (p. 261), it is difficult to understand what he has to whisper to her here. The context suggests the imparting of the same news; if that is the case, Wycherley may have forgotten that the job is already done. If there is no plot reason for the whisper, there is a dramatic one. Wycherley wants to pull Sir Jaspar and Lady Fidget aside so that Horner and Dorilant can play their brief approach scene with Dainty and Squeamish—really no more than a character-defining comic turn.

Act 3

1. Since Wycherley's references are usually to specific and well-known places, *Lewis's* is presumably a real tavern. Jacob Henry Burns lists a token, dated 1659, from an Edward Lewis in Bread Street, Cheapside. *A Descriptive Catalogue of the London Traders, Tavern, and Coffee-House Tokens,* London, 1855, p. 44. This is the only *Lewis's* I have come across and there is certainly no indication of the kind of popularity attached to the eating places Sparkish mentions in Act 1 (p. 268).

2. "If sack and sugar be a fault, God help the wicked!" So said Falstaff, *1 Henry IV,* II iv 464–465 (Arden). It was customary in the early part of the century to serve sugar with sack. Originally designating a dry wine, sack came to stand for any white wine from Spain or the Canary Islands. A sweet wine plus sugar might indeed be nauseous. Foh!

3. The Earl of Dorset began one of his songs: "Methinks the poor town has been troubled too long, / With Phillis and Chloris in every song." Yet he, too, rhymed to his Phillis ("Phillis, for shame let us improve"), as did the Earl of Rochester ("All my past Life is mine no more"), Sir Charles Sedley ("Phillis is my only Joy"), and almost every other

gentleman and/or poet who put verse to paper. *A Collection of English Poems, 1660–1800,* ed. Ronald S. Crane, New York, 1932, pp. 184, 183, 189, 173. Wycherley himself sang, "Why *Phillis!* shou'd you Rudeness call." Summers, III, 86.

4. The King dined in public about midday in the banqueting hall while the curious watched from the galleries. He supped in private. Sparkish is implying an intimacy that Harcourt's reply denies.

5. Clasp, who is not in the list of Persons, has only one line. It is unusual that such a character should be given a name; the doctor, after all, is called Quack. If there were no significance to the name, Clasp might be called simply Bookseller, as he is in Ward's edition. Since he is not, some joke may be intended; if so, it is a joke on the page only since the name would not be seen or heard in the theater. The first two of Wycherley's plays were printed for Henry Herringman, whose shop was in the Lower Walk of the New Exchange. On the second play, Herringman shared the publication with Thomas Dring, who is listed alone on the title page of *The Country-Wife.* If there was some difficulty between Herringman and Wycherley which would give point to an inside bookseller's joke, there is no record of it. Not that it helps in any way, but of the two plays Mrs. Pinchwife asks for, *Tarugo's Wiles* was printed for Herringman, *The Slighted Maid* for Dring.

6. *Covent Garden Drolery, or a Colection, Of all the Choice Songs, Poems, Prologues, and Epilogues,* (*Sung and Spoken at Courts and Theaters*) *never in Print before,* London, 1672. It contains "Since we poor slavish Women know" in a version slightly different from the one that is used at the end of Act II of *The Gentleman-Dancing-Master. Covent Garden Drollery,* London, 1927, pp. 21–22. Thomas St. Serfe's *Tarugo's Wiles* was performed in October 1667, and published in 1668. Robert Stapylton's *The Slighted Maid* was first performed on February 23, 1663, and published the same year; it was revived on July 28, 1668. Pepys reported of the first play that it was "the most ridiculous, insipid play that ever I saw in my life" (Wheatley, VII, 151), and of the second that "the play hath little good in it" (III, 51). If his opinion was a general one, the plays could hardly be considered popular items. The only reasonable explanation for their being used here is to indicate how country Mrs. Pinchwife is in her enthusiasm at seeing them. If we are going to be that subtle, however, we should remember that she is a young woman and that, unless there were unrecorded revivals, it is seven years since the plays had any kind of vogue, two facts which make unlikely her recognizing them at all. Her asking for the *Drollery* is

more acceptable. That volume does contain the Earl of Dorset's "To my friend, Master Tho. St. Serf" (pp. 65–66), which refers to *Tarugo's Wiles* without naming it, but that is hardly evidence that the play meant anything to anyone in 1675.

7. She is offstage. The Fujimura edition adds a stage direction to make this explicit.

8. There were two doors alongside one another on each side of the stage. See Nicoll, pp. 51–52. Sparkish and the others apparently entered from the same side that the Pinchwifes made their exit.

9. 1720 *Plays:* His. He.

10. This sounds as though it should be an aside although it has never been marked as such. Given Sparkish's wide-mouthed foolishness, he might speak it openly before Alithea.

11. This is not an acknowledgment of Horner's greeting; it is the form for ending a conversation.

12. 1675 Q: *Exit.* Hunt finally corrected this error.

Act 4

1. Fashionable places to live. The earls of Bristol and Sandwich lived in Lincoln's Inn Fields, of Clarendon and Oxford in St. James's Square, which had been laid out in St. James's Fields. Moll Davis, one of the King's mistresses, and Arabella Churchill, mistress of the Duke of York, also lived in St. James's. Although Sir William Temple and Robert Boyle both lived in Pall Mall, its most famous inhabitant at this time was Nell Gwynne. A brief scene in Act IV of *Love in a Wood* takes place in Pall Mall.

2. According to Canon LXII of the Anglican Book of Canons, 1604, re-established after the Restoration, ministers were forbidden to "join any persons . . . at any unseasonable times, but only between the hours of eight and twelve in the forenoon." *Synodalia,* ed. Edward Cardwell, I, Oxford, 1842, p. 282.

3. Plainly an aside; Churchill so marks it.

4. Churchill: *Aside.*

5. Presumably she almost hands him the wrong letter. This near mistake is simply an actor's (a playwright's) trick to emphasize for the audience the physical business involved in Mrs. Pinchwife's deception. It makes clear where the two letters are so that her switching of them will be quite apparent.

6. Since under the law of primogeniture the eldest son inherits the estate, younger brothers, on stage and off, are traditionally impecunious.

7. The castrati, whom chance or planning prepared for their trade, retained a soprano or alto voice after they had

grown to maturity; they were very popular in the seventeenth and eighteenth centuries. Baldassare Ferri, one of the most famous of the castrati, is supposed to have sung at Whitehall on June 3, 1669. Pepys reports on an unidentified singer, October 12, 1668, "we did hear the Eunuch (who, it seems, is a Frenchman, but long bred in Italy)" (Wheatley, VIII, 121).

8. In answer to the question, "What is a Row-Waggon?" R. J. Charleston, Keeper, Department of Ceramics, Victoria and Albert Museum, sent the following note to *Apollo*, LXV (June 1957), 251: "'Rollwaggon' (or however you care to spell it) is still used of the cylindrical-bodied vases of the type frequently found in Transitional or K'ang Hsi blue-and-white. The earliest reference which I know is in Wycherley's *Country Wife*. . . . The word 'rolwagens' appears in a Dutch inventory of 1689 (see T. Volker, *Porcelain and the East India Company*, Leiden, 1940, pp. 19–20, also footnote on p. 20)." Commenting on Charleston's note, Geoffrey Wills, editor of the ceramics column, points out that Horner's double entendre refers to the shape of the vase; a photograph on the same page confirms his suggestion.

9. The Lombard moneylender (see *Dancing-Master*, Epilogue, p. 235) would suspect the courtier of wanting a loan or wanting to welsh on one. Locket's was a popular ordinary at Charing Cross, known for its fancy foods and fancy prices. Lord Foppington in John Vanbrugh's *The Relapse* (1696): "I go to Dinner at *Lacket's;* where you are so nicely and delicately serv'd, that, stap my Vitals, they shall compose you a Dish no bigger than a Saucer, shall come to Fifty shillings" (London, 1697, p. 29).

10. An open arcade on two sides of Covent Garden, a fashionable place to live. The encounter between Sparkish and Alithea in Act 5 takes place there.

11. "To make sawce for a loyn of Veal, take all kind of sweet Pot herbs, and chopping them very small with the yelks of two or three Eggs, boyl them in Vinegar and Butter, with a few bread crums, and good store of sugar; then season it with Sugar and Cinnamon, and a Clove or two crusht, and so powre it upon the Veal, with the slices of Oranges and Lemons about the Dish." Gervase Markham, *The English House-Wife*, London, 1668, p. 77.

12. This speech is probably not to be heard by Sparkish. Perhaps the direct address to the doctor in it makes a specific stage direction unnecessary.

13. 1675 Q: Mrs. Pinchwife. The context and the style suggest that the line belongs to Mr. Pinchwife; following Hunt, I have assigned it to him.

14. Bell, probably correctly, marks this as an aside.

Act 5

1. 1695 Q-1: *aside*.

2. Plainly an aside; Bell so marks it.

3. A nightgown was a loose gown, something like a wrap. Although it was ordinarily worn informally, at home, there is nothing surprising in Margery (as Alithea) wearing it to go out. Evidence that it was worn to the theater can be found in Aphra Behn's *The Town-Fopp* (1676), although Sir Timothy belittles the inelegance of it: "Yes, and have the consolation, of seeing your frugal Huswifery Miss, sit in the Pit, at a Play, in a long Scarf, and Night-gown, for want of Points, and Garniture" (London, 1677, p. 3).

4. Plainly an aside; Churchill so marks it.

5. Presumably Horner is the whisperer and Pinchwife the *him* she motions away. Fujimura's stage direction makes this specific.

6. As Leigh Hunt indicates, an aside to Quack.

7. 1675 Q: Horner. 1695 Q-2 assigns the speech to Harcourt. The similarity between *Hor.* and *Har.* makes it surprising that there were not more confusions in the early editions.

8. Bell assigns this line to Horner; Hunt, Ward, and Churchill agree. Horner probably has more right to it than Harcourt, but since either might have spoken it, my reading follows 1675 Q.

9. Dueling was both common practice and against the law—or at least against the King's proclamation, August 13, 1660. See *Tudor and Stuart Proclamations, 1485–1714,* ed. Robert Steele, I, Oxford, 1910, pp. 389–390. False-swearing surgeons might well have been in demand to help keep fatal duels quiet.

10. In 1675 Q Lady Squeamish is usually identified as *Old La. Squeam.* when she speaks. This speech and the one below beginning *This you get* are assigned to *Old La. Fid.* in that edition. They are plainly Lady Fidget's lines; it is the *Old* and not the *Fid.* that is in error. The *Old* is finally dropped in 1720 *Plays.*

11. 1675 Q: Eew.

12. If this stage direction is to have any meaning for an audience, the dance would have to be to music that could be identified with cuckolds. Pepys reports on royal festivities, December 31, 1662: "Then to country dances; the King leading the first, which he called for; which was, says he, 'Cuckolds all awry,' the old dance of England" (Wheatley, II, 431). This was presumably "Cuckolds All a Row," a tune which, according to W. Chappell (*The Ballad Literature and Popular Music of the Olden Time,* I, London, 1859, p. 341), was in all editions of John Playford's *The Dancing Master.* Since

that work was published five times between 1652 and 1675, the tune was presumably well known. There is no record of what music was used in the Wycherley play, but "Cuckolds All a Row" is a possibility that might have given meaning to the dance. Since Pinchwife and Sir Jaspar have just been assured that they are not cuckolds, the use of a familiar tune would contradict the lines and provide a laugh.

Epilogue

1. 1675 Q: Mr. Hart. Plainly spoken by a woman. 1683 Q assigns it to Mrs. Knep.

2. Wycherley converts Falstaff's bragging in 1 *Henry IV*, II iv into sexual boasting. In that scene, Falstaff explains how he and his three companions, having just robbed sixteen men, were set upon by many more men and were themselves robbed; in his account, he keeps increasing the number of "rogues in buckram" whom he killed. The attackers were Prince Hal and Poins who, like the Falstaffs' friends of the Epilogue here, got the booty and the last laugh.

3. Since Flemish horses were imported during this century primarily for breeding purposes, the analogous use of Flanders mare for kept woman is all the sharper in the context of this sentence.

THE PLAIN-DEALER

The Plain-Dealer was performed on December 11, 1676, by the King's Company at the Theatre Royal, Drury Lane; it is uncertain whether this was the premiere. According to the title page of the first quarto, which is dated 1677, the play was licensed January 9, 1676 (i.e., 1677), and it was listed in *Term Catalogues*, May 28, 1677. There were at least two more editions of the play in 1677, labeled the second (wrongly dated 1678 on the title page) and the third. Churchill lists (p. 188) still another 1677 quarto, which he placed between the first quarto and the second edition. Although there is no mention of such an edition in Donald Wing, *Short-Title Catalogue, 1641–1700* (New York, 1945), the University Library, Cambridge, England, where Churchill consulted the rare quarto, confirms its existence. From their description of the title page and pagination, it sounds like a variation of the second edition. There were later editions in 1681, 1686, 1691, 1694, 1700, and 1709.

Molière's *Le Misanthrope* is the obvious source of Wycherley's play, but the extensive if superficial borrowing is so transformed by Wycherley that there is little resemblance between the two plays. For all their shared misanthropy, Manly and Alceste are not at all alike and the actions they take part in are totally different. The discussion on friendship between Manly and Freeman in Act I is a little like that between Alceste and Philinte in I i, and the Olivia-Novel gossip scene in Act II recalls Molière's II iv; in both cases Wycherley is much harsher in tone. Wycherley presumably borrowed and improved on Molière's letter scene (v iv) for the Novel-Plausible scene in Act IV, and, as Ward has pointed out (pp. 415, 480), there are obvious verbal echoes. Molière's *La Critique de l'École des Femmes* apparently gave Wycherley the idea for the discussion of *The Country-Wife* in Act II. Fidelia is a stereotype of romantic comedy and might have come from any number of sources, but the fact that she is attractive to a woman named Olivia suggests that *Twelfth Night* is the source and that Wycherley was making use of the contrast between the situation in his play and that in Shakespeare's.

The epigraph from Horace is from *Satires* I. x. 14–15: "Ridicule generally decides great matters more forcefully and better than severity." 1677 Q-2 corrected *acre* to *acri*. The comparison would seem to be between Manly's method and Wycherley's method in the presentation of Manly. The passage was apparently a favorite of Wycherley's for he used lines 7–8 as epigraph to *The Gentleman-Dancing-Master*.

The text for this edition is 1677 Q. I have also consulted the second and third editions (here called 1677 Q-2 and 1677 Q-3), as well as 1686 Q, 1691 Q, 1694 Q, and 1700 Q. The quartos I used are those in the University of Pennsylvania library. I have also made use of several other editions of *The Plain-Dealer: A Collection of the Best English Plays*, IV, London [1720], pp. 1–232 (printed for Thomas Johnson at The Hague; here called Hague); London, 1734; George B. Churchill (ed.), *The Country-Wife and The Plain-Dealer*, New York, 1924, pp. 188–434; Dougald MacMillan and Howard Mumford Jones (eds.), *Plays of the Restoration and Eighteenth Century*, New York, 1931, pp. 897–961; George H. Nettleton and Arthur E. Case, *British Dramatists from Dryden to Sheridan*, Boston, 1939, pp. 199–257.

THE
PLAIN-DEALER.
A
COMEDY.

As it is Acted at the

Theatre Royal.

Written by Mr WYCHERLEY.

HORAT.

—— *Ridiculum acre*
Fortius & melius magnas plerumque secat res.

Licensed *Jan.* 9. 1676.
ROGER L'ESTRANGE.

LONDON,

Printed by *T. N.* for *James Magnes* and *Rich. Bentley*
in *Russel Street* in *Covent-garden* near the *Piazza's.*
M.DC.LXXVII.

To my LADY B—[1]

Madam,

Tho I never had the Honour to receive a Favour from you, nay, or be known to you, I take the confidence of an Author to write to you a Billiet doux *Dedicatory; which is no new thing, for by most Dedications it appears, that Authors, though they praise their Patrons from top to toe, and seem to turn 'em inside out, know 'em as little, as sometimes their Patrons their Books, tho they read 'em out; and if the Poetical Daubers did not write the name of the Man or Woman on top of the Picture, 'twere impossible to guess whose it were. But you, Madam, without the help of a Poet, have made your self known and famous in the World; and, because you do not want it, are therefore most worthy of an Epistle Dedicatory. And this Play claims naturally your Protection, since it has lost its Reputation with the Ladies of stricter lives in the Play-house; and (you know) when mens endeavours are discountenanc'd and refus'd, by the nice coy Women of Honour, they come to you, To you the Great and Noble Patroness of rejected and bashful men, of which number I profess my self to be one, though a Poet, a Dedicating Poet; To you I say, Madam, who have as discerning a judgment, in what's obscene or not, as any quick-sighted civil Person of 'em all, and can make as much of a double meaning saying as the best of 'em; yet wou'd not, as some do, make nonsense of a Poet's jest, rather than not make it baudy: by which they show they as little value Wit in a Play, as in a Lover, provided they can bring t'other thing about. Their sense indeed lies all one way, and therefore are only*

*for that in a Poet which is moving, as they say; but what
do they mean by that word moving? Well, I must not put
'em to the blush, since I find I can do't. In short, Madam,
you wou'd not be one of those who ravish a Poet's innocent words, and make 'em guilty of their own naughtiness
(as 'tis term'd) in spight of his teeth; nay, nothing is secure from the power of their imaginations; no, not their
Husbands, whom they Cuckold with themselves, by
thinking of other men, and so make the lawful matrimonial embraces Adultery; wrong Husbands and Poets in
thought and word, to keep their own Reputations; but
your Ladyship's justice, I know, wou'd think a Woman's
Arraigning and Damning a Poet for her own obscenity,
like her crying out a Rape, and hanging a man for giving
her pleasure, only that she might be thought not to consent to't; and so to vindicate her honour forfeits her modesty. But you, Madam, have too much modesty to pretend
to't; tho you have as much to say for your modesty as
many a nicer she; for you never were seen at this Play, no,
not the first day; and 'tis no matter what Peoples lives have
been, they are unquestionably modest who frequent not
this Play: For, as Mr. Bays says of his,[2] that it is the only
Touchstone of Mens Wit and Understanding; mine is, it
seems, the only Touchstone of Womens Vertue and Modesty. But hold, that Touchstone is equivocal, and, by the
strength of a Lady's Imagination, may become something
that is not civil; but your Ladyship, I know, scorns to
misapply a Touchstone.[3] And, Madam, tho you have not
seen this Play, I hope (like other nice Ladies) you will
the rather read it; yet, lest the Chambermaid or Page
shou'd not be trusted, and their indulgence cou'd gain no
further admittance for it, than to their Ladies Lobbies or
outward Rooms, take it into your care and protection;
for, by your recommendation and procurement, it may
have the honour to get into their Closets: For what they
renounce in publick often entertains 'em there, with your
help especially. In fine, Madam, for these and many other
reasons, you are the fittest Patroness or Judge of this Play;
for you shew no partiality to this or that Author; for from*

*some many Ladies will take a broad jeast as chearfully
as from the Watermen,*[4] *and sit at some downright filthy
Plays (as they call 'em) as well satisfy'd, and as still, as a
Poet cou'd wish 'em elsewhere; therefore it must be the
doubtful obscenity of my Plays alone they take exceptions at, because it is too bashful for 'em; and indeed most
Women hate men, for attempting to halves on their
Chastity; and Baudy I find, like Satyr, shou'd be home,
not to have it taken notice of. But, now I mention Satyr,
some there are who say, 'Tis the Plain-dealing of the Play,
not the obscenity; 'tis taking off the Ladies Masks, not
offering at their Pettycoats, which offends 'em: and generally they are not the handsomest, or most innocent,
who are the most angry at being discover'd:*

—Nihil est audacius illis
Deprehensis; iram, atq; animos a crimine sumunt.[5]

*Pardon, Madam, the Quotation, for a Dedication can no
more be without ends of Latine, than Flattery; and 'tis
no matter whom it is writ to; for an Author can as easily
(I hope) suppose People to have more understanding and
Languages than they have, as well as more Vertues: But
why, the Devil! shou'd any of the few modest and handsome be alarm'd?* (*for some there are who as well as any
deserve those Attributes, yet refrain not from seeing
this Play, nor think it any addition to their Vertue to set
up for it in a Play-house, lest there it shou'd look too much
like acting.*) *But why, I say, shou'd any at all of the truly
vertuous be concern'd, if those who are not so are distinguish'd from 'em? For by that Mask of modesty which
Women wear promiscuously in publick, they are all alike,
and you can no more know a kept Wench from a Woman
of Honour by her looks than by her Dress; for those who
are of Quality without Honour (if any such there are)
they have their Quality to set off their false Modesty, as
well as their false Jewels, and you must no more suspect
their Countenances for counterfeit than their Pendants,
tho, as the Plain-dealer* Montaigne *says,* Els envoy leur
conscience au Bordel, & teinnent leur contenance en

regle:[6] *But those who act as they look, ought not to be scandaliz'd at the reprehension of others faults, lest they tax themselves with 'em, and by too delicate and quick an apprehension not only make that obscene which I meant innocent, but that Satyr on all, which was intended only on those who deserv'd it. But, Madam, I beg your pardon for this digression, to Civil Women and Ladies of Honour, since you and I shall never be the better for 'em; for a Comic Poet, and a Lady of your Profession, make most of the other sort, and the Stage and your Houses, like our Plantations,[7] are propagated by the least nice Women; and as with the Ministers of Justice, the Vices of the Age are our best business. But, now I mention Publick Persons, I can no longer defer doing you the justice of a Dedication, and telling you your own; who are, of all publick-spirited people, the most necessary, most communicative, most generous and hospitable; your house has been the house of the People, your sleep still disturb'd for the Publick, and when you arose 'twas that others might lye down, and you waked that others might rest; The good you have done is unspeakable; How many young unexperienc'd Heirs have you kept from rash foolish Marriages? and from being jilted for their lives by the worst sort of Jilts, Wives? How many unbewitched Widowers Children have you preserv'd from the Tyranny of Stepmothers? How many old Dotards from Cuckoldage, and keeping other mens Wenches and Children? How many Adulteries and unnatural sins have you prevented? In fine, you have been a constant scourge to the old Lecher, and often a terrour to the young; you have made concupiscence its own punishment, and extinguish'd Lust with Lust, like blowing up of Houses to stop the fire.*[8]

Nimirum propter continentiam, incontinentia
Necessaria est, incendium ignibus extinguitur.[9]

There's Latin for you again, Madam; I protest to you, as I am an Author, I cannot help it; nay, I can hardly keep my self from quoting Aristotle *and* Horace, *and talking to you of the Rules of Writing, (like the* French *Authors,)*[10] *to shew you and my Readers I understand 'em, in my Epistle, lest neither of you should find it out by the Play; and, according to the Rules of Dedications, 'tis no matter whether you understand or no, what I quote or say to you, of Writing; for an Author can as easily make any one a Judge or Critick, in an Epistle, as an Hero in his Play: But, Madam, that this may prove to the end a true Epistle Dedicatory, I'd have you know 'tis not without a design upon you, which is in the behalf of the Fraternity of* Parnassus, *that Songs and Sonnets may go at your Houses, and in your Liberties,*[11] *for Guinneys and half Guinneys; and that Wit, at least with you, as of old, may be the price of Beauty, and so you will prove a true encourager of Poetry, for Love is a better help to it than Wine; and Poets, like Painters, draw better after the Life, than by Fancy; Nay, in justice, Madam, I think a Poet ought to be as free of your Houses, as of the Play-houses;*[12] *since he contributes to the support of both, and is as necessary to such as you, as a Ballad-singer to the Pick-purse, in convening the Cullies at the Theatres, to be pick'd up, and carry'd to Supper and Bed at your houses. And, Madam, the reason of this motion of mine is, because poor Poets can get no favour in the Tiring Rooms, for they are no Keepers, you know; and Folly and Money, the old Enemies of Wit, are even too hard for it on its own Dunghill: And for other Ladies, a Poet can least go to the price of them; besides, his Wit, which ought to recommend him to 'em, is as much an obstruction to his Love, as to his wealth or preferment; for most Women now adays, apprehend Wit in a Lover, as much as in a Husband; they hate a Man that knows 'em, they must have a blind easie Fool, whom they can lead by the Nose, and as the* Scythian *Women of old, must baffle a Man, and put out his Eyes, ere they will lye with him,*[13] *and then too, like Thieves, when they have plunder'd and stript a Man, leave him. But if there shou'd be one of an hundred of those Ladies, generous enough to give her self to a Man that has more Wit than Money, (all things consider'd) he wou'd think it cheaper coming to you for a Mistress, though you made him pay his Guinney;*

as a Man in a Journey, (out of good husbandry) had better pay for what he has in an Inn, than lye on free-cost at
a Gentlemans House.

In fine, Madam, like a faithful Dedicator, I hope I have
done my self right in the first place, then you, and your
Profession, which in the wisest and most religious Government of the World, is honour'd with the publick allowance; and in those that are thought the most unciviliz'd
and barbarous, is protected, and supported by the Ministers of Justice; and of you, Madam, I ought to say no
more here, for your Vertues deserve a Poem rather than
an Epistle, or a Volume intire to give the World your
Memoirs, or Life at large, and which (upon the word of
an Author that has a mind to make an end of his Dedication) I promise to do, when I write the Annals of our
British Love, which shall be Dedicated to the Ladies
concern'd, if they will not think them something too obscene too; when your Life, compar'd with many that are
thought innocent, I doubt not may vindicate you, and me,
to the World, for the confidence I have taken in this Address to you; which then may be thought neither impertinent, nor immodest; and, whatsoever your Amorous
misfortunes have been, none can charge you with that
heinous, and worst of Womens Crimes, Hypocrisie; nay,
in spight of misfortunes or age, you are the same Woman
still; though most of your Sex grow Magdalens at fifty,
and as a solid French Author has it,

Apres le plaisir, vien't la peine,
Apres la peine la vertu;[14]

But sure an old sinner's continency is much like a Gamester's forswearing Play, when he has lost all his Money;
and Modesty is a kind of a youthful dress, which, as it
makes a young Woman more amiable, makes an old one
more nauseous; a bashful old Woman is like an hopeful
old man; and the affected Chastity of antiquated Beauties,
is rather a reproach than an honour to 'em, for it shews
the mens Vertue only, not theirs. But you, in fine, Madam,
are no more an Hypocrite than I am when I praise you;

therefore I doubt not will be thought (even by your's and the Play's Enemies, the nicest Ladies) to be the fittest Patroness for,

> *Madam,*
> Your Ladyship's most obedient, faithful, humble Servant, and
> THE PLAIN-DEALER.[15]

PROLOGUE,

Spoken by the

PLAIN-DEALER.

I The PLAIN-DEALER *am to Act to Day:*
And my rough Part begins before the Play.
First, you who Scrible, yet hate all that Write,
And keep each other Company in Spite,
As Rivals in your common Mistriss, Fame,
And, with faint Praises, one another Damn;
'Tis a good Play (we know) you can't forgive,
But grudge your selves, the pleasure you receive:
Our Scribler therefore bluntly bid me say,
He wou'd not have the Wits pleas'd here to Day.
Next, you, the fine, loud Gentlemen, o' th' Pit,
Who Damn all Playes; yet, if y'ave any Wit,
'Tis but what here you spunge,¹ and daily get;
Poets, like Friends to whom you are in Debt,
You hate: and so Rooks laugh, to see undone
Those Pushing Gamesters whom they live upon
Well, you are Sparks; and still will be i' th' fashion:
Rail then, at Playes, to hide your Obligation.
Now, you shrewd Judges who the Boxes sway,
Leading the Ladies hearts, and sense astray,
And, for their sakes, see all, and hear no Play;
Correct your Cravats, Foretops, Lock behind;

Foretop: a lock of hair, one's own or on a wig, arranged to ornament the forehead. The men in the boxes, pointing out to the ladies everything in theater except the play, would of course have worn periwigs.

The Dress and Breeding of the Play ne'r mind:
Plain-dealing *is, you'll say, quite out of fashion;*
You'll hate it here, as in a Dedication.
And your fair Neighbors, in a Limning Poet,
No more than in a Painter will allow it.
Pictures too like, the Ladies will not please:
They must be drawn too here, like Goddesses.
You, as at Lely's too, wou'd Truncheon wield,
And look like Heroes, in a painted Field;[2]
But the course Dauber of the coming Scenes,
To follow Life, and Nature only means;
Displays you, as you are: makes his fine Woman
A mercenary Jilt, and true to no Man;
His Men of Wit, and Pleasure of the Age,
Are as dull Rogues, as ever cumber'd Stage:
He draws a Friend, only to Custom just;
And makes him naturally break his trust.
I, only, Act a Part like none of you;
And yet, you'll say, it is a Fool's Part too:
An honest Man; who, like you, never winks
At faults; but, unlike you, speaks what he thinks:
The onely Fool who ne'r round Patron yet;
For Truth is now a fault, as well as Wit.
And where else, but on Stages, do we see
Truth pleasing; or rewarded Honesty?
Which our bold Poet does this day in me.
If not to th' Honest, be to th' Prosp'rous kind:
Some Friends at Court let the PLAIN-DEALER *find.*

round: in the sense of "to get
round a person."

MANLY
Mr. Hart.

Of an honest, surly, nice humor, suppos'd first, in the time of the *Dutch* War,[1] to have procur'd the Command of a Ship, out of Honour, not Interest; and choosing a Sealife, only to avoid the World.

FREEMAN
Mr. Kynaston.

MANLY's Lieutenant, a Gentleman well Educated, but of a broken Fortune, a Complyer with the Age.

VERNISH
Mr. Griffin.

MANLY's Bosome, and onely Friend.

NOVELL
Mr. Clark.

A pert railing Coxcomb, and an Admirer of Novelties, makes Love to OLIVIA.

MAJOR OLDFOX[2]
Mr. Cartwright.

An old impertinent Fop, given to Scribling, makes Love to the WIDOW BLACKACRE.

MY LORD PLAUSIBLE
Mr. Haines.

A Ceremonious Supple, Commending Coxcomb, in Love with OLIVIA.

JERRY-BLACKACRE
Mr. Charlton.

A true raw Squire under Age, and his Mothers Government, bred to the Law.

OLIVIA
Mrs. Marshall.

MANLY's Mistriss.

FIDELIA
Mrs. Boutell.

In Love with MANLY, and follow'd him to Sea in Man's Cloaths.

ELIZA
Mrs. Knep.

Cousin to OLIVIA.

LETICE
Mrs. Knight.

OLIVIA's Woman.

surly, nice: this odd combination of adjectives hold together if *surly* is taken in the sense of "arrogant" and *nice* as "strict." Of course, Manly is also *surly* as we use it today —"rude."

THE WIDOW BLACKACRE   A petulant, litigious Widow, al-
Mrs. Cory.   wayes in Law, and Mother to
                                          Squire JERRY.

*Lawyers, Knights of the Post, Bayliffs, an Alderman, a
    Booksellers Prentice, a Footboy, Sailors, Waiters, and
    Attendants.*

THE SCENE,

LONDON.

Blackacre: in litigation over land the label "black acre" was used to designate a particular parcel, to differentiate it from "white acre," "green acre," etc., as we might use *a, b, c*.

Knights of the Post: professional perjurers. In Samuel Butler's words, "a Retailer of Oaths, a Deposition-Monger, an Evidence-Maker that lives by the Labour of his Conscience. He takes Money to kiss the Gospel, as *Judas* did *Christ*, when he betrayed him." *Characters*, p. 154.

ACT I. SCENE I.

Captain MANLY's *Lodging.*

Enter Captain MANLY, *surlily; and my Lord* PLAUSIBLE *following him: and two* SAILORS *behind.*

MANLY. Tell not me (my good Lord *Plausible*) of your *Decorums,* supercilious Forms, and slavish Ceremonies; your little Tricks, which you the Spaniels of the World, do daily over and over, for, and to one another; not out of love or duty, but your servile fear.

PLAUSIBLE. Nay, i'faith, i'faith, you are too passionate, and I must humbly beg your pardon and leave to tell you, they are the Arts, and Rules, the prudent of the World walk by.

MANLY. Let 'em. But I'll have no Leading-strings, I can walk alone; I hate a Harness, and will not tug on in a Faction, kissing my Leader behind, that another Slave may do the like to me.

PLAUSIBLE. What will you be singular then, like no Body? follow Love, and esteem no Body?[1]

MANLY. Rather than be general, like you; follow every Body, Court and kiss every Body; though, perhaps at the same time, you hate every Body.

PLAUSIBLE. Why, seriously with your pardon, my dear Friend—

MANLY. With your pardon, my no Friend, I will not, as you do whisper my hatred, or my scorn, call a man Fool or Knave, by signs, or mouths over his shoulder, whil'st you have him in your arms: for such as you, like common Whores and Pickpockets, are onely dangerous to those you embrace.

PLAUSIBLE. Such as I! Heav'ns defend me—upon my Honour—

MANLY. Upon your Title, my Lord, if you'd have me believe you.

PLAUSIBLE. Well then, as I am a Person of Honour, I never attempted to abuse, or lessen any person, in my life.

MANLY. What, you were afraid?

PLAUSIBLE. No; but seriously, I hate to do a rude thing: no, faith, I speak well of all Mankind.

MANLY. I thought so; but know that speaking well of all Mankind, is the worst kind of Detraction; for it takes away the Reputation of the few good men in the World, by making all alike: now I speak ill of most men, because they deserve it; I that can do a rude thing, rather than an unjust thing.

PLAUSIBLE. Well, tell not me, my dear Friend, what people deserve, I ne'r mind that; I, like an Author in a Dedication, never speak well of a man for his sake, but my own; I will not disparage any man, to disparage my self; for to speak ill of people behind their backs, is not like a Person of Honour; and truly to speak ill of 'em to their faces, is not like a complaisant person: But if I did say, or do an ill thing to any Body, it shou'd be sure to be behind their backs, out of pure good manners.

MANLY. Very well; but I, that am an unmannerly Sea-fellow, if I ever speak well of people, (which is very seldom indeed) it shou'd be sure to be behind their backs; and if I wou'd say, or do ill to any, it shou'd be to their faces: I wou'd justle a proud, strutting, over-looking Coxcomb, at the head of his Sycophants, rather than put out my tongue at him, when he were past me; wou'd frown in the arrogant, big, dull face of an over-grown Knave of business, rather than vent my spleen against him, when his back were turn'd; wou'd give fauning Slaves the Lye, whil'st they embrace or commend me; Cowards, whil'st they brag; call a Rascal by no other title, though his Father had left him a Duke's; laugh at Fools aloud, before their Mistresses: And must desire people to leave me, when their visits grow at last as troublesom, as they were at first impertinent.

PLAUSIBLE. I wou'd not have my visits troublesom.

MANLY. The onely way to be sure not to have 'em troublesom, is to make 'em when people are not at home; for your visits, like other good turns, are most obliging, when made, or done to a man, in his absence. A pox why shou'd any one, because he has nothing to do, go and disturb another mans business?

PLAUSIBLE. I beg your pardon, my dear Friend. What, you have business?

MANLY. If you have any, I wou'd not detain your Lordship.

PLAUSIBLE. Detain me, dear Sir! I can never have enough of your company.

MANLY. I'm afraid I shou'd be tiresom: I know not what you think.

PLAUSIBLE. Well, dear Sir, I see you wou'd have me gone.

MANLY. But I see you won't.   [*Aside.*

PLAUSIBLE. Your most faithful—

MANLY. God be w'ye, my Lord.

PLAUSIBLE. Your most humble—

MANLY. Farewel.

PLAUSIBLE. And eternally—

MANLY. And eternally Ceremony—then the Devil take thee eternally.   [*Aside.*

PLAUSIBLE. You shall use no Ceremony, by my life.

MANLY. I do not intend it.

PLAUSIBLE. Why do you stir then?

MANLY. Only to see you out of doors, that I may shut 'em, against more welcomes.

PLAUSIBLE. Nay, faith that shan't pass upon your most faithful, humble Servant.

MANLY. Nor this any more upon me.   [*Aside.*

PLAUSIBLE. Well, you are too strong for me.

MANLY. I'de sooner be visited by the Plague; for that only wou'd keep a man from visits, and his doors shut.

[*Aside.*
[*Exit thrusting out my* LORD PLAUSIBLE.
Manent SAILORS.

1 SAILOR. Here's a finical Fellow *Jack!* What a brave fair weather Captain of a Ship he wou'd make!

2 SAILOR. He a Captain of a Ship! it must be when she's in the Dock then; for he looks like one of those that get the King's Commissions for Hulls to sell a Kings Ship,[2] when a brave Fellow has fought her almost to a Long-boat.

1 SAILOR. On my conscience then, *Jack,* that's the reason our Bully *Tar* sunk our Ship: not only that the *Dutch* might not have her, but that the Courtiers, who laugh at wooden Legs, might not make her Prize.

2 SAILOR. A pox of his sinking, *Tom,* we have made a base, broken, short Voyage of it.

1 SAILOR. Ay, your brisk dealers in Honour, always make quick returns with their Ship to the Dock, and their Men to the Hospitals; 'tis, let me see, just a Month since we set out of the River, and the Wind was almost as cross to us, as the *Dutch.*

2 SAILOR. Well, I forgive him sinking my own poor Truck, if he wou'd but have given me time and leave to have sav'd black *Kate* of *Wapping's* small Venture.

1 SAILOR. Faith I forgive him, since, as the Purser told me, he sunk the value of five or six thousand pound of his own, with which he was to settle himself somewhere in the *Indies,* for our merry Lieutenant was to succeed him in his Commission for the Ship back, for he was resolved never to return again for *England.*

2 SAILOR. So it seemed, by his Fighting.

1 SAILOR. No, but he was a weary of this side of the World here, they say.

2 SAILOR. Ay, or else he wou'd not have bid so fair for a passage into t'other.

1 SAILOR. *Jack,* thou think'st thy self in the Forecastle, thou'rt so waggish; but I tell you then, he had a mind to go live and bask himself on the sunny side of the Globe.

2 SAILOR. What, out of any discontent? for he's always as dogged, as an old Tarpaulin when hindred of a Voyage by a young Pantaloon Captain.[3]

1 SAILOR. 'Tis true, I never saw him pleas'd but in the

Wapping: downriver from the Tower of London, was an area frequented by sailors. For a colorful description, see the opening of Part XIV of Ned Ward's *The London-Spy Compleat,* London, 1706, pp.

322–329. 2 Sailor's *Kate* seems to have invested in the voyage.

the Indies: the East Indies. In her soliloquy (p. 406), Fidelia refers to the practice of suttee.

Fight, and then he look'd like one of us, coming from the Pay-table, with a new Lining to our Hats under our Arms.[4]

2 SAILOR. A pox he's like the *Bay of Biscay*, rough and angry, let the Wind blow where 'twill.

1 SAILOR. Nay, there's no more dealing with him, than with the Land in a Storm, No-near—

2 SAILOR. 'Tis a hurry-durry Blade; dost thou remember after we had tug'd hard the old leaky Long-boat, to save his Life, when I welcom'd him ashore, he gave me a box on the ear, and call'd me fawning Water-dog?

Enter MANLY, *and* FREEMAN.

1 SAILOR. Hold thy peace, *Jack,* and stand by, the foul weather's coming.

MANLY. You Rascals, Dogs, how cou'd this tame thing get through you?

1 SAILOR. Faith, to tell your Honour the truth, we were at Hob in the Hall, and whil'st my Brother and I were quarrelling about a Cast, he slunk by us.

2 SAILOR. He's a sneaking Fellow I warrant for't.

MANLY. Have more care for the future, you Slaves; go, and with drawn Cutlaces, stand at the Stair foot, and keep all that ask for me from coming up; suppose you were guarding the Scuttle to the Powder room: let none enter here, at your and their peril.

1 SAILOR. No, for the danger wou'd be the same; you wou'd blow them and us up, if we shou'd.

No-near: a command to the helmsman to come no closer to the wind. If the *no-near* here is taken as the culmination of the metaphor that compares Manly to a dangerous shoreline in a storm, the command would seem to be used as a warning not to come too close to the land. If, however, the metaphor ends with *Storm* and the speech takes a new tack after the comma, it is possible to read the *no-near* as a warning to 2 Sailor that he is about to wreck himself on the approaching wind (Manly). If we can assume that 1 Sailor has heard Manly's approach before his entrance, the *no-near* is a first attempt to get Jack to *Hold thy peace.* Certainly Manly is more wind than land in the passage as a whole, for he is *a hurry-durry Blade* and *foul weather. Hurry-durry:* a sailor's word for rough weather.

2 SAILOR. Must no one come to you, Sir?

MANLY. No man, Sir.

1 SAILOR. No man, Sir; but a Woman then, an't like your Honour—

MANLY. No Woman neither, you impertinent Dog. Wou'd you be Pimping? A Sea Pimp is the strangest Monster she has.

2 SAILOR. Indeed, an't like your Honour, 'twill be hard for us to deny a Woman any thing, since we are so newly come on shore.

1 SAILOR. We'll let no old Woman come up, though it were our Trusting Landlady at *Wapping*.

MANLY. Wou'd you be witty, you Brandy Casks you? you become a jest as ill, as you do a Horse. Be gone, you Dogs, I hear a noise on the Stairs. [*Exeunt* SAILORS.

FREEMAN. Faith, I am sorry you wou'd let the Fop go, I intended to have had some sport with him.

MANLY. Sport with him! A pox then why did you not stay? you shou'd have enjoy'd your Coxcomb, and had him to your self, for me.

FREEMAN. No, I shou'd not have car'd for him, without you neither; for the pleasure which Fops afford, is like that of Drinking, only good when 'tis shar'd; and a Fool, like a Bottle, which wou'd make you merry in company, will make you dull alone. But how the Devil cou'd you turn a man of his Quality down Stairs? You use a Lord with very little Ceremony, it seems.

MANLY. A Lord! What, thou art one of those who esteem men onely by the marks and value Fortune has set upon 'em, and never consider intrinsick worth; but counterfeit Honour will not be current with me, I weigh the man, not his title; 'tis not the King's stamp can make the Metal better, or heavier: your Lord is a Leaden shilling, which you may bend every way; and debases the stamp he bears, instead of being rais'd by't: Here again, you Slaves?

Enter SAILORS.

1 SAILOR. Only to receive farther instructions, an't like your Honour: What if a man shou'd bring you money, shou'd we turn him back?

MANLY. All men, I say; must I be pester'd with you too? you Dogs, away.

2 SAILOR. Nay, I know one man your Honour wou'd not have us hinder coming to you, I'm sure.

MANLY. Who's that? speak quickly, Slaves.

2 SAILOR. Why a man that shou'd bring you a Challenge; for though you refuse Money, I'm sure you love Fighting too well to refuse that.

MANLY. Rogue, Rascal, Dog. [*Kicks the* SAILORS *out.*

FREEMAN. Nay, let the poor Rogues have their Forecastle jests; they cannot help 'em in a Fight, scarce when a Ship's sinking.

MANLY. Dam their untimely jests; a Servant's jest is more sauciness than his counsel.

FREEMAN. But what, will you see no Body? not your Friends?

MANLY. Friends—I have but one, and he, I hear, is not in Town; nay, can have but one Friend, for a true heart admits but of one friendship, as of one love; but in having that Friend, I have a thousand, for he has the courage of men in despair, yet the diffidency and caution of Cowards; the secresie of the Revengeful, and the constancy of Martyrs: one fit to advise, to keep a secret: to fight and dye for his Friend. Such I think him; for I have trusted him with my Mistress in my absence: and the trust of Beauty, is sure the greatest we can shew.

FREEMAN. Well, but all your good thoughts are not for him alone? (I hope:) pray, what d'ye think of me, for a Friend?

MANLY. Of thee! Why, thou art a *Latitudinarian* in Friendship,[5] that is, no Friend; thou dost side with all Mankind, but wilt suffer for none. Thou art indeed like your *Lord Plausible*, the Pink of Courtesie, therefore hast no Friendship; for Ceremony, and great Professing, renders Friendship as much suspected, as it does Religion.

FREEMAN. And no Professing, no Ceremony at all in Friendship, were as unnatural and as undecent as in Religion; and there is hardly such a thing as an honest Hypocrite, who professes himself to be worse than he

is, unless it be your self; for, though I cou'd never get
you to say you were my Friend, I know you'll prove so.

MANLY. I must confess, I am so much your Friend, I
wou'd not deceive you, therefore must tell you (not
only because my heart is taken up) but according to
your rules of Friendship, I cannot be your Friend.

FREEMAN. Why pray?

MANLY. Because he that is (you'll say) a true Friend to a
man is a Friend to all his Friends; but you must pardon me, I cannot wish well to Pimps, Flatterers, De-
tractors, and Cowards, stiff nodding Knaves, and supple pliant kissing Fools: now, all these I have seen you
use, like the dearest Friends in the World.

FREEMAN. Hah, hah, hah— What, you observ'd me, I warrant, in the Galleries at *Whitehall*,[6] doing the business
of the place! Pshaw, Court Professions, like Court
Promises, go for nothing, man. But, faith, cou'd you
think I was a Friend to all those I hugg'd, kiss'd,
flatter'd, bow'd too? Hah, ha—

MANLY. You told 'em so, and swore it too; I heard you.

FREEMAN. Ay, but, when their backs were turn'd, did I not
tell you they were Rogues, Villains, Rascals, whom I
despis'd, and hated?

MANLY. Very fine! But what reason had I to believe you
spoke your heart to me, since you profess'd deceiving
so many?

FREEMAN. Why, don't you know, good Captain, that telling truth is a quality as prejudicial, to a man that wou'd
thrive in the World, as square Play to a Cheat, or true
Love to a Whore! Wou'd you have a man speak truth
to his ruine? You are severer than the Law, which requires no man to swear against himself; you wou'd
have me speak truth against my self, I warrant, and
tell my promising Friend, the Courtier, he has a bad
memory?

MANLY. Yes.

FREEMAN. And so make him remember to forget my business; and I shou'd tell the great Lawyer too, that he
takes oftner Fees to hold his tongue, than to speak!

MANLY. No doubt on't.

FREEMAN. Ay, and have him hang, or ruine me, when he shou'd come to be a Judge, and I before him. And you wou'd have me tell the new Officer, who bought his Employment lately, that he is a Coward.

MANLY. Ay.

FREEMAN. And so get my self cashiered, not him, he having the better Friends, though I the better Sword. And I shou'd tell the Scribler of Honour, that Heraldry were a prettier and fitter Study, for so fine a Gentleman, than Poetry!

MANLY. Certainly.

FREEMAN. And so find my self maul'd in his next hir'd Lampoon. And you wou'd have me tell the holy Lady too, she lies with her Chaplain.

MANLY. No doubt on't.

FREEMAN. And so draw the Clergy upon my back, and want a good Table to Dine at sometimes. And by the same reason too, I shou'd tell you, that the World thinks you a Mad-man, a Brutal,[7] and have you cut my throat, or worse, hate me! What other good success of all my *Plain-dealing* cou'd I have, than what I've mentioned?

MANLY. Why, first your promising Courtier wou'd keep his word, out of fear of more reproaches; or at least wou'd give you no more vain hopes: your Lawyer wou'd serve you more faithfully; for he, having no Honour but his Interest, is truest still to him he knows suspects him: The new Officer wou'd provoke thee to make him a Coward, and so be cashier'd, that thou, or some other honest Fellow, who had more courage than money, might get his place: the Noble Sonneteer wou'd trouble thee no more with his Madrigals: the praying Lady wou'd leave off railing at Wenching before thee, and not turn away her Chambermaid, for her own known frailty with thee: and I, instead of hating thee, shou'd love thee, for thy *Plain-dealing;* and in lieu of being mortifi'd, am proud that the World and I think not well of one another.

FREEMAN. Well, Doctors differ. You are for *Plain-dealing,* I find; but against your particular Notions, I have the practice of the whole World. Observe but any Morning what people do when they get together on the *Exchange,* in *Westminster-hall,*[8] or the Galleries in *Whitehall.*

MANLY. I must confess, there they seem to rehearse *Bays's* grand Dance:[9] here you see a *Bishop* bowing low to a gaudy *Atheist;* a Judge, to a Doorkeeper; a great Lord, to a Fishmonger, or a Scrivener with a Jack-chain about his neck; a Lawyer, to a Serjeant at Arms; a velvet *Physician,* to a thredbare *Chymist:* and a supple Gentleman Usher, to a surly Beef-eater; and so tread round in a preposterous huddle of Ceremony to each other, whil'st they can hardly hold their solemn false countenances.

FREEMAN. Well, they understand the World.

MANLY. Which I do not, I confess.

FREEMAN. But, Sir, pray believe the Friendship I promise you, real, whatsoever I have profest to others: try me, at least.

MANLY. Why, what wou'd you do for me?

FREEMAN. I wou'd fight for you.

MANLY. That you wou'd do for your own Honour: but what else?

FREEMAN. I wou'd lend you money, if I had it.

MANLY. To borrow more of me another time. That were but putting your money to Interest, a Usurer wou'd be as good a Friend. But what other piece of Friendship?

FREEMAN. I wou'd speak well of you to your Enemies.

MANLY. To encourage others to be your Friends, by a shew of gratitude: but what else?

FREEMAN. Nay, I wou'd not hear you ill spoken of behind your back, by my Friend.

MANLY. Nay, then thou'rt a Friend indeed; but it were unreasonable to expect it from thee, as the World goes now: when new Friends, like new Mistresses, are got by disparaging old ones.

Jack-chain: a jack chain is made of links consisting of double loops of wire resembling an 8. The name presumably comes from the roasting jack, the machine for turning a spit. The suggestion is that it is ostentatious, but its particular relevance to the scrivener escapes me.

Enter FIDELIA.

But here comes another, will say as much at least; dost not thou love me devilishly too, my little Voluntier, as well as he, or any man can?

FIDELIA. Better than any man can love you, my dear Captain.

MANLY. Look you there, I told you so.

FIDELIA. As well as you do Truth, or Honour, Sir; as well.

MANLY. Nay, good young Gentleman, enough, for shame; thou hast been a Page, by thy Flattering and Lying, to one of those praying Ladies, who love Flattery so well, they are jealous of it, and wert turn'd away for saying the same things to the old Housekeeper for Sweetmeats, as you did to your Lady; for thou flatterest every thing, and every Body alike.

FIDELIA. You, dear Sir, shou'd not suspect the truth of what I say of you, though to you; Fame, the old Lyar, is believ'd, when she speaks Wonders of you; you cannot be flatter'd, Sir, your Merit is unspeakable.

MANLY. Hold, hold, Sir, or I shall suspect worse of you, that you have been a Cushion-bearer to some State Hypocrite, and turn'd away by the Chaplains, for out flattering their Probation Sermons for a Benefice.[10]

FIDELIA. Suspect me for any thing, Sir, but the want of Love, Faith, and Duty to you, the bravest, worthiest of Mankind; believe me, I cou'd dye for you, Sir.

MANLY. Nay, there you lye, Sir; did I not see thee more afraid in the Fight, than the Chaplain of the Ship, or the Purser that bought his place?

FIDELIA. Can he be said to be afraid, that ventures to Sea with you?

MANLY. Fie, fie, no more, I shall hate thy Flattery worse than thy Cowardise, nay, than thy Bragging.

FIDELIA. Well, I own then I was afraid, mightily afraid; yet for you I wou'd be afraid again, an hundred times afraid: dying is ceasing to be afraid; and that I cou'd do sure for you, and you'll believe me one day. [*Weeps.*

FREEMAN. Poor Youth! believe his eyes, if not his tongue: he seems to speak truth with them.

MANLY. What, does he cry? A pox on't, a Maudlin Flatterer is as nauseously troublesom, as a Maudlin Drunkard; no more, you little Milk-sop, do not cry, I'll never make thee afraid again; for of all men, if I had occasion, thou shou'dst not be my Second; and, when I go to Sea again, thou shalt venture thy life no more with me.

FIDELIA. Why, will you leave me behind then?
(If you wou'd preserve my life, I'm sure you shou'd not.) [*Aside.*

MANLY. Leave thee behind! Ay, ay, thou art a hopeful Youth for the shore only; here thou wilt live to be cherish'd by Fortune, and the great ones; for thou may'st easily come to out-flatter a dull Poet, out-lye a Coffee-house, or Gazet-writer, out-swear a Knight of the Post, out-watch a Pimp, out-fawn a Rook, out-promise a Lover, out-rail a Wit, and out-brag a Sea-Captain: All this thou canst do, because thou'rt a Coward, a thing I hate, therefore thou'lt do better with the World than with me; and these are the good courses you must take in the World. There's good advice, at least, at parting; go, and be happy with't.

FIDELIA. Parting, Sir! O let me not hear that dismal word.

MANLY. If my words frighten thee, be gone the sooner; for, to be plain with thee, Cowardice and I cannot dwell together.

FIDELIA. And Cruelty and Courage never dwelt together sure, Sir. Do not turn me off to shame and misery; for I am helpless, and friendless.

MANLY. Friendless! there are half a score Friends for thee then; [*Offers her Gold.*] I leave my self no more: they'll help thee a little. Be gone, go, I must be cruel to thee (if thou call'st it so) out of pity.

FIDELIA. If you wou'd be cruelly pitiful, Sir, let it be with your Sword, not Gold. [*Exit.*

Enter first SAILOR.

1 SAILOR. We have, with much ado, turn'd away two Gentlemen, who told us forty times over, their names were Mr. *Novel,* and Major *Oldfox.*

MANLY. Well, to your Post again. [*Exit* SAILOR.
But how come those Puppies coupled alwayes together?

FREEMAN. O, the Coxcombs keep each other company, to shew each other, as *Novel* calls it; or, as *Oldfox* sayes, like two Knives, to whet one another.

MANLY. And set other peoples teeth an edge.

Enter second SAILOR.

2 SAILOR. Here is a Woman, an't like your Honour, scolds and bustles with us, to come in, as much as a Seamans Widow at the *Navy-Office:*[11] her name is Mrs. *Blackacre.*

MANLY. That Fiend too!

FREEMAN. The Widow *Blackacre,* is it not? that Litigious She-Pettyfogger, who is at Law and difference with all the World; but I wish I cou'd make her agree with me in the Church: they say she has Fifteen hundred pounds a Year Jointure, and the care of her Son, that is, the destruction of his Estate.

MANLY. Her Lawyers, Attornies and Solicitors have Fifteen hundred pound a Year, whil'st she is contented to be poor, to make other people so; for she is as vexatious as her Father was, the great Attorney, nay, as a dozen *Norfolk* Attornies,[12] and as implacable an Adversary, as a Wife suing for Alimony, or a Parson for his Tithes; and she loves an *Easter* Term, or any Term, not as other Countrey Ladies do, to come up to be fine, Cuckold their Husbands, and take their pleasure; for she has no pleasure, but in vexing others, and is usually cloath'd and dagled like a Baud in disguise, pursu'd through Alleys by Serjeants. When she is in Town, she lodges in one of the Inns of Chancery,[13] where she breeds her Son, and is her self his Tutoress in Law-French;[14] and for her Countrey abode, tho' she has no Estate there, she chooses *Norfolk.* But, bid her come in, with a pox to her; she is *Olivia's* Kinswoman, and may make me amends for her visit, by some discourse of that dear Woman.   [*Exit* SAILOR.

Enter Widow BLACKACRE *with a Mantle, and a green Bag, and several Papers in the other hand:* JERRY

---

bustles: struggles, scuffles.
Law-French: the corrupt variety of Norman French used in English law books.

green Bag: barristers carried their documents and papers in a green bag.

BLACKACRE *her Son, in a Gown, laden with green Bags, following her.*

WIDOW. I never had so much to do with a Judges Door keeper, as with yours; but—

MANLY. But the incomparable *Olivia,* how does she since I went?

WIDOW. Since you went, my Suit—

MANLY. *Olivia,* I say, is she well?

WIDOW. My Suit, if you had not return'd—

MANLY. Dam your Suit, how does your Cousin *Olivia?*

WIDOW. My Suit, I say, had been quite lost; but now—

MANLY. But now, where is *Olivia?* in Town? For—

WIDOW. For to morrow we are to have a Hearing.

MANLY. Wou'd you'd let me have a Hearing to day.

WIDOW. But why won't you hear me?

MANLY. I am no Judge, and you talk of nothing but Suits; but, pray tell me, when did you see *Olivia?*

WIDOW. I am no Visiter, but a Woman of Business; or, if I ever visit, 'tis only the *Chancery-lane* Ladies, Ladies towards the Law; and not any of your lazy, good-for-nothing Flirts, who cannot read Law-French, tho' a Gallant writ it. But, as I was telling you, my Suit—

MANLY. Dam these impertinent, vexatious people of Business, of all Sexes; they are still troubling the World with the tedious recitals of their Law-Suits: and one can no more stop their mouths, than a Wit's, when he talks of himself; or an Intelligencer's, when he talks of other people.

WIDOW. And a pox of all vexatious, impertinent Lovers; they are still perplexing the World with the tedious Narrations of their Love-Suits, and Discourses of their Mistresses: You are as troublesom to a poor Widow of Business, as a young Coxcombly Rithming[15] Lover.

Chancery-lane: Chancery Lane, runs between Holborn and Fleet, past Lincoln's Inn; Gray's Inn is not far away. This proximity to two of the Inns of Court made it a popular street for men (or Ladies, as the Widow says) connected with the law.

Intelligencer: Manly may be using it in the sense of "spy" or "informer," but more likely as "newsmonger."

MANLY. And thou art as troublesom to me, as a Rook to a losing Gamester, or a young putter of Cases to his Mistress and Sempstress, who has Love in her head for another.

WIDOW. Nay, since you talk of putting of Cases, and will not hear me speak, hear our *Jerry* a little; let him put our Case to you, for the Tryal's to morrow; and since you are my chief Witness, I wou'd have your memory refresh'd, and your judgment inform'd, that you may not give your evidence improperly. Speak out, Child.

JERRY. Yes, forsooth. Hemh! Hemh! *John-a-Stiles*—

MANLY. You may talk, young Lawyer, but I shall no more mind you, than a hungry Judge does a Cause, after the Clock has struck One.

FREEMAN. Nay, you'll find him as peevish too.

WIDOW. No matter. *Jerry,* go on. Do you observe it then, Sir, for I think I have seen you in a Gown once. Lord, I cou'd hear our *Jerry* put Cases all day long! Mark him, Sir.

JERRY. *John-a-Stiles*—no— There are first, *Fitz, Pere,* and *Ayle;*— No, no, *Ayle, Pere,* and *Fitz; Ayle* is seized in Fee of *Blackacre;*[16] *John-a-Stiles* disseises *Ayle; Ayle* makes Claim, and the Disseisor dyes; then the *Ayle*—no the *Fitz.*

WIDOW. No, the *Pere,* Sirrah.

JERRY. O, the *Pere:* ay, the *Pere,* Sir, and the *Fitz*—no the *Ayle;* no, the *Pere* and the *Fitz,* Sir, and—

MANLY. Dam *Pere, Mere* and *Fitz,* Sir.

WIDOW. No, you are out, Child; hear me, Captain then; there are *Ayle, Pere* and *Fitz, Ayle* is seised in Fee of

John-a-Stiles: a fictitious name for one of the parties in a legal action, comparable to our John Doe.
Fitz ("fils"), *Pere,* and *Ayle* (a corruption of "aieul"): are son, father, and grandfather in law-French. The case seems to make sense, once the Widow straightens it out, which it should since Wych-erley was, for a time, a member of the Inner Temple and his father was as notoriously litigious as the Widow Black-acre. Summers even suggests (I, 9) that the Widow is Daniel Wycherley in skirts. In the theater, of course, the effect should be that the legal speeches are gibberish.

Blackacre; and being so seised, *John-a-Stiles* disseises the *Ayle, Ayle* makes Claim, and the Disseisor dyes; and then the *Pere* re-enters, the *Pere* Sirrah, the *Pere—* [*To* JERRY.] And the *Fitz* enters upon the *Pere,* and the *Ayle* brings his Writ of Disseizen, in the *Post;* and the *Pere* brings his Writ of Disseizen, in the *Pere,* and—

MANLY. Canst thou hear this stuff, *Freeman?* I cou'd as soon suffer a whole noise of Flatterers at a great man's Levy in a morning; but thou hast servile complacency enough to listen to a Quibling Statesman, in disgrace, nay, and be before hand with him, in laughing at his dull No-jest; but I—   [*Offering to go out.*

WIDOW. Nay, Sir, hold. Where's the *Sub-pœna, Jerry?* I must serve you, Sir. You are requir'd, by this, to give your testimony—

MANLY. I'll be forsworn, to be reveng'd on thee.

[*Exit* MANLY, *throwing away the* Subpœna.

WIDOW. Get you gone, for a Lawless companion. Come, *Jerry,* I had almost forgot we were to meet at the Masters at three: let us mind our business still, Child.

JERRY. I, forsooth, e'en so let's.

FREEMAN. Nay, Madam, now I wou'd beg you to hear me a little, a little of my business.

WIDOW. I have business of my own calls me away, Sir.

FREEMAN. My business wou'd prove yours too, dear Madam.

WIDOW. Yours wou'd be some sweet business, I warrant: What, 'tis no *Westminster-Hall* business? Wou'd you have my advice?

FREEMAN. No, faith, 'tis a little *Westminster-Abby* business: I wou'd have your consent.

WIDOW. O fie, fie, Sir; to me such discourse, before my dear Minor there!

JERRY. Ay, ay, Mother, he wou'd be taking Livery and Seizen of your Jointure, by digging the Turf; but I'll

---

Writ of Disseizen in the Post: a post disseisin is a writ for one who, having recovered lands, is again disseised by the former disseisin.

Livery and Seizen: livery of seisin: delivery of possession. "Livery in *deed* is thus performed. . . . And then the feoffer, if it be of land, doth

watch your waters,[17] Bully, ifac. Come away, Mother.

[*Exit* JERRY, *haling away his Mother.*

Manet FREEMAN: *Enter to him* FIDELIA.

FIDELIA. Dear Sir, you have pity; beget but some in our Captain for me.

FREEMAN. Where is he?

FIDELIA. Within; swearing, as much as he did in the great storm, and cursing you, and sometimes sinks into calms and sighs, and talks of his *Olivia.*

FREEMAN. He wou'd never trust me to see her: is she handsom?

FIDELIA. No, if you'll take my word; but I am not a proper Judge.

FREEMAN. What is she?

FIDELIA. A Gentlewoman, I suppose, but of as mean a Fortune as Beauty; but her Relations wou'd not suffer her to go with him to the *Indies:* and his aversion to this side of the World, together with the late opportunity of commanding the Convoy, wou'd not let him stay here longer, tho' to enjoy her.

FREEMAN. He loves her mightily then.

FIDELIA. Yes, so well, that the remainder of his Fortune (I hear about five or six thousand pounds) he has left her, in case he had dy'd by the way, or before she cou'd prevail with her Friends to follow him, which he expected she shou'd do; and has left behind him his great bosom Friend to be her Convoy to him.

FREEMAN. What Charms has she for him, if she be not handsom?

FIDELIA. He fancies her, I suppose, the onely Woman of Truth and Sincerity in the World.

FREEMAN. No common Beauty, I confess.

FIDELIA. Or else sure he wou'd not have trusted her with

---

deliver to the feoffee, all other persons being out of the ground, a clod or turf, or a twig or bough there growing . . ." (William Blackstone, *Commentaries on the Laws of England,* 13th edi-

tion, London, 1800, Book II, No. 314). To make the livery, the Widow Blackacre would have to dig the turf, but if Jerry were accurate he would lose his double entendre.
ifac: in faith.

so great a share of his Fortune, in his absence; I suppose (since his late loss) all he has.

FREEMAN. Why, has he left it in her own custody?

FIDELIA. I am told so.

FREEMAN. Then he has shew'd Love to her indeed, in leaving her, like an old Husband that dyes as soon as he has made his Wife a good Jointure; but I'll go in to him, and speak for you, and know more from him of his *Olivia.* [*Exit.*

Manet FIDELIA *sola.*

FIDELIA. His *Olivia* indeed, his happy *Olivia,*
Yet she was left behind, when I was with him;
But she was ne'r out of his mind or heart.
She has told him she lov'd him; I have shew'd it,
And durst not tell him so, till I had done,
Under this habit, such convincing Acts
Of loving Friendship for him, that through it
He first might find out both my Sex and Love;
And, when I'd had him from his fair *Olivia,*
And this bright World of artful Beauties here,
Might then have hop'd, he wou'd have look'd on me
Amongst the sooty *Indians;* and I cou'd
To choose there live his Wife,[18] where Wives are forc'd
To live no longer, when their Husbands dye:
Nay, what's yet worse, to share 'em whil'st they live
With many Rival Wives. But here he comes,
And I must yet keep out of his sight, not
To lose it for ever. [*Exit.*

Enter MANLY *and* FREEMAN.

FREEMAN. But pray what strange Charms has she that cou'd make you love?

MANLY. Strange Charms indeed! She has Beauty enough to call in question her Wit or Virtue, and her Form wou'd make a starved Hermit a Ravisher; yet her Virtue, and Conduct, wou'd preserve her from the subtil Lust of a pamper'd Prelate. She is so perfect a Beauty, that Art cou'd not better it, nor Affectation deform it; yet all this is nothing. Her tongue as well as face, ne'r knew artifice; nor ever did her words or looks contradict her heart: She is all truth, and hates the lying, masking, daubing World, as I do; for which I love her, and for which I think she dislikes not me: for she has often shut out of her conversation for mine, the gaudy fluttering Parrots of the Town, Apes, and Echoes of men only, and refus'd their common place pert chat, flattery, and submissions, to be entertain'd with my sullen bluntness, and honest love. And, last of all, swore to me, since her Parents wou'd not suffer her to go with me, she wou'd stay behind for no other man; but follow me, without their leave, if not to be obtain'd. Which Oath—

FREEMAN. Did you think she wou'd keep?

MANLY. Yes; for she is not (I tell you) like other Women, but can keep her promise, tho' she has sworn to keep it; but, that she might the better keep it, I left her the value of five or six thousand pound: for Womens wants are generally their most importunate Solicitors to Love, or Marriage.

FREEMAN. And Money summons Lovers, more than Beauty, and augments but their importunity, and their number; so makes it the harder for a Woman to deny 'em. For my part, I am for the *French* Maxim, if you wou'd have your Female Subjects Loyal, keep 'em poor: but, in short, that your Mistress may not marry, you have given her a Portion.

MANLY. She had given me her heart first, and I am satisfi'd with the security; I can never doubt her truth and constancy.

FREEMAN. It seems you do, since you are fain to bribe it with Money. But how come you to be so diffident of the Man that sayes he loves you, and not doubt the Woman that sayes it?

MANLY. I shou'd (I confess) doubt the Love of any other Woman but her, as I do the friendship of any other Man but him I have trusted; but I have such proofs of their faith, as cannot deceive me.

FREEMAN. Cannot!

MANLY. Not but I know, that generally, no Man can be a great Enemy, but under the name of Friend; and if you are a Cuckold, it is your Friend only that makes you so; for your Enemy is not admitted to your house:

if you are cheated in your Fortune, 'tis your Friend that does it; for your Enemy is not made your Trustee: if your Honour, or Good Name be injur'd, 'tis your Friend that does it still, because your Enemy is not believ'd against you. Therefore I rather choose to go where honest, downright Barbarity is profest; where men devour one another like generous hungry Lyons and Tygers, not like Crocodiles; where they think the Devil white, of our complexion, and I am already so far an *Indian:* but, if your weak faith doubts this miracle of a Woman, come along with me, and believe, and thou wilt find her so handsom, that thou, who art so much my Friend, wilt have a mind to lie with her, and so will not fail to discover what her faith and thine is to me.

> *When we're in Love, the great Adversity,*
> *Our Friends and Mistresses at once we try.*

FINIS ACTUS PRIMI.

Act II. Scene i.

OLIVIA's *Lodging.*

Enter OLIVIA, ELIZA, LETTICE.

OLIVIA. Ah, Cousin, what a World 'tis we live in! I am so weary of it.

ELIZA. Truly, Cousin, I can find no fault with it, but that we cannot alwayes live in't; for I can never be weary of it.

OLIVIA. O hideous! you cannot be in earnest sure, when you say you like the filthy World.

ELIZA. You cannot be in earnest sure, when you say you dislike it.

OLIVIA. You are a very censorious Creature, I find.

ELIZA. I must confess I think we Women as often discover where we love, by railing; as men when they lye, by their swearing; and the World is but a constant Keeping Gallant, whom we fail not to quarrel with, when any thing crosses us, yet cannot part with't for our hearts.

LETTICE. A Gallant indeed, Madam, whom Ladies first make jealous, and then quarrel with it for being so, for if, by her indiscretion, a Lady be talk'd of for a Man, she cryes presently, *'Tis a Censorious World;* if, by her vanity, the Intrigue be found out, *'Tis a prying, malicious World;* if, by her over-fondness, the Gallant proves unconstant, *'Tis a false World;* and if, by her nigardliness, the Chambermaid tells, *'Tis a perfidious World:* but that, I'm sure, your Ladyship cannot say of the World yet, as bad as 'tis.

OLIVIA. But I may say, *'Tis a very impertinent World.* Hold your peace. And, Cousin, if the World be a Gallant, 'tis such an one as is my aversion. Pray name it no more.

ELIZA. But is it possible the World, which has such variety of Charms for other Women, can have none for you? Let's see—first, what d'ye think of Dressing, and fine Cloaths?

OLIVIA. Dressing! Fie, fie, 'tis my aversion. But, come hither, you Dowdy, methinks you might have open'd this Toure better: O hideous! I cannot suffer it! d'ye see how't sits?

ELIZA. Well enough, Cousin, if Dressing be your aversion.

OLIVIA. 'Tis so: and for variety of rich Cloaths, they are more my aversion.

LETTICE. Ay, 'tis because your Ladyship wears 'em too long; for indeed a Gown, like a Gallant, grows one's aversion, by having too much of it.

OLIVIA. Insatiable Creature! I'll be sworn I have had this not above three dayes, Cousin, and within this month have made some six more.

ELIZA. Then your aversion to 'em is not altogether so great.

OLIVIA. Alas! 'tis for my Woman only I wear 'em, Cousin.

LETTICE. If it be for me only, Madam, pray do not wear 'em.

ELIZA. But what d'ye think of Visits—Balls—

OLIVIA. O, I detest 'em.

Toure: from the French "taure" (also called a "bullhead") a forehead fringe of thick curls (sometimes artificial), popular in the late 1670s. Olivia's locks are apparently too tightly curled.

ELIZA. Of Playes?

OLIVIA. I abominate 'em: filthy, obscene, hideous things?

ELIZA. What say you to *Masquerading* in the Winter, and *Hide-park* in the Summer?[1]

OLIVIA. Insipid pleasures I taste not.

ELIZA. Nay, if you are for more solid pleasure, what think you of a rich, young Husband?

OLIVIA. O horrid! Marriage! what a pleasure you have found out! I nauseate it of all things.

LETTICE. But what does your Ladyship think then of a liberal, handsom, young Lover?

OLIVIA. A handsom, young Fellow, you Impudent! Be gone, out of my sight; name a handsom young Fellow to me! Foh, a hideous handsom young Fellow I abominate.   [*Spits.*

ELIZA. Indeed! But let's see—will nothing please you? what d'ye think of the Court?

OLIVIA. How? the Court! the Court, Cousin! my aversion, my aversion, my aversion of all aversions.

ELIZA. How? the Court! where—

OLIVIA. Where Sincerity is a quality as out of fashion, and as unprosperous, as Bashfulness; I cou'd not laugh at a Quibble, tho' it were a fat Privy Counsellor's; nor praise a Lord's ill Verses, tho' I were my self the Subject; nor an old Lady's young looks, tho' I were her Woman; nor sit to a vain young *Simile-maker*, tho' he flatter'd me: In short, I cou'd not glote upon a man when he comes into a Room, and laugh at him when he goes out; I cannot rail at the absent, to flatter the standers by, I—

ELIZA. Well, but Railing now is so common, that 'tis no more Malice, but the fashion; and the absent think they are no more the worse for being rail'd at, than the present think they are the better for being flatter'd: and for the Court—

OLIVIA. Nay, do not defend the Court; for you'll make me rail at it, like a trusting Citizen's Widow.

ELIZA. Or like a *Holborn* Lady,[2] who cou'd not get into the last Ball, or was out of countenance in the Drawing-room[3] the last Sunday of her appearance there; for

glote: gloat: look admiringly.

none rail at the Court, but those who cannot get into it, or else who are ridiculous when they are there: and I shall suspect you were laugh'd at, when you were last there, or wou'd be a Maid of Honour.

OLIVIA. I a Maid of Honour! To be a Maid of Honour were yet of all things my aversion.

ELIZA. In what sense am I to understand you? But, in fine, by the word Aversion, I'm sure you dissemble; for I never knew Woman yet that us'd it, who did not. Come, our tongues belie our hearts, more than our Pocket-glasses do our faces; but methinks we ought to leave off dissembling, since 'tis grown of no use to us; for all wise observers understand us now adayes, as they do Dreams, Almanacks, and *Dutch Gazets*,[4] by the contrary: And a Man no more believes a Woman, when she sayes she has an Aversion for him, than when she sayes she'll Cry out.

OLIVIA. O filthy, hideous! Peace, Cousin, or your discourse will be my Aversion; and you may believe me.

ELIZA. Yes; for, if any thing be a Womans Aversion, 'tis *Plain-dealing* from another Woman: and perhaps that's your quarrel to the World; for that will talk, as your Woman sayes.

OLIVIA. Talk not of me sure; for what Men do I converse with? what Visits do I admit?

Enter BOY.

BOY. Here's the Gentleman to wait upon you, Madam.

OLIVIA. On me! you little, unthinking Fop, d'ye know what you say?

BOY. Yes, Madam, 'tis the Gentleman that comes every day to you, who—

OLIVIA. Hold your peace, you heedless little Animal, and get you gone. This Countrey Boy, Cousin, takes my Dancing-master, Taylor, or the spruce Millener, for Visiters.   [*Exit* BOY.

LETTICE. No, Madam, 'tis Mr. *Novel*, I'm sure, by his talking so loud: I know his voice too, Madam.

OLIVIA. You know nothing, you Buffle-headed, stupid Creature you; you wou'd make my Cousin believe I

Buffle-headed: blockheaded.

receive Visits: but if it be Mr.—what did you call him?

LETTICE. Mr. *Novel*, Madam, he that—

OLIVIA. Hold your peace, I'll hear no more of him; but if it be your Mr.— (I can't think of his name again) I suppose he has follow'd my Cousin hither.

ELIZA. No, Cousin, I will not rob you of the Honour of the Visit: 'tis to you, Cousin, for I know him not.

OLIVIA. Nor did I ever hear of him before, upon my Honour, Cousin; besides, ha'nt I told you, that Visits, and the business of Visits, Flattery, and Detraction, are my Aversion? D'ye think then I wou'd admit such a Coxcomb as he is? who, rather than not rail, will rail at the dead, whom none speak ill of; and, rather than not flatter, will flatter the Poets of the Age, whom none will flatter; who affects Novelty as much as the Fashion, and is as fantastical as changeable, and as well known as the Fashion; who likes nothing, but what is new; nay, wou'd choose to have his Friend, or his Title, a new one. In fine, he is my Aversion.

ELIZA. I find you do know him, Cousin; at least, have heard of him.

OLIVIA. Yes, now I remember, I have heard of him.

ELIZA. Well; but, since he is such a Coxcomb, for Heav'ns sake, let him not come up: tell him, Mrs. *Lettice*, your Lady is not within.

OLIVIA. No, *Lettice*, tell him, my Cousin is here, and that he may come up; for, notwithstanding I detest the sight of him, you may like his conversation; and tho' I wou'd use him scurvily, I will not be rude to you, in my own Lodging; since he has follow'd you hither, let him come up, I say.

ELIZA. Very fine! Pray let him go to the Devil, I say, for me: I know him not, nor desire it. Send him away, Mrs. *Lettice*.

OLIVIA. Upon my word, she sha'nt: I must disobey your commands, to comply with your desires. Call him up, *Lettice*.

ELIZA. Nay, I'll swear she shall not stir on that Errand.

[*Holds* LETTICE.

OLIVIA. Well then, I'll call him my self for you, since you will have it so. Mr. *Novel,* [*Calls out at the door*] Sir, Sir.

Enter NOVEL.

NOVEL. Madam, I beg your pardon, perhaps you were busie: I did not think you had company with you.

ELIZA. Yet he comes to me, Cousin!   [*Aside.*

OLIVIA. —Chairs there.   [*They sit.*[5]

NOVEL. Well, but Madam, d'ye know whence I come now?

OLIVIA. From some melancholy place I warrant, Sir, since they have lost your good company.

ELIZA. So.

NOVEL. From a place, where they have treated me, at dinner, with so much civility and kindness, a pox on 'em, that I cou'd hardly get away to you, dear Madam.

OLIVIA. You have a way with you so new, and obliging, Sir.

ELIZA. You hate Flattery, Cousin!   [*Apart to* OLIVIA.

NOVEL. Nay faith, Madam, d'ye think my way new? then you are obliging, Madam. I must confess, I hate imitation, to do any thing like other people: all that know me, do me the Honour to say, I am an Original Faith; but as I was saying, Madam, I have been treated to day, with all the ceremony and kindness imaginable, at my Lady Autums; but the nauseous old Woman at the upper end of her Table—

OLIVIA. Revives the old *Grecian* custom, of serving in a Deaths head with their Banquets.[6]

NOVEL. Hah, ha! fine, just ifaith; nay, and new: 'tis like eating with the Ghost in the *Libertine;*[7] she wou'd frighten a Man from her dinner, with her hollow invitations, and spoil one's stomach—

OLIVIA. To Meat, or Women. I detest her hollow cherry cheeks; she looks like an old Coach new painted: affecting an unseemly smugness, whil'st she is ready to drop in pieces.

ELIZA. You hate Detraction I see, Cousin!

[*Apart to* OLIVIA.

NOVEL. But the silly old Fury, whil'st she affects to look like a Woman of this Age, talks—

OLIVIA. Like one of the last; and as passionately as an old Courtier, who has out-liv'd his Office.

NOVEL. Yes, Madam, but pray let me give you her character. Then, she never counts her age by the years, but—

OLIVIA. By the Masques she has liv'd to see.

NOVEL. Nay then, Madam, I see you think a little harmless railing too great a pleasure for any but your self, and therefore I've done.

OLIVIA. Nay, faith, you shall tell me who you had there at dinner.

NOVEL. If you wou'd hear me, Madam.

OLIVIA. Most patiently: speak, Sir.

NOVEL. Then, we had her daughter—

OLIVIA. Ay, her daughter, the very disgrace to good cloaths, which she alwayes wears, but to heighten her deformity, not mend it; for she is still most splendidly, gallantly, ugly, and looks like an ill piece of daubing in a rich Frame.

NOVEL. So! But have you done with her, Madam? And can you spare her to me a little now?

OLIVIA. Ay, ay, Sir.

NOVEL. Then, she is like—

OLIVIA. She is, you'd say, like a City Bride, the greater Fortune, but not the greater Beauty, for her dress.

NOVEL. Well: yet have you done, Madam? Then, she—

OLIVIA. Then she bestows as unfortunately on her face all the graces in fashion, as the languishing eye, the hanging or pouting lip; but as the Fool is never more provoking than when he aims at Wit, the ill-favor'd of our Sex are never more nauseous than when they wou'd be Beauties, adding to their natural deformity, the artificial ugliness of affectation.

ELIZA. So, Cousin, I find one may have a collection of all ones acquaintances Pictures as well at your house, as at Mr. *Lely's;* only the difference is, there we find 'em much handsomer than they are, and like; here, much uglier, and like: and you are the first of the profession of Picture-drawing I ever knew without flattery.

OLIVIA. I draw after the Life; do no Body wrong, Cousin.

ELIZA. No, you hate flattery and detraction!

OLIVIA. But, Mr. *Novel*, who had you besides at dinner?

NOVEL. Nay, the Devil take me if I tell you, unless you will allow me the priviledge of railing in my turn; but, now I think on't, the Women ought to be your Province, as the Men are mine: and you must know, we had him whom—

OLIVIA. Him, whom—

NOVEL. What? Invading me already? And giving the character, before you know the Man?

ELIZA. No, that is not fair, tho' it be usual.

OLIVIA. I beg your pardon, Mr. *Novel*, pray, go on.

NOVEL. Then, I say, we had that familiar Coxcomb, who is at home wheresoe're he comes.

OLIVIA. Ay, that Fool—

NOVEL. Nay then, Madam, your Servant: I'm gone. Taking a Fool out of ones mouth, is worse than taking the Bread out of ones mouth.

OLIVIA. I've done, your pardon, Mr. *Novel*, pray proceed.

NOVEL. I say, the Rogue, that he may be the onely Wit in company, will let no Body else talk, and—

OLIVIA. Ay, those Fops who love to talk all themselves, are of all things my Aversion.

NOVEL. Then you'll let me speak, Madam, sure. The Rogue, I say, will force his Jest upon you; and I hate a Jest that's forc'd upon a Man, as much as a Glass.

ELIZA. Why, I hope, Sir, he does not expect a Man of your temperance in jesting shou'd do him reason?

NOVEL. What, interruption from this side too! I must then—
[*Offers to rise,* OLIVIA *holds him.*

OLIVIA. No, Sir— You must know, Cousin, that Fop he means, tho' he talks only to be commended, will not give you leave to do't.

NOVEL. But, Madam—

OLIVIA. He a Wit! hang him, he's only an Adopter of stragling Jests, and fatherless Lampoons; by the credit of which, he eats at good Tables, and so, like the barren Beggar-woman, lives by borrow'd Children.

do him reason: do him justice. Here the phrase means "to keep up with him in drinking"; for a more conventional usage, see Lord Plausible's speech, p. 427.

NOVEL. Madam—

OLIVIA. And never was Author of any thing, but his News; but that is still all his own.

NOVEL. Madam, pray—

OLIVIA. An eternal Babler; and makes no more use of his ears, than a Man that sits at a Play by his Mistress, or in Fop-corner:[8] he's, in fine, a base detracting Fellow, and is my Aversion. But who else pr'ythee, Mr. *Novel*, was there with you? Nay, you sha'nt stir.

NOVEL. I beg your pardon, Madam, I cannot stay in any place, where I'm not allow'd a little Christian liberty of railing.

OLIVIA. Nay, pr'ythee, Mr. *Novel*, stay; and, tho' you shou'd rail at me, I wou'd hear you with patience: pr'ythee who else was there with you?

NOVEL. Your Servant, Madam.

OLIVIA. Nay, pr'ythee tell us, Mr. *Novel*, pr'ythee do.

NOVEL. We had no Body else.

OLIVIA. Nay, faith I know you had. Come, my Lord *Plausible* was there too, who is Cousin, a—

ELIZA. You need not tell me what he is, Cousin; for I know him to be a civil, good-natur'd, harmless Gentleman, that speaks well of all the World, and is alwayes in good humor, and—

OLIVIA. Hold, Cousin, hold, I hate Detraction; but I must tell you, Cousin, his civility, is cowardice; his good nature, want of wit; and has neither courage, or sense to rail: And for his being alwayes in humor, 'tis because he is never dissatisfi'd with himself. In fine, he is my Aversion; and I never admit his Visits beyond my Hall.

NOVEL. No, he visit you! Dam him, cringing, grinning Rogue; if I shou'd see him coming up to you, I wou'd make bold to kick him down again. Ha!—

Enter my Lord PLAUSIBLE.

My dear Lord, your most humble Servant.

[*Rises, and salutes* PLAUSIBLE, *and kisses him.*

ELIZA. So! I find kissing and railing succeed each other with the angry Men, as well as with the angry Women; and their quarrels are like Love-quarrels, since absence is the only cause of them; for, as soon as the Man appears again, they are over.   [*Aside.*

PLAUSIBLE. Your most faithful, humble Servant, generous
Mr. *Novel;* and, Madam, I am your eternal Slave, and
kiss your fair hands; which I had done sooner, according
to your commands, but—

OLIVIA. No excuses, my Lord.

ELIZA. What, you sent for him then, Cousin?   [*Apart.*

NOVEL. Ha! invited!   [*Aside.*

OLIVIA. I know you must divide your self; for your good
company is too general a good, to be ingross'd by any
particular Friend.

PLAUSIBLE. O Lord, Madam, my company! your most
obliged, faithful, humble Servant; but I cou'd have
brought you good company indeed, for I parted at your
door with two of the worthiest, bravest Men—

OLIVIA. Who were they, my Lord?

NOVEL. Who do you call the worthiest, bravest men, pray?

PLAUSIBLE. O the wisest, bravest Gentlemen! Men of such
Honour, and Virtue! of such good qualities! ah—

ELIZA. This is a Coxcomb, that speaks ill of all people a
different way, and Libels every body with dull praise,
and commonly in the wrong place, so makes his Panegyricks abusive Lampoons.   [*Aside.*

OLIVIA. But pray let me know who they were.

PLAUSIBLE. Ah! such patterns of Heroick Virtue! such—

NOVEL. Well, but who the Devil were they?

PLAUSIBLE. The honour of our Nation, the glory of our
Age, ah! I cou'd dwell a Twelvemonth on their praise;
which indeed I might spare by telling their names: *Sir
John Current*, and *Sir Richard Court-Title.*

NOVEL. *Court-Title!* Hah, ha.

OLIVIA. And *Sir John Current!* Why will you keep such a
Wretch company, my Lord?

PLAUSIBLE. Oh, Madam, seriously you are a little too severe; for he is a Man of unquestion'd reputation in every
thing.

OLIVIA. Yes, because he endeavors only with the Women,
to pass for a Man of Courage; and with the Bullies, for
a Wit; with the Wits, for a Man of Business; and with

the Men of Business, for a Favourite at Court; and at Court, for good City security.

NOVEL. And, for *Sir Richard,* he—

PLAUSIBLE. He loves your choice, pick'd company; persons that—

OLIVIA. He loves a Lord indeed; but—

NOVEL. Pray, dear Madam, let me have but a bold stroke or two at his Picture. He loves a Lord, as you say, tho'—

OLIVIA. Tho' he borrow'd his Money, and ne'r paid him again.

NOVEL. And wou'd bespeak a place three days before at the back-end of a Lords Coach, to *Hide-Park.*

PLAUSIBLE. Nay, i'faith, i faith, you are both too severe.

OLIVIA. Then, to shew yet more his passion for quality, he makes Love to that fulsom Coach-load of Honour, my *Lady Goodly;* for he is always at her Lodging.

PLAUSIBLE. Because it is the Conventickle-Gallant, the Meeting-house of all the fair Ladies, and glorious Superfine Beauties of the Town.

NOVEL. Very fine Ladies! there's first—

OLIVIA. Her Honour, as fat as an Hostess.

PLAUSIBLE. She is something plump indeed, a goodly, comly, graceful person.

NOVEL. Then there's my *Lady Frances,* what d'ye call'er? as ugly—

OLIVIA. As a Citizens lawfully begotten daughter.

PLAUSIBLE. She has wit in abundance; and the handsomest heel, elbow, and tip of an ear, you ever saw.

NOVEL. Heel, and elbow! hah, ha! And there's my *Lady Betty* you know—

OLIVIA. As sluttish, and slatternly, as an *Irish* Woman bred in *France.*

PLAUSIBLE. Ah, all she has hangs with a loose Air indeed, and becoming negligence.

ELIZA. You see all faults with Lovers eyes, I find, my Lord.

PLAUSIBLE. Ah, Madam, your most obliged, faithful, humble Servant to command! But you can say nothing sure against the Superfine Mistress—

OLIVIA. I know who you mean. She is as censorious and detracting a Jade, as a superannuated Sinner.

PLAUSIBLE. She has a smart way of Railery, 'tis confest.

NOVEL. And then, for Mrs. *Grideline*.

PLAUSIBLE. She I'm sure is—

OLIVIA. One that never spoke ill of any body, 'tis confest; for she is as silent in conversation as a Countrey Lover, and no better company than a Clock, or a Weatherglass; for if she sounds, 'tis but once an hour, to put you in mind of the time of day, or to tell you 'twill be cold or hot, rain or snow.

PLAUSIBLE. Ah, poor creature! she's extremely good and modest.

NOVEL. And for Mrs. *Bridlechin*, she's—

OLIVIA. As proud, as a Churchman's Wife.

PLAUSIBLE. She's a Woman of great spirit and honour, and will not make her self cheap, 'tis true.

NOVEL. Then Mrs. *Hoyden*, that calls all people by their Sirnames, and is—

OLIVIA. As familiar a Duck—

NOVEL. As an Actress in the Tyring-room. There I was once before-hand with you, Madam.

PLAUSIBLE. Mrs. *Hoyden!* A poor, affable, good-natur'd Soul! But the Divine Mrs. *Trifle* comes thither too: sure her beauty, virtue and conduct, you can say nothing too.

OLIVIA. No!

NOVEL. No!—pray let me speak, Madam.

OLIVIA. First, can any one be call'd beautiful that squints?

PLAUSIBLE. Her eyes languish a little, I own.

NOVEL. Languish! hah, ha.

OLIVIA. Languish! Then, for her conduct, she was seen at the *Countrey Wife*, after the first day. There's for you, my Lord.

PLAUSIBLE. But, Madam, she was not seen to use her Fan all the Play long, turn aside her head, or by a conscious blush, discover more guilt than modesty.

OLIVIA. Very fine! then you think a Woman modest, that

Grideline: gridelin (from "gris de lin": flax-gray) is pale purple. I have been able to find no special usage of the color that would convert the word into a significant name, giving, as so many names do in this conversation, the character of the person described.

sees the hideous *Countrey Wife*, without blushing, or publishing her detestation of it? D'ye hear him, Cousin?

ELIZA. Yes; and am, I must confess, something of his opinion, and think that as an over-conscious Fool at a Play, by endeavouring to shew the Author's want of Wit, exposes his own to more censure: so may a Lady call her own modesty in question, by publickly cavilling with the Poets; for all those grimaces of honour, and artificial modesty, disparage a Woman's real Virtue, as much as the use of white and red does the natural complexion; and you must use very, very little, if you wou'd have it thought your own.

OLIVIA. Then you wou'd have a Woman of Honour with passive looks, ears, and tongue, undergo all the hideous obscenity she hears at nasty Plays?

ELIZA. Truly I think a Woman betrays her want of modesty, by shewing it publickly in a Play-house, as much as a Man does his want of courage by a quarrel there; for the truly modest and stout say least, and are least exceptious, especially in publick.

OLIVIA. O hideous! Cousin, this cannot be your opinion; but you are one of those who have the confidence to pardon the filthy Play.

ELIZA. Why, what is there of ill in't, say you?

OLIVIA. O fie, fie, fie, wou'd you put me to the blush anew? call all the blood into my face again? But, to satisfie you then, first, the clandestine obscenity in the very name of *Horner*.

ELIZA. Truly, 'tis so hidden, I cannot find it out, I confess.

OLIVIA. O horrid! does it not give you the rank conception, or image of a Goat, a Town-bull, or a Satyr? nay, what is yet a filthier image than all the rest, that of an Eunuch?[9]

ELIZA. What then? I can think of a Goat, a Bull, or Satyr, without any hurt.

OLIVIA. I, but, Cousin, one cannot stop there.

ELIZA. I can, Cousin.

Town-bull: wencher. According to Robert Nares in his *Glossary* (London, 1859), "It was formerly the custom to keep a bull for the common use of the town."

OLIVIA. O no; for when you have those filthy creatures in your head once, the next thing you think, is what they do; as their defiling of honest Mens Beds and Couches, Rapes upon sleeping and waking Countrey Virgins, under Hedges, and on Haycocks: nay, farther—

ELIZA. Nay, no farther, Cousin, we have enough of your Coment on the Play, which will make me more asham'd than the Play it self.

OLIVIA. O, believe me, 'tis a filthy Play, and you may take my word for a filthy Play, as soon as anothers; but the filthiest thing in that Play, or any other Play, is—

ELIZA. Pray keep it to your self, if it be so.

OLIVIA. No, faith, you shall know it, I'm resolv'd to make you out of love with the Play: I say, the lewdest, filthiest thing, is his *China;*[10] nay, I will never forgive the beastly Author his *China:* he has quite taken away the reputation of poor *China* it self, and sully'd the most innocent and pretty Furniture of a Ladies Chamber; insomuch, that I was fain to break all my defil'd Vessels. You see I have none left; nor you, I hope.

ELIZA. You'll pardon me, I cannot think the worse of my *China,* for that of the Play-house.

OLIVIA. Why, you will not keep any now sure! 'tis now as unfit an ornament for a Ladies Chamber, as the Pictures that come from *Italy,* and other hot Countries, as appears by their nudities, which I alwayes cover, or scratch out, wheresoe're I find 'em. But *China!* out upon't, filthy *China,* nasty, debauch'd *China!*

ELIZA. All this will not put me out of conceit with *China,* nor the Play, which is Acted to day, or another of the same beastly Author's, as you call him, which I'll go see.

OLIVIA. You will not sure! nay, you sha'not venture your reputation by going, and mine by leaving me alone with two Men here: nay, you'll disoblige me for ever, if—   [*Pulls her back.*

ELIZA. I stay!—your Servant.   [*Exit* ELIZA.

OLIVIA. Well—but my Lord, tho' you justifie every body, you cannot in earnest uphold so beastly a Writer, whose Ink is so smutty, as one may say.

PLAUSIBLE. Faith, I dare swear the poor Man did not think to disoblige the Ladies, by any amorous, soft, passionate, luscious saying in his Play.

OLIVIA. Foy, my Lord; but what think you, Mr. *Novel*, of the Play? tho' I know you are a Friend to all that are new.

NOVEL. Faith, Madam, I must confess, the new Plays wou'd not be the worse for my advice, but I cou'd never get the silly Rogues, the Poets, to mind what I say; but I'll tell you what counsel I gave the surly Fool you speak of.

OLIVIA. What was't?

NOVEL. Faith, to put his Play into Rithme; for Rithme, you know, often makes mystical Nonsence pass with the Criticks for Wit, and a double meaning saying with the Ladies, for soft, tender, and moving passion.[11] But, now I talk of passion, I saw your old Lover this morning—Captain—   [*Whispers.*

Enter Captain MANLY, FREEMAN *and* FIDELIA
standing behind.

OLIVIA. Whom?—nay, you need not whisper.

MANLY. We are luckily got hither unobserv'd:— How! in a close conversation with these supple Rascals, the Outcasts of Sempstresses shops?

FREEMAN. Faith, pardon her, Captain, that, since she cou'd no longer be entertain'd with your manly bluntness, and honest love, she takes up with the pert chat and common place flattery of these fluttering Parrots of the Town, Apes and Echoes of Men only.

MANLY. Do not you, Sir, play the Echo too, mock me, dally with my own words, and shew your self as impertinent as they are.

FREEMAN. Nay, Captain—

FIDELIA. Nay, Lieutenant, do not excuse her, methinks she looks very kindly upon 'em both, and seems to be pleas'd with what that Fool there sayes to her.

MANLY. You lye, Sir, and hold your peace, that I may not be provok'd to give you a worse reply.

Foy: faith.

OLIVIA. *Manly* return'd, d'ye say! And is he safe?

NOVEL. My Lord saw him too. Heark you, my Lord.

[*Whispers to* PLAUSIBLE.

MANLY. She yet seems concern'd for my safety, and perhaps they are admitted now here but for their news of me; for Intelligence indeed is the common Passport of nauseous Fools, when they go their round of good Tables and Houses. [*Aside.*

OLIVIA. I heard of his fighting only, without particulars, and confess I alwayes lov'd his Brutal courage, because it made me hope it might rid me of his more Brutal love.

MANLY. What's that? [*Apart.*

OLIVIA. But is he at last return'd, d'ye say, unhurt?

NOVEL. Ay faith, without doing his business; for the Rogue has been these two years pretending to a wooden Leg, which he wou'd take from Fortune, as kindly, as the Staff of a Marshal of *France,* and rather read his name in a *Gazet*—

OLIVIA. Than in the Entail of a good Estate.

MANLY. So!— [*Aside.*

NOVEL. I have an Ambition, I must confess, of losing my heart, before such a fair Enemy as your self, Madam; but that silly Rogues shou'd be ambitious of losing their Arms, and—

OLIVIA. Looking like a pair of Compasses.

NOVEL. But he has no use of his Arms, but to set 'em on Kimbow, for he never pulls off his Hat, at least not to me, I'm sure; for you must know, Madam, he has a fanatical hatred to good company: he can't abide me.

PLAUSIBLE. O, be not so severe to him, as to say he hates good company; for I assure you he has a great respect, esteem and kindness for me.

MANLY. That kind, civil Rogue has spoken yet ten thousand times worse of me, than t'other.[12]

OLIVIA. Well, if he be return'd, Mr. *Novel,* then shall I be

Gazet: in this case, a battle report. According to de Beer (I, 102), *The London Gazette* published supplements covering the battles during the Dutch wars.

on Kimbow: akimbo.

pester'd again with his boistrous Sea-love; have my Alcove smell like a Cabin, my Chamber perfum'd with his Tarpaulin Brandenburgh, and hear vollies of Brandy sighs, enough to make a Fog in ones Room. Foh! I hate a Lover that smells like *Thames-street!*[13]

MANLY. I can bear no longer, and need hear no more.

[*Aside.*

But, since you have these two Pulvillio Boxes, these Essence Bottles, this pair of Musk-Cats here, I hope I may venture to come yet nearer you.

OLIVIA. Overheard us then?

NOVEL. I hope he heard me not.   [*Aside.*

PLAUSIBLE. Most noble and heroick Captain, your most oblig'd, faithful, humble Servant.

NOVEL. Dear Tar, thy humble Servant.

MANLY. Away—Madam—

OLIVIA. Nay, I think I have fitted you for listning.

[*Thrusts* NOVEL *and* PLAUSIBLE *on each side.*[14]

MANLY. You have fitted me, for believing you cou'd not be fickle, tho' you were young; cou'd not dissemble Love, tho' twas your interest; nor be vain,[15] tho' you were handsom; nor break your promise, tho' to a parting Lover; nor abuse your best Friend, tho' you had Wit: but I take not your contempt of me worse, than your esteem, or civility for these things here, tho' you know 'em.

NOVEL. Things!

PLAUSIBLE. Let the Captain Railly a little.

MANLY. Yes, things: canst thou be angry, thou thing?

[*Coming up to* NOVEL.

NOVEL. No, since my Lord sayes you speak in Raillery; for, tho' your Sea-raillery be something rough, yet I confess we use one another to as bad every day, at *Lockets*, and never quarrel for the matter.

Brandenburgh: morning gown. *Pulvillio:* men used puvilio, a perfumed powder, on their wigs. *Musk-Cats,* a general term for the musk-bearing animals, commonly used, as all

Manly's epithets are here, to mean "stinking fop."
Lockets: a fashionable restaurant. See *Country-Wife,* Act 4, n. 9.

PLAUSIBLE. Nay, noble Captain, be not angry with him: A word with you, I beseech you.— [*Whispers to* MANLY.

OLIVIA. Well, we Women, like the rest of the Cheats of the World, when our Cullies or Creditors have found us out, and will, or can trust no longer; pay Debts, and satisfie Obligations, with a quarrel, the kindest Present a Man can make to his Mistress, when he can make no more Presents: for oftentimes in Love, as at Cards, we are forc'd to play foul, only to give over the game; and use our Lovers, like the Cards, when we can get no more by 'em, throw 'em up in a pet, upon the first dispute.   [*Aside.*

MANLY. My Lord, all that you have made me know by your whispering, which I knew not before, is, that you have a stinking breath: there's a secret, for your secret.

PLAUSIBLE. Pshaw! pshaw!

MANLY. But, Madam, tell me, pray, what was't, about this spark, cou'd take you? was it the merit of his fashionable impudence, the briskness of his noise, the wit of his laugh, his judgment, or fancy in his garniture? or was it a well-trim'd Glove, or the scent of it that charm'd you?[16]

NOVEL. Very well, Sir, 'gad these Sea-Captains make nothing of dressing: but let me tell you, Sir, a man by his dress, as much as by any thing, shews his wit and judgment, nay, and his courage too.

FREEMAN. How his courage, Mr. *Novel?*

NOVEL. Why, for example, by red Breeches, tuck'd up Hair or Perruke, a greasie broad Belt, and now adayes a short Sword.[17]

MANLY. Thy courage will appear more by thy Belt than thy Sword, I dare swear. Then, Madam, for this gentle piece of courtesie, this Man of tame honour, what cou'd you find in him? was it his languishing affected tone? his mannerly look? his second-hand flattery, the refuse of the Play house tiring-rooms? or his slavish obsequiousness, in watching at the door of your Box at the Playhouse, for your hand to your Chair? or his janty way of playing with your Fan? or was it the Gunpowder

spot on his hand, or the Jewel in his ear, that pur-
chas'd your heart?

OLIVIA. Good jealous Captain, no more of your—

PLAUSIBLE. No, let him go on, Madam, for perhaps he
may make you laugh: and I wou'd contribute to your
pleasure any way.

MANLY. Gentle Rogue!

OLIVIA. No, noble Captain, you cannot sure think any
thing cou'd take me more than that heroick Title of
yours, Captain; for you know we Women love honour
inordinately.

NOVEL. Hah, ha, faith she is with thee, Bully, for thy
Raillery.

MANLY. Faith so shall I be with you, no Bully, for your
grinning.   [*Aside to* NOVEL.

OLIVIA. Then, that noble Lyon-like meen of yours, that
Soldier-like weather beaten complexion, and that manly
roughness of your voice; how can they otherwise than
charm us Women, who hate Effeminacy!

NOVEL. Hah, ha! faith I can't hold from laughing.

MANLY. Nor shall I from kicking anon.   [*Aside to* NOVEL.

OLIVIA. And then, that Captain-like carelesness in your
dress, but especially your Scarf; 'twas just such another,
only a little higher ty'd, made me in love with my
Taylor, as he past by my Window the last Training
day;[18] for we Women adore a Martial Man, and you
have nothing wanting to make you more one, or more
agreeable, but a wooden Leg.

PLAUSIBLE. Nay, i'faith there your Ladyship was a Wag,
and it was fine, just, and well Railly'd.

NOVEL. Ay, ay, Madam, with you Ladies too, Martial Men
must needs be very killing.

MANLY. Peace, you *Bartholomew-Fair Buffoons;*[19] and be
not you vain that these laugh on your side, for they will
laugh at their own dull jests: but no more of 'em, for I

Gunpowder spot: a beauty
spot impressed by gunpowder.
One of Wycherley's *Miscellany Poems* is "*Upon the* Gunpowder Spot *on a* Lady's
Hand" (Summers, III, 75–
76). For Manly, the spot, like
the earring, is an indication of
Lord Plausible's effeminacy.

will only suffer now this Lady to be witty and merry.

OLIVIA. You wou'd not have your Panegyrick interrupted. I go on then to your humor. Is there any thing more agreeable, than the pretty sullenness of that? than the greatness of your courage? which most of all appears in your spirit of contradiction, for you dare give all Mankind the Lye; and your Opinion is your onely Mistress, for you renounce that too, when it becomes another Mans.

NOVEL. Hah, ha! I cannot hold, I must laugh at thee Tar, faith!

PLAUSIBLE. And i'faith, dear Captain, I beg your pardon, and leave to laugh at you too, tho' I protest I mean you no hurt; but, when a Lady Raillies, a stander by must be complaisant, and do her reason in laughing: Hah, ha.

MANLY. Why, you impudent, pitiful Wretches, you presume sure upon your Effeminacy to urge me; for you are in all things so like Women, that you may think it in me a kind of Cowardice to beat you.

OLIVIA. No Hectoring, good Captain.

MANLY. Or, perhaps, you think this Ladies presence secures you; but have a care, she has talk'd her self out of all the respect I had for her; and by using me ill before you, has given me a priviledge of using you so before her: but if you wou'd preserve your respect to her, and not be beaten before her, go, be gone immediately.

NOVEL. Be gone! what?

PLAUSIBLE. Nay, worthy, noble, generous Captain.

MANLY. Be gone, I say.

NOVEL. Be gone again! to us be gone!

MANLY. No chattering, Baboons, instantly be gone. Or—

[MANLY *puts 'em out of the Room:* NOVEL *struts,*
PLAUSIBLE *cringes.*

NOVEL. Well, Madam, we'll go make the Cards ready in your Bed-chamber; sure you will not stay long with him.

[*Exeunt* PLAUSIBLE, NOVEL.

OLIVIA. Turn hither your rage, good Captain Swaggerhuff, and be saucy with your Mistress, like a true Captain; but be civil to your Rivals and Betters, and do not

threaten any thing but me here; no, not so much as
my Windows, nor do not think your self in the Lodgings
of one of your Suburb Mistresses beyond the *Tower*.[20]

MANLY. Do not give me cause to think so, for those less
infamous Women part with their Lovers, just as you did
from me, with unforc'd vows of constancy, and floods
of willing tears; but the same winds bear away their
Lovers, and their vows: And for their grief, if the
credulous unexpected Fools return, they find new Com-
forters, fresh Cullies, such as I found here. The mercenary love of those Women too suffer shipwrack, with
their Gallants fortunes; now you have heard *Chance* has
us'd me scurvily, therefore you do too. Well, persevere
in your ingratitude, falshood, and disdain; have constancy in something, and I promise you to be as just to
your real scorn, as I was to your feign'd love: And hence
forward will despise, contemn, hate, loath, and detest
you, most faithfully.

Enter LETTICE.

OLIVIA. Get the Hombre Cards ready in the next Room,
Lettice, and—   [*Whispers to* LETTICE.[21]

FREEMAN. Bravely resolv'd, Captain.

FIDELIA. And you'll be sure to keep your word, I hope, Sir.

MANLY. I hope so too.

FIDELIA. Do you but hope it, Sir? if you are not as good as
your word, 'twill be the first time you ever brag'd sure.

MANLY. She has restor'd my reason with my heart.

FREEMAN. But, now you talk of restoring Captain, there
are other things which, next to one's heart, one wou'd
not part with; I mean your Jewels and Money, which
it seems she has, Sir.

MANLY. What's that to you, Sir?

FREEMAN. Pardon me, whatsoever is yours, I have a share
in't, I'm sure, which I will not lose for asking, tho' you
may be too generous, or too angry now to do't your self.

FIDELIA. Nay, then I'll make bold to make my claim too.
                    [*Both going towards* OLIVIA.

MANLY. Hold, you impertinent, officious Fops—
How have I been deceiv'd!   [*Aside.*

FREEMAN. Madam, there are certain Appurtenances to a Lover's heart, call'd Jewels, which alwayes go along with it.

FIDELIA. And which, with Lovers, have no value in themselves, but from the heart they come with; our Captain's, Madam, it seems you scorn to keep, and much more will those worthless things without it, I am confident.

OLIVIA. A Gentleman, so well made as you are, may be confident—us easic Women cou'd not deny you any thing you ask, if 'twere for your self; but, since 'tis for another, I beg your leave to give him my Answer. (An agreeable young Fellow this!— And wou'd not be my Aversion!) [Aside.] Captain, your young Friend here has a very persuading Face, I confess; yet you might have ask'd me your self, for those Trifles you left with me, which (heark you a little, for I dare trust you with the secret: you are a Man of so much Honour I'm sure;) I say then, not expecting your return, or hoping ever to see you again, I have deliver'd your Jewels to—

[Aside to MANLY.

MANLY. Whom?

OLIVIA. My Husband.

MANLY. Your Husband!

OLIVIA. Ay, my Husband; for, since you cou'd leave me, I am lately, and privately marry'd to one, who is a Man of so much Honour and Experience in the World, that I dare not ask him for your Jewels again, to restore 'em to you; lest he shou'd conclude you never wou'd have parted with 'em to me, on any other score, but the exchange of my Honour: which rather than you'd let me lose, you'd lose I'm sure your self, those Trifles of yours.

MANLY. Triumphant Impudence! but marry'd too!

OLIVIA. O, speak not so loud, my Servants know it not: I am marry'd; there's no resisting one's Destiny, or Love, you know.

MANLY. Why, did you love him too?

OLIVIA. Most passionately; nay, love him now, tho' I have marry'd him, and he me: which mutual love, I hope you are too good, too generous a Man to disturb, by any

future claim, or visits to me. 'Tis true, he is now absent
in the Countrey, but returns shortly; therefore I beg of
you, for your own ease and quiet, and my Honour, you
will never see me more.

MANLY. I wish I never had seen you.

OLIVIA. But if you shou'd ever have any thing to say to me
hereafter, let that young Gentleman there, be your Messenger.

MANLY. You wou'd be kinder to him: I find he shou'd be
welcome.

OLIVIA. Alas, his Youth wou'd keep my Husband from suspicions, and his visits from scandal; for we Women may
have pity for such as he, but no love: And I already
think you do not well to spirit him away to Sea, and the
Sea is already but too rich with the spoils of the shore.

MANLY. True perfect Woman!—If I cou'd say any thing
more injurious to her now, I wou'd; for I cou'd out-rail
a bilk'd Whore, or a kick'd Coward: but, now I think
on't, that were rather to discover my love, than hatred;
and I must not talk, for something I must do.   [*Aside.*

OLIVIA. I think I have given him enough of me now, never
to be troubled with him again.—   [*Aside.*

Enter LETTICE.

Well, *Lettice*, are the Cards and all ready within? I
come then. Captain, I beg your pardon: You will not
make one at Hombre?

MANLY. No, Madam, but I'll wish you a little good luck
before you go.

OLIVIA. No, if you wou'd have me thrive, Curse me; for
that you'll do heartily, I suppose.

MANLY. Then, if you will have it so, May all the Curses
light upon you, Women ought to fear, and you deserve; first may the Curse of loving Play attend your
sordid Covetousness, and Fortune cheat you, by trusting
to her, as you have cheated me; the Curse of Pride, or a
good Reputation, fall on your Lust; the Curse of Affectation on your Beauty; the Curse of your Husbands
company on your Pleasures; and the Curse of your Gallant's disappointments in his absence; and the Curse of

scorn, jealousie, or despair, on your love: and then the Curse of loving on.

OLIVIA. And, to requite all your Curses, I will only return you your last; May the Curse of loving me still, fall upon your proud hard heart, that cou'd be so cruel to me in these horrid Curses: but Heaven forgive you.

[*Exit* OLIVIA.

MANLY. Hell, and the Devil, reward thee.

FREEMAN. Well, you see now, Mistresses, like Friends, are lost, by letting 'em handle your Money; and most Women are such kind of Witches, who can have no power over a Man, unless you give 'em Money; but when once they have got any from you, they never leave you, till they have all: therefore I never dare give a Woman a farthing.

MANLY. Well, there is yet this comfort by losing one's Money with one's Mistress, a Man is out of danger of getting another; of being made prize again by love; who, like a Pyrat, takes you by spreading false Colours: but when once you have run your Ship aground, the treacherous Picaroon loofs, so by your ruine you save your self from slavery at least.[22]

Enter BOY.

BOY. Mrs. *Lettice,* here's Madam *Blackacre* come to wait upon her Honour.[23]

MANLY. D'ye hear that? let us be gone, before she comes; for hence forward I'll avoid the whole damn'd Sex for ever, and Woman as a sinking Ship.

[*Exeunt* MANLY *and* FIDELIA.

FREEMAN. And I'll stay, to revenge on her your quarrel to the Sex; for out of love to her Jointure, and hatred to business, I wou'd marry her, to make an end of her thousand Suits, and my thousand engagements, to the comfort of two unfortunate sorts of people; my Plaintiffs, and her Defendants; my Creditors, and her Adversaries.

Enter Widow BLACKACRE *led in by Major* OLDFOX,
and JERRY BLACKACRE *following, laden with green Bags.*

WIDOW. 'Tis an arrant Sea-Ruffian, but I am glad I met with him at last, to serve him again, Major, for the last service was not good in Law. *Boy, Duck, Jerry,* where is my Paper of *Memorandums?* give me Child: so. Where is my Cousin *Olivia*, now, my kind Relation?

FREEMAN. Here is one that wou'd be your kind Relation, Madam.

WIDOW. What mean you, Sir?

FREEMAN. Why, faith (to be short) to marry you, Widow.

WIDOW. Is not this the wild rude person we saw at Captain *Manly*'s?

JERRY. Ay, forsooth, an't please.

WIDOW. What wou'd you? what are you? Marry me!

FREEMAN. Ay faith, for I am a younger Brother, and you are a Widow.[24]

WIDOW. You are an impertinent person, and go about your business.

FREEMAN. I have none, but to marry thee, Widow.

WIDOW. But I have other business, I'd have you to know.

FREEMAN. But you have no business anights, Widow; and I'll make you pleasanter business than any you have: for anights, I assure you, I am a Man of great business; for the business—

WIDOW. Go, I'm sure you're an idle Fellow.

FREEMAN. Try me but, Widow, and employ me as you find my abilities, and industry.

OLDFOX. Pray be civil to the Lady, Mr.—she's a person of quality, a person that is no person—

FREEMAN. Yes, but she's a person that is a Widow: be you mannerly to her, because you are to pretend only to be her Squire, to arm her to her Lawyers Chambers; but I will be impudent and baudy, for she must love and marry me.

WIDOW. Marry come up, you saucy familiar *Jack!* You think with us Widows, 'tis no more than up, and ride. Gad forgive me, now adayes, every idle, young, hectoring, roaring Companion, with a pair of turn'd red Breeches,

---

roaring: bullying, boisterous. It means the same as *hectoring;* the shade of meaning depends on whether the speaker takes hectors and roaring boys as high-spirited fellows or destructive troublemakers. See Olivia's attack on Manly in the scene immediately preceding for a harsher view of hectoring.

turn'd Breeches: if "turned

and a broad Back, thinks to carry away any Widow, of the best degree; but I'd have you to know, Sir, all Widows are not got, like places at Court, by Impudence and Importunity only.

OLDFOX. No, no, soft, soft, you are a young Man, and not fit—

FREEMAN. For a Widow? Yes sure, old Man, the fitter.

OLDFOX. Go to, go to, if others had not laid in their claims before you—

FREEMAN. Not you, I hope.

OLDFOX. Why not I, Sir? Sure I am a much more proportionable match for her, than you, Sir; I, who am an elder Brother, of a comfortable Fortune, and of equal Years with her.

WIDOW. How's that? You unmannerly person, I'd have you to know, I was born but in *Ann' undec' Caroli prim'*.[25]

OLDFOX. Your pardon, Lady, your pardon; be not offended with your very Servant.— But I say, Sir, you are a beggarly younger Brother, twenty Years younger than her; without any Land or Stock, but your great stock of Impudence: therefore what pretension can you have to her?

FREEMAN. You have made it for me; first, because I am a younger Brother.

WIDOW. Why, is that a sufficient Plea to a Relict? How appears it, Sir? by what foolish custom?

FREEMAN. By custom, time out of mind only. Then, Sir, because I have nothing to keep me after her death, I am the likelier to take care of her life. And, for my being twenty Years younger than her, and having a sufficient stock of Impudence, I leave it to her whether they

---

breeches" is a phrase indicating a particular style or cut, I have been unable to find it out. There are two possible readings of "turned" in this context. Either the breeches are well-turned, well-fashioned—a comment on the idle young man's concern with clothes—or they are altered (perhaps even newly dyed: one use of "turn" involves color change)—a comment on his poverty.

Ann' undec' Caroli prim': the eleventh year of Charles I's reign: 1636.

will be valid exceptions to me, in her Widow's Law or Equity.

OLDFOX. Well, she has been so long in *Chancery*, that I'll stand to her Equity and Decree between us. Come, Lady, pray snap up this young Snap at first, or we shall be troubled with him; give him a City Widow's Answer: (that is, with all the ill breeding imaginable.)

[*Aside to the* WIDOW.

Come, Madam.

WIDOW. Well then, to make an end of this foolish Wooing, for nothing interrupts business more; first, for you, Major—

OLDFOX. You declare in my favour then?

FREEMAN. What, direct the Court? (Come, young Lawyer, thou sha't be a Counsel for me.) [*To* JERRY.

JERRY. Gad, I shall betray your Cause then, as well as an older Lawyer, never stir.

WIDOW. First, I say, for you Major, my walking Hospital of an ancient Foundation, thou Bag of Mummy, that wou'dst fall asunder, if 'twere not for thy Cere-cloaths—

OLDFOX. How, Lady?

FREEMAN. Hah, ha—

JERRY. Hey, brave Mother! use all Suitors thus, for my sake.

WIDOW. Thou wither'd, hobling, distorted Cripple; nay, thou art a Cripple all over; wou'dst thou make me the Staff of thy Age, the Crutch of thy Decrepidness? Me—

FREEMAN. Well said Widow! faith, thou wou'dst make a Man love thee now, without dissembling.

WIDOW. Thou sensless, impertinent, quibling, driveling, feeble, paralytic, impotent, fumbling, frigid Nicompoop.

JERRY. Hey, brave Mother, for calling of names, ifac!

WIDOW. Wou'dst thou make a Caudlemaker, a Nurse of me? Can't you be Bed-rid, without a Bed-fellow? Won't your Swan-skins Furrs, Flannels, and the scorch'd

snap up this young Snap:
tell off this young rogue.

Trencher keep you warm there? Wou'd you have me
your Scotch-warming Pan, with a Pox to you? Me!—

OLDFOX. O Heav'ns!

FREEMAN. I told you I shou'd be thought the fitter Man,
Major.

JERRY. Ay, you old Fobus, and you wou'd have been
my Guardian, wou'd you? to have taken care of my Estate, that half of't shou'd never come to me, by letting
long Leases at Pepper-corn Rents.

WIDOW. If I wou'd have marry'd an old Man, 'tis well
known I might have marry'd an Earl; nay, what's more,
a Judge, and been cover'd the Winter-nights with the
Lamb-skins,[26] which I prefer to the Ermins of Nobles:
And dost thou think I wou'd wrong my poor Minor
there, for you?

FREEMAN. Your Minor is a chopping Minor, God bless him.
                    [*Strokes* JERRY *on the head.*

OLDFOX. Your Minor may be a Major of Horse or Foot, for
his bigness; and, it seems, you will have the cheating
of your Minor to your self.

WIDOW. Pray, Sir, bear Witness; Cheat my Minor! I'll
bring my Action of the Case for the slander.

FREEMAN. Nay, I wou'd bear false Witness for thee
now, Widow, since you have done me justice, and have
thought me the fitter Man for you.

WIDOW. Fair, and softly Sir, 'tis my Minor's Case, more
than my own: And I must do him justice now on you.

Trencher: a flat circular board, presumably here warmed and used to heat a bed.

Scotch-warming Pan: a woman to take to bed.

old Fobus: apparently an epithet about as strong as "old fogey." No one seems to know what it means or where it comes from, although Summers guesses (II, 302) that it derives from "to fob," meaning "to trick." In the late nineteenth century "fobus" was a slang word for "pu-

denda." Such a reading would not be inappropriate in this context; perhaps the vulgar usage is older than Eric Partridge thinks it is. See *A Dictionary of Slang* (London, 1961).

Pepper-corn Rents: nominal rents.

Action on *the Case:* a remedy under common law to recover damages for wrongs not committed with force. It is applicable to a charge of slander.

FREEMAN. How?

OLDFOX. So then.

WIDOW. You are first, (I warrant) some Renegado from the Inns of Court, and the Law; and thou'lt come to suffer for't, by the Law: that is, be hang'd.

JERRY. Not about your neck, forsooth, I hope.

FREEMAN. But, Madam—

OLDFOX. Hear the Court.

WIDOW. Thou art some debauch'd, drunken, leud, hectoring, gaming Companion, and want'st some Widow's old Gold to nick upon; but, I thank you, Sir, that's for my Lawyers.

FREEMAN. Faith, we shou'd ne'r quarrel about that; for Guineys wou'd serve my turn: but, Widow—

WIDOW. Thou art a foul-mouth'd Boaster of thy Lust, a meer Bragadochio of thy strength for Wine and Women, and wilt belie thy self more than thou dost Women, and art every way a base deceiver of Women: And wou'd deceive me too, wou'd you?

FREEMAN. Nay faith, Widow, this is Judging without seeing the Evidence.

WIDOW. I say, you are a worn-out Whoremaster, at five and twenty both in Body and Fortune: And cannot be trusted by the common Wenches of the Town, lest you shou'd not pay 'em; nor by the Wives of the Town, lest you shou'd pay 'em: so you want Women, and wou'd have me your Baud, to procure 'em for you.

FREEMAN. Faith, if you had any good Acquaintance, Widow, 'twou'd be civilly done of thee; for I am just come from Sea.

nick: gamble.

Guineys: guineas, which were first coined in 1663, were new gold compared to the *old Gold* of the Widow's line. In fact, there were even newer guineas, for in 1675 a new coining had added a castle to the elephant that decorated the first ones.

pay 'em: apparently in the sense of "give them what they deserve." The *"worn-out . . . in Body and Fortune"* that opens the speech suggests that the desert might be either the pox or a failure to perform. Since Freeman is a sailor, one specialized meaning of *pay* is worth considering: cover with tar.

WIDOW. I mean, you wou'd have me keep you, that you might turn Keeper; for poor Widows are only us'd like Bauds by you; you go to Church with us, but to get other Women to lie with. In fine, you are a cheating, chousing Spendthrift: And, having sold your own Annuity, wou'd waste my Jointure.

JERRY. And make havock of our Estate personal, and all our old gilt Plate; I shou'd soon be picking up all our mortgag'd Apostle-Spoons, Bowls and Beakers, out of most of the Ale-houses, betwixt *Hercules Pillars* and the *Boatswain* in *Wapping:* nay, and you'd be scouring amongst my Trees, and make 'em knock down one another, like routed reeling Watchmen at midnight. Wou'd you so, Bully?

FREEMAN. Nay, pr'ythee, Widow, hear me.

WIDOW. No, Sir, I'd have you to know, thou pitiful, paltry, lath-back'd Fellow, if I wou'd have marry'd a young Man, 'tis well known, I cou'd have had any young Heir in *Norfolk;* nay, the hopefull'st young Man this day at the *Kings-Bench Bar;* I that am a Relict and Executrix of known plentiful Assits and Parts, who understand my self and the Law: And wou'd you have me under Covert Baron again? No, Sir, no Covert Baron for me.

Apostle-Spoons: silver spoons with the apostles on the handles.

Hercules Pillars: Hercules' Pillars, an inn at Hyde Park Corner, the western entrance into London. Squire Western left his horses "at that Inn, which was the first he saw on his Arrival in Town." Henry Fielding, *Tom Jones,* VI, London, 1749, p. 5. The Wapping taverns mentioned in Jacob Henry Burns' *A Descriptive Catalogue of the London Traders, Tavern, and Coffee-House Tokens* (London, 1855) have conventional non-maritime names, like Sun and Cock, but Boatswain, whether Wycherley recorded or invented it, is a suitable public-house name for a seamen's town. The line means all the alehouses from one end of London to the other.

Kings-Bench Bar: King's Bench was the superior of the three common-law courts in Westminster Hall. See Act III, n. 7.

Covert Baron: wife. The wife was legally under the control and/or protection (covert) of the husband (baron).

FREEMAN. But, dear Widow, hear me. I value you only, not your Jointure.

WIDOW. Nay, Sir, hold there; I know your love to a Widow, is covetousness of her Jointure: And a Widow, a little stricken in Years, with a good Jointure, is like an old Mansion-house in a good Purchase, never valu'd; but take one, take t'other: And perhaps, when you are in possession, you'd neglect it, let it drop to the ground, for want of necessary repairs, or expences upon't.

FREEMAN. No, Widow, one wou'd be sure to keep all tight, when one is to forfeit one's Lease by dilapidation.

WIDOW. Fie, fie, I neglect my Business, with this foolish discourse of love. *Jerry,* Child, let me see the List of the Jury: I'm sure my Cousin *Olivia* has some Relations amongst 'em. But where is she?

FREEMAN. Nay, Widow, but hear me one word only.

WIDOW. Nay, Sir, no more, pray; I will no more hearken again to your foolish Love motions, than to offers of Arbitration.   [*Exeunt* WIDOW *and* JERRY.

FREEMAN. Well, I'll follow thee yet; for he that has a pretension at Court, or to a Widow, must never give over for a little ill usage.

OLDFOX. Therefore I'll get her by Assiduity, Patience, and Long-sufferings, which you will not undergo; for you idle young Fellows leave off Love, when it comes to be Business; and Industry gets more Women, than Love.

FREEMAN. Ay, Industry, the Fool's and old Man's merit; but I'll be industrious too, and make a business on't, and get her by Law, Wrangling, and Contests, and not by Sufferings: And, because you are no dangerous Rival, I'll give thee counsel, Major.

> *If you Litigious Widow e'r wou'd gain,*
> *Sigh not to her; but by the Law complain:*
> *To her, as to a Baud, Defendant Sue*
> *With Statutes, and make Justice Pimp for you.*
>   [*Exeunt.*

FINIS ACTUS SECUNDI.

Act III. Scene i.

Westminster-Hall.

Enter MANLY *and* FREEMAN, *two Sailors behind.*

MANLY. I hate this place, worse than a Man that has inherited a *Chancery* Suit:[1] I wish I were well out on't again.

FREEMAN. Why, you need not be afraid of this place: for a Man without Money, needs no more fear a croud of Lawyers, than a croud of Pick-pockets.

MANLY. This, the Reverend of the Law wou'd have thought the Palace or Residence of Justice; but, if it be, she lives here with the State of a *Turkish* Emperor, rarely seen; and besieg'd, rather than defended, by her numerous black Guard[2] here.

FREEMAN. Methinks, 'tis like one of their own Halls, in *Christmas* time,[3] whither, from all parts, Fools bring their Money, to try, by the Dice, (not the worst Judges) whether it shall be their own, or no: but, after a tedious fretting and wrangling, they drop away all their Money, on both sides; and finding neither the better, at last, go emptily and lovingly away together, to the Tavern, joining their Curses against the young Lawyers Box, that sweeps all, like the old ones.[4]

MANLY. Spoken, like a Revelling *Christmas* Lawyer.

FREEMAN. Yes, I was one, I confess; but was fain to leave the Law, out of Conscience, and fall to making false Musters; rather chose to Cheat the King, than his Subjects;[5] Plunder, rather than take Fees.

MANLY. Well, a Plague, and a Purse Famine, light on the Law; and that Female limb of it, who drag'd me hither to day: but pr'ythee go see if, in that croud of dagled Gowns there, thou canst find her.

[*Pointing to a croud of Lawyers, at the end of the Stage.*
[*Exit* FREEMAN.

Manet MANLY.

How hard it is to be an Hypocrite!
At least to me, who am but newly so.

I thought it once a kind of Knavery,
Nay, Cowardice, to hide ones faults; but now
The common frailty, Love, becomes my shame.
He must not know I love th' ungrateful still,
Lest he contemn me, more than she: for I,
It seems, can undergo a Womans scorn,
But not a Mans—

Enter to him FIDELIA.

FIDELIA. Sir, good Sir, generous Captain.

MANLY. Pr'ythee, kind Impertinence, leave me. Why shou'dst thou follow me, flatter my Generosity now, since thou know'st I have no Money left? if I had it, I'd give it thee, to buy my quiet.

FIDELIA. I never follow'd yet, Sir, Reward or Fame, but you alone; nor do I now beg any thing, but leave to share your miseries: You shou'd not be a Niggard of 'em, since, methinks, you have enough to spare. Let me follow you now, because you hate me, as you have often said.

MANLY. I ever hated a Coward's company, I must confess.

FIDELIA. Let me follow you, till I am none then; for you, I'm sure, will through such Worlds of dangers, that I shall be inur'd to 'em; nay, I shall be afraid of your anger more than danger, and so turn valiant out of fear. Dear Captain, do not cast me off, till you have try'd me once more: do not, do not go to Sea again without me.

MANLY. Thou to Sea! to Court, thou Fool; remember the advice I gave thee: thou art a handsom Spaniel, and canst faun naturally; go, busk about, and run thy self into the next great Man's Lobby: first faun upon the Slaves without, and then run into the Ladies Bed-chamber; thou may'st be admitted, at last, to tumble her Bed: go, seek, I say, and lose me; for I am not able to keep thee: I have not Bread for my self.

FIDELIA. Therefore I will not go, because then I may help and serve you.

MANLY. Thou!

busk about: tack, change course.

FIDELIA. I warrant you, Sir; for, at worst, I cou'd beg or steal for you.

MANLY. Nay, more bragging! dost thou not know there's venturing your life, in stealing?[6] Go, pr'ythee, away: thou art as hard to shake off, as that flattering effeminating mischief, Love.

FIDELIA. Love, did you name? Why, you are not so miserable as to be yet in Love, sure!

MANLY. No, no, pr'ythee away, be gone, or—
I had almost discover'd my Love and Shame; well, if I had? that thing cou'd not think the worse of me:—or if he did?—no—yes, he shall know it—he shall—but then I must never leave him, for they are such secrets, that make Parasites and Pimps Lords of their Masters; for any slavery or tyranny is easier than Love's. [*Aside.*
Come hither. Since thou art so forward to serve me, hast thou but resolution enough to endure the torture of a secret? for such, to some, is insupportable.

FIDELIA. I wou'd keep it as safe, as if your dear precious life depended on't.

MANLY. Dam your dearness. It concerns more than my life, my honour.

FIDELIA. Doubt it not, Sir.

MANLY. And do not discover it, by too much fear of discovering it; but have a great care you let not *Freeman* find it out.

FIDELIA. I warrant you, Sir. I am already all joy, with the hopes of your commands; and shall be all wings, in the execution of 'em: speak quickly, Sir.

MANLY. You said you wou'd beg for me.

FIDELIA. I did, Sir.

MANLY. Then you shall beg for me.

FIDELIA. With all my heart, Sir.

MANLY. That is, Pimp for me.

FIDELIA. How, Sir?

MANLY. D'ye start! thinkst thou, thou cou'dst do me any other service? Come, no dissembling honour: I know you can do it handsomly, thou wert made for't: You have lost your time with me at Sea, you must recover it.

FIDELIA. Do not, Sir, beget your self more Reasons for your Aversion to me, and make my obedience to you a fault: I am the unfittest in the World, to do you such a service.

MANLY. Your cunning arguing against it, shews but how fit you are for it. No more dissembling: here, (I say) you must go use it for me, to *Olivia*.

FIDELIA. To her, Sir?

MANLY. Go flatter, lie, kneel, promise, any thing to get her for me: I cannot live, unless I have her. Didst thou not say thou wou'dst do any thing, to save my life? And she said you had a persuading face.

FIDELIA. But, did not you say, Sir, your honour was dearer to you, than your life? And wou'd you have me contribute to the loss of that, and carry love from you, to the most infamous, most false, and—

MANLY. And most beautiful!—   [*Sighs aside.*

FIDELIA. Most ungrateful Woman, that ever liv'd; for sure she must be so, that cou'd desert you so soon, use you so basely, and so lately too: do not, do not forget it, Sir, and think—

MANLY. No, I will not forget it, but think of revenge: I will lie with her, out of revenge. Go, be gone, and prevail for me, or never see me more.

FIDELIA. You scorn'd her last night.

MANLY. I know not what I did last night; I dissembled last night.

FIDELIA. Heavens!

MANLY. Be gone, I say, and bring me love or compliance back, or hopes at least, or I'll never see thy face again: by—

FIDELIA. O do not swear, Sir, first hear me.

MANLY. I am impatient, away, you'll find me here till twelve.   [*Turns away.*

FIDELIA. Sir—

MANLY. Not one word, no insinuating Argument more, or soothing persuasion; you'll have need of all your Rhetorick with her: go, strive to alter her, not me; be gone.
          [*Exit* MANLY *at the end of the Stage.*

Manet FIDELIA.

FIDELIA. Shou'd I discover to him now my Sex,
 And lay before him his strange cruelty,
 'Twou'd but incense it more.— No, 'tis not time.
 For his Love, must I then betray my own?
 Were ever Love or Chance, till now, severe?
 Or shifting Woman pos'd with such a task?
 Forc'd to beg that which kills her, if obtain'd;
 And give away her Lover not to lose him.

[*Exit* FIDELIA.

Enter Widow BLACKACRE *in the middle of half a dozen
 Lawyers, whisper'd to by a Fellow in black,*
 JERRY BLACKACRE *following the croud.*

WIDOW. Offer me a Reference, you saucy Companion
 you! d'ye know who you speak to? Art thou a Solicitor
 in *Chancery,* and offer a Reference? A pretty Fellow!
 Mr. Serjeant *Ploddon,* here's a Fellow has the impudence
 to offer me a Reference.

PLODDON. Who's that has the impudence to offer a Reference within these Walls?

WIDOW. Nay, for a Splitter of Causes to do't!

PLODDON. No, Madam, to a Lady learned in the Law, as
 you are, the offer of a Reference were to impose upon
 you.

WIDOW. No, no, never fear me for a Reference, Mr. Serjeant. But, come, have you not forgot your Brief? Are
 you sure you shan't make the mistake of— Hark you—
 [*Whispers.*] Go then, go to your Court of *Common-
 Pleas,*[7] and say one thing over and over again: You do
 it so naturally, you'll never be suspected for protracting
 time.

Reference: a reference, in the Court of Chancery, was the act of sending matter to the Masters in Ordinary, who would then ascertain the facts and refer back to the court. In effect, a kind of arbitration, which, from the Widow's point of view, would take too much of the litigious fun out of the case.

Splitter of Causes: lawyer. To split a cause was to bring action for only a part of the cause of that action. The result might be multiple suits instead of a single one—an increase in business for the lawyer—so it is not difficult to see how the slang title came into being.

PLODDON. Come, I know the course of the Court, and your
    business.   [*Exit* PLODDON.

WIDOW. Let's see, *Jerry,* where are my Minutes? Come,
    Mr. *Quaint,* pray go talk a great deal for me in *Chan-*
    cery; let your words be easie, and your Sense hard, my
    Cause requires it: Branch it bravely, and deck my
    Cause with flowers, that the Snake may lie hidden. Go,
    go, and be sure you remember the Decree of my Lord
    Chancellor *Tricesimo quart'* of the Queen.

QUAINT. I will, as I see cause, extenuate, or examplifie[8]
    Matter of Fact; baffle Truth, with Impudence; answer
    Exceptions, with Questions, tho' never so impertinent;
    for Reasons, give 'em Words; for Law and Equity,
    Tropes and Figures: And so relax and enervate the
    sinews of their Argument, with the oyl of my Elo-
    quence. But when my Lungs can reason no longer, and
    not being able to say any thing more for our Cause, say
    every thing of our Adversary; whose Reputation, though
    never so clear and evident in the eye of the World, yet
    with sharp Invectives—

WIDOW. (Alias *Belin'sgate.*)

QUAINT. With poinant and sowre Invectives, I say, I will
    deface, wipe out, and obliterate his fair Reputation,
    even as a Record with the juice of Lemons; and tell
    such a Story, (for, the truth on't is, all that we can
    do for our Client, in *Chancery,* is telling a Story) a
    fine Story, a long Story, such a Story—

WIDOW. Go, save thy breath for the Cause; talk at the
    Bar, Mr. *Quaint:* You are so copiously fluent, you can
    weary any ones ears, sooner than your own tongue.
    Go, weary our Adversaries Counsel, and the Court: Go,
    thou art a fine-spoken person: Adad, I shall make thy
    Wife jealous of me: if you can but court the Court into
    a Decree for us. Go, get you gone, and remember—
                  [*Whispers. Exit* QUAINT.
    Come, Mr. *Blunder,* pray baul soundly for me, at the

Tricesimo quart' of the Queen: *Belin'sgate:* billingsgate.
in the thirty-fourth year of
Elizabeth's reign: 1591/92.

Kings-Bench; bluster, sputter, question, cavil; but be sure your Argument be intricate enough, to confound the Court: And then you do my business. Talk what you will, but be sure your tongue never stand still; for your own noise will secure your Sense from Censure: 'tis like coughing or heming when one has got the Belly-ake, which stifles the unmannerly noise. Go, dear Rogue, and succeed; and I'll invite thee, ere it be long, to more souz'd Venison.

BLUNDER. I'll warrant you, after your Verdict, your Judgment shall not be Arrested, upon if's and and's.

WIDOW. Come, Mr. *Petulant,* let me give you some new instructions, for our Cause in the *Exchequer:* Are the Barons sate?

PETULANT. Yes, no; may be they are, may be they are not: what know I? what care I?

WIDOW. Hey day! I wish you wou'd but snap up the Counsel on t'other side anon, at the Bar, as much; and have a little more patience with me, that I might instruct you a little better.

PETULANT. You instruct me! What is my Brief for, Mistress?

WIDOW. Ay, but you seldom read your Brief, but at the Bar, if you do it then.

PETULANT. Perhaps I do, perhaps I don't, and perhaps 'tis time enough: pray hold your self contented, Mistress.

WIDOW. Nay, if you go there too, I will not be contented, Sir, tho' you, I see, will lose my Cause for want of speaking, I wo'not: You shall hear me, and shall be instructed. Let's see your Brief.

PETULANT. Send your Solicitor to me, instructed by a Woman! I'd have you to know, I do not wear a Bargown—

WIDOW. By a Woman! And I'd have you to know, I am no common Woman; but a Woman conversant in the Laws of the Land, as well as your self, tho' I have no Bargown.

Barons: the judges of the
Court of Exchequer.

PETULANT. Go to, go to, Mistress, you are impertinent, and there's your Brief for you: instruct me!

[*Flings her Breviate at her.*

WIDOW. Impertinent to me, you saucy *Jack* you! You return my Breviate, but where's my Fee? You'll be sure to keep that, and scan that so well, that if there chance to be but a brass Half-crown in't, one's sure to hear on't again: wou'd you wou'd but look on your Breviate half so narrowly. But pray give me my Fee too, as well as my Brief.

PETULANT. Mistress, that's without Precedent. When did a Counsel ever return his Fee, pray? And you are impertinent, and ignorant, to demand it.

WIDOW. Impertinent again, and ignorant to me! Gadsbodikins, you puny Upstart in the Law, to use me so, you Green Bag Carrier, you Murderer of unfortunate Causes, the Clerks Ink is scarce off of your fingers, you that newly come from Lamblacking the Judges shooes, and are not fit to wipe mine; you call me impertinent and ignorant! I wou'd give thee a Cuff on the ear, sitting the Courts, if I were ignorant.[9] Marry gep, if it had not been for me, thou hadst been yet but a hearing Counsel at the Bar.   [*Exit* PETULANT.

Enter Mr. BUTTONGOWN, *crossing the Stage in haste.*

Mr. *Buttongown,* Mr. *Buttongown,* whither so fast? what, won't you stay till we are heard?

BUTTONGOWN. I cannot, Mrs. *Blackacre,* I must be at the Council, my Lord's Cause stays there for me.

WIDOW. And mine suffers here.

BUTTONGOWN. I cannot help it.

WIDOW. I'm undone.

BUTTONGOWN. What's that to me?

Breviate: brief.
Gadsbodikins: God's body.
Marry gep (or "marry gip"): a mild interjection, like "marry come-up," which the Widow uses on p. 432, presumably a corruption of "by Mary Gipcy" (St. Mary of Egypt). See OED.

hearing Counsel: a counsel without a case, standing around the courts in hope of business.

WIDOW. Consider the five pound Fee, if not my Cause: that was something to you.

BUTTONGOWN. Away, away, pray be not so troublesom, Mistress, I must be gone.

WIDOW. Nay, but consider a little, I am your old Client, my Lord but a new one; or, let him be what he will, he will hardly be a better Client to you, than my self: I hope you believe I shall be in Law as long as I live? therefore am no despicable Client. Well, but go to your Lord, I know you expect he shou'd make you a Judge one day; but I hope his promise to you will prove a true Lord's promise: But, that he might be sure to fail you, I wish you had his Bond for't.

BUTTONGOWN. But what will you yet be thus impertinent, Mistress?

WIDOW. Nay, I beseech you, Sir, stay; if it be but to tell me my Lord's Case: come, in short.

BUTTONGOWN. Nay, then—   [*Exit* BUTTONGOWN.

WIDOW. Well, *Jerry*, observe Child, and lay it up for here-after: These are those Lawyers who, by being in all Causes, are in none; therefore if you wou'd have 'em for you, let your Adversary fee 'em; for he may chance to depend upon 'em: and so, in being against thee, they'll be for thee.

JERRY. Ay, Mother, they put me in mind of the uncon-scionable Woers of Widows, who undertake briskly their Matrimonial business for their money; but when they have got it once, let who's will drudge for them; there-fore have a care of 'em, forsooth: there's Advice for your Advice.

WIDOW. Well said, Boy, come, Mr. *Splitcause*, pray go see when my Cause in *Chancery* comes on; and go speak with Mr. *Quillet* in the *Kings-Bench*, and Mr. *Quirk* in the *Common-Pleas*, and see how our matters go there.

Enter Major OLDFOX.

OLDFOX. Lady, a good and propitious morning to you; and may all your Causes go as well, as if I my self were Judge of 'em.

WIDOW. Sir, excuse me, I am busie, and cannot answer

Complements in *Westminster-hall.* Go, Mr. *Splitcause,* and come to me again, to that Booksellers, there I'll stay for you, that you may be sure to find me.

OLDFOX. No, Sir, come to the other Booksellers, I'll attend your Ladiship thither. [*Exit* SPLITCAUSE.

WIDOW. Why to the other?

OLDFOX. Because he is my Bookseller, Lady.

WIDOW. What to sell you Lozenges for your Catarrh? or Medicines for your Corns? what else can a Major deal with a Bookseller for?

OLDFOX. Lady, he Prints for me.

WIDOW. Why, are you an Author?

OLDFOX. Of some few Essayes; deign you, Lady, to peruse 'em. (She is a Woman of parts, and I must win her by shewing mine.) [*Aside.*

The Bookseller's BOY.

BOY. Will you see *Culpepper,* Mistress? *Aristotle's Problems?* The *Compleat Midwife?*[10]

WIDOW. No, let's see *Dalton, Hughs, Shepherd, Wingate.*[11]

BOY. We have no Law-books.

WIDOW. No? You are a pretty Bookseller then.

OLDFOX. Come, have you e're a one of my Essayes left?

BOY. Yes, Sir, we have enough, and shall alwayes have 'em.

OLDFOX. How so?

BOY. Why, they are good, steady, lasting Ware.

OLDFOX. Nay, I hope they will live, let's see. Be pleas'd, Madam, to peruse the poor endeavors of my Pen; for I have a Pen, tho' I say it, that— [*Gives her a Book.*

JERRY. Pray let me see *St. George for Christendom,* or, *The Seven Champions of England.*[12]

WIDOW. No, no, give him, *The Young Clerk's Guide.*[13] What, we shall have you read your self into a humor of Rambling, and Fighting, and studying Military Discipline, and wearing red Breeches!

OLDFOX. Nay, if you talk of Military Discipline, shew him my Treatise of *The Art Military.*

WIDOW. Hold, I wou'd as willingly he shou'd read a *Play.*

JERRY. O pray, forsooth Mother, let me have a *Play.*

WIDOW. No, Sirrah, there are young Students of the Law

enough spoil'd already, by *Playes;* they wou'd make
you in love with your Landress, or what's worse, some
Queen of the Stage, that was a Landress; and so turn
Keeper before you are of age.

[Several crossing the Stage.

But stay, *Jerry,* is not that *Mr. what-d' y' call-him,* that
goes there: he that offer'd to sell me a Suit in *Chancery*
for five hundred pound, for a hundred down, and only
paying the Clerks Fees?

JERRY. Ay, forsooth, 'tis he.

WIDOW. Then stay here, and have a care of the Bags,
whil'st I follow him: have a care of the Bags, I say.

JERRY. And do you have a care, forsooth, of the Statute
against *Champertee,* I say.   *[Exit* WIDOW.

Enter FREEMAN to them.

FREEMAN. So, there's a limb of my Widow, which was
wont to be inseparable from her: she can't be far.

[Aside.

How now, my pretty Son-in-law that shall be, where's
my Widow?

JERRY. My Mother, but not your Widow, will be forthcoming presently.

FREEMAN. Your Servant, Major; what, are you buying
Furniture for a little sleeping Closet, which you miscall
a Study? For you do only by your Books, as by your
Wenches, bind 'em up neatly, and make 'em fine, for
other people to use 'em: And your Bookseller is properly
your Upholster; for he furnishes your Room, rather than
your Head.

OLDFOX. Well, well, good Sea-Lieutenant, study you your
Compass, that's more than your head can deal with.
(I will go find out the Widow, to keep her out of his
sight, or he'll board her, whil'st I am treating a Peace.)

[Aside.

[Exit OLDFOX.

Champertee: champerty was a
bargain made with a party to
a suit whereby the champertor
(a lawyer, usually) paid the
costs in exchange for a portion of whatever was at stake
(money, lands) if the case
were successful. As Jerry indicates, it was illegal.

Manent FREEMAN, JERRY.

JERRY. Nay pr'ythee, Friend, now, let me have but the *Seven Champions*, you shall trust me no longer than till my Mothers Mr. *Splitcause* comes; for I hope he'll lend me wherewithall to pay for't.

FREEMAN. Lend thee! here, I'll pay him. Do you want Money, Squire? I'm sorry a Man of your Estate shou'd want Money.

JERRY. Nay, my Mother will ne'r let me be at Age: And till then, she sayes—

FREEMAN. At Age! Why, you are at Age already, to have spent an Estate, Man; there are younger than you, have kept their Women these three Years, have had half a dozen Claps, and lost as many thousand pounds at Play.

JERRY. Ay, they are happy Sparks! nay, I know some of my School-Fellows, who, when we were at School, were two Years younger than me; but now, I know not how, are grown Men before me, and go where they will, and look to themselves: but my Curmudgeonly Mother wo'nt allow me wherewithall to be a Man of my self with.

FREEMAN. Why there 'tis, I knew your Mother was in the fault: Ask but your School-Fellows what they did, to be Men of themselves.

JERRY. Why, I know they went to Law with their Mothers; for they say, there's no good to be done upon a Widow Mother, till one goes to Law with her: but mine is as plaguy a Lawyer, as any's of our Inn. Then wou'd she marry too, and cut down my Trees: Now I shou'd hate, Man, to have my Father's Wife kiss'd, and slap'd, and t'other thing too, (you know what I mean) by another Man; and our Trees are the purest, tall, even, shady twigs, by my fa—

FREEMAN. Come, Squire, let your Mother and your Trees fall as she pleases, rather than wear this Gown, and carry green Bags all thy life; and be pointed at for a Tony: But you shall be able to deal with her yet the common way; thou shalt make false Love to some Lawyer's daughter, whose Father, upon the hopes of thy marrying her, shall lend thee Money, and Law, to pre-

Tony: simpleton.

serve thy Estate and Trees; and thy Mother is so ugly, no Body will have her, if she cannot cut down thy Trees.

JERRY. Nay, if I had but any Body to stand by me, I am as stomachful as another.

FREEMAN. That will I, I'll not see any hopeful young Gentleman abus'd.

BOY. By any but your self.   [*Aside.*

JERRY. The truth on't is, mine's as arrant a Widow-Mother, to her poor Child, as any's in *England:* She wo'nt so much as let one have six-pence in one's Pocket, to see a Motion, or the Dancing of the Ropes, or—

FREEMAN. Come, you sha'nt want Money, there's Gold for you.

JERRY. O Lurd, Sir, two Guineys! d'ye lend me this? is there no trick in't? Well, Sir, I'll give you my Bond, for security.

FREEMAN. No, no, thou hast given me thy face for security: Any Body wou'd swear, thou dost not look like a Cheat. You shall have what you will of me; and, if your Mother will not be kinder to you, come to me, who will.

JERRY. By my fa— he's a curious fine Gentleman!— [*Aside.* But, will you stand by one?

FREEMAN. If you can be resolute.

JERRY. Can be resolv'd! Gad, if she gives me but a cross word, I'll leave her to night, and come to you. But, now I have got Money, I'll go to *Jack of All Trades,* at t'other end of the *Hall,* and buy the neatest, purest things—

FREEMAN. And I'll follow the great Boy, and my blow at his Mother: steal way the Calf, and the Cow will follow you.   [*Exit* JERRY, *follow'd by* FREEMAN. *Enter, on the other side,* MANLY, *Widow* BLACKACRE, *and* OLDFOX.

MANLY. Dam your Cause; can't you lose it without me? which you are like enough to do, if it be as you say, an honest one: I will suffer no longer for't.

---

stomachful: spirited.
Motion: puppet play. For testimony to the popularity of puppets and ropedancers during the Restoration, see Evelyn's *Diary* (de Beer, III, 27, 30, 197–198, 256, 492; IV, 362).

WIDOW. Nay, Captain, I tell you, you are my prime Witness, and the Cause is just now coming on, Mr. *Split-cause* tells me. Lord, methinks you shou'd take a pleasure in walking here, as half you see now do; for they have no business here, I assure you.

MANLY. Yes, but I'll assure you then, their business is to persecute me; but d'ye think I'll stay any longer, to have a Rogue, because he knows my name, pluck me aside, and whisper a Newsbook-secret to me, with a stinking breath? A second come piping angry from the Court, and sputter in my face his tedious complaints against it? A third Law-Coxcomb, because he saw me once at a Reader's dinner,[14] come and put me a long Law-Case, to make a discovery of his indefatigable dulness, and my weari'd patience? A fourth, a most barbarous civil Rogue, who will keep a Man half an hour in the croud with a bow'd body, and a hat off, acting the reform'd Sign of the *Salutation* Tavern,[15] to hear his bountiful professions of service and friendship; whil'st he cares not if I were damn'd, and I am wishing him hang'd out of my way? I'd as soon run the Gantlet, as walk t'other turn.

Enter to them JERRY BLACKACRE *without his Bags; but laden with Trinkets, which he endeavors to hide from his Mother: and follow'd at a distance by* FREEMAN.

WIDOW. O, are you come, Sir? But where have you been, you Ass? And how come you thus laden?

JERRY. Look here, forsooth Mother, now here's a Duck, here's a Boarcat, and here's an Owl.

> [*Making a noise with Cat-calls, and other such like Instruments.*

WIDOW. Yes, there is an Owl, Sir.

OLDFOX. He's an ungracious Bird, indeed.

WIDOW. But go, thou Trangame, and carry back those Trangames, which thou hast stol'n or purloin'd; for no Body wou'd trust a Minor in *Westminster-hall* sure.

JERRY. Hold your self contented, forsooth, I have these Commodities by a fair Bargain and Sale; and there stands my Witness, and Creditor.

Boarcat: male cat.   *Trangame:* toy, gewgaw.

WIDOW. How's that! What, Sir, d'ye think to get the Mother, by giving the Child a Rattle? But where are my Bags, my Writings, you Rascal?

JERRY. O Law! Where are they indeed? [*Aside.*

WIDOW. How, Sirrah? speak, come—

MANLY. You can tell her, *Freeman,* I suppose?

[*Apart to him.*

FREEMAN. 'Tis true, I made one of your Salt-water Sharks steal 'em, whil'st he was eagerly choosing his Commodities, as he calls 'em, in order to my design upon his Mother. [*Apart to him.*

WIDOW. Wo'nt you speak? Where were you, I say, you Son of a—an unfortunate Woman? O, Major, I'm undone; they are all that concern my Estate, my Jointure, my Husband's Deed of Gift, my Evidences for all my Suits now depending! What will become of them?

FREEMAN. I'm glad to hear this. [*Aside.*

They'll be safe, I warrant you, Madam.

WIDOW. O where? where? Come, you Villain, along with me, and shew me where.

[*Exeunt* WIDOW, JERRY, OLDFOX.
Manent MANLY, FREEMAN.

MANLY. Thou hast taken the right way to get a Widow, by making her great Boy Rebel; for, when nothing will make a Widow marry, she'll do't to cross her Children. But canst thou in earnest marry this Harpy, this Volume of shrivel'd blur'd Parchments and Law, this Attornies Desk?

FREEMAN. Ay, ay, I'll marry, and live honestly: that is, give my Creditors, not her, due Benevolence, pay my Debts.

MANLY. Thy Creditors, you see, are not so barbarous, as to put thee in Prison, and wilt thou commit thy self to a noisom Dungeon for thy life? which is the only satisfaction thou canst give thy Creditors, by this match.

FREEMAN. Why, is not she rich?

MANLY. Ay, but he that marries a Widow, for her Money, will find himself as much mistaken, as the Widow, that marries a young Fellow for due Benevolence, as you call it.

FREEMAN. Why, d'ye think I sha'nt deserve Wages? I'll drudge faithfully.

MANLY. I tell thee again, he that is the Slave in the Mine, has the least propriety in the Ore: You may dig, and dig; but, if thou wou'dst have her Money, rather get to be her Trustee, than her Husband; for a true Widow will make over her Estate to any Body, and cheat her self, rather than be cheated by her Children, or a second Husband.

Enter to them JERRY, *running in a fright.*

JERRY. O Law! I'm undone, I'm undone, my Mother will kill me: You said you'd stand by one.

FREEMAN. So I will, my brave Squire, I warrant thee.

JERRY. Ay, but I dare not stay till she comes; for she's as furious, now she has lost her Writings, as a Bitch when she has lost her Puppies.

MANLY. The comparison's handsom!

JERRY. O, she's here!

Enter Widow BLACKACRE, *and* OLDFOX.

FREEMAN. [*To the Sailor.*]¹⁶ Take him, *Jack,* and make haste with him, to your Master's Lodging; and be sure you keep him up, till I come.

[*Exeunt*¹⁷ JERRY *and* SAILOR.

WIDOW. O my dear Writings! Where's this Heathen Rogue, my Minor?

FREEMAN. Gone to drown, or hang himself.

WIDOW. No, I know him too well, he'll ne'r be *Felo de se* that way; but he may go and choose a Guardian of his own head, and so be *Felo de ses beins:*¹⁸ for he has not yet chosen one.

FREEMAN. Say you so? And he sha'nt want one.   [*Aside.*

WIDOW. But, now I think on't, 'tis you, Sir, have put this Cheat upon me; for there is a saying, *Take hold of a Maid by her Smock, and a Widow by her Writings, and they cannot get from you:* But I'll play fast and loose with you yet, if there be Law; and my Minor and Writings are not forthcoming, I'll bring my Action of Detinue or Trover.¹⁹ But first, I'll try to find out this Guardian-less, graceless Villain. Will you jog, Major?

MANLY. If you have lost your Evidence, I hope your Causes cannot go on, and I may be gone?

WIDOW. O no, stay but a making Water while, (as one may say) and I'll be with you again.

[*Exeunt* WIDOW, *and* OLDFOX.

Manent MANLY, FREEMAN.

FREEMAN. Well, sure I am the first Man that ever began a Love Intrigue, in *Westminster-hall.*

MANLY. No, sure; for the Love to a Widow generally begins here: And as the Widow's Cause goes against the Heir or Executors, the Jointure Rivals commence their Suit to the Widow.

FREEMAN. Well, but how, pray, have you past your time here, since I was forc'd to leave you alone? You have had a great deal of patience.

MANLY. Is this a place to be alone, or have patience in? But I have had patience indeed; for I have drawn upon me, since I came, but three Quarrels, and two Law-Suits.

FREEMAN. Nay, faith, you are too curst to be let loose in the World; you shou'd be ty'd up again, in your Sea-kennel, call'd a Ship. But how cou'd you quarrel here?

MANLY. How cou'd I refrain? A Lawyer talk'd peremptorily and saucily to me, and as good as gave me the Lye.

FREEMAN. They do it so often to one another at the Bar, that they make no Bones on't elsewhere.

MANLY. However, I gave him a Cuff on the Ear; whereupon he jogs two Men, whose Backs were turn'd to us, (for they were reading at a Booksellers) to Witness I struck him sitting the Courts; which office they so readily promis'd that I call'd 'em Rascals and Knights of the Post: one of 'em presently calls two other absent Witnesses, who were coming towards us at a distance; whil'st the other, with a Whisper, desires to know my name, that he might have satisfaction by way of Challenge, as t'other by way of Writ; but if it were not rather to direct his Brother's Writ, than his own Challenge: there you see is one of my Quarrels, and two of my Law-Suits.

FREEMAN. So:—and the other two?

MANLY. For advising a Poet to leave off Writing, and turn Lawyer, because he is dull, and impudent, and sayes or writes nothing now, but by Precedent.

FREEMAN. And the third Quarrel?

MANLY. For giving more sincere Advice, to a handsom, well-drest, young Fellow (who ask'd it too) not to marry a Wench, that he lov'd, and I had lay'n with.

FREEMAN. Nay, if you will be giving your sincere advice to Lovers, and Poets, you will not fail of Quarrels.

MANLY. Or, if I stay in this place; for I see more Quarrels crouding upon me: let's be gone, and avoid 'em.

Enter NOVEL, *at a distance, coming towards them.*

A Plague on him, that Sneer is ominous to us; he is coming upon us, and we shall not be rid of him.

NOVEL. Dear Bully, don't look so grum upon me; you told me just now, you had forgiven me a little harmless Raillery upon wooden legs last night.

MANLY. Yes, yes, pray be gone, I am talking of business.

NOVEL. Can't I hear it? I love thee, and will be faithful, and alwayes—

MANLY. Impertinent! 'Tis Business that concerns *Freeman* only.

NOVEL. Well, I love *Freeman* too, and wou'd not divulge his secret: pr'ythee speak, pr'ythee, I must—

MANLY. Pr'ythee let me be rid of thee, I must be rid of thee.

NOVEL. Faith, thou canst hardly, I love thee so. Come, I must know the business.

MANLY. So, I have it now.   [*Aside.*

Why, if you needs will know it, he has a quarrel, and his Adversary bids him bring two Friends with him: now, I am one; and we are thinking who we shall have for a third.

Several crossing the Stage.

NOVEL. A Pox, there goes a Fellow owes me an Hundred pound, and goes out of Town to morrow: I'll speak with him, and come to you presently.   [*Exit* NOVEL.

grum: morose, surly.

MANLY. No but you wo' not.

FREEMAN. You are dextrously rid of him.

Enter OLDFOX.

MANLY. To what purpose, since here comes another, as impertinent? I know, by his grin, he is bound hither.

OLDFOX. Your Servant, worthy, noble Captain: Well, I have left the Widow, because she carry'd me from your company; for, faith Captain, I must needs tell thee, thou art the only Officer in *England*, who was not an *Edg-hill*[20] Officer, that I care for.

MANLY. I'm sorry for't.

OLDFOX. Why, wou'dst thou have me love them?

MANLY. Any body, rather than me.

OLDFOX. What, you are modest I see! therefore too, I love thee.

MANLY. No, I am not modest, but love to brag my self, and can't patiently hear you fight over the last Civil War; therefore go look out the Fellow I saw just now here, that walks with his Stockings and his Sword out at heels,[21] and let him tell you the History of that scar on his cheek, to give you occasion to shew yours, got in the field at *Bloomsbury*,[22] not that of *Edg-hill*: go to him, poor Fellow, he is fasting, and has not yet the happiness this morning to stink of Brandy and Tobacco; go, give him some to hear you, I am busie.

OLDFOX. Well, ygad, I love thee now, Boy, for thy surliness: thou art no tame Captain, I see, that will suffer—

MANLY. An old Fox.

OLDFOX. All that sha'nt make me angry: I consider thou art peevish, and fretting at some ill success at Law. Pr'ythee tell me what ill luck you have met with here.

MANLY. You.

OLDFOX. Do I look like the Picture of ill Luck? Gadsnouns, I love thee more and more; and shall I tell thee what made me love thee first?

MANLY. Do: that I may be rid of that damn'd quality, and thee.

Gadsnouns: God's wounds.

OLDFOX. 'Twas thy wearing that broad Sword there.

MANLY. Here, *Freeman,* let's change: I'll never wear it more.

OLDFOX. How! You wo' not sure. Pr'ythee don't look like one of our Holyday Captains now adayes, with a Bodkin by your side, your Martinet Rogues.

MANLY. (O, then there's hopes.)   [*Aside.*
What, d'ye find fault with Martinet?[23] let me tell you, Sir, 'tis the best exercise in the World; the most ready, most easie, most graceful exercise that ever was us'd, and the most—

OLDFOX. Nay, nay, Sir, no more, Sir, your Servant, if you praise Martinet once, I have done with you, Sir. Martinet! Martinet!   [*Exit* OLDFOX.

FREEMAN. Nay, you have made him leave you as willingly, as ever he did an Enemy; for he was truly for the King and Parliament: for the Parliament, in their List; and for the King, in cheating 'em of their Pay, and never hurting the King's party in the Field.

Enter a Lawyer towards them.

MANLY. A Pox! this way; here's a Lawyer I know threatning us with another greeting.

LAWYER. Sir, Sir, your very Servant; I was afraid you had forgotten me.

MANLY. I was not afraid you had forgotten me.

LAWYER. No, Sir, we Lawyers have pretty good memories.

MANLY. You ought to have, by your Wits.

LAWYER. O, you are a merry Gentleman, Sir; I remember you were merry, when I was last in your company.

MANLY. I was never merry in thy company, Mr. Lawyer, sure.

LAWYER. Why, I'm sure you jok'd upon me, and shamm'd me all night long.

MANLY. Shamm'd! pr'ythee what barbarous Law-term is that?

LAWYER. Shamming! Why, don't you know that? 'tis all our way of Wit Sir.

MANLY. I am glad I do not know it then: Shamming! What does he mean by't, *Freeman?*

FREEMAN. Shamming, is telling you an insipid, dull Lye with a dull Face, which the slie Wag the Author only laughs at himself; and making himself believe 'tis a good Jest, puts the Sham only upon himself.

MANLY. So, your Lawyers Jest, I find, like his Practice, has more Knavery than Wit in't. I shou'd make the worst Shammer in *England;* I must alwayes deal ingeniously, as I will with you, Mr. Lawyer, and advise you to be seen rather with Attornies and Solicitors, than such Fellows as I am; they will credit your practice more.

LAWYER. No, Sir, your company's an honour to me.

MANLY. No, faith, go this way,²⁴ there goes an Attorney, leave me for him: let it be never said, a Lawyers Civility did him hurt.

LAWYER. No, worthy honour'd Sir, I'll not leave you for any Attorney sure.

MANLY. Unless he had a Fee in his hand.

LAWYER. Have you any business here, Sir? try me: I'd serve you sooner than any Attorney breathing.

MANLY. Business!— So, I have thought of a sure way.

                                  [*Aside.*

Yes, faith, I have a little business.

LAWYER. Have you so, Sir? in what Court, Sir? what is't, Sir? tell me but how I may serve you, and I'll do't, Sir; and take it for as great an honour—

MANLY. Faith, 'tis for a poor Orphan of a Sea-Officer of mine, that has no Money; but if it cou'd be follow'd *in Forma Pauperis;* and when the Legacy's recover'd—

LAWYER. *Forma Pauperis,* Sir!

MANLY. Ay, Sir.

              Several crossing the Stage.

LAWYER. Mr. *Bumblecase,* Mr. *Bumblecase,* a word with you; Sir, I beg your pardon at present, I have a little business—

---

ingeniously: he means "ingenuously"; the two words were often confused at the time. 1694 Q prints *ingenuously.*

in Forma Pauperis: if one could be declared a pauper, he might sue without court costs and be assigned free counsel.

MANLY. Which is not *in Forma Pauperis.* [*Exit* LAWYER.

FREEMAN. So, you have now found a way to be rid of people without quarrelling.

Enter ALDERMAN.

MANLY. But here's a City Rogue will stick as hard upon us, as if I ow'd him Money.

ALDERMAN. Captain, noble Sir, I am yours heartily d'ye see: Why shou'd you avoid your old Friends?

MANLY. And why shou'd you follow me? I owe you nothing.

ALDERMAN. Out of my hearty respects to you; for there is not a Man in *England.*

MANLY. Thou wou'dst save from hanging, with the expence of a shilling only.

ALDERMAN. Nay, nay, but Captain, you are like enough to tell me—

MANLY. Truth, which you wo'nt care to hear; therefore you had better go talk with some body else.

ALDERMAN. No, I know no body can inform me better, of some young Wit, or Spendthrift, that has a good dip'd Seat and Estate in *Middlesex, Hartfordshire, Essex,* or *Kent,* any of these wou'd serve my turn: now, if you knew of such an one, and wou'd but help—

MANLY. You to finish his ruine.

ALDERMAN. Ifaith, you shou'd have a snip—

MANLY. Of your Nose; you thirty in the hundred Rascal, wou'd you make me your Squire Setter, your Baud for Mannors? [*Takes him by the Nose.*

ALDERMAN. Oh!

FREEMAN. Hold, or here will be your third Law-Suit.

---

dip'd: dipped: mortgaged.
thirty in the hundred Rascal: one who lends money at 30% interest. As 6% was the highest legal interest, Manly is calling him a usurer.
Setter: OED lists it as a cant word for a sharper's confederate, a decoy, which is possible within this sentence. Set-ter must also have meant "pimp," however, which would fit even better in this context, strengthening the appositional *Baud.* Setter, Vainlove's servant in William Congreve's *The Old Batchelour,* (London, 1693), is identified in the Personae Dramatis simply as "a Pimp."

ALDERMAN. Gads precious, you hectoring person you, are you wild? I meant you no hurt, Sir; I begin to think (as things go) Land security best, and have, for a convenient Mortgage, some ten, fifteen, or twenty thousand pound by me.

MANLY. Then go lay it out upon an Hospital, and take a Mortgage of Heaven, according to your City custom; for you think, by laying out a little Money, to hook in that too hereafter: do, I say, and keep the Poor you've made, by taking forfeitures, that Heaven may not take yours.

ALDERMAN. No, to keep the Cripples you make this War; this War spoils our Trade.

MANLY. Dam your Trade, 'tis the better for't.

ALDERMAN. What, will you speak against our Trade?

MANLY. And dare you speak against the War, our Trade?

ALDERMAN. Well, he may be a Convoy of ships I am concern'd in.   [*Aside.*
Come, Captain, I will have a fair correspondency with you, say what you will.

MANLY. Then pr'ythee be gone.

ALDERMAN. No, faith; pr'ythee, Captain, let's go drink a Dish of Lac'd Coffee, and talk of the Times: Come, I'll treat you; nay, you shall go, for I have no business here.

MANLY. But I have.

ALDERMAN. To pick up a Man to give thee a Dinner? Come, I'll do thy business for thee.

MANLY. Faith, now I think on't, so you may, as well as any Man; for 'tis to pick up a Man, to be bound with me, to one who expects City security, for—

ALDERMAN. Nay, then your Servant, Captain; business must be done.

MANLY. Ay, if it can; but hark you, Alderman, without you—

ALDERMAN. Business, Sir, I say, must be done; and there's an Officer of the Treasury I have an Affair with—
                 [*Exit* ALDERMAN.

MANLY. You see now what the mighty friendship of the World is; what all Ceremony, Embraces, and plentiful

Professions come to: You are no more to believe a professing Friend, than a threatning Enemy; and as no Man
hurts you, that tells you he'll do you a mischief, no man,
you see, is your Servant, who sayes he is so. Why, the
Devil, then shou'd a Man be troubled with the flattery
of Knaves, if he be not a Fool, or Cully; or with the
fondness of Fools, if he be not a Knave, or Cheat?

FREEMAN. Only for his pleasure; for there is some in laughing at Fools, and disappointing Knaves.

MANLY. That's a pleasure, I think, wou'd cost you too dear,
as well as marrying your Widow to disappoint her; but,
for my part, I have no pleasure by 'em, but in despising
'em, wheresoe'r I meet 'em; and then, the pleasure of
hoping so to be rid of 'em. But now my comfort is, I am
not worth a shilling in the World, which all the World
shall know; and then I'm sure I shall have none of 'em
come near me.

FREEMAN. A very pretty comfort, which I think you pay
too dear for: But is the twenty pound gone since the
morning?

MANLY. To my Boats Crew: Wou'd you have the poor,
honest, brave Fellows want?

FREEMAN. Rather than you, or I.

MANLY. Why, art thou without Money? thou who art a
Friend to every Body?

FREEMAN. I ventur'd my last stake upon the Squire, to
nick him of his Mother; and cannot help you to a dinner,
unless you will go dine with my Lord—

MANLY. No, no, the Ordinary is too dear for me, where
flattery must pay for my dinner: I am no Herald, or
Poet.

FREEMAN. We'll go then to the Bishops—

MANLY. There you must flatter the old Philosophy: I cannot renounce my reason for a dinner.

FREEMAN. Why, then let's go to your Aldermans.

MANLY. Hang him, Rogue! that were not to dine; for he
makes you drunk with Lees of Sack before dinner, to
take away your stomach: and there you must call Usury
and Extortion, Gods blessings, or the honest turning of

the Penny; hear him brag of the leather Breeches in which he trotted first to Town; and make a greater noise with his Money in his Parlor, than his Casheers do in his Counting house, without hopes of borrowing a shilling.

FREEMAN. Ay, a pox on't, 'tis like dining with the great Gamesters; and, when they fall to their common Dessert, see the heaps of Gold drawn on all hands, without going to twelve. Let us go to my Lady *Goodly's.*

MANLY. There, to flatter her looks, you must mistake her Grandchildren for her own; praise her Cook, that she may rail at him: and feed her Dogs, not your self.

FREEMAN. What d'ye think of eating with your Lawyer then?

MANLY. Eat with him! Dam him; to hear him employ his barbarous eloquence in a Reading upon the two and thirty good Bits in a shoulder of Veal;[25] and be forc'd your self to praise the cold Bribe pye, that stinks; and drink Law-French Wine, as rough and harsh, as his Law-French. A pox on him, I'd rather dine in the Temple Rounds, or Walks, with the Knights without Noses, or the Knights of the Post; who are honester Fellows, and better company. But let us home, and try our Fortune; for I'll stay no longer here, for your damn'd Widow.

FREEMAN. Well, let us go home then; for I must go for my damn'd Widow, and look after my new damn'd

going to twelve: the precise meaning of this phrase is not known. Perhaps "the twelve" means a pair of dice, but several of the dice games of the period were played with more than two dice. In any case, the line plainly means that it is difficult to see the money pile up without getting into the game.

Knights without Noses: presumably the statues of the Knights Templar that sat, cross-legged, in the Round Church of the Temple. This was a place where lawyers met clients, and willing witnesses could be found. Samuel Butler in *Hudibras,* III, iii, writes of ". . . Witnesses / That ply i' th' *Temples,* under Trees. / Or walk the Round, with Knights o' th' Posts / About the Cross-leg'd Knights, their Hosts." London, 1709, p. 190.

Charge; three or four hundred Year ago, a Man might
have din'd in this Hall.[26]

MANLY. *But now, the Lawyer only here is fed:*
   And, Bully-like, by Quarrels gets his Bread.

                                              [*Exeunt.*

FINIS ACTUS TERTII.

ACT IV. SCENE I.

MANLY'S *Lodging.*

Enter MANLY, *and* FIDELIA.

MANLY. Well, there's success in thy face; hast thou prevail'd? say.

FIDELIA. As I cou'd wish, Sir.

MANLY. So, I told thee what thou wert fit for, and thou
wou'dst not believe me. Come, thank me for bringing
thee acquainted with thy Genius. Well, thou hast molli-
fi'd her heart for me?

FIDELIA. No, Sir, not so; but what's better.

MANLY. How? what's better!

FIDELIA. I shall harden your heart against her.

MANLY. Have a care, Sir, my heart is too much in earnest
to be fool'd with, and my desire at heighth, and needs
no delays to incite it; what, you are too good a Pimp
already, and know how to endear pleasure, by with-
holding it? but leave off your Pages, Baudy-house tricks,
Sir, and tell me, will she be kind?

FIDELIA. Kinder than you cou'd wish, Sir.

MANLY. So then: well, pr'ythee what said she?

FIDELIA. She said—

MANLY. What? thou'rt so tedious; speak comfort to me:
what?

FIDELIA. That, of all things, you were her aversion.

MANLY. How?

FIDELIA. That she wou'd sooner take a Bedfellow out of
an Hospital, and Diseases, into her Arms, than you.

MANLY. What?

FIDELIA. That she wou'd rather trust her Honour with a dissolute, debauch'd Hector; nay worse, with a finical baffled Coward, all over loathsom with affectation of the fine Gentleman.

MANLY. What's all this you say?

FIDELIA. Nay, that my offers of your Love to her, were more offensive, than when Parents wooe their Virgin Daughters, to the enjoyment of Riches onely; and that you were, in all circumstances, as nauseous to her, as a Husband on compulsion.

MANLY. Hold; I understand you not.

FIDELIA. So, 'twill work I see.   [*Aside.*

MANLY. Did not you tell me—

FIDELIA. She call'd you ten thousand Ruffins.

MANLY. Hold, I say.

FIDELIA. Brutes—

MANLY. Hold.

FIDELIA. Sea-Monsters—

MANLY. Dam your intelligence: hear me a little now.

FIDELIA. Nay, surly Coward she call'd you too.

MANLY. Won't you hold yet? hold, or—

FIDELIA. Nay, Sir, pardon me; I cou'd not but tell you she had the baseness, the injustice, to call you Coward, Sir, Coward, Coward, Sir.

MANLY. Not yet?—

FIDELIA. I've done. Coward, Sir.

MANLY. Did not you say she was kinder than I cou'd wish her?

FIDELIA. Yes, Sir.

MANLY. How then?—O—I understand you now. At first, she appear'd in rage, and disdain, the truest sign of a coming Woman; but, at last, you prevail'd it seems: did you not?

FIDELIA. Yes, Sir.

MANLY. So then, let's know that only; come, pr'ythee, without delays: I'll kiss thee for that News before hand.

FIDELIA. So; the Kiss, I'm sure, is welcom to me, whatsoe're the News will be to you.   [*Aside.*

baffled: disgraced.   *coming:* ready, eager.

MANLY. Come, speak, my dear Voluntier.

FIDELIA. How welcome were that kind word too, if it were not for another Womans sake! [*Aside.*

MANLY. What, won't you speak? You prevail'd for me, at last, you say?

FIDELIA. No, Sir.

MANLY. No more of your fooling, Sir; it will not agree with my impatience, or temper.

FIDELIA. Then, not to fool you, Sir, I spoke to her for you, but prevail'd for my self; she wou'd not hear me when I spoke in your behalf; but bid me say what I wou'd in my own, tho' she gave me no occasion, she was so coming: and so was kinder, Sir, than you cou'd wish; which I was only afraid to let you know, without some warning.

MANLY. How's this? Young man, you are of a lying age; but I must hear you out, and if—

FIDELIA. I wou'd not abuse you, and cannot wrong her by any report of her, she is so wicked.

MANLY. How, wicked! had she the impudence, at the second sight of you only—

FIDELIA. Impudence, Sir! Oh, she has impudence enough to put a Court out of countenance, and debauch a Stews.

MANLY. Why, what said she?

FIDELIA. Her tongue, I confess, was silent; but her speaking Eyes gloted such things, more immodest, and lascivious, than Ravishers can act, or Women under a confinement think.

MANLY. I know there are whose Eyes reflect more Obscenity, than the Glasses in Alcoves; but there are others too who use a little Art with their looks, to make 'em seem more beautiful, not more loving: which vain young Fellows, like you, are apt to interpret in their own favor, and to the Lady's wrong.

FIDELIA. Seldom, Sir; pray have you a care of gloting Eyes; for he that loves to gaze upon 'em, will find, at last, a thousand Fools and Cuckolds in 'em, instead of *Cupids*.

MANLY. Very well, Sir: but, what, you had only eye-kindness from *Olivia*?

Stews: brothel.

FIDELIA. I tell you again, Sir, no Woman sticks there: Eye-promises of Love they only keep; nay, they are Contracts which make you sure of 'em. In short, Sir, she, seeing me, with shame and amazement dumb, unactive, and resistless, threw her twisting arms about my neck, and smother'd me with a thousand tasteless Kisses: believe me, Sir, they were so to me.

MANLY. Why did you not avoid 'em then?

FIDELIA. I fenced with her eager Arms, as you did with the grapples of the Enemy's Fireship;[1] and nothing but cutting 'em off, cou'd have freed me.

MANLY. Damn'd, damn'd Woman, that cou'd be so false and infamous! And damn'd, damn'd heart of mine, that cannot yet be false, tho' so infamous! What easie, tame, suffering, trampled things does that little God of talking Cowards make of us! but—

FIDELIA. So! it works I find as I expected.   [Aside.

MANLY. But she was false to me before, she told me so her self, and yet I cou'd not quite believe it; but she was, so that her second falseness is a favor to me, not an injury, in revenging me upon the Man that wrong'd me first of her Love. Her Love!—a Whores, a Witches Love!— But, what, did she not kiss well, Sir? I'm sure I thought her Lips—but I must not think of 'em more—but yet they are such I cou'd still kiss,—grow to—and then tear off with my teeth, grind 'em into mammocks, and spit 'em into her Cuckolds face.

FIDELIA. Poor man, how uneasie he is! I have hardly the heart to give him so much pain, tho' withall I give him a cure; and to my self new life.   [Aside.

MANLY. But, what, her Kisses sure cou'd not but warm you into desire at last, or a compliance with hers at least?

FIDELIA. Nay more, I confess—

MANLY. What more? speak.

FIDELIA. All you cou'd fear had pass'd between us, if I cou'd have been made to wrong you, Sir, in that nature.

MANLY. Cou'd have been made! you lie, you did.

FIDELIA. Indeed, Sir, 'twas impossible for me; besides, we were interrupted by a visit; but, I confess, she would

mammocks: bits, shreds.

not let me stir, till I promis'd to return to her again, within this hour, as soon as it shou'd be dark; by which time, she wou'd dispose of her visit, and her servants, and her self, for my reception: which I was fain to promise to get from her.

MANLY. Ha!

FIDELIA. But if ever I go near her again, may you, Sir, think me as false to you, as she is; hate, and renounce me; as you ought to do her, and I hope will do now.

MANLY. Well, but now I think on't, you shall keep your word with your Lady. What, a young Fellow, and fail the first, nay, so tempting an assignation!

FIDELIA. How, Sir?

MANLY. I say you shall go to her when 'tis dark, and shall not disappoint her.

FIDELIA. I, Sir! I shou'd disappoint her more by going; for—

MANLY. How so?

FIDELIA. Her impudence, and injustice to you, will make me disappoint her Love; loath her.

MANLY. Come, you have my leave; and if you disgust her, I'll go with you, and act Love, whil'st you shall talk it only.

FIDELIA. You, Sir! nay, then I'll never go near her. You act Love, Sir! You must but act it indeed, after all I have said to you. Think of your Honour, Sir, Love—

MANLY. Well, call it Revenge, and that is Honourable: I'll be reveng'd on her; and thou shalt be my second.

FIDELIA. Not in a base action, Sir, when you are your own Enemy: O go not near her, Sir, for Heav'ns sake, for your own, think not of it.

MANLY. How concern'd you are! I thought I shou'd catch you. What, you are my Rival at last, and are in Love with her your self; and have spoken ill of her, out of your Love to her, not me; and therefore wou'd not have me go to her!

FIDELIA. Heav'n witness for me, 'tis because I love you only, I wou'd not have you go to her.

disgust: dislike.

MANLY. Come, come, the more I think on't, the more I'm satisfi'd you do love her: those Kisses, young Man, I knew were irresistible; 'tis certain.

FIDELIA. There is nothing certain in the World, Sir, but my Truth, and your Courage.

MANLY. Your Servant, Sir. Besides false, and ungrateful, as she has been to me; and tho' I may believe her hatred to me, great as you report it; yet I cannot think you are so soon, and at that rate, belov'd by her, tho' you may endeavor it.

FIDELIA. Nay, if that be all, and you doubt it still, Sir, I will conduct you to her; and, unseen, your Ears shall judge of her falseness, and my Truth to you: if that will satisfie you.

MANLY. Yes, there is some satisfaction in being quite out of doubt: because 'tis that alone with-holds us from the pleasure of Revenge.

FIDELIA. Revenge! What Revenge can you have, Sir? Disdain is best reveng'd by scorn; and faithless Love, by loving another, and making her happy with the others losings: which, if I might advise—

Enter FREEMAN.

MANLY. Not a word more.

FREEMAN. What are you talking of Love yet, Captain? I thought you had done with't.

MANLY. Why, what did you hear me say?

FREEMAN. Something imperfectly of Love, I think.

MANLY. I was only wond'ring why Fools, Rascals, and desertless Wretches, shou'd still have the better of Men of Merit, with all Women; as much as with their own common Mistress, Fortune!

FREEMAN. Because most Women, like Fortune, are blind, seem to do all things in jest, and take pleasure in extravagant actions; their love deserves neither thanks, or blame, for they cannot help it: 'tis all sympathy; therefore the noisie, the finical, the talkative, the cowardly and effeminate, have the better of the brave, the reasonable, and Man of Honour; for they have no more reason in their love, or kindness, than Fortune her self.

MANLY. Yes, they have their reason. First, Honour in a

Man they fear too much to love; and Sence in a Lover,
upbraids their want of it; and they hate any thing that
disturbs their admiration of themselves; but they are of
that vain number, who had rather shew their false generosity, in giving away profusely to worthless Flatterers,
than in paying just Debts: And, in short, all Women,
like Fortune, (as you say) and Rewards, are lost, by too
much meriting.

FIDELIA. All Women, Sir! sure there are some, who have
no other quarrel to a Lovers merit, but that it begets
their despair of him.

MANLY. Thou art young enough to be credulous; but we—

Enter 1 SAILOR.

1 SAILOR. Here are now below, the scolding, daggled Gentlewoman, and that Major Old—old—Fop, I think you
call him.

FREEMAN. *Oldfox:* pr'ythee bid 'em come up, with your
leave, Captain, for now I can talk with her upon the
square; if I shall not disturb you.

MANLY. No; for I'll be gone. Come, Voluntier.

FREEMAN. Nay, pray stay; the Scene between us will not
be so tedious to you, as you think: besides, you shall
see, how I have rigg'd my Squire out, with the remains
of my shipwrack'd Wardrobe; he is under your *Sea-Valet
de Chambre*'s hands, and by this time drest, and will
be worth your seeing. Stay, and I'll fetch my Fool.

MANLY. No; you know I cannot easily laugh: besides, my
Voluntier and I have business abroad.

[*Exeunt* MANLY, FIDELIA *on one side,* FREEMAN *on t'other.*
Enter Major OLDFOX, *and Widow* BLACKACRE.

WIDOW. What, no body here! Did not the Fellow say he
was within?

OLDFOX. Yes, Lady; and he may be perhaps a little busie
at present; but, if you think the time long till he comes,
[*Unfolding Papers*] I'll read you here some of the fruits
of my leisure, the overflowings of my fancy and Pen.
(To value me right, she must know my parts.)   [*Aside.*
Come—

WIDOW. No, no; I have reading work enough of my own,
in my Bag, I thank you.

OLDFOX. I, Law, Madam; but here is a Poem, in blank Verse, which I think a handsom Declaration of one's Passion.

WIDOW. O! if you talk of Declarations, I'll shew you one of the prettiest pen'd things, which I mended too my self you must know.

OLDFOX. Nay, Lady, if you have us'd your self so much to the reading of harsh Law, that you hate smooth Poetry; here is a Character for you, of—

WIDOW. A Character! Nay, then I'll shew you my Bill in Chancery here, that gives you such a Character of my Adversary, makes him as black—

OLDFOX. Pshaw; away, away, Lady. But if you think the Character too long, here is an Epigram not above 20 Lines, upon a cruel Lady; who Decreed her Servant shou'd hang himself, to demonstrate his Passion.

WIDOW. Decreed! if you talk of Decreeing, I have such a Decree here, drawn by the finest Clerk—

OLDFOX. O Lady, Lady, all interruption, and no sence between us, as if we were Lawyers at the Bar! But I had forgot, *Apollo* and *Littleton* never lodge in a head together. If you hate Verses, I'll give you a cast of my Politics in Prose: 'tis a Letter to a Friend in the Countrey; which is now the way of all such sober, solid persons as my self, when they have a mind to publish their disgust to the Times; tho' perhaps, between you and I, they have no Friend in the Countrey. And sure a Politic, serious person may as well have a feign'd Friend in the

Character: a brief, satirical, prose description of a particular person or a type: lawyer, soldier, proud man. The genre, borrowed from Theophrastus, was popular during the Restoration. The best of the character-writers of the period was probably Samuel Butler although his characters, some of which have been cited in the footnotes to this volume, were not published until 1759.

Apollo and Littleton: art and law. Sir Thomas Littleton (1422–81) was an English jurist whose treatise on tenures (c. 1481), written in law-French, became a standard work on the subject. Part of its reputation derived from the fact that Sir Edward Coke wrote a commentary on it. An edition of *Littleton's Tenures, in French and English* had been published as recently as 1671.

Countrey to write to, as well as an idle Poet a feign'd Mistress to write to. And so here is my Letter to a Friend, or no Friend, in the Countrey, concerning the late conjuncture of Affairs, in relation to Coffee-houses:[2] or the Coffee-man's Case.

WIDOW. Nay, if your Letter have a Case in't, 'tis something; but first I'll read you a Letter of mine, to a Friend in the Countrey, call'd a Letter of Attorney.

Enter to them FREEMAN, *and* JERRY BLACKACRE, *in an old gaudy Suit, and Red Breeches of* FREEMAN'S.

OLDFOX. What, Interruption still? O the plague of Interruption! worse to an Author, than the plague of Critics!
　　　　　　　　　　　　　　　　　　　　　　　[*Aside.*

WIDOW. What's this I see, *Jerry Blackacre,* my Minor, in Red Breeches! What, hast thou left the modest seemly Garb of Gown and Cap, for this? And have I lost all my good Inns of Chancery breeding upon thee then? And thou wilt go a breeding thy self, from our Inn of *Chancery* and *Westminster-hall,* at Coffee-houses and Ordinaries, Play-houses, Tennis-courts, and Baudy-houses.

JERRY. Ay, ay, what then? perhaps I will; but what's that to you? here's my Guardian and Tutor now forsooth, that I am out of your Hucksters hands.

WIDOW. How? thou hast not chosen him for thy Guardian yet?

JERRY. No, but he has chosen me for his Charge, and that's all one; and I'll do any thing he'll have me, and go all the World over with him; to Ordinaries, and Baudy-houses, or any where else.

WIDOW. To Ordinaries and Baudy-houses! have a care, Minor, thou wilt infeeble there thy Estate, and Body: do not go to Ordinaries and Baudy-houses, good *Jerry.*

JERRY. Why, how come you to know any ill by Baudy-houses? You never had any hurt by 'em, had you, forsooth? Pray hold your self contented; if I do go where Money and Wenches are to be had, you may thank your self; for you us'd me so unnaturally, you wou'd never

Letter of Attorney: a written instrument empowering one person to act lawfully in place of another.

let me have a Penny to go abroad with; nor so much as come near the Garret, where your Maidens lay; nay, you wou'd not so much as let me play at Hotcockles with 'em, nor have any Recreation with 'em, tho' one shou'd have kist you behind, you were so unnatural a Mother, so you were.

FREEMAN. Ay, a very unnatural Mother, faith, Squire.

WIDOW. But, *Jerry*, consider thou art yet but a Minor; however, if thou wilt go home with me again, and be a good Child, thou shalt see—

FREEMAN. Madam, I must have a better care of my Heir under age, than so; I wou'd sooner trust him alone with a stale Waiting-woman and a Parson, than with his Widow Mother and her Lover or Lawyer.

WIDOW. Why, thou Villain, part Mother and Minor! Rob me of my Child and my Writings! but thou shalt find there's Law; and as in the Case of Ravishment, of Guard—*Westminster* the Second.[3]

OLDFOX. Young Gentleman, Squire, pray be rul'd by your Mother, and your Friends.

JERRY. Yes, I'll be rul'd by my Friends, therefore not by my Mother, so I won't: I'll choose him for my Guardian till I am of age; nay, may be for as long as I live.

WIDOW. Wilt thou so, thou Wretch? And when thou'rt of age, thou wilt Sign, Seal, and Deliver too, wilt thou?

JERRY. Yes marry will I, if you go there too.

WIDOW. O do not squeeze Wax, Son; rather go to Ordinaries, and Baudy-houses, than squeeze Wax: if thou dost that, farewell the goodly Mannor of *Blackacre*, with all its Woods, Underwoods, and Appurtenances whatever. Oh, oh! [*Weeps.*

FREEMAN. Come, Madam, in short, you see I am resolv'd

Hotcockles: an innocent game in which the person who is "it," blind-folded, tries to guess who has hit him, but from the context Jerry sounds as though he has some other kind of play in mind. According to Partridge, "cockles" came to mean the labia minora in the eighteenth century, and "to play at hot cockles" became a slang phrase for sexual manipulation. This, surely, is an early instance of that usage.

to have a share in the Estate, yours or your Sons; if I
cannot get you, I'll keep him, who is less coy you find;
but, if you wou'd have your Son again, you must take
me too. Peace, or War? Love, or Law? You see my
Hostage is in my hand: I'm in possession.

WIDOW. Nay, if one of us must be ruin'd, e'en let it be him.
By my Body, a good one! Did you ever know yet a
Widow marry or not marry for the sake of her Child?
I'd have you to know, Sir, I shall be hard enough for
you both yet, without marrying you: if *Jerry* won't be
rul'd by me, what say you, Booby, will you be rul'd?
speak.

JERRY. Let one alone, can't you?

WIDOW. Wilt thou choose him for Guardian, whom I refuse
for Husband?

JERRY. Ay, to choose, I thank you.

WIDOW. And are all my hopes frustrated? Shall I never
hear thee put Cases again to *John* the Butler, or our
Vicar? Never see thee amble the Circuit with the
Judges; and hear thee, in our Town-Hall, louder than
the Cryer?

JERRY. No; for I have taken my leave of Lawyering, and
Pettifogging.

WIDOW. Pettifogging! thou prophane Villain, hast thou so?
Pettifogging!—then you shall take your leave of me, and
your Estate too; thou shalt be an Alien to me and it for
ever. Pettifogging!

JERRY. O, but if you go there too, Mother, we have the
Deeds, and Settlements, I thank you: Wou'd you cheat
me of my Estate, ifac?

WIDOW. No, no, I will not cheat your little Brother *Bob;*
for thou wert not born in Wedlock.

FREEMAN. How's that?

JERRY. How? What Quirk has she got in her head now?

WIDOW. I say thou canst not, shalt not inherit the *Blackacres* Estate.

JERRY. Why? Why, forsooth? What d' ye mean, if you
go there to?

WIDOW. Thou art but my base Child; and, according to

the Law, canst not inherit it: nay, thou art not so much as Bastard eigne.

JERRY. What, what? Am I then the Son of a Whore, Mother?

WIDOW. The Law says—

FREEMAN. Madam, we know what the Law says; but have a care what you say: do not let your Passion, to ruine your Son, ruine your Reputation.

WIDOW. Hang Reputation, Sir, am not I a Widow? Have no Husband, nor intend to have any? Nor wou'd you, I suppose, now have me for a Wife. So, I think now I'm reveng'd on my Son and you, without marrying, as I told you.

FREEMAN. But, consider, Madam.

JERRY. What, have you no shame left in you, Mother?

WIDOW. Wonder not at it, Major, 'tis often the poor prest Widows case, to give up her Honour to save her Jointure; and seem to be a light Woman, rather than marry: as some young men, they say, pretend to have the filthy Disease, and lose their credit with most Women, to avoid the importunities of some.   [*Aside, to* OLDFOX.

FREEMAN. But one word with you, Madam.

WIDOW. No, no, Sir. Come, Major, let us make haste, now to the Prerogative Court.

OLDFOX. But, Lady, if what you say be true, will you stigmatize your Reputation on Record? And, if it be not true, how will you prove it?

WIDOW. Pshaw! I can prove any thing; and for my Reputation, know, Major, a wise Woman will no more value her Reputation in disinheriting a Rebellious Son, of a good Estate; than she wou'd in getting him, to inherit an Estate.   [*Exeunt* WIDOW *and* OLDFOX.

FREEMAN. Madam— We must not let her go so, Squire.

JERRY. Nay, the Devil can't stop her tho' if she has a mind to't. But come, Bully Guardian, we'll go and advise with three Attornies, two Proctors, two Solicitors, and a

---

Bastard eigne: when the older of two children was born before the marriage of his parents, he is known in law as the *Bastard eigne* (elder).

shrewd man of *White Friers*,[4] neither Attorney, Proctor, or Solicitor, but as pure a Pimp to the Law as any of 'em; and sure all they will be hard enough for her: for I fear, Bully Guardian, you are too good a Joker, to have any Law in your head.

FREEMAN. Thou'rt in the right on't, Squire; I understand no Law: especially that against Bastards, since I'm sure the Custom is against that Law; and more people get Estates by being so, than lose 'em. [*Exeunt.*

The Scene changes to OLIVIA's *Lodging.*

Enter Lord PLAUSIBLE, *and* BOY *with a Candle.*

PLAUSIBLE. Little Gentleman, your most obedient, faithful, humble Servant: where, I beseech you, is that Divine person your Noble Lady?

BOY. Gone out, my Lord; but commanded me to give you this Letter. [*Gives him a Letter.*

Enter to him NOVEL.

PLAUSIBLE. Which he must not observe.

[*Aside.*] [*Puts it up.*[5]

NOVEL. Hey, Boy, where is thy Lady?

BOY. Gone out, Sir; but I must beg a word with you.

[*Gives him a Letter, and Exit.*

NOVEL. For me? So. [*Puts up the Letter.*

Servant, Servant, my Lord; you see the Lady knew of your coming, for she is gone out.

PLAUSIBLE. Sir, I humbly beseech you not to censure the Lady's good breeding: she has reason to use more liberty with me, than with any other man.

NOVEL. How, Vicount, how?

PLAUSIBLE. Nay, I humbly beseech you, be not in choler; where there is most love, there may be most freedom.

NOVEL. Nay, then 'tis time to come to an eclercisment with you, and to tell you, you must think no more of this Lady's love.

PLAUSIBLE. Why, under correction, dear Sir?

NOVEL. There are Reasons, Reasons, Vicount.

PLAUSIBLE. What, I beseech you, Noble Sir?

NOVEL. Pr'ythee, pr'ythee be not impertinent, my Lord;

some of you Lords are such conceited, well-assur'd, impertinent Rogues.

PLAUSIBLE. And you noble Wits, are so full of shamming, and droling, one knows not where to have you, seriously.

NOVEL. Well, you shall find me in Bed, with this Lady, one of these dayes.

PLAUSIBLE. Nay, I beseech you, spare the Lady's Honour; for her's and mine will be all one shortly.

NOVEL. Pr'ythee, my Lord, be not an Ass: dost thou think to get her from me? I have had such encouragements—

PLAUSIBLE. I have not been thought unworthy of 'em.

NOVEL. What, not like mine! Come to an eclercisment, as I said.

PLAUSIBLE. Why, seriously then, she has told me, Vicountess sounded prettily.

NOVEL. And me, that *Novel* was a name she wou'd sooner change her's for, than for any Title in *England*.

PLAUSIBLE. She has commended the softness, and respectfulness of my behaviour.

NOVEL. She has prais'd the briskness of my Railery of all things, Man.

PLAUSIBLE. The sleepiness of my Eyes she lik'd.

NOVEL. Sleepiness! dulness, dulness. But the fierceness of mine she ador'd.

PLAUSIBLE. The brightness of my hair she lik'd.

NOVEL. The brightness! No, the greasiness, I warrant. But the blackness, and lustre of mine, she admires.

PLAUSIBLE. The gentleness of my smile.

NOVEL. The subtilty of my leer.

PLAUSIBLE. The clearness of my complexion.

NOVEL. The redness of my lips.

PLAUSIBLE. The whiteness of my teeth.

NOVEL. My janty way of picking them.

PLAUSIBLE. The sweetness of my breath.

NOVEL. Hah ha!— Nay then she abus'd you, 'tis plain; for you know what *Manly* said: the sweetness of your Pulvillio she might mean; but for your breath! ha, ha, ha. Your breath is such, Man, that nothing but Tobacco can perfume: and your Complexion nothing cou'd mend, but the Small Pox.

PLAUSIBLE. Well, Sir, you may please to be merry; but, to put you out of all doubt, Sir, she has receiv'd some Jewels from me, of value.

NOVEL. And Presents from me; besides what I presented her jantily, by way of 'Ombre, of three or four hundred pound value, which I'm sure are the earnest Pence for our Love bargain.

PLAUSIBLE. Nay then, Sir, with your favor, and to make an end of all your hopes, look you there, Sir, she has writ to me.— [*Deliver to each other their Letters.*[6]

NOVEL. How! how! Well, well, and so she has to me: look you there.—

PLAUSIBLE. What's here!

NOVEL. How's this?

Reads out.

My dear Lord,

You'll excuse me, for breaking my word with you, since 'twas to oblige, not offend you; for I am only gone abroad but to disappoint Novel, *and meet you in the Drawing-room;*[7] *where I expect you, with as much impatience, as when I us'd to suffer* Novel's *Visits, the most impertinent Fop, that ever affected the name of a Wit, therefore not capable, I hope, to give you jealousie; for, for your sake alone, you saw, I renounc'd an old Lover, and will do all the World. Burn the Letter, but lay up the kindness of it in your heart, with your*

OLIVIA.

Very fine! but pray let's see mine.

PLAUSIBLE. I understand it not; but sure she cannot think so of me.

Reads the other Letter.

NOVEL. *Humh! ha!—meet—for your sake—umh—quitted an old Lover—World—Burn—in your heart, with your*

OLIVIA.

Just the same, the names only alter'd.

PLAUSIBLE. Surely there must be some mistake; or some body has abus'd her, and us.

NOVEL. Yes, you are abus'd, no doubt on't, my Lord; but I'll to *Whitehall,* and see.

PLAUSIBLE. And I, where I shall find you are abus'd.

NOVEL. Where, if it be so, for our comfort, we cannot fail of meeting with Fellow-sufferers enough; for, as *Freeman* said of another, she stands in the Drawing-room, like the Glass, ready for all Comers to set their Gallantry by her: and, like the Glass too, lets no man go from her, unsatisfi'd with himself.   [*Exeunt Ambo.*

Enter OLIVIA *and* BOY.

OLIVIA. Both here, and just gone?

BOY. Yes, Madam.

OLIVIA. But are you sure neither saw you deliver the other a Letter?

BOY. Yes, yes, Madam, I am very sure.

OLIVIA. Go then to the *Old Exchange,* to *Westminster, Holbourn,* and all the other places I told you of; I shall not need you these two hours:[8] Be gone, and take the Candle with you, and be sure you leave word again below, I am gone out, to all that ask.

BOY. Yes, Madam.   [*Exit.*

OLIVIA. And my new Lover will not ask I'm sure; he has his Lesson, and cannot miss me here, tho' in the dark: which I have purposely design'd, as a remedy against my blushing Gallant's modesty; for young Lovers, like game Cocks, are made bolder, by being kept without light.

Enter her husband VERNISH, *as from a Journey.*

VERNISH. Where is she? Darkness everywhere!   [*Softly.*

OLIVIA. What, come before your time? my Soul! my Life! your haste has augmented your kindness; and let me thank you for it thus, and thus— [*Embracing and kissing him.*] And tho' (my Soul) the little time since you left me, has seem'd an Age to my impatience, sure it is yet but seven—

VERNISH. How! who's that you expected after seven?

OLIVIA. Ha! my Husband return'd! and have I been throwing away so many kind Kisses on my Husband, and wrong'd my Lover already?[9]

VERNISH. Speak, I say, who was't you expected after seven?

OLIVIA. What shall I say?—oh—   [*Aside.*
Why, 'tis but seven days, is it, dearest, since you went out of Town? and I expected you not so soon.

VERNISH. No, sure, 'tis but five days since I left you.

OLIVIA. Pardon my impatience, dearest, I thought 'em seven at least.

VERNISH. Nay then—

OLIVIA. But, my life, you shall never stay half so long from me again; you shan't, indeed, by this kiss, you shan't.

VERNISH. No, no; but why alone in the dark?

OLIVIA. Blame not my melancholy in your absence— But, my Soul, since you went, I have strange News to tell you: *Manly* is return'd.

VERNISH. *Manly* return'd! Fortune forbid.

OLIVIA. Met with the *Dutch* in the Channel, fought, sunk his ship, and all he carri'd with him: he was here with me yesterday.

VERNISH. And did you own our Marriage to him?

OLIVIA. I told him I was marry'd, to put an end to his love, and my trouble; but to whom, is yet a secret kept from him, and all the World: And I have us'd him so scurvily, his great spirit will ne'r return, to reason it farther with me; I have sent him to Sea again, I warrant.

VERNISH. 'Twas bravely done. And sure he will now hate the shore more than ever, after so great a disappointment. Be you sure only to keep awhile our great secret, till he be gone: in the mean time, I'll lead the easie honest Fool by the Nose, as I us'd to do; and, whil'st he stays, rail with him at thee; and, when he's gone, laugh with thee at him. But have you his Cabinet of Jewels safe? Part not with a Seed Pearl to him, to keep him from starving.

OLIVIA. Nor from hanging.

VERNISH. He cannot recover 'em; and, I think, will scorn to beg 'em again.

OLIVIA. But, my life, have you taken the thousand Guineys he left in my name, out of the Goldsmiths hands?

VERNISH. Ay, ay, they are remov'd to another Goldsmiths.

OLIVIA. Ay but, my Soul, you had best have a care he find not where the money is; for his present wants (as I'm inform'd) are such, as will make him inquisitive enough.

VERNISH. You say true, and he knows the man too: but I'll remove it to morrow.

OLIVIA. To morrow! O do not stay till to morrow: go to night, immediately.

VERNISH. Now I think on't, you advise well, and I will go presently.

OLIVIA. Presently! instantly: I will not let you stay a jot.

VERNISH. I will then, tho' I return not home till twelve.

OLIVIA. Nay, tho' not till morning, with all my heart: go, dearest, I am impatient till you are gone—

[*Thrusts him out.*

So, I have at once now brought about those two grateful businesses, which all prudent Women do together, secur'd money and pleasure; and now all interruptions of the last are remov'd. Go Husband, and come up Friend; just the Bucket's in the Well: the absence of one brings the other; but I hope, like them too, they will not meet in the way, justle, and clash together.

Enter FIDELIA, *and* MANLY *treading softly, and staying behind at some distance.*

So, are you come? (but not the Husband-bucket, I hope, again.) Who's there? my dearest?   [*Softly.*

FIDELIA. My life—

OLIVIA. Right, right: where are thy lips? here, take the dumb, and best Welcomes, Kisses and Embraces; 'tis not a time for idle words. In a Duel of Love, as in others, Parlying shews basely. Come, we are alone; and now the Word is only Satisfaction, and defend not thy self.

MANLY. How's this? Wuh, she makes Love like a Devil in a Play; and in this darkness, which conceals her Angels face; if I were apt to be afraid, I shou'd think her a Devil.   [*Aside.*

OLIVIA. What, you traverse ground, young Gentleman.

[FIDELIA *avoiding her.*

FIDELIA. I take breath only.

MANLY. Good Heav'ns! how was I deceiv'd!   [*Aside.*

OLIVIA. Nay, you are a Coward; what are you afraid of the fierceness of my Love?

FIDELIA. Yes, Madam, lest its violence might presage its change; and I must needs be afraid you wou'd leave me

traverse ground: move from
side to side in fencing.

quickly, who cou'd desert so brave a Gentleman as
Manly.

OLIVIA. O! name not his Name; for in a time of stol'n joys,
as this is, the filthy name of Husband were not a more
alaying sound.

MANLY. There's some comfort yet.   [*Aside.*

FIDELIA. But did you not love him?

OLIVIA. Never. How cou'd you think it?

FIDELIA. Because he thought it, who is a Man of that sence,
nice discerning, and diffidency, that I shou'd think it
hard to deceive him.

OLIVIA. No; he that distrusts most the World, trusts most
to himself, and is but the more easily deceiv'd, because
he thinks he can't be deceiv'd: his cunning is like the
Coward's Sword, by which he is oftner worsted, than
defended.

FIDELIA. Yet, sure, you us'd no common Art, to deceive
him.

OLIVIA. I knew he lov'd his own singular moroseness so
well, as to dote upon any Copy of it; wherefore I feign'd
an hatred to the World too, that he might love me in
earnest: but, if it had been hard to deceive him, I'm
sure 'twere much harder to love him. A dogged, ill-
manner'd—

FIDELIA. D'ye hear her, Sir? pray hear her.

[*Aside, to* MANLY.

OLIVIA. Surly, untractable, snarling Brute! he! a Masty
Dog were as fit a thing to make a Gallant of.

MANLY. Ay, a Goat, or Monky were fitter for thee. [*Aside.*

FIDELIA. I must confess, for my part, (tho' my Rival) I
cannot but say, he has a Manly handsomness in's face
and meen.

OLIVIA. So has a Saracen in the sign.[10]

FIDELIA. Is proper, and well made,

OLIVIA. As a Drayman.

FIDELIA. Has Wit,

OLIVIA. He rails at all Mankind.

FIDELIA. And undoubted Corage,

Masty: mastiff.

OLIVIA. Like the Hangman's, can murder a Man when his hands are ty'd. He has Cruelty indeed; which is no more Corage, than his Railing is Wit.

MANLY. Thus Women, and Men like Women, are too hard for us, when they think we do not hear 'em; and Reputation, like other Mistresses, is never true to a Man in his absence.   [*Aside.*

FIDELIA. He is—

OLIVIA. Pr'ythee no more of him; I thought I had satisfi'd you enough before, that he cou'd never be a Rival for you to apprehend; and you need not be more assur'd of my aversion to him, but by the last testimony of my love to you: which I am ready to give you. Come, my Soul, this way—   [*Pulls* FIDELIA.

FIDELIA. But, Madam, what cou'd make you dissemble Love to him, when 'twas so hard a thing for you, and flatter his Love to you?

OLIVIA. That which makes all the World flatter and dissemble, 'twas his Money: I had a real passion for that. Yet I lov'd not that so well, as for it to take him; for, as soon as I had his Money, I hastened his departure: like a Wife, who, when she has made the most of a dying Husband's breath, pulls away the Pillow.

MANLY. Damn'd Money! it's Master's potent Rival still; and, like a saucy Pimp, corrupts, it self, the Mistress it procures for us.

OLIVIA. But I did not think with you, my life, to pass my time in talking. Come hither, come; yet stay, till I have lock'd a door in the other Room, that might chance to let us in some interruption; which reciting Poets, or losing Gamesters, fear not more than I at this time do.
                                              [*Exit* OLIVIA.

FIDELIA. Well, I hope you are now satisfi'd, Sir, and will be gone, to think of your Revenge.

MANLY. No, I am not satisfi'd, and must stay to be Reveng'd.

FIDELIA. How, Sir? You'll use no violence to her, I hope, and forfeit your own life, to take away hers? That were no Revenge.

MANLY. No, no, you need not fear: my Revenge shall only be upon her honour, not her life.

FIDELIA. How, Sir? her honour? O Heav'ns! Consider, Sir, she has no honour. D'ye call that Revenge? Can you think of such a thing? But reflect, Sir, how she hates and loaths you.

MANLY. Yes, so much she hates me, that it wou'd be a Revenge sufficient, to make her accessary to my pleasure, and then let her know it.

FIDELIA. No, Sir, no; to be Reveng'd on her now, were to disappoint her. Pray, Sir, let us be gone. [*Pulls* MANLY.

MANLY. Hold off. What, you are my Rival then; and therefore you shall stay, and keep the door for me, whil'st I go in for you: but, when I'm gone, if you dare to stir off from this very Board, or breathe the least murmuring Accent, I'll cut her Throat first, and if you love her, you will not venture her life; nay, then I'll cut your Throat too; and I know you love your own life at least.

FIDELIA. But, Sir, good Sir.

MANLY. Not a word more, lest I begin my Revenge on her, by killing you.

FIDELIA. But are you sure 'tis Revenge, that makes you do this? how can it be?

MANLY. Whist.

FIDELIA. 'Tis a strange Revenge indeed.

MANLY. If you make me stay, I shall keep my word, and begin with you: no more.

> [*Exit* MANLY, *at the same door* OLIVIA *went.*
> *Manet* FIDELIA.

FIDELIA. O Heav'ns! is there not punishment enough
In loving well, if you will have't a Crime;
But you must add fresh Torments daily to't,
And punish us like peevish Rivals still,
Because we fain wou'd find a Heaven here?
But did there never any love like me,
That, untry'd Tortures, you must find me out?
Others, at worst, you force to kill themselves;
But I must be Self-murd'ress of my love,

peevish: spiteful.

Yet will not grant me pow'r to end my life,
My cruel life; for when a Lover's hopes
Are dead, and gone, life is unmerciful.

[*Sits down and weeps.*
Enter MANLY *to her.*

MANLY. I have thought better on't, I must not discover
my self now, I am without Witnesses; for if I barely
shou'd publish it, she wou'd deny it with as much impudence, as she wou'd act it again with this young Fellow here. Where are you?

FIDELIA. Here—oh—now I suppose we may be gone.

MANLY. I will, but not you; you must stay, and act the
second part of a Lover: that is, talk kindness to her.

FIDELIA. Not I, Sir.

MANLY. No disputing, Sir, you must: 'tis necessary to my
design, of coming again to morrow night.

FIDELIA. What, can you come again then hither?

MANLY. Yes, and you must make the appointment, and an
Apology for your leaving her so soon; for I have said
not a word to her, but have kept your counsel, as I expect you shou'd do mine: do this faithfully, and I promise you here, you shall run my Fortune still, and we will
never part as long as we live; but, if you do not do it,
expect not to live.

FIDELIA. 'Tis hard, Sir; but such a consideration will make
it easier: you won't forget your promise, Sir?

MANLY. No, by Heav'ns. But I hear her coming.   [*Exit.*
Enter OLIVIA *to* FIDELIA.

OLIVIA. Where is my life? run from me already! you do
not love me, dearest; nay, you are angry with me; for
you wou'd not so much as speak a kind word to me
within: What was the reason?

FIDELIA. I was transported too much.

OLIVIA. That's kind; but come, my Soul, what make you
here? let us go in again; we may be surpriz'd in this
Room, 'tis so near the stairs.

FIDELIA. No, we shall hear the better here, if any body
shou'd come up.

OLIVIA. Nay, I assure you, we shall be secure enough
within: Come, come—

FIDELIA. I am sick, and troubled with a sudden diziness; cannot stir yet.

OLIVIA. Come, I have spirits within.

FIDELIA. Oh!—don't you hear a noise, Madam?

OLIVIA. No, no, there is none: Come, come.   [*Pulls her.*

FIDELIA. Indeed there is; and I love you so much, I must have a care of your Honour, if you wo' not, and go; but to come to you to morrow night, if you please.

OLIVIA. With all my Soul; but you must not go yet: Come, pr'ythee.

FIDELIA. Oh!—I am now sicker, and am afraid of one of my Fits.

OLIVIA. What Fits?

FIDELIA. Of the Falling-sickness: and I lie generally an hour in a trance; therefore pray consider your honour, for the sake of my love, and let me go, that I may return to you often.

OLIVIA. But will you be sure then to come to morrow night?

FIDELIA. Yes.

OLIVIA. Swear.

FIDELIA. By our past kindness.

OLIVIA. Well, go your wayes then, if you will, you naughty Creature you.   [*Exit* FIDELIA.
These young Lovers, with their fears and modesty, make themselves as bad as old ones to us; and I apprehend their bashfulness, more than their tatling.

FIDELIA returns.

FIDELIA. O, Madam, we're undone! there was a Gentleman upon the stairs, coming up, with a Candle; which made me retire. Look you, here he comes!

Enter VERNISH, and his Man with a Light.

OLIVIA. How! my Husband! Oh, undone indeed! This way.
    [*Exit.*

VERNISH. Ha! You shall not scape me so, Sir.
    [*Stops* FIDELIA.

FIDELIA. O Heav'ns! more fears, plagues and torments yet in store!   [*Aside.*

VERNISH. Come, Sir, I guess what your business was here; but this must be your business now. Draw.   [*Draws.*

FIDELIA. Sir—

VERNISH. No Expostulations: I shall not care to hear of't. Draw.

FIDELIA. Good Sir.

VERNISH. How, you Rascal! not Courage to draw, yet durst do me the greatest injury in the World? Thy Cowardice shall not save thy life.   [*Offers to run at* FIDELIA.

FIDELIA. O hold, Sir, and send but your Servant down, and I'll satisfie you, Sir, I cou'd not injure you, as you imagine.

VERNISH. Leave the light, and be gone.   [*Exit Servant.* Now quickly, Sir, what you've to say, or—

FIDELIA. I am a Woman, Sir, a very unfortunate Woman.

VERNISH. How! A very handsom Woman I'm sure then: here are Witnesses of't too, I confess—
                [*Pulls off her Peruke, and feels her breasts.*
(Well, I'm glad to find the Tables turn'd, my Wife in more danger of Cuckolding, than I was.   [*Aside.*

FIDELIA. Now, Sir, I hope you are so much a Man of Honour, as to let me go, now I have satisfi'd you, Sir.

VERNISH. When you have satisfi'd me, Madam, I will.

FIDELIA. I hope, Sir, you are too much a Gentleman, to urge those secrets from a Woman, which concern her Honour: You may guess my misfortune to be Love, by my disguise; but a pair of Breeches cou'd not wrong you, Sir.

VERNISH. I may believe Love has chang'd your outside, which cou'd not wrong me; but why did my Wife run away?

FIDELIA. I know not, Sir; perhaps because she wou'd not be forc'd to discover me to you, or to guide me from your suspitions, that you might not discover me your self: which ungentleman-like curiosity I hope you will cease to have, and let me go.

VERNISH. Well, Madam, if I must not know who you are, 'twill suffice for me only to know certainly what you are: which you must not deny me. Come, there is a Bed within, the proper Rack for Lovers; and if you are a Woman, there you can keep no secrets, you'll tell me there all unask'd. Come.   [*Pulls her.*

FIDELIA. Oh! what d'ye mean? Help, oh—

VERNISH. I'll show you; but 'tis in vain to cry out: no one dares help you, for I am Lord here.

FIDELIA. Tyrant here; but if you are Master of this House, which I have taken for a Sanctuary, do not violate it your self.

VERNISH. No, I'll preserve you here, and nothing shall hurt you, and will be as true to you, as your disguise; but you must trust me then. Come, come.

FIDELIA. Oh! oh! rather than you shall drag me to a death so horrid, and so shameful, I'll die here a thousand deaths: but you do not look like a Ravisher, Sir.

VERNISH. Nor you like one wou'd put me to't, but if you will—

FIDELIA. Oh! oh! help, help—

Enter Servant.

VERNISH. You saucy Rascal, how durst you come in, when you heard a Woman squeak? that shou'd have been your Cue to shut the door.

SERVANT. I come, Sir, to let you know, the Alderman coming home immediately after you were at his house, has sent his Casheer with the money, according to your Note.

VERNISH. Dam his money! money never came to any sure unseasonably, till now. Bid him stay.

SERVANT. He sayes, he cannot a moment.

VERNISH. Receive it you then.

SERVANT. He sayes, he must have your Receit for it: he is in haste, for I hear him coming up, Sir.

VERNISH. Dam him. Help me in here then with this dishonorer of my Family.

FIDELIA. Oh! oh!

SERVANT. You say she is a Woman, Sir.

VERNISH. No matter, Sir: must you prate?

FIDELIA. Oh Heav'ns! is there—

[*They thrust her in, and lock the door.*

VERNISH. Stay there, my Prisoner; you have a short Reprieve.

I'll fetch the Gold, and that she can't resist;
For with a full hand 'tis we Ravish best.   [*Exeunt.*

FINIS ACTUS QUARTI.

Act V. Scene i.

ELIZA's *Lodging.*

Enter OLIVIA, *and* ELIZA.

OLIVIA. Ah, Cousin, nothing troubles me, but that I have
given the malicious World its Revenge, and Reason now
to talk as freely of me, as I us'd to do of it.

ELIZA. Faith, then, let not that trouble you; for, to be
plain, Cousin, the World cannot talk worse of you, than
it did before.

OLIVIA. How, Cousin? I'd have you to know, before this
faux pas, this trip of mine, the World cou'd not talk of
me.

ELIZA. Only, that you mind other peoples actions so much,
that you take no care of your own, but to hide 'em;
that, like a Thief, because you know your self most
guilty, you impeach your Fellow Criminals first, to clear
your self.

OLIVIA. O wicked World!

ELIZA. That you pretend an aversion to all Mankind, in
publick, only that their Wives and Mistresses may not
be jealous, and hinder you of their conversation, in
private.

OLIVIA. Base World!

ELIZA. That, abroad, you fasten quarrels upon innocent
men, for talking of you, only to bring 'em to ask you
pardon at home, and to become dear Friends with 'em,
who were hardly your acquaintance before.

OLIVIA. Abominable World!

ELIZA. That you condemn the obscenity of modern Plays,
only that you may not be censur'd for never missing
the most obscene of the old ones.

OLIVIA. Damn'd World!

ELIZA. That you deface the nudities of Pictures, and little Statues, only because they are not real.

OLIVIA. O fie, fie, fie; hideous, hideous, Cousin! the obscenity of their Censures makes me blush.

ELIZA. The truth of 'em, the naughty World wou'd say now.

Enter LETTICE *hastily.*

LETTICE. O! Madam, here is that Gentleman coming up, who now you say is my Master.

OLIVIA. O! Cousin, whither shall I run? protect me, or—
            [OLIVIA *runs away, and stands at a distance.*
                    Enter VERNISH.

VERNISH. Nay, nay, come—

OLIVIA. O, Sir, forgive me.

VERNISH. Yes, yes, I can forgive you being alone in the dark with a Woman in Mans cloaths; but have a care of a Man in Womans cloaths.

OLIVIA. What does he mean? he dissembles, only to get me into his power: Or has my dear Friend made him believe he was a Woman? My Husband may be deceiv'd by him, but I'm sure I was not.   [*Aside.*

VERNISH. Come, come, you need not have lay'n out of your House for this; but perhaps you were afraid, when I was warm with suspitions, you must have discover'd who she was: And pr'ythee, may I not know it?

OLIVIA. She was— (I hope he has been deceiv'd: and, since my Lover has play'd the Card, I must not renounce.)[1]
                                                            [*Aside.*

VERNISH. Come, what's the matter with thee? If I must not know who she is, I'm satisfi'd without. Come hither.

OLIVIA. Sure you do know her; she has told you her self, I suppose.

VERNISH. No, I might have known her better, but that I was interrupted, by the Goldsmith you know, and was forc'd to lock her into your Chamber, to keep her from his sight; but, when I return'd, I found she was got away, by tying the Window-curtains to the Balcony, by which she slid down into the street: for, you must know, I jested with her, and made her believe I'd ravish her; which she apprehended, it seems, in earnest.

OLIVIA. Then she got from you?

VERNISH. Yes.

OLIVIA. And is quite gone?

VERNISH. Yes.

OLIVIA. I'm glad on't—otherwise you had ravish'd her, Sir?
but how dar'st you go so far, as to make her believe you
wou'd ravish her? let me understand that, Sir. What!
there's guilt in your face, you blush too: nay, then you
did ravish her, you did, you base Fellow. What, ravish
a Woman in the first Month of our Marriage! 'Tis a
double injury to me, thou base ungrateful Man; wrong
my Bed already, Villain! I cou'd tear out those false
Eyes, barbarous unworthy Wretch.

ELIZA. So, so!—

VERNISH. Pr'ythee hear, my Dear.

OLIVIA. I will never hear you, my plague, my torment.

VERNISH. I swear—pr'ythee hear me.

OLIVIA. I have heard already too many of your false Oaths
and Vows, especially your last in the Church. O wicked
Man! And wretched Woman that I was! I wish I had
then sunk down into a Grave, rather than to have given
you my hand, to be led to your loathsom Bed. Oh-oh-
                              [Seems to weep.

VERNISH. So, very fine! just a Marriage quarrel! which, tho'
it generally begins by the Wives fault, yet, in the conclusion, it becomes the Husbands; and whosoever offends at first, he only is sure to ask pardon at last. My
Dear—

OLIVIA. My Devil—

VERNISH. Come, pr'ythee be appeas'd, and go home; I
have bespoken our Supper betimes: for I cou'd not eat,
till I found you. Go, I'll give you all kind of satisfactions;
and one, which uses to be a reconciling one, Two hundred of those Guineys I receiv'd last Night, to do what
you will with.

OLIVIA. What, wou'd you pay me for being your Baud?

VERNISH. Nay, pr'ythee no more; go, and I'll thoroughly
satisfie you, when I come home; and then, too, we will
have a fit of laughter, at *Manly,* whom I am going to

find at the *Cock* in *Bow-street*,[2] where, I hear, he din'd. Go, dearest, go home.

ELIZA. A very pretty turn, indeed, this! [*Aside.*

VERNISH. Now, Cousin, since by my Wife I have that honour, and priviledge of calling you so, I have something to beg of you too; which is, not to take notice of our Marriage, to any whatever, yet awhile, for some reasons very important to me: and next, that you will do my Wife the honour to go home with her, and me the favour, to use that power you have with her, in our reconcilement.

ELIZA. That, I dare promise, Sir, will be no hard matter. Your Servant. [*Exit* VERNISH.

Well, Cousin, this I confess was reasonable hypocrisie; you were the better for't.

OLIVIA. What hypocrisie?

ELIZA. Why, this last deceit of your Husband was lawful, since in your own defence.

OLIVIA. What deceit? I'd have you to know, I never deceiv'd my Husband.

ELIZA. You do not understand me, sure; I say, this was an honest come-off, and a good one: but 'twas a sign your Gallant had had enough of your conversation, since he cou'd so dextrously cheat your Husband, in passing for a Woman?

OLIVIA. What d'ye mean, once more, with my Gallant, and passing for a Woman?

ELIZA. What do you mean? You see your Husband took him for a Woman.

OLIVIA. Whom?

ELIZA. Hey-day! Why, the Man he found you with, for whom last Night you were so much afraid; and who you told me—

OLIVIA. Lord, you rave sure!

ELIZA. Why, did not you tell me last night—

OLIVIA. I know not what I might tell you last night, in a fright.

ELIZA. Ay, what was that fright for? for a Woman? besides, were you not afraid to see your Husband just now? I warrant, only for having been found with a Woman!

nay, did you not just now too own your false step, or trip, as you call'd it? which was with a Woman too! Fie, this fooling is so insipid, 'tis offensive.

OLIVIA. And fooling with my Honour will be more offensive. Did you not hear my Husband say, he found me with a Woman, in Mans cloaths? And d'ye think he does not know a Man from a Woman?

ELIZA. Not so well, I'm sure, as you do; therefore I'd rather take your word.

OLIVIA. What, you grow scurrilous, and are I find more censorious, than the World! I must have a care of you, I see.

ELIZA. No, you need not fear yet, I'll keep your secret.

OLIVIA. My secret! I'd have you to know, I have no need of Confidents, tho' you value your self upon being a good one.

ELIZA. O admirable confidence! You show more in denying your wickedness, than other people in glorying in't.

OLIVIA. Confidence, to me! to me such language! nay, then I'll never see your face again. (I'll quarrel with her, that people may never believe I was in her power; but take for malice all the truth she may speak against me. [*Aside.*] *Lettice*, where are you? let us be gone from this censorious, ill Woman.

ELIZA. Nay, thou shalt stay a little, to damn thy self quite.
[*Aside.*

One word first, pray Madam; can you swear that whom your Husband found you with—

OLIVIA. Swear! ay, that whosoever 'twas that stole up, unknown, into my Room, when 'twas dark, I know not whether Man or Woman, by Heav'ns, by all that's good; or, may I never more have joyes here, or in the other World: nay, may I eternally—

ELIZA. Be damn'd. So, so, you are damn'd enough already, by your Oaths; and I enough confirm'd: and now you may please to be gone. Yet take this advice with you, in this Plain-dealing Age, to leave off for-swearing your self; for when people hardly think the better of a Woman for her real modesty, why shou'd you put that great constraint upon your self to feign it?

OLIVIA. O hideous! hideous advice! Let us go out of the hearing of it: She will spoil us, *Lettice.*

> [*Exeunt* OLIVIA *and* LETTICE *at one door,*
> ELIZA *at t'other.*

The Scene changes to the Cock *in* Bow-street.

A Table, and Bottles.

MANLY *and* FIDELIA.

MANLY. How! sav'd her Honour, by making her Husband believe you were a Woman! 'twas well, but hard enough to do sure.

FIDELIA. We were interrupted, before he cou'd contradict me.

MANLY. But can't you tell me, d'ye say, what kind of man he was?

FIDELIA. I was so frightned, I confess, I can give no other account of him, but that he was pretty tall, round fac'd, and one I'm sure I ne'r had seen before.

MANLY. But she, you say, made you swear to return to night?

FIDELIA. But I have since sworn, never to go near her again; for the Husband wou'd murder me, or worse, if he caught me again.

MANLY. No, I'll go with you, and defend you to night, and then I'll swear too, never to go near her again.

FIDELIA. Nay, indeed Sir, I will not go, to be accessary to your death too: besides, what shou'd you go again, Sir, for?

MANLY. No disputing, or advice, Sir; you have reason to know I am unalterable. Go, therefore, presently, and write her a Note to enquire if her assignation with you holds; and if not to be at her own house, where else? and be importunate to gain admittance to her to night: let your Messenger, ere he deliver your Letter, enquire first, if her Husband be gone out. Go, 'tis now almost six of the clock; I expect you back here before seven, with leave to see her then. Go, do this dext'rously, and expect the performance of my last nights promise, never to part with you.

FIDELIA. Ay, Sir: but will you be sure to remember that?

MANLY. Did I ever break my word? go, no more replies, or doubts.   [*Exit* FIDELIA.

Enter FREEMAN, *to* MANLY.

Where hast thou been?

FREEMAN. In the next Room, with my *Lord Plausible* and *Novel*.

MANLY. Ay, we came hither, because 'twas a private house; but with thee indeed no house can be private, for thou hast that pretty quality of the familiar Fops of the Town, who, in an eating house, always keep company with all people in't, but those they came with.

FREEMAN. I went into their Room, but to keep them, and my own Fool the Squire, out of your Room; but you shall be peevish now, because you have no Money: but why the Devil won't you write to those we were speaking of? since your modesty, or your spirit, will not suffer you to speak to 'em, to lend you Money, why won't you try 'em at last, that way?

MANLY. Because I know 'em already, and can bear Want, better than Denials; nay, than Obligations.

FREEMAN. Deny you! they cannot: all of 'em have been your intimate Friends.

MANLY. No, they have been people only I have oblig'd particularly.

FREEMAN. Very well; therefore you ought to go to 'em the rather sure.

MANLY. No, no: those you have oblig'd most, most certainly avoid you, when you can oblige 'em no longer; and they take your Visits like so many Duns: Friends, like Mistresses, are avoided, for Obligations past.

FREEMAN. Pshaw! but most of 'em are your Relations; Men of great Fortune, and Honour.

MANLY. Yes; but Relations have so much Honour, as to think Poverty taints the blood; and disown their wanting Kindred: believing, I suppose, that, as Riches at first makes a Gentleman, the want of 'em degrades him. But, damn 'em, now I'm poor, I'll anticipate their contempt, and disown them.

FREEMAN. But you have many a Female acquaintance,

whom you have been liberal to, who may have a heart to refund to you a little, if you wou'd ask it: they are not all *Olivia's*.

MANLY. Dam thee! how cou'dst thou think of such a thing? I wou'd as soon rob my Footman of his Wages: Besides, 'twere in vain too; for a Wench is like a Box in an Ordinary, receives all peoples Money easily; but there's no getting, nay shaking any out again: and he that fills it, is sure never to keep the Key.

FREEMAN. Well, but noble Captain, wou'd you make me believe that you, who know half the Town, have so many Friends, and have oblig'd so many, can't borrow fifty or an hundred pound?

MANLY. Why, noble Lieutenant, you who know all the Town, and call all you know Friends, methinks shou'd not wonder at it; since you find Ingratitude too: for how many Lords Families (tho' descended from Blacksmiths, or Tinkers) hast thou call'd Great, and Illustrious? how many ill Tables call good eating? how many noisie Coxcombs, Wits? how many pert Coaching[3] Cowards, stout? how many taudry affected Rogues, well drest? how many Perukes admir'd? and how many ill Verses applauded? and yet canst not borrow a shilling; dost thou expect I, who always spoke truth, shou'd?

FREEMAN. Nay, now you think you have paid me; but hark you, Captain, I have heard of a thing call'd grinning Honour, but never of starving Honour.[4]

MANLY. Well, but it has been the fate of some brave Men: and if they wo' not give me a Ship again, I can go starve any where, with a Musket on my shoulder.

FREEMAN. Give you a Ship! why, you will not solicit it.

MANLY. If I have not solicited it by my services, I know no other way.

FREEMAN. Your Servant, Sir: nay then I'm satisfi'd, I must solicit my Widow the closer, and run the desperate fortune of Matrimony on shore.   [*Exit.*

Box in an Ordinary: the box in which the house receives its cut on a dice or card game. See Act III, n. 4. Ordinaries were often gambling houses as well as restaurants. See Cotton, pp. 1–20.

Enter, to MANLY, VERNISH.

MANLY. How!— Nay, here is a Friend indeed; and he that
has him in his arms, can know no wants.

[*Embraces* VERNISH.

VERNISH. Dear Sir! and he that is in your arms, is secure
from all fears whatever; nay, our Nation is secure by
your defeat at Sea, and the *Dutch* that fought against
you, have prov'd enemies to themselves only, in bringing you back to us.

MANLY. Fie, fie; this from a Friend? and yet from any
other 'twere unsufferable: I thought I shou'd never have
taken any thing ill from you.

VERNISH. A Friends privilege is to speak his mind, tho' it
be taken ill.

MANLY. But your tongue need not tell me you think too
well of me; I have found it from your heart, which
spoke in actions, your unalterable heart: but *Olivia* is
false, my Friend, which I suppose is no News to you.

VERNISH. He's in the right on't.   [*Aside.*

MANLY. But cou'dst thou not keep her true to me?

VERNISH. Not for my heart, Sir.

MANLY. But cou'd you not perceive it at all, before I went?
cou'd she so deceive us both?

VERNISH. I must confess, the first time I knew it, was three
dayes after your departure, when she receiv'd the
Money you had left in *Lombard-street,* in her name;
and her tears did not hinder her it seems from counting
that. You wou'd trust her with all, like a true generous
Lover!

MANLY. And she, like a mean Jilting—

VERNISH. Traytrous—

MANLY. Base—

VERNISH. Damn'd—

MANLY. Covetous—

VERNISH. Mercenary Whore—

(I can hardly hold from laughing.)   [*Aside.*

Lombard-street: the street
where the majority of the
bankers (goldsmiths) had
their headquarters. See *Dancing-Master,* Epilogue, p. 235.

MANLY. Ay, a Mercenary Whore indeed; for she made me pay her, before I lay with her.

VERNISH. How!— Why, have you lay'n with her?

MANLY. Ay, ay.

VERNISH. Nay, she deserves you shou'd report it at least, tho' you have not.

MANLY. Report it! by Heav'n, 'tis true.

VERNISH. How! sure not.

MANLY. I do not use to lie, nor you to doubt me.

VERNISH. When?

MANLY. Last night, about seven or eight of the clock.

VERNISH. Ha!— Now I remember, I thought she spake as if she expected some other, rather than me: a confounded Whore indeed!   [*Aside.*

MANLY. But, what, thou wonder'st at it! nay, you seem to be angry too.

VERNISH. I cannot but be enrag'd against her, for her usage of you: damn'd, infamous, common Jade.

MANLY. Nay, her Cuckold, who first Cuckolded me in my Money, shall not laugh all himself; we will do him reason, shan't we?

VERNISH. Ay, ay.

MANLY. But thou dost not, for so great a Friend, take pleasure enough in your Friends Revenge, methinks.

VERNISH. Yes, yes; I'm glad to know it, since you have lay'n with her.

MANLY. Thou canst not tell me who that Rascal, her Cuckold, is?

VERNISH. No.

MANLY. She wou'd keep it from you, I suppose.

VERNISH. Yes, yes—

MANLY. Thou wou'dst laugh, if thou knewst but all the circumstances of my having her. Come, I'll tell thee.

VERNISH. Dam her; I care not to hear any more of her.

MANLY. Faith, thou shalt. You must know—

Enter FREEMAN *backwards, endeavouring to keep out*
NOVEL, LORD PLAUSIBLE, JERRY *and* OLDFOX,
who all press in upon him.

FREEMAN. I tell you, he has a Wench with him, and wou'd be private.

MANLY. Dam 'em! a Man can't open a Bottle, in these eating houses, but presently you have these impudent, intruding, buzzing Flies and Insects, in your Glass.— Well, I'll tell thee all anon. In the mean time, pr'ythee go to her, but not from me, and try if you can get her to lend me but an hundred pound of my Money, to supply my present wants; for I suppose there is no recovering any of it by Law.

VERNISH. Not any; think not of it: nor by this way neither.

MANLY. Go, try, at least.

VERNISH. I'll go; but I can satisfie you before hand, 'twill be to no purpose: You'll no more find a refunding Wench—

MANLY. Than a refunding Lawyer; indeed their Fees alike scarce ever return: however, try her, put it to her.

VERNISH. Ay, ay, I'll try her, put it to her home, with a vengeance.   [*Exit* VERNISH.

Manent cœteri.

NOVEL. Nay, you shall be our Judge, *Manly.* Come, Major, I'll speak it to your teeth: if people provoke me to say bitter things, to their faces, they must take what follows; tho', like my *Lord Plausible,* I'd rather do't civilly behind their backs.

MANLY. Nay, thou art a dangerous Rogue, I've heard, behind a Mans back.

PLAUSIBLE. You wrong him sure, noble Captain; he wou'd do a Man no more harm behind his back, than to his face.

FREEMAN. I am of my Lord's mind.

MANLY. Yes, a Fool, like a Coward, is the more to be fear'd behind a Man's back, more than a witty Man: for, as a Coward is more bloody than a brave Man, a Fool is more malicious than a Man of Wit.

NOVEL. A Fool, Tar—a Fool! nay, thou art a brave Seajudge of Wit! a Fool! pr'ythee when did you ever find me want something to say, as you do often?

MANLY. Nay, I confess, thou art always talking, roaring, or making a noise; that I'll say for thee.

NOVEL. Well, and is talking a sign of a Fool?

MANLY. Yes, alwayes talking; especially too if it be loud and fast, is the sign of a Fool.

NOVEL. Pshaw! Talking is like Fencing, the quicker the better; run 'em down, run 'em down; no matter for parrying; push on still, sa, sa, sa: no matter whether you argue in form, push in guard, or no.

MANLY. Or hit, or no; I think thou alwayes talk'st without thinking, *Novel.*

NOVEL. Ay, ay; study'd Play's the worse, to follow the Allegory, as the old Pedant sayes.

OLDFOX. A young Fop!

MANLY. I ever thought the Man of most Wit, had been, like him of most Money, who has no vanity in shewing it everywhere; whil'st the beggarly pusher of his Fortune, has all he has about him still, only to show.

NOVEL. Well, Sir, and makes a very pretty show in the World, let me tell you; nay, a better than your close Hunks: A Pox, give me ready Money in Play; what care I for a Mans reputation? what are we the better for your substantial thrifty Curmudgeon in Wit, Sir?

OLDFOX. Thou art a profuse young Rogue indeed.

NOVEL. So much for talking; which I think I have prov'd a mark of Wit; and so is Railing, Roaring, and making a noise: for, Railing is Satyr, you know; and Roaring and making a noise, Humor.

Enter to them, FIDELIA, *taking* MANLY *aside,*
and shewing him a paper.

FIDELIA. The hour is betwixt seven and eight exactly: 'tis now half an hour after six.

MANLY. Well, go then to the Piazza, and wait for me; as soon as it is quite dark, I'll be with you: I must stay here yet awhile, for my Friend. But is Railing Satyr, *Novel?*   [*Exit* FIDELIA.

FREEMAN. And Roaring, and making a noise, Humor?

NOVEL. What, won't you confess there's Humor in Roaring, and making a noise?

FREEMAN. No.

---

sa, sa, sa: so, so, so.

the Piazza: in Covent Garden. See *Love in a Wood,* I, p. 15.

NOVEL. Nor in cutting Napkins, and Hangings?

MANLY. No, sure.

NOVEL. Dull Fops!

OLDFOX. O Rogue, Rogue, insipid Rogue! Nay, Gentlemen, allow him those things for Wit; for his parts lie only that way.

NOVEL. Peace, old Fool, I wonder not at thee; but that young Fellows shou'd be so dull, as to say, there's no Humor in making a noise, and breaking Windows![5] I tell you, there's Wit and Humor too, in both: And a Wit is as well known by his Frolick, as by his Simile.

OLDFOX. Pure Rogue! there's your modern Wit for you! Wit, and Humor, in breaking of Windows! There's Mischief, if you will; but no Wit, or Humor.

NOVEL. Pry'thee, pr'ythee peace, old fool. I tell you, where there is Mischief, there's Wit. Don't we esteem the Monky a Wit amongst Beasts, only because he's mischievous? And let me tell you, as good Nature is a sign of a Fool, being Mischievous is a sign of Wit.

OLDFOX. O Rogue, Rogue! pretend to be a Wit, by doing Mischief and Railing!

NOVEL. Why, thou, old Fool, hast no other pretence to the name of a Wit, but by Railing at new Playes.

OLDFOX. Thou, by Railing at that facetious, noble way of Wit, quibling.

NOVEL. Thou call'st thy dulness, gravity; and thy dozing, thinking.

OLDFOX. You, Sir, your dulness, spleen: And you talk much, and say nothing.

NOVEL. Thou read'st much, and understand'st nothing, Sir.

OLDFOX. You laugh loud, and break no Jest.

NOVEL. You rail, and no body hangs himself: And thou hast nothing of the Satyr, but in thy face.

OLDFOX. And you have no jest, but your face, Sir.

NOVEL. Thou art an illiterate Pedant.

OLDFOX. Thou art a Fool, with a bad Memory.

MANLY. Come, a Pox on you both, you have done like Wits now; for you Wits, when you quarrel, never give over, till you prove one another Fools.

NOVEL. And you Fools have never any occasion of laugh-

ing at us Wits, but when we quarrel: therefore, let us
be Friends, *Oldfox*.

MANLY. They are such Wits as thou art, who make the
name of a Wit as scandalous, as that of Bully; and sig-
nifie a loud-laughing, talking, incorrigible Coxcomb; as
Bully, a roaring, hardned Coward.

FREEMAN. And wou'd have his noise and laughter pass for
Wit; as t'other his huffing and blustring, for Courage.

Enter VERNISH.

MANLY. Gentlemen, with your leave, here is one I wou'd
speak with, and I have nothing to say to you.

[*Puts 'em out of the Room.*

Manent MANLY, VERNISH.

VERNISH. I told you 'twas in vain, to think of getting Money
out of her: she sayes, if a shilling wou'd do't, she wou'd
not save you from starving, or hanging, or what you
wou'd think worse, begging or flattering; and rails so at
you, one wou'd not think you had lay'n with her.

MANLY. O, Friend, never trust, for that matter, a Womans
railing; for she is no less a dissembler in her hatred,
than her love: And as her fondness of her Husband is
a sign he's a Cuckold, her railing at another Man is a
sign she lies with him.

VERNISH. He's in the right on't: I know not what to trust to.
[*Aside.*

MANLY. But you did not take any notice of it to her, I
hope?

VERNISH. So!— Sure he is afraid I shou'd have disprov'd
him, by an enquiry of her: all may be well yet. [*Aside.*

MANLY. What hast thou in thy head, that makes thee
seem so unquiet?

VERNISH. Only this base, impudent Womans falsness: I
cannot put her out of my head.

MANLY. O my dear Friend, be not you too sensible of my
wrongs, for then I shall feel 'em too, with more pain,
and think 'em unsufferable. Dam her, her Money, and
that ill-natur'd Whore too, Fortune her self; but if thou
wou'dst ease a little my present trouble, pr'ythee go
borrow me somewhere else, some Money: I can trouble
thee.

VERNISH. You trouble me indeed, most sensibly, when you command me any thing I cannot do: I have lately lost a great deal of Money at Play, more than I can yet pay; so that not only my Money, but my Credit too is gone, and know not where to borrow; but cou'd rob a Church for you. (Yet wou'd rather end your wants, by cutting your throat.)   [*Aside.*

MANLY. Nay, then I doubly feel my poverty, since I'm incapable of supplying thee.   [*Embraces* VERNISH.

VERNISH. But, methinks, she that granted you the last favour, (as they call it) shou'd not deny you any thing—

NOVEL. Hey, Tarpaulin, have you done?

[NOVEL *looks in, and retires again.*

VERNISH. I understand not that point of kindness, I confess.

MANLY. No, thou dost not understand it, and I have not time to let you know all now, for these Fools, you see, will interrupt us; but anon, at Supper, we'll laugh at leisure together, at *Olivia's* Cuckold; who took a young Fellow, that goes between his Wife and me, for a Woman.

VERNISH. Ha!

MANLY. Sensless, easie Rascal! 'twas no wonder she chose him for a Husband; but she thought him, I thank her, fitter than me, for that blind, bearing Office.

VERNISH. I cou'd not be deceiv'd in that long Womans hair ty'd up behind; nor those infallible proofs, her pouting, swelling breasts: I have handled too many sure not to know 'em.   [*Aside.*

MANLY. What, you wonder the Fellow cou'd be such a blind Coxcomb!

VERNISH. Yes, yes—

NOVEL. Nay, pr'ythee come to us, *Manly;* Gad, all the fine things one sayes, in their company, are lost, without thee.   [NOVEL *looks in again, and retires.*

MANLY. Away, Fop; I'm busie yet.

You see we cannot talk here at our ease; besides, I must be gone immediately, in order to meeting with *Olivia* again to night.

VERNISH. To night! it cannot be sure—

MANLY. I had an appointment just now from her.

VERNISH. For what time?

MANLY. At half an hour after seven precisely.

VERNISH. Don't you apprehend the Husband?

MANLY. He! sniveling Gull! he a thing to be fear'd! a Husband, the tamest of creatures!

VERNISH. Very fine! [*Aside.*

MANLY. But, pr'ythee, in the mean time, go try to get me some Money. Tho' thou art too modest to borrow for thy self, thou canst do any thing for me I know. Go; for I must be gone to *Olivia:* go, and meet me here anon.— *Freeman,* where are you! [*Exit* MANLY.

Manet VERNISH.

VERNISH. Ay, I'll meet with you, I warrant; but it shall be at *Olivia's.* Sure it cannot be; she denies it so calmly, and with that honest, modest assurance, it can't be true —and he does not use to lye—but belying a Woman, when she won't be kind, is the onely lye a brave Man will least scruple. But then the Woman in Mans cloaths, whom he calls a Man!— Well, but, by her Breasts, I know her to be a Woman:— But then, again, his appointment from her, to meet with him to night! I am distracted more with doubt, than jealousie. Well, I have no way to disabuse or revenge my self, but by going home immediately, putting on a riding Sute, and pretending to my Wife the same business which carry'd me out of Town last, requires me again to go Post to *Oxford* to night; then, if the appointment he boasts of be true, it's sure to hold; and I shall have an opportunity either of clearing her, or revenging my self on both. Perhaps, she is his Wench, of an old date, and I am his Cully, whil'st I think him mine; and he has seem'd to make his Wench rich, only that I might take her off of his hands: or if he has but lately lay'n with her, he must needs discover, by her, my treachery to him; which I'm sure he will revenge with my death, and which I must prevent with his, if it were only but for fear of his too just reproaches; for, I must confess, I never had till now any excuse, but that of int'rest, for doing ill to him.

[*Exit* VERNISH.

Re-enter MANLY *and* FREEMAN.

MANLY. Come hither, only I say be sure you mistake not the time; you know the house exactly where *Olivia* lodges: 'tis just hard by.

FREEMAN. Yes, yes.

MANLY. Well then, bring 'em all, I say, thither, and all you know that may be then in the house; for the more Witnesses I have of her infamy, the greater will be my revenge: and be sure you come strait up to her Chamber, without more ado. Here, take the Watch: you see 'tis above a quarter past seven; be there in half an hour exactly.

FREEMAN. You need not doubt my diligence, or dexterity; I am an old Scowrer, and can naturally beat up a Wenches quarters that won't be civil. Sha'nt we break her Windows too?

MANLY. No, no: be punctual only.   [*Exeunt Ambo.*

Enter Widow BLACKACRE, *and two Knights of the Post: a Waiter with Wine.*

WIDOW. Sweetheart, are you sure the door was shut close, that none of those Roysters saw us come in?

WAITER. Yes, Mistriss; and you shall have a privater Room above, instantly.   [*Exit* WAITER.

WIDOW. You are safe enough, Gentlemen, for I have been private in this house ere now, upon other occasions, when I was something younger. Come, Gentlemen, in short, I leave my business to your care and fidelity: and so, here's to you.

1 KNIGHT. We were ungrateful Rogues, if we shou'd not be honest to you; for we have had a great deal of your Money.

WIDOW. And you have done me many a good job for't: and so, here's to you again.

2 KNIGHT. Why, we have been perjur'd, but six times for you.

1 KNIGHT. Forg'd but four Deeds, with your Husband's last Deed of Gift.

2 KNIGHT. And but three Wills.

1 KNIGHT. And counterfeited Hands and Seals to some six Bonds; I think that's all, Brother.

WIDOW. Ay, that's all, Gentlemen; and so, here's to you again.

2 KNIGHT. Nay, 'twou'd do one's heart good to be forsworn for you: you have a conscience in your wayes, and pay us well.

1 KNIGHT. You are in the right on't, Brother; one wou'd be damn'd for her, with all ones heart.

2 KNIGHT. But there are Rogues, who make us forsworn for 'em; and when we come to be paid, they'll be forsworn too, and not pay us our wages which they promis'd with Oaths sufficient.

1 KNIGHT. Ay, a great Lawyer, that shall be nameless Bilkt me too.

WIDOW. That was hard, methinks, that a Lawyer shou'd use Gentlemen Witnesses no better.

2 KNIGHT. A Lawyer! d'ye wonder a Lawyer shou'd do't? I was Bilk'd by a Reverend Divine, that preaches twice on Sundayes, and prayes half an hour still before dinner.

WIDOW. How? a Conscientious Divine, and not pay people for damning themselves! Sure then, for all his talking, he does not believe damnation. But come, to our business: pray be sure to imitate exactly the flourish at the end of this name.   [*Pulls out a Deed or two.*

1 KNIGHT. O he's the best in *England* at untangling a flourish, Madam.

WIDOW. And let not the Seal be a jot bigger: observe well the dash too, at the end of this name.

2 KNIGHT. I warrant you, Madam.

WIDOW. Well, these, and many other shifts, poor Widows are put to sometimes; for every body wou'd be riding a Widow, as they say, and breaking into her Jointure: they think marrying a Widow an easie business, like leaping the Hedge, where another has gone over before; a Widow is a meer gap, a gap with them.

        Enter to them MAJOR OLDFOX, *with two Waiters.*

        [*The Knights of the Post huddle up the Writings.*

What, he here! go then, go, my hearts, you have your instructions.   [*Exeunt Knights of the Post.*

OLDFOX. Come, Madam, to be plain with you, I'll be fob'd

off no longer. I'll bind her and gag her, but she shall
hear me. [*Aside.*

Look you, Friends, there's the Money I promis'd you;
and now do you what you promis'd me: here are my
Garters, and here's a Gag: you shall be acquainted with
my parts, Lady, you shall.

WIDOW. Acquainted with your parts! A Rape, a Rape—
What, will you ravish me?

[*The Waiters tye her to the Chair, and gag her;
and Exeunt.*

OLDFOX. Yes, Lady, I will ravish you; but it shall be
through the ear, Lady, the ear onely, with my well-
pen'd Acrostics.

Enter to them, FREEMAN, JERRY BLACKACRE, *three Bayliffs,
a Constable and his Assistants, with
the two Knights of the Post.*

What, shall I never read my things undisturb'd again?

JERRY. O Law! my Mother bound hand and foot, and
gaping, as if she rose before her time to day!

FREEMAN. What means this, *Oldfox?* But I'll release you
from him: you shall be no Mans Prisoner, but mine.
Bayliffs, execute your Writ. [FREEMAN *untyes her.*

OLDFOX. Nay, then I'll be gone, for fear of being Bayl, and
paying her Debts, without being her Husband.

[*Exit* OLDFOX.

1 BAYLIFF. We Arrest you, in the King's Name, at the
Suit of Mr. *Freeman,* Guardian to *Jeremiah Blackacre*
Esq; in an Action of Ten thousand pounds.

WIDOW. How! how! in a Choak-Bayl Action! What, and
the Pen and Ink Gentlemen taken too! Have you confest, you Rogues?

1 KNIGHT. We needed not to confess; for the Bayliffs
dog'd us hither to the very door, and overheard all that
you and we said.

WIDOW. Undone, undone then! no Man was ever too hard
for me, till now. O, *Jerry,* Child, wilt thou vex again the
womb that bore thee?

Choak-Bayl Action: choke-
bail action: one so serious that
bail is not allowed.

JERRY. Ay, for bearing me before Wedlock, as you say: But I'll teach you to call a *Blackacre* a Bastard, tho' you were never so much my Mother.

WIDOW. Well, I'm undone: not one trick left? no Law-Meush imaginable? [*Aside.*
Cruel Sir, a word with you I pray.

FREEMAN. In vain, Madam; for you have no other way to release your self, but by the Bands of Matrimony.

WIDOW. How, Sir, how! that were but to sue out a *Habeas Corpus,* for a removal from one Prison to another. Matrimony!

FREEMAN. Well, Bayliffs, away with her.

WIDOW. O stay, Sir, can you be so cruel as to bring me under Covert Baron again? and put it out of my power to sue in my own name. Matrimony, to a Woman, worse than Excommunication, in depriving her of the benefit of the Law: and I wou'd rather be depriv'd of life. But hark you, Sir, I am contented you shou'd hold and enjoy my person by Lease or Patent; but not by the spiritual Patent, call'd a Licence; that is, to have the priviledges of a Husband without the dominion; that is, *Durante beneplacito:* in consideration of which, I will, out of my Jointure, secure you an Annuity of Three hundred pounds a Year, and pay your debts; and that's all you younger Brothers desire to marry a Widow for, I'm sure.

FREEMAN. Well, Widow, if—

JERRY. What, I hope, Bully Guardian, you are not making Agreements, without me?

FREEMAN. No, no. First, Widow, you must say no more that he is the Son of a Whore; have a care of that: And then, he must have a setled Exhibition of Forty pounds a Year, and a Nag of Assizes, kept by you,

---

Meush: Meuse: loophole.
Durante beneplacito: during good pleasure. The tenure of English judges used to be durante bene placito, at the king's pleasure.
Exhibition: maintenance.

Nag of Assizes: Assizes were ordinances establishing weights and measures for particular commodities. A nag of assizes, then, would be a horse of standard size and quality.

but not upon the Common; and have free ingress, egress, and regress to and from your Maids Garret.

WIDOW. Well, I can grant all that too.

JERRY. Ay, ay, fair words butter no Cabage; but, Guardian, make her Sign, Sign and Seal: for, otherwise, if you knew her as well as I, you wou'd not trust her word for a farthing.

FREEMAN. I warrant thee, Squire. Well, Widow, since thou art so generous, I will be generous too; and if you'll secure me Four hundred pound a Year, but during your life, and pay my debts, not above a thousand pound; I'll bate you your person, to dispose of as you please.

WIDOW. Have a care, Sir, a Settlement without a Consideration, is void in Law: you must do something for't.

FREEMAN. Pr'ythee then let the Settlement on me be call'd Alimony; and the Consideration our Separation: Come, my Lawyer, with Writings ready drawn, is within, and in haste. Come.

WIDOW. But, what, no other kind of Consideration, Mr. Freeman? Well, a Widow, I see, is a kind of a *sine cure*, by custom of which the unconscionable Incumbent enjoyes the profits, without any duty, but does that still elsewhere.   [*Exeunt Omnes.*

The Scene changes to OLIVIA's *Lodging.*

Enter OLIVIA, *with a Candle in her hand.*

OLIVIA. So, I am now prepar'd once more for my timorous young Lover's reception: my Husband is gone; and go thou out too, thou next interrupter of Love:— [*Puts out the Candle.*] Kind darkness, that frees us Lovers from scandal and bashfulness, from the censure of our Gallants and the World. So, are you there?

Enter to OLIVIA, FIDELIA, *follow'd softly by* MANLY.

Come, my dear punctual Lover, there is not such another in the World; thou hast Beauty and Youth to please a Wife; Address and Wit, to amuse and fool a Husband; nay, thou hast all things to be wish'd in a Lover, but your Fits: I hope, my Dear, you won't have one to night; and, that you may not, I'll lock the door, tho' there be no need of it, but to lock out your Fits; for my Husband is just gone out of Town again. Come, where are you?   [*Goes to the door, and locks it.*

MANLY. Well, thou hast impudence enough to give me Fits too, and make Revenge it self impotent, hinder me from making thee yet more infamous, if it can be.   [*Aside.*

OLIVIA. Come, come, my Soul, come.

FIDELIA. Presently, my Dear: we have time enough sure.

OLIVIA. How! time enough! True Lovers can no more think they ever have time enough, than love enough: You shall stay with me all night; but that is but a Lover's moment. Come.

FIDELIA. But won't you let me give you and my self the satisfaction of telling you, how I abus'd your Husband last night?

OLIVIA. Not when you can give me, and your self too, the satisfaction of abusing him again, to night. Come.

FIDELIA. Let me but tell you how your Husband—

OLIVIA. O name not his, or *Manly's* more loathsom name, if you love me; I forbid 'em last night: and you know I mention'd my Husband but once, and he came. No talking pray; 'twas ominous to us. You make me fancy a noise at the door already, but I'm resolv'd not to be interrupted. [*A noise at the door.*] Where are you? Come; for, rather than lose my dear expectation now, tho' my Husband were at the door, and the bloody Ruffian *Manly* here in the room, with all his awful insolence, I wou'd give my self to this dear hand, to be led away, to Heavens of joys, which none but thou canst give. But, what's this noise at the door? So, I told you what talking wou'd come to.

        [*The noise at the door increases.*
Ha!—O Heavens, my Husbands voice!—

        [OLIVIA *listens at the door.*

MANLY. *Freeman* is come too soon.   [*Aside.*

OLIVIA. O 'tis he!— Then here is the happiest minute lost, that ever bashful Boy, or trifling Woman fool'd away! I'm undone! my Husbands reconcilement too was false,

as my joy, all delusion: but, come this way, here's a
Back-door.   [*Exit, and returns.*
The officious Jade has lock'd us in, instead of locking
others out; but let us then escape your way, by the Balcony; and, whil'st you pull down the Curtains, I'll fetch,
from my Closet, what next will best secure our escape:
I have left my Key in the door, and 'twill not suddenly
be broke open.

      [*Exit.*] *A noise as it were, people forcing the door.*

MANLY. Stir not, yet fear nothing.

FIDELIA. Nothing, but your life, Sir.

MANLY. We shall now know this happy Man she calls
Husband.

            OLIVIA *Re-enters.*

OLIVIA. Oh, where are you? What, idle with fear? Come,
I'll tie the Curtains, if you will hold. Here, take this
Cabinet and Purse, for it is thine, if we escape;

      [MANLY *takes from her the Cabinet and Purse.*
therefore let us make haste.   [*Exit* OLIVIA.

MANLY. 'Tis mine indeed now again, and it shall never
escape more from me: to you at least.

The door broken open, Enter VERNISH *alone, with a dark
Lanthorn and a Sword, running at* MANLY; *who draws,
puts by the thrust, and defends himself awhile:*

    FIDELIA *runs at* VERNISH *behind.*

VERNISH. So, there I'm right sure—   [*With a low voice.*

MANLY. *Softly.* Sword and dark Lanthorn, Villain, are
some odds; but—

VERNISH. Odds! I'm sure I find more odds than I expected:
What, has my insatiable two Seconds at once? but—

              [*With a low voice.*

      [*Whil'st they fight,* OLIVIA *re-enters,
tying two Curtains together.*

OLIVIA. Where are you now?— What, is he entered then,
and are they fighting! O do not kill one that can make
no defence.— [MANLY *throws* VERNISH *down, and dis-
arms him.*] How! but I think he has the better on't:
here's his Scarf, 'tis he. So, keep him down still: I hope
thou hast no hurt, my dearest?   [*Embracing* MANLY.

Enter to them FREEMAN, LORD PLAUSIBLE, NOVEL,
    JERRY BLACKACRE, *and the* WIDOW BLACKACRE,
    lighted in by the two Sailors with Torches.

Ha!— What?— *Manly!* And have I been thus concern'd
for him, embracing him? And has he his Jewels again
too? What means this? O 'tis too sure, as well as my
shame! which I'll go hide for ever.

> [*Offers to go out,* MANLY *stops her.*

MANLY. No, my dearest, after so much kindness as has
past between us, I cannot part with you yet. *Freeman,*
let no body stir out of the Room; for, notwithstanding
your lights, we are yet in the dark, till this Gentleman
please to turn his face.— [*Pulls* VERNISH *by the sleeve.*
How! *Vernish!* Art thou the happy Man then? Thou!
Thou! Speak, I say; but thy guilty silence tells me all.—
Well, I shall not upbraid thee; for my wonder is striking
me as dumb, as thy shame has made thee. But, what?
my little Volunteer hurt, and fainting!

FIDELIA. My wound, Sir, is but a slight one, in my Arm:
'tis only my fear of your danger, Sir, not yet well over.

MANLY. But what's here? more strange things!

> [*Observing* FIDELIA's *hair unty'd behind, and*
> *without a Peruke, which she lost in the scuffle.*

What means this long Womans hair? and face, now all
of it appears, too beautiful for a Man; which I still
thought Womanish indeed! What, you have not deceiv'd
me too, my little Volunteer?   [*Aside.*

OLIVIA. Me she has I'm sure.

MANLY. Speak.

          Enter ELIZA, *and* LETTICE.

ELIZA. What, Cousin, I am brought hither by your Woman,
I suppose, to be a witness of the second vindication of
your Honour?

OLIVIA. Insulting is not generous: You might spare me, I
have you.

ELIZA. Have a care, Cousin, you'll confess anon too much;
and I wou'd not have your secrets.

MANLY. Come, your blushes answer me sufficiently, and
you have been my Volunteer in love.   [*To* FIDELIA.

FIDELIA. I must confess I needed no compulsion to follow

you all the world over; which I attempted in this habit, partly out of shame to own my love to you, and fear of a greater shame, your refusal of it: for I knew of your engagement to this Lady, and the constancy of your nature; which nothing cou'd have alter'd, but her self.

MANLY. Dear Madam, I desir'd you to bring me out of confusion, and you have given me more: I know not what to speak to you, or how to look upon you; the sense of my rough, hard, and ill usage of you, (tho' chiefly your own fault) gives me more pain now 'tis over, than you had, when you suffer'd it: and if my heart, the refusal of such a Woman, [*Pointing to* OLIVIA] were not a Sacrifice to prophane your love, and a greater wrong to you than ever yet I did you; I wou'd beg of you to receive it, tho' you us'd it, as she had done; for tho' it deserv'd not from her the treatment she gave it, it does from you.

FIDELIA. Then it has had punishment sufficient from her already, and needs no more from me; and, I must confess, I wou'd not be the onely cause of making you break your last nights Oath to me, of never parting with me: if you do not forget, or repent it.

MANLY. Then, take for ever my heart, and this with it; [*Gives her the Cabinet*] for 'twas given to you before, and my heart was before your due; I only beg leave to dispose of these few— Here, Madam, I never yet left my Wench unpaid.

[*Takes some of the Jewels, and offers 'em to* OLIVIA; *she strikes 'em down:* PLAUSIBLE *and* NOVEL *take 'em up.*

OLIVIA. So it seems, by giving her the Cabinet.

PLAUSIBLE. These Pendents appertain to your most faithful humble Servant.

NOVEL. And this Locket is mine; my earnest for love, which she never paid: therefore my own again.

WIDOW. By what Law, Sir, pray? Cousin *Olivia*, a word: What, do they make a seizure on your Goods and Chattels, *vi & armis?* Make your demand, I say, and bring

vi & armis: with force and arms.

your Trover, bring your Trover: I'll follow the Law
for you.

OLIVIA. And I my revenge.   [*Exit.*

MANLY *to* VERNISH. But 'tis, my Friend, in your consideration most, that I wou'd have return'd part of your Wives
portion; for 'twere hard to take all from thee, since thou
hast paid so dear for't, in being such a Rascal: yet thy
Wife is a Fortune without a Portion; and thou art a man
of that extraordinary merit in Vilany, the World and
Fortune can never desert thee, tho' I do; therefore be
not melancholy. Fare you well, Sir.

[*Exit* VERNISH, *doggedly.*

Now, Madam, I beg your pardon, [*Turning to* FIDELIA]
for lessening the Present I made you; but my heart
can never be lessen'd: this, I confess, was too small for
you before; for you deserve the *Indian* World; and I
wou'd now go thither out of covetousness for your sake
only.

FIDELIA. Your heart, Sir, is a Present of that value, I can
never make any return to't; [*Pulling* MANLY *from the
company.*] but I can give you back such a Present as
this, which I got by the loss of my Father, a Gentleman
of the North, of no mean Extraction, whose onely Child
I was, therefore left me in the present possession of Two
thousand pounds a Year; which I left, with multitudes
of Pretenders, to follow you, Sir; having in several
publick places seen you, and observ'd your actions
throughly, with admiration, when you were too much
in love to take notice of mine, which yet was but too
visible. The name of my Family is *Grey;* my other,
Fidelia: the rest of my Story you shall know, when I
have fewer Auditors.

MANLY. Nay, now, Madam, you have taken from me all
power of making you any Complement on my part; for
I was going to tell you, that for your sake onely, I wou'd
quit the unknown pleasure of a retirement; and rather
stay in this ill World of ours still, tho odious to me, than
give you more frights again at Sea, and make again too
great a venture there, in you alone. But if I shou'd tell
you now all this, and that your virtue (since greater

than I thought any was in the World) had now reconcil'd me to't, my Friend here wou'd say, 'tis your Estate that has made me Friends with the World.

FREEMAN. I must confess I shou'd; for I think most of our quarrels to the World, are just such as we have to a handsom Woman: only because we cannot enjoy her, as we wou'd do.

MANLY. Nay, if thou art a *Plain-dealer* too, give me thy hand; for now I'll say I am thy Friend indeed: And, for your two sakes, tho' I have been so lately deceiv'd in Friends of both Sexes;

> *I will believe, there are now in the World*
> *Good-natur'd Friends, who are not Prostitutes,*
> *And handsom Women worthy to be Friends:*
> *Yet, for my sake, let no one e're confide*
> *In Tears, or Oaths, in Love, or Friend untry'd.*
> *[Exeunt Omnes.*

FINIS.

EPILOGUE,

Spoken by the WIDOW BLACKACRE.

To you, the Judges learned in Stage Laws,
Our Poet now, by me, submits his Cause;
For with young Judges, such as most of you,
The Men by Women best their bus'ness do:
And, truth on't is, if you did not sit here,
To keep for us a Term throughout the Year,
We cou'd not live by'r Tongues; nay, but for you,
Our Chamber-practice wou'd be little too.
And 'tis not only the Stage Practiser
Who, by your meeting, gets her living here;
For, as in Hall of Westminster,
Sleek Sempstress vents, amidst the Courts, her Ware:
So, while we Baul, and you in Judgment sit,
The Visor-Mask sells Linnen too i'th' Pit.
O many of your Friends, besides us here,

Do live, by putting off their sev'ral Ware.
Here's daily done the great affair o'th' Nation:
Let Lòve, and Us then, ne'r have Long-vacation.
But hold; like other Pleaders, I have done
Not my poor Client's bus'ness, but my own.
Spare me a word then, now, for him. First know,
Squires of the Long Robe, he does humbly show
He has a just Right in abusing you;
Because he is a Brother-Templer *too:*
For, at the Bar, you Railly one another;
And Fool, and Knave, is swallow'd from a Brother:
If not the Poet here, the Templer *spare;*
And maul him, when you catch him at the Bar.
From you, our common modish Censurers,
Your Favor, not your Judgment, 'tis he fears:
Of all Loves begs you then to Rail, find fault;
For Playes, like Women, by the World are thought
(When you speak kindly of 'em) very naught.

NOTES

1. A well-known procuress, also called Mother Bennet. Richard Steele, in *The Spectator*, No. 266 (January 4, 1712): "These Directors of Sin, after they can no longer commit it, makes up the Beauty of the inimitable Dedication to the *Plain Dealer*, and is a Master-piece of Raillery on this Vice." Pepys (September 22, 1660) describes the lady in action: "he told me how the pretty woman that I always loved at the beginning of Cheapside that sells child's coats was served by the Lady Bennett (a famous strumpet), who by counterfeiting to fall into a swoon upon the sight of her in her shop, became acquainted with her, and at last got her ends of her to lie with a gentleman that had hired her to procure this poor soul for him" (Wheatley, I, 246).

2. Bayes is the poet of George Villiers' *The Rehearsal* (1671). He says, "I know you have wit by the judgement you make of this Play; for that's the Measure I go by: my Play is my Touch-stone" (London, 1672, p. 23).

3. MacMillan and Jones suggest that there is a double meaning in *Touchstone* of which the significance is lost. Since we know that "touch-hole" was the pudenda and "touch-trap" the penis in seventeenth-century slang, one might make a stab at the equivocation.

4. As an example of the broadness of the jests of the Thames boatmen and the cheerfulness with which some ladies took them, here is a passage from Tom Brown's *A Walk round London and Westminster*: "No sooner had we put off into the middle of the Stream, but our *Charon* and his Assistant (being jolly Fellows) began to scatter their verbal Wild-fire on every side of them, their first Attack being on a couple of fine Ladies with a Footman in the Stern as follows, *viz. How now you two Confederate Brimstones, Where are you swimming with your Fine Top-knots, to invite some Irish Bully or Scotch Highlander, to scour your cloven Furbiloes for a Petti-coat Pension? I'll warrant your poor Cuckolds are hovering about Change, to hear what News from Flanders, whilst you like a couple of hollow-belly'd Wh---s, are sailing up to Spring-Garden to cram one end with roasted Fowls, and the other with raw Saussages.* One of the Ladies taking Courage, pluck'd up a Female Spirit of Revenge, and facing us with the Gallantry

of an *Amazon*, made the following return, *viz. Get you home you old Cuckold, look under your Wives Bed, and see what a lusty Gardener has been planting, a Son of a Wh--e in your Parsley-Bed. . . ."* And there is more. Thomas Brown, *Works*, III, London, 1708, pp. 58–59.

5. Juvenal *Satires* vi. 284–285. Usually printed *Deprensis* for *Deprehensis.* A. F. Cole's translation is hardly literal, but it seems appropriate here: "When once surprised, the sex all shame forego; / And more audacious, as more guilty, grow." *The Satires of Juvenal*, New York, 1906, p. 117.

6. Montaigne, *Essais*, III, 5 (Paris, 1828, V, p. 61). Since his attack is on the ladies, Wycherley changed the sex of Montaigne's *ils*; 1677 Q-2 corrected *envoy* to *envoyent.* In John Florio's translation: "They send their conscience to the stews, and keepe their countenance in order." New York, n.d. (Modern Library), p. 761.

7. Any number of entries in the *Calendar of State Papers, Colonial* testify to the common practice of transporting the poor and the criminal, female as well as male, to the Plantations. A proposal concerning Jamaica, dated uncertainly November 1660: "To send over women for planters' wives; Newgate and Bridewell to be spared as much as may be, and poor maids instead, with which few parishes in England are unburdened, sent over" (I, London, 1860, pp. 491–492). Newgate and Bridewell were prisons, the latter particularly noted for its hospitality to prostitutes. A message from Nicholas Blake, Bilbao Plantation, Barbadoes, to the King, October 20, 1670: "his Majesty may also have 2000 acres laid out in four large sugar works, which may be peopled at an easy rate by sending over poor miserable people who have forfeited their lives for offences less than treason, murder, witchcraft, and the like, or vagrant and idle people who are continually put into Bridewell . . ." (VII, London, 1889, p. 115). As a single example of many see the case of Margaret Griffith (or Gryffyth), who chose to be transported rather than otherwise punished after being convicted for felony; she made her petition on January 21, 1669; it was granted on January 29 (VII, p. 6).

8. This may be more than a general metaphor; it perhaps recalls the actual practice during the Great Fire of London (September 2–6, 1666). John Evelyn reports (September 4) that authorities "began to consider that nothing was like to put a stop, but the blowing up of so many houses, as might make a wider gap, than any had yet ben made by the ordinary method of pulling them downe with Engines . . ." (de Beer, III, 455).

9. Tertullian *De Pudicita* 1. 16. Wycherley apparently got it from the Montaigne essay he quoted earlier for he repeats

Montaigne's use of *extinguitur* for *extinguetur*. *Essais,* V, p. 84. The passage is prose, not verse as it is set here. Florio translates it (p. 773), "Belike we must be incontinent that we may be continent, burning is quenched by fire."

10. Wycherley is probably thinking of Pierre Corneille, a prodigious writer of prefaces and directions *au lecteur.* In the 1660 edition of his plays one of the three *Discours* appears in each volume and there are *Examens* for the early plays. References to *Discours* in Dryden's *Of Dramatick Poesie* (1668) indicate that the Restoration dramatists were concerned with Corneille's theoretical writing. By 1677 Racine too had piled up an impressive stack of prefaces. Molière, on the other hand, wrote very few; his comments on the drama occasionally took dramatic form: *La Critique de l'École des Femmes* (1663) and *L'Impromptu de Versailles* (1663). Wycherley goes that road in Act II when he lets Olivia and Eliza discuss *The Country-Wife.*

11. The liberties were districts lying outside the city but still under municipal control. The suggestion is that Mother Bennet runs things in a few houses not apparently hers.

12. Some of the playwrights, by way of fringe benefit, were granted free admission to the theaters.

13. Montaigne, in that much rifled essay, refers to the Scythian women: "The Scythian women were wont to thrust out the eies of all their slaves and prisoners taken in warre, thereby to make more free and private use of them." *Essais,* V, p. 99. Florio, p. 780.

14. Although the sentiments are familiar enough (as any collection of quotations or adages is likely to show), I have been no more successful than previous editors in discovering who the *solid French author* is.

15. After the success of this play, the label, *The Plain-Dealer,* stuck to Wycherley for the rest of his life. He even used it himself: in signing the Preface to *Miscellany Poems* (Summers, III, 13); in letters to John Dennis (Summers, II, 199) and Alexander Pope (Sherburn, I, 55, 66, 69). Dryden did not help matters, when in his poem to William Congreve in praise of *The Double-Dealer,* he called the playwright "Manly Witcherly." *The Poems of John Dryden,* II, ed. James Kinsley, Oxford, 1958, p. 852. The equating of the author with his hero perhaps began when Wycherley signed the dedication *The Plain-Dealer.* For an example of the flourishing critical fallacy see F. W. Bateson's Introduction to *The Works of Congreve* in which, in praising Congreve's ability to generalize his experience, he speaks of Wycherley's use of "concealed autobiography" and of "an unexplained residuum of personal bitterness" in *The Plain-Dealer.* New York, 1930, p. xii. The confusion of author and hero is particularly ironic if it occurred as a result of the signature to the Epistle Dedica-

tory, for that essay is built on a double entendre and almost every line is packed with multiple meaning. An obvious example near the beginning: his attack on the mistaken assumption of double meaning in his work in a passage which makes the most of *moving*.

PROLOGUE

1. Although it was contrary to a direct order of the Lord Chamberlain, it was customary for men to escape paying at the theater by arriving late or leaving before the play was over. See *The London Stage*, I, lxxii–lxxiv. Summers suggests (II, 297) that Wycherley here refers to that custom. Since the freeloaders were a popular target of the playwrights, he may well be correct. The theater itself is the victim of this kind of cheating, however, and the line implies that the poets are the ones being used. It would be possible to read the line to mean that the gentlemen of the pit, even if they have paid their 2s. 6d. to get in, are sponging on the poets by borrowing their lines.

2. Sir Peter Lely was a fashionable portrait painter. Pepys reports (March 24, 1666): "I had occasion to follow the Duke [of York] into his lodgings, into a chamber where the Duchesse was sitting to have her picture drawn by Lilly, who was then at work" (Wheatley, V, 254–255). Wycherley, too, had his portrait done by Lely; the frontispiece to Connely's biography reproduces the engraving that I. Smith made of the Lely portrait for use in *Miscellany Poems* (1704). See Connely, p. 266. As for Lely as a painter of *Heroes,* Pepys mentions (April 18, 1666) going to the painter's to see "the heads, some finished, and all begun, of the Flaggmen [admirals] in the late great fight with the Duke of Yorke against the Dutch" (Wheatley, V, 272–273).

THE PERSONS

1. The most recent Dutch War is the third one, 1672–74. Nettleton and Case suggest (p. 206) that the second one, 1665–67, is intended. They assume that the discussion between the two sailors about their losses and Manly's (p. 392) refers to trading, and that the second Dutch War provided the greater opportunity for mixing naval duty with incidental profit-making. It is true that after the defeat of the Dutch by the English fleet under the Duke of York, the English ships ranged the seas with comparative freedom, but if the opportunity-providing second Dutch War is intended, why in the world are the soundly defeated Dutch attacking Manly's convoy in the English Channel? Contrariwise, to strengthen Nettleton

and Case's choice of war, there is the reference in the Prologue to Lely and the painting of the heroes. So far as the play is concerned, the particular war needs no identification. In fact, no war is necessary. Although we learn piecemeal of Manly's disastrous encounter with the Dutch and although his conversation with the Alderman in Act III (p. 461) indicates that a war is presently in progress, it has nothing to do with the action of the play. It is little more than an excuse to provide Manly with a calling which separates him from London society. Samuel Butler in his character of "A Sailor" writes, "The boysterous ruggedness of the element he lives in alters his nature, and he becomes more rude and barbarous than a land man, as water dogs are rougher than land spaniels." *Characters and Passages from Note-Books*, Cambridge, 1908, p. 254.

2. Nettleton and Case suggest (p. 206) that "fox" in this case means "sword." Their reading is strengthened not only by the discussion about swords between Oldfox and Manly in Act III (p. 458), but also by the joke about Oldfox—that, in comparison to Freeman, he is an aging fop.

ACT I

1. Hague: follow, love and esteem no body. Nettleton and Case make a determined but unconvincing effort to explain the phrase *follow Love* in this context. Although all the quartos print *Love* as a noun, I suspect that it was an error in 1677 Q repeated in the later editions. *Love* as a verb not only makes more sense, but it balances *hate* as a verb in Manly's answer. Hunt, Ward, and Churchill follow the Hague edition in printing it as a verb.

2. The King could and did give away the rights to ships taken out of service. See Wheatley, X, 249–250, for a defense of Pepys for having asked and received such a commission. Wheatley justifies Pepys on the grounds that "the King was extending those gifts to people having small claim on him, and had done little in the public service."

3. This refers to a continuing quarrel between the professional seamen and the gentlemen (pantaloon-wearing) captains. It was particularly virulent during the second Dutch War. Pepys records meeting Sir W. Pen and Sir W. Coventry on June 29, 1667: "Then we to talk of the loss of all affection and obedience now in the seamen, so that all power is lost." The reason, according to Sir W. Coventry, was "the having of gentlemen Captains, who discourage all Tarpaulins, and have given out that they would in a little time bring it to that pass that a Tarpaulin should not dare to aspire to more than to be a Boatswain or a gunner. That this makes the Sea Captains to lose their own good affections to the service, and to instil it into

the seamen also, and that the seamen do see it themselves and resent it" (Wheatley, VI, 400). See also, VI, 29–30, 104.

4. "in steps another of the *Tarpauling Fraternity*, with his Hat under his Arm, half full of Money . . ." (Ned Ward, p. 327).

5. Given Manly's view of friendship, his use of *Latitudinarian* to describe Freeman makes a nice theological point. The word was used originally to describe liberal churchmen who were willing to acknowledge as Christian any sect that accepted the Apostles' Creed. It came to be used as a label for the Cambridge Platonists (Latitude Men), a group of theologians who attempted to separate religion from dogma. What Manly is saying, in effect, is that a man can no more believe in friendship if he has many friends than he can believe in Christianity if he accepts as possible many concepts of God.

6. On April 13, 1666, Pepys met John Hales and "he and I presently resolved of going to White Hall, to spend an houre in the galleries there among the pictures, and we did so to my great satisfaction, he shewing me the difference in the payntings . . ." (Wheatley, V, 268). This would have been the Stone Gallery, the chief gathering place within the royal palace. Pepys must have been one of the few people to come to look at the pictures, for—as Freeman's line implies—it was a place to see and be seen, to hear rumors, to seek preferment.

7. A short space follows *Brutal* in 1677 Q as though a word had been left out; I have added the comma, following 1677 Q-2.

8. The Law Courts were in Westminster Hall, as were a great many shops. Act III takes place there. The Exchange may mean either the New Exchange, the arcade of shops where Mrs. Pinchwife had such a grand time in Act 3 of *The Country-Wife*, or the Royal Exchange, where the merchants and bankers plied their trade.

9. When the two Kings of Brentford descend from the clouds in Bayes's play in *The Rehearsal*, the 1st King says, "Come, now, to serious counsel we'l advance." The 2nd King answers, "I do agree; but first, let's have a Dance." The stage direction is "Dance a grand dance." London, 1672, p. 45.

10. Before receiving an appointment to a living, an ecclesiastical office with revenues, a candidate was expected to preach a probation sermon. John Evelyn reports (November 3, 1661), "Our *Mr. Breton* preached his probation sermon at our Parish Church, & indeede made an excellent sermon . . . so as I could not but recommend him to the Patron" (de Beer, III, 302).

11. Seamen's widows were entitled to a small payment (Ogg, I, p. 276), but they must sometimes have had trouble collecting it. "Petition of the Wives and Widows of 12 Seamen, whose names are subscribed, to the King, for order to the pay-

master speedily to pay them the money due to them; are in great distress, their husbands being prisoners, wounded, or dead." August 6, 1666, *Calendar of State Papers, Domestic, 4*, VI (London, 1864), p. 15. If widows were forced to petition the king, they might as easily make a scene at the Navy Office.

12. According to Summers (II, 299), John Ozell, in his translation (1708) of Boileau's *Le Lutrin*, explains a change he made: *"In the Original it is* Men of Normandy, *who like our* Norfolk Men *are remarkably Litigious."* The 1708 edition that I consulted, the one in the Columbia University library, does not use Norfolk in the line Summers cites, nor does it have such a note. Summers' reading of Norfolk may well be sounder than his factual accuracy. If not from Ozell, then certainly from the context, we can accept Norfolk as a litigious county.

13. The Inns of Chancery were attached to the four Inns of Court, where students were required to live for a number of Terms before they could be admitted to the bar. By staying at the Inns of Chancery, where presumably students not yet admitted to the Inns of Court might be living, Mrs. Blackacre gets as close as she ever can to being a barrister.

14. *Law-French.* "A mere Fustian Jargon which no Part of Mankind meddles with, but themselves [lawyers], whom it serves only for Tearmes of Art, though words of no manner of Intention, and yet is sufficient to Containe in so short, and rude a Compass, the greatest, and most Difficult Curiositys, (as they say) of all Human Sense and Reason, like Lully's Ars brevis which none but children or those who had been twice such, Ignorant old Dotards, were ever the wiser for. And yet those of the Dullest Capacitys are able to instruct themselves in, without the Assistance of a Tutor: a Broken Gibberish that has no Part of Speech in it, like Spanish morisco." Samuel Butler may be overstating the case, for apparently Jerry Blackacre does need a tutor. *Characters*, pp. 427–428.

15. 1686 Q: riming.

16. See The Persons, p. 388.

17. A familiar saying, meaning "to keep a sharp eye on." Thus Goldingham in Thomas Shadwell's *The Miser* (1672): "This design was well scaped; but I'le watch your waters I warrant you" (London, 1691, p. 48). For two reasons, the phrase as Jerry uses it may be particularly appropriate in the immediate context. (1) The phrase apparently originated from the idea of examining one's urine for complications, so there may be an implied contiguousness between Freeman's waters and the turf he is expected to dig. (2) There are legal difficulties involved in water since, like light and air, it is not subject to claim. "if a body of water runs out of my pond into an-

other man's, I have no right to reclaim it." Blackstone, II, No. 18. Jerry has cause to watch waters.

18. 1720 *Plays* adds commas after *cou'd* and *choose* which clarifies the lines. Fidelia intends to say: "I could, if I had my choice, there live as his wife."

Act II

1. "Hyde-park, everyone knows, is the promenade of London: nothing was so much in fashion, during the fine weather, as that promenade, which was the rendezvous of magnificence and beauty: every one, therefore, who had either sparkling eyes, or a splendid equipage, constantly repaired thither; and the king seemed pleased with the place." Anthony Hamilton, *Memoirs of Count Grammont*, I, London, 1811, p. 206.

2. Here used in much the same sense as *Citizen's Widow* in Olivia's speech. Holborn was one of the main streets leading into the City; although Sir Kenelm Digby had built some presumably attractive houses there a half-century earlier, it was not a fashionable address.

3. At Whitehall. John Evelyn reports (May 14, 1661), "His *Majestie* was pleased to discourse with me . . . as he sat at Supper in the withdrawing roome to his Bed-Chamber" (de Beer, III, 288). Anyone with any sense of his own importance wanted to be seen in the drawing room of either the king or the queen, particularly at mealtime.

4. An entry in Pepys (March 24, 1667) indicates the English interest in what was being said in Dutch gazettes: "for when by and by my Lord Arlington come in with letters, and seeing the King and Duke of York give us and the officers of the Ordnance directions in this matter, he did move that we might do it as privately as we could, that it might not come into the Dutch Gazette presently, as the King's and Duke of York's going down the other day to Sheerenesse was, the week after, in the Harlem Gazette" (Wheatley, VI, 236). That interest and a suspiciousness about the truth of the items can be seen in two notes from the *Calendar of State Papers, Domestic,* one from the period of the second Dutch War, the other from the third. June 15, 1666: "The Dutch Gazette, speaking dishonorably of the Prince, offers occasion for a word or two. Cannot imagine greater courage, conduct, and presence of mind than he showed all the day, in the midst of the showers of balls." Ser. 4, V (London, 1864), p. 441. March 4, 1673: "a Dutch skipper had the enclosed *Gazette* . . . I believe you will meet with impudent falsities in it." Ser. 4, XV (London, 1902), p. 11. The Dutch, of course, reported the wars from their point of view and the English necessarily read the gazettes by contraries; for instance, the first *CSPD* note above

was written by Prince Rupert's secretary, who must have had as strong a motivation to see the Prince's courage as the Dutch had to be blind to it.

5. Churchill: *exit Lettice*. She must leave the stage at some point between Eliza's holding her above and her entrance on p. 428; this is the logical moment.

6. Perhaps she is thinking of a Greek reporter rather than a Greek custom. Herodotus reports of the Egyptians: "At rich men's banquets, after dinner a man carries round an image of a corpse in a coffin, painted and carved in exact imitation, a cubit or two cubits long. This he shows to each of the company, saying, 'Drink and make merry, but look on this; for such shalt thou be when thou art dead.'" Book II, 78. Translated, A. D. Godley, I, London, 1926, p. 365.

7. There are two scenes involving ghosts and dining in Thomas Shadwell's *The Libertine* (1675). At the end of Act IV, Don Pedro's Ghost comes in while Don John and his friends are eating; he declines their hospitality, but invites them to dine with him in his tomb. In Act V, when Don John and his friends arrive at the church, they meet the ghosts of many of their victims, are offered blood to drink and given a diabolic floor show. Novel's analogy breaks down because Don John, although he declines to drink the blood, refuses to be frightened; only his servant is afraid. Shadwell's play had been performed by the Duke's Company as recently as October 5, 1676.

8. *Fop-corner* was apparently a designation for the part of the theater where the self-styled wits and gallants gathered. It was used in the Epilogue to Aphra Behn's *The City-Heiress* (1682). Summers says (IV, 301) that it was the part of the pit nearest the stage; Nettleton and Case suggest the side-box (p. 217). It seems probable that no fixed place is intended. James Wright indicates in *The Humours and Conversations of the Town* that the fops were ubiquitous: "Are not your Fops in the Pit and Boxes incorrigible to all the Endeavours of your Writers, in their Prologues and Epilogues, or the variety of Characters that have been made to reform them?" London, 1693, pp. 105–106. (Facsimile, Gainesville, Florida, 1961.)

9. Horner pretends to be an eunuch to gain easy access to willing wives.

10. For the famous china scene, see pp. 326–329.

11. Wycherley may have intended this as a joke at the expense of his friend John Dryden. Dryden, particularly in his continuing debate with Sir Robert Howard, was the chief proponent of the use of rhyme in serious drama. See the prefatory essays to *The Rival Ladies* (1664), the second edition of *The Indian Emperour* (1668), and *The Conquest of Granada*

(1672); and *Of Dramatick Poesie* (1668), in which Neander (Dryden) defends rhyme against Crites (Howard).

12. Plainly an aside. Hague so marks it. Churchill says (p. 263) that the stage direction was added in an earlier edition (1710) in which the place of publication is not identified.

13. Thames Street ran along the north bank of the river. If it smelled to Olivia as it smelled to John Gay forty years later, the insult is a penetrating one: "Or who that rugged Street would traverse o'er, / That stretches, O *Fleet-ditch,* from thy black Shore / To the Tow'rs moated Walls? Here Steams ascend / That, in mix'd Fumes, the wrinkled Nose offend." *Trivia,* London [1716], p. 29.

14. The problem here is who does the thrusting and when. As the stage direction stands, Olivia pushes her way past Novel and Lord Plausible to confront Manly; she is quite capable of such an action. Hague places the stage direction after Manly's *Madam* and Hunt after *Away;* both readings transfer the action to Manly.

15. 1677 Q: in vain. 1686 Q drops the in.

16. Men's gloves were often embroidered with silver or gold thread, trimmed with ribbons, lace, or fur. They were frequently perfumed or made out of leather that had a scent of its own.

17. Although there was no prescribed uniform at the time, Novel is apparently describing military dress. The red breeches can be found in Widow Blackacres' mouth (p. 448) where she is afraid Jerry is going to take to *Rambling, and Fighting, and studying Military Discipline* and the short sword is the occasion for Oldfox's anger in Act III (p. 458). Elsewhere in the play (p. 472), where the connection between Freeman and red breeches is emphasized, they suggest the roistering young man.

18. Her tailor presumably belongs to a train-band, a company of citizen soldiers, and was wearing a scarf as an indication of his rank. *Training day* was a day legally appointed for the drilling of the militia.

19. Bartholomew Fair, held from August 22 to September 2 in Smithfield, was not noted for the subtlety of its entertainments, as Ben Jonson's play of that name testifies. Ned Ward describes a Merry Andrew and his partner doing a turn outside a droll-booth in an attempt to draw in a paying audience: "Between these two the clod-skul'd Audience were lug'd by the Ears for an Hour; the Apes blundering over such a parcel of Insignificant Nonsense, that none but a true *English* unthinking Mob could have laugh'd, or taken Pleasure at any of their empty Drollery . . ." pp. 238–239.

20. Wapping lay beyond the tower. See Act I, p. 392.

21. Leigh Hunt adds "who goes out"; of course, Lettice's exit is implicit in Olivia's lines.

22. Pirates did often use false signal flags to approach a ship to begin an engagement. Manly's piratical metaphor is a bit confusing. It is not a developing metaphor built on a continuing action, a pirate's showing false colors and then luffing to avoid going aground. The colon divides it into two different comments on love. Love, like a pirate, operates under false colors. Love, like a pirate, alters course when he sees that his target is a ruin, not a prize. The second metaphor breaks down because a ship aground is still a prize; the pirate might luff to save his ship, but he would send in the longboat to plunder.

23. Hunt adds a stage direction: *Exeunt* Lettice *and* Boy.

24. Since under the law of primogeniture the eldest son inherits the estate, a younger son must look elsewhere, as to a profitable marriage, to provide for himself.

25. Nettleton and Case suggest (p. 224) that the joke lies in her lying about her age, an assumption that depends on the play's being set during the second Dutch War, when she would be less than thirty with a twenty-one-year-old son. Wycherley was not that rigid about his time setting, for there are obvious references in the play to events of the 1670s. The age joke in the line, judging by what follows, is aimed at Oldfox as much as at the Widow. The joke, in relation to her, is that she cannot name a year, true or false, without using law Latin, in which, as Samuel Butler says, the lawyer "has but one Termination for all *Latin* Words, and that's a Dash. He is very just to the first Syllables of Words, but always bobtails the last, in which the Sense most of all consists . . ." (*Characters*, p. 73).

26. Judges were called lamb-skin-men because lambskin was used in their robes.

Act III

1. Among other things, the Court of Chancery dealt with the administration of estates of deceased persons. The delays of the court were notorious, so an inheritance might become, as Manly implies, an unending headache. "As we were thus squeezing along towards the *Chancery-Bar*, a couple of Country Fellows met, and Greeted one another after the following manner, *How d'ye, Neighbour*, says the one, *Is your Suit ended yet? No, trowly*, says the other, *nor can any Body tell when it wool.*" Ned Ward, p. 189.

2. The lawyers wore black. See stage direction, p. 443. The comparison, of course, calls lawyers, "blackguards," but Wycherley may also have been thinking of the homeless street urchins who traveled in bands. "*We . . . are the City* Black-Guard *marching to our Winter Quarters . . . give us a Penny or a Half-penny amongst us, and you shall hear any of us (if you please) say the* Lords-Prayer *backwards, Swear the* Com-

pass *round; give a new Curse to every Step in the* Monument, *call a* Whore *as many proper Name as a* Peer *has Titles."* Ned Ward, pp. 36–37. In their way, the urchins were as articulate as the lawyers and as willing to sell their words.

3. Gambling was permitted in the Inns of Court during the Christmas celebrations, from Christmas to Epiphany.

4. Freeman's comparison is complicated by the problem of plurals and possessives in the sentence. 1713 *Works* says "Lawyer's" and Hunt and Ward follow that usage. Churchill reverts to "lawyers" in his text, but in a note on the passage (p. 424), he assumes that the lawyer is singular and that the box is a dice-box which has defeated the gamblers. When it is compared with the old lawyers' cash-box, as he admits, there is a confusion in point of view. This can be removed if we take *Lawyers* as a plural possessive, and the box that belongs to them all not as a dice-box, but as the box which received the house cut. John Strype in his enlargement of John Stow's *A Survey of London* writes: "To the Dicing all Comers are admitted; and it is so excessive, having such abundance of Tables placed in the Hall, that what comes to the Box generally amounts to 50£. a Day and Night : So that by this, with a small Contribution from each Student, the great charge of the whole *Christmas* is defrayed." *A Survey of the Cities of London and Westminster*, I, London, 1720, p. 123. *The Nicker Nicked; or, The Cheats of Gaming Discovered* (London, 1669) cites the dangers of the house cut: "I have seen . . . three persons sit down and each draw forty shillings a piece; and, in little more than two hours, the box has had three pounds of the money; and all the three gamesters have been losers, and laughed at for their indiscretion." Quoted, John Ashton, *The History of Gambling in England*, Chicago, 1899, p. 45. What Freeman is saying is that rival gamblers at the Inns, like the rival litigants, both lose in the end and that only the boxes of the legal middle-men stand to gain.

5. Officers were paid so much subsistence for each soldier for each day of a muster. One way of making money was to pad out the muster lists with false names or with passe-volants, who were dismissed as soon as they were counted. For a brief description of ways of cheating on musters see J. W. Fortescue, *The History of the British Army*, I, 1899, pp. 319–320. In his character of "A Lawyer," Samuel Butler made even better use of the false-muster comparison than Freeman does: "For when he draws up a Business, like a Captain that makes false Musters, he produces as many loose and idle Words as he can possibly come by, until he has received for them, and then turns them off, and retains only those that are to the Purpose—" *Characters*, p. 73.

6. Grand larceny (anything over 12 pence) and robbery were both death felonies. See Michael Dalton, *The Countrey Justice*, London, 1677, pp. 361–363. It was a book which, in earlier editions, the Widow would have used; see n. 11, below.

7. Aside from the Court of Chancery, the three central tribunals in Westminster Hall, in all of which Widow Blackacre has cases pending, were Common Pleas, King's Bench, and Exchequer. Common Pleas was supposed to deal with cases involving subject against subject; King's Bench with pleas of the crown; Exchequer with revenue cases. In fact, they were all common-law courts whose jurisdictions were not clearly defined; the bulk of the cases in all three courts were those that might nominally have belonged to Common Pleas.

8. 1677 Q-2: amplifie. Whether *examplifie* is taken as an old form of "amplify" or in the sense of "exemplify," it is a way of killing time in the court.

9. The penalty for hitting someone in Westminster Hall while the courts were in session was life imprisonment and the confiscation of one's goods.

10. Nicholas Culpeper was a medical writer, whose best-known book was *The English Physician* (1652), of which an enlarged version was published five times between 1661 and 1676. He was also the author of *A Directory for Midwives* (1651; also published, 1660, 1671, 1675) and *Culpeper's Directory for Midwives: or, a Guide for Women, the second part* (1662, 1671). There were editions of *The Problems of Aristotle* (1597), which was not by Aristotle at all, in 1666 and 1670. *The Compleat Midwifes Practice*, by T.C., was published in 1656; Churchill records (p. 427) a third edition (1663), and Summers attributes (II, 304) it to Culpeper. Nettleton and Case assume (p. 229) that the bookseller's boy is pushing two bogus Aristotle items, but the first date I can find for *Aristotle's Compleat and Experienc'd Midwife* is 1700.

11. Michael Dalton's *The Countrey Justice*, which first appeared in 1618, was published in a variety of editions throughout the century; an issue of the sixth edition had been published as recently as 1666. Williams Hughes of Gray's Inn, as he billed himself, wrote a number of legal books. *The Parsons Law* (1641) was most often reprinted; *Hughes's Quaeries* (1675), the most recently published. William Sheppard was the most prolific of the writers mentioned. His *The Court-Keepers Guide* (1649) was most often reprinted; he published two books, *Actions upon the Case for Deeds* and *A Grand Abridgment of the Common and Statute Law*, in 1675. Edmund Wingate, who was better known as a mathematician, was the author of *The Body of the Common Law* (1655), which had been reissued as recently as 1670.

12. Jerry gets *Christendom* and *England* turned around in his title. He is probably asking for Richard Johnson's *The Most Famous History of the Seven Champions of Christendom* (1596). There were editions of this very popular book, with "Most" dropped from the title, in 1660, 1670, and 1675. On the title page (1596), Saint George gets top billing among the heroes.

13. There was an edition, labeled the fourteenth, of Sir Richard Hutton's much reprinted *The Young Clerk's Guide* in 1673. The second edition, the first known one, was published in 1650.

14. There were two Readers appointed each year in the Inns of Court to lecture to the members on whatever statutes they chose. In the last week of each Reader's term, a feast was held, to which dignitaries from outside the inn were invited. Such feasts could be very elaborate. John Evelyn reports (August 2, 1668): "Mr. *Bramstone* (son to *Judge Bramstone*) my old acquaintance & fellow travelor, now Reader at the middle Temple invited me to his feast which was so very extravagant & greate as the like had not ben seene at any time" (de Beer, III, 512).

15. A common name for a tavern. The best-known one, perhaps because Pepys visited it (March 5, 1660; Wheatley, I, 80), was in Billingsgate. Burns lists five others. The reformed sign would have been of two men bowing, a substitution for the original St. Gabriel and Mary. Burns quotes Richard Flecknoe's *Aenigmatical Characters* (1665): "as for the signs, they have pretty well begun their reformation already, changing the sign of the Salutation of the Angel and our Lady into the Souldier and Citizen . . ." (p. 27).

16. There is no stage direction to indicate when the sailor enters. If Jack is 2 Sailor of Act I, then Tom (1 Sailor) may be the "salt-water shark" who steals the Widow's bags at Freeman's instructions. If the pair are parted to do Freeman's business, Tom may go off with the bags and Jack come on stage with Freeman and Jerry when they return loaded with trinkets. In any case, the stage is very busy throughout this act with supernumeraries passing back and forth to suggest the traffic of Westminster Hall. Some characters are presumably on stage throughout the act, only occasionally taking notice of the main action. For example, there are no stage directions to provide for either the entrance or the exit of the bookseller's boy; he and his shop must be at hand when the lines require them. Presumably the conversations of the main characters would be played on the forestage and the inner stage could be used for peripheral action suggested by the conversations or a general depiction of Westminster Hall.

17. 1677 Q: *Exit.*

18. "But by the Common Law, if a man kill himself (either with a mediate hatred against his own life, or out of distraction, or other humour) he is called *Felo de se*." Dalton, p. 341. His goods were then forfeit to the state. In saying that Jerry is more likely to commit a felony against his goods than against himself, the Widow is saying that she does not fear losing his estate by his death but by his life. Since "biens" (*beins*) means property other than estates and inheritances, she may have achieved the balance of the two *Felo* phrases at the expense of her legal terminology.

19. Detinue is an action to recover property lawfully obtained but unlawfully detained and trover an action to recover the value of such property when it is wrongfully used by the possessor. Nettleton and Case suggest (p. 232) that the Widow's law is faulty here, that her correct action is replevin, to recover property unlawfully taken and held. Since Freeman may be said to have found the bags rather than to have stolen them and since finding is one of the lawful ways of gaining possession, the Widow is probably correct.

20. Edgehill, on the border of Warwickshire and Oxfordshire, was the scene of the first big battle of the civil war, October 23, 1642. Nettleton and Case assume (p. 233) that Oldfox is speaking of Cavalier officers, but Freeman's speech at the end of this scene, if it is taken as more than a joke, puts Oldfox with the Parliament men.

21. 1713 *Works:* with his Sword and Stockings out at Heels. Certainly this makes better sense, but Manly may have intended the unlikely reversal to emphasize that the man's bravery is as shabby as everything else about him.

22. Summers guesses (II, 307) that Manly is referring to the fields behind Southampton House, Bloomsbury, as dueling grounds. Churchill assumes (p. 429) that the reference is to the pitched battles often fought in Southampton Fields, a Sunday rendezvous for the lower classes. The latter makes the better insult.

23. Under Louis XIV and his minister of war, the Marquis de Louvois, the French developed in the decade 1660–70 a modernized military system that was to serve for years as a model for all of Europe. One element in that development was a uniform system of drilling and training, introduced by Lt. Col. Jean Martinet. Although the English army was still far from becoming a working organization, some officers must have been adopting parts of Martinet's drill, although I can find no confirmation of this outside Oldfox's speech. Presumably the drill involved a short sword (Oldfox's "bodkin" I take as an overstatement), which the Major finds less manly than Manly's broadsword. If we take Oldfox as an old Parliament man (see n. 20), his distaste for Martinet may lie in its being a

borrowing from France. That is not his primary characterization however.

24. 1677 Q-2: go thy wayes. I prefer this reading, but since the original makes sense I did not change it.

25. The point of the phrase does not lie in the number of bits. In *A Collection of English Proverbs*, John Ray lists "In a shoulder of *veal* there are twenty and two good bits," and then he explains: "This is a piece of country wit. They mean by it, There are twenty (others say forty) bits in a shoulder of veal, but two good ones." Cambridge, 1678, p. 83.

26. Formerly used as a royal banqueting hall on special occasions. "In the yeare 1316. *Edward* the second did solemnize the feast of Penticost at Westminster, in the great hall, where sitting royally at the table with his Pears about him. . . ." John Stow, *A Survey of London*, II, London, 1908, p. 114.

ACT IV

1. Since "fireship" is slang for "whore," Fidelia's simile is particularly appropriate.

2. On December 29, 1675, a royal proclamation announced the suppression of coffeehouses after January 10. On January 8, a second proclamation provided an extension until June 24, but made the proprietor responsible for what was said in his house. See *Tudor and Stuart Proclamations*, ed. Robert Steele, I, Oxford, 1910, p. 439. The suppression, which never took place, was aimed at the supposedly seditious talk that went on in coffeehouses. See *Love in a Wood*, II, n. 7.

3. 13 Edward I, 1285, Statute 1, was known as Westminster 2. Cap. xxxv of that statute concerns Ravishment of Ward: "Concerning Children Males or Females (whose Marriage belongeth to another) taken and carried away . . ." *The Statutes at Large*, I, London, 1763, p. 101. Although Freeman seems to have no intention of marrying Jerry with or without his mother's permission, he might conceivably be subject to punishment under Westminster 2 if Jerry really were a minor.

4. Until the privilege of sanctuary was abolished in 1697, the precinct of Whitefriars was a refuge for debtors and lawbreakers who formed a community of their own, called Alsatia, with its own cant language. Thomas Shadwell's *The Squire of Alsatia* (1688) is the best portrait of the area. Presumably the inhabitants knew the law as well as their neighbors in the Temples. Cheatly, in Shadwell's play, knows the terminology at least, although in this speech to Lolpoop he is talking legal gibberish: "Why, put the Case you are indebted to me 20£. upon a *Scire facias :* I extend this up to an Outlawry, upon Affidavit upon the *Nisi prius :* I plead to all this matter, *Non est inventus* upon the Pannel; what is there to be done more

in this Case, as it lies before the Bench, but to award out Execution upon the *Posse Comitatus,* who are presently to issue out a *Certiorari.*" London, 1688, p. 7.

5. The stage direction was printed in roman in 1677 Q, as though it were part of Plausible's speech. 1691 Q changed to italics.

6. Both Hague and 1720 *Plays* place this stage direction after Novel's speech rather than before it, a more sensible placing in terms of stage action.

7. In Whitehall, as Novel's line below indicates. See Act II, n. 3.

8. The boy's errands are taking him to such widely scattered places that Olivia's emphasis of *two hours* is hardly necessary.

9. 1677 Q-2 correctly marks this an aside.

10. "When our Countrymen come home from fighting ag[ains]t the Saracens & were beaten by them, they pictur'd them with huge, bigg terrible faces (as you still see the Signe of the Saracen's head is) . . ." *Table Talk of John Selden* [1689], London, 1927, p. 136.

Act V

1. According to Charles Cotton, in ombre, which is Olivia's game (see p. 428), "in playing Trumps, if any plays an ordinary one, and you have only the three best Cards or *Matadors* singly or jointly in your hands, you may refuse to play them without renouncing, because of the priviledge which these Cards have, that none but commanding Cards can force them out of your hand." Olivia also knows that "If you renounce you are to double the Stake . . ." *The Compleat Gamester,* London, 1674, p. 102.

2. Something of the character of the Cock in Bow Street, also known as Oxford Kate's, can be assumed by the events that take place there later in this act—the willingness of the waiters to bind and gag the Widow, the presence of the bailiffs listening at the door (p. 507). For outside testimony to the liveliness of the Cock, here is Samuel Pepys, July 1, 1663: "Mr. Batten telling us of a late triall of Sir Charles Sydly the other day, before my Lord Chief Justice Foster and the whole bench, for his debauchery a little while since at Oxford Kate's, coming in open day into the Balcone and showed his nakedness, . . . and abusing of Scripture and as it were from thence preaching a mountebank sermon from the pulpit, saying that there he had to sell such a powder as should make all the [women] in town run after him, 1,000 people standing underneath to see and hear him, and that being done he took a glass of wine . . . and then drank it off, and then took another and

drank the King's health" (Wheatley, III, 191). There are a number of versions of the same incident; for an account that uses them all, see Vivian de Sola Pinto, *Sir Charles Sedley*, London, 1927, pp. 61–66.

3. 1677 Q-2: *cocking*. There may be such a thing as a coaching coward, one who somehow displays his cowardice by the way he behaves in his coach, but a cocky, strutting coward better fits the context.

4. They might well be the same thing. When Falstaff says, "I like not such grinning honour as Sir Walter hath," Sir Walter is dead. *1 Henry IV*, v iii 58–59 (Arden).

5. In Act 1 of Thomas Shadwell's *The Scowrers* (1690) a glazier, hearing that Sir William's regular glazier is dead, comes in to solicit his business. That play provides a good portrait of the pointless, violent fun of the hectoring, roaring, scouring boys.